THE TREE & THE COLUMN

A volume in the series

MEDIEVAL SOCIETIES, RELIGIONS, AND CULTURES

Edited by M. Cecilia Gaposchkin and Anne E. Lester

A list of titles in this series is available at cornellpress.cornell.edu.

THE TREE & THE COLUMN

The Bronze Door of Hildesheim

Isabelle Marchesin

Translated from the French
by Janice Bertrand Owen and Ester Zago

Foreword by Herbert L. Kessler

Cornell University Press | Ithaca and London

Originally published in France as *L'Arbre et la Colonne. La porte de bronze d' Hildesheim*, Isabelle Marchesin

For information, address Cornell University Press, Sage House, 512 East State Street, Ithaca, New York 14850. Visit our website at cornellpress.cornell.edu.

First published 2024 by Cornell University Press

Printed in China

Library of Congress Cataloging-in-Publication Data

Names: Marchesin, Isabelle, author. | Owen, Janice Bertrand, translator. | Zago, Ester, translator.

Title: The tree and the column : the bronze door of Hildesheim / Isabelle Marchesin, translated by Janice Bertrand Owen and Ester Zago.

Other titles: Arbre & la colonne. English

Description: Ithaca [New York] : Cornell University Press, 2024. | Series: Medieval societies, religions, and cultures | Includes bibliographical references.

Identifiers: LCCN 2023024319 | ISBN 9781501768668 (paperback)

Subjects: LCSH: Bernward, Bishop of Hildesheim, approximately 960-1022. | Dom zu Hildesheim. | Bronze doors, Medieval—Germany—Hildesheim. | Bronze doors, Romanesque—Germany—Hildesheim. | Relief (Sculpture), Romanesque—Germany—Hildesheim. | Relief (Sculpture), German—Germany—Hildesheim. | Christian art and symbolism—Germany—Hildesheim. | Church decoration and ornament—Germany—Hildesheim.

Classification: LCC NB1287.H5 M3713 2024 | DDC 739.5/120943595—dc23/eng/20230727

LC record available at https://lccn.loc.gov/2023024319

All photos are from Bildarchiv Monheim except:
Figures 9, 10, 133, 136: Isabelle Marchesin.
Figures 4, 85, 92, 151, 198: Dom Museum Hildesheim.
Figure 2, 3, 84, 135: from *L'Europe de l'An Mil*, dir. P. Riche, Zodiaque, 2001.
Figure 122: Naples, Bibliotheque Nationale. Used by permission.
Figure 134: *L'Art paléochrétien*, Zodiaque, 1998.

Dedicated to the memory of my dearest friends, † Jan Owen and † Ester Zago (without whom this book would not exist), with all my love and gratitude. My thanks also to Sally Pane for her kind help in completing the work.

I am the vine, you the branches.
—John 15:5

CONTENTS

FOREWORD BY HERBERT L. KESSLER
"CONVENIENTIAE QUASI PICTUAE CORPORIS SUNT EXPONENDE"

Sixty years after the publication of Rudolf Wesenberg's magisterial *Bernwardinische Plastik*,[1] nearly a quarter century since the magnificent exhibition in Hildesheim,[2] and concurrent with the reinstallation of the Diözesanmuseum, Isabelle Marchesin represtinates with the intellectual content of Bishop Bernward's great bronze doors. Seamlessly integrating the previous discussions of the original destination, technique, authorship, and pictorial models into a sustained and elegant visual analysis, she teases out the doors' meaning and function, which she shows, are at once complex but unified, targeted but intentionally elusive.

In the very structure of opposing narrative sequences from the Book of Genesis and the Gospels hanging at the entrance to a sacred space, Bernward's "valvas fusiles in facie [m] templi suspendi" offer a multivalent introduction to the history of salvation as Bernward understood it that simultaneously introduces the sacrality beyond and closes it off. Their basic syntax has long been recognized. Beginning with the Creation of Humankind at the top of the left door, eight panels trace the Fall of Adam and Eve through Cain's rebuke for murdering Abel; and continuing from the bottom up on the right valve, eight other panels track Christian salvation, from the Holy Spirit's entering flesh at the Annunciation and Christ's infancy through the Passion and Resurrection (the Savior's public life is narrated on Bernward's bronze column). Motival repetitions, variations, and juxtapositions weave a net of associations within and between the separate sequences, for instance, Eve nursing Abel abutting Mary presenting the Child to the Magi.

Grosso modo, all modern scholars accept the basic structure of interwoven historical and exegetic sequences in Bernward's doors. More important, the concept is paralleled in medieval theology, for instance, in Anselm of Canterbury's influential *Cur deus homo*:

> For it was appropriate that, just as death entered the human race through a man's disobedience, so life should be restored through a man's obedience; and that, just as the sin which was the cause of our damnation originated from a woman, similarly the originator of our justification and salvation should be born of a woman. Also that the devil, who defeated the man whom he beguiled through the taste of a tree, should himself similarly be defeated by a man through tree-induced suffering which he, the devil, inflicted. . . . Then, in order that the physical reality of the truth, so to speak, may shine forth all the more, these harmonies may be set out as pictorial representations of this physical reality.[3]

---

1 R. Wesenberg, *Bernwardinische Plastik. Zur Ottonischen Kunst unter Bischof Bernward von Hildesheim*, Berlin, 1955.

2 *Bernward von Hildesheim und das Zeitalter der Ottonen*, ed. Michael Brandt and Arne Eggebrecht, Hildesheim and Mainz, 1993.

3 "Oportebat namque ut sicut per hominis inobedientiam mors in humanum genus intraverat, ita per hominis obedientiam vita restitueretur; et quemadmodum peccatum, quod fuit causa nostrae damnationis, initium habuit a femina, sic nostrae justitiae et salutis auctor nasceretur de femina; et ut diabolus, qui per gustum ligni quem persuasit,

It should be noted that Anselm wrote his powerful tract in 1096–98, more than eight decades after Bernward completed his doors; and although he drew on a long tradition of exegesis going back to Augustine that Bernward would also have known, no earlier writing offers so comprehensive an interpretation of sacred history. Indeed, it is telling that the precedent typological texts—Prudentius, Paulinus of Nola, Helpidius Rusticus, and Bede—are all descriptions of picture sequences.[4] What Marchesin's intense visual analysis reveals, then, is that, when read with sensitivity to detail and a conviction that artistic nuance is no mere whim, the Hildesheim doors are, themselves, a form of sophisticated exegesis that may not only have preceded but perhaps also have influenced written expositions. Among this book's numerous important contributions is its overturning of the priority usually accorded texts over pictures and its suggestion that the typological structure of so much medieval art may, in fact, be based on images not words. Anselm himself recognized typology's fundamentally visual aspect when he noted: "All these are beautiful notions, and are to be viewed like pictures."[5]

The well-traveled Bernward had famously responded to the ancient triumphal columns and to the more recent doors at Aachen and Mainz; and he made use of a frontispiece from a Touronian Bible to fashion the Genesis door. The intricate interweaving of Old Testament narratives and Gospel scenes at Hildesheim may owe as much to Bernward's reactions to the Early Christian doors of Santa Sabina he saw in Rome as to any written treatise (although the overall selection of scenes is quite different, Marchesin recognizes a possible connection in the representation of the Adoration of the Magi). As Ivan Foletti has recently disclosed, the fifth-century wood doors deploy narratives and typologies in many of the same ways Marchesin proposes for the Hildesheim;[6] and, indeed, the syncopation of visual simplicity and theological complexity that she reveals evokes the rhetoric of styles Foletti discerns at Santa Sabina. In short, Bernward was probably not only an author of works of art but also an appreciator who constructed the doors from pictures and monuments he had encountered and understood.

As in Santa Sabina, art's inherent polysemia enabled its appeal to diverse audience. Citing Pope Gregory the Great's dictum repeated throughout the Middle Ages, that art serves persons unable to read (Latin, Christian) Scripture and innately attracted to physical objects, Marchesin proposes that the Hildesheim panels were designed, on one level, simply to be "read." In fact, the paired doors evoke book covers and figured frontispieces that need to be turned to reveal their contents; and it is perhaps no mere chance that the Old Testament scenes are based on frontispieces in ninth-century pandects that, exceptionally in comprehensive single volumes contain the "testamenta duo quod relegenda gerit."[7] Pope Gregory's putative simple persons, especially those who lived their lives in Hildesheim and participated in church rituals (including scriptural readings), would have been able to pick up at least the basic associations Marchesin identifies in the visual means used to portray the biblical stories. They need not have been able to read Isidore of Seville or Hrabanus Maurus (as Bernward was) to discern the meaning of humankind's primordial androgyny transformed when Adam and Eve sinned, nor would they have missed the overall impression of order and geometry ceding to disarray that Marchesin puts into high relief. Furthermore, those who scrutinized the doors might well have pondered such meaningful juxtapositions as Eden's Tree of Life with the roughhewn cross on which Christ is shown dying, or discerned the enormous cross formed by the two doors' seam intersected by the horizontal frame bearing the dedicatory inscription. And perhaps the most curious and very attentive would even have noted the fact that the devil in the scene of the Fall occupies the same position as the angel in the Creation scene and that his evil hybridity is like no creature they had ever encountered in their lives. Marchesin

hominem vicerat, ita per passionem ligni, quam intulit, ab homine vinceretur. . . . Deinde, ut ipsum quasi corpus veritatis plus niteat, istae convenientiae quasi picturae corporis sunt exponendae." *Cur deus homo*, Book I, chaps. 3–4; PL 158.364–65; trans. B. Davies and G. R. Evans, Oxford, 1998, pp. 268–69. See: T. A. Heslop, "St Anselm, Church Reform and the Politics of Art," *Anglo-Norman Studies*, 33 (2011), pp. 103–24; and Herbert L. Kessler, "'Aliter enim videtur pictura, aliter videntur litterae': Reading Medieval Pictures," *Scrivere e leggere*, Settimana di studio LIX, 2012, Spoleto: CISAM. 2012, pp. 701–29; Vojtech Novótny, *Cur homo?: A History of the Thesis of Man as a Replacement for Fallen Angels*, Prague, 2014.

4 See: Arwed Arnulf, *Versus ad Picturas. Studien zur Titulusdichtung als Quellengattung der Kunstgeschichte von der Anitke bis zum Hochmitelalter*, Berlin, 1997.

5 Omnia haec pulchra et quasi quaedam picturae suscipienda sunt.

6 Ivan Foletti and Manuela Gianandrea, *Zona liminare. Il nartece di Santa Sabina a Roma, la sua porta e l'iniziazione cristiana*, Rome, 2015.

7 See Paul Edward Dutton and Herbert L. Kessler, *The Poetry and Paintings of the First Bible of Charles the Bald*, Ann Arbor, 1997, p. 104.

makes a compelling case that not only the events but also how they are rendered visually provided significance.

That said, few simple people, even those who meditated on the doors over a lifetime, would have comprehended the most profound meanings Marchesin teases out in her analysis of the conceits of resemblance, alternation, ambiguity, and absence; indeed, she shows that even the most sober renderings mask complex references that could only have been understood fully by the learned, in the first instance, by Bernward himself. For example, even if the responsiveness of the depicted trees animates the interpretation of the Introduction of Eve to Adam (and throughout the doors) in a purely pictorial way, the visual punning that evokes "virago" from vir and radix demands a knowledge of Latin.[8]

In Marchesin's reading, many of the depicted things are simultaneously alive and inert, vegetal or animal and human, mathematical and organic, material and spiritual; and the very ambivalence allows them to move from Old Testament to New. Finding significance in the rendering of plants or earth, Marchesin quite literally leaves no leaf or stone unturned; and her archaeological analysis of clothing, architecture, and attributes also implies profoundly sophisticated viewers. Small details in the Genesis cycle allude to God's goodness even after the Fall and hence to the promise of ultimate restoration; and features in the New Testament series allude back to the cause or forward to salvation.

Thus, the branch Mary grasps in the Annunciation is Sapientia's virga, a reference to the Tree of Life and an antonym of Cain's club; the sudarium involutum within Christ's tomb in the depiction of the Three Maries refers to Christ's body as sanctuary; and the tiny portal in the depiction of the Noli me tangere provides both a reference back to the Annunciation and a furtive eschatological allusion. Represented throughout the reliefs, doors are among the details that establish a web of interconnections, some open, some closed, some ambiguous; and like the actual doors on which they appear, they, too, mark both a physical obstruction and a rupture leading to a higher stage of human awareness.[9]

By intensely excavating profound spiritual significance in the literal, material pictures, Marchesin demonstrates that, like Scripture, the Hildesheim doors must be read and reread so that their unifying message in Christ might shine forth. Citing the cross that occupies one of the "portae paradisi" depicted on the Marian page of Bernward's precious Gospelbook in Hildesheim (Dom- und Diözesanmuseum, Domschatz MS 61), she bolsters the basic argument that the typologies are themselves keys for reopening Eden's gates. The hand of God in the fiery mandorla beneath the lion knob in the scene of the Sacrifice of Cain and Abel is a metonym of the doors made of metal fired in a furnace and replete with the Lord's spirit; engaging the very processes Marchesin so beautifully details, it attests to Bernard's hope that his own offering in Hildesheim might, like Abel's, find God's favor, and provide him, too, with a door into Paradise.

8 Marchesin's reading of the plants as spiritualized matter is supported by Ittai Weinryb's quite different argument in *The Bronze Object in the Middle Ages*, Cambridge, 2016, pp. 70–73.

9 The same kind of self-referentiality is a characteristic of the eleventh-century Salerno ivories; see: *The Salerno Ivories: Objects, Histories, Contexts*, eds. Anthony Cutler, et al., Berlin, 2016.

THE TREE & THE COLUMN

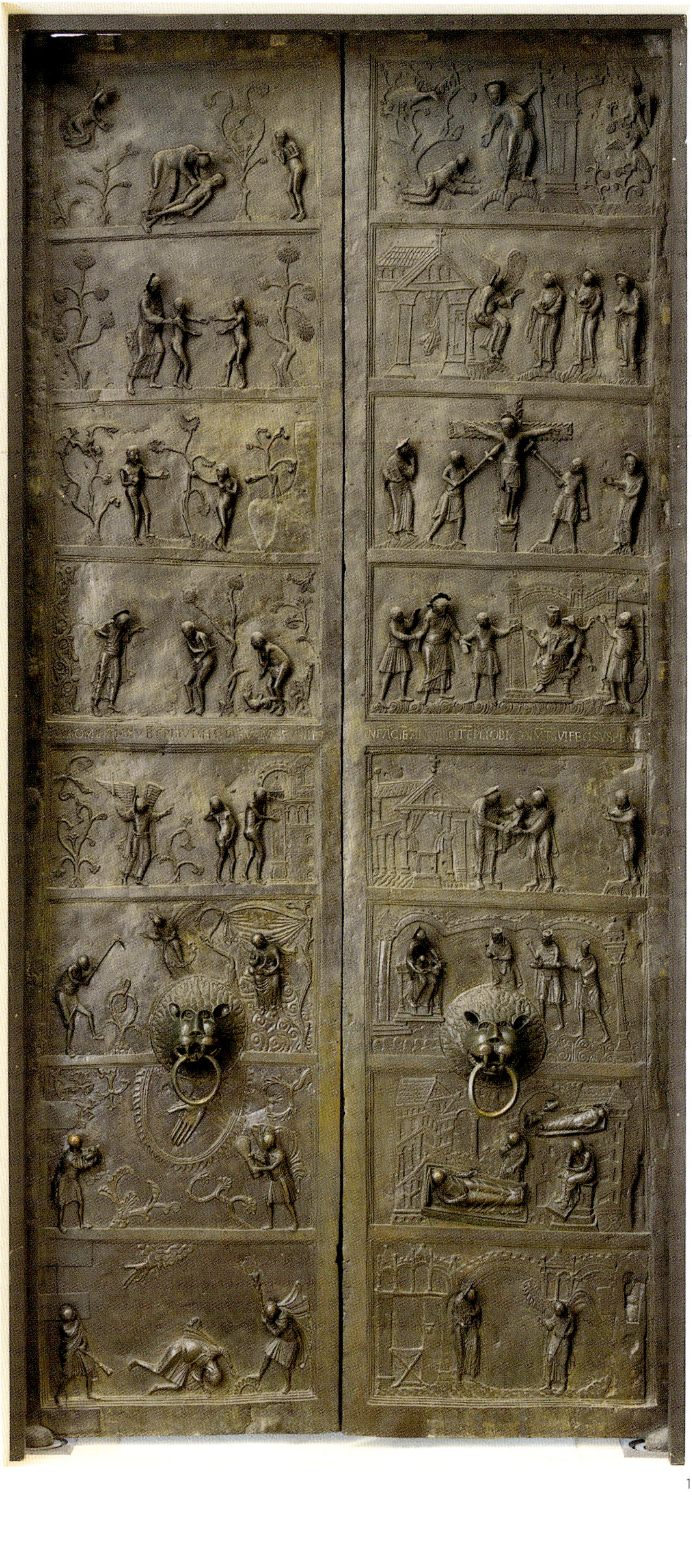

1. *The bronze door. Author's note: No photograph can reproduce, without some distortion, the panels of a 4.7-meter-tall door, particularly when affected by factors of casting methods, wear, and presentation (the two door leaves are not contiguous). We have rendered their formats as accurately as possible, while taking into account that the original format was intended to be rectangular and uniform, and was therefore meant to be presented as such.*

1

FACING THE DOOR

The beginning of the eleventh century, South Saxony, about thirty-five kilometers southeast of present-day Hanover (fig. 2). Around 1000 CE the episcopal town of Hildesheim was a large village, covering an area probably no larger than 130 meters by 165 meters, or two hectares (fig. 3). Dwarfed in size by the ancient towns in Romanized Europe, the settlement was roughly comparable to the contemporaneous Germanic bishoprics of Paderborn or Osnabrück [Kruse 1987, 111].

Founded in 815 on the site of what was probably already a fairly large settlement, Hildesheim was chosen by the Carolingian emperor Louis the Pious from his own domains to serve as an outpost in the conquest and Christianization of Saxon territory. The location was ideal. Nestled in the heart of rich agricultural land near a ford, the village stood on top of a hill contoured by a bend of the river Treibe. The watercourse ran along the town's south and east sides, protecting it from the old riverbed to the west. Hildesheim lay at the crossroads of several interregional routes, especially the great east–west trade route connecting the Rhineland with the Slavic regions and the Baltic Sea [Kruse 1987, 109].

In the decades following its foundation in 815, the episcopal village was enlarged, protected by walls from the Viking invasions. Later, merchants and craftsmen settled in its suburbs. But it was only at the time of Bernward's episcopate, at the beginning of the millennium, that the town acquired considerable importance. By that time political conditions had changed. The Christian empire founded by Charlemagne at the beginning of the ninth century had collapsed; with the coronation in 962 of Otto I, son of Henry the Fowler, Duke of Saxony and King of East Francia, the crown passed to the Ottonian dynasty. The town of Hildesheim was in the heart of Saxon territory, the land of the new imperial dynasty. It was located about 60 kilometers northwest of the fortress of Goslar, one of the court's main residences, and 150 kilometers from the archbishopric of Magdeburg on the eastern border of the empire. It was also close to great abbeys such as Gandersheim, Quedlinburg, and a little farther south, Fulda, all cultural centers where Ottonian princes enjoyed residing.

The geographic location of Hildesheim, as well as its wealth and increasing strategic importance, explain why, in 993, its diocese was entrusted to Bernward, a Saxon aristocrat with strong ties to the imperial court. Since bishops played a major role in supporting the emperor who appointed them, Bernward's mission was obviously not only pastoral and administrative but also included supervising political, military, and public works. He is credited with completing Hildesheim's cathedral, as well as with the construction of a new stone rampart with evenly spaced round towers to protect the town [Kruse 1987, 111; Boockmann 1993]. At the end of his life, he devoutly founded and personally financed a monastery dedicated to St. Michael, which he endowed with lavish liturgical furnishings; the building was located about three hundred meters north of the town on a small hill overlooking a hollow (fig. 4).

By the time the bronze door was cast in 1015 (fig. 1), Hildesheim's appearance had been considerably changed by the bishop's construction projects. In addition to the cathedral, the city walls now enclosed the episcopal palace to the south, a hospice

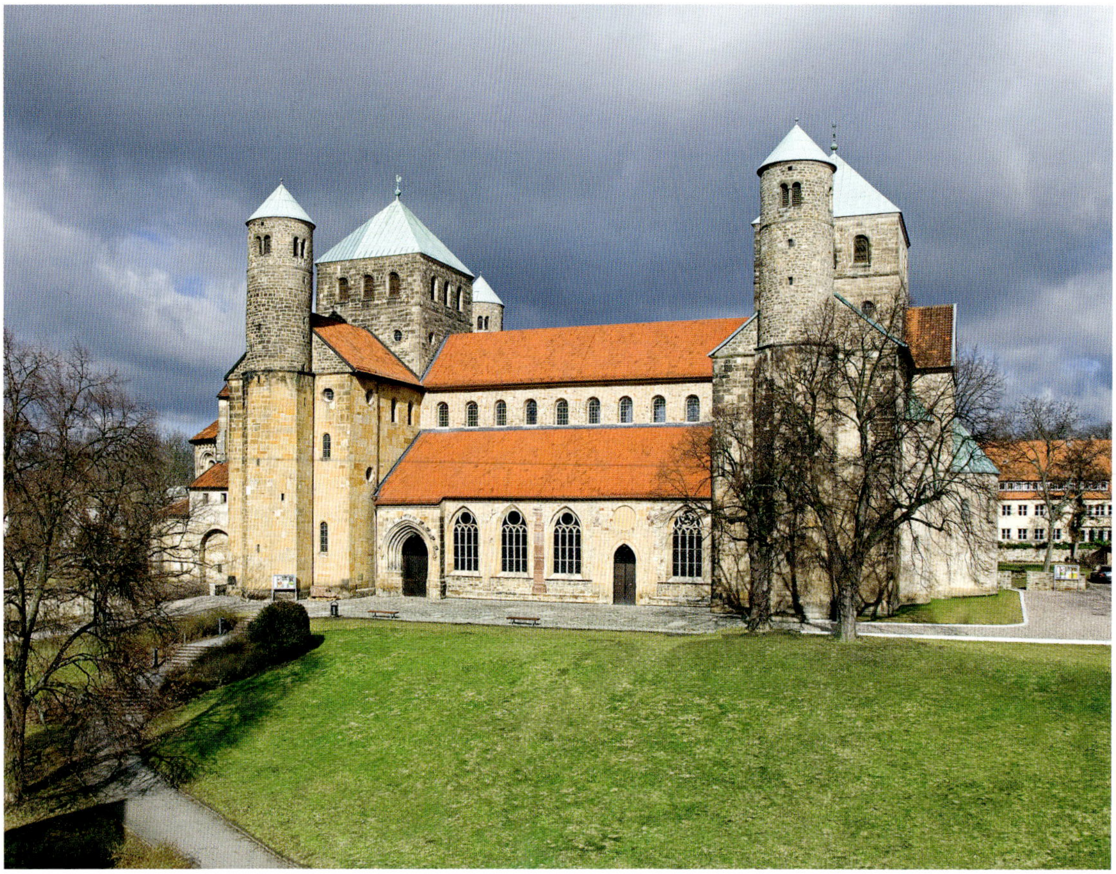

2

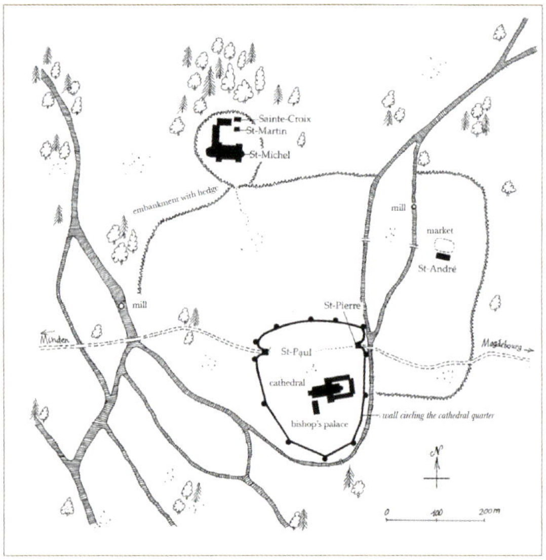

3

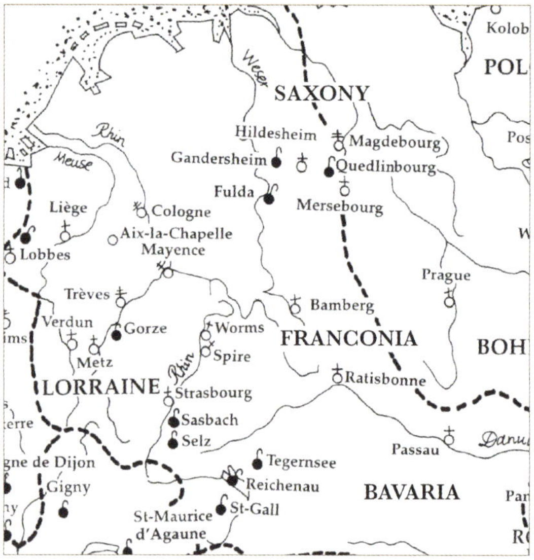

4

2. *St. Michael's of Hildesheim.*

3. *Map of Hildesheim in the year 1000.*

4. *Ottonian Saxony.*

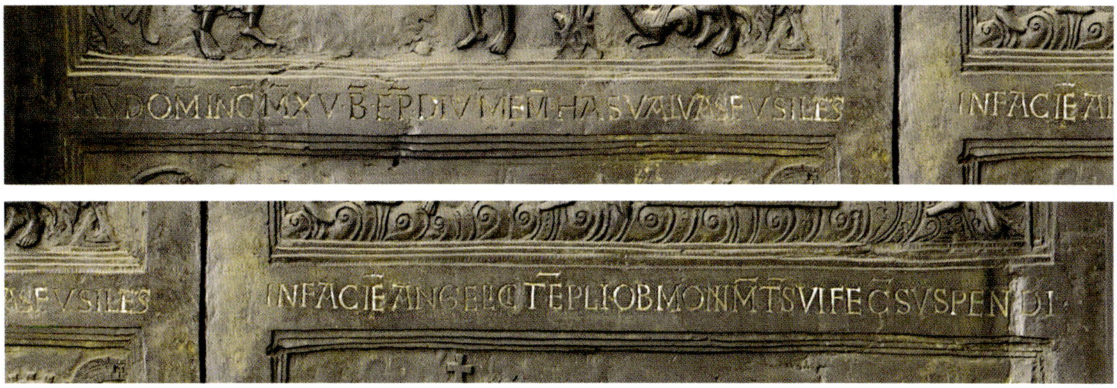

5

5. *The door's dedicatory inscription.*

to the north as well as craftsmen's shops. The great east–west communication route running north of the town entered the enclosure by means of two gates, each with a chapel on the second floor: the western one was dedicated to St. Paul; the eastern one, dedicated to St. Peter, opened directly onto the river crossing, either a ford (or bridge), of the Treibe [Kruse 1987, 108].

North of the city walls, work was in progress on a second urban center developing around St. Michael's Monastery and its two adjoining chapels dedicated to St. Martin and Sainte-Croix. This new district was protected by a circular hedge which would later enclose the dwellings around St. Andrew's Church and its adjoining market. It is possible, as well, that another settlement was established north of the enclosure around the mills already installed there. It was in this small episcopal village in full economic and architectural development that the oldest historiated bronze door of the Middle Ages was created. But for which building and for what purpose?

The question of the initial location of the door has been much debated, an issue that requires distinguishing between Bernward's original intent and what became of the door later. The most recent historical and archeological research reinforces the old hypothesis that the door was first conceived for the Church of St. Michael, perhaps for the south entrance [Schütz 1994; Kruse 2012], which is precisely what my iconographic analysis tends to confirm. A monumental work, included in a devotional building program, the door would thus have faced the town of Hildesheim.

However, there is nothing to confirm that the door was ever installed in the church [Schulz-Mons 2010, 280–330]. Bernard died before St. Michael's construction was finished; he had time only to consecrate the liturgical choir and crypt. Moreover, a fire destroyed the church shortly after its completion. The only reliable evidence for the fate of the door's two wings comes from the fact that Bernward's successor, Godehard, was so struck by their beauty and grandeur that he requested that they be installed in Hildesheim Cathedral in the town center, rather than outside the walls.

Viewers standing in front of the bronze door are struck first by its massiveness before appreciating its visual impact. It is extremely large—more than 4.70 meters high by 2.40 meters wide—an immense metal surface reflecting light. Only a bronze craftsman could estimate its weight; its 3.7 tons exceed what a human being can imagine in relation to their own body. The door is a permanent and structural part of the architectural elements surrounding it. What is especially impressive is the fact that each of the door's two wings was cast as a single piece rather than assembled by riveting, as was the practice for many ancient and early Christian doors, even those later than Hildesheim's.

Each of the massive, hinged wings has a large frame enclosing eight panels delineated by narrow ledges on which are carved figures in low and high relief, a door handle in the form of a lion's head, and a band bearing a dedicatory inscription. Hans Drescher's research [Drescher 1988], recently confirmed by epigraphic studies, proved that the latter were contemporary with the casting (fig. 5).

The bronze door of Hildesheim, conceived as a component of the monumental complex rather than as furnishings, is an integral part of the church, defining the space as much as the space defines it. Its location designates it as a threshold controlling access to an ecclesiastic space that it can just as easily close as open. Made of pure bronze rather than wood, a less noble or durable material, the door is incorruptible, highly resistant, and potentially eternal. The outstanding qualities of this metal, associated with Christ, are mentioned by Gregory the Great in his Homilies on Ezekiel, a work Bernward had in his library [Gallistl 1999, 109]. Its cost, power, and immutable place in time are signs of the authority the door embodies, an authority less related to the building itself than to the structured community it protects and of which the bishop is both leader and pastor. In the same way that the powerful figures of Roman antiquity had the signs of their might and ancestral prestige engraved in monumental stone, it is in the monumentality of the bronze that the Christian pontiff engraved his name and memory (fig. 5).

> AN(NO) DOM(INI),INC(ARNATIONIS) MXV
> B(ERNWARDUS) EP(ISCOPUS) DIVE MEM(ORIAE)
> HAS VALVAS FUSILES/IN FACIE(M) ANGELICI
> TE(M)PLI OB MONIM(EN)T(UM) SUI FECIT SESPENDI

> In the year of our Lord Incarnate 1015,
> Bishop Bernward of blessed memory had the
> two wings of the door cast and placed on
> the facade of the temple of the angels in his
> perpetual commemoration.

The door is a signifier not only because of its location, its weight, the material of which it is made, and the message it delivers but also because of its formal configuration (fig. 1). The symmetrical play between the two wings is so perfect, the continuity of the inscription underscoring the panels so patent, that the two wings convey the image of a functionally articulated whole. Furthermore, nothing disturbs the overall systematic and plastically homogenous sequence of the sixteen historiated scenes, with the result that the Hildesheim door is a signifier not only as an object per se but also as a coherent, symbolic narrative. Being and narrating merge into a single discursive system and the entire door, as a unity, offers itself to the gaze as a gigantic sign.

In addition to its signifying qualities, the bronze door also compels our admiration on technical grounds. Its closest models are the door of Aachen, cast in Charlemagne's time, and the door of the Mainz Cathedral that Archbishop Willigis had made before 1009 by a certain Master Bérenger [Mende 1994, 25–26]. Those doors, however, were not cast as one solid piece but consisted instead of a frame in which were mounted panels without images and door handles in the form of lion heads.

In an effort to explain Bernward's exceptional achievement, it has been suggested that the bishop possessed a copy of Ar-Razi's *Secreta secretorum*, a work of practical alchemy treating metallic salts, a hypothesis difficult to defend. No translation of this treatise is known to have existed at the beginning of the eleventh century. It is true, however, that Adam of Bremen relates that an alchemist from Greece was practicing his art shortly afterward at the court of Archbishop Adalbert of Bremen (1045–1072), which suggests that Byzantine craftsmen may have introduced certain Eastern skills to northern Germany [Gallistl 1999, 108]. In addition, it is possible that the art of casting had been perfected in foundries of Germanic bells, even though the monk Theophilous described this activity only a century later [Drescher 1993, 337–339].

In any case, in the Hildesheim workshop each of the sixteen historiated panels was sketched, drawn to scale, molded in high relief in a wax block, then assembled within the framework of the door wings, also in wax. Once assembled, the entire piece was coated with a layer of slurry reinforced by iron lattice work whose trace remains visible on the back of the door; then it was fired [Drescher 1993, 339–340]. Into this clay mold, buried deeply in the ground to provide resistance to internal pressure, several tons of molten metal were poured all at once. The process either succeeded or failed altogether, producing either impressive high reliefs or irretrievable loss of material in the areas most remote from the pouring point, or subjected to some disruption in the casting process caused by air bubbles.

Once the casting was completed, the cleaning process could begin by first removing the bronze from its dark shell and then polishing the metal. This was followed by the meticulous work of finishing: scraping, chipping, skillful chiseling and scratching. The traces of this labor endure even today in the extreme finesse of the morphological detail of the historiated panels, such as in clothes, plants, and architectural elements [Drescher 1993]. The entire process was completed with remarkable speed. Thangmar, Bernward's biographer, who recounts the entirety of artistic production linked to the bishop until 1008, makes no mention of this ambitious project; moreover, the cooling of the molten metal undoubtedly took a long time, at least a year. By 1015 the door was completed.

The modeling of the bronze sculptures was partly determined by the height of the wings and by the angle from which they would be viewed. The higher the panels, the more prominent or rounded the sculptures, especially the heads of the divine figures, thus rendering them more visible from below. The different height of the reliefs does not, however, diminish in any way the iconographic expressiveness. Regardless of their placement, each of the bronze panels contain more or less the same number of people, plants or architectural elements, as well as about the same number of signifying details and profusion of analogical signs and symbols, which we will study at length. Certain features are very small, at times measuring only a few centimeters, such that they would be barely perceptible if they did not usually appear in graphic form, modeled or engraved in low relief on the metal. The lines forming these details are more clearly visible in strong lateral lighting or under particularly intense lights, conditions that would have been favored by the original position of the door with the historiated side facing outward, all the more so if it was indeed intended for the south entrance, the sunlit side of the Abbey Church of St. Michael.

Although the modeling of the door enhances the legibility of the iconographic discourse, this syntactic function does not diminish the particularly expressive power of the figures. The high relief lends them a marked vitality and intense presence, felt especially when viewed at eye level. That impression is borne out by the touch, perhaps of children's hands, that through the centuries have polished the heads of Abel and his lamb, of the infant Jesus or of the animals that warmed him in the manger. The lower panels have attracted hands as much as eyes, eliciting an empathy that contributes to the iconographic discourse.

The interconnection between structure, spatial organization and modeling, and the unfolding of meaning testifies to a remarkable level of rigor in the planning and aesthetic execution of the historiated panels. By taking significant technical and financial risks and by giving so much attention and care to the production of the bronze door, Bernward belongs to a long tradition of builders.

The inhabitants of Hildesheim around the year 1000 were doubtless unaware that a thousand years earlier a similarly imposing door had been built at the entrance to the Roman Curia; although they may have heard tell from travelers or their bishop of the silver door, embellished with precious stones, that gave access to the Basilica of St. Peter in Rome. Rare, costly, and permeated with collective memory, metal doors appear as signs of political supremacy, of a sacred power of government that Charlemagne claimed when he had bronze doors placed in his Palatine chapel, a power also claimed by Archbishop Willigis when he referred to Charlemagne in the dedication of his own cathedral door in Mainz [Mende 1994, 25–26].

The Hildesheim bronze door affirms Bernward's memory and implies a similar desire on the part of the bishop to present himself as the leader of a community. However, since the panels are historiated—which was unprecedented—with a biblical narrative, they also recall Bernward's apostolic mission. As an aristocrat and Christian pastor, the bishop belongs fully to the culture of his world and his time. At the beginning of the eleventh century, the political strategy of the Ottonian emperors was based on the ideal of the *renovatio imperii*. Perpetuating the Christian Roman Empire, they protected monastic reforms and promoted evangelizing missions east of their borders [Oexle 1993].

Bernward too embraces this *translatio*, but he understands it on an even larger time scale. An indication of his personal participation in history appears in the dedication appended to the bronze door. The inscription describes the church destined to house the door as *templum*. While the term *templum* was sometimes used in the Middle Ages to designate an ecclesial building, in the patristic tradition it refers primarily to the Old Testament sanctuary preceding and announcing the Church founded by Christ, a prophetic prefiguration to which the historiated narrative of the door gives great importance.

Bernward's motivation is more explicit in the charter he edited to explain the context and reasons for his monastic foundation. As successor to the apostles, the bishop claims a direct filiation with the visionary founders and biblical builders who contributed to the establishment of God's kingdom on earth, and especially with Solomon, builder of the temple in Jerusalem:

> Clear as daylight is the evidence of the holy Solomon, who after building the temple of God, cleansed himself in accordance with the laws of his religion, and brought himself closer to God by participating in cultic mysteries, he who was found to be without equal as a penitent. To all of them God revealed the special nature of their merits through their respective manner of deeds, so that in time they will remain different from all others, always, by virtue of merit and deed, and in eternity they will be equal to the angels . . . I wanted to carry out in deed that which I had long been planning in my heart, that is, I wanted to prepare a felicitous memorial to my name as someone who had built churches, instituted the service of God in them, and donated all his possessions to the Lord. Now God's decrees are hidden but always just. I therefore began, with the joyous consent of the faithful, to construct a new house of God, and in doing so both fulfilled my own promise and served the best interests of Christendom, to the praise and glory of the name of the Lord, by settling monks there, beloved of God. (from the *Testament of Bernward*, edited by Wolfram Von Den Steinen; I provide a full translation at the end of this chapter.)

It is therefore impossible to understand Bernward's work if we underestimate the spiritual dimension of his activities in favor of too political a reading: these two aspects are, for the bishop as for his contemporaries, intimately linked. This desire to be counted among the builders of Christ's church on earth is made clear by Bernward's personality, which is less accessible through his letters and charters than in the biography his former teacher Thangmar dedicated to him (*Vita Bernwardi,* MGH, SS IV, 758–785) [Schuffels 1993].

Bernward was born around 960 into an aristocratic Saxon family. He was educated in the Ottonian cathedral schools, which trained not only future clerics but also children of great families destined for a secular career, as prescribed by Charlemagne two centuries earlier. Bernward began his apprenticeship at Hildesheim, where two future emperors, Otto III and Henry II, would be educated [Crivello 2004, 43].

Under the strict discipline of the schoolmaster Thangmar, he studied the liberal arts of the *trivium* and *quadrivium*, that is, the foundations of literary and mathematical knowledge. The quality of that apprenticeship was undoubtedly remarkable. Like so many Germanic dioceses, Hildesheim had a long scholarly tradition, setting the standard for excellence in Saxony. Its library owed its reputation to the many religious and secular works that Bishop Otwin brought from Italy in the second half of the tenth century [Wesenberg 1955, 11]. In addition, the episcopal city benefited from all the knowledge accumulated and reorganized during the Carolingian Renaissance, thanks to its succeeding prelates, who had been trained at Fulda, Corvey, or Reichenau [Riché 1983, 125–173; Tschan 1951, 7–15].

We shall not dwell too long on the intellectual and spiritual qualities, both remarkable and precocious, that Thangmar attributed to his student. Although there is no particular reason to doubt them, we can also recognize in them traits that would support a future hagiography. In addition, the *Vita*, begun during Bernward's lifetime, probably underwent later interpolations intended to promote the prelate's canonization in 1192 [Crivello 2004, 45]. One detail, however, has not escaped historians' attention. Thangmar mentions that the young Bernward studied what we would call crafts or mechanical skills: "He devoted himself to the study of simpler practical skills [*mechanicas*]. He first distinguished himself in writing [*scribendo*]; he also displayed acumen in the art of images [*picturam*, drawing or painting]; he excelled extraordinarily in the science of metallurgy [*fabrili*], in locksmithing [*arte clusoria*] and in all areas of building [*structura*], as well as most construction work [*aedificia*]."

The acquisition of these skills, not included in the classical liberal arts curriculum, was perhaps linked to Thangmar's particular competencies [Schuffels 1993, 29–30], but it also stems from the relationships Bernward had established with clerks working in the chancery and the scriptorium, as well as with artisans employed by the diocese, especially goldsmiths. From the second half of the tenth century, and in connection with the nearby mines of Goslar, Hildesheim's bishops had become accustomed to having some of the liturgical furnishings cast in precious metals [Wesenberg 1955, 13; Tschan 1951, 13–15]. Both the learned and technological traditions that Bernward embraced were therefore quite ancient and well-rooted in this small Saxon town.

Once his education in Hildesheim was completed, Bernward attended the prestigious cathedral school of Willigis in Mainz in order to broaden his theological knowledge. While there he was first anointed as deacon, then as priest; as many art historians have emphasized, he was also able to observe the cathedral's many ongoing building projects. It was perhaps there that the young man broadened his knowledge of casting [Tschan 1951, 30–31].

After staying with his grandfather, Count Athelboro, Bernward joined the court of Otto II and Theophano in 977. Following in the footsteps of his uncle Folcmar, he became imperial secretary and notary. Between 980 and 983 he accompanied Otto II to Italy, a journey that took him to Milan and Ravenna but also to Rome and even to the south of the peninsula. A leading figure—Bernward liked to call himself *aulicus scriba doctus*, learned court doctor—he was appointed tutor to the future Otto III in 987–88, then consecrated as bishop and assigned to the Hildesheim Cathedral on January 15, 993. Between September 996 and the end of 997, he obtained from the emperor a substantial land grant, the renewal of episcopal privileges, and in addition, the right of immunity and the right to choose the diocesan bailiff [Schuffels 1993, 33].

The years 1000 and 1001 were largely taken up by the conflict with Willigis of Mainz over the jurisdiction of the Gandersheim Monastery [Schuffels 1993, 33–35]. The quarrel was so complex and tense that it led Bernward to return to Rome in January and February 1001 to plead his case with Otto III. The issue was eventually settled in his favor, although without resolving the problem, by a synod under the aegis of Pope Sylvester II, also known as Gerbert of Aurillac, a great scholar and brilliant mathematician of his time.

Thangmar's narrative allows the reader to follow

the peregrinations of Hildesheim's bishop, sometimes associated with diplomatic missions, to Pavia, Vercelli, and Saint-Maurice-d'Agaune in the Valais. Bernward made another important trip a few years later, in 1006–7. Beginning as a military campaign in Flanders, this long journey would become a pilgrimage, taking Bernward to the royal abbey of Saint-Denis, to Saint-Martin-de-Tours, and perhaps even to Saint-Benoît-sur-Loire [Parisse].

Back in Germany, Bernward actively devoted himself to the fortifications and urban planning of Hildesheim, as well as founding St. Michael's Monastery. The first stone was laid in 1010, but the monastic church would not be consecrated until 1022, the year of the bishop's death. In the meantime, Bernward became a patron of the arts on a scale comparable to that of his contemporaries, Willigis of Mainz, Mainwerk of Paderborn, or even Emperor Henry II in Bamberg.

While the devotional work of Hildesheim's bishop is not surprising in itself—every donor expects to benefit from the support of the religious community he has founded or helped during his lifetime—it is nonetheless particularly varied and original. Several of the manuscripts Bernward commissioned for St. Michael's Monastery fortunately still survive, preserved today in the Hildesheim Cathedral museum: a richly illuminated book of the Gospels (DS 33), a lavishly decorated Gospel (DS 18), and a Bible ornamented with an illuminated frontispiece (DS 61). In addition, between 1007 and 1022, the bishop commissioned the sculpting and casting of some important liturgical furnishings: a silver crucifix and a small crucifix of bronze, two partially gilded silver candelabra, as well as the famous bronze column inspired in form, if not in size, by Trajan's Column in Rome (fig. 10). Decorated with scenes from the public life of Christ, this column was originally placed behind the altar of the Cross in St. Michael's Church [Gallistl 1993]. Finally, the bishop also had his own sarcophagus sculpted and engraved, to be placed in the crypt under the west choir [Kahsnitz 1993].

Like his contemporaries, Bernward was keenly aware of the importance of *memoria*. As evidenced by the carefully selected dedications he had appended to his oeuvre, he was anxious to secure his salvation, and perhaps also to lay the groundwork for future sainthood [Wulf 2008]. His monogram appears virtually everywhere in St Michael's, even on the foundation stone, discovered at the beginning of the twentieth century. It was this extraordinary artistic and building production that provided the context for the genesis of the bronze door.

Like every aristocrat of his time, the bishop of Hildesheim involved himself extensively in the choice of works and craftsmen, going so far as to control the form and content of his initiatives [Bergmann 1985], as evidenced by his dedicatory inscriptions. The degree of his involvement appears in many aspects of the bronze door: numerous features resonate with his intellectual education, scientific knowledge, breadth of reading, the typological and aesthetic models he encountered during his travels, and his access both to manuscripts and monumental works. Still, it remains difficult to determine his precise role in the making of the bronze door.

As stated earlier, there is no doubt that the bishop acted as commissioner, financier, creator, and overseer of the enterprise. Thangmar duly underscored his knowledge of construction techniques but was Bernward the prime designer and maker of the work itself? The dedications stating that he "made" (*fecit*), or that he "constructed" (*aedificavit*) the door do not guarantee his technical contribution, since they refer primarily to his role as sponsor. In light of these uncertainties, it would seem judicious to concur with the prudent reserve of most historians. However, in his glowing portrait of Bernward, at once conventional and original, Thangmar stated that the bishop practiced both the art of writing and that of drawing images. Some have attributed to him the miniatures of his Gospel Book, but even if this is not the case, his involvement in the manuscript program is beyond doubt [Kingsley 2014]. If he did not actually make the wax models of the door, for which as many as six different modelers have been identified [Mende 1994, 31], this excerpt from the *Vita* allows for the hypothesis that he himself may have drawn, if only schematically, the composition as well as the formal outline of the various bronze panels. This inference is not drawn merely for the sake of attribution. Rather, it permits the explanation of the impressive complexity and radical organicity of the door's discourse. The expressiveness of line and the signifying force of both forms and composition depend inherently on an idea and a plastic discourse coherent from beginning to end, together with the intensity of perfectly chiseled and insightful pastoral preaching. The power of these traits is the equivalent of a Christian theological treatise whose meaning is embedded in the depth of its successive layers. Such a result could have been obtained only by a quasi-symbiotic complicity between the creator of the concept and the craftsman, implying perfect articulation between the idea and its agency, and by very close supervision of the modeling procedures as well as of the finishing touches to the bronze panels.

Each wing displays eight panels (fig. 1). They are rectangular in format and the narrative composition is clear and rational, with well-defined figures against a neutral background. All historians agree that the panels show the influence of the cycle of Genesis as illustrated in the great Carolingian Bibles. In addition to the fact that Bernward might have seen one of these manuscripts on his journey through Tours in 1007, the philological studies of Karl Nordenfalk [1971] have shown that a Bible from Tours provided the basic text for the bishop's Bible.

Resembling an immense open book, the narrative and chronological development of the bronze door begins on the upper left of the left wing with the creation of Adam and Eve. As in the other fifteen panels, the scene shows a great unity of time and place. It functions in a mode less diegetic than mimetic, which means that it does not so much "tell" the biblical story as it "shows" the viewer an identifiable episode. Intelligible independently of each other, the panels therefore exist first individually, constituting systems of autonomous signification.

Once the beginning point of the door's narrative is identified, viewers might be tempted to let their gaze glide horizontally toward the uppermost panel of the right wing. In doing so, they would be impressed by the imposing figure of Christ risen from Hell and would understand that this is a *terminus ad quem* related to the New Testament and not a scene placed in chronological continuity with panel 1. The spectators' gaze then descends along the left wing, recognizing the episodes of the Old Testament that Bernward wanted to have represented, such as original sin. Viewers then resume the course of their reading, from bottom to top of the right wing, discovering episodes from the New Testament along the way. The iconographic program is thus split into two historical time periods oriented from top to bottom and then from bottom to top (fig. 6). This second reading mode, U-shaped, literal, and chronological, has determined the numbering of the panels now uniformly adopted by art historians (fig. 7).

Viewers have a third reading option, to let the gaze circulate horizontally between the panels belonging to the same register (fig. 8). This axial symmetry is underscored by formal analogies, especially noticeable between panels 6 and 11; placed at the same level, besides identical ring holders in the form of a lion's head, they present two "mothers with child," whose visual impact is enhanced by their proximity.

The elaboration of an iconographic discourse in interconnected panels was not in itself a new idea in Christian art. It had already been used for the wooden door of the fifth-century Santa Sabina Basilica in Rome, a church that Bernward knew since he had lived on the Aventine at the time of his second Roman stay. There are other, later examples such as the mid-ninth-century St. Ambrose altar, wrought in precious metal in Milan, another city Bernward had visited. In both arrangements, the interrelated placement of the scenes constructs part of the meaning: it is still discernable in Santa Sabina despite the disorganization and approximate reassembling of the wooden panels [Kemp 1994, ch. 7; Spieser 1991], and it is clearly visible in the altar where the spatial distribution of the scenes guides the direction of the gaze, making it converge toward Christ [Capponi 1996]. The same ambitious control of the gaze determines the configuration of the bronze door. Although it is admirably inscribed into this programmatic tradition, its originality lies elsewhere, in the combinatorial effect it has with historical chronology.

The idea of devoting each wing to a single Testament, and then of articulating the two wings in order to produce a new meaning, comes from a very ancient discursive technique based on the model of interpretation that the Church Fathers used in order to clarify the biblical text: the *concordia veteris et novi testamenti*, or biblical typology. This system of correspondence had already been used in Rome's fifth-century mural paintings [Garrison 1953–62, IV, 201 *ff.*], in the great Carolingian iconographic programs [Lammers 1971], and by the Ottonians, at least since the end of the tenth century [Hughes 2001, 185]. With Bernward's door, biblical typology unfolds for the first time in a monumental work of art.

A quick glance at the panels suffices to identify the scenes and grasp their main reading keys. Previous historians have also identified them, insofar as the essential core of historiography focuses on identifying the scenes and their iconographic origins on the one hand, and on the typological articulation between the two wings—original sin and the Crucifixion that effaces it; Eve and Mary's pregnancies; Abel's death and the conception of Jesus. Yet historians may have failed to point out the extent to which the narrative framework of the door was itself organically structured.

On the left wing are eight episodes portraying the history of Adam and Eve and their children, Cain and Abel (fig. 1). Beyond its linearity, the Old Testament narrative is articulated in pairs of panels. It begins with the presentation of humanity, featuring the creation and Presentation of Eve to Adam (panels 1 and 2); it continues with original sin, represented in two phases, the transgression and its denial (panels 3 and 4); sanction follows with the expulsion from Eden and entrance into the non-Edenic world on earth, as obverse and reverse of the same drama (panels 5 and 6). The left wing's last panels tell the story of

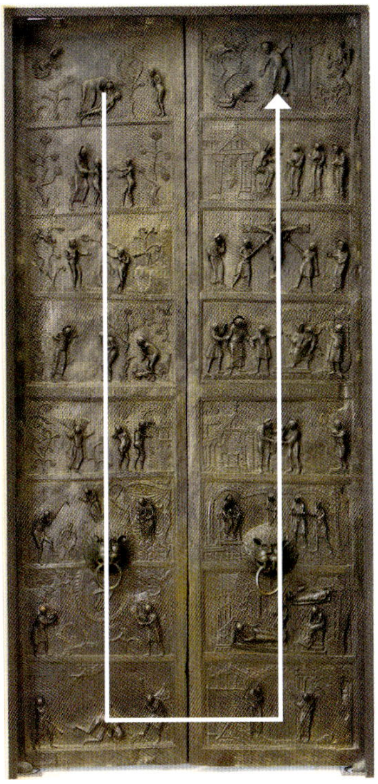

6

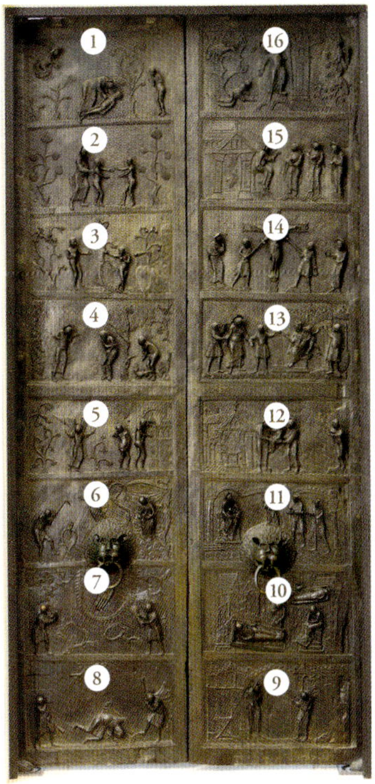

7

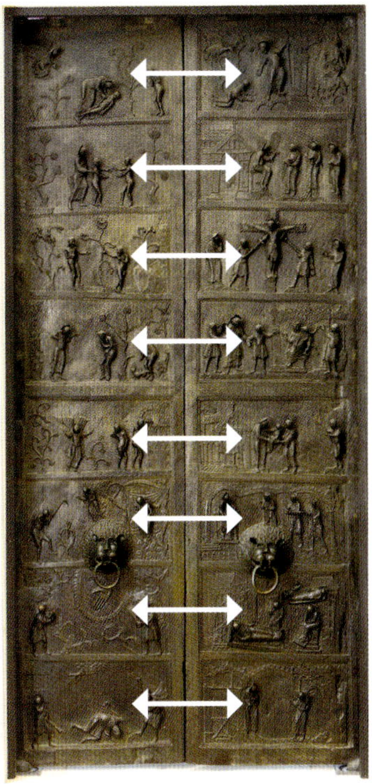

8

6. *Direction in which the story is read.*

7. *Conventional numbering.*

8. *Typological relations between the door leaves.*

Adam and Eve's two sons, concluding the narrative with Abel's death, the first in history (panels 7 and 8).

The same binary structure is found in the panels of the right wing. The Incarnation is depicted in two scenes, the Annunciation and the Nativity (panels 9 and 10). The creation of a religious community around Christ also unfolds in two phases, the Epiphany and the Presentation at the Temple (panels 11 and 12). The ensuing death of Christ includes both the Trial and the Crucifixion (panels 13 and 14). Finally, the Resurrection is told in two complementary episodes, showing the disappearance and then the reappearance of Christ's body in the scenes of the visit to the sepulcher and the Apparition of Christ to Mary Magdalene (panels 15 and 16).

These eight pairs of panels can be seen as four clearly visible rectangles since the wings themselves are divided horizontally in half by the inscription that runs through the middle of the door. The four central themes of the Economy of Salvation are displayed here: sinful humanity, death as punishment, incarnation as the foundation of a new community, and sacrifice as a condition for eternal life. These themes can themselves be reduced to two essential notions embodied by each of the two wings: the Fall and Salvation. Thus, the bronze door addresses the simple and fundamental question of the nature of death.

To answer this question, Bernward discloses the reasons for and the interconnection of the Fall and the Resurrection, offering viewers a long visual journey through the history of the world and humanity. Each form, each substance, each composition, and each movement is a vector of reflection and a bearer of meaning resonating with wide-ranging scientific and theological knowledge. This profound hermeneutical unveiling was familiar to clerics and monks who had been trained in the study of the scriptures. Yet I would argue that it does not appear to be out of reach of ordinary believers. Indeed, the knowledge underpinning the iconographic program is not the same as that required to understand the images. The first comes from impressive intellectual learning, the second emerges from the gaze of the spectator who, by examining the panels at length, can grasp their rigorous syntactic logic. The process is certainly daunting. Bernward may have conceived the coherence of the door at varying levels of complexity, but he may just as well have anticipated the interaction between the faithful and their surroundings. Perhaps the *illiteratti*, those who could not read Latin, were guided by clerical teaching. Or perhaps the common knowledge progressively organized around the images was instrumental in enlightening the members of the community.

Such hypotheses take nothing away from my argument. The door speaks to every Christian, showing them the path to liberation from death, which may be achieved by adhering in full consciousness to communal practices and to the personal transformations they bring about. In addition, the images develop a Christian spirit that responds less to the expectations of monks or clerics than to those of lay people within the ecclesial community. Bernward is a bishop, and far from asserting the superiority of his scholarly erudition or displaying an excessive ambition to be remembered, he offers the faithful a profoundly generous pastoral guide, serving first and foremost their own needs. Unlike ephemeral images, this visual discourse is so powerful that it could serve as a guide to Christians for a lifetime of contemplation and meditation. As such, it is not different from the great programmatic works found in early medieval manuscripts or murals.

The form I have chosen for this work should not, therefore, come as a surprise. The breadth and careful progression of the analysis respect, as much as possible, the intention and working mode of the bronze door such as it was conceived. Nor should anyone be surprised that I have included so few scholarly references in my analysis. My predecessors have unveiled some of the major aspects of its iconography, but they have not been interested in Bernward's discursive strategies, nor have they delved into the deepest ontological meaning of the images. Due to their research methods, they have compared a body of knowledge and identified the convergences suggested by the texts, but they have not truly looked into the monumental work for itself.

My research is different in nature. It considers the door as an autonomous discourse, concentrating on the semiotic functioning of the images; that is, on the extraordinary manipulation of forms and signifying temporalities put forward by the bishop of Hildesheim. And if in my analysis I did not think it appropriate or courteous to underscore what my predecessors had not seen, it is because they could not see what they were not looking for. However, I will gladly state that I am not the first to have identified the scenes of the sixteen bronze panels, nor to have understood the issues of the wings' placement and their functioning. By the same token, I readily acknowledge the importance of the work that has been done on Bernward's personality and the context in which he commissioned his works. Without this research, mine would have been impossible.

The historiography of the door goes back a long way. It was first treated as a topic of art history when Adolf Bertram compared it to the door of Santa Sabina in Rome in a comparative study published in 1892. This filiation, supplemented by others, was never questioned. In 1907, Franz Dibelius dedicated the first monograph to the door, *Die Bernwardstür zu Hildesheim*, a work still relevant in many respects. He identified the sixteen scenes and proposed an analysis of its structural and typological narrative—later clarified by Michael Fehr's 1978 dissertation—which is still widely accepted today. He also defended the idea that the door was conceived as two joined wings for the Monastery of St. Michael, with which most historians agree (except for some scholars who favor a hypothesis proposed by Rudolf Wesenberg in 1955).

In addition to the destination and placement of the door, part of the historiography has concentrated on the potential literary sources of the images. Dibelius suggested associating them with Slavonic texts; Gisela Nowak has added some Hebrew apocryphal texts, Konrad Algermissen a corpus of Germanic texts. This approach is legitimate, but it seems to me quite futile in this case, since the Bible and the apocryphal Gospel of the Pseudo-Matthew, the very same one that was put into verse by Hrostvitha of Gandersheim around 950, are sufficient to explain the images. In the same way, the theological contents of the panels often, and quite commonly for the early Middle Ages, converge with the great tradition of biblical interpretation established by the Church Fathers, in particular with two great texts redacted by St. Augustine, both known to Bernward: the first on Genesis, *De Genesi ad litteram*, and the second on the Church, *De Civitate Dei*. This patristic tradition is surprisingly absent from Aloys Butzkamm's recent work, a useful but anachronistic pastoral commentary published in 2004.

The debate around questions of identification and iconographic filiation is clearly richer. No one has questioned the presence of Roman references on the bronze panels, although they have been studied mainly with regard to the composition of the images rather than their iconographic content. New research appeared during the 1950s with Francis Tschan's and Rudolf Wesenberg's books and later, in 1966, with Ursula Storm's dissertation, which has, among other merits, that of giving the vegetation more attention than her predecessors. However, the real turning point in this historiography occurred in the 1980s. Following Herbert Kessler's landmark studies on the connection between the bronze door and certain Carolingian frontispieces, and Gerd Bauer's historiographical synthesis, the debate essentially became an evaluation of the Anglo-Saxon and Carolingian influence on the door. William Tronzo (1983) treated the issue especially well, as did Soren Von Kaspersen (1988), whose article seems to me to offer the most conclusive conceptual approach to the historiographical question. Kurd Fleige's article (1993), more questionable because it is indemonstrable, suggests a reverse filiation between the Hildesheim door, completed in 1015, and the door of San Zeno in Verona, whose lost original would go back to the year 1000.

Other contemporary studies have sought to situate the program of the door in political or conjunctural contexts that might clarify its nature. However, these suggestions turn out to be of little use in understanding the level of discourse I am studying, since they historicize universal issues. In his 1993 article, Reinhart Staats cites a dynastic quarrel in order to identify the king in panel 13 as Henry II; Adam Cohen and Anne Derbes, in their 2001 publication, attribute to Bernward a misogyny exacerbated by his difficult relationship with the female abbey of Gandersheim. Otto Karl Werckmeister's anthropological approach suggests that the door's two wings mirror a process of transformation from the savage to the sacramental, which has no connection with the theological content of the sixteen panels and the symbolic use of the vegetal and architectural settings.

Many of the important articles dealing with the iconographic debate come from two major collective works, the first edited in 1988 by Martin Gosebruch and Frank N. Steigerwald, *Bernwardische Kunst*, and the second, even richer, presented as a volume appended to the catalog of an exhibition organized in 1993 at Hildesheim, *Bernward von Hildesheim und das Zeitalter der Ottonen*, under the supervision of Thomas Giessmann, Arne Eggebrecht, and Michael Brandt, to whom we owe a number of syntheses. These collective works have the virtue of offering a contextualization that is indispensable to understanding the door. They also include valuable information about the cathedral of Hildesheim, the Church of St. Michael, the urban setting of that episcopal town (Hartmut Boockmann) as well as the history of the techniques in working precious metal (Hermann Fillitz) and casting in Ottonian times (Hans Drescher).

Biographical works about Bernward are equally useful. The oldest, in English, is by Francis Tschan [1951], the only relevant work not written in German, to which one should add the work of Gerhard Oexle [1995], who skillfully puts into perspective the bishop's memorializing euergetism, as well as the interesting studies by Günther Binding [1987; 1988] on Bernward's scientific background and Thomas Vogtherr's remarkable 1993 synthesis, extended by the publications of Hans Jacob Schuffels [1993] and Uwe Wolff [1996].

The relationship between the program, the monumental complex containing it, and the Ottonian liturgy has been the object of a particularly erudite study by Bernhard Gallistl. In addition, Gallistl has offered one of the best popularizations to date, among the dozen or so of little scholarly interest that have been published on the door, the bronze column, St. Michael's Church, and Hildesheim's cathedral. Finally, this impressive bibliographical corpus should not fail to include research dedicated to medieval doors—such as that by Hermann Leisinger in 1956, Ute Götz's 1971 dissertation, and Ursula Mende's 1994 book—and to medieval metalwork, especially Ittai Weinryb's studies [2013; 2016]. Also worthy of acknowledgement are general works on Ottonian literary culture and art, notably those by Hans Jantzen [1947], Henry Mayr-Harting, Rosamond McKitterick, and Jennifer Kingsley [2014]. Among the great works on Christian iconography, the following were particularly useful to me: *Eva und Maria* by Ernst Guldan [1966] and *Ikonologie der Genesis* by Hans Martin von Erffa [1995].

Last, many works published on the occasion of St. Michael's millennium take into consideration the archeological excavations done in 2006, which help to put into perspective the historiographical analyses of the building and Bernward's artistic productions. Special mention should be made of *1000 Jahre St. Michael in Hildesheim* [2012].

All this research has greatly broadened my understanding of the door, providing the framework within which my own inquiry could unfold. The iconographic interpretations I suggest rest primarily and systematically on analysis of the images as well as on the biblical text to which they refer. Only then will these interpretations be placed in relation to other literary or visual contexts supporting them, thus reinscribing them into the historiography.

Bernward's Text of Foundation

Every creature with the name "human being" was made by his Creator in such a way that, in accordance with the law of nature, he prefers to serve his Creator rather than the creature. It is true that association with things distracts him; yet this fundamental constitution, to the extent that the person is in possession of his reason, keeps guiding him back to the path of his original destiny. However, the greater the corrections a person experiences by the grace of God, the more fervently he feels united to God in all things. This would not be possible if God did not draw everyone toward Himself with his mighty hand. Thus the succoring mercy of God finds its expression in the human longing for grace, and adapts itself to the individual person. If we look for examples of this we immediately find a divine answer: after Adam's fall and the long age of exile Abraham believed the Lord, and precisely that was counted to him for righteousness. By contrast Moses, who gave the Law, became a leader and teacher of the people of Israel both by God's outreaching grace and through his own merit. And Elijah, worker of miracles, gave evidence of a similar holiness in that he did not experience the limit of human years but was carried away in a fiery chariot to eternal judgment. It surpasses our understanding, and we would never be finished if we wanted to penetrate these questions more deeply with our reason. Enough evidence is found in the example of David, who with a strong hand rose up mightily in battle. Clear as daylight is the evidence of the holy Solomon, who after building the temple of God, cleansed himself in accordance with the laws of his religion, and brought himself closer to God by participating in cultic mysteries, he who was found to be without equal as a penitent. To all of them God revealed the special nature of their merits through their respective manner of deeds, so that in time they will remain different from all others, always, by virtue of merit and deed, and in eternity they will be equal to the angels.

In view of this I, Bernward, appointed bishop by God's election and not of my own merit, have given long thought to how I, learned court clerk, tutor and keeper of documents of Emperor Otto III of blessed memory, might be deserving of heaven, by what architecture of merit, by what achievement. Seized by God's grace, trembling at the excess of my sins, and at the same time filled with longing for divine grace, I considered first one thing, then another, as a means to satisfy eternal mercy and achieve salvation for my soul. But with my modest resources I had to fear that whatever I might intend, I would either not be able to begin it at all or in any case would never be able to complete it. Nevertheless the wish to carry out my intention grew stronger and stronger inside me, even if my circumstances at the time did not allow me to undertake anything. But behold, God's will and ancient decree singled me out to be raised up to the glorious throne of a bishop. And so that the flock of the Lord would not be thrown into confusion for lack of a shepherd, or our Mother Church become a widow, as it were, the Spirit of Peace caused everyone to be of one heart and one mind at the election of the new bishop. Then, having ascended the throne of the church of Bennopolis [Hildesheim], I wanted to carry out in deed that which I had long been planning in my heart, that is, I wanted to prepare a felicitous memorial to my name as someone who had built churches, instituted the service of God in them, and donated all his possessions to the Lord. Now God's decrees are hidden but always just. I therefore began, with the joyous consent of the faithful, to construct a new house of God, and in doing so both fulfilled my own promise and served the best interests of Christendom, to the praise and glory of the name of the Lord, by settling monks there, beloved of God. However, when the foundations of the building had been laid, and the outlines of the individual rooms were already visible, I was stricken with fever and was ill for five years, so that no digression into earthly matters—praise be to thee, Christ!—would delay the progress of the undertaking. But since nothing on earth occurs without a reason, I believe and trust that the Lord was chastising me with his chastisements, yet he did not deliver me up unto death, and thus prevented the work of my hope from being interrupted because of my absence. I caused monks to occupy this place, which was dedicated to God, the holy cross, the ever pure Virgin Mary and the holy archangel Michael. I united them here according to the principle that, being removed from the activity of this world as laid down in the rule of monks, they might be free of all hindrances of wordly duties.

Therefore, with the consent of the Lord and Emperor Henry and of my superior, the archbishop Erkanbald, whom I, together with my fellow brothers, consecrated as archbishop, I gave away everything I had inherited or acquired by my private means in wordly goods, estates, farms, lands, fields, pastures, waters, forests, meadows, churches, relics, books, gold, and silver, and whatever else there might be. Aside from what I bequeathed to the altar of the blessed Mary in the cathedral in form of golden crowns, chalices, candlesticks, vestments, and other paraments, I made over everything by the hand of my testamentary guardian to God and his saints for the use and benefit of the brothers. I have bequeathed it for the salvation of my aforementioned Lords and Emperors, of myself and my successors, as well as of all those from whom I have acquired inheritances, so that the servants of Christ, free of all earthly duties, secure in the protection of my successors, may enjoy peaceful times and devote themselves to the life of pious contemplation for the salvation of all men.

If, however, someone should come after me, cleric or lay person, who tries to infringe on this or is even so bold as to seize this property by force, I ban him with the sword of the Word of God and His saints; all curses will break upon him, all blessings flee from him. He will thus be blotted out in heaven and on earth and will have his part with Judas and with those who wanted to possess the temple of God as their inheritance. Moreover the heirs shall attempt, on the authorization of God and myself, to regain possession of the property when they see an intruder residing on their portion of the inheritance. And in order for it to remain stable and impregnable, all the people surrounding it must attempt at obtaining God's grace by means of constant prayers.

Written at Hildesheim, on the calends of November of the year of the Incarnation 1009 by Bernward, most venerable bishop of this church on the twenty-seventh year of his ordination.

(Translated by B. Gallistl and published in his article, "Bernward of Hildesheim: A Case of Self-planned Sainthood?" in *The Invention of Saintliness,* eds. H. J. W. Drijvers and A. B. Mulder-Bakker, 2002, 146–148.)

(Overleaf spread)

9. *St. Michael's of Hildesheim, nave.*

10. *St. Michael's of Hildesheim, column.*

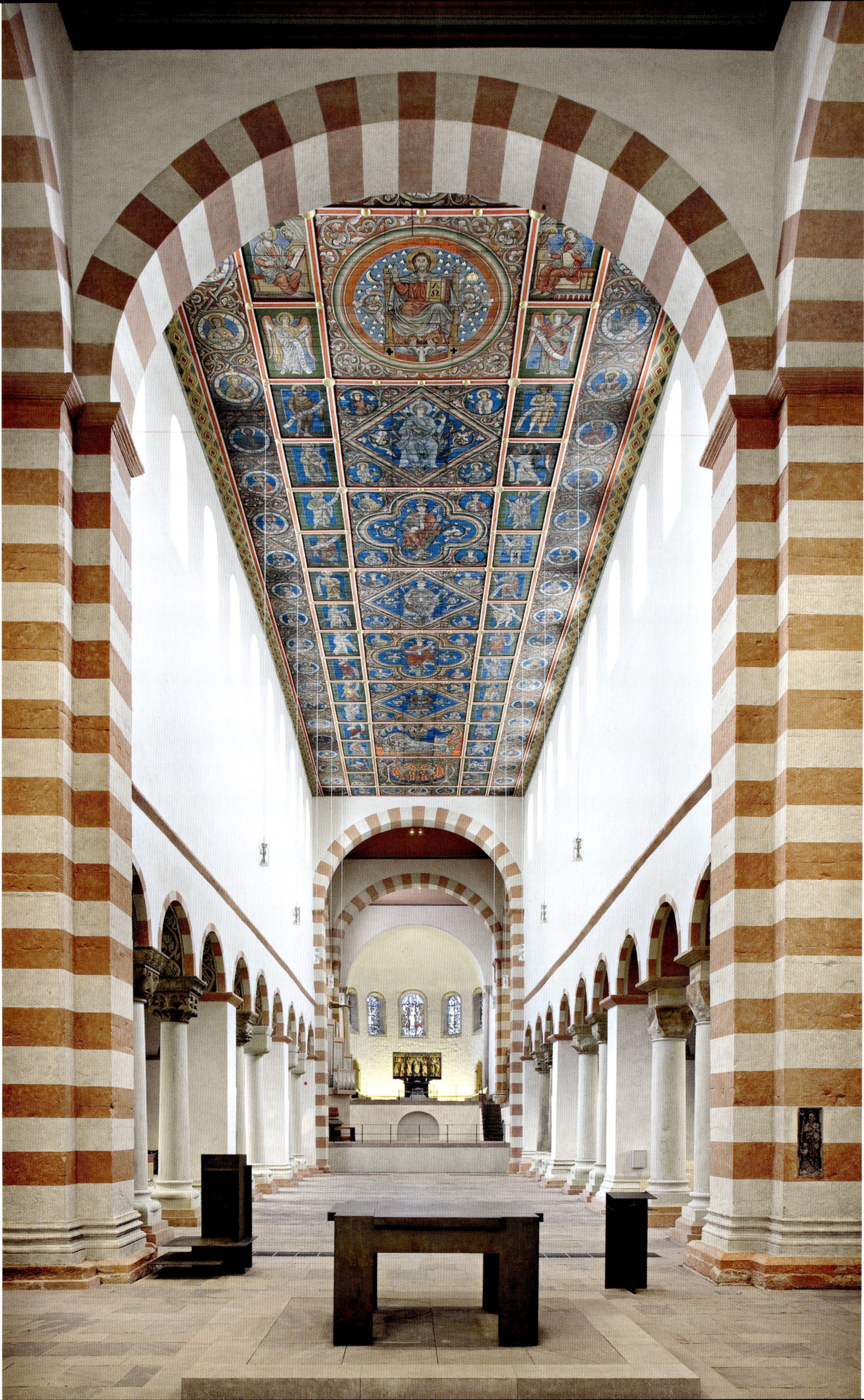

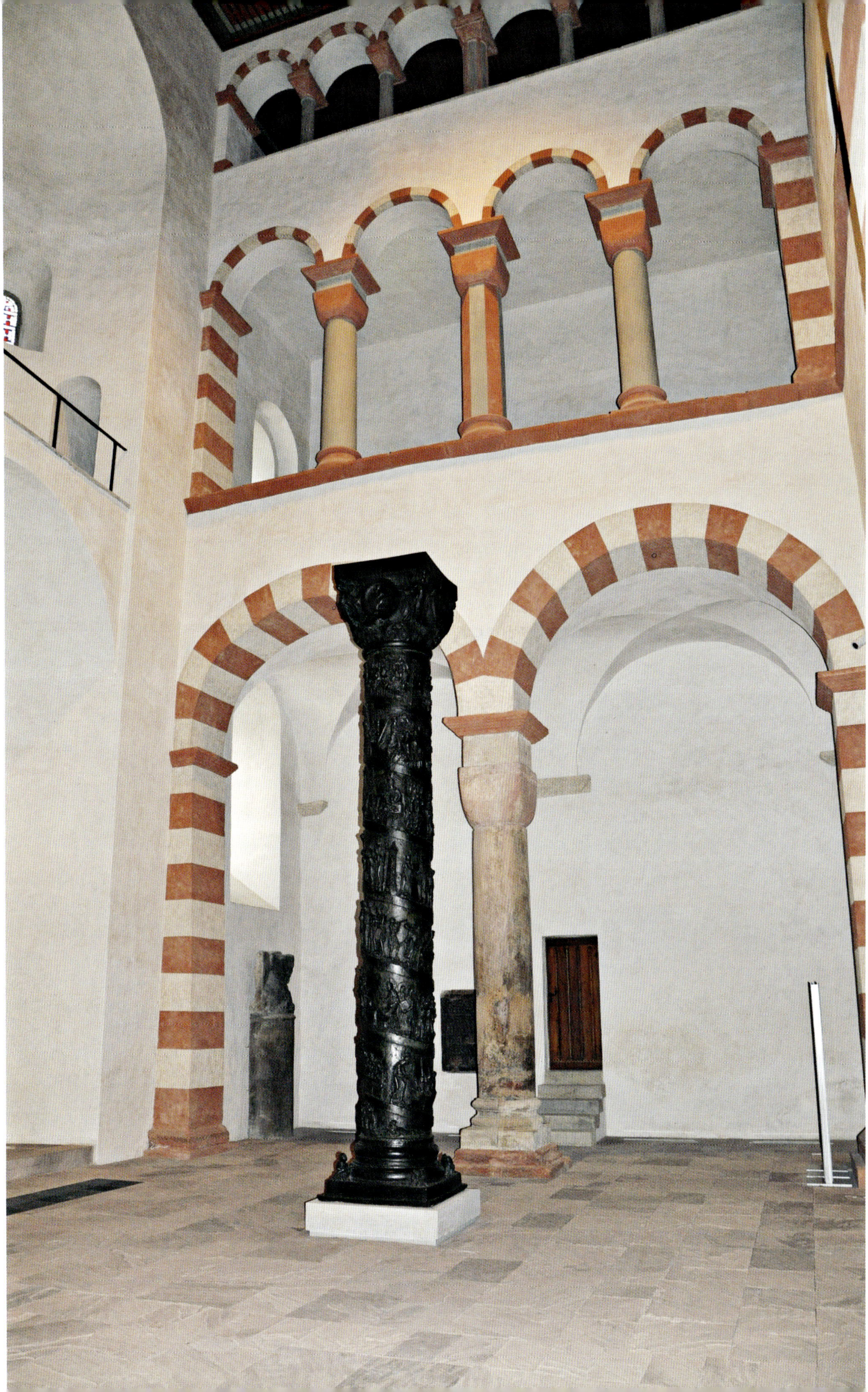

10

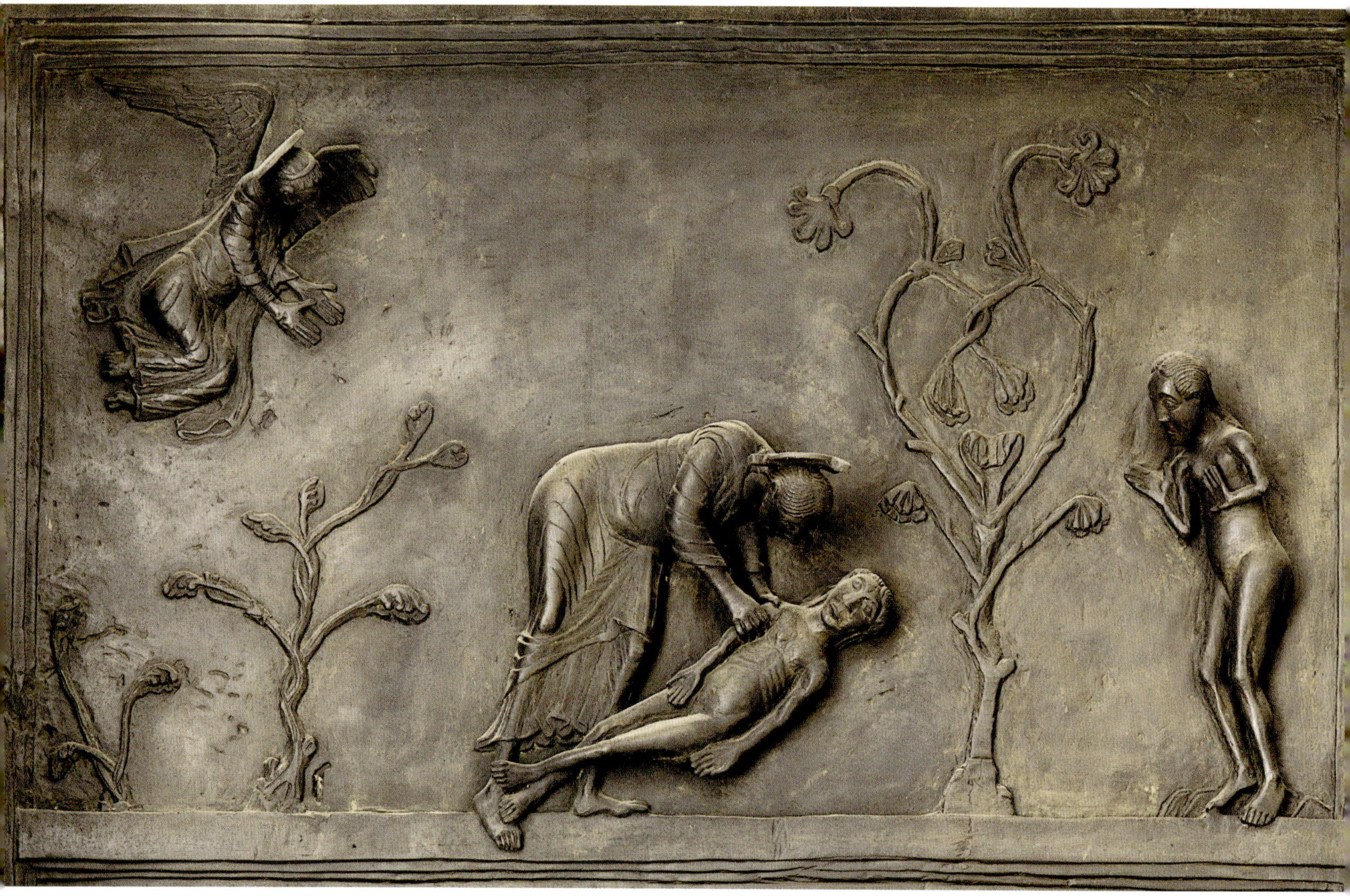

Panel **1**

LIFE

> I am well aware that many people have said many things about Paradise. There are however, three generally held opinions about this topic; one held by those who think Paradise should only be understood in the literal material sense, another by those for whom only the spiritual sense is true, the third by those who take Paradise in each way, differently though in the material, differently in the spiritual sense. So then, in a word, I admit that it is the third opinion which I favor.
> —Augustine, *The Literal Meaning of Genesis* (*De Genesi ad litteram*), in *On Genesis*, Book VIII, 1, 1, trans. Edmund Hill, O.P., New City Press/Augustinian Heritage Institute, 2002, 346. This translation, hereafter as *De Genesi ad litteram*, will be used throughout

In the upper left corner of the first panel of the bronze door, an angel is flying, wings outspread, body weightless. Isolated from the other figures, he reaches out toward the scene unfolding on the ground below: the creation of man (fig. 11). Having been created when the world began, our celestial onlooker gazing out on this fertile paradise is not made of the clay from which God gave life to humans and plants. The book of Genesis does not mention his presence at the moment of Man's creation; indeed, he is not mentioned at all until the third book of Exodus when he appears to Moses in the burning bush. It was only in the later prophetic tradition that it was firmly established that man was created after the angels to replace those who had fallen. Anglo-Saxon artists were depicting angels in Creation scenes as early as the tenth century [Tronzo 1983, 163]. Furthermore, earlier historians have suggested that an apocryphal Jewish text, the *Vita Adae et Evae*, was responsible for spreading the notion of an angel adoring Adam among Christians [Dibelius 1907; Wesenberg 1955; and, for the text, Pettorelli 1999]. That legend may have contributed to the persistence of the motif. Yet a serious problem remains: how could an early eleventh-century viewer have established a link between the angelic figure and an Anglo-Saxon miniature or Jewish text? The reuse of this motif is itself meaningful, and an iconographic analysis must take that meaning into account.

11. *Panel 1.*

An iconographic source does not mean the same thing for the "artist" of the early Middle Ages as it does for the historian. Craftsmen and the clerics or monks who commissioned them could search for and find all they needed to express their meaning in their religious, literary, or visual culture, as well as in their liturgical practices, experiences, and travels. They reworked, left out, or transformed this heritage, using known or innovative themes, even on occasion taking up a motif but changing its significance by adapting it to a new context. What they produced or reproduced made sense in its context; the iconographic source was merely a tool to transform a thought into plastic form. Historians look more readily for filiations, origins, or models, whether the artist acknowledges them or not. As taxonomists, they reconstitute a lineage of authoritative sources and references, classifying them according to their likelihood. Their rational inquiry is partly subject to the necessity of calling attention to the modalities of filiation and elements of analogical recognition.

The learned studies of previous scholars have determined that Bernward, the door's likely designer, was as well acquainted with Carolingian images—

more precisely the Tours miniatures—as he was with Anglo-Saxon ones. Yet no one can establish or quantify these contributions with any degree of certainty, leaving the issue to be debated by specialists. What we do know from his biography, though, is that the bishop traveled extensively in Italy, particularly in Milan, Ravenna, and Rome, but also to Saint-Denis, Tours, Aix-la-Chapelle, and throughout the Ottonian Empire. He certainly must have drawn inspiration from his travels.

To what extent does such scholarly knowledge shed light on the door's narrative? It allows us to delimit the field of possible meanings but does not on its own constitute a sufficient argument in the interpretive process. Each work is unique and deserves to be read in its historical context, as it would have been by the addressees of its message. If the challenge is to understand the angel's raison d'être in the panel's system of signification, the fundamental question is not so much the origin of the motif but the reasons and conditions leading to its reuse or adaptation. No longer a topic of investigation, tradition becomes the substratum, its role in the germination of the idea and its plastic realization to be plumbed for insights. At the risk of appearing remiss, this analysis will retain from the valuable and distinguished historical studies only what helps clarify the door's meaning.

The panel's configuration into zones, masses, groups, and interactions binds and unbinds the figures together, inviting the viewer to look, to question, to probe the meaning, in order to then reassemble the findings in a coherent whole. The angel is there and yet quickly slips from view (fig. 11). Our gaze glides on, following the movement of the figure's gracefully extended arms and the direction of its gaze. (The angelic countenance is rendered in high relief.) The angel desires and celebrates God alone. Our inquisitive eyes follow his lead to the central figures on the ground, searching for the essence of the story that will henceforth be the object of our inquiry. We lose sight of the angel because he is only an epigraph, an introduction to the story and because, from his ethereal position floating in light, focusing intently on the mystery of Creation, he does not see us either. Yet, as the first witness of the divine work, the angel is presented as a conscious and knowing figure, a noetic archetypal Creature turned toward its Creator. He urges the viewer to follow him and enter the narrative unfolding on the door's sixteen panels. As indelible and silent as a memory, unobtrusively relegated to the background of the visual adventure, the angel accompanies the viewers' gaze from the very start, showing the way. In a very real sense, then, he is the one who opens our eyes to the possibility of seeing, just as, at the end of the visual adventure, he is the one who completes our understanding of the discourse.

If the angel in the upper left corner serves as an entry point, it is inarguably the great figure of God

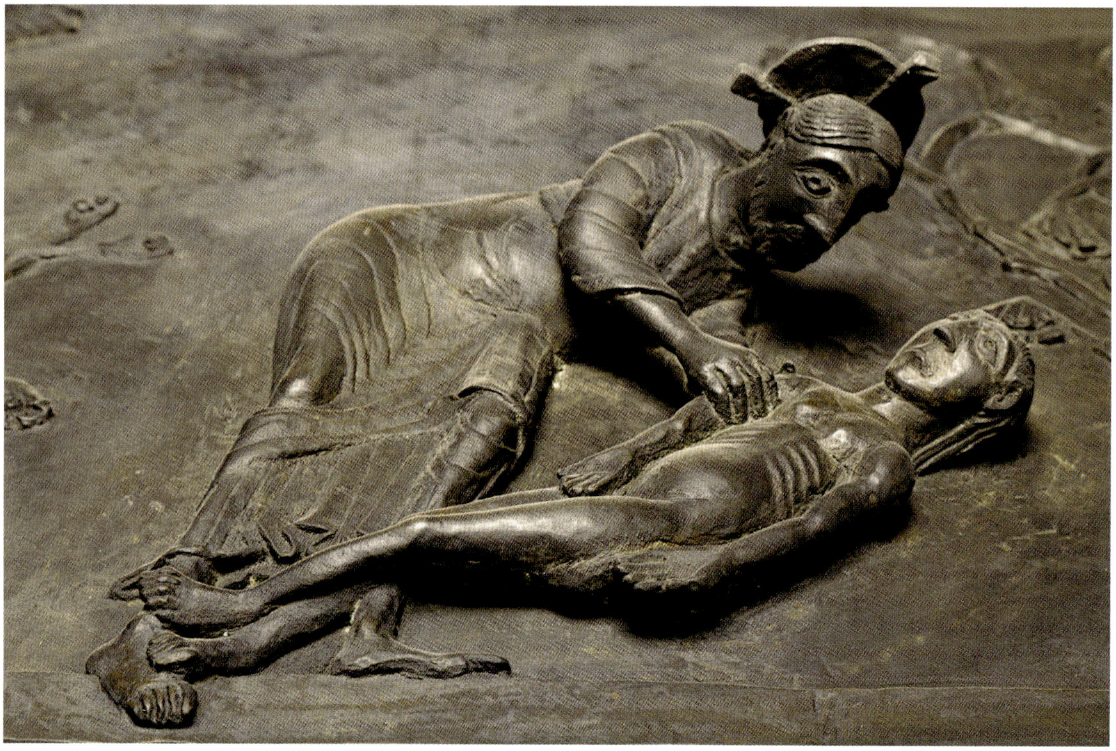

12

12. *Panel 1, viewed from the foot of the door.*

that commands our attention. Placed in the center of the panel, God is immediately identifiable due to his imposing size and cruciform halo—the Father can be neither seen nor represented except through the image of Christ the Son. What a frontal photograph can only partially show emerges strongly when viewed from the foot of the door. Placed more than four meters above the ground, sculpted in very high relief and clearly detached from the background, God's visage dominates the entire right wing (fig. 12). Unlike the angel's head, equally prominent yet tilted toward the panel's center, the face of God is oriented toward the observer, who can only accept the bond offered to them: the viewer is prisoner of the cognitive reflex that leads every one of us to respond to the gaze of another, in life as in images. If the angel acts as a vector of attention, it is the figure of God the Creator, inaccessible, that first summons the viewer.

Bent over in his effort, God firmly holds the shoulder of the figure lying beneath him in his left hand while clasping its upper-right arm in the other. The two figures are intimately bound by this contact, constituting a scene in themselves that the vegetation isolates further by partitioning the image into distinct spaces, just as was already done in the frontispieces of Carolingian manuscripts. The identity of the human figure that God holds under him has given rise to numerous controversies, even though the general consensus is, logically, that it could only be Adam or Eve. The episode of Adam's creation, as told in Genesis, mentions the modeling clay and the insufflation of life:

> And the Lord God formed man of the slime of the earth [*limo terrae*] and breathed into his face the breath of life [*spiraculum vitae*], and man became a living soul [*animam viventem*]. (Gen. 2:7)
>
> Then the Lord God cast a deep sleep upon Adam and when he was fast asleep, he took one of his ribs [*unam de costis eius*], and filled up flesh for it. And the Lord God built the rib which he took from Adam into a woman [*mulierem*] and brought her to Adam. (Gen. 2:21–22 [*The Holy Bible: Douay-Rheims Version*; this version will be used throughout])

Given the biblical text, it is tempting to identify the supine figure with Adam being formed by God [Kaspersen 1988, 81]. Yet this hypothesis becomes problematic when set against the rest of the panel, since a second human being stands on the right, separated from the central group by a tree. Naked and leaning slightly forward, right hand outstretched in sign of wonder and left hand with open palm against the chest, possibly a gesture of reception, this figure looks attentively at the central scene while taking no part in the action. Like the angel, it is an involved spectator.

Even if we assume that the panel represents two different stages of the story, for reasons of both chronological and narrative coherence, the artist could not possibly have meant to depict Eve watching the creation of Adam; thus, the figure on the right must be Adam (fig. 13). As for the figure lying at the feet of God, some consider it Eve, others Adam. This is not surprising since in medieval iconography it is not unusual for a character to be represented twice in the same image, appearing in two scenes where the actions or situations either take place one after the other or in a different setting. Is that the case in the bronze panel? Does Adam contemplate his own creation, as Herbert Schade [1958] and Michael Fehr [1978] have suggested, the former basing his conclusion on the *Vita Adae et Evae,* the latter underscoring the two phases of Adam's creation? If that were the case, the panel would be an exceptional *unicum* because, as some scholars have noted, throughout Christian tradition whenever two humans are represented in the Creation episode they are consistently identified as Adam and Eve [Kaspersen 1988, 82]. Formulated in this way, the debate appears insoluble, especially since the arguments of either side are weakened by Bernward's numerous iconographic innovations, as will be argued in the following analyses. Only a comparative study can resolve the issue, but it will have to be done within the visual program of the bronze door.

While in Paradise (panels 1 through 5), the two humans share a common nudity, head and facial hair, as well as invisible genitalia. In contrast, their chests are treated differently beginning with panel 2, where Eve's nipples become discretely visible (fig. 39). This difference does not appear in panel 1, where the chests of the supine and standing figures

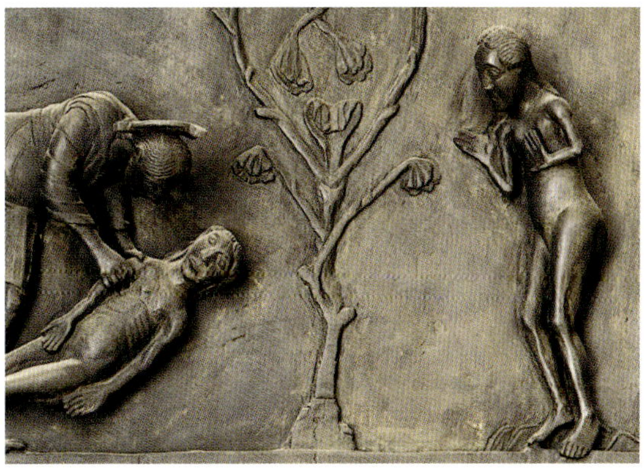

13

13. *Panel 1, lower right.*

are equally prominent but without nipples. If Bernward had wished to establish a gender distinction so high on the door, he would have emphasized the size and anatomy of the chest. The obvious conclusion is that in panel 1 the two human figures conform strictly to each other since they are not gendered. Identification based on physical attributes is therefore impossible.

This impossibility constitutes what we might call an iconic knot, the first focal point of the viewer's analytical reasoning. The iconographic program guides the gaze by the questions it elicits, thus directing the intellective process as well. The question of the two humans' identity, a question raised by the very form of the discourse, invites the viewer to examine the images in their most minute details. The similarity of the two humans does not go beyond their anatomical identity since their morphology differs radically. The body of the figure on the ground is rigid, almost cadaverous, a stiffness emphasized by the inert arms extending along the length of the torso, palms open, as if to signify surrender into the hands of God; the eyes, fixed and vacant, do not gaze up at the Creator, they are inert like the tightly pressed lips of the figure's closed mouth (fig. 12). Finally, and this detail is important, although no genitalia are visible, the thoracic cage is carefully shaped. Even at a height of four meters one can count the ribs attached to the sternum. Widely spaced, as if expanded by breath from the lungs, they rise above a swollen abdomen. The figure stretched out on the ground appears both dead and alive.

The position of the two humans is also quite different (fig. 11). The standing figure's legs are parallel, whereas those of the figure on the ground are crossed and placed between God's legs with the soles of the feet on either side of the divine ankle. Confined in this position, the legs can neither uncross nor straighten themselves; God's right foot, however, already functions as a pivot: only a little pressure combined with the tension applied to the shoulders would allow the figure to be raised. In fact, the erect position is already anticipated in the image, as is apparent in the alignment of the deceptively inert body. The raised torso is not aligned on the legs' axis but rather along the great diagonal that cuts across the image, as shown in the overall composition of the bronze panel (fig. 14). It should be noted that this new axis also corresponds to the alignment of the asymmetrical branch sprouting like an incongruous sucker from the bush just behind God. Construction mishap? Concern for the internal order of the image? Or does it possess a more elaborated signifying function? Even a cursory glance at the strongly differentiated configuration of trees and bushes invites speculation about the role they might play in the development of the visual discourse.

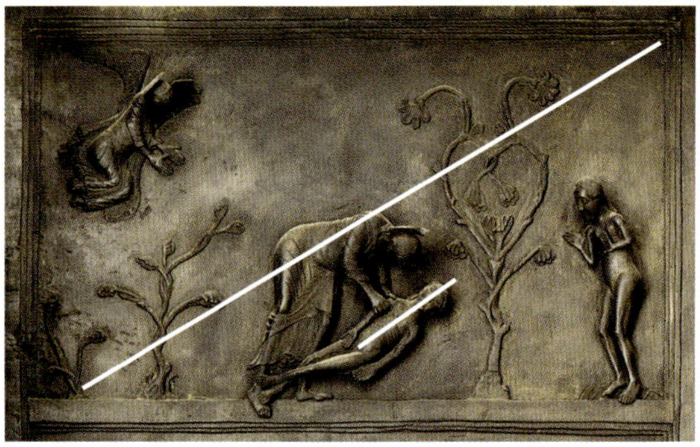

14

14. *Panel 1, diagonal of life.*

Besides the diegetic function of certain trees identified and named in the biblical text, such as the Tree of Knowledge of Good and Evil or the burning bush, it is widely known among those familiar with Carolingian or Byzantine miniatures that plants play a role in the overall organization of the image and in clarifying the scenes, as well as serving to visually balance the figures. That role, however, does not suffice in itself to explain the presence, the positioning, and especially the various forms of the door's trees and bushes, a variety also found in the frontispieces of Genesis produced in Carolingian workshops: folio 7 v of the *Bible of Saint Paul Outside the Walls,* folio 10 v of the *Bible of Charles the Bald* (Paris, BnF, Ms. Lat. 1) and especially folio 7 v of the *Bamberg* Bible (Bamberg, Staat., Ms. Bibl. 1). One of these images might have inspired Bernward.

In addition to their considerable formal variety, the plants are not of equal importance in the door's two wings, appearing in inverse proportion to the presence of architectural elements. Trees and bushes are present in seven of the eight panels of the left wing, those recounting episodes from the Old Testament, but are absent in the first seven panels of the right wing, before reappearing in the very last panel in the door's upper right. Conversely, in seven of the eight panels of the right wing, we find architectural elements as varied and complex as the plants, whereas they appear only in panel 5 of the left wing (fig. 1).

It is generally acknowledged that the antinomic placing of vegetation and architecture is compatible with the settings of the biblical episodes under consideration. The Old Testament scenes, ending with Abel's murder, take place in the countryside, whereas those from the New Testament are situated either in cities (Bethlehem and Jerusalem) or in front of buildings (the Temple, the palace of the governor of Judea, and the tomb represented in panel 5 in the form of an aedicule, as in Carolingian iconography). The fact remains that these different scenes were chosen from a vast biblical panorama; the presence of vegetal and architectural elements, as important as we think it is, could have been just as decisive in contributing to the selection of the scenes and their staging. There are two panels with neither vegetation nor buildings: panel 8, Abel's death; and panel 14, the death of Christ. Both portray a killing and are composed around a victim isolated in the center. Panels 5 and 16, featuring both plants and architecture, share a change of setting: panel 5 depicts the expulsion of Adam and Eve from Paradise, announcing the arrival of the human race on earth, whereas panel 16 represents the return of Christ from the Harrowing of Hell, announcing by his Resurrection the return to heaven. The place of return, which for the moment we will call Paradise, appears on the right, constituting the only circumscribed space on the door, where everything appears together: tower, door, walls, bushes and birds, thus closing the narrative with an unprecedented synthesis.

The arrangement of vegetation and architecture on the bronze door could not possibly have been done at random, even though it is still too early to explain their interconnection and significance. We are faced with a problem: we cannot theorize about the signifying function of the vegetation and architecture before studying the panels in question; but we cannot understand even the first panel without taking into account the symbolic potential of the plants. I propose to solve this problem by taking up the postulate formulated by Harvey Stahl, who suggests that the trees of the Hildesheim door have some sort of behavior and that they are "built like bodies"; however, as my arguments will soon show, I cannot follow him when he suggests that the trees have a "mimetic function, lending strength to the emotions" and that they "broaden . . . the signifying field by acting as an ancient chorus" [Stahl, 167 *ff.*]. For the moment I suggest thinking of the plants as actors in the image, lending their plasticity, individuality, and dynamism to the body of the discourse.

Let us return to the first panel. Three plants differing in size and form mark the rhythm of the space. The first bush, on the left, is very small (fig.15). It sprouts from a split stump that it seems to perforate, just as a young shoot might cut through a clump of soil. ("Let the earth bring forth grass," Gen. 1:11.) Extremely schematic, this bush has three dissimilar branches ending in curled leaves. They undulate slightly as if to indicate, as in fern fronds, a growing process. Throughout their length the three stems show a long and narrow groove extending up to the leaves. This vein indicates a circulating liquid, a sap

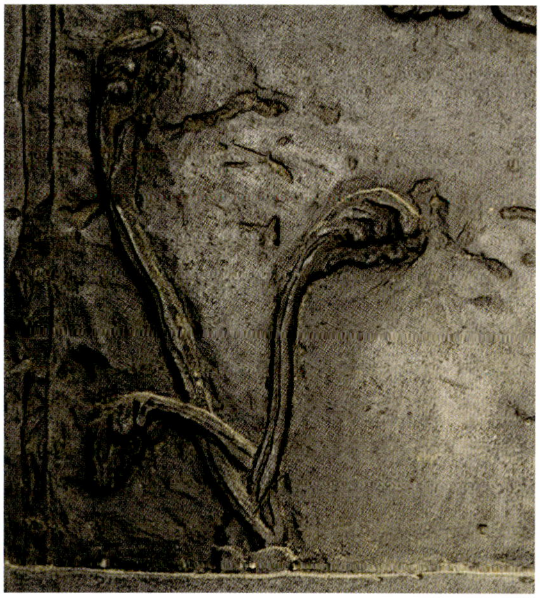

15

15. *Panel 1, shrub, lower left.*

derived from a life-giving water whose presence on the paradisical ground just before the appearance of vegetation is attested in Genesis (Gen. 1:10–11) and whose importance will be strongly affirmed in the subsequent panels.

> Even bushes are moved not only by some external force acting on them, as when they are being shaken by winds, but also by that inner motion which drives whatever belongs to the growth and beauty of a tree, by which sap is drawn into the root, and there turned into all that constitutes the nature of the herb or tree. None of this happens, after all, without internal movement. (Augustine, *De Genesi ad litteram*, Book VII, 16, 22, 375)

The three branches of the first bush vary in vigor: the smallest seems weak, listless, the middle one still uncertain, almost receding, whereas the one on the right appears vital and vigorous (fig. 15).

The second bush is larger and more structured. It is irrigated by roots that have made their way into the earth and its size is almost double that of the first bush (fig. 16). Its general outline is very similar to the latter, but its branches spread in a symmetrical, almost vectorial, way. Two small perfectly balanced branches sprout midway up its central axis while two quite disproportionate ones grow from the top: a single leaf on the left, a long asymmetric branch on the right. The torso of the reclining figure is aligned with the latter. We should also note that beginning with its first interweaving branches, its multiple stems intertwine three times, twice on the trunk and once on the elongated branch.

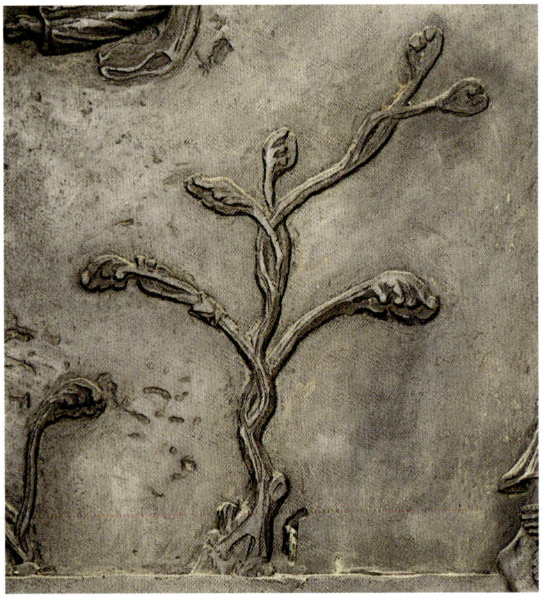

16

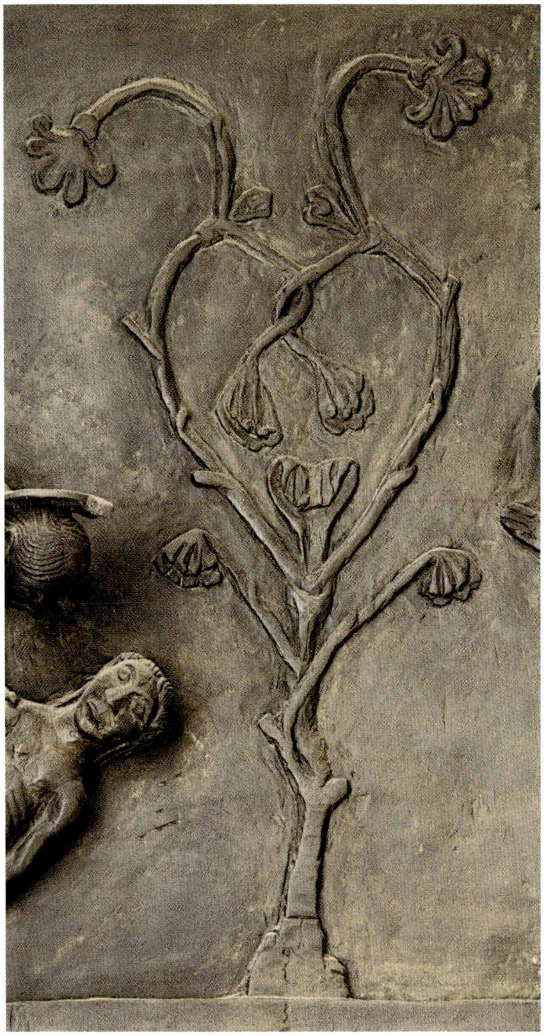

17

The largest of the three plants, on the panel's right side, has two different kinds of foliage (fig. 17). At the end of the two main branches are vigorous palm-shaped clusters of leaves. Just like the tree's structure, of which they are a component, they attest to the plant's successful growth. In contrast, the tree's lower branches end in small leaves resembling bindweed, which share neither the form of the fern fronds of the previous plants nor the vitality of the palms at the top. Veined and arranged in the round, the leaves are so tender that they appear to bend under their own weight, as much like petals as leaves. These tender leaves correspond to a second stage in the tree's growth, namely, the development of its vegetal matter rather than its structure. Perhaps they are meant to evoke the freshness of young foliage, while symbolically denoting a subtle, delicate, almost ethereal nature. Numerous arguments support this hypothesis. The foliage—balanced and harmonious, symmetrical and elegantly arranged—appears alongside the tree's tripartite structure, which is more geometric than naturalistic. This schematic and rational perception of the plant is in keeping with a scientific culture also expressed in the botanic images in the few remaining early medieval copies of the Pseudo Apuleius's *Herbarius* (for example, Oxford Bod. Lib. Ms. Ashmole 1431, eleventh century).

Sprouting from the base of the trunk, two small leafy branches echo the pair of branches opposite each other on the middle plant. They also underscore the curved and perfectly symmetrical double growth axis of the two main branches. The latter's upper extremities are extended by the palmette tips and are linked at midpoint by two elegantly entwined branches to form a heart. The human heart already appears in this shape in ancient, early Christian, and medieval art, although it could be represented differently, particularly in treatises of anatomy [Vinken 2000, 13 *ff.*]. On a different scale, these two large branches repeat the pattern of intertwining stems so evident in the central bush; indeed, they are even structurally similar to its asymmetrical branch, of which they are a greatly enlarged version.

Considered together, these three plants evoke the three growing stages of a single shrub, a shrub that takes root in the soil, becomes established, grows, develops in structure, then expands into the formal blossoming of splendid maturity. It is at this point that it acquires a particularly significant quality, which will be discussed later. The link between the three plants is underscored not only by their upper extremities' common alignment along the panel's great diagonal but also by their proportions: the dimensions of the first and second shrubs are geometrically inscribed in the heart of the third.

16. *Panel 1, shrub, center.*

17. *Panel 1, tree, right.*

The vital force that brings matter to life and makes it grow is the first expression of a metamorphic principle at work in the bronze door. It certainly constitutes its most fundamental and original visual aspect. Embodied in the vegetation offered to the gaze from the very first panel, this vital force appears from the outset as a divine act. Not only are there three bushes in the panel, the first is composed of three stems, the second has as many interlacings, and the third as many levels. Without necessarily plunging into the perilous register of arithmology, we must note that the number three is too charged with meaning in Christianity to be incidental: it corresponds to the number of hypostases of the Trinity's creative power. In addition, this vital force is presented as the principle that drives rigorously determined growth within Creation. It confers a more geometric and symmetric aspect to visible forms and proceeds in distinct phases, each new plant amplifying and revealing the potential characteristics of the previous one. It is an agent of connection, of continuity, of motion; it is God acting on the world as *pneuma*, the spirit of life, that is to say, the Holy Spirit.

The Trinitarian organization of Creation and its diffusion in the orthonormal space containing it refers explicitly to the ontological order that God commanded for his Creation: "[The wisdom of God] has ordered all things in measure, and number, and weight" (Gen. 11:21). In addition to this fundamental biblical formulation, some patristic works, known to have been in Bernward's possession [Gallistl 1999, 109], may have inspired the bishop architect to use geometric forms for his bronze door. The first of these texts is the *Homilies on Ezekiel* by Gregory the Great. In this lengthy treatise on Christian meditation and hope, Gregory reflects several times on the bronze man standing by the threshold of the temple in Jerusalem and holding a measuring rod (Ezek. 40: 3). The bronze man thus prefigures the referential Word of Christ and His Church—the Bible as Law—to which Christians must conform (Bk II, 1 and 2). However, it is in Augustine's *De Genesi ad litteram* that the idea of a universal mathematical order functioning as a natural law is developed and applied to the vegetal world.

> So let us consider then the beauty of any kind of tree you like, in its trunk, its branches, its leaves, its fruits. This admirable sight did not of course suddenly spring into being in its full stature and glory, but in the order with which we are also familiar. Thus it rose from its roots, which the first sprig had fixed in the earth, and from there grew all these parts in their distinct forms and shapes. That sprig, furthermore, came from a seed; so it was in the seed that all the rest was originally to be found, not in the mass of full material growth, but in the potentiality of its causative virtue. That full growth, you see, was built up from a supply of earth and moisture. But much more wonderful and remarkable is that virtue in a tiny grain which enabled the surrounding moisture mixed with earth to be turned as the basic material into the specific wood of that tree, into the spread of the branches, into the green and the shape of the leaves, into the succulent form of the fruit and the wonderfully disposed order of all these. (*De Genesi ad litteram,* Book V, 22, 44, 331)

One cannot overstate the importance during the early Middle Ages of the mathematical cosmology rooted in the Book of Wisdom. It appears quite early in the Insular and Carolingian geometric patterns [Marchesin 2000; 2010; 2014]. Architecture was another major locus of meaningful proportion, evident, for example, in the modular design of St. Gall's Abbey or in Charlemagne's palace and chapel at Aachen. The application of geometric proportions to visible forms is therefore neither a conceit nor a secret method but a broadly shared aesthetic approach, like the one found in Christian musical forms and liturgical texts: it tells and reflects the structure of the world. As such, it is both heir to ancient science and to the Christianization of the entire sensible universe proposed by St. Augustine in his *De Doctrina christiana.* For the bishop of Hippo, as for his medieval successors, identifying and understanding the mathematical order of the world is the specific condition for the possibility of comprehending God the Creator, insofar as the Creation contains traces of the divine laws that presided over its configuration. These natural laws stand as a source of teaching and divine messages complementary to those of the Bible; in Christian culture their very existence legitimized the permanent place of the quadrivium in the curriculum of medieval learned people.

Regarding scientific culture, the Ottonians had no reason to envy the Carolingians. They held *De Doctrina christiana* in high esteem. It is among the first citations of Ruotger, the biographer of Bruno the Great, brother of Otto I [Mayr-Harting 2007, 78]. It belongs to a culture well versed in classic Latin literature [McKitterick 1992] and particularly interested in sciences and their applications. At a time of extraordinary technological and mathematical development, scientific thinking was fundamental. Both Abbo of Fleury, whose work Bernward had perhaps known at Saint-Benoît-sur-Loire, and Gerbert

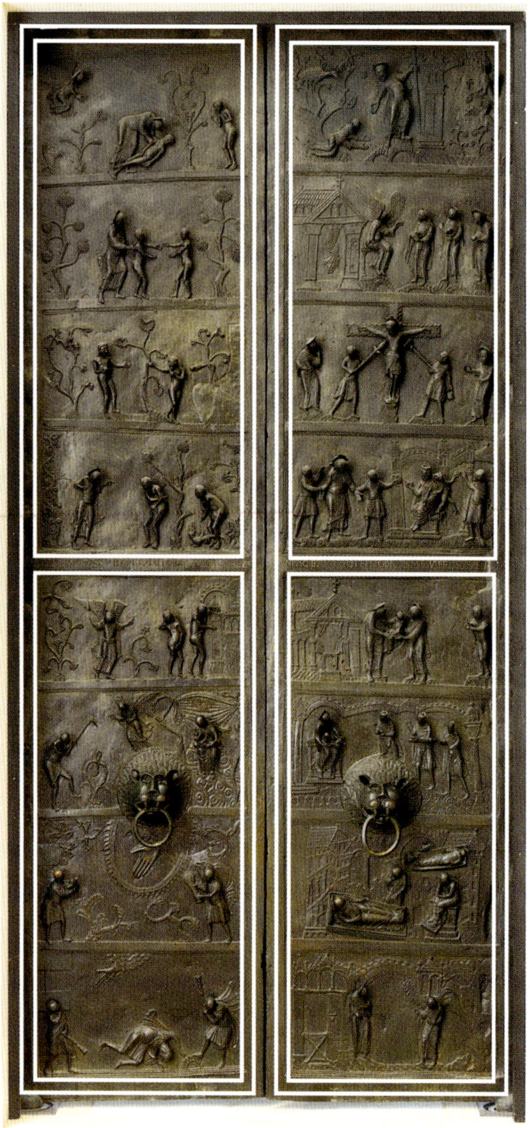

18

18. *Door, structure of the story.*

of Aurillac, the future Pope Sylvester II, whom Bernward met in Rome at the time of the conflict over the Gandersheim Monastery [Poulle 2005], embodied this mindset. Bernward was one of the most brilliant representatives of the generation of learned scholars trained in the cathedral schools, a generation that was very involved in the artistic productions of their time. Even though Thangmar, his biographer, may have exaggerated his merits, let us not forget that, given what is known, Bernward was credited with original skills in metallurgy, architecture, and drawing; he was the future emperor Otto III's tutor (*didascalus*) before becoming his counselor and first archivist (*primiscrivus*). In addition, it is known that the bishop of Hildesheim had a copy made in his scriptorium of the *De arithmetica* by Boethius with Vitruvian interpolations [Hildesheim, Dom. Ms. 31; Guillaumin 1995, LXXII]. Having read Calcidius's fifth-century annotated translation of the *Timaeus* [Rädle 2002], Bernward was familiar with Plato's mathematical cosmology with its analogies between the proportional soul of the world and the human soul.

Bernward thinks, describes, and conceives of the world like a scientist, and theology, which now replaces ancient wisdom as the fundamental end and aim of liberal studies, is, for him, at the highest degree, a matter of logical operations, of reason applied to understanding of the Bible and the whole created world. All this knowledge was put into practice at the Abbey of St. Michael, his monastic foundation: as several studies have shown, the bishop had conceived of his abbey as a holistic structure, integrally configured at the geometrical and symbolical level [Binding 1987, 1988; 1998; Hiscock 2000; Rottlander 1990; Overesch and Alfhart 2009]. The same mechanisms are at work in the bronze door whose discourse takes a mathematically formal, mechanical, and dynamic approach to Creation.

The mathematical organicity of the formal discourse corresponds to a geometric arrangement of the bronze wings, which is articulated not only on its surface but also in its depth (fig. 18). The first level of the geometric plan concerns the door writ large. It is made up of the rectangular structure of each wing and the broad band bearing the dedicatory inscription. The layout shows the general form of a cross. This effect is not original: crosses appear on many medieval bronze doors, either formed by the structure's ornamentation—as for instance at the Basilica of Saint Paul Outside the Walls in Rome—or used as a form of decoration. However, in the Hildesheim door the cross linking the two wings is also the formal paradigm of all the forms displayed in Creation. From a historical perspective, the Word is Christ the Savior, connecting the Old and New Testaments. Structurally and ontologically, the orthonormal cross, signifying the Word-Wisdom, outlines the two paradigmatic axes of the ordered world within which the diagonal of the first panel unfolds, and the forms are elaborated.

The second level of the geometric arrangement concerns the depth of the door and is formed by the framing of the panels. It is composed of three stepped moldings and provides the connection between the framework (including the inscription) and the panels. When the panels rest directly on the wing's framework, as is the case for numbers 4 and 13 above the dedicatory inscription, and 8 and 9 at the bottom of the door, three thin moldings of equal size appear on the lower edge. When two panels are adjacent Bernward replaces one of the moldings with a larger strip—allowing a regular placement of the rectangles within the wings. All connections between panels, as well as those between panels and structure, are therefore threefold, evoking the divine organization of the world's forms and their relative placement. Following the Father as vital principle, the Word as formal principle, and the Holy Spirit as dynamic principle, it is now the Trinity that determines the general placement of the panels: composed of the Father and the Son and connected by the Holy Spirit, the Trinity constitutes a paradigm of the concept of linkage. This Trinitarian theology is applied to Creation in St. Augustine's *City of God,* a fundamental text in Carolingian and Ottonian culture. Bernward had an early and profound exegetic knowledge of this work, probably gained from pouring over the copy in the bishop of Mainz's library while attending Willigis's lectures [Mayr-Harting 1999, II, 86].

> We believe and hold, and faithfully preach, that the Father begat the Word, that is, Wisdom, by Which all things were made: His only begotten Son, one as He is one, eternal as He is eternal, supremely good as He is equally good. We believe also that the Holy Spirit is simultaneously the Spirit of the Father and the Son, and is Himself one in substance and co-eternal with both. (Augustine, *The City of God against the Pagans*, ed. R. Dyson, Cambridge University Press, 1998, Book XI, XXIV, 480–481. This translation, hereafter as *De civitate Dei*, will be used throughout.)

The deepest recesses of the door are made up of the bare and neutral backgrounds of the panels framing the figures. These rectangular panels are configured by the number four which, through its link with the number three in Christian culture, represents the materiality of the created world, its elements, its cardinal points, and its flow of time. It is within these rectangular frames that the story takes place. These neutral and rectangular spaces make up the prescribed order within which life created by God develops, life that unfolds in the material thickness of sculpture in the round and in the metamorphic temporality of its growth and diffusion.

> So this God, then, living in unchanging eternity, *created all things simultaneously* [Sirach 18:1], from which point times would run their course and places would be filled and the ages would unroll with movement in time and space. Some of these things he created were spiritual, some corporeal, and he set them up by forming or shaping a basic material which none other but he himself had put in place as shapeless, and capable of being formed or shaped. (*De Genesi ad litteram*, Book VIII, 20, 39, 416)

Let us return now to the first panel (fig. 11 and 14). The geometric structure of the central scene is organized along the great diagonal tracing the growth axis of the plant and the rising axis of the supine figure. To what does it refer? It might be opportune to recall here that the right-angled rectangle is the first shape describing the solid elements of the earth in the Platonic tradition [Davy et al. 1976, 197–199]; Calcidius's commentary on the Timaeus reached the height of its popularity precisely during the eleventh century [Calcidius 2011, 57], especially in the milieu of Gerbert and his Ottonian followers [Somfai 2002]. That being the case and considered simply at the iconographic level, the diagonal represents the vital force that sets the parameters for Eve's insertion into the image; it is therefore consistent with the insufflation that God performs on His creature, who is filled with air swelling the abdomen. A human being, according to the biblical text, is an *anima vivens.* In both classic and medieval Latin, the term *anima* signifies breath, air, what breathes, and consequently life and the living.

"Air or wind may also be called 'breath'; but, because it is corporeal, it is not the Breath of life. And the Breath of life Which quickens all things and is the Creator of every body and of every created spirit is God Himself, the wholly uncreated Spirit" (*De civitate Dei*, Book V, 9, 202). In Augustine, as in the broad patristic tradition, the *anima* insufflated into man is made of two components whose terminology is somewhat elusive, even if the bipartite system is not; Augustine distinguishes between *spiritus vitae,* life spirit, and *mens* or *ratio,* the rational soul conceived in God's image. Although the vital principle animates all living things, vegetal and animal alike, the rational soul is specific to Man [Gilson 1987, 56 *ff.*; Agaësse and Solignac 1970, I, 624–630].

> Giving us to understand, evidently, that it was in the very factor in which he surpasses non-rational animate beings that man was made to God's image. That, of course, is reason itself [*ratio*], or mind [*mens*], or intelligence [*intelligentia*], or whatever other word it may more suitably be named by. That is why the apostle too says "Be renewed in the spirit of your minds and put on the new man, who is being renewed for the recognition of God according to the image of him who created him" [Eph. 4:23–24; Col. 3:10], where he makes it plain enough just in what part man was created to God's

image—that is not in the features of the body but in a certain form of the illuminated mind [*mens inluminata*]. (*De Genesi ad litteram,* Book III, 20, 30, 261)

In the first panel the insufflation of the vital breath is accompanied by insufflation of the other component of the soul that will bring Man, Adam at the right, closer toward truly resembling God. To understand this process of conformation, it is necessary to turn to the large tree standing between Adam and God, prism of understanding and archetype of the human condition.

Unlike the two preceding plants this huge tree, much larger than the humans or the angel, is represented as an autonomous and self-sufficient creature (fig. 19). It is anchored in a smooth mound and is set neither on a clump of earth nor on powerful roots like those at the base of the bushes' trunks. The tree does not even need to be vivified by earth water, of which there is no trace on the wood; it culminates in the widely open palms, regarded since early Christian times as signs of Edenic eternity [Manns 2002, 280]. What is it then that makes the tree so independent of the matter in the Garden of Eden? For Bernward, as for ancient and medieval science writ large, approaching things (*res*) from a scientific perspective meant considering them as *forma* and *materia* ("rebus ex materia et forma constantibus," Porphyry, *Isagoge* [Erismann 2011, 91]).

Understood as a link between form and matter, the tree reveals its essence and, in fact, its identity. Indeed, the figure of the heart as central and structuring organ of the plant's metabolism is proof that the Creator has instilled the vital principle, the spirit of life, namely the Holy Spirit, within the plant's configuration. In fact, in concluding the long chapter in *De Genesi ad litteram* devoted to the verse on the insufflation of the soul, St. Augustine posits an equivalence between this spirit/spirit of life (*spiritus vitae*) and *anima* (Book VII, 21, 30, 380). At this point we must underscore a very important fact: the spiritual vivification of the tree bends the entire plant to its own law, imposing its geometric reason on physical matter. The soul's total dominance over the body yields an eternal vitality of foliation manifesting itself through the substance composing it. This substance is certainly corporeal but also spiritualized—the delicate ethereal leaves in corolla—and eternal—the palms at the top. In this first panel, Bernward places the viewer in the presence of the perfect form taken by corporeal matter. Once completely spiritualized, matter is superimposed on the form of the soul, becoming one with it (we shall return later to the question of the soul's form).

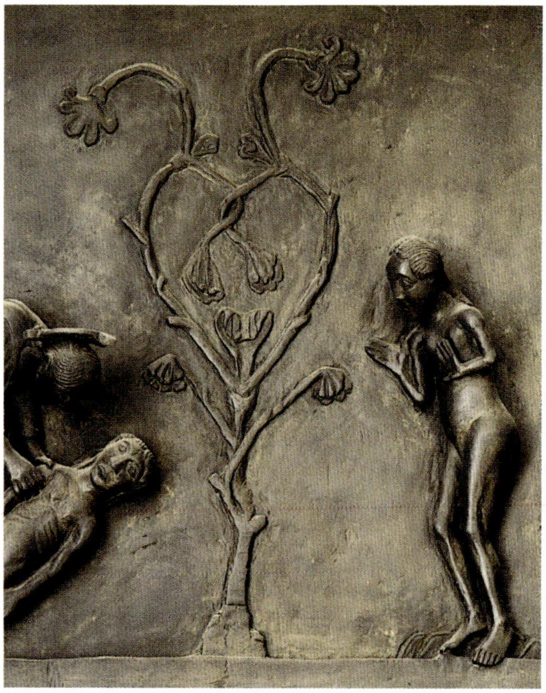

19

19. *Panel 1, Adam and right-hand tree.*

Taken together, these considerations suggest that the tree in the first panel is the "wood of life," the *lignum vitae* placed at the center of the Garden of Eden (Gen. 2:9). An immortal figure that encloses the source of its own immortality, the tree is transformed by the Spirit into a unified form of matter in a three-stage process according to the divine laws of geometry and proportion. In the general scheme of the bronze door, this Tree of Life serves as the archetype of the perfect formal and substantial configuration of the body by the soul. It is from this wood of life that humans draw both their life's breath (*spiritus vitae*) and the template for using their rational soul (*mens*) to dominate their body and acknowledge their Creator.

In the biblical text, the vivification effected by the *anima* is spread through the body by the blood, starting from the heart: "Because the life of the flesh [*anima carnis*] is in the blood [*sanguine*]" (Lev. 17:11), and again "Only beware of this, that thou eat not the blood, for the blood is for the soul" (Deut. 12:23). One finds similar principles in the anatomy of Hippocrates, Aristotle, and Galen, the latter's theories transmitted at least to the Byzantine world, in which the heart is the source not only of body heat but also of the vital force carried by the blood and ruling the body [Vinken 2000, 311]; the heart is even classified among the respiratory organs [Pigeaud 2003, 15].

Just as the two bushes on the left share their vital principle with the human being into whom God insufflated life, the large tree on the right is the spiritual fountain of the man leaning toward it. Adam stretches his right hand in the direction of the plant's heart/vital principle and makes it his own with his left by placing his open palm on his heart (fig. 19). By this gesture, man draws from the Tree of Life not only the substance that nourishes him eternally but also the formal model of the configuration of his external being (the body) and his internal being (the soul). The *City of God*, the other great Augustinian text that inspired Bernward's system of theological demonstration, offers the clearest description of this double operation:

> For man is not a body alone nor a soul alone; rather, he is composed of both soul and body. It is indeed true that the soul is not the whole man, but the better part of man, and the body is not the whole man, but the inferior part of man; it is when both are joined together that they receive the name of man. . . . calling the soul "the inward man" and the body "the outward man," as if there were two men even though both parts together make one man. (*De civitate Dei*, Book XIII, 24, 575)

It should be noted, however, that Adam does not gaze at the plant that serves as his life source and model; instead, he inclines his head as if to contemplate his Creator. This attitude, which has led to much speculation among historians, seems to me to bring Bernward's system of portraying the Edenic human nature to completion. While contemplating the Creator insufflating his soul, which is an act of recollection, an awareness arises in Adam that allows him to understand himself rationally as a creature and thus to complete his resemblance to God.

> Here we must not neglect that other point either, that after saying "to our image," he [God] immediately added: "and let him have authority over the fishes of the sea and the flying things of heaven," and of the other animals which lack reason, giving us to understand, evidently, that it was in the very factor in which he surpasses non-rational animate beings that man was made to God's image. That, of course, is reason itself, or mind, intelligence, or whatever other word it may more suitably be named by. . . . Man was created to God's image—that it was not in the feature of the body, but in a certain form of the illuminated mind. . . . Human nature too is intellectual like that light, and that is why being made is the same thing for it as recognizing the Word of God by whom it is being made. (*De Genesi ad litteram,* Book III, 20, 30–31, 251–252)

The faculty of knowledge that allows Man to understand himself as creature (*ratio,* reason, or *mens*, intelligence, set in the *spiritus*, the spirit) is inseparable from the formation of the bond of love, whose seat too is the heart, as had been firmly established throughout Christian culture through the concept of *caritas* [Guerreau-Jalabert 2003]. The reception of the Tree of Life-Wisdom is therefore in accord with the loving reception of God. This loving and knowing gaze is the final condition for fulfilling the likeness to God; indeed, the original soul, not yet completed since it is still formable, can only be realized in God's image when it has turned to its Creator, transforming itself through its knowledge.

> The Son, after all, the Word, does not have an unformed life. . . . A creature, on the other hand, even a spiritual and intelligent or rational one, which seems to be closer to that Word than others, can have an unformed life, because, while for it also to be is the same as to live, to live is not the same as to live wisely and blessedly; if it turns away from the unchangeable Wisdom, after all, it lives foolishly and miserably. It is formed, however, by turning to the unchangeable light of Wisdom, the Word of God. . . . Eternal Wisdom, of course, is the origin or beginning of the intelligent creation. (*De Genesi ad litteram*, Book I, 5, 10, 177–178)

Turned toward Wisdom, the soul's intellectual part attains an understanding of truth, a discernment of which the double reading that could be done of the size of God on whom Adam is gazing gives a better account than any other: seen as he appears, the Creator is so tall that he exceeds in size the Tree of Life, even reaching the size of the panel itself, of which he becomes a sort of principled module; nevertheless, the horizontal line of his bent back makes God seem smaller.

> And so the human mind first experiences through the senses of the body the things that have been made and from them gains such knowledge of them as its human weakness allows; and then it looks for their causes, if by any manner of means it may attain them where they abide primordially and unchangingly in the Word of God, and may

> thus come to an *understanding of his invisible things through those that have been made* [Rom. 20]. Is anyone unaware of how slow and dull the mind is at doing this . . . and what a long time it takes . . . even when it is being hurried along by its fervent and eager desire to persevere in pressing on to this goal? (*De Genesi ad litteram*, Book IV, 32, 49, 294)

To summarize, and contrary to what historiography has generally suggested, the central scene of the first panel does not represent the creation of corporeal man from the dust of the ground but rather the creation of spiritual man according to the image, that is, of man as a soul vivifying and organizing a body. The scene does not refer to the second but rather to the first, brief passage of the book of Genesis concerning the creation of human beings: "And God created man to his own image: to the image of God he created him: male and female he created them" (Gen. 1: 27). This explains the absence of sexual differentiation between the two human figures in the first panel. Yet this does not mean that man and woman were not biologically distinct from the very beginning. The text of the first creation clearly states this otherness; moreover, the creation of the soul and the formation of the body must not be understood as succeeding one another but as two levels of the same demiurgic operation rendered by two distinct verbs. St. Augustine, inspired by Philo of Alexandria, makes it clear: *fecit* (he made) for the soul, and *finxit* (he fashioned) for the body (*De Genesi ad litteram,* III, 22, 34).

> But on account of their being joined in one, *God made* the Scripture says, *man to the image of God*. And in case anyone should think it was only the spirit of man that was made . . . it says *male and female* [Gen. 1:27] to give us to understand that the body was also being made now. Again, in case anyone should suppose that it was made in such a way as to represent each sex in a single person, like those called hermaphrodites who are found occasionally, he shows that he put it in the singular on account of their being joined in one, and because the woman was made from the man. (*De Genesi ad litteram*, Book III, 22, 34, 255)

By depriving the human figures of sexual characterization in the first panel but making it apparent in the second, Bernward calls attention to the essential uniqueness of the body animated by the soul. However, this body already contains the potential of future distinction between the sexes. The heart, formed by the large branches of the tree on the right, defines the creation of the soul as a pneumatic operation containing characteristics that will allow life to fructify. Indeed, if humans are indebted to the Tree of Life for their immortality, they also owe their proliferation throughout the world to it. Two details of the tree on the right's structure have so far gone unnoticed (fig. 19). The first is the knot tied by the two middle branches fashioning the upper part of the heart. The second is the entwining of the two lower branches that, in turn, emphasizes the interlacing of the branches in the central bush, thus echoing the original crossing at the base of the very first bush on the left. I would argue that a second principle can be joined to the principle of vitality: a fertility that is conditioned by a dual nature in which it is logical to identify the masculine and the feminine. This duality is literally cited in the only biblical injunction stated by God in the passage describing Man's coming to life: "And [God] said: 'Let us make man to our image and likeness and let him have dominion over the fishes of the sea, and the fowls of the air, and the beasts, and the whole earth, and every creeping creature that moveth upon the earth.' And God created man to his own image, to the image of God he created him, male and female he created them. And God blessed them, saying: 'Increase and multiply'" (Gen. 1: 26–28).

If Bernward does not portray the difference between male and female by the indicating the sex of the human bodies, he clearly implies its potential presence in the branches of the Tree of Life.

> [These things] already made received the characteristic activities of their own proper time, which came forth in manifest forms and natures from the secret formulae that are causally latent in creation; things like grass which sprang up over the earth, and the man made into a living soul, and other things of this sort, whether shrubs or animals, which belong to that work of God at which he is working until now. But these things too carry within them a repetition, so to say, of their very selves, invisible in some hidden power of reproduction, derived from those primordial causes of theirs, in which they were inserted into the world that was created *when the day was made*, before they ever burgeoned into the visible manifestations of their specific natures. (*De Genesi ad litteram*, Book VI, 10, 17, 344–345)

The Tree of Life, whose creation occurs in three phases in the first panel, is not only a principle of vitality and a model of the configuration of body and soul but also an assertion of the possibility of fructification, the paradigm of the entire human species.

The two human beings appearing in the panel are at the same time "Man" and man and woman, meaning that on one level the image can be read as depicting Adam on the right and Eve in the hands of God.

Yet the marvelous gift of life is not without constraints. Even if Man is untainted by carnal drive—as evidenced by his nudity—his corporeal nature requires staying near the tree in order to live; his gazing at God is subject to the mediation of the tree, separating him from the Creator while at the same time connecting him to God; his immortality depends on remaining in Paradise.

> The first man, however, "of the earth, earthy" was made a living soul, not a quickening spirit, for the latter condition was reserved for him as a reward of obedience. His body therefore had need of food and drink in order not to be weakened by hunger and thirst, and it possessed no absolute and indestructible immortality. Rather, protected as it was from the necessity of dying by the tree of life . . . it was beyond doubt an animal rather than a spiritual body. It would, however, not have died had not man, by offending, incurred the vengeance of which God had forewarned him. And though he was indeed not denied nourishment even outside Paradise, yet, being forbidden the tree of life, he was handed over to the wasting of time and old age, at least in respect of that life which, had he not sinned, he could have retained perpetually in Paradise. (*De civitate Dei*, Book XIII, 23, 570)

The creatures' dependence is signified by the image's hierarchy of size, with the human figures smaller than the tree and smaller than God. It is also evident from the presence of the navel (fig. 23). With no anatomical legitimacy, since neither Adam nor Eve was born of a mother, the navel is a pure sign. It may evoke, on the part of the creatures, the acknowledgement of their link to his Creator—the most likely hypothesis—without excluding the possibility that the navel signifies also the generating power delegated by the Creator to his living creatures. The navel reappears on all the door's nude bodies.

Finally, the creatures' dependence in relation to God is signaled by Adam's assigned position: the ground. Formed of small mounds in low relief on a plateau appearing neither under God's figure nor under the plants, this substratum is absent from the rest of the left wing, but it reappears on the right wing, charged with a considerable symbolic weight that will be analyzed in due time. This is the earth on whose surface runs nourishing water (Gen. 2:6), and at the same time it is both the clay of which man is

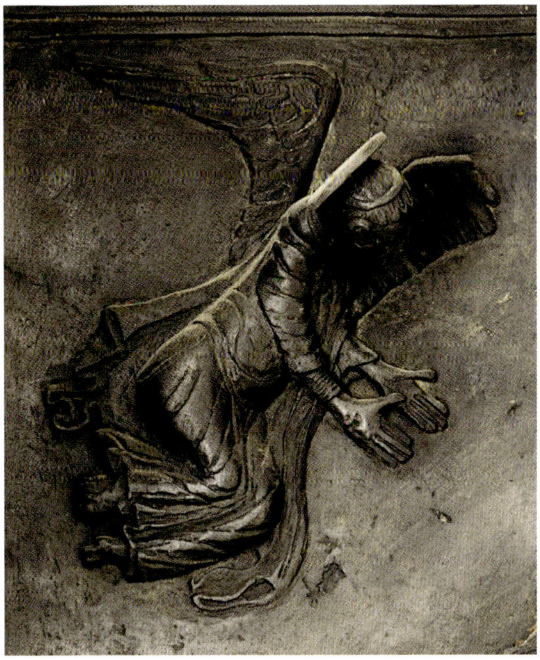

20

made and the mound that elevates him, as befitting a creature that will dominate the other animals (Gen. 1:26). It is the place, in the most material meaning of the word, that humans occupy in the Garden of Eden.

The place granted to Adam is simultaneously symmetrical with and diametrically opposed to that of the flying angel in the upper left corner of the panel (fig. 20). Humans share the angel's size but not his nature. His halo symbolizes the celestial creature's elevation to the same height as the Tree of Life's eternal palms, his diadem his belonging to the order of light. The angel's body, including the flowing clothes that underscore his ethereal quality, is inscribed in the panel's diagonal. His hands follow the axis of the opposite diagonal, completing the geometric structuring of the image's internal space (fig. 21). In this mathematical, orthonormal, and polarized space, the celestial being does not appear to depend on the Tree of Life or on God's hands. He is perfectly aligned,

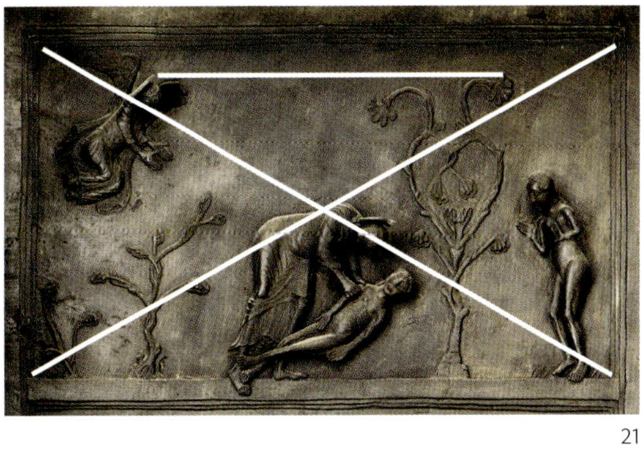

21

20. *Panel 1, angel.*

21. *Panel 1, positioning of the angel.*

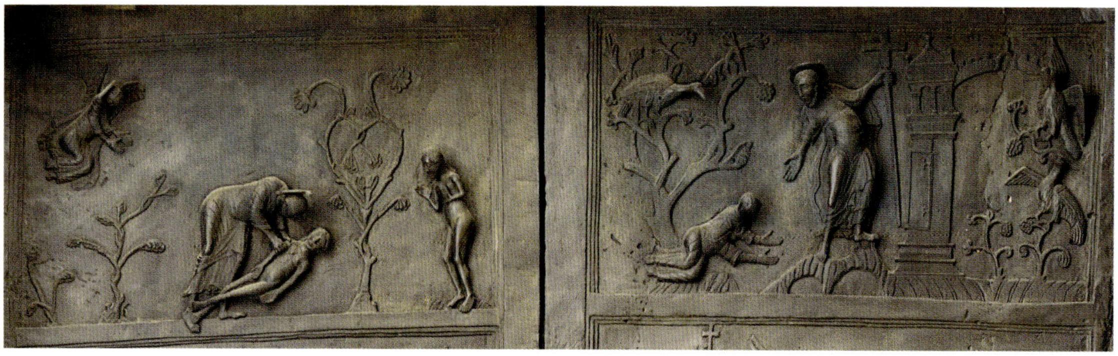

22

gazing on his Creator without any intermediary or mediation. He has no vital necessity other than to eternally contemplate the Creator and his œuvre to the point, as St. Augustine explains, that this direct knowledge is his raison d'être (*De Genesi ad litteram,* IV, 23, 41 and 32, 49). In other words, the angel knows God naturally because, by his nature, he partakes of the divine.

> Light was first fashioned in the Word of God in terms of the formula by which it is fashioned, that is, in the Wisdom co-eternal with the Father, and next in the actual fashioning of light in terms of the nature which was fashioned. At the first stage it was not made but begotten; here in the second stage, however, it is made, because formed out of formlessness. . . . Angels, after all, do not see these sensible material things just by the senses of the body, as animals do; but even if they do not make use of such senses, it is rather a case of their recognizing such things, which they have a better knowledge of inwardly, in the very Word of God, by which they are enlightened in order to live wisely, since there is in them that light which was the first thing to be made, if we understand it as a spiritual light that was made on that day. . . . Angels, you see, did not progress like us to the gaining of wisdom, to "behold the invisible things of God by understanding them through the things that have been made" [Rom. 1:20]. No, from the moment they were created they have been enjoying the eternity of the Word in holy and devout contemplation; from there they look back—over their shoulders, as it were—at these material things, and according to what they see within the Word they either approve of good deeds or condemn the sins. . . . Nor is it to be wondered at that God should first show his holy angels, formed in that primal fashioning of light, what he was going to create from then on. (*De Genesi ad litteram,* Book II, 8, 16–18, 199–200)

Man's vision is much more limited than the angel's because it is subject to the mediation of the Tree of Life. In addition to the assimilation of the tree to the organizing Wisdom in *De Genesi ad litteram* (II, 29, 29), the perfect plant also prefigures Christ who, as a new paradigm and new life source, will enable man to recapture his lost condition, forcefully highlighted by the typological structure of the panels on the bronze door.

In fact, panel 16—the panel opposite panel 1 and its depiction of the quickening of Man—portrays the encounter between Mary Magdalene and the resurrected Christ on Easter Sunday (John 20:15–17) (fig. 22). Renewing the demiurgic act of the Creator, the Savior, placed at the center of the image, beckons Mary Magdalene to rise, promising her eternal life by the mere fact of his Resurrection. On the right a lush Edenic garden replaces the mound on which Man was standing in the first panel. On the left, a bird perched on a tree branch has taken the place of the angel, who has disappeared. Mary Magdalene, the new Eve, is not naked—her flesh is not visible—but wears a finely pleated garment that looks exactly like the one worn by the angel in the first panel; furthermore, she reproduces his silhouette, floating position, outstretched arms, and direct vision of God.

The key to the visual discourse lies in the close parallelism between the angel and Mary Magdalene. Christ's promise of resurrection is here the promise of an ultimate metamorphosis: "For in the resurrection they shall neither marry nor be married; but shall be as the angels of God in heaven [*erunt sicut angeli Dei*]" (Matt. 22:30). It is the story of this miracle that the bronze door narrates. This idea, as central to Christian theology and baptismal liturgy as it was to Bernward's personal life, is mentioned in the founding charter of St. Michael's Abbey in Hildesheim: "To all of them (Moses, Elijah, David, Solomon, his models), God revealed the special nature of their merits, so that they would always, over the course of

22. *Panel 1 and Panel 16.*

time, be different from all others in virtue and deed, but especially so that they could become eternally similar [*coaequales*] to the angels."

Once again, Bernward is faithful to St. Augustine's interpretations of this passage in St. Matthew, found throughout the Christian patristic tradition:

> Again, a question often raised is whether it was an embodiment of soul that was first formed for the **animal body** [*animale corpus*], such as we now have, or a **spiritualized body** [*spiritale corpus*], such as we shall have when we rise again. For although this sort of body will be changed into that: *it is sown* ***animal body*** *and it rises* ***spiritualized body*** [1 Cor. 15:44] . . . we will not receive again what we lost in **it** [**the animal body**] but something altogether better to the extent that spirit surpasses soul, when we shall be *equal to the angels of God* [Luke 20:36]. (*De Genesi ad litteram,* Book VI, 19, 30, 353–354; passages in bold character are author's corrections)

> So how, they ask, are we said to be renewed if we don't get back what was lost by the first man, *in whom we all sinned* [Rom. 5:12]? . . . We shall be renewed from the staleness of sin, not to the original **animal body** [**corpus animale**] which Adam had, but to something better, that is, to a **spiritualized body** [**corpus spiritale**], when we are made *equal to the angels of God* [Luke 20:36], fit for heavenly mansions, where we will not need any food that decays. So then, we shall *be renewed in the spirit of our minds* [Eph. 4:23], *according to the image of him who created us* [Col. 3:10], which Adam lost by sinning. We shall also be renewed in the flesh, though, *when this perishable thing puts on imperishability* [1 Cor. 15:54] so that it may be a **spiritualized body**, into which Adam had not yet been changed, but into which he was to have been changed if he had not earned the death of his **spiritualized body** by sinning. (*De Genesi ad litteram*, Book VI, 24, 35, 321; see also *De civitate Dei*, Book XIII, 23, 570–71)

Even though Bernward's burial would have taken place later [Lasko 1987], the bishop of Hildesheim believed so strongly in this metamorphosis that he asked for the angelic hierarchies to be represented on his own tomb next to an eschatological citation evoking the vision of God through the mediation of the resurrected individual carnal body (Job 19:25–27) [Bergmann 1985, 125]. Bernward also had his funerary crypt consecrated and placed in the Church of St. Michael on the third day of the calends of October, the feast day of the archangel of the Last Judgment, patron saint of the monastery [Wulf 2008]. Finally, in the dedicatory inscription on his monumental bronze door, he qualified the church that was to receive it not only as a "temple," but more precisely as a *templum angelicum* (temple of the angels) quite naturally identifiable as the abbatial church of St. Michael. Like a look-out post dominating the episcopal town toward which the historiated door turns, this angelic church, filled with relics and unveiling the path leading Man to resurrection, functions as an immaterial wall, a spiritual protection keeping safe the city and its inhabitants.

To summarize, the doctrinal principles encoded in the first panel are not original, even though they show great theological depth; they belong to a vast patristic tradition, but it is obvious that Bernward's direct sources are *De Genesi ad litteram* and *De civitate Dei*—St Augustine's thought having nurtured Ottonian culture [Mayr-Harting 2007, 77*ff*.]. In the future, however, I will seldom quote from these texts, preferring simpler references: these texts support the iconographic demonstrations more than they clarify them. On the other hand, the body of scientific knowledge underlying Bernward's position will be called on throughout the analysis; just like the biblical text, it allows us to identify and understand the nature of the iconic unities displayed in the images. Such was the case for Boethius and Aristotle in the first panel: by playing with the two plastic pivots of form and substance, Bernward arranges his interpretation of the world according to the material, accidental, generic, and ontological categories so closely associated with the Aristotelian heritage valued by Ottonian culture.

To this it should be added that the concrete form of the discourse established by Bernward is just as remarkable as its naturalistic and scientific dimension. The visual vocabulary, taken from the sensible world and from well-known passages of the Bible, is designed to be accessible to all perceptive inquiry. This cognitive prerequisite adheres very strictly to the criteria and conditions for the use of images that Gregory the Great set down in a letter written in 599 for bishop Serenus of Marseille. This text, well known in the Ottonian world [Mayr-Harting 1989, II, 75] was well known to the Carolingians. Walafrid Strabo, abbot of Reichenau, for example, quoted it in his work when he insisted that images, in addition to their contemplative virtues, must lead "the *simplices* and the *ignaros*" to "the love of invisible things," namely the knowledge of God (*De exordiis*, MGH Capit. Reg. Franc. II, c. 8, 483).

Finally, the syntactical structure of the discourse consists in progressively exposing the viewer to content through a variety of forms, materials, personifications, and symbolic gestures arranged in analogical and converging layers. Here, the exegetical technique—first developed by the Church Fathers and used by medieval scholars when confronted by obscurities and seeming contradictions in the Bible [De Lubac 1959–64, especially 60 *ff.*]—is applied to the visible in an exemplary fashion. More than a simple interpretative technique, analogical thought is a relationship with the world shared by the entire community of medieval Christians; it establishes a cosmology in which everything is connected and potentially signifying. The same is true of the bronze door, which becomes a mirror of the world and of the Word that created and rebuilt it by its incarnation.

23. *Panel 1, Adam.*

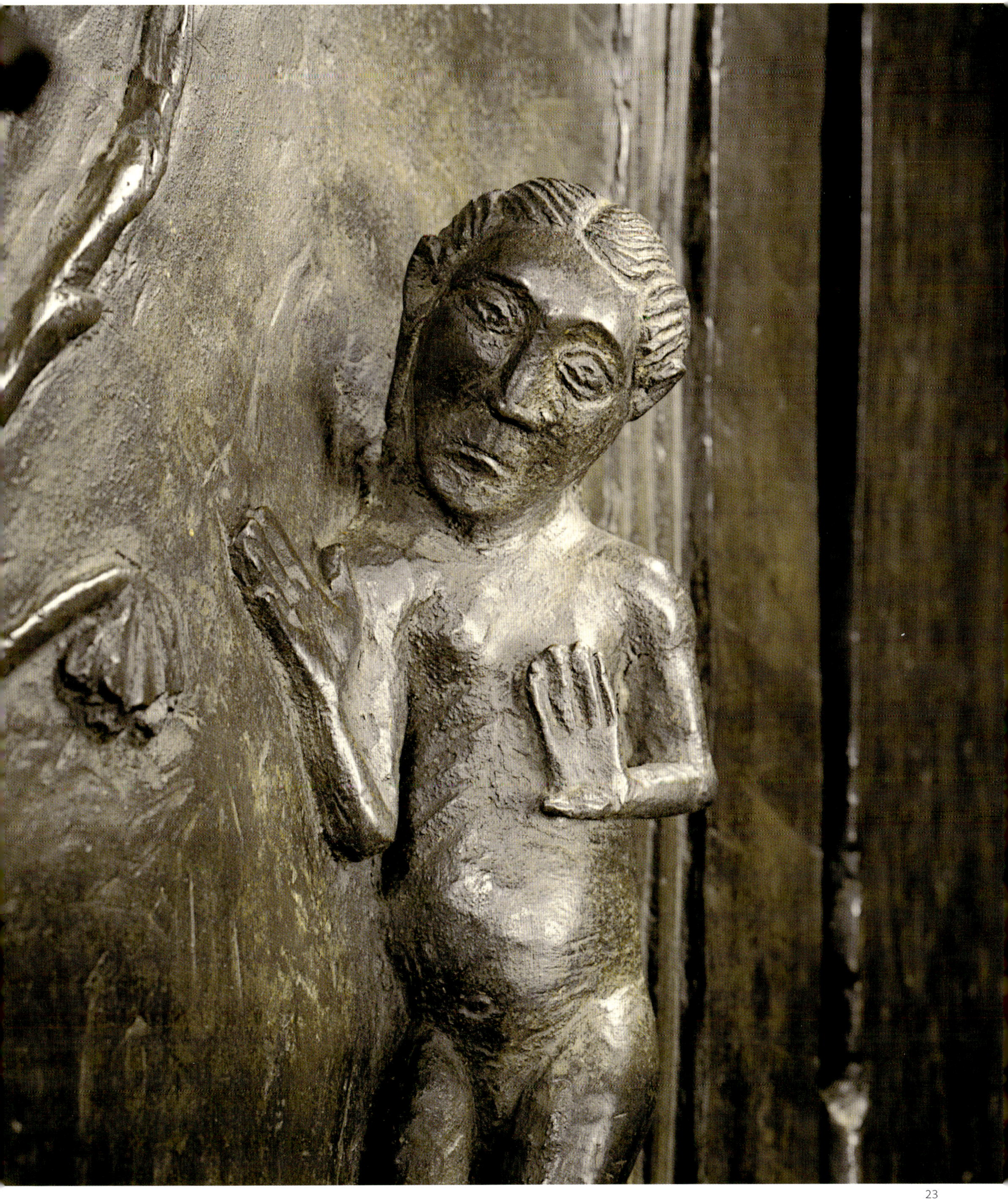

23

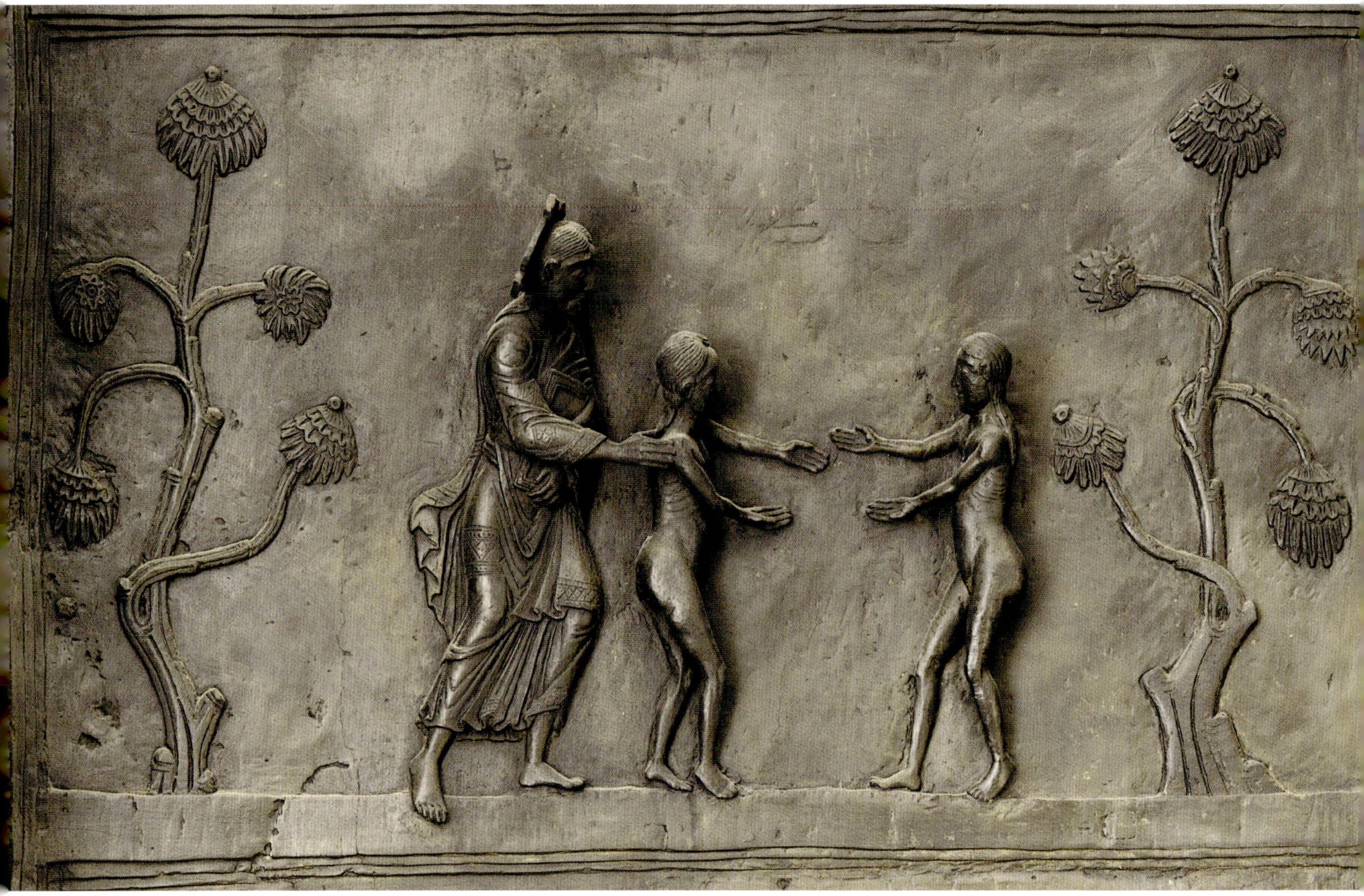

Panel **2**

LOVE

The richness of the door's first panel sets the stage for the story's beginning and gives a glimpse of its ending. The seeming simplicity of the second panel, clearer and better structured than the first, is misleading: the spectator is invited to plunge knowingly into the abyss separating the human from the divine (fig. 24).

A single scene unfolds between the two large trees that unify the space. With a firm but gentle gesture God ushers in a small nude figure, introducing her to a second person. The Bible says: "And the Lord God built the rib which he took from Adam into a woman and brought her to Adam" (Gn. 2:22). The two humans occupy the same relative positions as those conferred on them in the preceding panel by the reading suggesting sexual difference. Can we then rightly identify them as Adam and Eve?

The question is not as anodyne as one might think. Latin Bibles are not all identical, to say nothing of the considerable differences that may exist between twenty-first century vernacular Bibles. Like all his contemporaries, the bishop was part of a long tradition that sought to penetrate the hidden meaning of the divine message by studying concordances, assonances, and verbal etymologies. This commitment to the biblical thus moves beyond the narrative content to take in words as highly signifying forms. In the Latin Vulgate, elaborated by St. Jerome working from the Septuagint, a more-or-less fixed version in Carolingian times [Riché 1984, 55 ff.], man is first named Adam in Genesis 2:20—the passage where he names the animals—while in the Hebrew Bible, the basis for the many vernacular translations, man is not named before Genesis 4.

24. *Panel 2.*

Happily, the Carolingian version of the Vulgate Bernward used has been preserved, allowing us to read the very text on which the program of the bronze door is based (Hildesheim, Dombibliothek, Ms. 61). In Bernward's Bible, Adam is already named when God presents him with a companion (folio 6); the same cannot be said for the woman, whose name is mentioned only in Genesis 3:20 (folio 6v) after the scene of the original sin. Readers should bear in mind that the woman is referred to as Eve only to facilitate our analysis; we shall return later to the important nuance that her generic qualification introduces into the biblical episode represented in panel 2.

A very strict axial symmetry governs the panel's general structure, a symmetry suggested in the previous image by the upper branches of the Tree of Life, evoking a dual matter. The two great trees framing the scene, as well as Adam and Eve—represented face to face, eye to eye, at the precise moment when they first become aware of one another—mirror each other. The vegetal/vital principle is divided in half; each human must now be considered individually according to their analogic relationship with the Tree of Life in the background.

As they gaze at each other, Adam and Eve see themselves as we do: similar and dissimilar at the same time (fig. 26). The tension of their mutual desire is palpable in the empty space defined by their outstretched arms and almost touching hands. Their gestures correspond perfectly to one another, even interconnecting. Adam's slightly elevated arm suggests an embrace just as the position of his left leg implies a perfect interlocking of the bodies. This complementarity increases the confusion between the two fig-

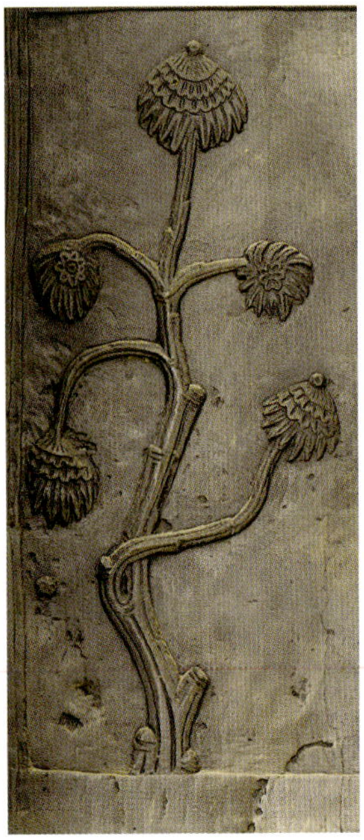

25

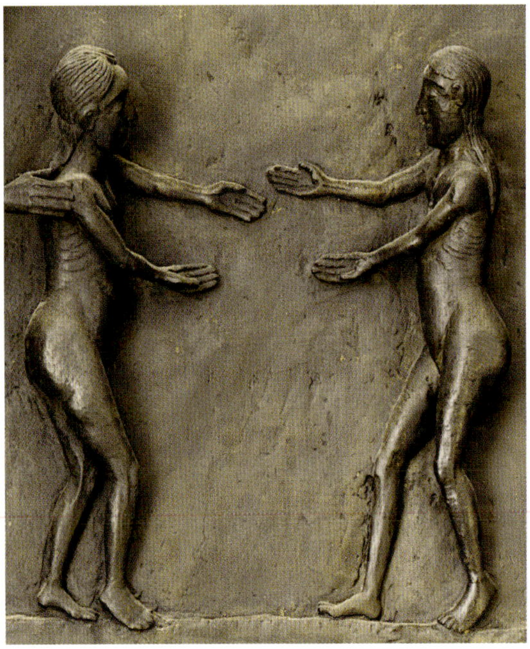

26

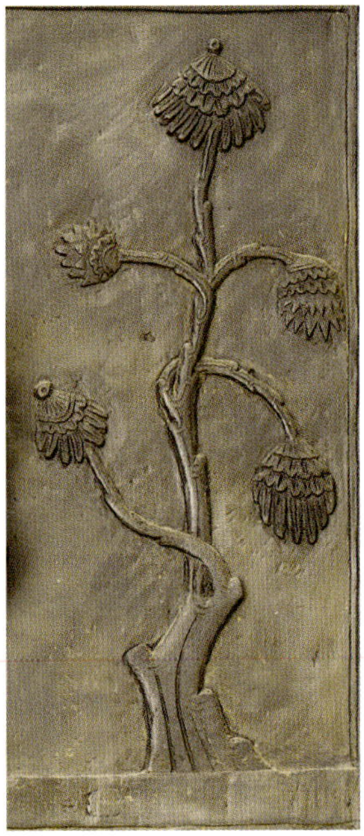

27

25. *Panel 2, Eve's tree.*

26. *Panel 2, Eve and Adam.*

27. *Panel 2, Adam's tree.*

ures, whose anatomy is identical, with the significant exception, already noted in the analysis of panel 1, of the presence of breasts on the woman (cf. fig. 39): in both figures we see the same long hair, the same slim legs and slender arms, the same visible ribs and erect torso, and of course the absence of genitalia, since Adam and Eve become gendered only after the Fall.

A more thorough observation of these two bodies' remarkable plasticity reveals that their gestures are not exactly identical. Eve's back is slightly more arched than Adam's, due less to her anatomy than to a slight twist of the torso accompanying the inclined head. In addition to his slightly raised arm, Adam's stride is longer than Eve's. We shall return to these differences.

The two trees appear as similar to each other as Adam and Eve: same size, same single trunk, same number of levels, each one ending with a cluster of leaves (fig. 25 and 27). This magnificent arrangement contributes to the panel's sense of harmony. However, the morphological identity is broken by details of such subtlety that very lengthy scrutiny is necessary to reveal their presence.

The first differences are seen in the tree trunks, beginning from the base, or roots, the part of the plant described by the Latin word *radix*. Although of similar shape, the roots are different in width and height. The power emanating from the root mass behind Adam is greater (fig. 31). In addition to its massive framework, this root mass is made more prominent on the right-hand side by a flow of undulating matter, like a surge from the soil whose thrust is emphasized by vertical lines, each topped by two small horizontal half-moons.

This is mirrored on the left side of Eve's tree's root bundle by a little figure appended to the trunk. Oblong, supple, just slightly curved, bipartite and marked by two deep horizontal lines, it is topped by a rounded outgrowth (fig. 29). The two trunks exhibit another notable difference. Although continuous lines starting from the ground ascend both trees, recalling their irrigation in the first panel, it is only on Eve's tree, that we spot a thick elongated branch divided into more-or-less equal sections and tied to the trunk with knots (fig. 28). The branch goes up the trunk, adapting itself perfectly to its wooden curves and extending itself to the main branches, surrounding them with the same rigorous precision. Does this represent another circulatory system, which of course would lead one to think of sap?

Distinguishing between water and sap seems as little pertinent to the physiological understanding of the plants as distinguishing between water and blood would be for the human body; to the extent that water as source of life is identified with Christ's blood in the right wing, such a hypothesis is incompatible with the vital principle of Adam's tree, whose modalities of survival are exactly the same as those of Eve's. We must turn, then, to the biblical text Bernward considered the sacred fountain of Revelation for answers:

> And the Lord God formed man of the slime of the earth. (Gn. 2:7)

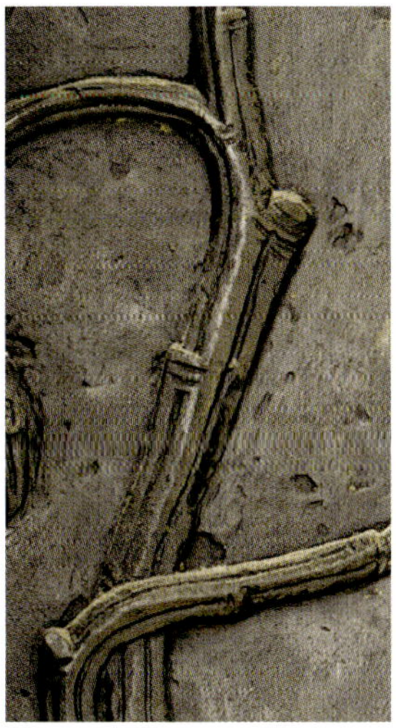

28

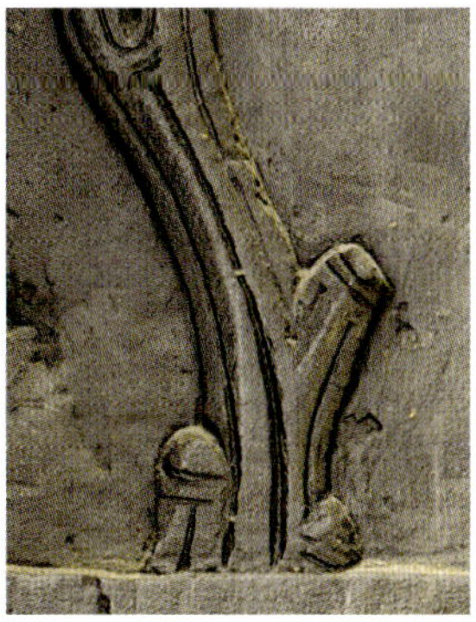

29

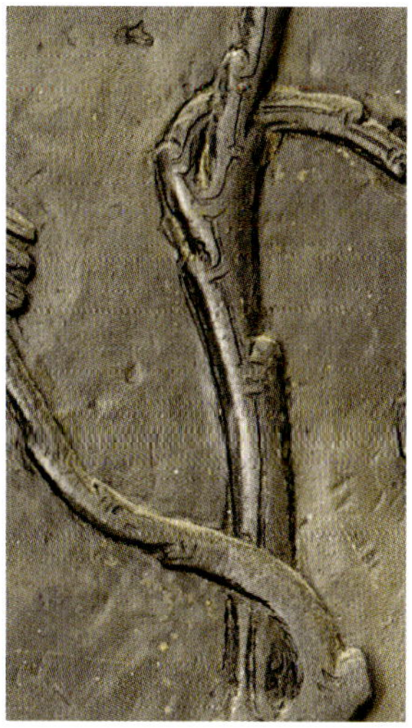

30

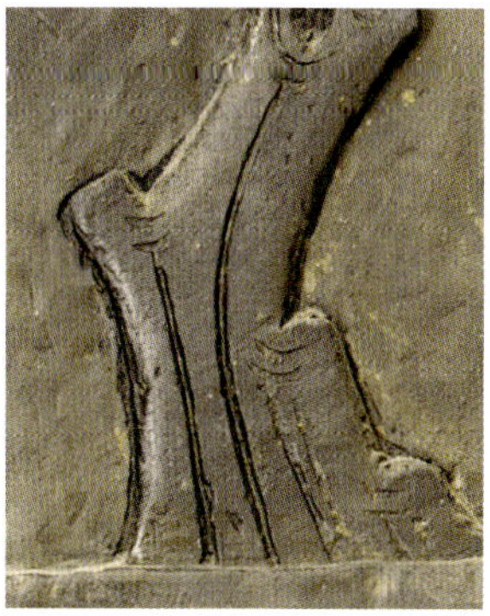

31

> Then the Lord God . . . took one of his ribs, and filled up flesh for it. And the Lord God built the rib which he took from Adam into a woman: and brought her to Adam. And Adam said: This now is bone of my bones, and flesh of my flesh; she shall be called woman, because she was taken out of man. (Gn. 2: 21–23)

At this point in the story, it is important to recall that the woman is not yet called Eve but *virago*, a term that the text says explicitly comes from the root *vir*, man. The same Latin word, *radix*, designates both plant roots and the etymological root of words. Clearly, I am arguing that the roots' morphology depicts the different geneses of the two human bodies. Adam's body is homogeneous, formed from the clay of the earth, as shown by the undulating flow of matter rising from the ground. Eve's body, made from Adam's rib, is composite and is represented by the little oblong shape inscribed in the root mass. This rib contains in potentiality the two great principles that will transform it into a human being: matter, incarnated in the upper excrescence (*caro de carne*), and shape, since the initial orientation along the bole is taken over by the supernumerary stem that, when applied to the tree, constitutes its skeleton (*os ex ossibus*).

28. *Panel 2, structure of Eve's tree.*

29. *Panel 2, roots of Eve's tree.*

30. *Panel 2, structure of Adam's tree.*

31. *Panel 2, roots of Adam's tree.*

Unlike the Tree of Life in the first panel, which was shared by both humans, the two Trees of Life in the second panel represent both the divergence of their respective geneses and the similarity in the matter and structure with which they are made. This assumption inevitably gives rise to paradox: why insist on this difference if Adam and Eve turn out alike at the end of the process?

Let us quote *in extenso* the biblical passage about the creation of woman:

> And the Lord God said: It is not good for man to be alone: let us make him a help like unto himself [*faciamus ei adiutorium similem sui*]. . . . Then the Lord God cast a deep sleep upon Adam: and when he was fast asleep, he took one of his ribs, and filled up flesh for it. And the Lord God built the rib which he took from Adam into a woman: and brought her to Adam. And Adam said: This now is bone of my bones, and flesh of my flesh; she shall be called woman, because she was taken

out of man. Wherefore a man shall leave father and mother, and shall cleave to his wife: and they shall be two in one flesh [*duo in carne una*]. (Gn 2: 18–24)

Adam and Eve are certainly similar, but they must necessarily be different in order to become one flesh. The plants' branches are used to develop this discourse on the crucial otherness of man and woman (fig. 32 and 33).

Tensions and orientations arranged in axial symmetry dominate the two trees' lower and middle branches. The former, centripetal and extended toward one another, are quite vigorous. As if themselves mutually attracted, they seem to conform to the image of Adam's and Eve's arms and legs and their desire to come together. Conversely, the centrifugal middle branches just above fall heavily toward the ground. Their terminal leaf clusters hang equally lifeless, emphasizing the vital tension that lies in the two tree's attraction for one another.

The clusters of leaves at the end of the "desiring branches" are identical to those at the top. Their conical form when stretched, as well as the silhouette traced by their withering, evoke the Eastern palms that Romans of early Christian times depicted on their sarcophagi and on the great paradisiac mosaics of their basilicas. As we shall see, this hypothesis is strengthened by the trees' "behavior." Moreover, they are very similar to vegetation in Carolingian miniatures evoking biblical places (for example, in the *Bamberg Bible*, Bamberg, Staat., Ms. Bibl 1, f 7 v, or in the *Bible of St. Paul Outside the Walls,* f 7 v).

Although the two trees express the same desire, there is a major difference between their opposing upper branches. In Eve's tree each of the leaf clusters contains an open flower revealing a pistil and petals that form a crown. If the trees are indeed palm trees, these flowers may be an erroneous figuration of bunches of dates. Regardless, the flowers do not appear on Adam's tree. The distinction does not concern the structure of the two trees but rather their anatomy; like the two breasts perceptible on the woman's chest the flowers function as a way to distinguish between two almost identical figures. This attributive dissimilarity respects the ontological uniqueness of nature and form between the two creatures, yet distinguishes them by gender.

The admittedly sketchy anatomical descriptions that the early Middle Ages inherited distantly from Hippocrates and Aristotle and more directly from the Romans Galen and Pliny (in zoology), regarded the male and female organs as being inversely similar, that is, the same yet different [Thomasset 1990, 58; Bonnet-Cadilhac 1997, 110]. The shift from the vegetal to the human, expressed in the figuration of the genesis of the bodies and the assertion of their sexual difference, is no mere metaphor here. In spite of the warnings of Theophrastus, the first Greek botanist to be aware of the risk in applying the Aristotelian vocabulary for animal topologies to plants, the ancient and subsequent medieval classification of plants developed analogically from that of other domains of living things [Morton 1981, 33]. The consequence of these confusions, so characteristic of the systemic approach favored by ancient science, is that the sexual traits of plants are based on anatomical and behavioral distinctions borrowed from human beings; this is particularly true for Latin writers, who equate vegetal pairing to that of the social couple [Bretin-Chabrol 2007]. One finds the most striking expression of such inappropriate analogies in Pliny, where books XII to XXI of his *Natural History* are entirely devoted to plants. The emblematic species of this vegetal reproduction is unquestionably the date palm of Judea and Arabia (*Phoenix dactylifera*), a tree already cited by Theophrastus; Pliny describes its extraordinary longevity, noted also by Isidore of Seville (*Etymologies, XVII, VII*), and describes its sexual union as an actual coitus (bk. XIII, c. VI). Thus, the likelihood of the palm tree as a model for the configuration of the Tree of Life in panel 2 appears even more justified. Let us continue with the comparison.

The uppermost leaf clusters of the two Trees of Life differ in that the one on Eve's tree is rounder, more developed, while Adam's is more outstretched and dynamic. On Eve's tree, the two inner flowers are not strictly identical (fig. 32): the small heart of the left flower is more developed than the one on the right; its tiny central circle has expanded, its notched crown has thickened, as if it had grown by spreading its substance, while simultaneously the leaf cluster bearing it has sagged, as if drained of the energy that nourished the leaves.

The difference between Eve's two leaf clusters could seem fortuitous were those on Adam's Tree of Life not identical (fig. 33). The tall branch turned toward Eve's tree is permeated by an intense and polarized tension that stiffens the wood and bristles the leaves, like the bracts of a thistle. In contrast, its leaf cluster is less substantial than its symmetrical counterpart, equivalent to a whole layer of leaves: some residual traits remain, engraved on the bronze and visible under low-angled light (fig. 35). Fuller but lifeless, the right branch collapses, just like its thick foliage. Therefore, specific conditions connect the leaf clusters on Adam's and Eve's trees two by two.

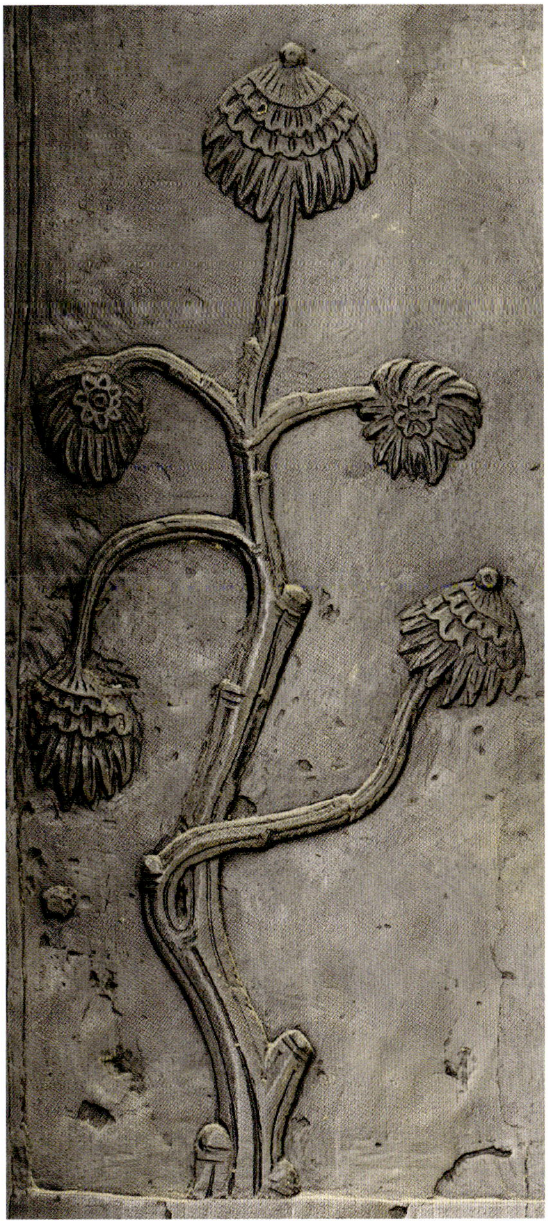

32

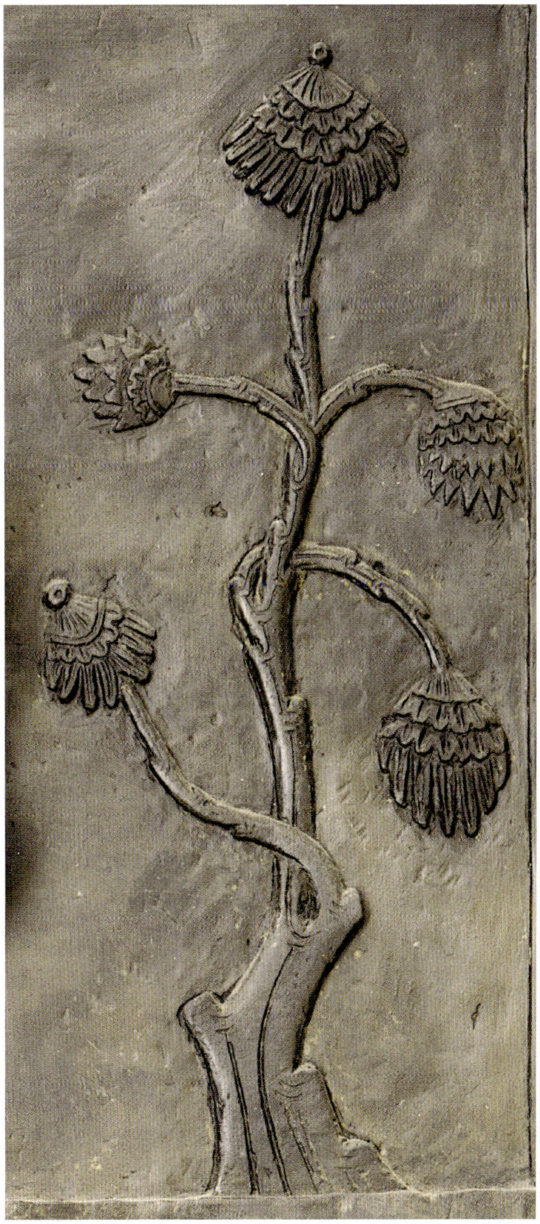

33

32. *Panel 2, Eve's tree.*

33. *Panel 2, Adam's tree.*

The first concerns the vigorous central clusters, one of which shelters the finely detailed flower, the other the foliage, bristly but with one amputated layer. I suggest interpreting this as the seeding process that transfers the male matter to the female matrix, a process achieved through an organic tension described by Pliny in his presentation of the Judean palm.

> It is asserted that in a forest of natural growth the female trees will become barren if they are deprived of the males, and that many female trees may be seen surrounding a single male with downcast heads and a foliage that seems to be bowing caressingly towards it; while the male tree, on the other hand, with leaves all bristling and erect, by its exhalations, and even the very sight of it and the dust from off it, fecundates the others. (Pliny, *Natural History*, Book XIII, c. VII, Perseus Digital Library translation)

I wonder whether it is judicious to insist further on the correspondence between the image and Pliny's text, but it is worth noting that the left side of the root of Eve's tree, which we suggested identifying with Adam's rib, looks remarkably like a phallus (fig. 30). Christians certainly incorporated this law of living and fructifying into the divine order: "From Him comes everything which exists in nature . . . the seeds of forms and the forms of seeds and the movements of seeds and forms. He gave also to flesh its origin,

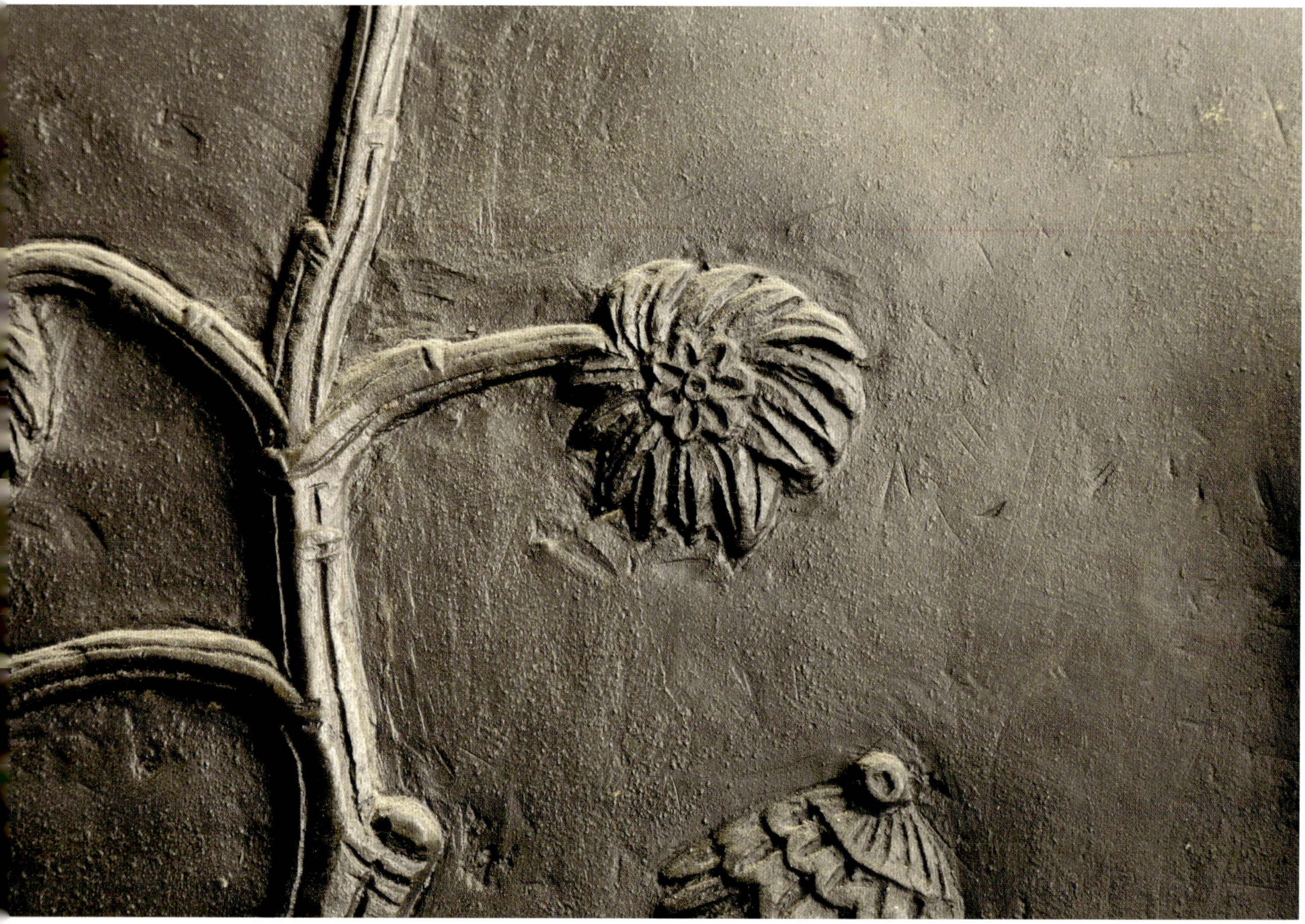

34

34. *Panel 2, Eve's tree, close up.*

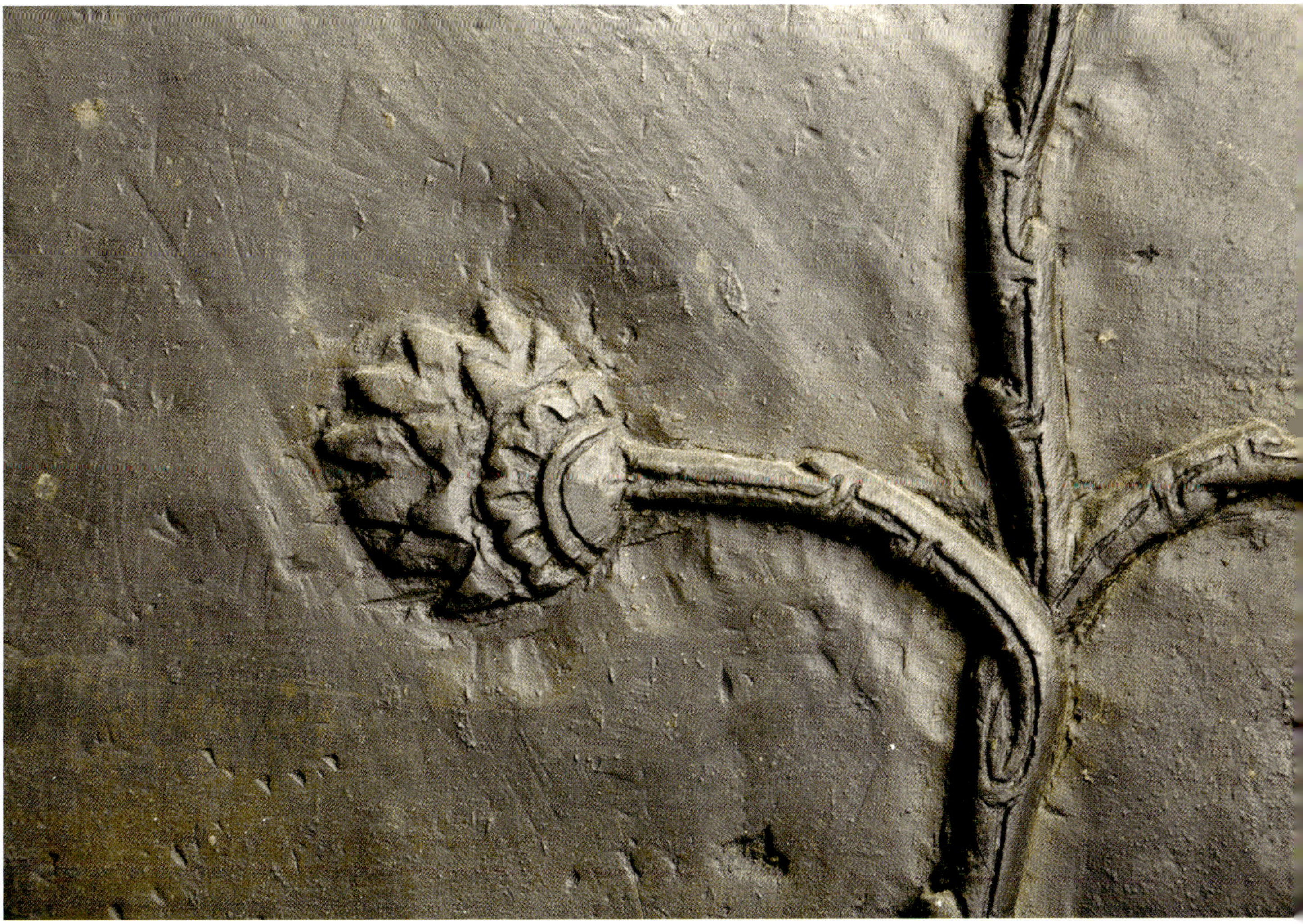

35

35. *Panel 2, Adam's tree, close up.*

beauty, health, fruitfulness in propagation, and the disposition and wholesome concord of its members" (Augustine, *De civitate Dei,* V, 11, 206).

There remain the two external leaf clusters on the opposing upper branches: if they serve as a useful reverse shot to the central action, it is probable that they represent a time different from that of fertilization (fig. 32 and 33). Their absence of vigor and increased matter suggest that they present themselves as matrixes at a postcoital state, Eve's cluster henceforth sheltering a life that it nourishes—we must remember that the flower is fuller—while Adam's is restoring its seeding capability. Regardless of how far we may wish to push the analogy, it must be agreed that, at the very least, it emerges from the visual adventure suggested by Bernward: although man and woman are, in conformity with divine Law, ontologically identical, the fruits resulting from intermixing the masculine and the feminine are to be born from the anatomically female body.

Contrary to the primordial androgyny of platonic culture and the absence of gender distinction proposed by Gregory of Nyssa [Angliviel de la Beaumelle 2001, 72], Bernward prefers the original view defended by St. Augustine in his *De Genesi ad litteram* (Book III, 22,34, 254–255). The bishop of Hippo suggests that there was a principled polarization between masculine and feminine in the Creation, existing potentially in the first biblical passage concerning Man (he speaks of the *informatio* of creatures) and activated at the time of the second formation of the bodies and their presentation to each other (*formatio*) [Angliviel de la Beaumelle 2001, 73]. Avoiding precisely describing the conditions of Adam's and Eve's union in Eden, he suggests instead to model them on those that took place later, giving them a spiritual form without the "troubling ardors of concupiscence," a stance that Bernward takes up again on the door. Finally, in a statement that will become a veritable commonplace in Christian thought, Augustine explains that Eve was created for Adam for the sole purpose of becoming a mother. In that regard, the Bible presents a strong argument. The first mention of the woman's name is concomitant with the affirmation of her maternal quality: "The man called the name of his wife Eve: because she was the mother of all the living" (Gn. 3: 20, Bernward's Bible, f. 6v).

Just as the Tree of Life in the first panel represented a twofold vital principle serving as a paradigm for humans and the rest of Creation, the two Trees of Life in the second panel show and explain the principles of vitality embodied, in the literal sense of the term, in the bodies of the man and the woman. The trees reveal the two humans' ontological identity, their parity established by the same matter and structure, while presenting their anatomical differences as the sine qua non of a fertile complementarity. Therefore, the Trees of Life in the second panel serve as models for not one but two ways of creating bodies. The first, a divine action, is the transformation of the man's rib into a woman; the second, which follows from it, transfers the vitality principle from masculine to feminine bodies, establishing the latter as "creators" of life. This very common denomination appears especially in Isidore of Seville's *Etymologies* (book XI, I, 15), an encyclopedic text used extensively by Rabanus Maurus, a Carolingian abbot from Fulda, in his *De universo* (Book VI, I): "The flesh [*caro*] is thus called because of [its root], 'creating' [*creando*]. *Crementum* [the principle of growth] is the male seed from which the bodies of men and animals are conceived. Hence, the parents are called *genitores* [*creatores*]."

We shall point out here, and this clarification will become important in the following panels, that in animal generation as described by Isidore and Rabanus Maurus, the female too is endowed with a seed that she mingles with the male's in order to be able to give life.

To summarize, just as Bernward's employed his knowledge of geometry to delineate how form was inscribed in the laws of divine creation in the first panel, he carries out an identical scientific synthesis in the second that enables him to better define the reproduction it depicts. He applies his botanical knowledge to the biblical story of the Tree of Life, to which he gives certain characteristics of the *Phoenix dactylifera*—the most "eternal" of trees—and shows how the vital drive acts within a gendered and homogeneous nature in its fructification principles. This detailed explanation of reproduction mechanisms brings the visual discourse back to a concrete level with which all viewers would be familiar without, however, slipping into an erotic plane that would be both pointless and especially inappropriate when depicting Eden. Moreover, the vegetal fertilization paradigmatic of human creation at the beginning of time is associated with a mutual desire, a love willed by God, which seeks and accomplishes the fertile mix of masculine and feminine. These modalities of fruitful union, which differ greatly from those that will appear after the original sin, are made clear by the figures' position in the image.

In comparison to the preceding panel, the second panel depicts a standing Creator who has moved back a step, without modifying the position of his feet on the ground (fig. 37). At the same time the supine creature of the first panel has been set upright, though not at the expected place, namely at the level of his

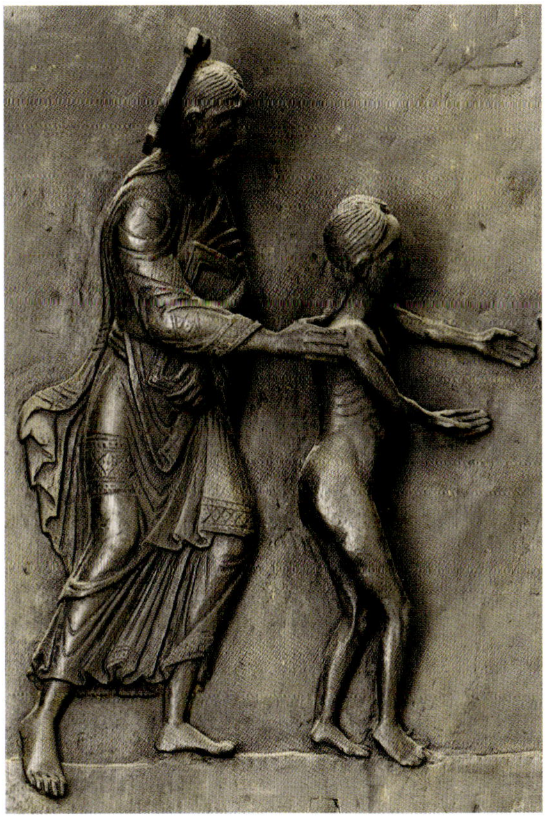

36

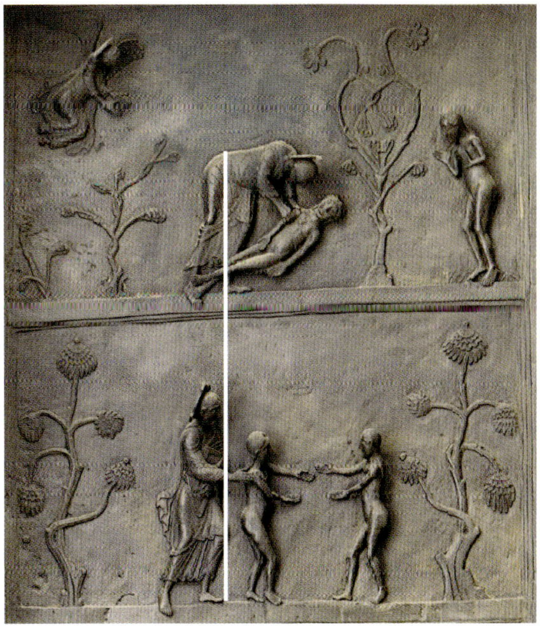

37

36. *Panel 2, God and Eve.*

37. *Panels 1 and 2.*

crossed ankles but in front of the Creator. This new iconic knot, perceptible only under close scrutiny, is of great importance: from one panel to the other, God has stepped back, he has withdrawn from the center of the image in order to foreground the creature he has raised up, the Eve of the second panel.

To this astonishing phenomenon is added an equally unexpected mimesis. In his centripetal movement toward Eve, Adam imitates God's step. The relation between Eve and God is slightly more complex. Visually the Creator stimulates the woman's movement by the weight of his lofty presence and the dynamic force of his displacement (fig. 36). In fact, he touches her shoulder, without the slightest pressure, only with his fingertips, the shoulder being where her arm stretched toward Adam begins. The movement of this arm literally imitates the movement of God's arm. In other words, the Creator does not exert any external constraint on Eve, any more than he does on Adam; he acts by stimulation and by suggestion and the humans imitate him, conforming to His image. God's archetypal gestures, encouraging but not coercive, reveal a new dimension in the narration. In the space still separating the two humans, there is an immediate future during which the contact between Eve and God will be interrupted: by giving Eve to Adam the Creator relinquishes his power over his creature, he liberates her; by giving humans the gift of freedom, he places them face to face with himself in the literal sense of the term. Man and woman, made in God's image, are now complete.

Freedom, however, is not autonomy, and the link established between Adam and Eve remains as dependent on God as eternity was on the Tree of Life in the first panel. Here God holds an oblong book, seen with him also in panel 4 where he condemns Adam and Eve after original sin (fig. 58). Three more books will be placed on the door's right wing: in the hands of the Virgin, the Christ child, and St. John. Subsequent to the panel of the Incarnation, however, they take on a particular significance, to which we will return in due time. The book appears only twice in the narrative of the Old Testament, and always as a divine attribute whose meaning requires further study. In the two panels under scrutiny, the book is pressed against God's body, underscoring his gesture: here it is placed behind his prompting, liberating arm; in panel 4, it is aligned with the axis, practically above the accusing finger he projects forward. In these depictions of God, it thus functions as the starting point for movements of which it is also the source.

Moreover, in both panels the book is pressed identically against God's body, aligned with the figurative codes of the divine garment against which it rests. In panel 2 (fig. 38) the book is decorated with an ornate binding, bordered by a row of studs or set stones, as was customary in Ottonian time [Krug 1993]. As for God's attire, it is adorned with fine embroidery, probably of precious metal, arranged in strips and lattice patterns on the sleeves, the thighs,

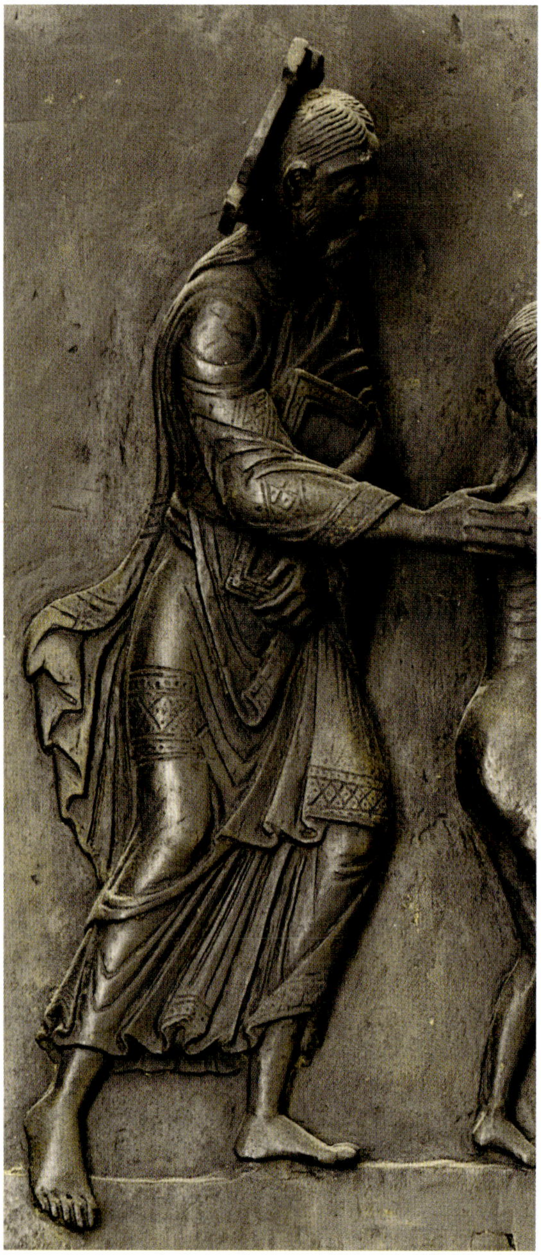

38

and the border of the tunic and toga. None of these ornaments appear on the book or on God's garment in panel 4 (cf. fig. 68). In fact, they will disappear altogether from the rest of the bronze door, hereafter characterized by austere simplicity. Only the lattice work, a multiplication of the cross motif, placed from the narrative's beginning on the Creator's cruciform nimbus, will have a recurring symbolic function in the following panels.

These comparisons are instructive. The visual identity between the book and the garment on which it is superimposed suggests that, in both panels, the book is much more than a circumstantial attribute, instead becoming an ontological component of the divine person. Associated with the gestures of which it is the source, it transmits a performative language, namely, a body of divine words that accomplish what they state: here by suggestion and in panel 4 by constraint. In other words, in these images the book refers to God's words, that is, his Word. But in which of its functions?

To understand this, we must recall the divine figure of the door's first panel. Through his cruciform nimbus, God already appeared there with the characteristics of the Son, of the first Word identical to the Creator, explicitly identified with Christ by Christians in theological dogma since the first Council of Nicaea, as well as in images since Carolingian times [Von Erffa 1995, 46]. It is through this very Word ("And God *said*: Be light made. And light was made," Gn. 1:3) that the Father created the world, spreading Wisdom, his life-giving and ordering impetus.

In the second panel the creating Word has left the center of the image and, in a way, the image itself. God has not withdrawn from the world, but here he no longer acts as demiurge. The laws he has established suffice to create an orderly proliferation of life. The dynamic principles he placed in the two creatures in the first panel take form naturally, their sexualized bodies allowing humans to mate, grow, and multiply, to give life in their turn, as foreseen by Divine Providence. By eluding its demiurgic quality, from being creator according to divine will *in action,* the Word becomes *signified* divine will, the world's law for humans. And since the humans imitate it freely—Eve with her arm, Adam with his step—it has become specifically intelligible and contractual law. The form through which the Word chooses to address Adam and Eve, however, is not articulated language; that is, the conventional and limited words humans will use after the Fall. Rather, it is light. This light is God's fundamental attribute: "For she [Wisdom] is the brightness of eternal light, and the unspotted mirror of God's majesty, and the image of his goodness" (Sg 7, 26).

It is also, of course, Christ at the beginning of John's Gospel: "In the beginning was the Word, and the Word was with God, and the Word was God. The same was in the beginning with God. All things were made by him: and without him was made nothing that was made. In him was life, and the life was the light of men" (Jn. 1:1–4).

For the first and last time on the door God's visible image—the book as garment—shines with ornaments rich in evocative power, even more so for Bernward since he was himself a goldsmith and had varied and rich liturgical furnishings executed for his

38. *Panel 2, God.*

church. [On the general and central theme of light in Christianity, see Davy et al. 1976; on the theme of ornamentation see Bonne, 1996; 1997.] God presents himself to be comprehended by this shining light: it is because they comprehend him—in the literal sense of the term, *cum-prendere,* meaning to take on oneself—that Adam and Eve act in his image and fulfill what God wills for them, namely, that they be and behave like him. Freedom, completing the resemblance to God, is thus contained within the limits of knowledge and respect for divine will.

This knowledge of God is no more direct here than it was in the first panel. The book, placed behind the woman, is not visible to humans; in an even more paradoxical manner, Adam and Eve gaze into each other's eyes in such a way that they do not look at the Word. As in the previous panel, the knowledge of God requires mediation. The representation of this mediation is extremely subtle. Since God is much taller than Eve, the light he releases illuminates the woman, surrounding her with a halo, so that Adam sees Eve in God's light and is able to see God's light when gazing at Eve. Therefore, Adam does not see the woman for what she is "visibly," physically, with the body's eyes. Illuminated by divine light, he sees her spiritually with the heart's eyes (*De civitate Dei,* Book XI, 27, 486). [On vision, see Klein; Marchesin 2007]. That is why the two humans are not ashamed of being naked. Furthermore, Adam does not see God where he "really" stands in the image—and where the spectators see him—but in the spot where he stood in the previous panel, in the middle, where he shines spiritually. And since, in seeing Eve, Adam sees God, it is God he desires when desiring Eve, thus uniting himself with God in uniting with Eve. The fertile love between man and woman is not the carnal and fatal bond of the next panel but a love connecting with God. It is the covenant, the exclusive mutual love willed by God, of which the book seals the contract and decrees the rules.

We now face the very essence of both the Hebrew and the Christian liturgy. In addition, because the renewal of the covenant between God and humans is enacted and reenacted, panel 15, placed opposite panel 2, develops a subject perfectly articulated with the idea of God's loving desire (the Holy Women come to Christ's tomb to take care of his corpse). In the same way panel 15 prolongs the meditation on God's visibility (the absent Christ is replaced by an immense drapery focusing our attention on a visible absence and an invisible presence) (fig. 1).

We shall not go further in presenting the typological connections between the two wings. Too many elements are missing for the comprehension of panel 15; they will be included in the analysis of the left wing and the beginning of the right wing. Bernward programmed the reading of the door as a pathway occasionally enlightened by facing images, but he did not use typology as the driving force of signification. In fact, the strongest links between the panels are the ones articulating their succession. Thus, in panel 2 the Word-book has taken the place of the Word-creator in order to fully realize what had been initiated in panel 1: Man in the likeness and image of God—that is, free and life giving—loving his creator and himself through the love for the other as a creature of God. This emancipation without autonomy intrinsically includes the possibility of sin. Since God wanted a covenant, albeit an asymmetrical one, he has turned his love for humanity into a bond that the latter has the power to break. Thus the second panel announces the third, just as the first panel announced the second. It sheds light on what will happen not by weaving a causal link between facts but by calling attention to their dialectic articulation: it is not because God has determined the basis for an alliance that such a pact will be violated; rather, because it exists, it can be transgressed.

These connections of anticipation and resolution between the successive panels give a new coherence to the chronological reading of the door, a level of comprehension that allows the viewer to understand the signifying position of the episodes in relation to one another. The biblical narrative therefore appears in its sacred depth: it is not written by humans but by God, and the events recounted become his message. The "Book of the Covenant," like the Tree of Life earlier, calls attention to the fact that in its structuring temporality is the fruit of a divine, omniscient and providential will that defines the framework of human freedom. The trees attest to the fact that natural law is an expression of divine Law, just as history is.

Bernward's narrative discourse is therefore much more than a recollection: it reorganizes biblical material, unveiling the motivations of history and raising understanding of the factual *pagina* to the level of divine reasons—that is, to the knowledge, albeit partial, of God. The reading of the door constantly oscillates between two interpretative levels: an immediate comprehension, recognizing the event in its relation to the biblical narration, the *historia*, and a lengthy decoding of the signs tracing the depth of their meaning.

Both these levels are intimately interwoven through an interpretative relationship arranged by a visual syntax that the self-reflexive door also exhibits. This set of rules, this syntax, is not merely a discursive device. It contains per se a considerable symbolic dimension, like the metamorphosis that is both the active visual principle, the richest in meaning of the door's images, and the main subject of the door. Here the story is told of the transformation of human into angel, and of the conversion of the Christian in front of the door, preparing for this metamorphosis.

It is not only the biblical events acting as signifiers but also the visual means by which they are represented. It is the combination of contained and container in the visual message that restores it to the plenitude of its meaning; in the same way the words of the Bible recover their quality of divine truth only by means of their formulation, their composition, in the liturgical and/or musical word as well as in the calligraphy and rich ornamental system pertaining to it. When we stand in front of the bronze door, we face a completely Christianized universe in which the visual signs are iconic (their container and their content participate identically in what they designate). The images, including the door itself, are an incarnation of the divine Word, and their components function as signs in the fullest, Peircean sense of the term.

39. *Panel 2, God and Eve.*

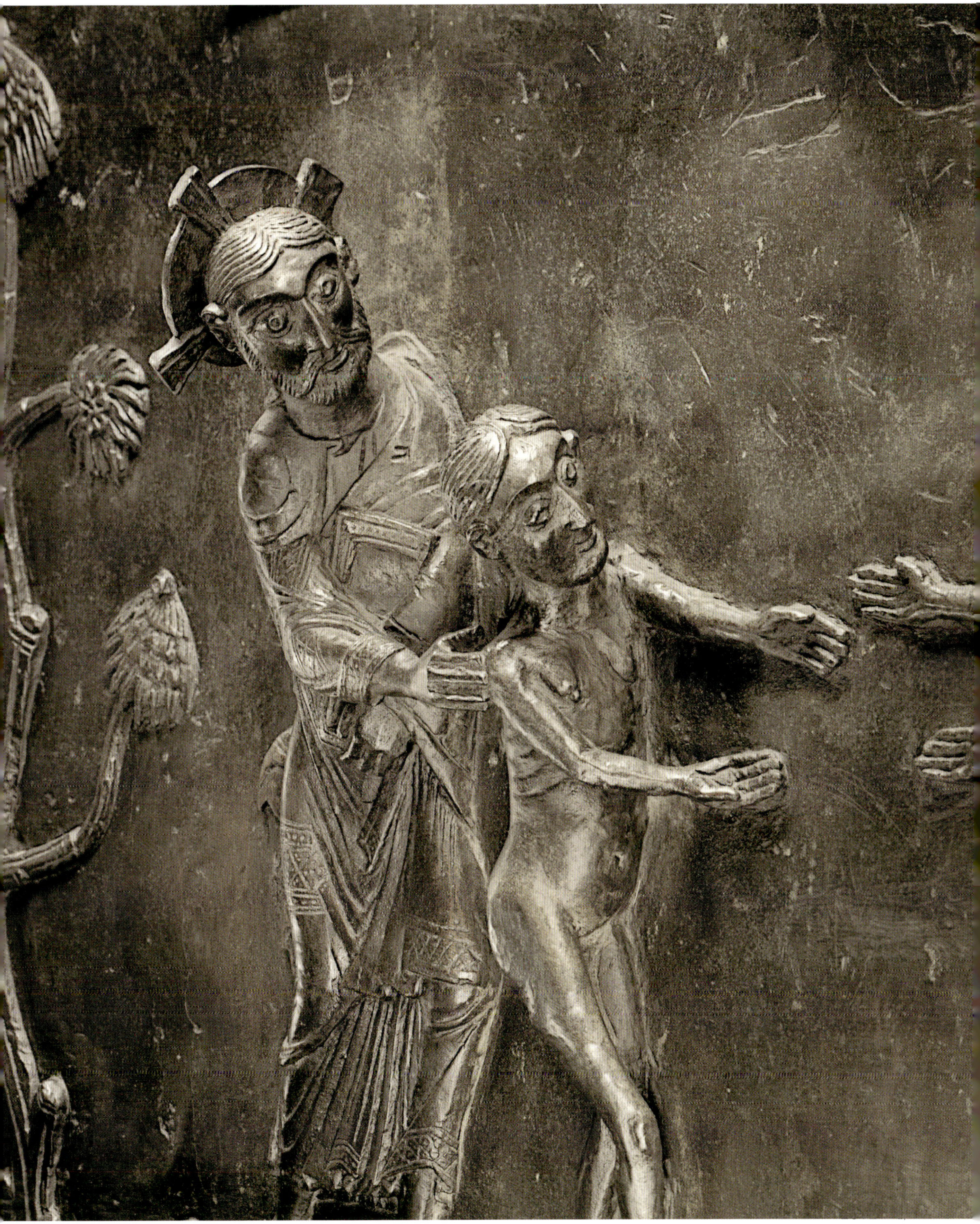

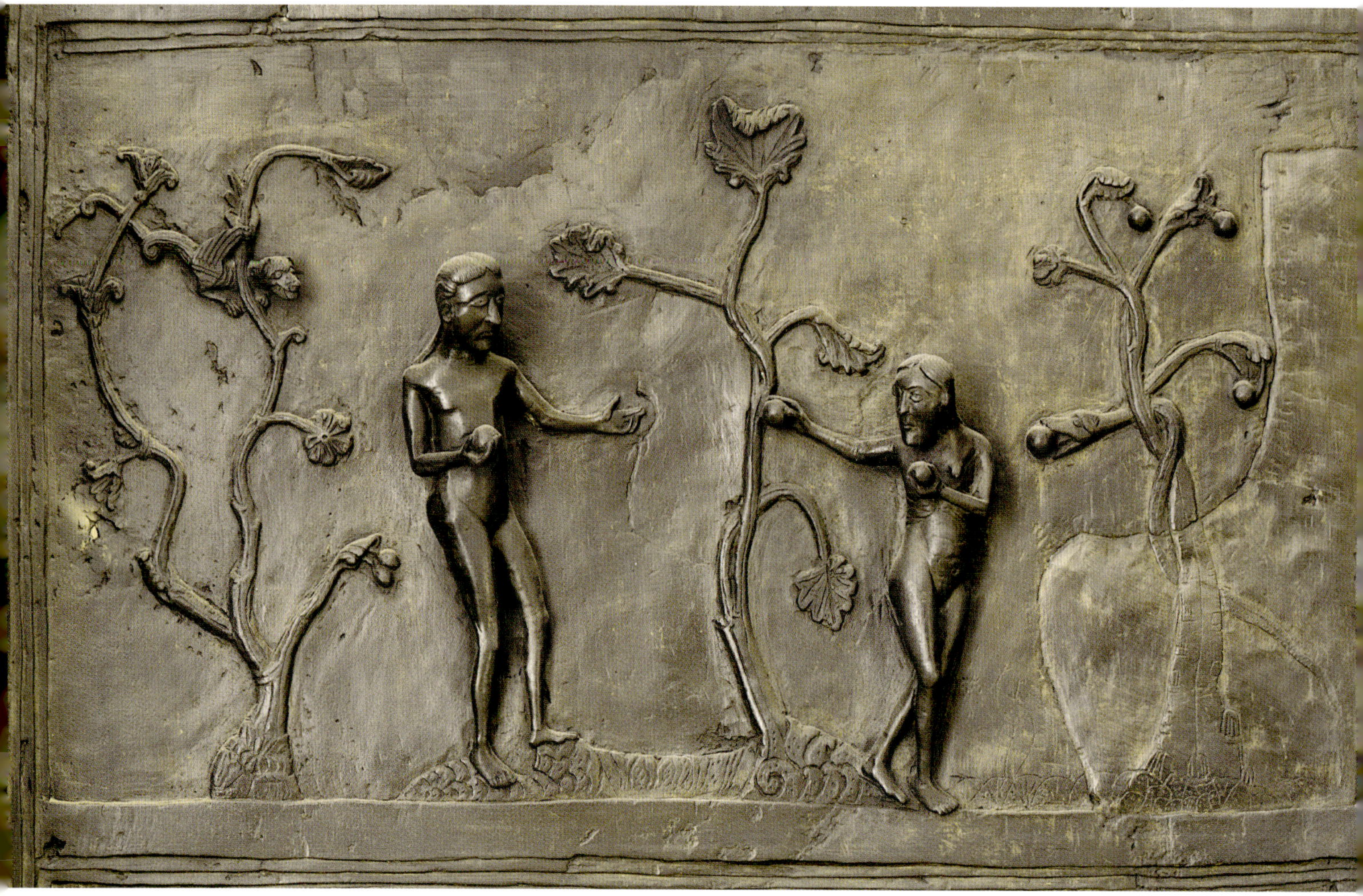

Panel 3

DEFORMATION

The door's third panel depicts original sin, the most famous and terrible episode in the Old Testament (fig. 40). God has disappeared. Two humans and three plants are arranged alternately on the image's surface. (The large patch that appears to be added on the right is most likely a crack caused by a cooling accident after casting.) Instead of the similarity and symmetry of the previous panel, Bernward has established visible and profound differences between the new protagonists. These differences primarily concern the trees, which are as dissimilar as the foliage. They also concern Adam and Eve, who are differentiated in their physical appearance for the first time: Eve is obviously smaller than her spouse and is placed at a lower level in the image. A residual symmetry remains, an outstretched arm and a bent elbow, but it is very clearly broken by her body language: Eve holds out an apple to Adam, who points at it with his index and middle fingers while opening his hand to receive the fruit; Eve's legs are crossed whereas Adam's are parallel; lastly, her movement is centrifugal, while Adam's is centripetal.

This interruption in the arrangement of the bodies is articulated with a deceptively symmetrical topography. In the center of the image stands a large, thick, monolithic mound. It consists of two knolls separated by a wide depression, a river, as we shall see later; it supports the middle tree on one side and Adam on the other. It is now possible to suggest that the scene represents the Garden of Eden at whose center, as the biblical text says, God placed the Tree of Life (Gen. 2:9). The garden is not in the exact middle of the panel but, instead, has slipped noticeably to the left, while the Tree of Life, which appears to be at the center of the image, has in fact slightly displaced toward the right. Their double function as an expected but unrealized symmetrical axis increases the instability of the whole scene.

40. *Panel 3.*

This visual disarray is intensified by the difficulty of drawing any connection between the supernumerary trees and the humans. Far from clarifying the reading, as they have done so far, the plants almost become a source of confusion. The panel's only intelligible action, the gift of the apple, is just as bewildering: the relative position of the two humans has been reversed, and although Eve moves toward the right, she turns to the left.

What is immediately striking about the panel is an individualization of the forms and an atomization of the visual space, as well as the diegetic space that contains the narrative. The panel is presented as introducing a chaotic disorder within the divine creation. In fact, the narrative is organized visually and chronologically around seven apples, constituting a sort of formal rhyme within the panel: one in Adam's right hand, two held by Eve, and four on the tree at the extreme right.

The biblical text is silent regarding the nature of the forbidden fruit taken by the two humans. The Christian East sees it as a fig, whereas the West prefers to identify it as an apple, a fruit both very much appreciated and widespread in the West; moreover, through homonymy it is a signifier of the evil it symbolizes. In classical as well as medieval Latin, the apple is called *pomum* and *malum* [Pastoureau 1993]. In the integrally meaningful world of the Christian universe, the deep truth of an object can be found also, and perhaps first of all, in the word designating

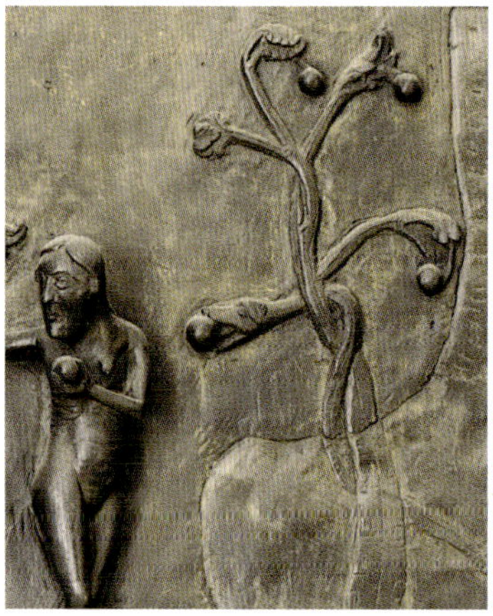

41

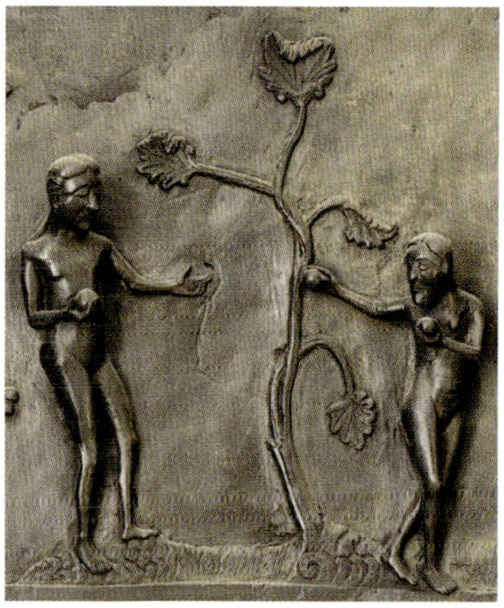

42

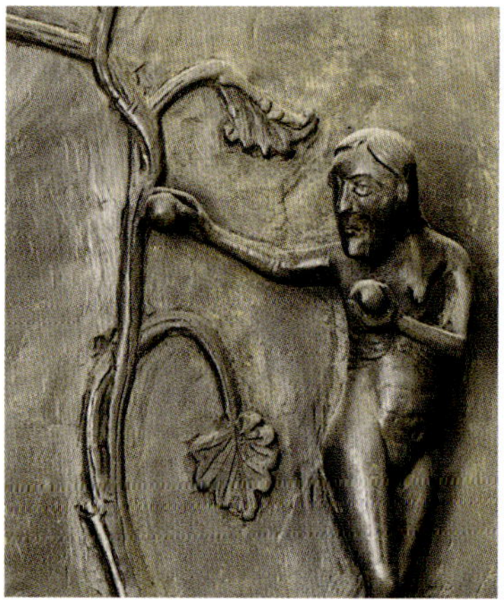

43

it. Thus, the apple is the archetype of both the desired fruit and the forbidden fruit.

The tree that produces the apple is designated by God as the Tree of the Knowledge of Good and Evil. Cited together with the Tree of Life, from which it does not greatly differ in exegesis or iconography [Von Erffa 1995, 105 ff.], in Genesis 1:9, it is the only tree from which God has strictly forbidden to eat, on pain of death (Gen. 2:16–17). By contravening his injunction, Eve commits the first sin, original sin. Just like the biblical text, the panel depicts the episode's unfolding in great detail. Read from right to left, the scene reverses the order of the first panel depicting the growth of the Tree of Life, in other words, an order counter to divine will and life itself.

The apple tree is placed behind Eve, not between Adam and Eve, as was frequently the case in previous iconography. Three apples hang from its branches (fig. 41). A fourth appears on the left side of the tree, tightly held in the jaws of a snake wound around the trunk, the front of its body merging with one of the plant's branches in a perfectly illusionistic way. This tree, as pure as anything that God placed in his Paradise (*De Genesi ad litteram*, Book VIII, 13, 28, 409), is one of the multiple forms assumed by the Tree of Life. Marked by the seal of the Trinity since it carries three fruits, it behaves like a character in a story, resisting the aggression of which it is the victim by retracting its foliage. If it leans slightly to the left, it is solely because of the pressure exerted by the serpent's body on its trunk. Finally, the tree explicitly turns its fruits to the right, thus putting them out of Eve's reach and signifying, in so doing, that it is not the woman's tempter. This tree, naturally good as a creature and image of God, has acquired a harmful appendage, a false graft making human sin possible. Could the serpent, which Genesis qualifies as the most clever and skillful animal on earth ("*callidior cunctis animantibus terrae*," Gen. 3:1), be the source of evil? By entwining its body with the tree, the serpent gives Eve the illusion that the Tree of Knowledge is offering her its apple. That is its only fault. Eve's fault is on an entirely different scale, extending the meditation on the vision put forward by Bernward in the first panel of the bronze door.

By the illusion it produces, the serpent is just as mendacious in the image as it is in the Bible, leading Eve to believe that humans will not die if they eat of its fruit but will instead become "like gods who know good and evil" (Gen. 3:5, Bernward's Bible, f. 6). The serpent embodies the most dangerous and most reprehensible of vices in medieval culture [Casagrande and Vecchio 1987]. It is here that Bernward ties a "semiotic knot," a system of gazing that engenders an intense meditation.

The Tree of Knowledge is shown simultaneously for what it is—pure and triune, since it actually bears only three apples—and as illusion distorts it: tempting and quadruple in that it seems to offer a supernumerary apple. Like the viewers of the door, Eve can see the sign as divine truth, not as its sham. She does not look at the tree; in fact, she turns away from it, preferring instead the serpent's venomous lie.

Thus, the animal is merely a part of evil: temptation. Eve, however, gives it substance, constructing it as sin when, having been created with freedom of choice, she shares the fallacious appearances with Adam instead of God's image and truth.

Indeed, she becomes as much an illusionist (Gen. 3:6) as the serpent (fig. 42). Although this is a recurrent trait of the iconography of original sin [Von Erffa 1995, 180], Eve generally plays a much less elaborated role than she does in this panel.

With her right hand she offers Adam the forbidden fruit, covering its upper part with outstretched fingers so that, by a distortion of perspective, Adam, like the viewer (as well as some historians obviously deceived by the artifice) has the impression that

41. *Panel 3, the Tree of Knowledge.*

42. *Panel 3, Adam and Eve.*

43. *Panel 3, Eve.*

the fruit comes from the tree in the center of the background (fig. 43). Contrary to appearances, the central tree clearly has no apple. Of the three plants represented in the panel, this tree is actually the one that adheres most closely to the form of the previous ones, even if its large leaves, unprecedented in size and shape, liken it to a fig tree, the very tree that, according to the text of Genesis, provides the leaves with which Adam and Eve cover themselves (*folia ficus*, Gen 3:6). A living wood, incorporated into the continuity of previous plants, this tree would even be in line with the orthonormal arrangement of the Tree of Life in the first panel if its withered right branch did not turn toward the ground and if, at the base of the trunk, there were not a leaf of such weight that it vertically bends the branch carrying it, in a troubling premonition of the Fall.

It is worth noting that the distortion of the tree is lateralized. It involves only its right side, as if Eve had contaminated her surroundings with some kind of poison. What happened, or is happening, to the woman that does not affect the man? The two humans are equally sinners in that they have both broken their covenant with God. However, their involvement in the process triggered by the rupture of the covenant is different. Adam is holding just one apple; his hand, stretched toward the fruit Eve is offering, is the manifestation of either a query or a desire. Either way, the man has not yet eaten the forbidden fruit, which is not the case for Eve.

Indeed, if the woman reproduces the serpent's illusionist act, she also repeats its body language: her body turns in snakelike fashion, her arm twists sinuously as she holds out the apple. In other words, her gestures mark her out as the mediator of evil, a far cry from the previous panel, where her gestures imitated her Creator's. The downfall is enormous. If Eve was blind to God's presence in the Tree of Knowledge, she had no difficulty in spotting the mendacious animal. With biting irony, the animal told the truth when it claimed that from now on, she would have the ability to see good *and* evil. The woman's gaze has been ontologically modified by sin, becoming strictly physical (*De Genesi ad litteram*, Book XII, 24, 52, 565–566).

Thus, the woman's transgression unfolds in four stages. First, she believed the serpent's lie since she was incapable of seeing God in the tree. Second, she ate the apple and saw evil. Third, she imitated evil in order to make Adam her accomplice in sin. And fourth, she offered the apple to her spouse so that he would eat it too. It is the third stage—the reason why Eve caused Adam to yield to temptation—that is the basis of the Christian perception, so troubling in our time, that woman was responsible for original sin. In addition, it is what introduces inequality between the two creatures that God had conceived as a complementary pair.

Let us make clear, however, that Bernward's position is not axiological. Morality prescribes but does not explain, and it is not the bishop's objective to impose certain norms but rather to persuade the faithful in order to create the conditions for an inner conversion. As mentioned earlier, the symbolic images set up by Bernward derive from an understanding of biblical literality as the source of an unveiling of meanings dealing with reasons and essences, which Christian authors, depending on the time and classifications, qualified as the spiritual or allegorical meaning of the Bible, a meaning that "derives solely from the structure of things and, consequently, [that] God alone can establish in the very nature of the real" [De Bruyne 1998, II, 680].

Bernward does not shift strategy to explain Eve's role in original sin. He applies a logical demonstration to the sequence of events, and if many Christian authors remain vague about the reasons for sin or apply a moral interpretation to it, the bishop explains its process rationally, finding, as did St. Augustine, that the episode's only blind spot was the reason why God allowed humans to lose sight of him. This will never be explained, even if good can come from evil. Everything else is comprehensible and pertains only to the nature that God gave humankind.

Let us return to the scene. The Tempter who slithered onto the Tree of the Knowledge of Good and Evil is an animal, and it is by playing with this archetypal animality that Bernward makes explicit the link between sin and sexuality. The apple that Eve holds against her chest is placed just in front of her right breast and it would appear that her sex, unlike Adam's smooth lower abdomen, is evoked by three small lines, unless they are the result of accidental chisel blows, which is doubtful (fig. 44).

As for the extra branch of the central Tree of Life, its leaf is set at the level of the woman's genitals (fig. 45). Open, widely spread and split in the middle, it appears like a metonymic figure of the genitals it will cover. Nothing like it appears on Adam's side of the tree; he has not yet eaten the apple, but this serves only to shift the phenomenon to the tree on the left of the panel. What Eve seeks in Adam is found on the lower branch of the plant: a stiff trunk raised like an erect penis. From the uppermost leaf hang two small round fruits resembling testicles; they are aligned with the man's lower abdomen (fig. 46). In addition, the base of the tree takes on the shape of a swollen sheath, possibly a visual citation of a canker draining the strength of a considerably shortened trunk.

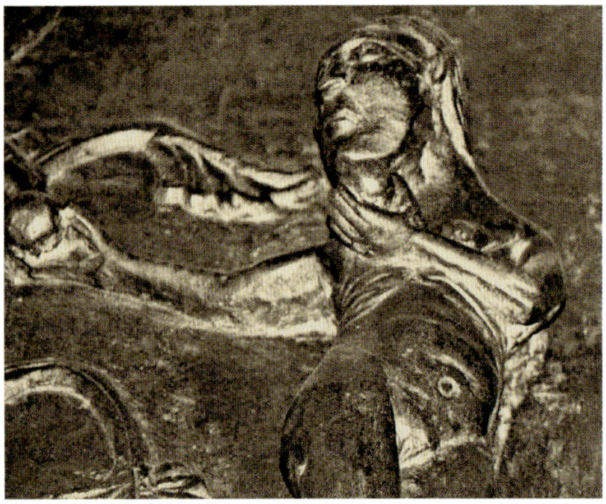

44

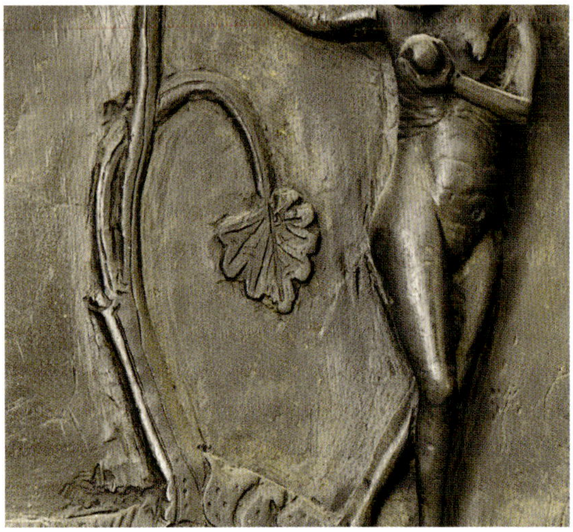

45

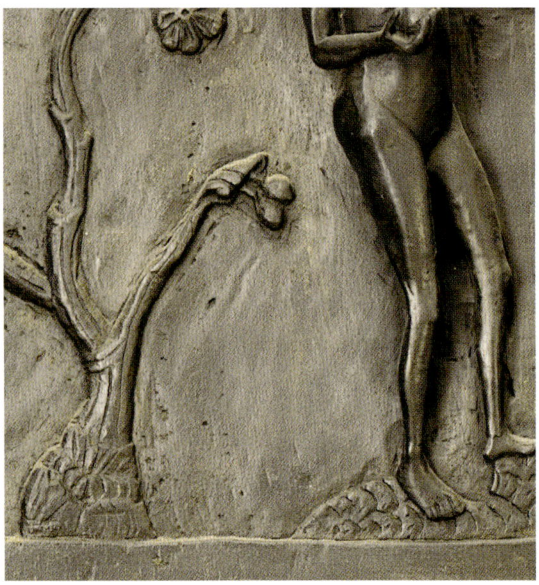

46

Incongruously attached to the tree like an obscene graft, the sex-like appendage acts on the plant like the serpent intertwining with the Tree of Knowledge of Good and Evil. It inscribes carnal sexuality thoroughly into the structure of the plant. In its absence, the other two gnarled and contorted branches would be so unbalanced that the whole thing would fall (fig. 47).

The tree has been disfigured by sin; certain exegetes describe its ugliness after the Fall, and at least one Carolingian artist represented it in an altered form on a frontispiece of Genesis (Bamberg, Misc. class. Bibl. I, f 7v). The plant here becomes the plastic expression of a new vital principle made explicit by its morphology. Its two great branches maintain the initial quality of the first great Tree of Life, signifying the masculine on the left and the feminine on the right, as shown by the presence of two isolated details in the middle register. The first is a flower (fig. 48), different from those found in Eve's tree in panel 2 (fig. 49) in that it is deprived of its setting of palm leaves. This is the last flower to appear on the bronze door.

On the masculine branch, symmetrical to this flower, are attached two rolled up leaves enclosing a third one, thin, flat, and striated (fig. 50). Contrary to expectations, this vegetal element does not resemble the cluster of leaves on Adam's Tree of Life in panel 2; rather it more closely resembles the young bindweed leaves on the Tree of Life in panel 1 (fig. 51), not only in its inverted position and general funnel shape but also in the subtle and polarized striation of its central leaf. I suggest that here the plant takes on the opposite of its model in order, like the sickly swelling of the trunk, to take into account the confinement of the spiritual material in the stifling gangue of the thick and coarse lateral leaves.

Whatever the hypothesis, the feminine flower seems deprived of matter, whereas the masculine leaf lacks vitality. The fertility resources of the trees in the second panel have been morphologically altered. It is difficult to know if Bernward was thinking of the anatomical descriptions by Isidore of Seville and Rabanus Maurus of the quality of masculine and feminine seeds. Regardless, these two authors explain that feminine infertility is due to lack of seed, which is assimilated into menstrual blood, and that masculine infertility comes from the fact that the man's seed is too thick (Isidore of Seville, *Etymologies,* Book XI, I, 139 and 142; Rabanus Maurus, *De universo,* Book VI, I).

The top of the plant will reveal the productive mixture of these barren flowers and leaves but only after the gaze and the narration have encountered

44. *Panel 3, Eve.*

45. *Panel 3, Eve's branch.*

46. *Panel 3, Adam's branch.*

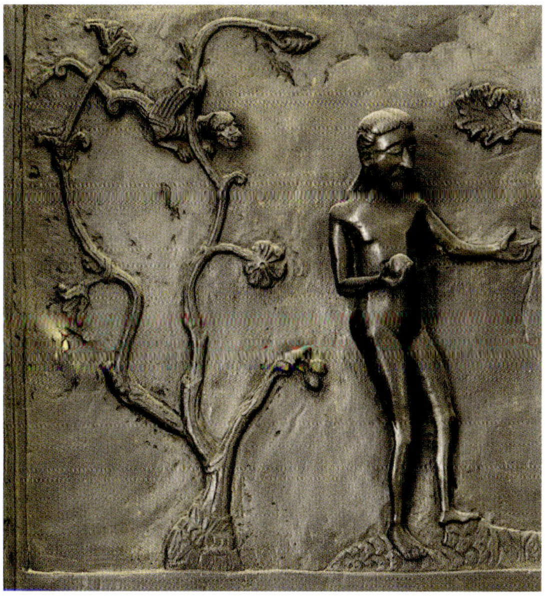

47

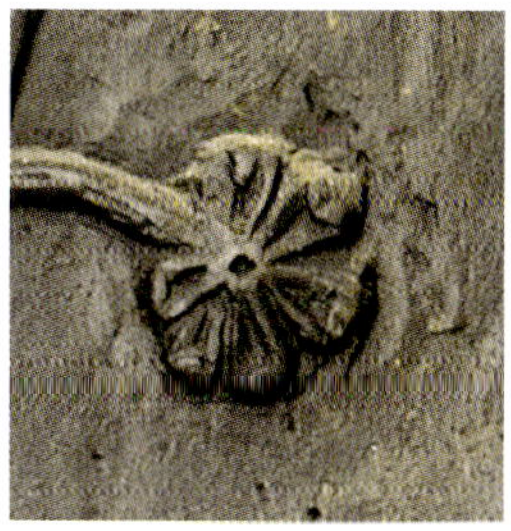

48

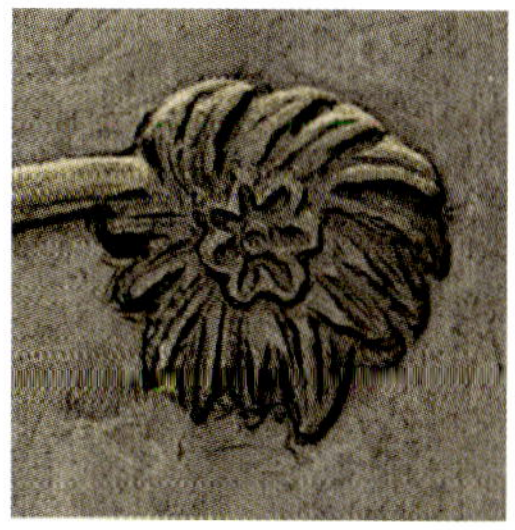

49

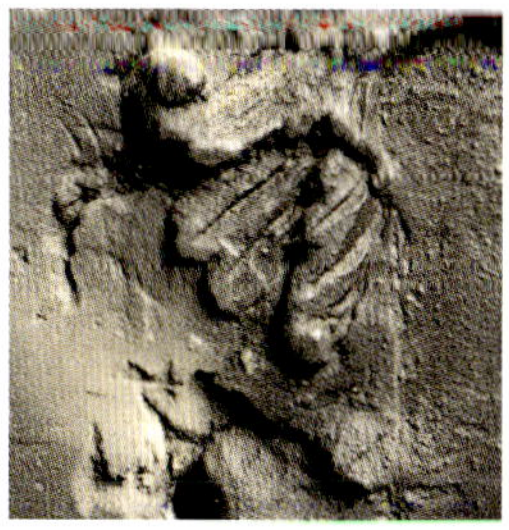

50

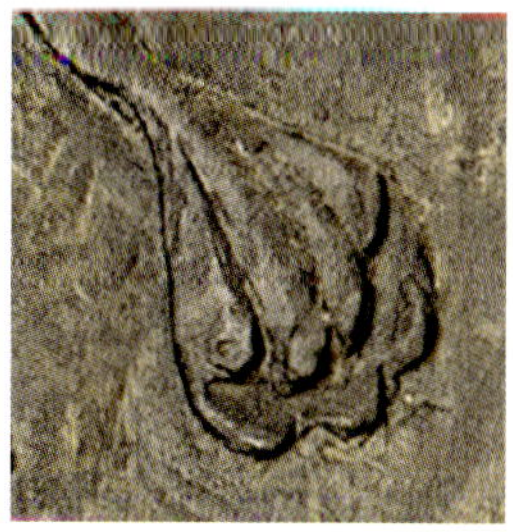

51

the monstrous beast draped astride the two branches of this new Tree of Life, or rather, this tree of a new life (fig. 52).

The beast does not correspond to anything mentioned in Genesis—which, it should be noted, mentions neither devil nor demon—but its distant template is the serpent appearing on the right of the panel, to which, God had given, as to all of Nature, a formal order, an inner coherence. The hybrid is a profoundly modified version of this serpent; it is composed of a canine head, clawed paws, bird wings and a tail with the naturalistic curls of an asp; the tail's tip, distinct from the body, holds up an appendage in the shape of a bristly hook, half-animal, half-vegetal. In this menacing beast is concentrated a total blurring of species, a disorganization of living beings contrary to the natural laws decreed by God. Where does it come from if it is not part of the Creation?

Its position in the upper left corner of the panel, identical to that of the angelic figure in the first panel, is doubtless significant (cf. fig. 1). Winged and dominating the scene toward which it extends its paws, the hybrid is no longer the spiritual light shining on and celebrating the divine work but rather its absolute opposite: a being made of thick matter, incoherent and foreign to God, contemplating the development of an evil in which it participates: original sin infecting the whole panel.

Further, by occupying this position and acting in the same way as the angel, the first of God's creatures, the hybrid also presents itself as a created being; created, however—at least this is the hypothesis I am defending—by Adam and Eve of whom he is, in a way, their first offspring. In contrast to the angel's noetic gaze, the hybrid exhibits the concupiscent gaze that binds fallen humans to their animal bodies in such a way that, in the image, evil reveals itself as endogenous to humanity and, therefore, external to the Creator, from whom humankind is now separated. Straddling the two branches of the tree, the carnal hydrid gaze replaces the spiritual bond through which Adam and Eve saw each other in panel 2, redesigning, in a grotesque and cruel parody, the destroyed heart that was the source of the eternal life of the Tree of Life in panel 1 (cf. fig. 19).

In other words, concupiscence now plays the role of a vital principle, a driving force within fallen humanity that is made explicit by the metamorphosis of the plant's sexual markers. Appearing first in the lower part of the tree below the hybrid as a loss of resemblance, it extends itself above the hybrid, as the invention of a new model of generation (fig. 52).

The upper part of the masculine branch on the left crosses over the hybrid's tail, displaying a new

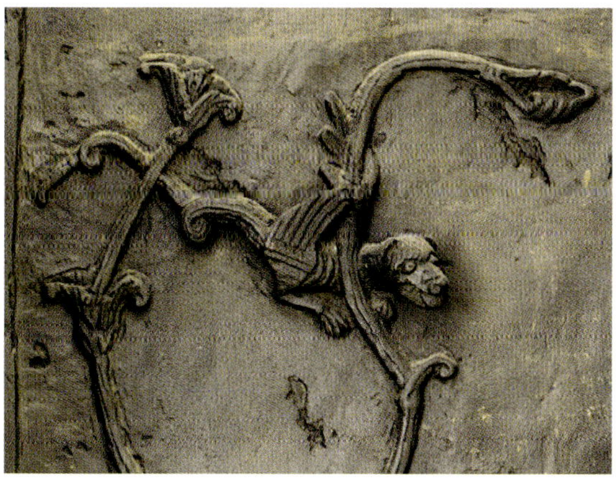

52

47. *Panel 3, sexualized tree.*

48. *Panel 3, sexualized tree, close up.*

49. *Panel 2, center of Eve's tree, close up.*

50. *Panel 3, center of sexualized tree, close up.*

51. *Panel 1, center of right-hand tree, close up.*

52. *Panel 3, upper portion of sexualized tree.*

(Overleaf spread)

53. *Panel 3, Adam.*

54. *Panel 3, Eve.*

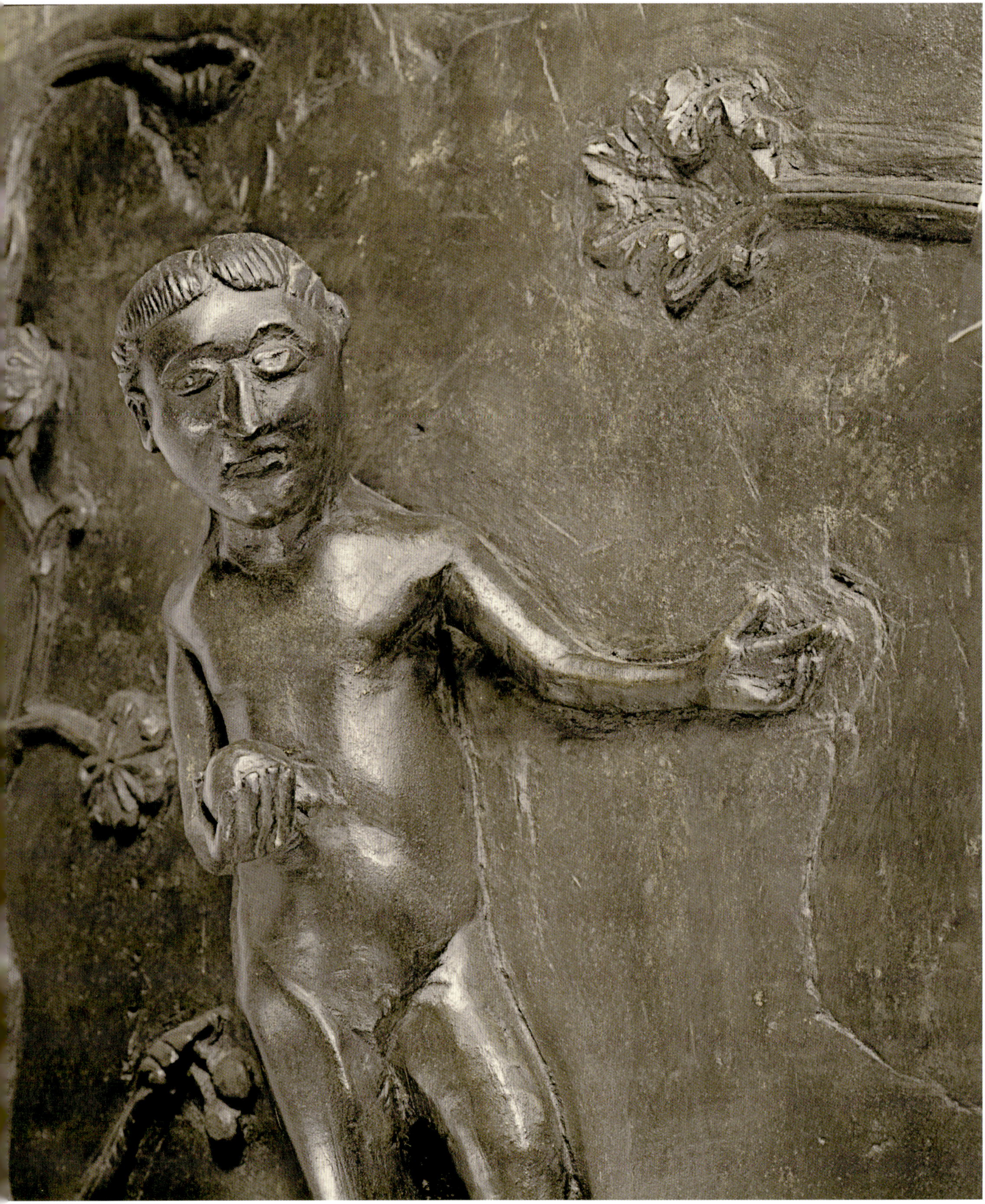

53

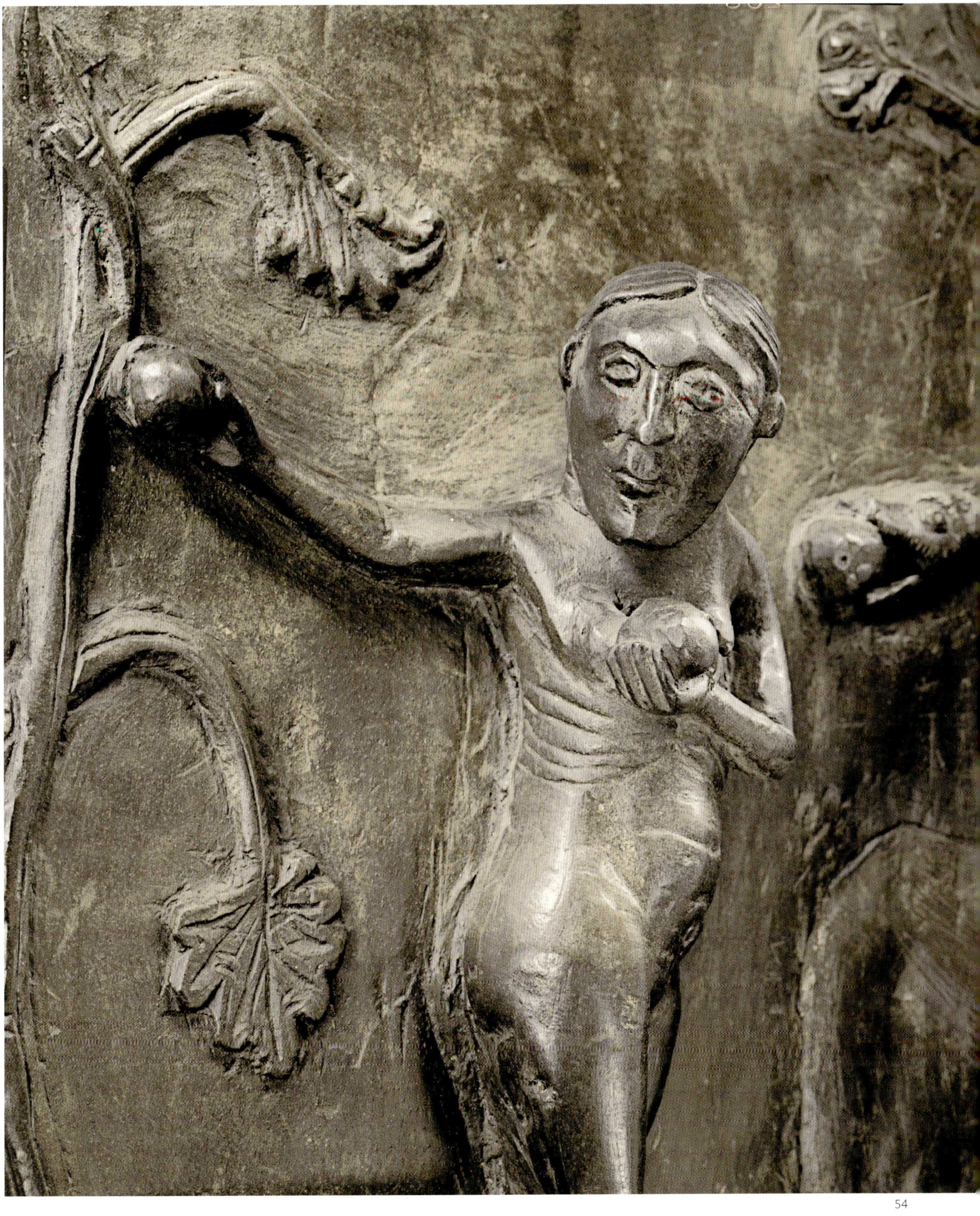

54

leaf cluster emerging from a little ball not unlike the coils of the monstrous beast's tail. The transformation is completed in the heart of this cluster. The foliage, arranged as an enveloping corolla, reveals in the center the small, veined leaves found at the lower level, although they are now covered with asperities, bristling like the hybrid's tail. They form a sort of kernel or seed. The abstract vegetal principle of spiritual generation is embodied here in the guise of a material seed, as unfamiliar, poisonous, and foreign to divine morphogenesis as the hybrid animal.

On the right, Eve's branch passes between the wing and the body of the monstrous beast. Past this point of contact, a flat, notched leaf emerges, the shape of which evokes the fig leaf hanging at the level of the woman's genitals, and then ends in a new leaf. This leaf is the same as the previous one, but it has retracted and assumed a cuplike shape. In fact, it constitutes a receptacle capable of receiving the bristling seed of Adam's branch.

The reader may wonder at the anatomical-botanical precision and the attention to linearity through which I suggest we interpret the plants' progressive configuration. However, all of this is in preparation for the apotheosis of the history of the world as portrayed in the door's final panel. There is, to be sure, a hypothetical component to my interpretation. The system of communication in the bronze panels is so complex, so inventive, and the signifying range of plastic forms so intricate to negotiate that it is difficult to avoid misunderstandings and the omission of details, especially since the grid underlying the door's visual staging represents the whole of Christian cosmology. However, by steady work on the syntactic and semantic coherence of the discourse and in support of a famous maxim attributed to William of Ockham that "essential things should not be needlessly multiplied," by focusing on what is strictly represented and by avoiding the projection of heterogeneous elements of iconographic identification, it is possible to determine which of the semiotic system's resolutions is the simplest and most efficient. One can then verify if it is compatible with the overall discourse of the door and with the culture of its time, which is revealed by the convergences between sources.

In this case, the study of the left tree in panel 3 simply reapplies the visual formula that Bernward utilized for the trees in panel 2, shifting them, as required by patristic interpretation, from the spiritual to the carnal. The transformation process of the two fertility principles is identical for the two branches, thus placed at parity. It first passes through the loss of resemblance to the divine model. What remains of the initial material is then deformed/reformed through contact with the hybrid animal; at the end of the process and despite the transitional disorder, it again finds a principled complementarity between the masculine and the feminine that is active even in evil.

This visual discourse has two aspects. It gives an account of Adam and Eve's responsibility in the deformation of their Tree of Life, a deformation that is due both to their distancing from the divine model and to the replacement of the latter by a carnal paradigm: the way they gaze at each other. At the same time, it shows that the process of deformation/reformation remains within the divine Law of fructification, even if it now applies to humans reduced to the rank of animals (*De Genesi ad litteram*, Book VI, XII, 21, 348). What the encounter between this Law and this flesh will produce will be the subject of the door's fourth panel; the third panel offers only an exploration of the mysteries of these new forms and substances.

Indeed, the formal alteration resulting from sin concerns not only the souls of humans, that is their vision represented by the hybrid as well as their flesh, which has become animal and instinctual; it also concerns the entire earthly Paradise, as stated in the Bible: "The earth will be cursed [*terra maledicta*] because of you" (Gen. 3:18, Bernward's Bible, f. 6). Antonym of Creation, the genesis of this degeneration, of this destruction of the world, begins at the very place where evil appears, on the serpent that has insinuated itself into the Tree of Knowledge of Good and Evil. It appears under the emblematic form of small chisel marks that Bernward undoubtedly meant as an iconic gesture, an agitation of worldly matter as much as that of the door. These marks will reappear on later figures on the door who embody illusion and death: the hybrid serpent of panel 4, the anthropomorphic demon of panel 13 (cf. fig. 1).

A mark of devastating and deforming illusion, this venom contaminates the Tree of Knowledge but only from the place where the serpent's body wraps itself around the branch, not above it (fig. 55). The trunk undergoes a first transformation by twisting and dividing itself longitudinally like the serpent's body. On the right side of the trunk, blotches become increasingly larger on the lower part of the tree. On the left, the side where the apple is clamped in the serpent's jaws, a longitudinal band cuts into the trunk, initially unblemished and then covered with chisel strokes where it comes into contact with the animal's body. Then, still following a descending axis, some clawlike marks appear, as if weighed down by heaviness, clinging to the venomous band.

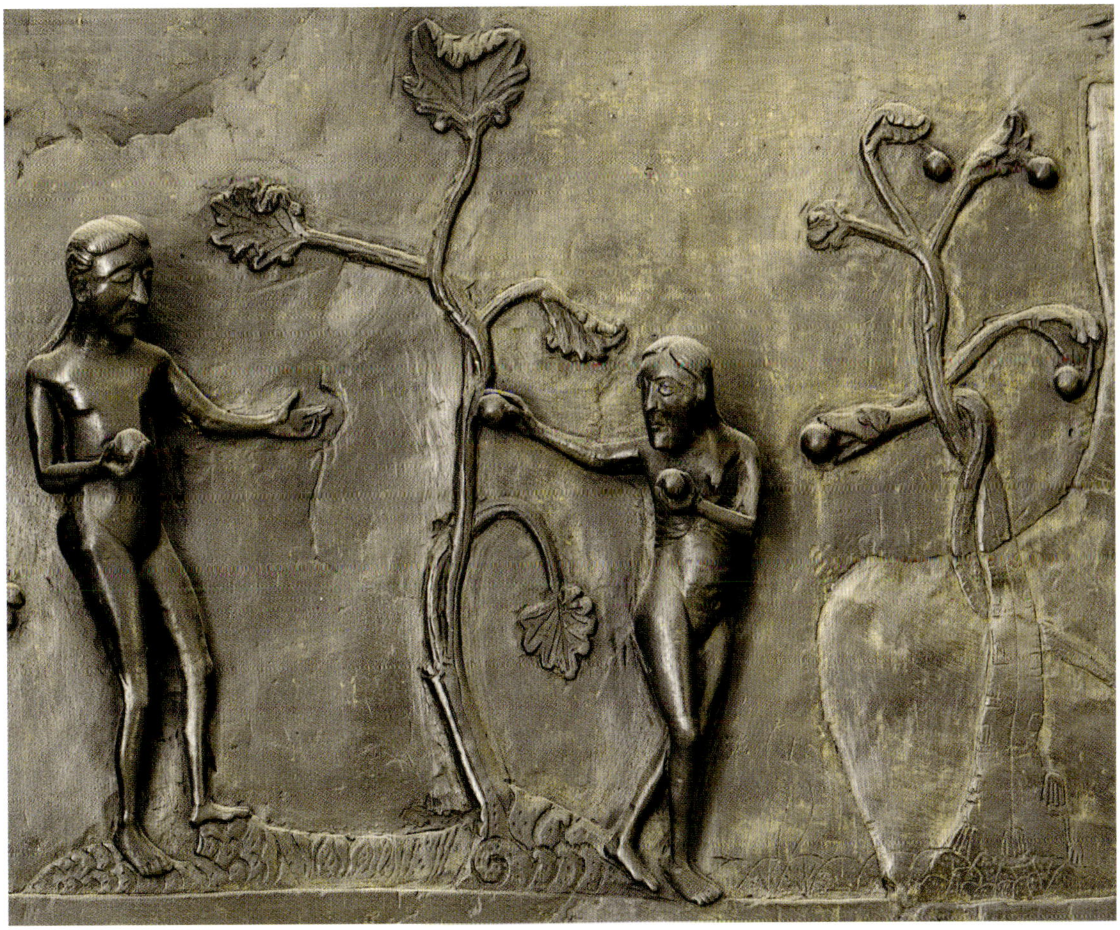

55

55. *Panel 3, transformation of plants and ground.*

I suggest that these figures represent dead leaves, stiff and withered, their schematization distinguishing them from the model of the ethereal, spiritual, and eternally living leaves of the very first Tree of Life (fig. 19). The lower part of the trunk is covered with these lifeless leaves, to which it is possible to retrospectively reattach the misshapen seed of the tree on the left. On contact with the soil, they release their substance into the clods of earth supporting the tree (fig. 55). There they morph into patches bearing chisel marks like cracks in dried up soil. The venomous spots disappear on the tree's left side where the arid clumps give way to large palmate leaves, from which spring three stems of fine grass so schematic and lightly carved that they give the impression of fading (fig. 56). This interruption, to which we shall return, is even more striking because the chisel strokes reappear at the center of the image on the base depicting the closed garden of Paradise (fig. 55). On the right, they cover clods of earth, curving up progressively in form of curls identical in shape to those of the serpent and hybrid's tails. They are found again on the left side of the base. Marked by the formal and substantial seal of evil—the curve and the chisel marks—these curls end up resembling one of the conventional representations of rocks in medieval art, as demonstrated by the mound that elevates nursing Eve in panel 6 (cf. fig. 88). The dried up and cracked earth has thus become mineralized.

The chisel marks also affect the depression located between the two lateral mounds of the garden. Covered with fine meandering lines, this depression represents the river that God made to flow in the garden ("a river went out of the place of pleasure to water paradise," Gen. 2:10) and whose water is now poisoned. The entire schema prepares the time of the world's revivification by the blood of Christ, as we will analyze in our study of panel 12. A last geomorphic event marks the disintegration of the Garden of Eden. The mound on the left is an altered version of the mound on the right. It has been lowered, its curls are smaller and more blurred, and even more visibly, it has cracked. Between the feet of Adam, who completes original sin by eating the apple, the mineral bedrock splits, creating a chasm. By a single human transgression, Hell was born of Paradise, completing the destruction begun by humanity.

One part of the image, however, escapes this

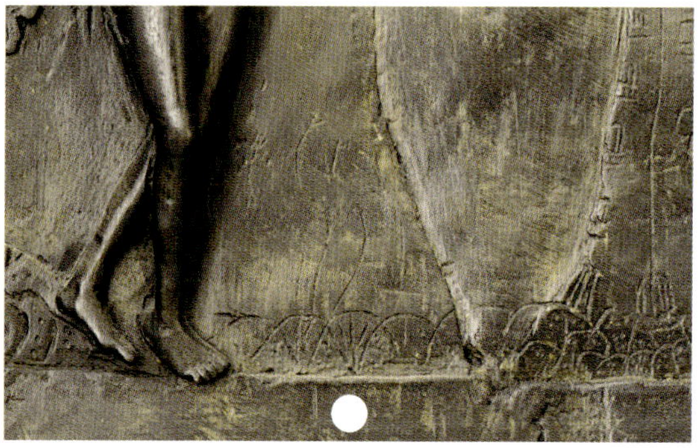

56

contaminating evil: the plants—unpoisoned, well ordered, and growing—that appear between the Tree of Knowledge and the Garden of Eden (fig. 56, white spot). Very stylized, without thickness and therefore without matter, they are not really plants, rather the matrix and spiritual form of plants. If humans brought chaos into Creation, it did not reach the depth of its structure. Humanity's future lies in the hope of the restoration of the world's original form; after studying all the panels, a rereading of the images allows us to identify in this evanescent vegetal motif the signs of a possible reparation. The three long, grassy stems reappear as a regular pattern under Mary's feet in panel 9, portraying the Annunciation (cf. fig. 115). As for the veined motif of the lightly etched large leaves, it will be taken up again, in a thicker shape, under the throne of the Virgin and Child in panel 11 (cf. fig. 139). Finally, the well-ordered and symmetric form of the Tree of Life will be restored and even completed by Christ's cross, represented in the Crucifixion panel on the right wing opposite panel 3 (cf. fig. 1).

If the typological connection between original sin and the Crucifixion is a commonplace in iconography, exegesis, and Christian liturgy, Bernward here gives it a strictly ontological dimension. The body of Christ, which vivifies the cross's dead wood, as shown in the border of living leaves running along the rim of the boards, becomes the new Tree of Life, which will save humans and give them back eternal life (cf. fig. 169). Thus, the narrative of the Fall contains the elements that will allow for the attainment of salvation in the right wing. This providential story, as told in the biblical text, seems to me to correspond not only to the typological organization of the episodes from the Old and New Testaments but also to the diegetic structure of the events recounted in each of the bronze panels.

Let us consider how the action displayed in the door's first panel unfolds from left to right (fig. 57). This natural movement, aligned with the meaning of the textual reading, determines the reappearance of God and Eve in panel 2, the direction of God's accusing gestures in panel 4, the expulsion from Eden in panel 5, and finally, in symmetry with the first panel, the panel of the *Noli me tangere* where Christ brings Mary Magdalene into Eden. Only one panel belonging to Edenic history unfolds its action in a direction contrary to the axis of life set up in the first panel: it is precisely that of original sin, whose narration begins on the right with the Tree of Knowledge and ends on the left with the tree of carnal life. We shall find the same reading direction for the panels concerning earthly history, with the exception of panel 16 and two panels on the right wing that have a nonuniform and particularly signifying orientation: panel 13, the Trial of Christ, whose shifting axes are in conflict, as befits the confrontation between divine truth and men's mendacity, and the Crucifixion panel which follows it and is entirely centered.

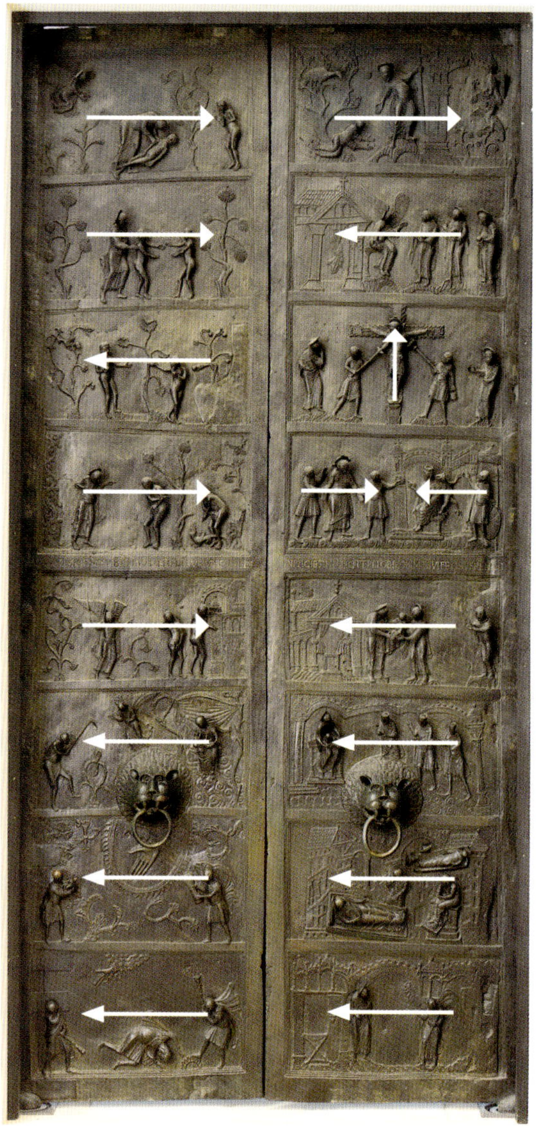

57

56. *Panel 3, matrix forms of plant life.*

57. *Panel 3, orientation of action.*

Two complementary interpretations may be suggested for this arrangement of narrative sequences. The first considers that sin and humans' immoral life on earth unfold in opposition to divine Law because they are contrary to what had been initially contemplated as a perpetual movement of life's expansion. Apart from the fact that life on earth was set up not with but against life's axis in panel 1, it collides with it in an eternal spinning on itself, a circular process that can also express the life principle by successive mortal generations. The second interpretation considers that the orientation from right to left necessitates the earthly narrative's return to its point of origin. This process is particularly striking in the two panels on the right wing that depict a procession, that of the Epiphany (panel 11), and that of the visit of the Holy Women to the tomb (panel 15). The biblical narrative after the Fall would thus be presented as a long return toward the beginning of the world and toward the Creator. As a conversion toward God, human history would be just as dynamic and woven with successive metamorphoses as the history of its distancing from the Creator, but it would operate in the opposite direction.

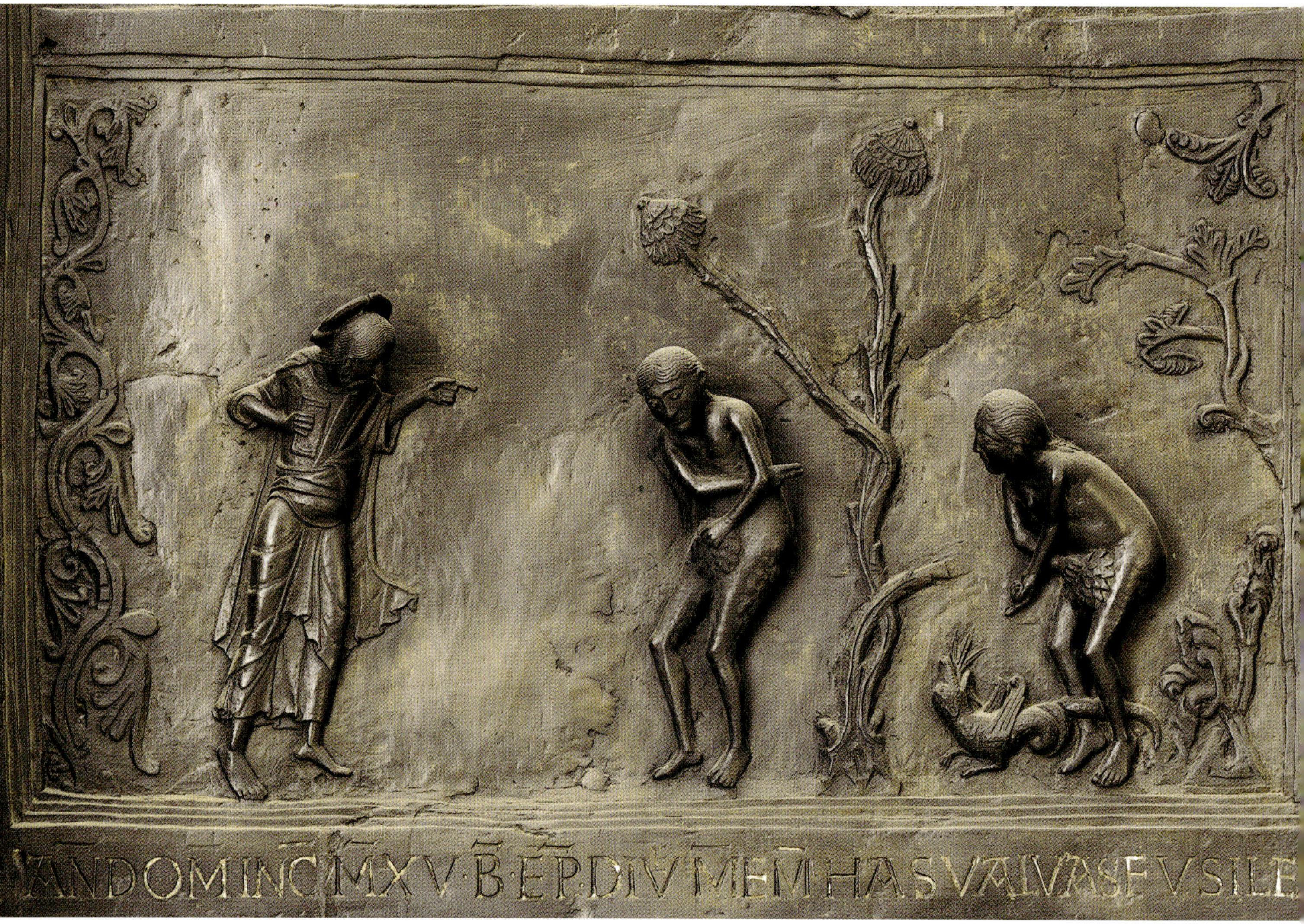
ANDOM INC MXV·B·EP·DIV MEM HAS VALVAS FVSILE

Panel 4

DIVISION

Absent when humans sinned, God reappears in the door's fourth panel (fig. 58). Leaning forward while holding a book tightly against his chest, he points an accusing finger toward Adam and Eve. Most historians have interpreted the panel as depicting anger, reproaches, or divine judgment, especially since the episode of Christ's trial corresponds to this scene on the right wing (cf. fig. 1). The typological link between the panels is particularly clear: in the two images, the divinity is placed at the left. Contrary to what has been suggested [Stahl 2002, 165], there is no irony in the reversal of roles between accusers and accused but rather the most unfathomable mystery for Christians: the all-powerful God, who punishes humans' transgressions, manifests himself on the right wing in the sacrificial annihilation of the human nature he has chosen to assume.

Two judgments, one punishment: death, of which the second will invalidate the first. The prophecy is in itself very powerful, but we should not stop at the interpretative level, first of all because Christian typology is neither a subject nor an end in itself but rather a dialectic component of Revelation that attests to Divine Providence and wisdom. Thus, while panel 1 reveals the laws of Creation, it does so to provide the viewer with the conceptual material necessary to understand the re-creation of a new humanity in panel 16. Panel 2, while conveying the modalities of the covenant between humans and God, draws a relational schema for understanding the complex nature of the covenant that is restored between the Church and the body of Christ in panel 15. And in panel 3, original sin presents itself as the antonym of Christ's sacrifice in panel 14, just as the deformation of the Tree of Life announces its own future restoration, since the rebuilding of a universal order has become necessary only because of its previous disappearance.

The great simplicity and discursive efficacy of the visual typology might conceal the fact that the events by themselves do not lead to knowledge of the principles acting in things, but by their chains of logic and dissemination as echoes through the course of time, they set up the bases for another level of discourse and comprehension: ontological and teleological. In Bernward's Augustinian Christianity, the mirror is not the light it reflects: the essence of the phenomena does not come from history, which only provides the stage, but from the systems' operating mode, from the divine Law acting in the world such as God created it.

The reading of the panels ultimately gives access to this strictly spiritual dimension, to this comprehension of the world illuminated by the spirit from within. In short, panel 1 unveils the very principles of life; panel 2 elucidates the nature of love, the bond between the created and the Creator; panel 3 portrays sin's visage, the alteration and deformation of substances following the rupture of the loving and specular relationship with God. In continuity with the images preceding it, and beyond its typological link with panel 13 (cf. fig. 160), panel 4 describes the nature and modalities of the transmission of sin, in order to set down the precise terms of a future redemption.

Several episodes of the biblical narrative are intertwined in the panel. They correspond to the dialogues of Genesis chapter 3, verses 9–15. God searches for man: "Where are you?" (Gen. 3:9). Adam explains

58. *Panel 4.*

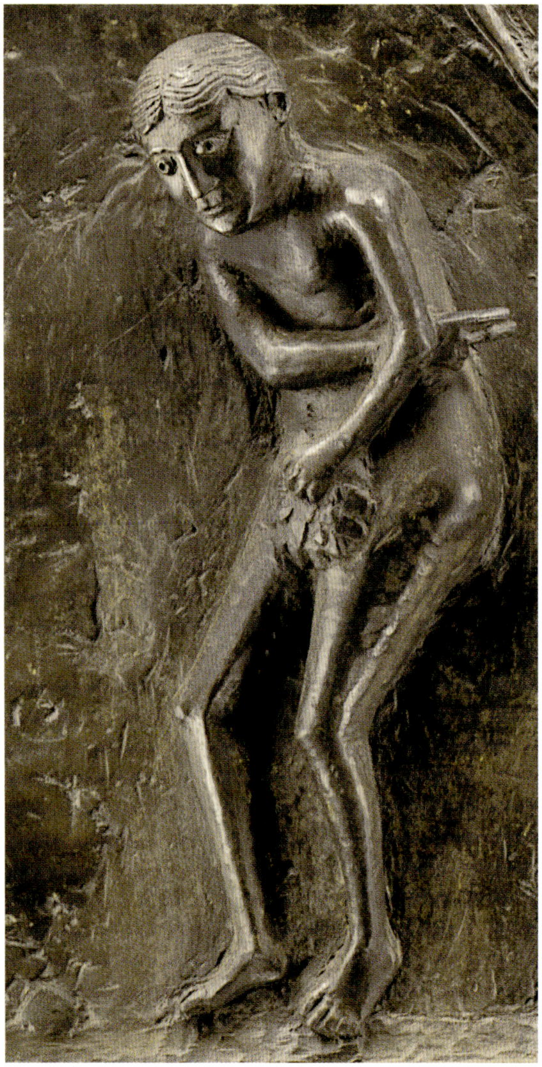

59

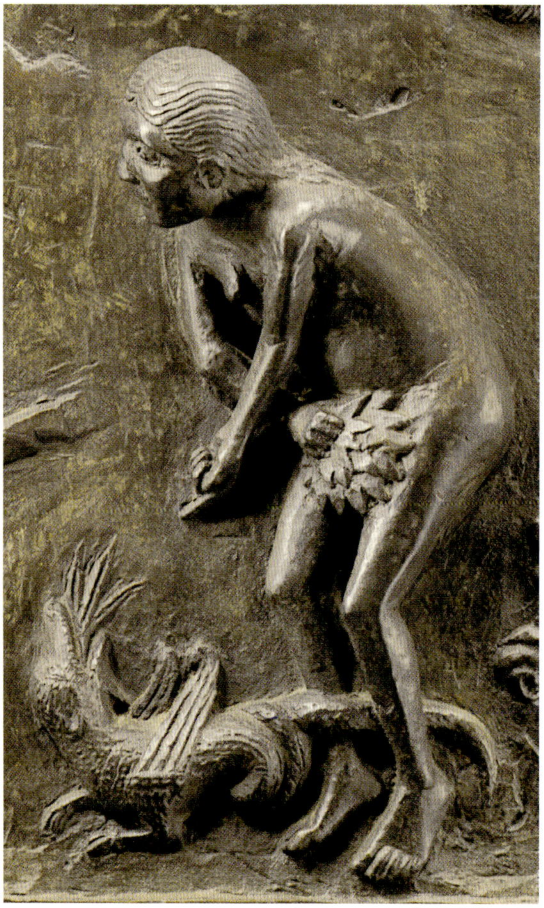

60

that he is afraid because he knows he is naked and so he is hiding (Gen. 3:10). As in almost the entire iconographic tradition dealing with this theme, Eve and Adam conceal their genitals by covering them with leaves. Besides the fact that these leaf clusters are particularly thick, and thus heavy and dense, it should be noted that by reversing their association, their form takes on the shape of the fertile leaf clusters of the trees of spiritual life in the second panel (cf. fig. 32 and 33): the pointed leaves supporting the seeds projected by Adam's tree are placed over Eve's genitals, while the concentric cluster that harbored the sown flower is now placed on Adam's. Bernward explicitly evokes the level at which the union between man and woman is played out; biblical prudishness is here understood as the sudden shame felt before the irrepressible impulses leading to contact between the sexes and the mixing of animal flesh (*De Genesi ad litteram,* Book XI, 32, 42, 518).

God then asks accusingly: "Thou hast eaten of the tree whereof I commanded thee that thou shouldst not eat?" (Gen. 3:11). Adam blames Eve (fig. 59), who in turn shifts the responsibility to the serpent (Gen. 3:12–13) (fig. 60). The image shows the sin's development. All the gestures of the protagonists are connected: God's index finger is extended by Adam's accusing gesture and then by that of Eve, who points to the serpent placed between her legs (fig. 58). The serpent is not represented as an animal, such as it appeared in the Tree of Knowledge. Contaminated by the evil pervading the previous panel, it is dotted with chisel marks, taking on some of the traits of the hybrid conceived by Adam and Eve—wings, clawed paws, snout, and coiled tail (fig. 54). It differs from the latter, however, in that it looks like a reptile and spits venom. In the second panel, the book that God held tightly against his chest already functioned as performative Law. In panel 4, the Creator—Word in action—has regained control of Creation: "Upon thy breast shalt thou go, and earth shalt thou eat all the days of thy life" (Gen. 3:14).

The serpent interacts with the humans. Ever since the original sin, it has replaced God in humans' eyes.

59. *Panel 4, Adam.*

60. *Panel 4, Eve and serpent.*

Paradigmatic of the animality to which the latter have been reduced, the monstrous animal once again becomes a behavioral model. Adam's and Eve's crossed arms, a sign of duplicity, are borrowed from the coils formed by the reptile's body, themselves derived from those of the serpent and the hybrid in panel 3 (fig. 63); this maleficent arm crossing affects even the lower branch of the tree in panel 4 (fig. 61). Beyond this mimetic relationship, the serpent is also directly associated with the woman (fig. 60). Lying flat on the ground, it has slid its tail between Eve's legs ("I will put enmities between thee and the woman, and thy seed and her seed: she shall crush thy head, and thou shalt lie in wait for her heel," Gen. 3:15). Although later, at the end of the Book of Revelation, in a passage much studied by exegetes, the woman crushes the animal under her feet, thus manifesting the Church's victory, here she is threatened by the serpent's poisoned skin as it unwinds from around her calves. The implicitly sexual character of this aggression is explicitly underscored by the three streams of poison spewing from the reptile's throat. These streams of venom spew back at the woman the sin that humans denied in later times.

The jet of venom on the left is aimed at Eve's face, more precisely at her eyes. Symbolically, it reminds us that the woman's polluted gaze was the first factor of the Fall; in reality, it blinds Eve who, although looking in the direction of God, cannot see him. The equivalent of this blindness can be found in Adam. From his stooped shoulders, tilted head, but also from his posture in retreat, the man is represented staring at the ground, probably at an apple that cuts him off from God, as if it were an insurmountable obstacle (fig. 59). By associating the denial of the transgression with bodies that are physically incapable of seeing God, Bernward perhaps calls attention to the fact that the carnal is blind to the spiritual. Indeed, God will disappear from the left wing. In addition, this stage setting announces the right wing, and the operative power Christ will have there once he assumes the bodies' thick matter to become a visible God. On the condition of the faithful's inner conversion—recognizing Christ as the God he truly is—this single vision, of which the symmetrical panel of Jesus's trial represents the antonym, will be the bodies' first redemption.

The second and third jets of venom spewed by the serpent are directed toward Eve's chest and lower abdomen (fig. 60). According to a tradition going back to Galen, there is a genuine connection between the breasts and womb of the mother, progenitor and nurturer [Bonnet-Cadilhac 1997, 84]. It is not Eve, therefore, but the child she carries who is, in fact, placed at the end of a chain of denials of responsibility for the Fall. The sin not acknowledged by the parents thus falls on their descendants until Christ, as he appears in the opposite panel, interrupts the transmission. One might legitimately wonder how a sin that does not seem to be reproducible could be incorporated into a genetic lineage. Losing sight of God and breaking the covenant affecting the whole

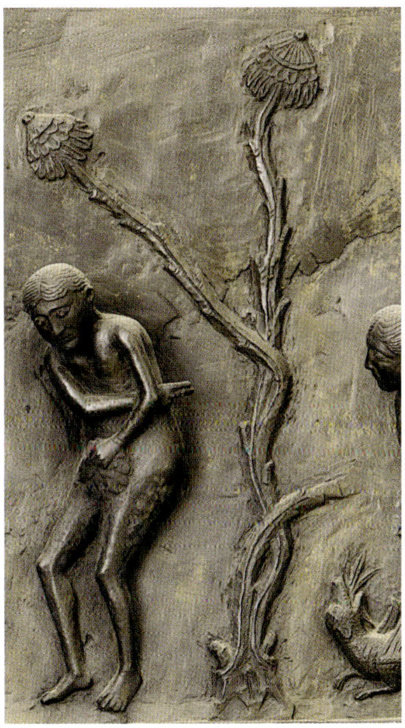

61

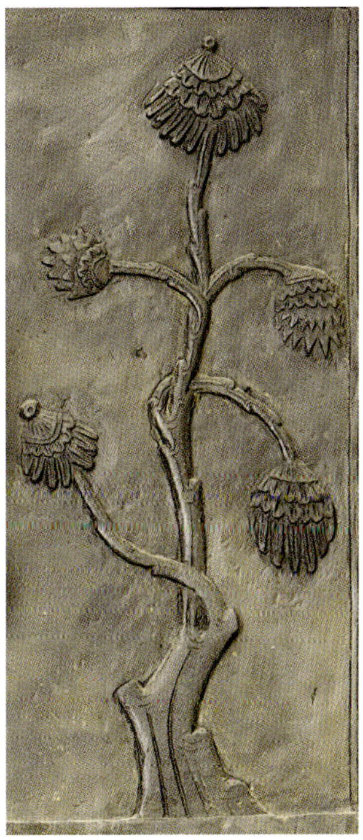

62

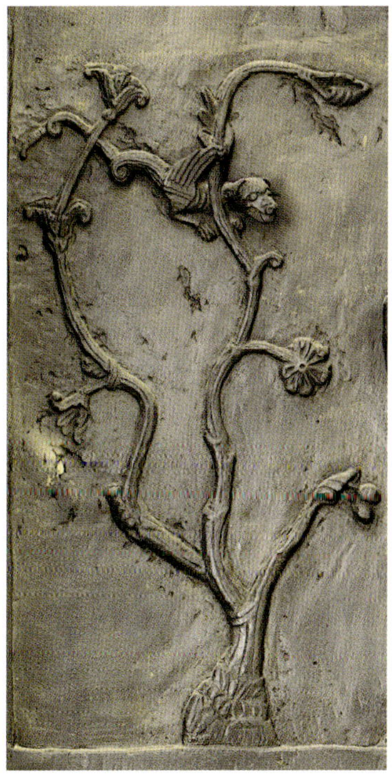

63

61. *Panel 4, tree, center.*

62. *Panel 2, Adam's tree.*

63. *Panel 3, sexualized tree.*

of humanity are in fact, as Bernward clarifies, consequences of the flesh's new condition.

Apart from the winged reptile, there is no evidence of chisel marks in panel 4, nor do they appear on the wood of the tree of gendered reproduction in panel 3 (fig. 63). One can therefore deduce that these chisel marks designate exclusively the deformation of creatures such as God had initially conceived them: if the tree of carnal reproduction is not affected by chisel marks, it is because it did not result from destruction of Paradise but was generated by humans. All the plants of panel 4 are the same as this tree: they are the expression of a postlapsarian humanity whose vitality is strictly carnal.

The first and most visible of these trees is placed between Adam and Eve (fig. 61). It combines many traits borrowed from plants in the preceding panels. It borrows the height, the verticality, and the top foliage from the two Trees of Life in panel 2 that traced the modalities of the union between Adam and Eve (fig. 62). From the tree of carnal reproduction in panel 3, it retains the imbalance and general structure composed of two main branches and a side sucker (fig. 63). Barbed and phallic, pointed at Eve's womb, the latter constitutes a visual analogy of the snake's venom spurts. The generation of human life is here represented as a begetting of death, which is also attested to by the thorny desiccation of the trunk and branches, and the multiple stumps resulting from the section of suckers and branches discarded just after their birth. The sucker, whose extremity is literally filed down on the bronze, bears the emblematic memory of this violence. If the tree placed at the center of panel 4 highlights Adam and Eve's desire to be united, it is to insist on the joint component of vitality and morbidity characterized by this carnal drive.

It should be noted that the only vigorous part of the tree is found in the upper foliage. The semiotic knot of the figuration derives from the fact that the foliage is now placed, not on two symmetrical and complementary trees but on one tree only. The enduring vital principle no longer concerns humans as individuals but the whole of humanity as the product of mixing masculine and feminine. Life has become a succession of generations within the species. The new tree, although ugly, deformed, and dry remains, all the same, the Tree of Life, but the humanity's Tree of Life is no longer Adam or Eve's. This reduction of the vital principle and the irremediable dilution of life into a programmed animal death are no more a divine punishment than the sin of the flesh. In an almost mechanical way, these two factors stem from the Law laid down at the time of Creation, the primary and constant injunction of which, addressed

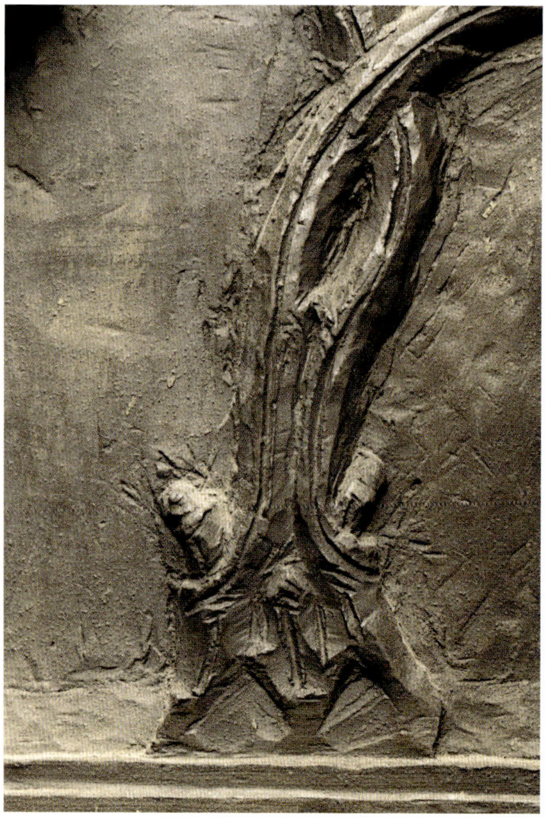

64

both to humans and animals, was to grow and multiply: "Be fruitful and increase in number; fill the earth and subdue it" (Gen. 1:28). What should therefore be understood is that while Adam and Eve have lost the ability to see the divine image in themselves, they remain subject to the Law of the living. Their desire of being united remains, and since they no longer can realize it according to the terms of the covenant contracted with God in panel 2, they act with the only life force left to them, a fecundity inscribed in the flesh of their animal body, the only possible response to individual death; the driving force, as necessary as it is pathetic, is concupiscence.

The conditions of this procreation by the flesh are traced by the roots of the plants, especially by those of the central tree (fig. 64). As usual, Bernward states what the tree no longer is before explaining what it has become. Because of its desiccation, the channels that could have brought life-giving water from the soil up to its trunk have been carefully severed. In addition, its root mass has been hollowed out by powerful oblique strokes, leaving sharp edges on the trunk. However, the vascularity of the tree has not completely disappeared. Two irrigation channels extend the length of the trunk; one irrigates the trunk carrying the two clusters of leaves, the other irrigates the branch that will engender life in Eve's womb. This configuration of the root mass and the circulatory

64. *Panel 4, roots of center tree.*

system establishes a significant fact: humanity's Tree of Life is not animated either by vivifying water or by the soil of the earthly Paradise. What is the matter that replaces them?

I suggest that the animal flesh itself is represented at the center of the root mass in the trunk's axis as a strange composite form, both organic and geometric, too structured to be merely the consequence of residual metal. In the absence of any comparative example in the iconographic tradition, this image is particularly challenging to study.

The modeling technique revealing the composite figure is itself an initial source of information. The flesh was preexistent in the tree and has become visible, by default, only when the matter of the earthly Paradise, which constituted its perfection and immortality, disappeared. A first hypothesis suggests that it is the result of a combination of a masculine seed and a feminine seed. In this case, we would not be dealing with an anatomical figure, since nothing like it exists in nature but with the schematic representation of a sexual act presented as life source at the base of the tree. Apart from the somewhat coarse frontal view of a redundant elucidation, the problem comes from the fact that the schematic figure would then refer to the sexual union and not to the matter that forms it.

I favor a second hypothesis that suggests that the composite figure evokes the two human substances at the origin of generation, of which Bernward has already given a vegetal image in the carnal tree in the previous panel: a spermatic substance replacing water, having the form of a split and elongated seed, and a feminine matter represented as a triangular vase with two handles in the form of a uterus and constituting a matrix of flesh, destined to protect and nurture the development of the male seed. In addition to the fact that spermatic matter has already been evoked through the seed of the tree in panel 3, it should be emphasized, again with reference to the only anatomical text of which we can be fairly certain that Bernward knew—the Isidorian tradition taken up by Rabanus Maurus—that this spermatic matter at the same time provides the principle of vitality and the form of the progeny. This matter would thus be in the direct line of the rib/phallic form that appeared at the foot of Eve's tree in panel 2, when the human body was for the first time a source of new life (cf. fig. 30). The suggested association between the vase and the uterus is more difficult to defend. It is doubtful that Bernward was aware of the numerous debates in which the physicians of antiquity were engaged regarding the form and internal subdivisions of this organ. Still, the fact remains that the uterus is often represented in the form of a bladder, while insisting, ever since Aristotle, on its similarity with the male genitals [Bonnet Cadilhac 1997, 48–53]. We should also note that the oldest Western medieval image of a uterus appears in a ninth-century copy of a treatise addressed to midwives and written by Moschion, a sixth-century Roman physician (Brussels, Bibliothèque Royale, Ms. 3701–14). Moschion represents it as a goatskin with two handles containing a tiny human form [Bonnet-Cadilhac 1997, 55].

The last argument supporting the hypothesis of a root mass representing the mixture of seeds comes from the configuration of the bush behind Eve on the very right of the panel (fig. 65). The clearly geometric lower part of the plant is a triangular block separated from the ground by a small base. The two offshoots of the crossed stems enclose an oblong orifice, as if the matrix triangle of the previous block, turned upside down, had literally absorbed Adam's seed, keeping only its vertical structure.

I propose identifying the final stage of the process begun at the root level of the central tree, the Tree of Life of Adam and Eve's potential offspring, or rather a part of that tree, as its formal development and its association with the two plants surmounting it will make clear. Furthermore, at this point it should be noted that the specificity of the vegetal sucker implies

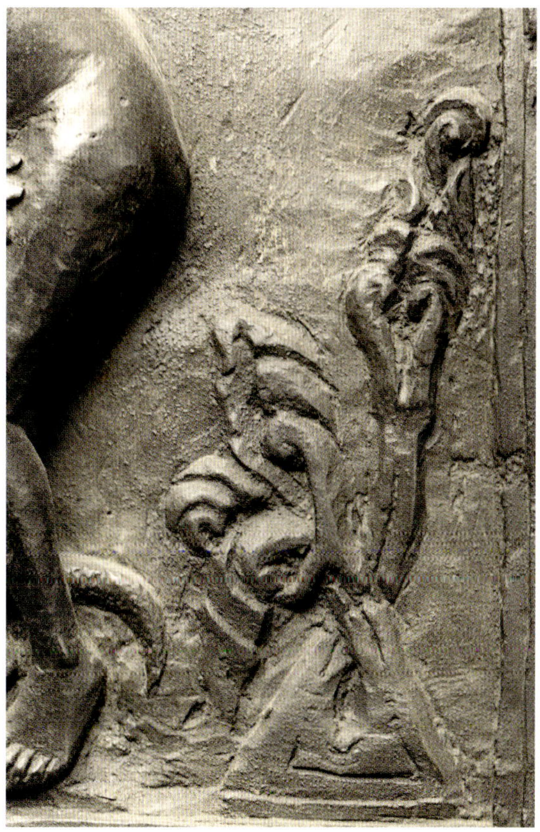

65

65. *Panel 4, plant, lower right.*

(overleaf spread)

66. *Panel 4, God.*

67. *Panel 4, Adam.*

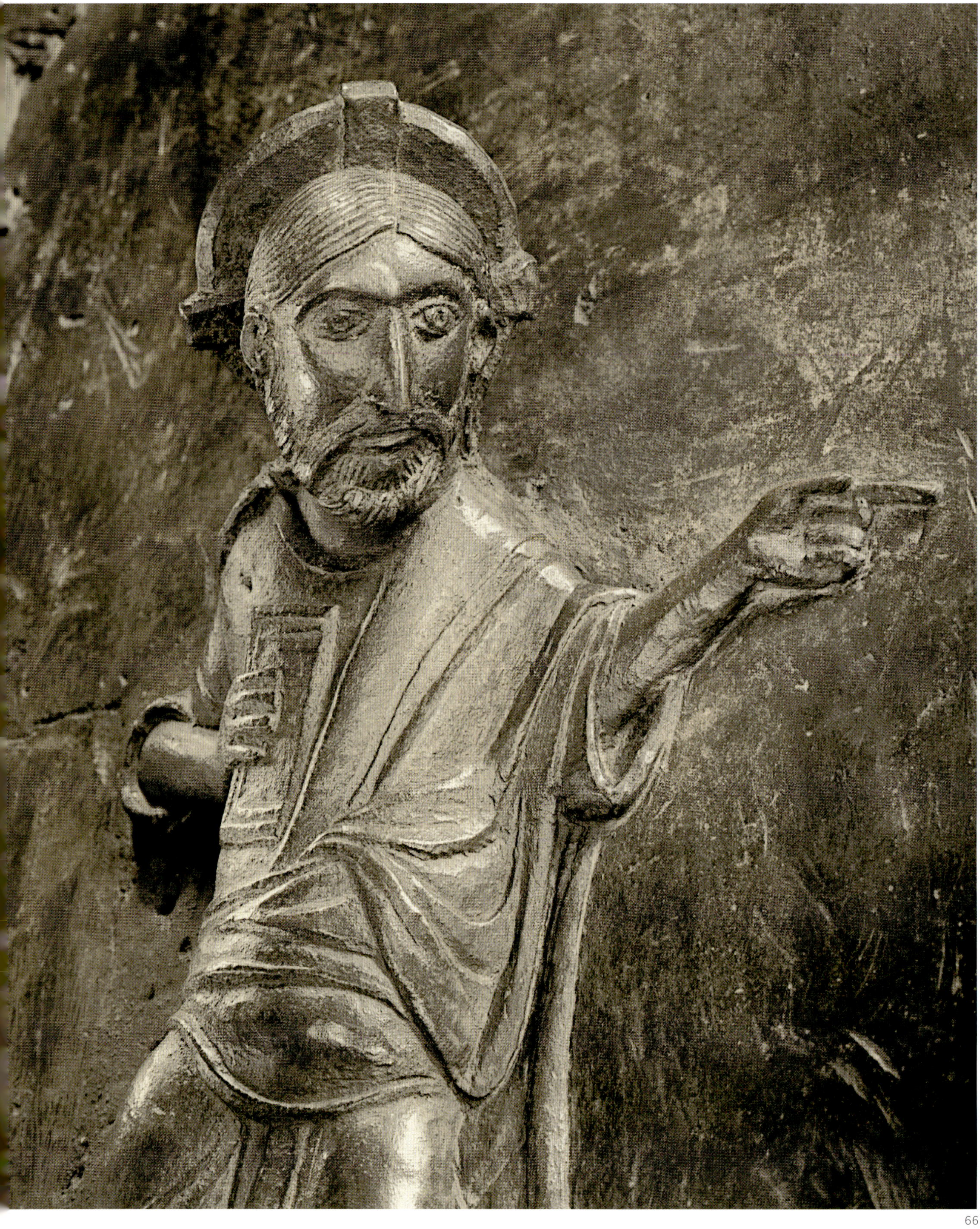

66

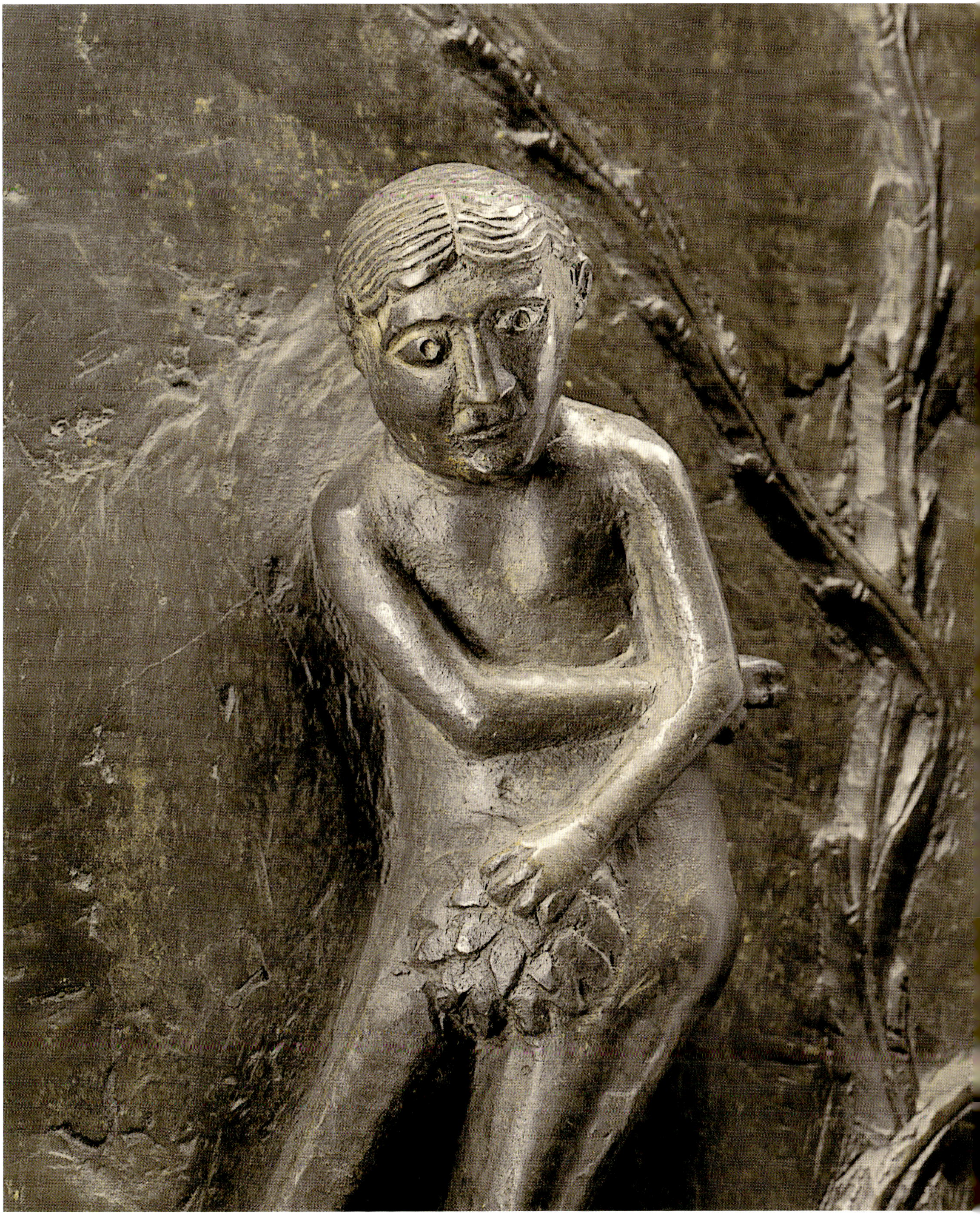

67

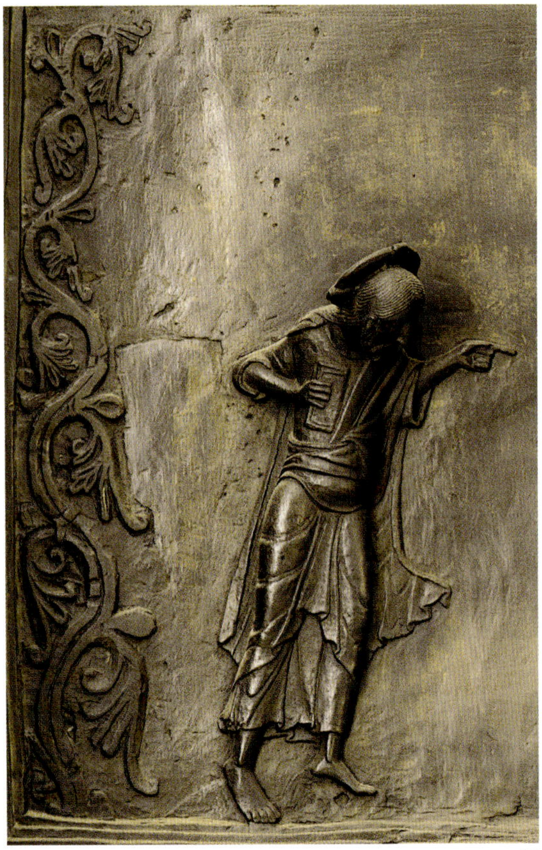

68

that it can break away from the trunk bearing it and constitute an autonomous plant.

Whereas the root mass of the central Tree of Life was deprived of matter, the plant in the ground behind Eve pours out matter in magmatic profusion. Each of its short stems forms a pair of heart-shaped pincers, extending in the lower one into a leaf subdivided into thick, small, curled-up leaves, while the taller one forms an almost vertical spear-shaped leaf. The plant seems to give life to its own matter, and perhaps the differentiation of its leaves is designed to exhibit the two physiological forms of the masculine and feminine it contains in principle. Restive and unsettled, this plant seems to evoke the distant paradigm of fern fronds of the door's very first bush. The latter showed the birth of living matter, but the triangle drawn in the first demiurgic moment came from the intertwining of three stems (cf. fig. 15), not from the fusion of the flesh of two animals, as is the case in panel 4.

Such meticulous care to let none of the Edenic material—water as well as earth—enter the carnal trees of life, while at the same time attributing to them fertility in process, can only have one function: to demonstrate that the animal bodies of humans now function in an autonomous manner. They no longer draw from the resources that God had placed in the earthly Paradise that will allow them to live after leaving the Garden of Eden, while explaining that the flesh nourishes its vitality only by itself, so that it engenders nothing other than flesh.

This new ontological order, corresponding to the growth sequence of the plants in the first panel, is epitomized by the two diametrically opposed vegetal groups rising along the frame on either side of the panel. On the left, behind God, there is an ornamental foliage motif that has no equivalent in the door (fig. 68). Its single undulating stem, rising from a triple base and irrigated throughout its length, ascends regularly and harmoniously up to the sky, while its leaves mirror the pattern of the palms of eternity. This vegetal ornamental motif, frequently found in depictions of Paradise in early Christian mosaics, as well as in sculpted or painted ornamental patterns of the High Middle Ages, here evokes God's uniqueness and perfection.

In contrast to this motif, emblematic of the divine, a vegetal cluster broken up into three bushes is placed symmetrically along the right frame of the panel (fig. 69). Together they represent humanity's constitutive parts that sin has separated. We have already studied the lower bush and its profusion of flesh. The middle bush is better arranged. Consisting of only one hook-shaped branch, it is anchored onto the frame, displaying its matter in a coherent albeit constrained way, with leaves rising from a distinctly woody skeleton. Its curvature is similar to the divine ornamental motif, and several details recall the foliage, although in a truncated and deformed way. In my opinion, the middle bush models the principle of formal development imposed by the vegetative soul on the flesh, a law common to all animals inscribing in themselves a movement leading life to growth and then to death.

The third bush on the panel's right side is very different from the ones below it. It exhibits formal attributes taken more from the spiritual than the carnal domain. Besides being triple and well balanced, it even forms a discreet cross at the junction of its stem and three leaves. In addition, it is anchored on the right and upper frames, thus relating it both to the order of nature and to a superior principle. I suggest viewing it, in line with the carnal matter and the vitality driven by the vegetative soul, as the visualization of the rational soul. Created in God's image, the latter imparts to the body the formal connections and principles permitting resemblance to the Creator.

This triple component, carnal and doubly spiritual, of the new human being becomes the main subject of the subsequent images on the left wing. In panel 4, Bernward interrupts his demonstration with

68. *Panel 4, God with ornamental foliage.*

two prophetic statements. The first echoes the matrixlike permanence of Edenic perfection, resistant to sin and represented in the background of panel 3 (cf. fig. 56) by the destruction of the Garden of Eden. Even though unsettled and deformed, the flesh, the vegetative soul, and the rational soul survive in the child born of sin. These conditions are necessary for a possible reunification that would reestablish the perfection of the divine image in Man. None of the panels of the left wing is ever sealed in on itself, and hope persists in even the darkest of episodes.

At the same time, Bernward insists on the terrifying consequence of applying the divine Law to worldly forms and substances. Almost all scholars have interpreted the hunched posture of Adam and Eve, as well as the strained features of their faces—Adam, frozen, his eyes wide open, and Eve, her mouth pinched, the corners of her eyes downcast—as a manifestation of the terror that the divine judgment inspired in them. Pathos is a salient trait of Bernward's images and of Ottonian illumination [Mayr-Harting 1999, I, 103; Fisher]. This analysis is acceptable on the condition that these affects be considered not as personality traits but as manifestation of the awareness that, from now on, humans will have of their own nature. In contrast to panel 2, the Law no longer offers the choice of freedom and love but imposes itself on humanity's flesh as a constraint. The left branch of the central tree is parallel to Adam's stooped back, a pressure echoed by the hook-shaped bush dominating Eve (fig. 69). As in panel 3, evil is concupiscence—a transgressive desire for the forbidden fruit—but the object of desire has changed. The apple is replaced by the body of the other. The violence of this evil destined to affect all the descendants of Adam and Eve places all of humanity under the yoke of sin, as elucidated in a passage of Paul's Epistle to the Romans:

> Is the law sin? God forbid. But I do not know sin, but by the law, for I had not known concupiscence [*concupiscentiam*], if the law did not say: "Thou shalt not covet." But sin taking occasion by the commandment, wrought in me all manner of concupiscence [*omnem concupiscentiam*]. For without the law sin was dead. And I lived some time without the law; but when the commandment came, sin revived, and I died: the commandment that was ordained to life, the same was found to be unto death to me. For sin, taking occasion by the commandment, seduced me, and by it killed me. . . . For we know that the law is spiritual; but I am carnal, sold under sin. For that which I work, I understand not. For I do not that good which I will; but the evil which I hate, that I do. If then I do that which I will not, I consent to the law, that it is good. Now then it is no more I that do it, but sin that dwelleth in me. . . . For I am delighted with the law of God, according to the inward man [*secundum interiorem hominem*]; but I see another law in my members, fighting against the law of my mind, and captivating me in the law of sin [*in lege peccati*], that is in my members. Unhappy man that I am, who shall deliver me from the body of this death? The grace of God, by Jesus Christ our Lord. Therefore, I myself, with the mind serve the law of God; but with the flesh, the law of sin. (Rom. 7:7–25)

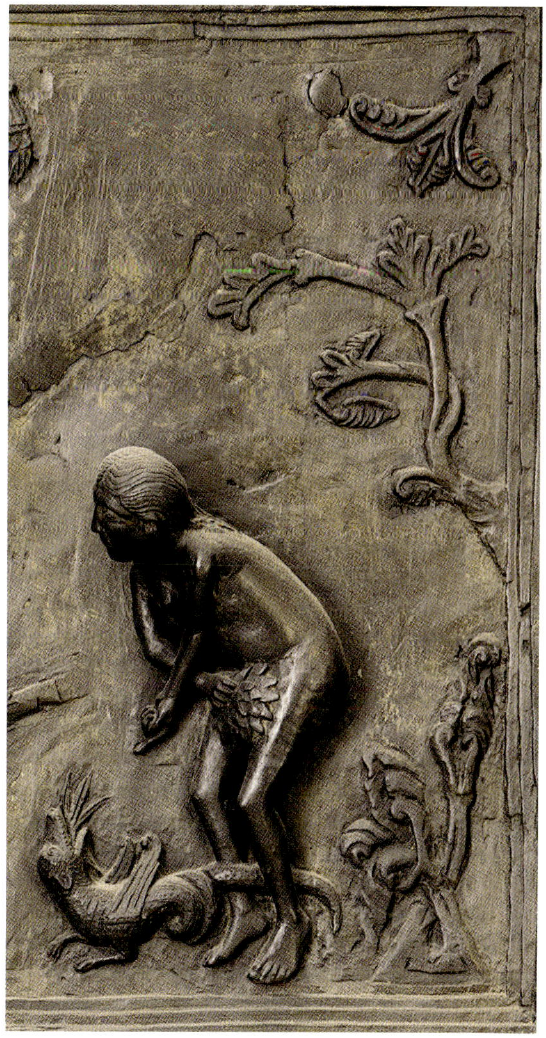

69

69. *Panel 4, Eve's plants.*

The stooped posture of the figures, a sign of submission to sin, is concomitant with the disappearance of the vertical and orthonormal position, so rich in meaning, in the door's first panel. It is especially important here since it distinguishes humans from animals in Christian culture (Isidore of Seville,

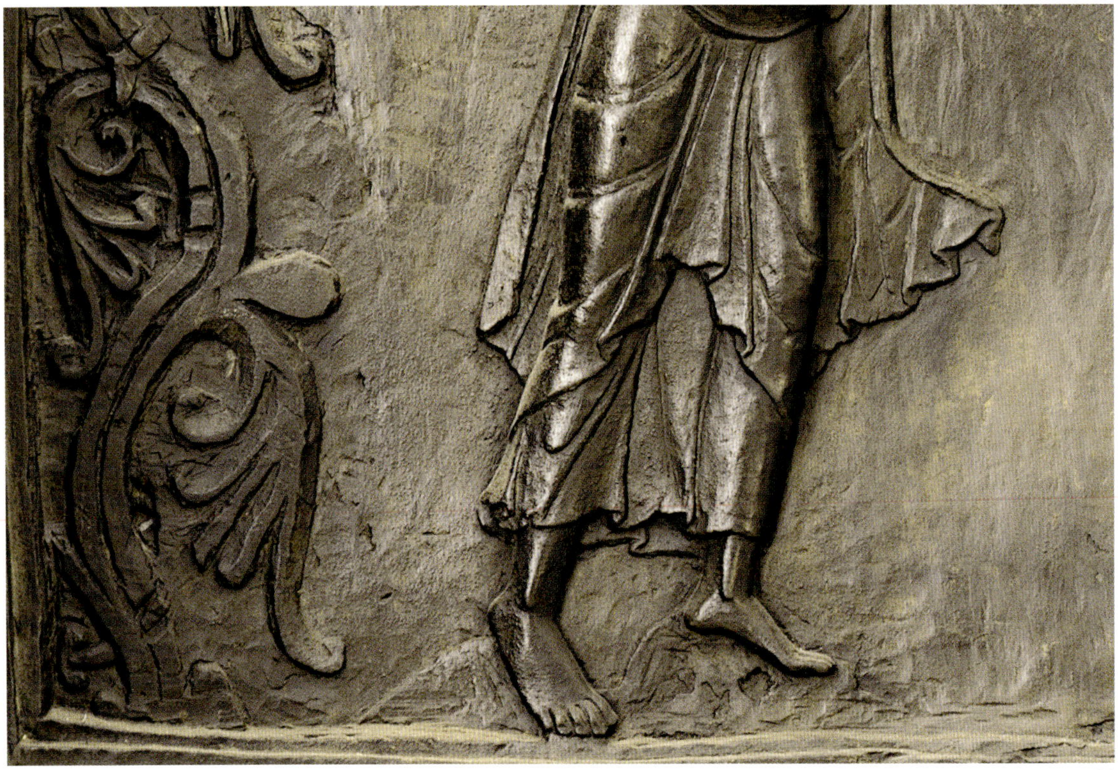

70

Etymologiae XI, 1; Rabanus Maurus, *De universo*, VI, 1). The change in the ontological status of humanity brings about a new hierarchy of the living. It does indeed show Adam smaller than God, but also Eve smaller than Adam, and the serpent smaller than Eve. This reduction in size draws an axis of degradation ending in the substance shaped by hand that covers the ground on the right side of the panel. This strip of supple, thick matter begins in front of Adam and continues to the seeded matrix behind Eve (fig. 71). It is absent from the area occupied by God who, moreover, stands on two little knolls, while still maintaining physical contact with the edge of the panel (fig. 70). The matter-territory on which humans are confined and which prefigures a land without God is undoubtedly the clay from which they were formed and to which they are destined to return: "By the sweat of your brow you will eat your food until you return to the ground, since from it you were taken; for dust you are and to dust you will return" (Gen. 3:13).

We have reached the end of the analysis of panel 4. Within a general framework that is and will forever be configured by divine Law, the initial concupiscence distorted the whole of Creation, not only the beings and the interrelationships uniting them but also the driving force and life's orientation. All the attributes characterizing Adam and Eve—their nudity, the atomization of their components, their submissive posture, the size and substance of their bodies—signify humanity's collapse into an ever-increasing animality, and then its dilution in the inanimate clay from which it was formed. The chain of events is the fruit of the Law, but it places exclusive responsibility on Adam and Eve for the evil they will transmit to their progeny; the Creator's coherence and absolute goodness are thus entirely preserved.

It may seem that the theological demonstration through images is of such great complexity that it could not have been understood by an eleventh-century lay person. I have already suggested that the door's interpretation, even though it encourages a personal journey, could have been guided by clerics' words unknown to us. However, at this stage of the inquiry, I would like to call attention to an important distinction. The visual elaboration of the discourse, probably one of the most subtle that Western Christian art has ever produced, is certainly complex, but its vocabulary and syntax come, in the first place, from the experience that everyone can draw from the world of nature, even more so if one lives in a rural society. In addition, the amount of time necessary for comprehension must be considered in the particular context of a world containing very few images.

The theological content must be considered at another level. Even though it is formulated in an extraordinary Augustinian linearity, it remains basic. Learning what constitutes divine Creation, body, soul, sin, death, and then, as we shall see, the Church

70. *Panel 4, ground underneath God.*

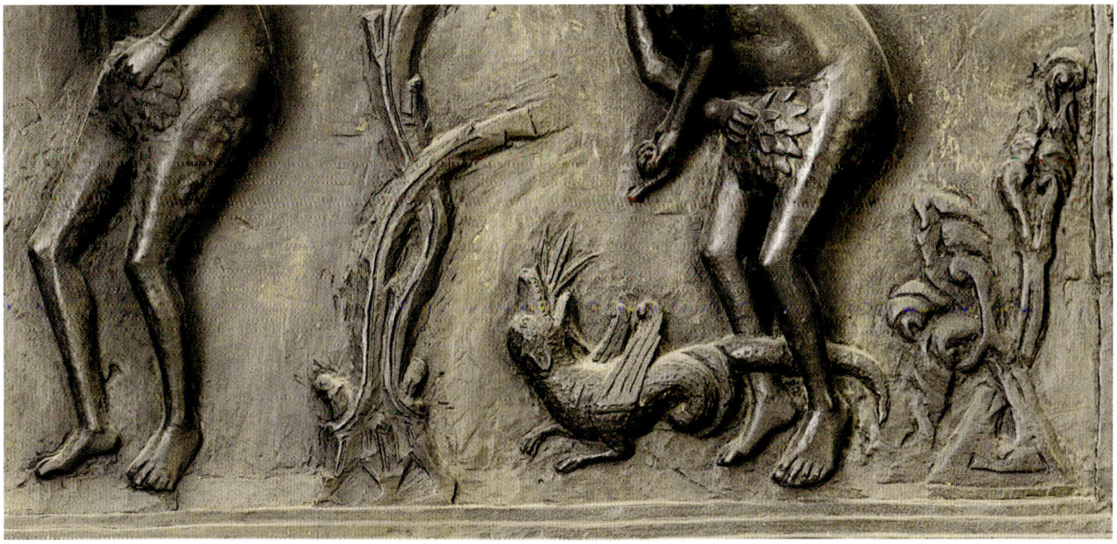

71

and salvation, is the cornerstone of a Christian education and is not at all exceptional. What may be surprising is that a pastoral hermeneutic is far removed from the morality and educational mores that spearheaded the history of the Western Church. Iconicity still reigns here. Through it, the discourse's semantic form and content correspond closely. Bernward offers the viewer of his door a conversion anchored in the discovery of the reason for things, a knowledge that rests on what the Creator has given and never taken away from his creatures: a life to be born into the world, a body to perceive it, and its inner image to comprehend it. Understanding the visual discourse is, per se, a path to atonement.

71. *Panel 4, ground underneath Adam and Eve.*

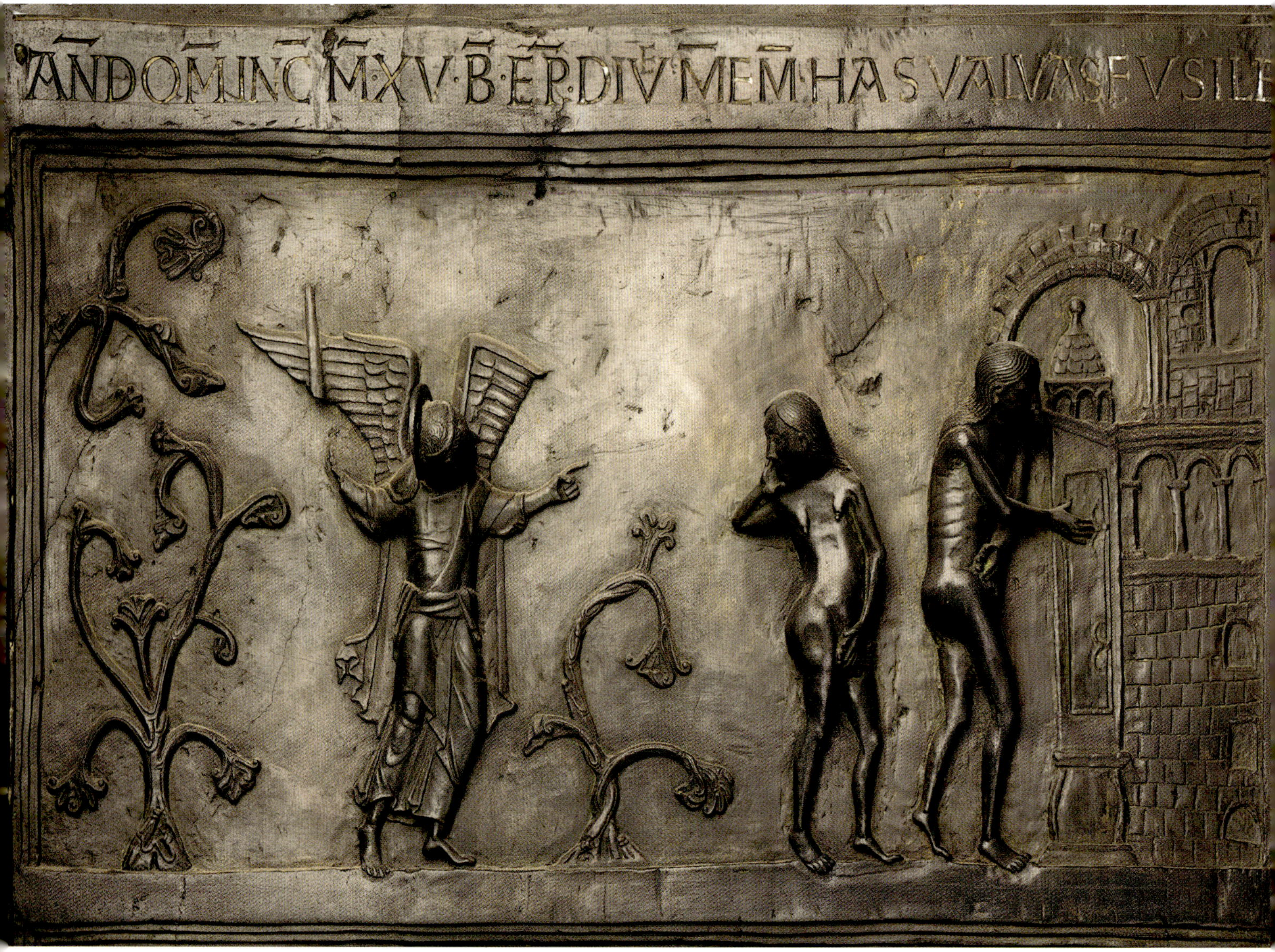
AN DOM INC M·XV·B·EP·DIV MEM·HAS VALVAS FVSIL

Panel 5

DEATH

The fifth panel, depicting Adam and Eve being forced to leave Eden under an angel's fiery sword, is bordered by a dedicatory inscription (fig. 72). Many examples, notably the doors of Byzantine tradition that flourished in Italy between 1060 and 1100, attest to the fact that it was not customary to place the dedicatory inscription in median position or to display its textual continuity across both wings. Therefore, the door Willigis commissioned for his cathedral in Mainz stands out even more strongly as the model for this particular arrangement.

Inscribed as an epigraph on the bronze itself, the dedication is an integral component of Bernward's general discourse, not only because it describes the door's origin (the bishop), its technique (the casting of the wings), its date (1015), its purpose (the sponsor's *memoria*), and its destination ("the temple of the angels"), but also because it functions as an image in itself, complementary to those on the panels. Two of the three major characteristics of the epigraphic band have already been mentioned. Placed without any textual interruption on the two wings, it is a major clue to the typological interpretation associating the images facing each other, transcending the division of the door, hence restoring its fundamental unity. From a geometric point of view, the band is in the middle of the door, but together with the vertical line seen when the door is closed, it forms a great cross. The phenomenon, even more noticeable on Willigis's aniconic door, recalls an early Christian tradition for identifying church entrances, as shown by the first bronze doors Pope Hilarius commissioned for the Lateran baptistery, which were covered with little crosses, a motif that can also be found on the Hagia Sophia, built in Constantinople during Justinian's reign [Mende 1994, 18].

72. *Panel 5.*

The third characteristic of the epigraphic band is that it introduces a visual break in the panels' unfolding narrative. This is not the case for the historiated doors that lend themselves to comparison: the late fourth-century door of St. Ambrose in Milan, which develops a cycle of David as a Christlike figure; the wooden door of St. Sabine in Rome with explicitly typological images; or Byzantine doors without any specific narrative. This peculiar scansion of the narration does not correspond to any articulation of the biblical text, and it must be emphasized that the two scenes on panels 4 and 5, separated by the dedicatory inscription, are drawn paradoxically from the same verse: "And he (God) cast out Adam, and placed before the paradise of pleasure Cherubims, and a flaming sword, turning every way, to keep the way of the Tree of Life" (Gen. 3:24).

Even though it may be bound by technical constraints, this division of the narrative is highly significant. It occurs just after panel 4 where human nature was described as atomized, composite, and heterogeneous to the divine. At the same time, it acts as a compensating factor on the scale of the door's system since, as a transverse section of the monumental cross, it announces that Christ will allow humans to renew their first unity in themselves and with God. The double action of the inscription, scission, and connection announces the main subject of the fifth panel.

Brandishing a sword, the angel stands on the left, like God in the previous panel. He enacts the same figural gestures, leaning forward on his left leg with

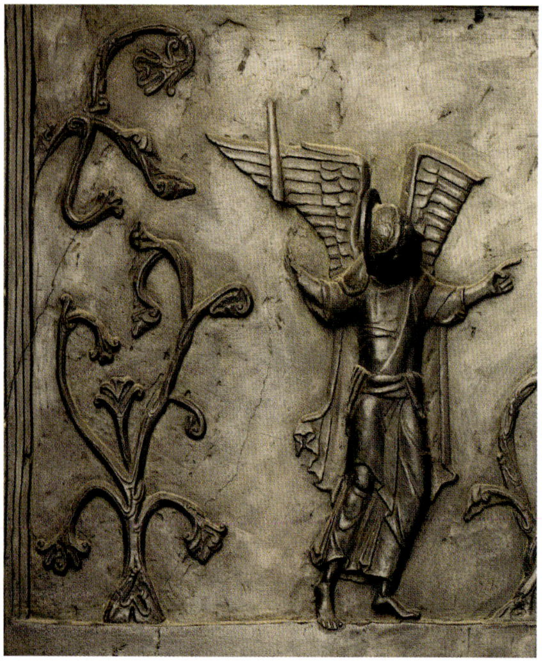

73

arm raised and finger pointing (fig. 73). The angel's feet stand on a ground that, this time, is the same for all protagonists. Playing his role as a guardian, the angel pushes man out of a Paradise that he aggressively appropriates in an iconography going back to early Christian images [LCI, *Adam und Eva* and *Vertreibung*]. Historians have unanimously considered this angel as a divine executor, placing this scene squarely within a Carolingian tradition (Bible of Charles the Bold, BnF lat. 1, f. 10v; Bamberg Bible, Msc Bibl. 1 f. 7v; Bible of Moutier-Grandval, British Lib. Add 10546, f. 5v). What has not been considered is that here, on first coming into contact with humans, the angel also assumes the ontological function associated with his name: he cuts humans from the Tree of Life, yes, but, as God's messenger, he also establishes a bond with them. Let us develop this topic.

Behind the angel are two bushes, one anchored to the ground, the other to the left side of the frame. Although these plants are indisputably distinct, the eye tends to bring them closer together. Their foliage and movements are similar, and they are placed vertically like the divine unified branch of panel 4. With their mass and volume, together they provide a visual counterweight to the architectural elements on the opposite side of the image. These two plants, linked and separated at the same time, generate a diffuse impression of cross-sectioning, compounded by the divergence of their growth and the close presence of the angel's sharp-edged sword.

The upper bush has the features of a spiritual material (fig. 77). Its high branch bears the palmette symbolizing eternity and the plant is composed of three stems echoing the plant on the upper-right spandrel of the previous panel, which I suggested interpreting as a figuration of the soul in the triune image of God (fig. 75).

The lower bush is fleshy but surprisingly lifeless. It resembles the lower and middle sections of the great Tree of Life in the first panel (fig. 74), but its branches are bent, loosened, just like the torn palmettes, bordering on spasm for lack of ligature. The plant's anatomical structure becomes literally undone. This general disunity leans back against a particular configuration of the root mass, whose double wooden skeleton, connected through a channel, traces the interrupted contour of a heart (fig. 76).

With this unprecedented iconography, Bernward refines his characterization of the vital principle in a distinction as essential to his cosmology as it is to the vitalist theory inspired by Aristotle's naturalism and developed by St. Augustine. The divine organizing dynamic, which arranges and coordinates the parts so as to confer on them a harmonious overall vitality, is not the same as the potentiality that God has given to corporeal matter enabling it to come to life and take shape. In other words, corporeal matter has the potential to become animated, but it has neither the driving force nor the model to do so. In panel 5, what is lacking in the lower bush is precisely the upper bush from which it has been separated, namely, the soul, that part of the being that organizes and moves the corporeal material in order to make life circulate in it (*De civitate Dei,* Book XIII, 15, 557). The bushes on the left are therefore the one and the same Tree of Life whose body (the lower segment) and soul (the upper segment) have come apart.

In turns growing, organized, immortal, gendered, fertile, victimized, poisoned, sexual, composite, and then separated, the Tree of Life, through its visual discourse, has underscored and subsumed the entirety of world history. In this botanical epic, it plays a paradigmatic role due as much to its prosopographic qualities as to its ability to emblematize the living faculty that St. Augustine, as Pliny's heir, attributes to the plant:

> Even bushes are moved not only by some external force acting on them, as when they are shaken by winds, but also by that inner motion which drives whatever belongs to the growth and beauty of a tree, by which sap is drawn into the root, and there turned into all that constitutes the nature of the herb or tree. None of this happens, after all, without internal movement. (*De Genesi ad litteram,* Book VII, 16, 22, 375)

73. *Panel 5, angel and left-hand tree.*

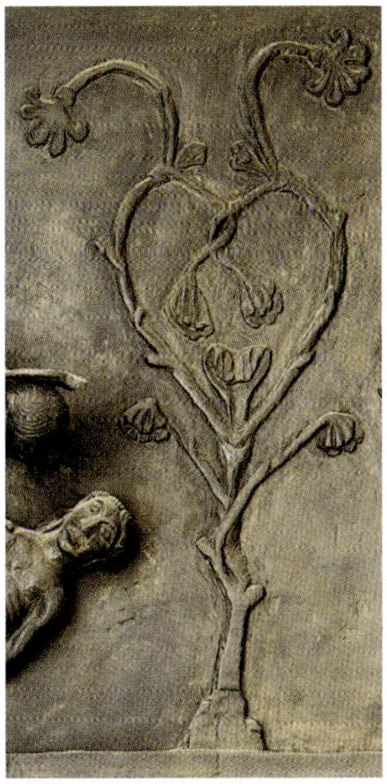

74

75

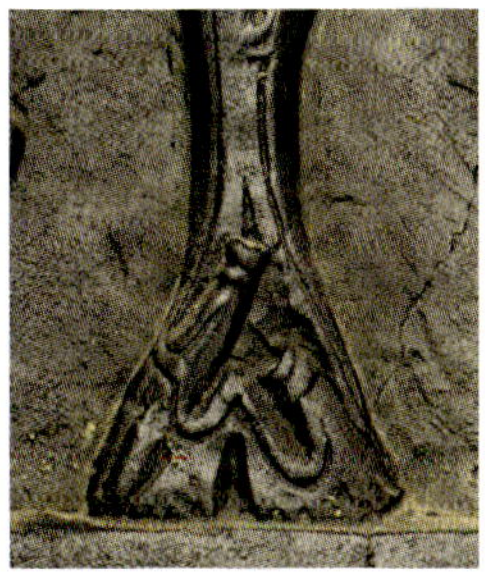

76

The tree in the first panel of the bronze door thus establishes all the morphological and substantial characteristics that make it possible to study subsequent plants on the basis of their similarities and contingent differences: distinction of species, structural configurations, specific tensions and components (foliage, roots, vascularization, masses, and wooden qualities). In the fifth panel, at the end of a considerable metamorphic journey, the viewer is placed before a portrayal of the separation of body and soul, a representation to my knowledge without equal, of death *in itself.*

The future of the soul is different from that of the body. By nature, it is immortal, being made of a spiritual and immaterial substance, which paradoxically does not prevent it from having a form, as St Augustine underscores (*De Genesi ad litteram,* Book VII, 6,9; 15, 21 and 19, 25, 367, 375 and 377). This is what allows depicting the plant differently in panel 5 than in panel 4 (fig. 75). Comparing the two yields rich information. By its being anchored only on the left side of the frame, the soul in panel 5 shows that it has lost its double reference to the earthly and the celestial world (fig. 77). The cross that determined the orientation and curled-up arrangement of the three leaves in the upper spandrel of panel 4 has also disappeared. In place of the cruciform support there is a loop motif identical to the hybrid's tail in panel 4 (cf. fig. 52). Due to the loss of its divine model, the soul suffers from the weakening of the link. Its constitutive elements, released and left to themselves, twist and turn in a disorderly way. The soul does not die but becomes distorted. Its chaotic state blurs the harmony of its parts, destroying the divine image underlying its spiritual disposition. Its matter is not altered in any way by contamination since inferior corporeal matter cannot act on superior spiritual matter. However, the soul has let the body's drives emerge within itself, as well as the restlessness of that part of the being that by nature it should dominate. The central leaf has become a magmatic excrescence, like the bubbling flesh behind Eve in panel 4 (cf. fig. 65), but it has also morphed into a deadly weapon. Aggressive and spearlike, this leaf evokes the angel's sword whose size it shares. The experience of the death of the flesh is extended here to a spiritual death, since it disappears from its own eyes as well as from those of the Creator. A soul "deprived of God" is a dead soul, as Augustine puts it simply (*De civitate Dei*, Book XIII, 12, 554).

The angel actualizes and signifies the double death of body and soul. Its "flaming sword flashing back and forth" (Gen. 3:24) forbids any hope of return to Paradise, but it must also be considered for what it is literally, a source of light, such as is underscored by a tradition of commentaries initiated by the Venerable Bede, whose profound influence on Germanic authors is well known (Bede, *In principium Genesis,* Book 1, III). With God's disappearance in panel 5, a new model of communication between the human and the divine is set in place.

On the bronze door all the angels, of course, wear a halo, but only three of them also possess a wrought diadem: twice in Eden (panels 1 and 5) and once in front of what is associated with Paradise (Christ's tomb in panel 15, to be discussed later at length) (cf. fig. 1). Regarding this point, I suggest that the an-

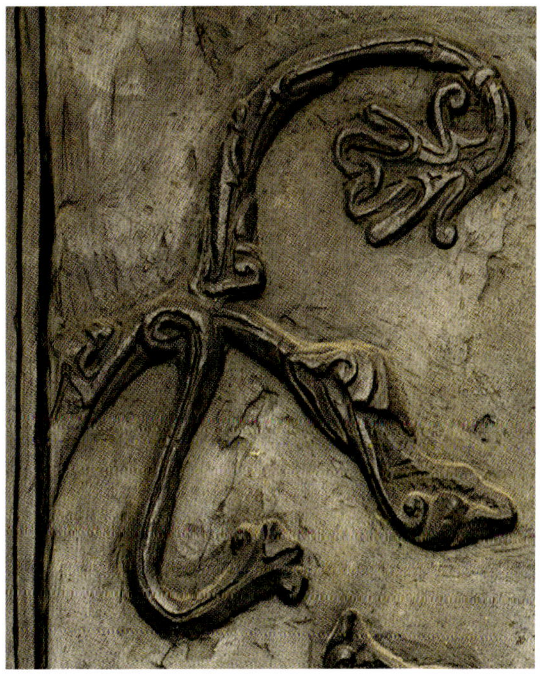

77

74. *Panel 1, paradigmatic tree.*

75. *Panel 4, plant, upper-right corner.*

76. *Panel 5, roots of left-hand tree.*

77. *Panel 5, plant, upper left.*

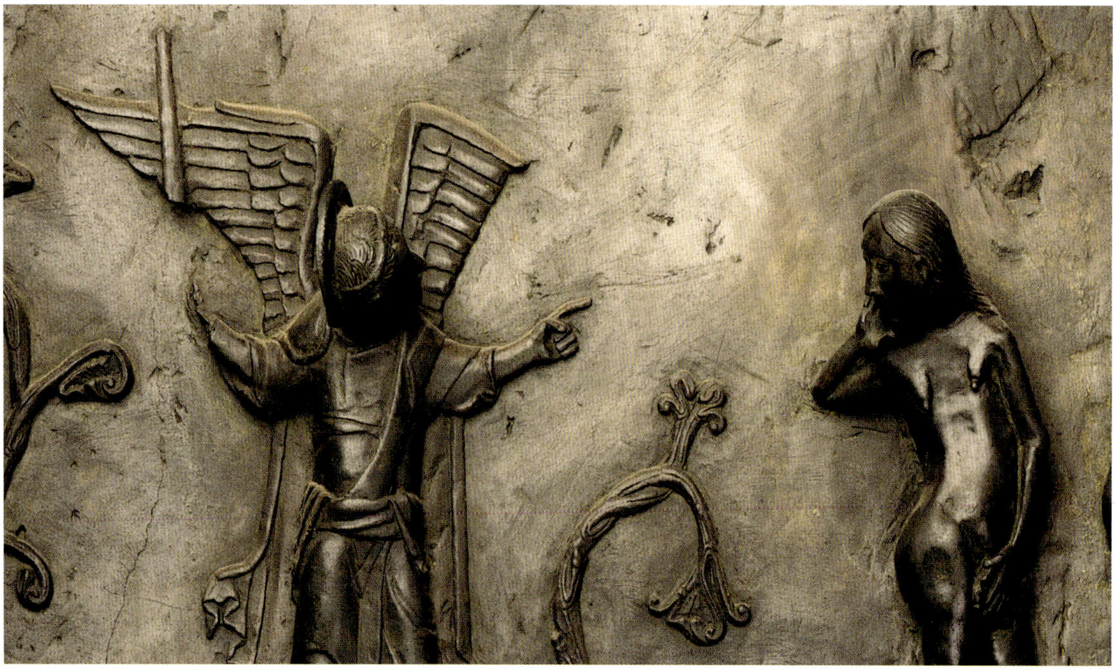

78

gelic diadem is a sign of the reflection of divine light acting in its plenitude, especially since its wrought ornamentation in the shape of small dots recalls the decoration of the divine book and garments that signaled the enveloping glory of the Creator's light in panel 2 (cf. fig. 39).

With his body, and especially with his glowing halo placed perpendicular to the door, the angel conceals the split tree, while illuminating its spiritual significance. His visage is placed in direct line with Eve's face and constitutes a mirror in which the woman sees and understands what she no longer is, all the more so since she sees and knows herself without God, a consciousness reinforced perhaps by the traditional association, in Christian commentaries, between the sword and God's Word penetrating the soul (fig. 78).

Both a divine soldier by his gesture (recalling the narrative of the *historia*) and an intellective light (in that he reveals the deepest meaning of the events), the angel is the messenger of a doubly signifying Word. It is this vision that explains Eve's tightly compressed lips, her hollowed-out eye sockets, and the hand she brings to her face as a sign of deep sorrow; and not, as it has almost always been interpreted, with a touch of romanticism, her regret over a lost Paradise. In the same way that her visage is distorted by suffering, her twisted body, as in the panel of the original sin, bears the marks of a future sorrow; worn out by maternities to come, her breasts have visibly sagged.

Adam's body is equally marked (fig. 79). A sharp hardness characterizes his nose, cheek bones and mouth, while his stooped torso, appearing to be crushed by the crenellated arc ending on his shoulder, is marked by deep slashes. They draw attention to his ribs, foreshadowing the painful toil to which man will be subjected in the next panel.

The two humans thus bear on their very flesh not the traces of what they are constrained to live, since they have not yet left Eden, but the stigmata of the anguished movements imposed on their tormented souls by the announcement of their terrifying future. In this perspective, more than physical pain itself, it is the fear and suffering in the face of death, linked to their self-awareness, solitude, and finiteness without God that Bernward places at the heart of the banished's condition. And yet, once more, a vision of hope is offered, and it is up to them to seize it.

Like Bede (*In principium Genesis,* Book I, III) and his successors, Bernward has taken into account the two epithets qualifying the angel's sword in Genesis 3. Its blaze, namely its light, but also its twirling, even though the translation does not quite reflect the Latin *versatilem*, which signifies a change of condition. What the sword forbade in the past, it will authorize one day as Word incarnate. This indication of a possible return to Eden is a fundamental theological point that Bernward deploys in the image by means of the plant standing between Eve and the angel (fig. 80).

The expressiveness and orientation of the plant's branches have led historians to suggest that the plant pushed the humans out of Eden (fig. 72). The point is valid, but the bush signifies much more than that:

78. *Panel 5, angel and Eve*

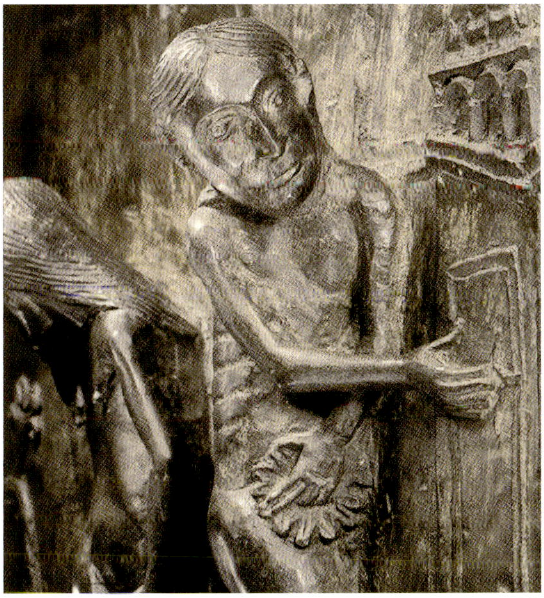

79

its configuration and position in the panel are as ambiguous as the sword.

It must be noted, first of all, that the bush is placed in front of the angel and not behind him, so that it does not act so much against the humans or defend itself against them, as it shows them the way out of Eden. The bush is the new Tree of Life, soul and body reunited, that will condition their life on earth. Its vitality remains connected to the flesh. Its triangular root mass, composite and hollowed at the core, owes its traits to the bush on the right in panel 4, where it signified a fertilized matrix (cf. fig. 65). However, contrary to all expectations, the bush's configuration is not a consequence of an internal application of the formal masculine principle. Unlike those of the previous shrubs, the skeleton's ligneous offshoots are split on both sides of the root mass, and therefore cannot grow strong enough to support the branches.

To understand the organizing source of this plant, one must turn to the attributes it inherits from the Tree of Life in the first panel, considered in its second growing phase (fig. 16). Somewhat orthonormal, it has the same structure, albeit toned down. Its two vascularized creepers intertwine allowing for the growth—although quite weakened—of a central branch-stem, to which a vegetal appendage, such as a bindweed, serves as a support. In the first panel the appendage's diagonal underscored the axis of life that God had established in Creation. In panel 5 it raises the quadrilobate leaf at the top to the geometric center of the image (fig. 72).

The principle embodied in this small leaf, of which there is no other occurrence on the bronze door, is characterized by the number four, not by the number three as one would more naturally expect. In medieval culture and in the exegetical tradition, four is the mark of the quaternities characterizing the earthly world, its space organized according to cardinal points, the temporality of its seasons, its constituent elements—the bodies themselves—or even the four Gospels coming to renew the Law. This quatrefoil leaf, qualified by its earthly materiality but whose power of action is spiritual, poses problems of consistency between substances. As mentioned earlier, according to the hierarchization of the species, corporeal matter, inferior and placed under the sign of four, cannot act on spiritual material, superior and placed under the sign of three. The only reasonable explanation for the quatrefoil comes from what God has left as seed in the soul, and consequently in the deformed bodies of men, something spiritual, although retaining a corporeal form. In my opinion, only one bit of matter, the apex of Christian history, corresponds to this criterion: the Word incarnate in human flesh, which it subsumes and transforms.

It may be difficult at this stage of the visual inquiry to explain in depth the raison d'être of this image of Christ hidden in the human soul, yet three converging traits in panel 5 already contribute to the credibility of this hypothesis.

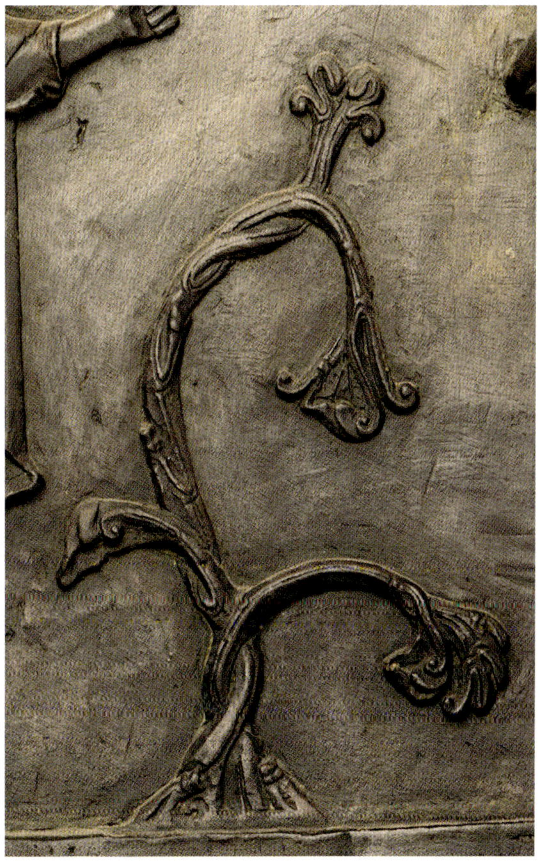

80

79. *Panel 5, Adam.*

80. *Panel 5, shrub between angel and Eve.*

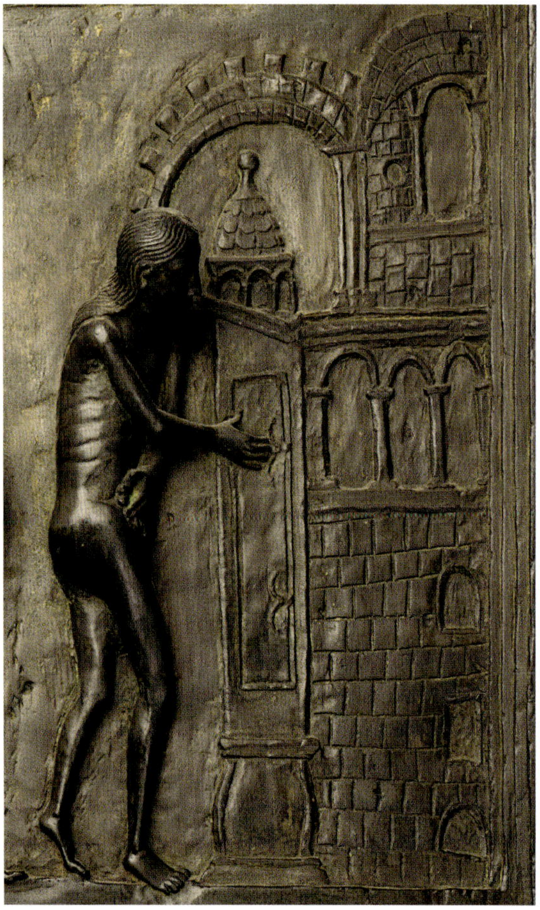

81

The first one comes from the fact that the little quatrefoil, almost insignificant visually, is the pivot around which the whole image is arranged: placed at the panel's center (fig. 72), it compensates for the lack of axes of symmetry and structuring diagonals, not to replace their function but rather to maintain a geometric logic, the possibility of understanding the space as a Euclidian plane. In other words, the central quatrefoil does not construct the preexisting space, the rectangular frame set in place by the Creator in the first panel. Rather, contained in the very matrix of the world, like the Word, it is the immobile and sole point of stability that gives order and intelligibility to the viewer's gaze.

A second feature of the arrangement, the quatrefoil foliage, is also illustrative. Indeed, it develops a subtle analogy with the unified structure of the perfect soul as represented in the upper-right corner of the previous panel (fig. 75). As spiritual matter taking a material, symmetrical, and orthonormal form, the quatrefoil potentially contains a factor of linkage, of unification, that seems to me to announce the orthonormal cross of the sacrifice, the very same cross that structures the bronze door in order to bestow on it a precise cosmological unity.

A third aspect of the image supports the hypothesis that the quatrefoil is the prophetic and residual trace within the human lineage of a Word destined to become incarnate. The cluster of leaves is the only vegetal element that Eve could grasp merely by stretching her arm and converting her gesture of despair into an act of faith. It is in the radicalism of the choice offered to her that the freedom reserved to humans to recognize or to ignore the presence in them of a veiled but indelible imprint of the Word is expressed. This imprint will be activated in a developed form in panel 7, above Abel, the first Righteous Man in history, a topic to which we will return later. It is the potential for an orderly growth, that, once incarnate, will oppose its saving cross to the maleficent spiral of evil, thus assuring the passage from Fall to Salvation. This future is intimately connected to the woman and her progeny; from a narrative perspective, Adam is not directly affected by the bush.

Turned away from the dramatic action, Adam is pushing against the door of an architectural complex with which he constitutes a theatrical unity (fig. 81); it introduces the viewer to another phase of the narration but also to a new speculative perception.

The Vulgate does not mention this building—the first artifact of the bronze door—it says only that the angel (some cherubs) stands *ante paradisum voluptatis.* No architectural structure appears in Carolingian miniatures depicting the episode. However, an enclosed garden, an aedicule, and a hinged door are represented in the *Caedmon Genesis* (Oxford, Bodl. Junius 11, 45 and 46), which could confirm the Anglo-Saxon influence cited by William Tronzo [1983] to explain other details of Bernward's iconography. This possible source of inspiration cannot be considered a model. At best, it could be interpreted as a suggestion, since the buildings in the illustrations of the *Caedmon Genesis* are totally different from those of the door, as are the relationships that the characters have with them. Rather, what interests us here is a symbolic staging of the space. By means of this device, Bernward qualifies the "places" between which the transition unfolds.

The building of panel 5 is composed of four large sections: a tower in the lower left; a large wall topped by a triple arcature in the lower right; a domed structure in the upper right; and a crenellated arch in the upper left. This architecture is represented with remarkable attention to detail. Immediately apparent are certain medieval features, many of which had previously been inherited from antiquity. The narrow tower rises from a rounded base defined by molding and placed on a beveled plinth, which gives it the general appearance of a column. The tower is sur-

81. *Panel 5, Adam and right-hand building.*

mounted by a small pinnacle resting on two oblique ridges, calling attention to a change in elevation. In the lower part, the pinnacle is composed of a triple semicircular arch supported by small twin columns; the upper part is covered by a conical roof decorated with fish scales; this section is topped by an orb, characteristics not of a column but of a church bell tower.

The tower is pierced by a door almost completely covering the central section. Like all my predecessors, I will call this door, for the moment, the "Door of Paradise." It constitutes a motif at once autonomous from and integral to the tower. Defined by framing that makes it stand out against the background, it is attached to the tower by carefully designed iron work extending onto the frame and functioning as hinges.

The wall juxtaposed against the tower is composed of bulky contiguous stones. It is pierced by three small, vertically placed bays, two round and one rectangular. They will reappear in the large symbolic constructions of the right wing (especially in panel 10). In addition, the wall is surmounted by an arcature supported by slender columns, each with base and capital. Higher still, placed on a sort of cylinder, is the rounded structure shaped like a dome, interrupted on the right by the panel frame and featuring an *oculus* (a small round bay) and a large window resting on two columns with base and capital.

The crenellated arch crowning the whole structure comprises a double row of stones that become increasingly smaller. Its right end appears to rest on the triple-columned pilaster supporting the left side of the dome but extends on the left to the level of Adam's shoulder.

Only the man's hand, observed from the wrist to the fingertips, reaches the tower, touching it. The thumb's end phalanx on which he leans is rounded off, much like the curvature and thickness of the door's ironwork. Visually the thumb constitutes a formal rhyme with the hinges. Mechanically it exerts a pressure on the left side of the door in such a way as to make the left wing of the door lean toward the interior. By his action, Adam becomes an involved participant in a mechanism to which he is implicitly assimilated.

Adam's other fingers press against the metal hinge. This carefully planned positioning, together with a spectacular disproportion, calls attention to a hand whose length, from wrist to fingertips, is equivalent to the width of the door inscribed in the tower. Perhaps this similarity is coincidental, but we must remember that God's stature served as a model for the configuration of the first panel portraying the divine Creation. In fact, almost all medieval units of measure are based on body dimension, especially those of the hand (palm, hand-span, or palm of the hand) and, equally important, the hand is humans' primary tool. All this seems sufficient to suggest the hypothesis that Adam lends his dimensions to an architecture that, in its quality as an artifact—the first of the bronze door—brings sin and death closer to previous human creations. To the extent that Adam's body comes between the outer wall and the tower's door, it could even be argued that he is contributing to the enclosure of the space he is penetrating. Therefore, the door at which the angel points is not the door of Paradise but the entrance to another space, enclosed and incarcerating, that Adam has built to create his own prison. His physical body? Certainly, but considered as lineage and therefore as human community, as we shall see.

Interpreting architecture is a challenge one cannot address without considering all the constructions appearing in the panel, or inquiring about their identification, their relationship to the sensible world, as well as their expressive and symbolic potential. These architectural elements are numerous and varied. They represent towers, aedicules, and parallelepipeds with clearly visible differences in elevation, enclosures, arches, piers and columns, foundations, and stylobates, but also pediments, windows of various shapes, and finely crafted roofing and pinnacles. Their precision is as remarkable as their variety, and even the ironwork and ornamentations are carefully thought out: cylinders and moldings decorate bases and capitals; stones are arranged in meticulously oriented alignment, and windows, round, rounded, or rectangular, are carefully placed on the edifices.

The plastic dimension of the modulation that introduces variety, movement, and therefore temporality into the narrative cannot be neglected, but it does not sufficiently explain the breadth of the phenomenon, nor does it take into account the evocative power of the forms. The presence of a lock modifies the quality of a door; a great arch, an arcature, or an enclosure do not evoke the same weights or the same tensions; a small tower, a steeple, an elevation level, an edifice, plain or with windows, covered by a dome or a roof, do not call to mind the same light, the same volume or even the same type of construction. The diversification of the architectural means of expression appeals to the judgment of the senses as well as to reason, leading viewers to interpret what they see in relation to their own experiences of monumental constructions, if only regarding the small town of Hildesheim.

Furthermore, the question of architectural identification brings together underlying referential systems more numerous and more complex than those required for the recognition of plants. The process used to identify trees and shrubs on the door relies on comparing their aspect with certain morphological characteristics found in nature (ferns, thistles, fig and palm trees, and, as we shall see later, grapevines). Bernward articulates these natural forms in light of his extensive knowledge of plant physiology in order to represent in the images living, dynamic, and credible beings. Perhaps stimulated by the inventiveness of Carolingian art on the subject, the bishop adds to this artifact a creative freedom that he puts to use for the elaboration of a discourse on forms.

Architecture must be examined through additional prisms. The problem is not in recognizing the presence of a building or laws determining the coherence of its configuration but rather in examining it from the perspective of the artist, the viewer, and the historian. This entails breaking down the inquiry into smaller components. Did Bernward want to represent one or several specific buildings, from which times and places, and for what purpose? One wonders whether every construction requires identification, and accordingly, classification: generic (as a principle of construction); typological (type of building); archeological (an existing edifice, or one no longer extant); spatial (structuring of an area accommodating figures); metaphorical (replacing an entity or a concept unrelated to architecture but having analogical links with construction). Would a Christian at the beginning of the eleventh century have been able to identify the buildings as such? And in what context: perceptual experience; a common culture rooted in biblical narrative; the accounts of travelers, warriors, merchants, or pilgrims? As we shall see, they all play a role to a varying degree in answering the question.

Let us begin our inquiry with the visual sources. The artist could rely on a long Christian tradition of representations of cities and buildings, whether secular or religious, if only in reference to holy places (cities like Jerusalem, Bethlehem, Nazareth, or Rome, but also temples, churches, and other buildings evoking the Holy Sepulcher, the Temple of Solomon, or even the celestial City described in prophetic visions). Despite stylistic evolutions, these architectural representations maintained through the centuries a certain number of characteristics inspired by what came before. They correspond to qualities inherent in the form or in what underlies it, but there remain sufficient characteristics for the prototype to be recognized in the copy [Bandmann 2005, 49–50]. Thus, cities can be identified by their fortified walls, towers, and gates, even sometimes by their interiors with two or three levels of elevation. The temples and the churches often have a basilica-type plan—an early Christian echo but also a reference to the Temple of Solomon—with a gabled roof and sometimes a pediment. The roundness and the dome of the Holy Sepulcher are retained.

In addition, biblical exegesis, liturgy, and medieval cosmology create constant parallels between heaven and earth but also between different moments of the world's history. One of the functions of these architectural representations—whether early Christian mosaics, early medieval illuminations, or ivories that served as binding covers for the most precious manuscripts—is to call attention to the spatial and temporal context of the events represented, by weaving links between buildings of different natures, times, and locations. In other words, a construction is seldom univocal: it pierces through the time and space of historia.

To understand a structure's symbolic power, it is necessary to recall some anthropological aspects of architecture. As Günter Bandmann clearly demonstrated in his seminal book, *Mittelalterliche Architektur als Bedeutungsträger* [1951], all major forms of architecture, particularly the dome and the column, carry symbolic significations since they cite not only major buildings in Christianity but also recall archetypal forms: the circularity of roundness, the verticality of supporting elements, the almost magical span of the vault, the natural weight of the stones, the harmony of static interdependence, majesty, solidity, among other qualities.

Additionally, in the Middle Ages wood and stone were thought to have a similar aptitude for animation, since buildings were fundamentally understood as the synthesis of the human beings involved with them [Wallis, in Bandmann 2005, 3]. Already in Vitruvius's *De Architectura,* a building is an organism comparable to the human body (or to a social body) occupying a space on the ground and whose mathematically arranged parts have a signifying organicity in themselves [Wallis, in Bandmann 2005, 30, 54]. Therefore, perceiving architecture in terms of animated matter (that is, signifying postures and gestures) presents no conceptual problem in medieval culture.

The architecture designed by Bernward functions in the same way. As we shall see, it draws from different types of construction, which the experience of the sensible world and biblical descriptions make recognizable without resorting to a learned tradition, although one might more accurately speak of suggestions and impressions rather than of formal identification. At the same time, this ambiguity leaves open the possibility of a symbolic arrangement of forms and substances, conferring on the constructions an aspect of almost autonomous shapes in the visual discourse.

In order to make this architecture readable and expressive, Bernward inscribes it into a thoughtfully organized representational system, as was the case for the "wood of life." The variety of buildings in the bronze door is in fact constantly monitored by a formal syntax that smooths the figuration while at the same time emphasizing its difference's subtle asperities. This syntax appears in two complementary ways. First, it presents a uniform realism of the construction going well beyond the approximate architectural imitations found in Carolingian and Ottonian images. Except for certain deliberate deviations, to which we shall return, Bernward displays an exceptional respect for the standards of professional practice in articulating architectonic components and arranging masses and thrusts in order to achieve balance or movement. For example, a *tas-de-charge* consisting of horizontal keystones and a dosseret are placed at the starting point of the double arch in panel 10 (fig. 127). In panel 9, the buttressing piers and their base support an arch's weight (fig. 118). Moreover, the lock behind the Virgin of the Annunciation is of extraordinary precision (fig. 117). This is not surprising since Bernward, who programmed and directed the beginnings of the construction of St. Michael's abbey, was an architect or rather (the title itself does not appear in Thangmar's text) that he was "expert in all domains of construction" (*omnique structura mirifice exelluit, ut in plerisque aedificiis*), as well as in the art of locksmithing (*ars clusoria*) (*Vita Bernwardi*, c. 6, MGH, SS, IV, 758).

The second aspect of architectural uniformity is the perspective used to represent the entire building on the door, even though these evocations of volume would be surprising to eyes used to receding perspective lines. Bernward makes very little use of the possibilities offered by high relief to construct spatial depth, contrary to the practice that he adopts for the bronze column around which the viewer must walk to follow the narrative (cf. fig. 10). In the panels, the metal parts of the construction are, at most, a few centimeters deep, that with the reflection of light emphasize minute details or particularly complex forms, as was the case for the plants. The high relief is reserved for the main characters and provides the salient surface of the biblical historia, used as a hermeneutic veil. As for the perspective, it is constructed in a different way depending on the context.

The early Middle Ages had its own canons of spatial representation. As we have seen, size ratios and textural precision are not used to create the illusion of distance but serve rather to hierarchize and qualify the elements composing the semiotic systems. In this tradition, conventions of perspective, more intuitive than canonical, combine low angle views, frontal and profile views (pseudo-axonometric at best), as well as simultaneous access to both the exterior and interior of a volume. Moreover, they present interconnected constructions and the surfaces arranged between them, each having an individual perspective different from the others and highly localized within the field of the image [De Rosa et al. 2000, 122–125].

These multiple perspectives, equally frequent in illuminations, affect not only the buildings of the bronze door but also their components. They bring into play a deliberately ambiguous perception of spaces that cannot be deciphered unequivocally [De Rosa et al. 2000, 127], thus permitting a very useful polysemy in the elaboration of the visual discourse. An edifice can be seen frontally or in profile at the same time, just as an arch can also be an enclosure, depending on whether it is perceived as being on the surface or in the image's depth.

Finally, and this feature is particularly noticeable in the bronze door, several planes are flattened or even overlapped. I would argue that this effect derives from three planar factors, the combination of which definitively distances the figures from optical mimesis. The first and most important is that the arrangement in vertical tiers signifies depth, according to one of the representational *habiti* most frequently used during the early Middle Ages [De Rosa et al. 2000, 128–131]. The second is the purely iconic treatment of the mass, which expresses its law on the surface and not in a fictitious three-dimensional space. The third is the double reading that can be done of the physical contacts established between architectural components: either they act as a connection having signifying valence on the surface, or they point to the superposition of constructions in depth.

Faithful to the medieval building, as far as its components are concerned, and structurally balanced in its masses and thrusts, the architecture figured on the door combines architectonic realism (architectonic signifying the technical and formal rules regarding construction) and architectural unrealism (architectural signifying what corresponds to a realistic arrangement, proportional but also conventional in contemporary constructions). In other words, the building's constituent elements, which are plausible and identifiable, are distributed in conformity with the standards of professional practice by Bernward the architect, but they are reconfigured and rearranged according to a strictly iconic syntax by Bernward the creator of images. Like plants, at once close to and distant from sensible reality, figurative

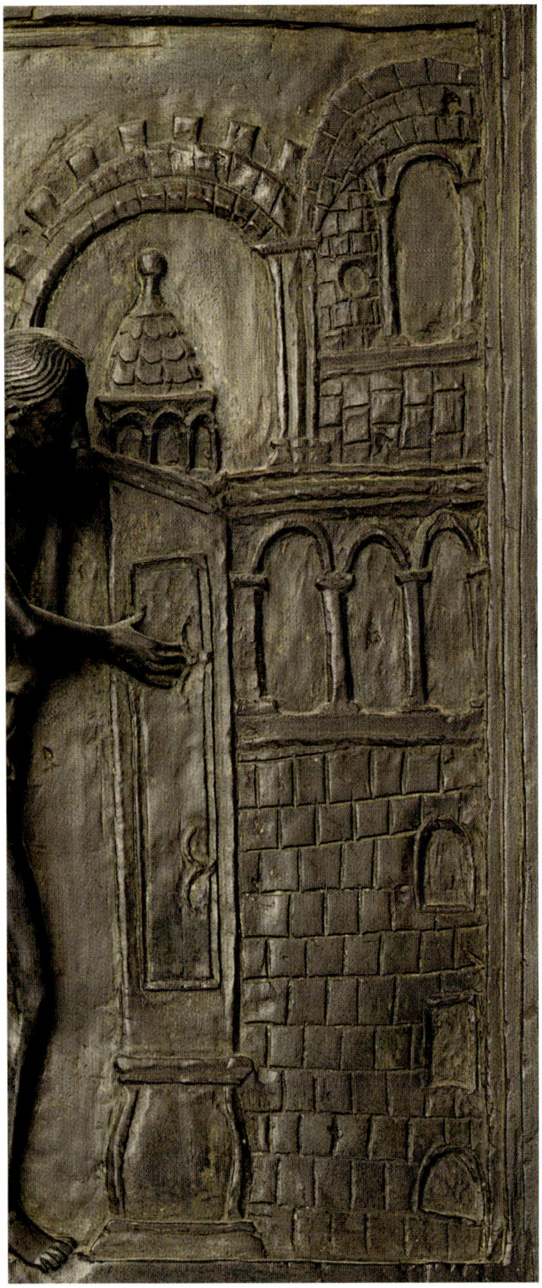

82

82. *Panel 5, right-hand building.*

architecture stands above the architectural inspiration in this respect that, far from being merely an illusionist quest, it brings into play the fundamental and organic principles of form-mass in order to provide access to the laws and essences of things, not to their appearance. Like wood, the stone will thus adopt various forms and substantial qualities apt to unveil the ontology hidden behind the historia, while maintaining a structure respectful of the constraints of materials, forces, and weight existing in perceptible reality, filtered through a semiotic treatment morphing the visible into the intelligible.

This is precisely what happens in panel 5, where we have temporarily set aside the analysis of the buildings. All these considerations may be a valid scientific argument, yet it was only after I had fully understood the typology of the buildings represented on the door and had then integrated and redistributed all their components in my memory that I was able to appreciate their organicity and signifying qualities. As Mary Carruthers argues [1998], in a biblical and exegetical culture whose cornerstone is the analogic articulation of methodically organized recollections, an intelligent vision can only result from an inner reconfiguration.

In the flat verticality of panel 5, the crenellated arc is buttressed by the triple column supporting the dome on the right (fig. 82). However, as shown by the orientation of its keystones and by its movement encircling the tower, the arc is seen also behind the buildings. It has been placed higher to signify that it is the furthest away from them and, in addition, it constitutes a low enclosure that begins in the image's depth.

Although visually interconnected with the arc-surrounding wall, the composite construction, reaching almost the height of the panel, exists as an autonomous structure. It is not subjected to a global perspective but is subdivided into many buildings rendered three-dimensionally in places by the play of textures, orientations, and arrangement of materials.

The large wall that rests directly on the panel's frame is made of large square blocks, carefully sealed and placed in staggered rows to ensure stability, as in the real world. In its upper part are three arched windows set crosswise on a bar, without any visible stone, which serves as a base for the small columns. Although the compound is strictly vertical, the arcature's abrupt interruption, as well as the decentering of the three bays on the wall's lower part, give the impression that the structure continues on the right side, beyond the panel's frame. As it appears, it is difficult to know if this wall is straight or whether it takes on the curved shape of an apse, as the mental reconstruction of its missing symmetrical section would suggest.

A band whose middle part is shaped like a thick cord tops the triple arcature. If it is a molding, it may imply the presence of an intermediate roof. The cord and the bar above it are placed all along the segmented band marking the elevation of the left tower, which is thus represented in oblique perspective. The arcature wall and the tower, visually and architecturally connected, are nonetheless disconnected on the framework since the tower is in front of the construction, as confirmed by the wall's interrupted stones.

The dome-shaped edifice surmounting the great

arcaded wall is set in yet another perspective. Its façade has been eliminated, thus rendering the interior structure visible. Dominating the whole complex, the semicircular edifice made of keystones aligned and decreasing in size delineates a vault abruptly interrupted by the panel's frame. Below it is a surface covered with stones placed not horizontally but rather offset by half a brick in relation to the others. It is impossible to raise a wall without aligning the stones horizontally, as shown in the lower wall. Hence this surface can only have been conceived as horizontal. It represents a floor moved up in height to indicate depth. Between the vault and the floor tiles, the optical illusion works, because it gives the impression that the left wall is pierced by an oculus as a lateral wall would be, and the large window appears as an open background wall.

The carefully staged perspective of the hall, dominated by the dome, completes the volumetric elaboration of the architecture in panel 5. One might wonder why Bernward took such care in representing a three-dimensionality that is partly mimetic, a view avoided in Ottonian illuminations, if it were not for the fact that it appears precisely at this point of the story, not only as a syntactical element but also as subject.

Indeed, the episode of the expulsion from Eden opposes two contiguous places evoking neither the same spatiality nor the same materiality. The perspective used on the panel's right side corresponds to the world to which humans are destined. It is absent from the image's left side, an Edenic garden whose planarity, which had hitherto never been questioned even though it was implicit in the orthonormal configuration of the first panel, now stands out due to the presence of the central quatrefoil that fixes the image's Euclidian plane.

The obvious hypothesis is that Bernward conceptualized the three-dimensionality inherent in architecture, which fundamentally distinguishes it from geometry, as a visual means of evoking the dense and perishable corporeal materiality, of fallen humanity's new abode. The tridimensional perspective renders the Paradise that humans leave behind even more ideal and spiritual. As Evgueni Zaitsev puts it, in the early Middle Ages, God the Creator is not so much an architect as he is a geometer [Zeitsev].

I agree that this unprecedented hypothesis, according to which a scholar at the beginning of the eleventh century envisioned places in terms of thickness and substance, may be disconcerting. However, apart from the strength of its simplicity and appropriateness to the Christian definition of the flesh, this proposition will subsequently be confirmed by several aspects of the iconographic program: the setting up of a vast visual meditation on the nature of the bodily sheath, the signifying use of differentiated perspectives in panel 10 (figs. 129 and 130), or the effacement of the edifice's materiality in panel 15 (cf. fig. 184).

The substantive transformation of the world after the Fall does not at all invalidate the rectangular format used as a background beginning with the first panel, nor does it efface past divine actions—those already seen in panel 3 (cf. fig. 56). The Word continues to act in the world, a subtle but present matrix. It is expressed in the quatrefoil, Christ's harbinger, which serves a geometric purpose and supports the Tree of Life for humans excluded from Paradise. It also explains the one patent incongruity that escapes the architectonic organization and rigorous perspective of the architecture on the panel's right side: the pillar composed of three columns placed between the dome and the crenellated wall (fig. 83).

In addition to its shape, this pillar occupies an unsuitable place since it rises above the totality of the inner space of the vaulted hall in which the floor does not appear. It also bears the virtual impact of the surrounding arch, as well as that of the vault and base of the aedicule's window, thus appearing at the same time as the outside and inside of the edifice. The unrealistic pillar functions in a strictly iconic way, in a purely intellective space. It creates an equilibrium of masses in the image's planarity, establishing the connection between the four distinct parts of the architecture; in other words, it visually ties the structure together. Now, as an echo of the triple semicircular arches, the pillar's shape is both one and triune. The three adjoined shafts rise from distinct bases appearing to be placed in a circle, but they are unified by a single capital. It is precisely this unification of three in one that explains the range of nonmimetic figuration of these columns and the function of organization and relationship that Bernward assigns to them. The entire right wing of the door will develop and make use of its full signifying potential.

I am arguing that we see in the door the first occurrence of the Christlike column, which will scan and organize the symbolic narration of the New Testament, an axis around which will be distributed the details composing the construction of panel 5. These details are designed to reappear as bearers of precise symbolic significations that do not need to be discussed here. At this point we will simply emphasize that the first architectural image of the bronze door will serve as a formal paradigm for all future constructions, in the same way that the Tree of Life

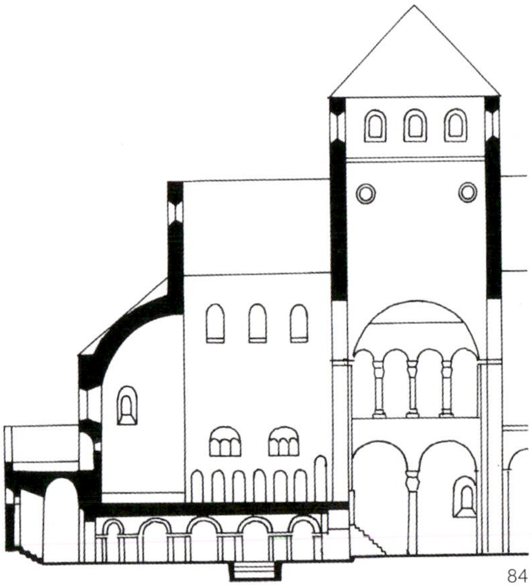

84

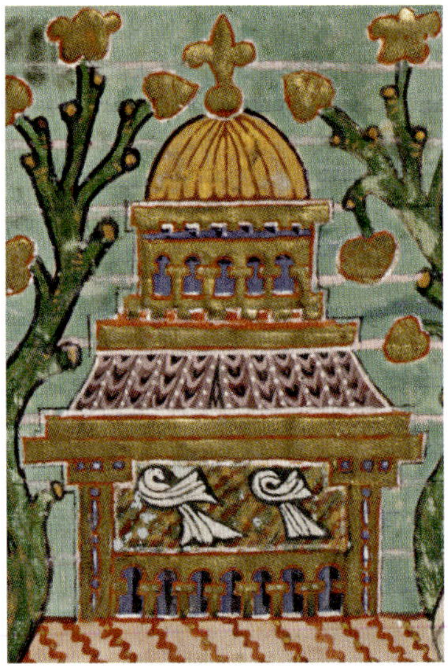

85

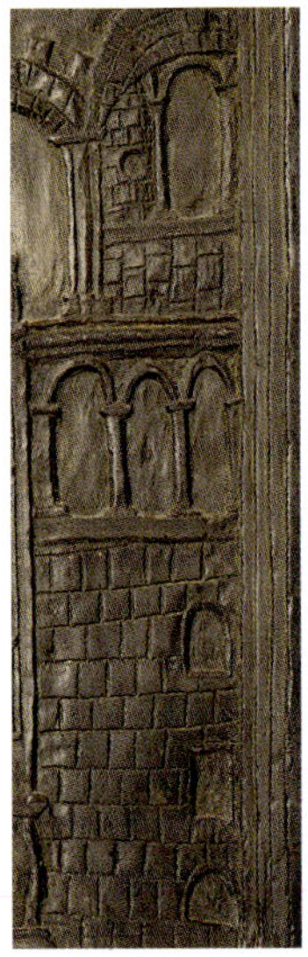

86

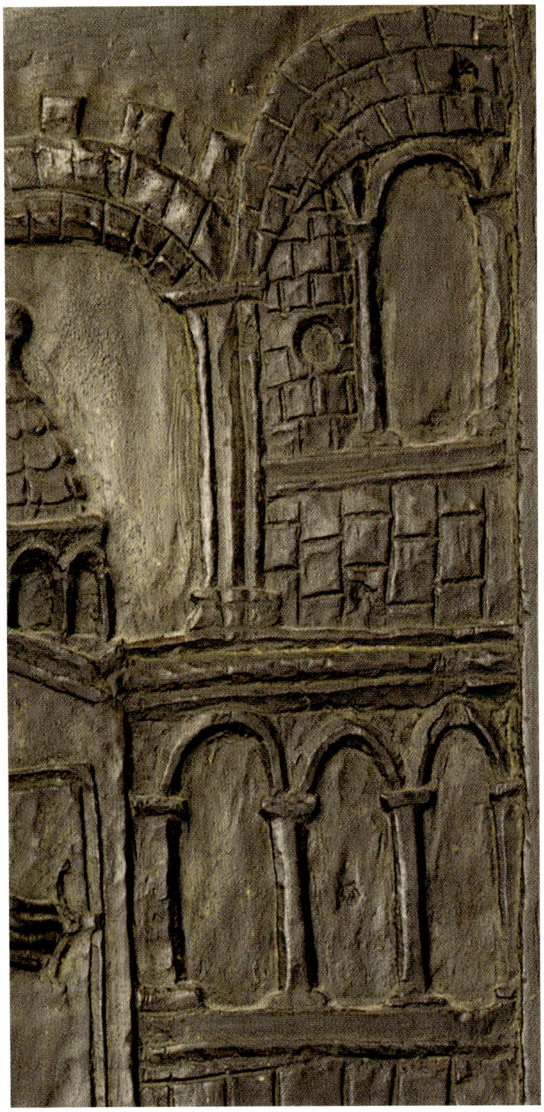

83

in the first panel was intended to serve as a reference point for the plants of the subsequent panels.

The time has come to synthesize this analysis and to ask what the building represents. The crenellated arc and the tower opened by a door refer both to the walls surrounding a closed city and its monumental, fortified entrance. There are still visible examples, such as the Aurelian wall in Rome or the ancient Porta Nigra in Trier (Trêves), but we also know that Bernward had a stone wall built around Hildesheim to replace the old wooden enclosure. As the city administrator, the bishop ordered the construction of two monumental gates, two towers-cum-porches that have since disappeared, which he called St. Peter's Gate and St. Paul's Gate, after the two patron saints of Rome. He must necessarily have known the Roman prototypes since he visited these Constantinian basilicas, two major pilgrimage centers in the holy city, namely St. Peter in the Vatican and St. Paul Outside the Walls.

As the tower of panel 5 bears little resemblance to a defensive building, the viewer is encouraged to engage in a second reading also involving the large wall and the small building above it. In Ottonian architecture, the apses are vaulted, so the buildings in panel 5 may very well refer to them. On this subject, it should be noted that the *Westwerk*, or the Western complex of St. Michael's Church of Hildesheim, although unfinished at the time of Bernward's death, was designed to enclose the bishop's funerary crypt. The choir, elevated and dedicated to St. Michael as well as to all saints [Mende 1994, 29], also opens on a vaulted transept framed by two small towers embellished by oculi and semicircular arched bays (fig. 84). The similarity may be disconcerting, but

83. *Panel 5, upper portion of building.*

84. *Cross-section of the western apse of St. Michael's.*

85. *F. 75v of Bernward's Gospel Book, Hildesheim, Dom Museum, DS 18, close up.*

86. *Panel 5.*

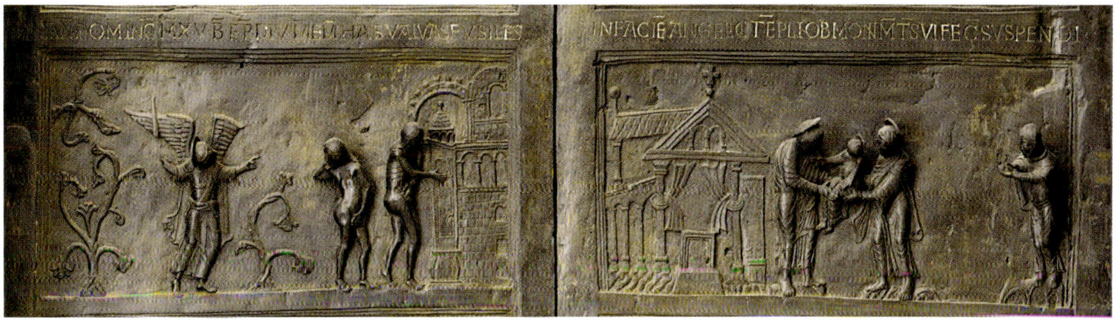

87

let us not be mistaken: if Bernward had wanted to refer precisely to the abbey he established, he would have given clearer visual clues. There remains an ambiguity that keeps the buildings in a fundamentally semantic and typological plasticity. In this instance, one might just as plausibly say that the domed aedicule above the great wall in panel 5 recalls Christ's tomb, the grotto of the *Anastasis* (the Resurrection) that was covered by a rotunda in the fourth century.

The Church of the Holy Sepulcher is the most important of all the symbolic buildings in the Christian world [Krautheimer 1942]. Its model dominates Byzantine culture, from its greatest monuments, such as Hagia Sophia in Constantinople, to its most delicate art objects. A reliquary representing it and dated at the end of the tenth century was probably brought back from the East for Theophano or for Otto III [Niehoff 1985, 88]. The Church of the Holy Sepulcher was just as famous in the West. Its round shape was used as a model for the chapel that Charlemagne ordered to be built at Aachen and that Bernward certainly knew, as he had been there. The same model is found in many Carolingian and Ottonian manuscripts, including Bernward's very own Gospel Book, in which there is a silhouette closely resembling the architecture of panel 5 (Dombibl. Hildesheim, Ms. 18, f. 75v) (fig. 85).

The commonalities between the different possible architectural sources in panel 5 converge with what emerges from the iconographical analyses: a similar reference to death (Adam enters the space destined to become humanity's tomb) and a similar emphasis on the upper parts of buildings as passages (here the triple column functions as a promise of reunification, a pledge of rebirth). However, the keystone of the demonstration is the typological connection that the viewer can establish between the architecture of panel 5 and the one corresponding to it horizontally, in panel 12 of the right wing (fig. 87). It insists on the idea of Christ's reorganizing death, the death of the Word that has not ceased to be present in the world before becoming incarnate in order to re-create it. Placed in strict axial symmetry with the sepulcher's apse, the Temple of Solomon is identically decentered in the image and is organized around a visible entrance where the sacrificial altar stands, a place of death surmounted this time by a large cross evoking the Resurrection. It is not yet the time to study this image, but we can be assured that this new passage will amend the expulsion in panel 5.

By using the quadruple morphological reference of a door, a walled city, a church apse, and a tomb, Bernward unveils the complex nature of what lies ahead outside of Paradise. It is a prisonlike abode, irremediably cut off from the Tree of Life, a prison incarcerating and crushing human existence, sanctioned by death. But at the same time, it is a place for building a community (indeed the primary meaning of the term *ecclesia*) within which there is the possibility of a way out, conditioned by the realization of a future completeness. Hence, the architecture of panel 5 represents the body: humans' carnal body and the body as a city of men and women. It is in these two bodies, both exhibited as transitory places, between life and death, death and life, that humanity's individual and collective destiny will be played out. Within this City of Man, the "column" will play the role of a framework, a law that will continue the function of the Tree of Life; but it is still too early to demonstrate it.

87. *Panels 5 and 12.*

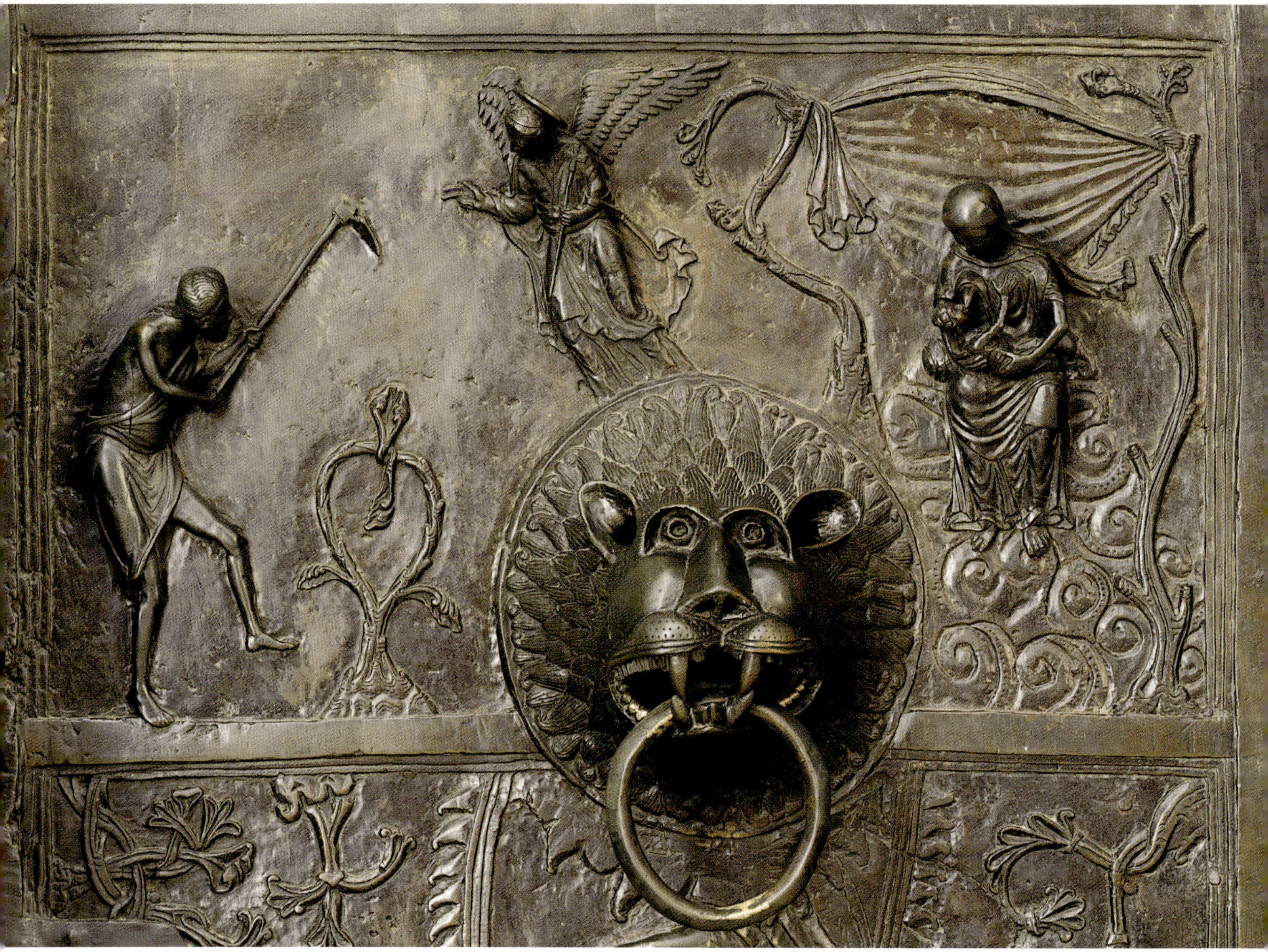

Panel 6

TIME

Panel 6 offers a vision of a new world, albeit one well known to viewers since it represents the non-Edenic land inhabited by Adam and Eve and all their descendants up to the present (fig. 88). The image includes the same protagonists as before, but they appear in three distinct areas and in different associations. Adam and the angel face each other and interact with each other. Isolated at the right, Eve concentrates on the child she is holding on her knees, a newcomer on stage. Adam is working the soil, as in all previous representations of the episode, but clearly under the angel's instructions, which is unprecedented. Protected by a curtain stretched above her, Eve is nursing her child. This configuration is very ancient. It is found in Carolingian illuminations (in the Moutier-Granval Bible, London, Br. Lib., Add. 10546, f. 5v and in the Bible of St. Paul Outside the Walls, f. 7v [Kessler 1971, 150–151, and Kaspersen 1988, 80]), but it ultimately derives from an earlier tradition, undoubtedly of Hebrew influence (the Pentateuch of Ashburnham, BnF, n.a.l.2334, f. 6, late sixth c. [Hoogland Verkerk 1995]). As mentioned earlier, Bernward had knowledge of a Tours Bible, from which he drew his inspiration. One example does not make a rule, but this tradition supplies comparative elements indispensable to understanding the creative process that may have guided the making of the image.

As with the whole door, the literalness of the story is scrupulously respected here. Adam accomplishes precisely the task to which divine sanction has condemned him: "To Adam he said: because thou hast hearkened to the voice of thy wife, and hast eaten of the tree, whereof I commanded thee that thou shouldst not eat, cursed is the earth in thy work; with labour and toil shalt thou eat thereof all the days of thy life. Thorns and thistles shall it bring forth to thee; and thou shalt eat the herbs of the earth" (Gen. 3:17–18).

88. *Panel 6.*

His back stooped, leaning on his left leg to add weight to his effort, Adam lifts a spade above a little bush. His body is wholly engaged in the labor imposed on him. Like his whole posture, the tool with which the man hoes the soil to prepare it for planting is extremely realistic. The handle fitting, the socket, and the flat triangular blade, details undoubtedly linked to Bernward's knowledge of metallurgical skills, are readily identifiable. The viewer cannot help identifying with the figure presented to them. Whether peasant or inhabitant of a rural and feudal milieu, they recognize the material conditions of agricultural work lived as a divine punishment; the medieval term *labor* encompassing the double notion of pain and need [Le Goff and Schmitt 1999, 1138].

Adam's body completes this realism. His appearance differs from that in the previous panels. Paradoxically, his emaciated visage and torso no longer reveal the angular bone structure or ribs. Instead—and these are such obvious observations that they have not attracted the historians' attention—Adam wears a clinging garment, almost soaked with sweat, as well as a beard. The representational range of the body has shifted.

In the previous panels, human morphology was based on the bone structure and its internal organization. In this respect, it corresponded to the representational mode of the Tree of Life established at the beginning of the narration and modified in

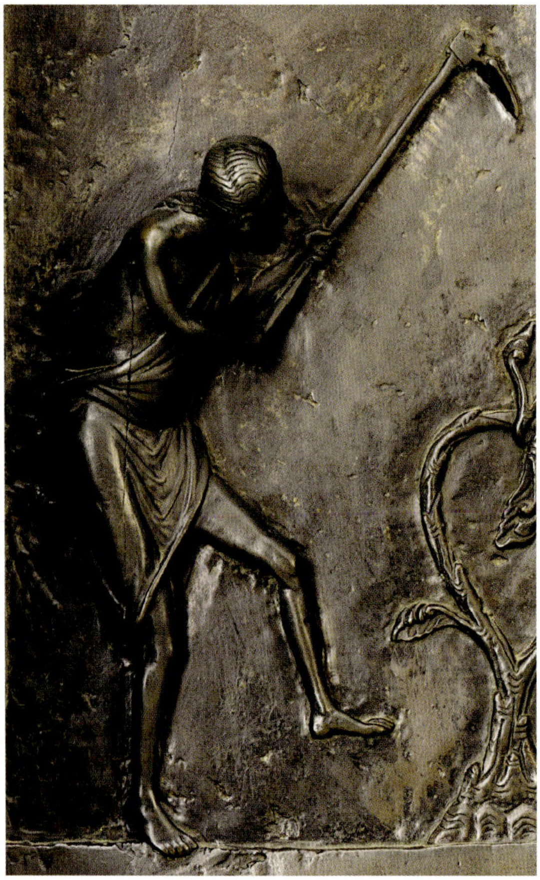

89

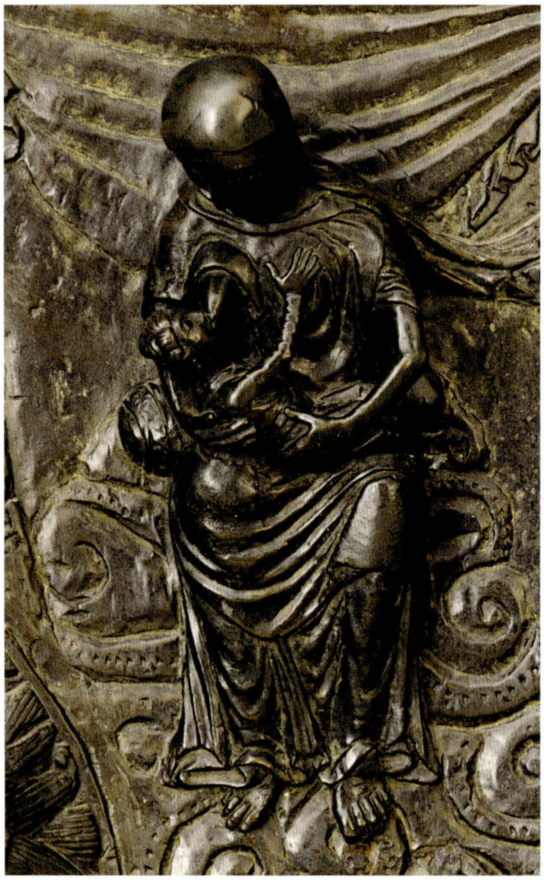

90

89. *Panel 6, Adam.*

90. *Panel 6, Eve.*

panel 5, in accordance with the emergence of the vital principle destined to accompany humans out of Eden. Quite logically, this skeleton is no longer visible in Adam's body in panel 6. It will reappear only in Christ's body in panel 14, at the precise moment—which is extremely important—when the Savior's sacrifice recasts the world's geometric order (cf. fig. 171).

While the structure of Adam's body becomes understated, its sheath of flesh stands out through the new addition of his clothing (fig. 89). The thin tunic, worn on his left shoulder, thickly folded and draped low on the thigh, underscores the strenuous work, while at the same time calling attention to his lean, gaunt flesh. The remarkable plastic artistry, made possible by the initial modeling of the wax block, creates the illusion of a fabric that is as clinging and heavy as it is thin and fragile, in complete contrast to the flowing, diaphanous garment that the angel wears here as well as in all the other panels. In this case, it should be remembered that the term *tunica*, designating a piece of clothing worn on the torso, is used in the Vulgate to describe the physical condition of the two humans expelled from Eden: "The Lord God made for Adam and his wife, garments of skins (*tunicas pelliceas*) and clothed them" (Gen. 3:21).

Both meaningful shroud and derisory protection, Adam's tunic displays all the flaws of animal skin: heaviness, tautness, fragility, vulnerability, but also absence of internal structure or at least of inner perceptible order. The level of expression and perception of the self within the creature has shifted. The residual consciousness the human being has of himself is expressed only in and by the flesh that lives to die and must suffer to live. The change of surroundings therefore follows a change of ontological paradigm. The inner order is about to be concealed by the turmoil superimposed on it. This process will be completed in the following panels with the story of Cain and Abel.

Like Adam's, Eve's body is only partially covered, befitting the representation of the female form in the early eleventh century. Her right breast is exposed, but she wears a tunic with short or rolled up sleeves, covered by a sleeveless robe clinging to the body. This particular attire is not found anywhere else on the door, but Eve's nudity is not new: she is represented bare-breasted in the Pentateuch of Ashburnham (f. 6) and in the Carolingian Moutier-Grandval Bible (f. 5v).

Christians did not invent a tradition representing the suffering of childbirth—"To the woman also he said: I will multiply thy sorrows, and thy conceptions: in sorrow shalt thou bring forth children." (Gen.

3:16)—but once again the scene has precedents. The great Carolingian frontispieces represent Eve nursing, thus associating her with Adam's penal labor. The swollen breasts that recall the sagging breasts in the previous panel, the mother's concentration on her child, and the bare arms of a peasant woman at work, all call attention to the fatigue of nursing and its profoundly carnal nature.

However, the impact of the representation goes beyond the mere narrative frame of the panel. The image of the nursing mother is an ancient topos seen in pagan antiquity, as well as in the Christian world. In mystery religions, it allows for the identification of universal mother figures such as Isis or Cybele. Bernward chose a mother pressing her twins against her breast as an allegory for the nurturing Earth in the Gospel Book that he commissioned and perhaps sketched or drew himself in the same years during which the door was built (Dombibl. Ms. 18, f. 174v). The scene's anthropological depth adds to the evocation of divine punishment and recalls another biblical verse from Genesis, the one in which Eve, called by name for the first time, is described as the mother of all living beings: "Adam called the name of his wife Eve because she was the mother of all the living" (Gen. 3:20).

The newborn, nursed by Eve, lays his hand on his mother's breast. To the best of my knowledge, the realism of this gesture is unprecedented in previous medieval iconography. It does not pertain merely to an anecdotal realism or a manifestation of love meant to elicit the viewer's empathy. Just like the laboring father, the son by pressing his hand on his mother's breast is intent in earning a food of which he is not the passive beneficiary. In addition, it should be noted that unlike the twins in Bernward's Gospel Book, the infant is not naked. He is not even swathed, going against the Carolingian representation of newborns that Bernward used for the infant Jesus in the Nativity scene of panel 12. The clothing chosen for the new human being extends the significance of his gesture. His short and clinging garment resembles that of his father and the absence of sleeves recalls that of his mother. The infant's clothes, resulting from the combination of those of his two parents, provide revealing details of his carnal inheritance.

It is difficult to identify the newborn. The iconographic tradition would opt for Cain, the first born of the two brothers, but there is also an earlier representation in which an inscription designates Abel as Eve's child (Pentateuch of Ashburnham, f. 6). The bronze door does not offer such decisive information, but it provides certain visual details guiding the interpretation.

To begin with, let us note that Eve is seated on a rocky knoll made up of serpentine volutes covered with regular chisel marks, identical to the ones representing life's destructive poison in panel 3 (fig. 55). The place occupied by mother and child is made of arid stone; that is, not only of the sterile material produced by the poison of original sin but also of the very matter of which the city-tomb in the previous panel is composed. The womb welcoming birth is a deadly loam. In fact, the first and only death in the left wing is that of Abel, not of Cain.

In addition, Eve is not seated on the bare stone but on a pillow decorated with a lattice pattern. The motif had already appeared on the door. It adorned the sleeves and border of God's garment in panel 2, indicating that the Word was the form under which the divinity let himself be understood (cf. fig. 38). The same lattice pattern is found in panel 10, where it embellishes Jesus's swaddling clothes (cf. fig. 138). Life and death are juxtaposed since the cross characterizing the Word is primarily the prophetic sign of the Crucifixion. While Abel is the only dead human being represented on the left wing, Jesus is the only child who will be seen going to his death on the right wing. The one announces the other in a prefigurative relationship underscored by the axial symmetry that Eve shares with the Virgin in panel 11. Indeed, they hold the same position, the same higher elevation, and are noticeably the same size, even though Mary is a little taller (fig. 91).

In all likelihood, panel 5 represents Eve and Abel, and not Eve and her first born, Cain, in a maternity scene foreshadowing that of the Virgin on the right wing. The symmetry between Eve and Mary in the two facing panels is represented without any ambiguity. The two mothers with child are identically separated from the other protagonists by the lion head door handles, and they constitute a major point of entry to the reading of the door, one both emotional and rational. The Marian cult was already well established in the empire around the year 1000, and maternal love has always appealed to the faithful. (Traces of wear on the bronze are a testimony to this cult.) At the same time the double representation of Eve and Mary invites the learned faithful, as well as anyone having a minimum of exegetical experience (thanks to sermons, for instance), to consider the Old and New Testaments as shedding light on each other according to patristic tradition and Christian culture as a whole. Such a preparation to reading the visual discourse is not exceptional in early medieval art. A large number of complex images (by which I mean images that are not objects of devotion but still need an interpretation through articulated layers of

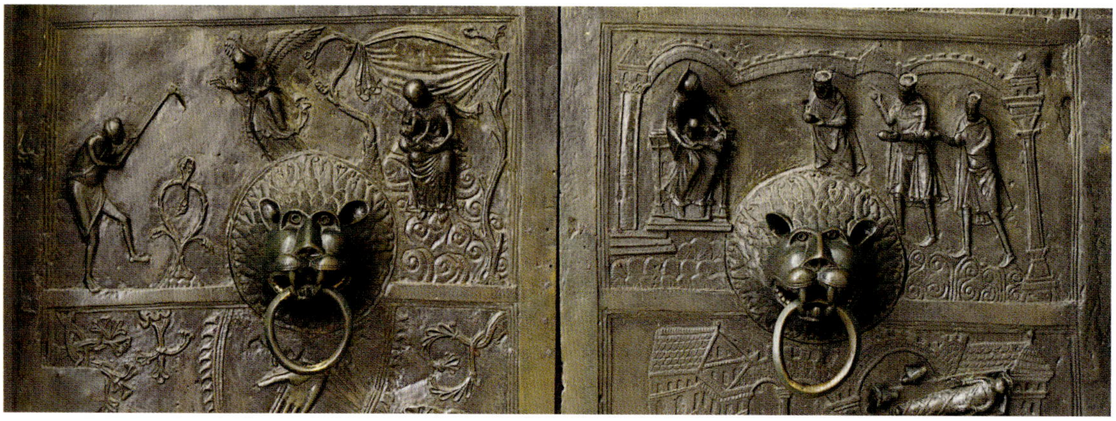

91

meaning) includes clues highlighting and guiding their reading.

It is obviously not by chance that the spiritual understanding of the bronze door grows out of the contemplation of these two mothers. Since 1966, Ernst Guldan's beautiful book, *Eva und Maria: Eine Antithese als Bildmotiv* [*Antithesis as Motif*] has put in perspective the ancient and seminal typological relationship between the mother of a sinful humanity and the mother of God the Savior [cf. also Thérel 1965 on the theme's origins]. At any rate, Bernward has taken an important step forward. Never before had this connection been so clearly established by an image. In order to understand its impact, it may be useful to turn, as Ernst Guldan did [1966, 13 *ff.*], to another representation of Eve and Mary found in Bernward's Gospel Book (Dombibl. Ms. 18, f. 17v), (fig. 92). The Virgin, queen of Heaven and *Theotokos* ("mother of God") is seated on a throne with the child on her lap between two angels who are crowning her under an arcature supporting the dedication and Marian hymns, a very rare iconography before the twelfth century [for a historical, material, and liturgical understanding of the image, cf. Kingsley 2014, ch. 1]. Two medallions, each placed at the base of the arc, enclose Mary's bust on the left and Eve's on the right. In the traditional reading direction, from left to right, as in the text, Mary appears before Eve in a sort of temporal inversion. This preeminence is confirmed by the large figure of the Virgin in Majesty placed at the center of the image.

Above the two medallions are two large vertical panels covered with inscriptions. The left panel continues up to the lower band whereas the right panel stops before reaching the border. On Eve's side, this panel is fixed with its hinges to the adjoining column as a sign of closure. On Mary's side a narrow vertical blue band (the color of the Marian halo) replaces the column and contains a cross-staff.

This type of cross was associated with the Virgin early in the Byzantine Empire before being adopted as an attribute of a *Virgo militans* around the year 800 in the West [Russo 1996, 217, 221]. A symbol of rebirth because of its victory over death, beginning in the tenth century it is found in Germanic illuminations where it is held by the angels of the Annunciation and of the Annunciation to the Shepherds, and particularly by Christ returning from the Harrowing of Hell, as in panel 16 of the bronze door.

In the Gospel Book's illumination, the cross-staff designates the blue strip as a door that Mary opens to heaven, as confirmed by the inscription on the two vertical panels: "porta paradisi primaeva(m) clausa per aevam/nunc est per s(an)c(t)am cunctis patefacta maria(m)" [The door of Paradise, closed though the

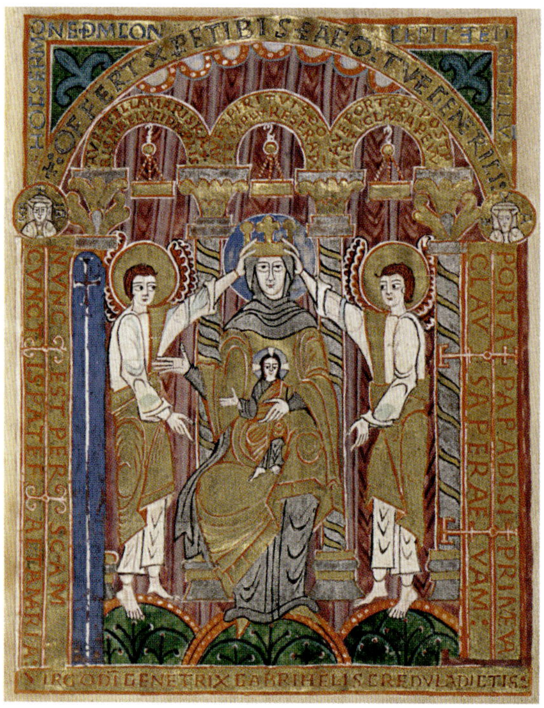

92

91. *Panel 6 and 11.*

92. *F. 17v of Bernward's Gospel Book.*

first Eve, is now though Holy Mary thrown open to all] [Kingsley 2014, 20].

In early medieval Marian commentaries, far less numerous than those appearing from the twelfth century forward, the cement binding Eve to Mary is not so much motherhood—indispensable but insufficient to associate them entirely—than their common link to the idea of passage. The dominant scriptural tradition, going back to the first centuries of the Church, underscores that Eve closes the door to Paradise and that Mary opens it again by giving birth to the Savior. This tradition is taken up by the Marian liturgy, particularly in the hymn *Ave Maris Stella,* attested from the ninth century but which probably appeared earlier, and whose fourth line designates the Virgin as "porta coeli" [Heaven's door]. However, Bernward's originality is not in the theme, since Mary had been called God's virgin mother since the Council of Ephesus (431 CE), and was already associated with Eve in patristic commentaries. The originality is in her configuration, of which we must try to understand the specific function.

Historiography goes no further than dwelling on the profound religiosity and devotion of Bernward and his contemporaries. In the Monastery of St. Michael, for which he may have intended his Gospel Book, Bernward had a crypt built, one that was later to receive his remains, as well as an altar dedicated to Mary. In addition, the Virgin had been the patron of Hildesheim's diocese ever since its foundation in 815, when the cathedral had been placed under her patronage. Bernward was particularly sensitive to the Mariology of his time. A notable example is the literary production of Hrosvitha of Gandersheim, who composed a Life of Mary in verse. It is quite possible that the bishop may have wanted to express his devotion through images. He may have drawn his inspiration from Carolingian figurative traditions, from sarcophagi, or from murals he had seen in Rome (as in St. Peter's or St. Paul's), or from the door of St. Sabina where the Virgin with Child can be seen. These suggestions may be persuasive in explaining the presence of the iconographic theme and the care with which Bernward strove to be understood. However, they may not sufficiently explain the quality of the supporting discursive strategy.

In the illuminations of the Gospel Book—a liturgical manuscript containing the passages read during mass—the typological relationship between Eve and Mary features only the Virgin, the central subject of an image that opens the manuscript and which outlines its symbolic and global impact. Mary is represented in her role as Mother of God and as the new mother of the living, with a shift from divine maternity to ecclesial maternity, the latter underscored by the inscription on the back cover of the manuscript (*spolium*/reuse of the book box housing the manuscript), which presents a new portrait of the Virgin: "Hoc opus eximium Bernwardi presulis arte/factum cerne Deus/mater et alma tua" [Look at God and at your nurturing mother, this magnificent work that was made (*factum*) by the art of the prelate Bernward] [North and Cutler 2003; Kingsley 2014, 18 and 103]. In the manuscript, therefore, Mary, the new Eve and temple of God, is also an *Ecclesia* who nourishes humanity with Christ's salvific word (the Gospels), making them reborn again and grow within her breast, thus allowing them to associate themselves with the heavenly destiny celebrated by Mary's coronation.

In the bronze door, the typological relationship between Eve and Mary is more than a Marian attribute; it articulates and qualifies the program as a whole. Indeed, the lion head fixtures isolating the women within their respective images hold the door handles that, very concretely, allow or forbid entrance to the ecclesial building. The two figures placed at the heart of the device become the pivot of a global iconicity in the sense that the discourse developed by the panels corresponds to what the door is by its very nature. The added meaning inferred from this iconicity qualifies the considerable spiritual impact that the very act of entering a church assumes, which is certainly not surprising. Christian theology and early medieval culture are deeply rooted in sensible reality. As they spread, they question their founding principles through experience of the world. By their inquiries, they animate here and now the hidden, albeit accessible nature of the signs with which God has saturated the universe. Liturgy is the most rigorously organized mirror of this divine order. Whether or not one passes through the door of an ecclesiastical building, metonymically joining or remaining apart from the community gathered around its priest conditions the possibility offered to the Christian to be born again. The believer's preparation for his inclusion in the Christlike body of the Church, presented here to the viewer in an intuitive fashion, will be revealed at the end of the visual analysis as the key to the bronze door's pastoral discourse.

Let us now analyze Eve and Abel in detail (fig. 93). Above the two figures is draped a large curtain already present in three of the four Anglo-Saxon and Carolingian representations of the scene. In the Pentateuch of Ashburnham, Eve and her child are covered by vegetal trellises held up by forked stakes; in the Moutier-Grandval Bible, the trellises are replaced by fine wooden roofing and a garland placed

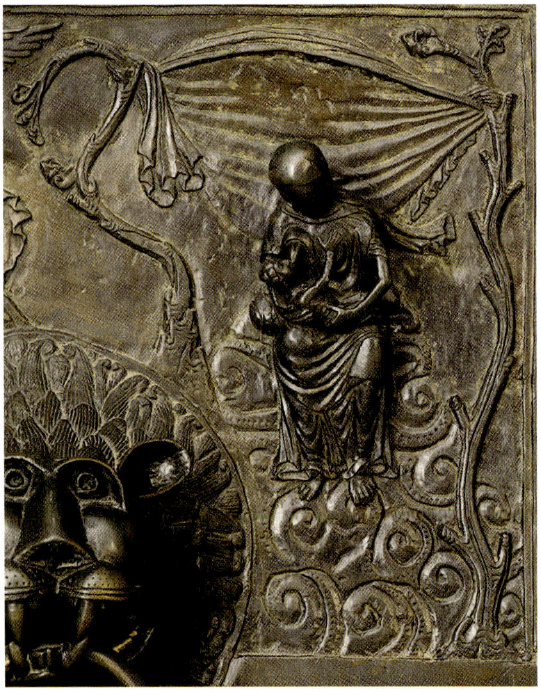

93

between two dead trees whose pruned branches define an elongated almond shaped form; in the Bible of St. Paul Outside the Walls a garland hangs from two forked poles.

The canopy in panel 6 reflects this heritage, but it is made of a cloth like that of the characters' own clothes. The supports of the little structure have also been modified. In earlier manuscripts the canopy's supports were arranged in pairs, putting together two poles or two dead trees in the shape of a fork. In panel 6 the two trees are alive, and they differ not only in size and growth pattern but also in vitality.

In the tree on the right, the stumps of severed branches are arranged in tiers along its length, and its trunk, divided longitudinally, is covered with chisel marks, reminders of the archetypal scission and poisoning of the Tree of Knowledge in panel 3 (cf. fig. 55). This tree also shares certain features with the central tree in panel 4 which, as I suggested, may represent the fusion of the two carnal seed matters involved in human reproduction (cf. fig. 61). Chiseled circular arcs isolate its root mass, while its top bears two distinct leaves, one, on the right, is tightly stretched; the other, on the left, is cup shaped. This plant, heir to both the poisoned Tree of Knowledge and the Tree of carnal/sexual union, is a dead tree with residual animal vitality. One wonders whether this theoretical construction within an image, appearing already weakened in panel 4, could be a repetition.

Bernward does not repeat himself: he prepares, announces, and proceeds with his visual demonstration. One cannot rule out the possibility that his creative genius sometimes struggled with the complex articulation of interpretive levels, yet the formal aspect of the images was so carefully and, undoubtedly, so lengthily pondered that the whole constitutes a program as coherent as it is holistic, capable of rendering visible the Word and Wisdom, which are the ontological foundations of Creation.

There is a major difference between the leaves of the Tree of carnal reproduction in panel 3 (cf. fig. 47) and those of the dead/living Tree in panel 6. Whereas the two "female" leaves have the shape of a cup, the "male" leaf bearing Adam's seed is replaced here by a leaf that again takes up the orthonormal aspect of the trilobed branch in the shape of a cross, previously used to represent the soul (cf. fig. 69); it should be noticed that its stalk and veins form a very visible skeleton.

Bernward adds a new element to his previous schema of sexual generation. The vertical and triune form bestowed on the body by the soul and transmitted patrilineally to the newborn is a divine gift that God has not withdrawn, despite the sin and disintegration of the Edenic order.

Transposed from the vegetal to the human realm, the image affirms that humans have not lost their primary quality of resemblance to God: "Faciamus hominem ad imaginem et similitudinem nostrum" [Let us make mankind to our image, to our likeness] (Gen. 1:26). Foreshadowed by the quatrefoil of the previous panel, the Word, creator, and architect, leaves his mark everywhere on the earthly world. That does not mean that he goes *naturally* from power to enactment as he did in Paradise. Far from it, the incompleteness and partial death of the plant are proofs of that.

The next phase of Bernward's demonstration is embodied in the tree supporting the canopy's left side. Two morphological differences distinguish it from the tree on the right. The first is quite visible. As vertical and stiff as the tree on the right is, the tree on the left is flexible and shapely. The second difference consists in the vigor of the branches. Although bearing the stumps of cut branches, the left tree presents a curled-up leaf in its middle section. Its fleshier root mass is covered with growth rings, indicating that matter has circulated there despite the poison applied to its trunk.

Neither tree supporting the canopy is dead but neither are they fully alive. One has appearance and therefore form but lacks matter; the other has matter but no structure. The little bush Adam is cultivating resolves this dichotomy by combining the two qualities of form and substance found in the canopy's trees

93. *Panel 6, Eve.*

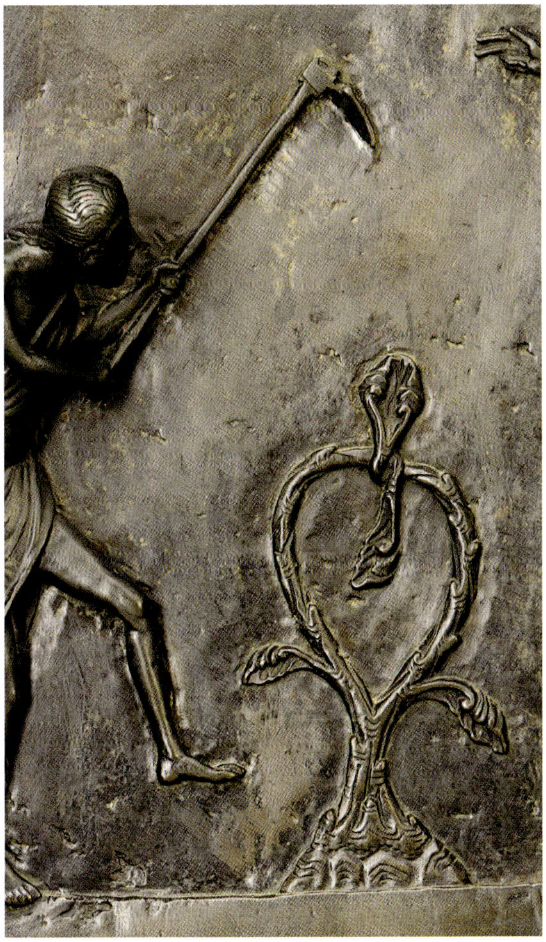

94

(fig. 94). Stung by the venom at the roots, it is not free of the evil that has contaminated the world: "Cursed is the ground because of you; through painful toil you will eat food from it all the days of your life. It will produce thorns and thistles for you, and you will eat the plants of the field" (Gen. 3:17–18). But even poisoned, this little bush is orthonormal, displaying two thick branches covered with growth rings and tender shoots. It owes its vitality to the terrain in which it is planted, no longer an arid mountain but fertile soil bathed by beneficial water flowing in small parallel waves under the root mass.

This water transforms the stone back into nourishing soil, and once it has become sap, it rises in the trunk and branches until it vitalizes the big, wide-open leaf at the top. Because of its power to overcome the poison's effects, the restorative water foreshadows the blood that will be spilled by Christ on the temple's altar in the scene symmetrically placed in panel 6 of the right wing (cf. fig. 156). In panel 6, it is simply the principle of life on earth.

With its symmetrical side branches and its two heart-shaped branches, the small irrigated bush is identical to the central part of the Tree of Life in the first panel (cf. fig. 11): life flows in it simply because form (male principle) and substance (female principle) are firmly linked in it.

94. *Panel 6, shrub in front of Adam.*

> All the primordial seeds . . . from which every kind of flesh or fruit is born, are moist and grow and develop out of moisture. But they have within them the most efficacious numbers [*temporales numeros*], which bring along with them potentialities [*primordia seminum*] consequent upon those perfect works of God, from which he rested on the seventh day. (*De Genesi ad litteram*, Book V, 7, 20, 314–315)

Even though the law of life is unchanged, it cannot efface the disparity between the Edenic model and its earthly imitation: reduced size, inferior quality of the foliage, absence of palms of eternity, and loss of autonomy and self-sufficiency. The tip of Adam's hoe, placed vertically in relation to the knot, shows that man must work tirelessly to maintain the connection between form and substance necessary for the circulation of life-water. God intervenes in the earthly world altered by sin only by means of the residual laws he has placed there. Work is less a divine punishment than a replacement activity that men impose on themselves for their survival.

As usual, Bernward further develops the conceptual element that he has just introduced into his visual discourse. The reinscription of life into the orderly framework that conditions it presupposes, on Adam's part, an a priori knowledge of the laws governing it. In other words, if he wants to live, Adam must know and respect the functioning principles of the earthly world. An incidental but masterful demonstration of the usefulness of knowledge, the image is articulated around laws stated by the angel, a promethean messenger intuited by Franz Dibelius more than a century ago, without knowing how to explain its workings. Three attributes are given to the angel in panel 6: the cross-staff held in the left hand, the gesture of the right hand, and the placement of the figure within the image (fig. 95).

The cross-staff is represented on two other occasions on the right wing, once in the hands of the Archangel Gabriel in the Annunciation panel (panel 9, cf. fig. 115), and again in the hand of the resurrected Christ in the door's last panel (panel 16, cf. fig. 185). Therefore, there is no doubt that the cross-staff functions here both as the citation of a Christ-Word destined to become incarnated and as the sign of victory over death. Thus, it is life that the angel brings to panel 6, *a contrario* of the previous panel where its sword, also held in the left hand, signified death.

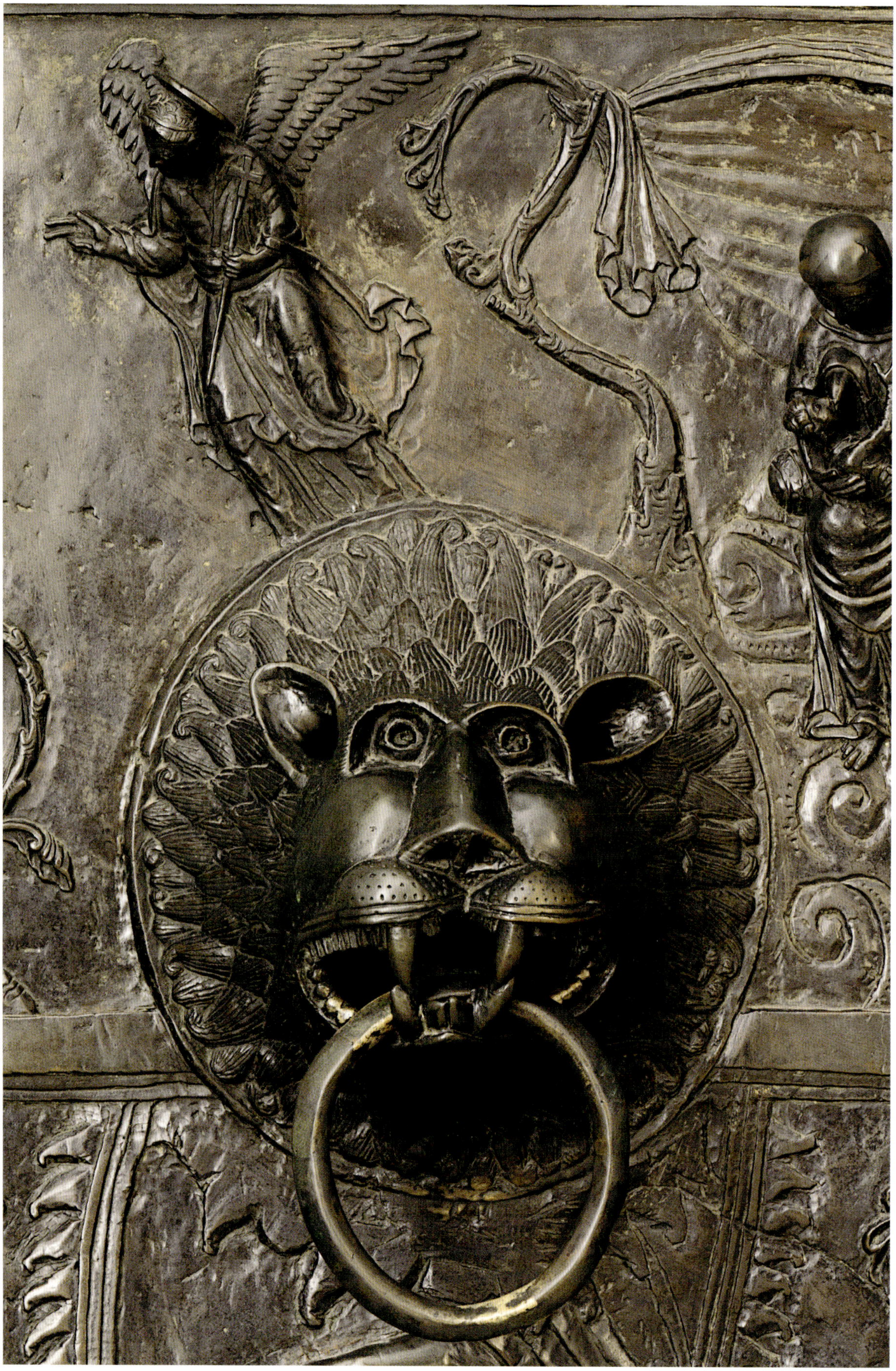

The gesture of the angel's right hand stands out clearly against the plain background of the panel. The middle finger, index finger, and thumb are extended, while the ring finger and the little finger are curled into the palm. This gesture, commonly interpreted as a benediction, deserves some clarification. In the West, benediction representations involve two or three extended fingers. In the case of two fingers, the thumb is bent into the palm of the hand, sometimes even touching the ring finger. In the case of three fingers, the middle finger and the index are raised, and either the thumb extends outward or the little finger remains raised according to the Eastern model. The benediction representations in Ottonian images display all these possibilities.

Several other finger positions appear on the bronze door. Let us set aside Adam's hand, its palm open to receive the fruit that Eve offers in the panel of original sin. We shall focus on the only gesture of the hand later displayed in panels 4 and 5: the pointing index finger of God, Adam, Eve, and then the angel, which are all gestures of designation. They will reappear in the Annunciation panel where Gabriel designates Mary as the chosen one, and in panel 15, where a king points an accusing finger toward Jesus (cf. fig. 1).

Although the position of the angel's fingers in panel 6 is unprecedented, the depiction of two other hands on the door shed light on its significance. The first is in panel 8, where the hand of God's justice—index and middle finger joined together, thumb apart—orders Cain to leave after having perpetrated his crime (cf. fig. 108). The second is the hand that Jesus stretches in blessing toward the aged Simeon in panel 12: two extended fingers and the thumb bent into the palm of the hand (cf. fig. 153). The angel's hand in panel 6, index and middle finger outstretched but not rigid, thumb slightly away from the palm, derives both from the benediction represented in the symmetrical panel (panel 12) and a more authoritative suggestion depicted two panels later. Given Bernward's formal and discursive mastery, we will assume that this ambiguity is deliberate, suggesting that the angel gives Adam an order functioning as a benediction for humans: what God leaves in the world after exiting its history is an imposed but benevolent law.

This law is substantiated within the image by means of the angel's third attribute, namely his position at the very center. This angel has not failed to attract historians' attention, for several reasons. There is no known equivalent in earlier representations of the scene, and the disc with the lion's head hides the lower part of the angel's body, to the extent that the door handle has sometimes been interpreted as a justification for the "mediocrity" of the composition [Dibelius 1907, 34]. Besides the fact that an artist must decide how to play with constraints, it appears here that the angel's size and position are deliberately articulated with the door handle in such a way as to constitute a dynamic system whose equivalent is found in the right wing.

95. *Panel 6, angel on ornamental fixture.*

The figure's oblique position, the wings pushed backward, the direction of the fluttering garments, all point to the fact that the angel seems to be hit by a powerful gust of wind, swelling the canopy's cloth behind him, and lifting Eve's veil. The angel transmits this animation to the disc supporting him and the lion head fixture seems to move like a wheel under his steps. This dynamic impression is increased by the position of the disc straddling two panels, and especially by the curvature of the trunk of the bush supporting the canopy: the upper part of the disc is curved toward the angel, while the robust root mass has shifted to the right, as if pulled by the rotating disc.

All the elements of this dynamic system—the gust of wind, the angel, and the disc—are very ancient symbolic figures that resonate as much with ancient and medieval cosmology as with the Old Testament heritage.

A powerful blast of air runs throughout the world (*pneuma* in Greek, *spiritus* in Latin), qualifying both the cosmic wind animating the universe and the Holy Ghost, *Spiritus Sanctus*, whom the Christians have designated as the artisan of the preservation of the world's dynamic order, oriented toward its end and at the same time moving in cadence with the astral and seasonal cycles.

The shape of the fixture of panel 6 is circular. This geometric form is new in the bronze door, transcending the rectangles of the panels and the orthonormal system governing them. Next to the earth, Edenic as well as poisoned, it delineates an alternative and contiguous place from which the angel addresses men. After the sin, God and his angelic creatures have withdrawn to a supralunar heaven, the empyrean, the highest sphere that contains the fixed stars. Cosmologic tradition, from the Greek astronomers to their Christian and Latin successors, states that it surrounds the world and turns eternally from east to west without corruption or alteration, conferring its rhythm mechanically to the earth at its center:

> The sphere [*sphaera*] of the sky is so named because it has a round shape in appearance. But anything of such a shape is called a *sphaera*. . . . Philosophers say that the sky is completely convex, in the shape of a sphere, equal on every side, enclosing

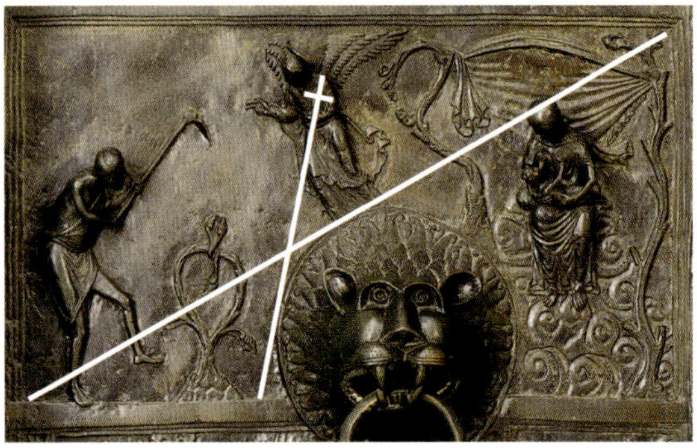

96

the earth, poised in the center of the world's mass. People say that the sky moves, and with its motion the stars fixed in it go around from east to west. (Isidore of Seville, *Etymologies*, XIII, V, 2. Trans. S. A. Barney, W. J. Lewis, J. A. Beach, and O. Berghof, Cambridge University Press, 2006, 272)

I suggest that the disc-shaped fixture is a metaphorical representation of the sphere.

As for the articulation between the fixture and the angel, we may recall that several literary traditions associate this sphere (or these spheres, according to their being separated into successive heavens) with beings moving it. The earliest pagan representation, going back to Roman times, is the image of the Wheel of Fortune showing the goddess perched on a sphere. Beginning with Boethius, Christian authors transmitted and adapted it to medieval morality [Schilling 1975; Bertrand 1997]. A few centuries later, Rabanus Maurus, whose influence on Ottonian culture was considerable, assimilated the hydraulic wheel into the *cursus vitae* [course of life] in his *De universo* (PL. 111, col. 612). There, the rotating wheel is a representation of the passing of time in changeable form, cyclic and linear at the same time, recording the events of human life.

The Bible is at the origin of a converging tradition. The wheel supporting celestial bodies is a major image in the Old Testament, found especially in Ezekiel's prophetic visions (Ezek. 1:15–21, God's chariot; 10:8–17, the cherubs' wheel). Ever since the fifth and sixth centuries (the oldest example is found in the *Vienna Genesis* [Vienna, Öst. Nb., cod. theol. Gr.31, f. 1, 2]), these visions have served as a basis for specific angelic representations in the iconography of the expulsion from Eden [Von Erffa 1995, 240]. The image of the wheel is also in the Psalms, where it evokes instability and mutability (Ps. 83:13). Later on, a vast Neoplatonic tradition associates the angels with the rotating movement of the celestial spheres, a tradition that Bernward certainly knew, since it characterizes the angelic hierarchies he had represented on his tomb [Bruderer-Eichberg 1998].

In summary, I would argue that Bernward's mathematical-formal perception of the world led him to represent not only space but also time, inasmuch as it is the measure and order of movement, an Aristotelian approach Christianized in Augustine: "It is the movement of creatures from one state to another, with things following each other as regulated by God managing everything he has created" (*De Genesi ad litteram*, Book V, 5,12, 310). These evolutions are evidenced in panel 6 by Adam's beard but also by a specific geometric construction allowing gestures to make visible the inclusion of creatures in the law of the new world. The celestial disc-sphere is decentered and confined to the lower right rectangle triangle of the panel (fig. 96). Its positioning is determined by the same great structuring diagonal as the one representing the growth axis in the door's first panel (cf. fig. 14).

While the contiguity of the diagonal and the circle dictates the height of the latter, it does not dictate its format, since Bernward could just as well have extended or reduced its diameter. Therefore, the compositional schema needed a complementary geometric reference point that would stabilize the shape. This additional parameter does not come from the door's first panel; it derives instead from the axis formed by the long staff of the cross held by the angel, or, to put it differently, from the Word of whom he is the messenger.

Placed within the vertical axis of the quatrifoil foliage of the upper panel (cf. fig. 1)—the quatrefoil that I earlier suggested was announcing the cross—the cross-staff defines the left edge of the fixture's circle, and therefore its diameter. The configuration can be understood in this way: through the intervention of his angelic messenger, the Word adds to the principled linear time the beneficent cyclic rhythm of the seasons. Earthly time, linear and cyclical, composes the new framework of the profusion of life: natural law henceforth defined and specified.

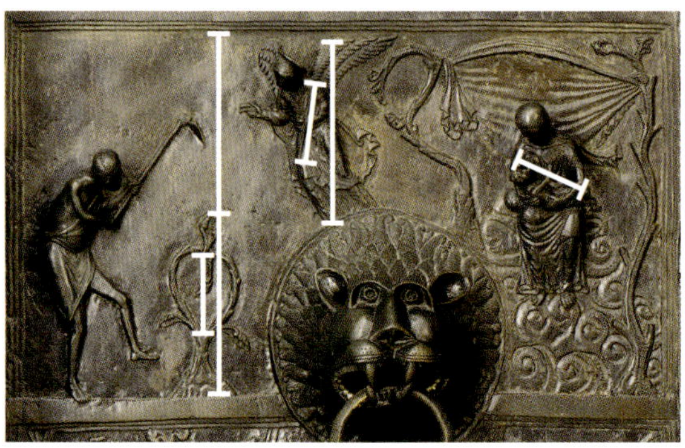

97

96. *Panel 6, panel structure.*

97. *Panel 6, equivalences in formatting.*

As in the first panel, the parameters for including plants in this natural law are mathematical. The dimension of the cross-staff is identical to that of the heart of the bush (and perhaps also to the child's size), whereas the angel's height is identical to that of the bush and doubled in order to establish the panel's height. This subtle difference is very significant. In panel 6, the divine, eternal messenger is no longer consubstantial with the perishable, terrestrial world; it is even exterior to it. The original unity between the angel, the Tree of Life, and the diagonal of panel 1 (linked by participation in the Creation) is replaced by the rule of proportionality, a distanced relationship that evokes the divine engine in creation as a source but not as a presence. In the bronze door, this proportion, which is at the heart of early medieval aesthetics, constitutes the new paradigm of the order of the matter of the world.

In panel 1, the inclusion of humans in the law was visualized by the alignment of the still-inert human body within the diagonal of the image (cf. fig. 14). In the same way, in panel 6, Adam's gestures are inscribed on the image's diagonal, reproducing those of the angel under Adam's intent gaze (fig. 98). The celestial creature is teaching the law of earthly life, offering a behavioral model to the fallen humans. The way back that begins here will lead them, at the end of the narrative, to an actual identification with the angel, although it cannot yet be explained.

In conclusion, Bernward has conceived his sixth panel as a new cosmology in which natural law is an extension of the Law of life but in the unprecedented version of a vital animation connected with time. As extrinsic motor of the celestial spheres, the angel is overseer of and messenger to humanity. It is only because he reveals its content and deep resources to Adam that the latter can restore nature to its vital

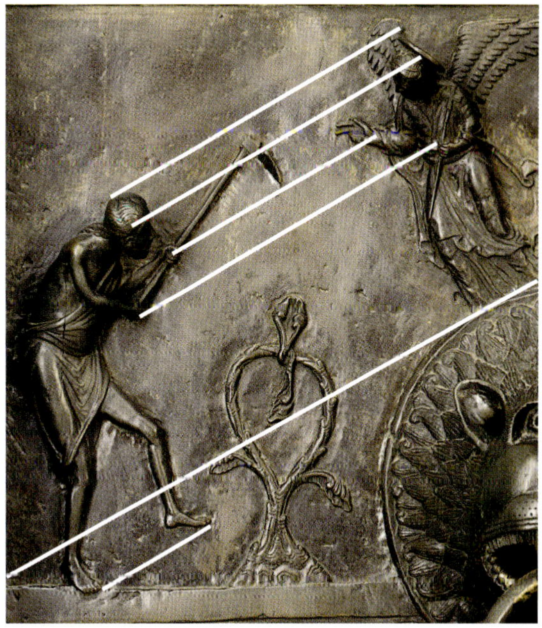

99

form and to extract from the soil what will help him to live. From this perspective, the labor of Adam, father of vegetation, is equivalent to the labor of Eve, earth-mother nurturing the child.

The analogy between the two similar and complementary activities of man and woman allows Bernward to broaden his discourse to all of humanity. And it is from this ordinary bush, just as from this ordinary child, similarly conceived according to earthly, postlapsarian law, that the possibility of the restoration of humans and of the world will arise. This is the discourse developed in the subsequent panel, confirming that if Eve is undoubtedly a figure announcing Mary, her child, Abel, is indeed the precursor of the Christ to come.

98. *Mimesis between Adam and angel.*

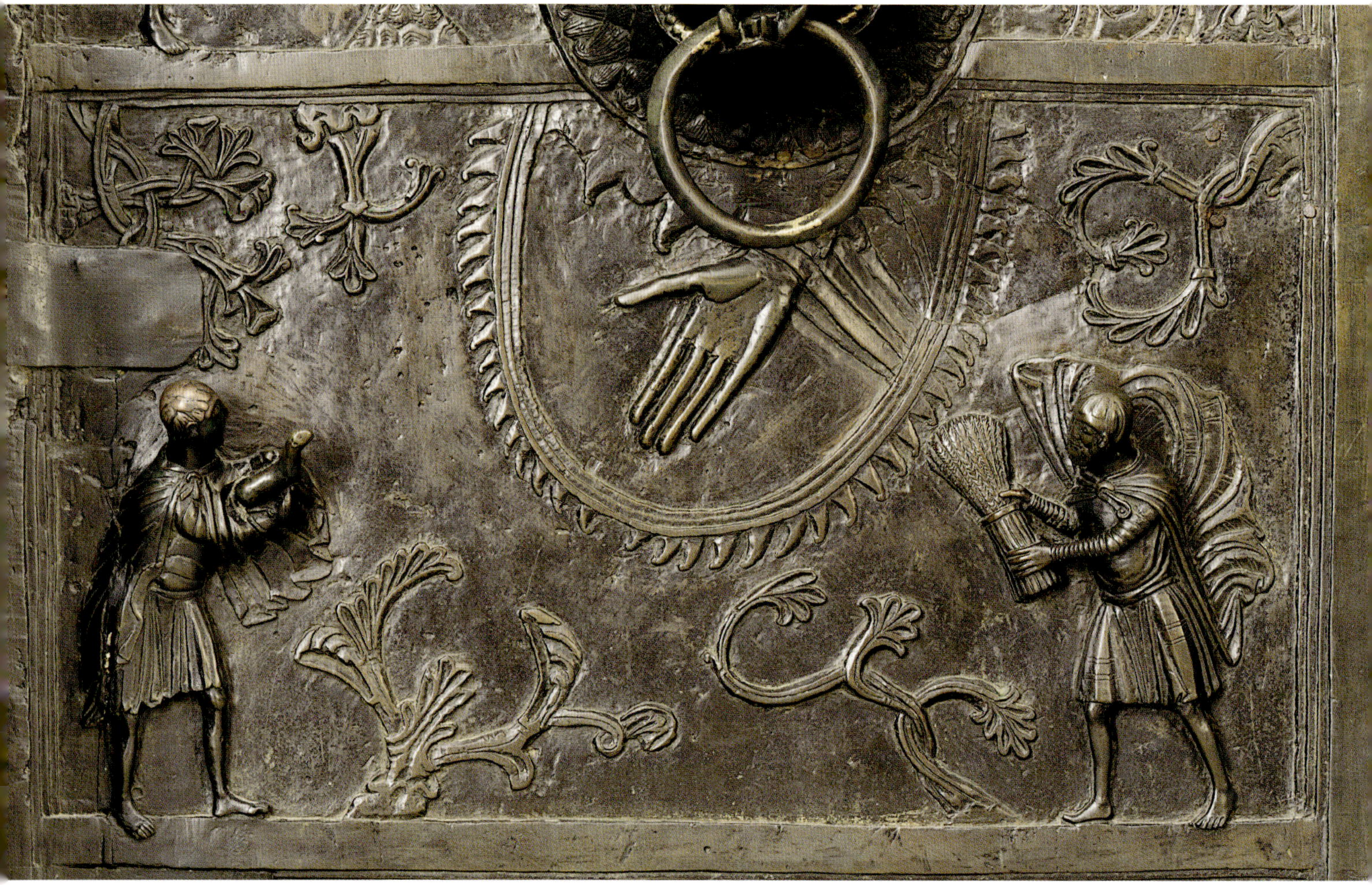

Panel 7

COVENANT

The last two panels of the left leaf tell the story of Cain and Abel, Adam and Eve's first two children (fig. 99 and 100). In panel 7, the young men give their offerings to God. In panel 8, Cain murders Abel and is condemned. Beyond this literal narrative, the two images prepare the shift from Old to New Testament that takes place at the base of the door.

The offering scene is dominated by a large hand extended in the middle of the panel, a *Dextera Domini*, found again in panel 8 (fig. 100). Appearing frequently in Carolingian and Ottonian iconography, God's right hand is traditionally considered a metonymic sign for his authority, order, and protection, be it in word or deed [Kirigin 1976, 98 *ff.*]. However, we cannot limit our analysis to this functional approach because the divine hand is not represented in the same way in these panels. In panel 8, the hand lies against the rectangular area of the image emerging from the clouds; in panel 7, it is isolated from the characters by a flaming mandorla that emerges from high flames originating in the circular lion head fixture defined as a celestial sphere in the previous panel. Such a strongly differentiated representation calls attention to the materials and spaces involved in these two theophanies.

Beyond their formal analogy with the lion's stylized mane, the large, lively, and irregular flames in panel 7 take on the medieval figurative tradition of the elements, especially that of fire, linked to the emblematic figure of the sun. They describe not so much a place as the material background from which the divine hand emerges. Its point of origin is, in fact, the fixture/sphere that vertically straddles the two panels. Hence, the mandorla appears as an extension of the

99. *Panel 7.*

100. *Panel 8.*

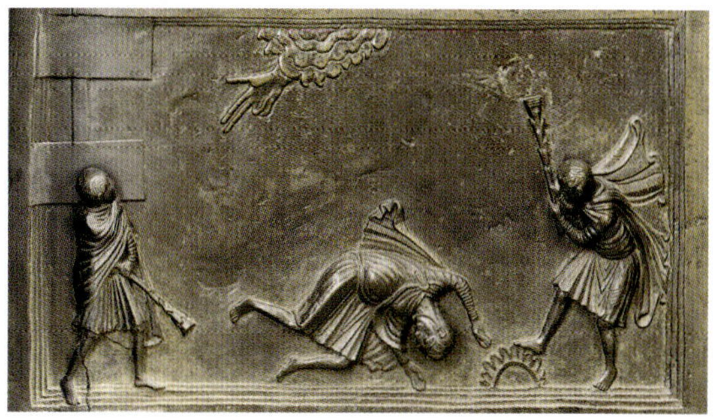

100

sphere in the infra-lunar sky and is set in an intermediary location between the empyrean and the earth.

Slightly slanted toward the left, a continuous triple line frames the delicate mandorla (fig. 101). Similar to the triple framing of the panels, which isolates the narratives while at the same time assuring their providential connection, this triple border defines two distinct and articulated spaces: an interior one where the divine Hand appears and an exterior one, beginning with the little flames evenly spaced along its rim, a diminished version of the celestial blaze. I suggest that this is a reduced and delimited version of the flaming matter originating in heaven, adapted to the capabilities of humans' physical perception.

It is difficult to be more precise about the nature of these substances connected with fire and/or light. Aristotle suggests that in the celestial supralunar world there is an incorruptible and eternal body—ether—a fifth, almost immaterial element functioning as a cosmic bath and constituting both place and matter. This celestial element is endowed with a physical property similar to fire without being identical to it. It is its own motor and moves in a

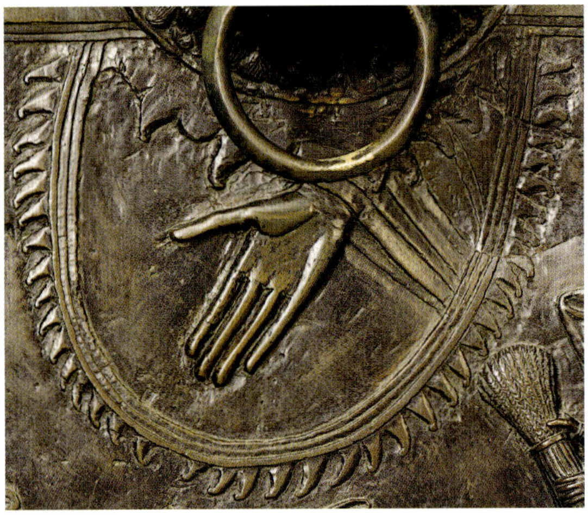

101

circular manner, conforming to its own nature; the further away it is from the elements of the earthly world, the more noble, pure, and divine [Taton 1957, 268–269]. Different from earthly matter, this celestial substance has the characteristic of not exhibiting any qualitative, quantitative, or substantive change, and of having a self-generated circular movement, rather than a generated and linear one, as is the case of all earthly movements [Grant 1996, 69]. Lastly, it is this celestial substance that, penetrating the earthly world, allows for the perception of bodies and colors because it enacts the transformation of the diaphanous into light in matter [Vasiliu 1997, 51].

Aristotle's cosmological thought did not reach the West before the twelfth century, and not without posing problems for Christian dogma, but there are traces of its physical description of matter and celestial movements in Lucretius (*De natura rerum*, Book I), in Apuleius (*De mundo,* c. 1), and in Cicero (*De natura Deorum,* Book II, par. 116). Even at a minimum level, these notions reached Bernward through the mediation of Isidore of Seville and Rabanus Maurus. Isidore's etymological analysis of the word *eternity* includes the root "ether," explaining that it is present in heaven where God resides (*Etymologies*, Book VII, 1, 22).

In medieval culture, no one questioned the existence of a matter analogous to fire and animated by a specific movement in the supralunar heaven [Grant 1996, 138–139]. However, the existence of a fifth element was not taken for granted. Augustine categorically rejects the idea of its presence in the world (*De Genesi ad litteram*, Book VII, 21, 27). And Isidore (*Etymologies,* XIII, V, 1), Rabanus Maurus (*De universo*, IX, 5), and Ambrose of Milan (*Hexameron, Dies* I, 6) mention the hypothesis of its existence without going any further. Given the absence of Christian consensus, we shall simply suggest that Bernward conceived the celestial matter-space, from which the hand of God emerges, as a flaming substance whose power diminishes as it approaches the earth. It is this spiritual atmosphere, both space and substance, that God causes to descend on the earth, through the mediation of the mandorla, in order to make himself known to the humans exiled below.

From a scriptural perspective, it must be underscored that no narrative concerning the history of Cain and Abel mentions any flaming theophany. In this biblical episode, God communicates uniquely through language. However, the divine fire is cited elsewhere in the Old Testament, especially in the book of Genesis at the time of the apparition to Abraham, which precedes his covenant with God (Gen. 15:16–17), and in the book of Exodus, in the episode of the burning bush when the Creator reveals himself as the sole God, protector of the Hebrews (Exod. 3:2–5). The Abrahamic and Mosaic models that lie behind this theophany, unprecedented in Cain's and Abel's iconography, underscore what Bernward has set visually in place: not a biblical quotation but the staging of a renewal of the covenant with God, depending, within limits that depend, as we shall see, on the compatibility and incompatibility of the substances involved in the offering.

The text of the Vulgate offers no explanation about God's choice between the two children of Adam and Eve:

> Abel was a shepherd, and Cain a husbandman. And it came to pass after many days, that Cain offered, of the fruits of the earth, gifts to the Lord. Abel also offered of the firstlings of his flock, and of their fat and the Lord had respect to Abel, and to his offerings. But to Cain and his offerings he had no respect and Cain was exceedingly angry, and his countenance fell. And the Lord said to him: Why art thou angry and why is thy countenance fallen? If thou do well, shalt thou not receive? But if ill, shall not sin forthwith be present at the door? But the lust thereof shall be under thee, and thou shalt have dominion over it. (Gen 4:2–7)

Nothing in the image gives any indication whatsoever that the intrinsic nature of the two offerings, the lamb and the wheat, factor into God's choice. On the other hand, and here Bernward adheres to a widespread exegetical tradition, the offering gestures are differentiated at the qualitative level, since they reflect the extent to which the two brothers involve themselves in carrying out the ritual.

The two young men do not keep the same distance

101. *Panel 7, Hand of God.*

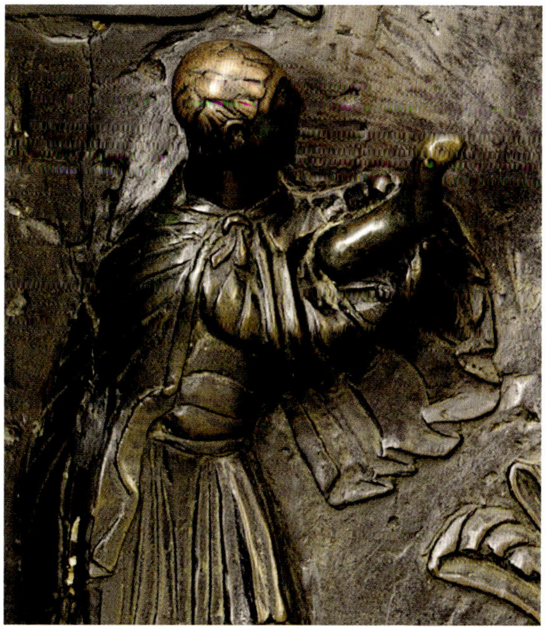

102. *Panel 7, Abel.*

from the flaming mandorla. Abel is set back, motionless, attentive, leaning on his right leg, several steps away from the theophany (fig. 99). He does not carry his offering in his bare hands; rather he has respectfully wrapped it in the front part of his cloak. Cain is much closer to the mandorla. He pushes himself forward, leaning on his right leg, and with outstretched hands holds his sheaf of wheat, which comes into contact with the little flames. His cloak rises above his head toward the divine hand, as if lifted by a gust of wind. Would feeling an intense and manifest desire for God be so sacrilegious as to lead the divine hand to reject Cain, preferring Abel to him?

A first answer can be found in the Old Testament law enjoining men not to defile the sacred through bodily contact. Besides the interdiction prohibiting Moses from walking into the burning bush, it is worth remembering the episode of Uzzah, struck dead because he tried to prevent the Ark of the Covenant from falling while it was being brought back in procession toward Jerusalem (2 Sam. 6:6–7). Considered legally binding, any deviation from proper ritual protocol merits punishment. As in the great frontispieces of Genesis, the episode reverberates like an echo of original sin, compounding human debt. However, in panel 7 Bernward asks the viewers to shift from this Old Testament perspective to that of the New, thus unveiling the process leading Cain to his loss and Abel to his election.

Whereas Cain's cloak swirls around, the only movement in Abel's cloak is in the piece with which he wraps the lamb (fig. 102). Concentrated on his sacrificial gesture, the young man puts himself entirely at the service of an offering that he renders sacred by separating it from his person. A carefully sculpted work refines the cloth of Abel's garments. The folds of his cloak and tunic are worked into a cloth that we can imagine being as soft and delicate as the lamb's now burnished fleece. The part of the cloak in which the offering is held morphs into a light, flowing veil; its loose and irregular folds tend to evoke the angel's tunic in the first panel (cf. fig. 20). By contrast, Cain's clothing is made up of thick pleats, naturalistically superimposed or deeply pleated as, for example, in the sleeves and on the abdomen.

The attitude of the two brothers, the fabric of their garments, and the nature of their offerings are elucidated by the configuration of the bushes surrounding them. In fact, a single semiotic system governs the panel's plants, with those in the lower part representing material bodies, while those in the upper part represent spiritual substances.

A bush by Abel's foot consists of two symmetrical branches that rise (a botanical incongruity) from a central leaf attached to a sort of husk to which we will return later (fig. 99). This large leaf is extended along the axis of God's hand. The bush is configured analogically to the sacred space toward which it extends itself as seen in its position at just the right distance from the fiery mandorla, its orientation toward the Hand, and the curvature of its branches, which forms a circular arc. Just as in the liturgy, this respectful, reflexive relationship, this mimetic dissymmetry, makes possible the exchange between humans and God. The bush only renders more explicit the quality of the offering gesture.

The plant placed in front of Cain is quite different from the previous one. Its three intertwined branches are visibly trying to reach the mandorla, which is closer to them than to Abel's bush. At the same time, their movement is hindered by their weight, their absence of organic connection, and by the attraction that Cain's figure seems to exert on their terminal leaves. This heavy, asymmetrical plant, turned toward the man, excludes all possibilities of exchange with the divine hand.

A similar opposition is found in the upper part of the panel. Both plants above Abel are organized according to the open model of a cross, whereas the bush associated with Cain bends its two branches to encircle its central palm.

This opening and this closing toward God have no psychological implications. Instead, they serve an ontological purpose that will be revealed by a detailed analysis.

Of the two upper bushes associated with Abel, the most stylized one is close to the divine mandorla

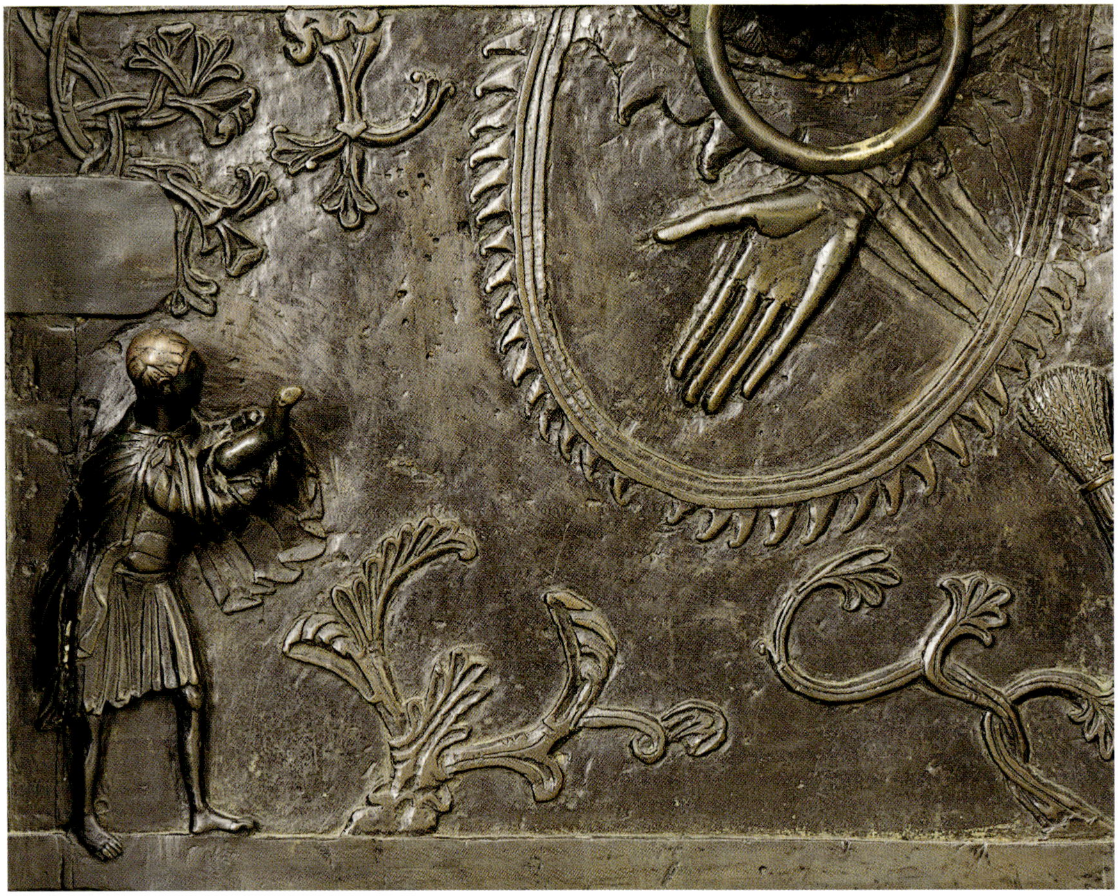

103

(fig. 103). It emerges from the clouds and has three branches ending in clusters of leaves. There is no need to remove or add anything to it to make it explicitly foreshadow Christ's sacrifice, which governs all the forms of the bronze door, including that of the souls. One should recall here the harmonious soul, in the upper-right spandrel of panel 4 (cf. fig. 69), as well as the detached and deformed soul fastened to the left side of the supporting frame in the panel of the expulsion from Eden (cf. fig. 77).

The plant in the upper left-hand corner, whose position identifies it once more as a soul, is more animated and more spread out than the cross-shaped plant on the right (fig. 103). Even though it is partially covered by the reinforcement plate riveted onto the door, one can see that its stems have been intertwined in order to conform to the cruciform model. By placing side by side the divine paradigm and the metamorphic process at work in Abel's soul, Bernward represents the activation of the divine image in the pious young man; that is, the fulfillment of the promise of salvation that had illuminated the darkness of the panel of the expulsion from Paradise.

The differences between the model and the imitation clarify the nature of the process. The divine paradigm, or *imago*, is a living cross with a double stem; it is fanning out in two axes. It is not intertwined, belonging to only one plant, and has three branches jointed in an intersection underscored by a small and very graphic angle bracket (fig. 104). Abel's soul has neither the same uniqueness, being composite, nor the same planar quality. Its thickness is constructed in two ways. First, by its general form, to the extent that the vertical stems and the horizontal sprigs are superimposed; and second, by the shaping of its substance, since at its base the left stem goes through the right stem like a thread through the eye of a needle.

This minimal yet forceful three-dimensionality is reminiscent not only of the Anglo-Saxon tradition [Bonne 1999] but also of the Ottonian practice of interlacing onto which it could shed new light. It is doubly built up, by the deployment of the archetypal matrix and by the matter folding back on itself. Or to put it another way, if the divine metamorphic mechanisms are of a purely geometric nature, they affect both the shape of the substance and the general form of the transformed object, which they arrange and coordinate in all its dimensions. In the door's last panel, the world's reunified matter, destined to celes-

103. *Panel 7, Abel's plants.*

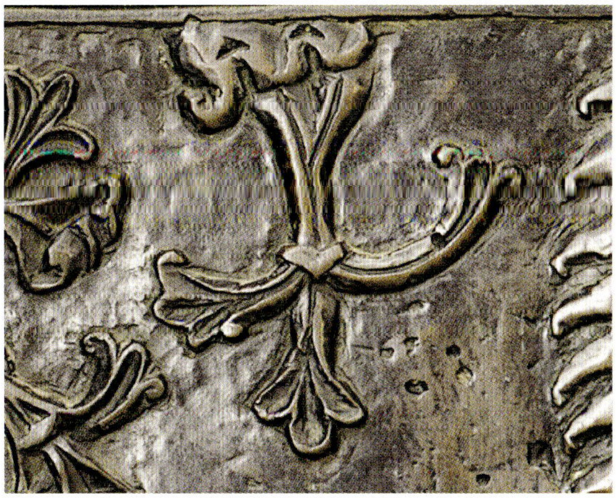

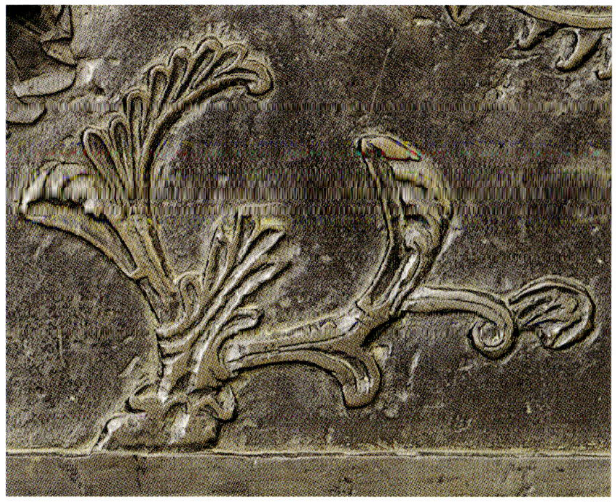

104. *Panel 7, plant neighboring the mandorla.*

105. *Panel 7, plant at Abel's feet.*

tial ascension, will even include a fractal pattern, the duplication of a unique matrix-module at all levels.

Let us return to panel 7. As mentioned earlier, by dissociating the soul from the body (fig. 73), the expulsion from Eden has taken on the spectacular form of entrance into death. Anchored in the solemn heights of heaven, the representation of Abel's soul is above him, but it marks a diagonal directed toward the bush set in front of the young man. It is because it submits itself to the soul's domination that this vegetal-body can, in turn, develop a mimetic relationship with the mandorla and the divine hand, thus conforming to God's expectations. As the immaterial image had its place of expression in the substantial soul, so the soul, itself incorporeal, has its place of expression in the body.

In order to visualize the dominance of the spiritual over the corporeal, Bernward chose to reutilize the diagonal that, in the bronze door as a whole, represents the spirit of life, breath and light. According to Augustine, the soul utilizes the closest sensible elements so that they may act on the body:

> While therefore we are inquiring where it comes from itself, that is from what material [*velut materie*] [—elsewhere Augustine says that the soul is made of a "spiritual material" [*spiritalis materies*], *De Genesi ad litteram*, Book VII, 6, 10, 367—] so to say, God made this puff which is called the soul, we ought not to think of any kind of body. Just as God, after all, surpasses every bodily creature. Nonetheless it administers the body through light and air, as being the kinds of body with the closest resemblance to spirit; in the world at large too, after all, they are the most excellent of the elements, better suited to acting than moisture and earth, whose mass makes them more liable to be acted upon. (*De Genesi ad litteram*, Book VII, 19, 25, 377)

If examined closely, the diagonal delineated by the intertwining of the stems of Abel's soul comes to rest precisely on the strange-looking root of the corporeal bush (fig. 105). The upper edge of this small swollen sheath exhibits a soft, undulating border. It is composed of a homogeneous, yet slightly hollowed-out material. It does not contain any geometric trait that might bring to mind a skeleton—it is uniquely substantial—but it resembles neither the earth nor the water that enlivened the base of the earlier plants of the door. With its shape of vaporous gangue, it might almost appear as a countermodel of the woody mass from which the twin-sexed Tree of Life emerges in the panel of the original sin (cf. fig. 46).

Having already depicted the celestial fire in this panel, would Bernward represent yet another unprecedented form of matter in the door? There is nothing here reminiscent of the vegetal trellis of Abel's soul. Nature's otherness is such that God does not give his own substance to the soul, just as the soul cannot give its own substance to the body. The small swollen sheath can be likened, in this panel, only to the clouds placed at the base of the cross/Word that represents the divine image. Here again, however, there is a difference since the celestial clouds are flat, whereas the earthly sheath is seen in perspective, and therefore as an earthly, though spiritualized, substance.

If we look closely at the base of this cross/Word, we will see that the unified double stem is underscored above by two chisel marks struck on the clouds (fig. 104). I would argue that this configuration evokes the double nature the Word will adopt by becoming incarnate in the world. In order to annul the substantial otherness separating the divine from the soul and the soul from the body, God will choose to go beyond natural laws by descending into poisoned matter in order to act directly on it. If my interpretation is correct, we are faced here with an

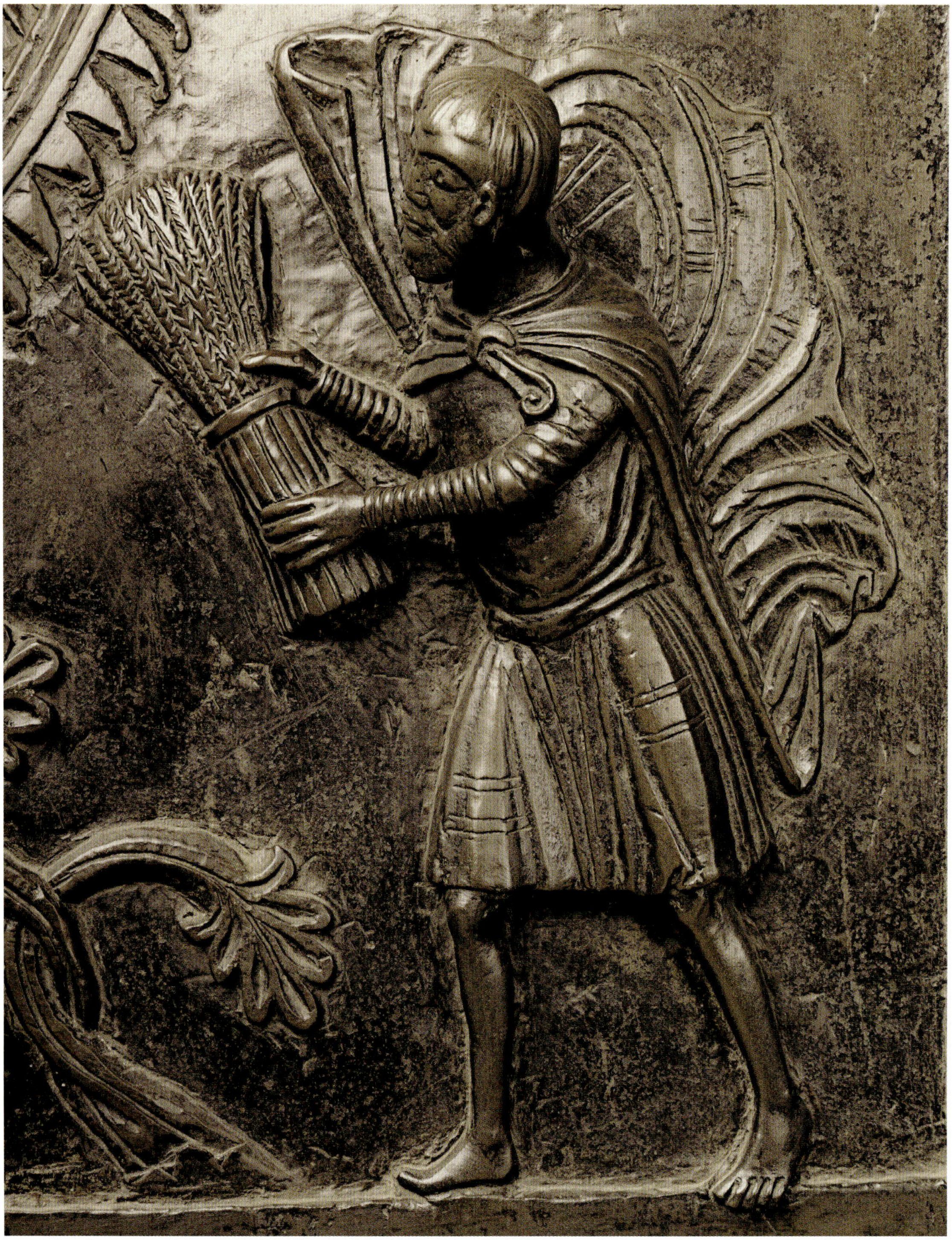

106

exceptional naturalistic and scientific explanation of the Incarnation.

The prophecy has not yet become a reality—it will happen only on the right wing of the bronze door—but Abel sees its image and understands it. By letting light come to him, by positioning himself to be open to God, he spiritualizes his body, nourishing it with celestial matter, just like his plant. He is thus preparing it to receive, in exchange for the lamb he is about to offer, the sacrificial and salvific lamb which will be returned to him, the body of Christ.

The mimesis at work between the great central palm of the vegetal-body and God's hand then takes on the magnitude of a corporeal refoundation, of a possibility for complete restoration, body and soul, of the divine image within humans, and of a prom-

106. *Panel 7, Cain.*

ise of reunification with the Father. This assertion is supported by the fine, continuous lines covering Abel's torso and cloak (fig. 103). As the rest of the narration, and especially the last two panels of the door, will confirm, these lines show the way in which the light moves and irrigates the flesh when the latter has been rendered apt to receive it because of its reconfiguration.

In contrast to the fine, long spiritual conduits on Abel's torso, Cain's tunic and cloak feature double parallel and segmented lines (fig. 106). Despite their erratic appearance, these graphic elements, also destined to reappear, are set in precisely placed and oriented pairs. Their purpose is to underscore movement. This can be easily seen on the thighs, although it is a bit harder to make them out on the cloak, where they call attention to the ascending dynamics of the cloth going up toward the shoulders, to be arranged in radiating fashion on the cloth forming the arc of a circle, a sort of halo around Cain's head.

What does it mean? I suggest that the double segmented lines—which, if aligned, would have constituted long linear channels—instead mark the flesh's residual vital drive; that is, the agitation of matter left to itself, incapable of organizing a vital flow within itself and preserving only the physical animation that makes it live, thus authorizing its movement. From now on I will call these double parallel lines, which we shall see again, "life channels."

This enunciative schema of orderly or disorderly circulation of vital liquids in the body is different from the spiritual quality of the flesh, which manifests itself through the clothes' relief and thickness. This should not be surprising. The metabolism of human bodies reproduces here the system of substance and irrigation of plants, and refers, like plants, to the life channels whose poisoning Bernward used to represent Edenic earth in the panel of the original sin (cf. fig. 55).

At this stage of human history, Abel keeps this sinful heritage within himself. He cannot entirely spiritualize his body nor restore its unity with his soul: his two plants remain apart, and the plant on the ground in front of him—the wood of spiritualized flesh—is still animated by uncontrolled driving movements, as shown by the little branch escaping from its plant's right, which is coiled like the serpent's tail and restless like Cain's bush toward which it reaches (fig. 103). It should be noted in this case that attached to the little branch is a large cup-shaped leaf—a female leaf (cf. fig. 63)—a reminder, if one were needed, of how original sin is transmitted. This insistence calls attention to the theological perspectives opened up by representing the cross as matrix of a new humanity.

It seems clear that in panel 7, Cain is presented as Abel's carnal opposite. This opposition concerns not only the condition of their bodies but also the quality of their souls. If Cain's soul, in the upper-right spandrel (fig. 99), remains immortal, as attested by the presence of the central palmette, it does not take on the cruciform schema of Abel's soul, nor does it keep the triune structure that characterized the souls in the previous panels. In an eminently paradoxical way, it is Cain's corporeal plant, on the ground, that contains three intertwined lianas; conversely, his "dead soul" above resembles the bush representing Abel's body but without the great central leaf analogous to God's hand (fig. 107). The visual method adopted by Bernward is particularly appropriate. By using only a part of the vegetal configuration of Abel's body as a model for Cain's soul, and by reversing how symbolic quantities are assigned to the soul and the body, the bishop reveals the source of Cain's inner turmoil: Cain thinks that the divine image is *in his body*, not in his soul, the latter being configured in turn according to a corporeal format, and therefore, incapable of dominating the sick flesh.

Why does Cain fail to understand what Abel could see so well? In medieval culture, vision, and corporeal perception more generally, was considered a double process. First, the images coming from the outside world are imprinted on the sensory organ, which is itself material. Then, the soul causes immaterial referential images to rise to the surface of this same organ, in order to permit the identification and intellectual analysis of what is perceived [Vinge 1975]. In panel 7, the divine image that structures Abel's soul, the cross, is missing in Cain. Not knowing the divine inside him, Cain cannot see it outside. Not possessing the spiritual vision to which Augustine devotes the entire Book XII of his *De Genesi ad litteram,* Cain's vision is corporeal; that is, his perception and understanding engage no other referential system in his soul other than what it knows of the world through bodily experience.

Cain's relationship to God is altogether perverted. Whereas Abel appealed to God's hand above the flaming arc and saw God's *hand gesture*—that is, he understood the will of God—Cain sees only the physically perceptible part of the theophany: the four large parallel pleats of the sleeve of the divine tunic, visible because they touch the edge of the mandorla in the axis of Cain's gaze and offering (fig. 107). Incapable of perceiving God spiritually, the young man addresses God's vestments, an illusory materiality into which he projects himself and on which he establishes his mimesis. It is because of this misunderstanding that he chooses his offering: parallel and artificially

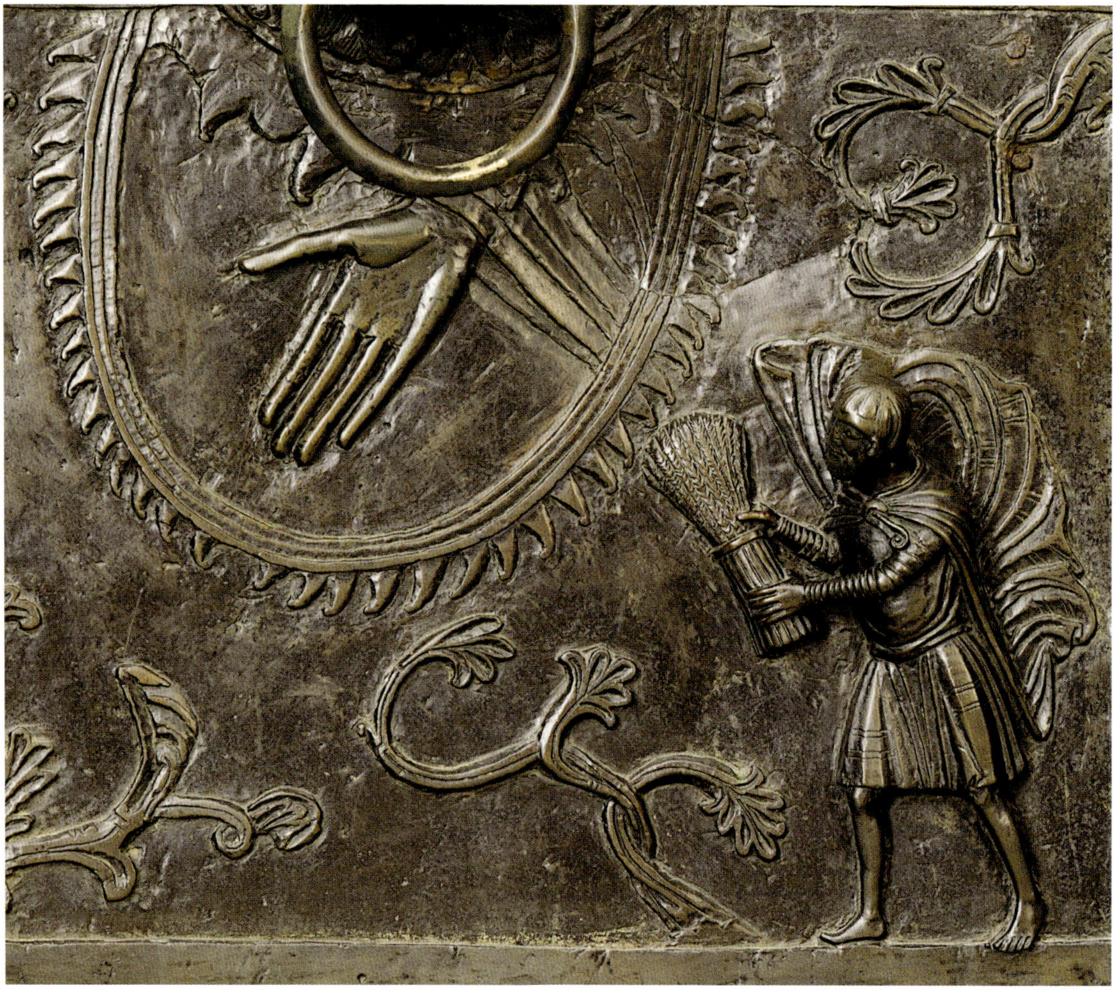

107

bound wheat stalks assertively extended toward the parallel pleats of God's sleeve. It is also on the basis of this illusion that he composes the face that he presents to God thinking it worthy of him: his hair is made up of stiff, parallel strands, like the wheat stalks with which he identifies, whereas his beard is arranged in neat parallel lines, a beard formally different from the one Adam had in the preceding panel and which will disappear in the next.

By stressing the young man's physical traits, Bernward calls attention not only to the way Cain glorifies his physicality, but also to the fact that in Cain the individual, troubled by his own particular story, has prevailed over the creature—the man conscious of his filiation with his creator. Driven, blinded, arrogant, imagining that he is equal to a God whose appearance he makes to his liking, Cain replays the same illusory and toxic game as his parents. In contrast to Abel the Righteous, he embodies the figure of the sinner lost "by the love of self extending even to the contempt of God" (Augustine, *De civitate Dei*, Book XIV, 28, 632).

From this first blindness—thinking of the offering and of himself in material terms and deeming them worthy of God—arises a second: Cain thinks he is giving but in reality he is not. As we have seen, the three lianas of the corporeal plant at his feet delineate a loop extending to the right, forcing each other to turn away from the mandorla toward Cain (fig. 107). In addition, the upper section of the cloak folds backward at head level, just as the soul above Cain turns inward.

Cain does not make his offering *for* God, he makes it expecting something for himself *from* God. To the best of my knowledge, Bernward is the first to visually establish this principle of opposition between intention and behavior as it is found in the biblical text of the *Vetus latina* (a corpus of Latin translations based on the Septuagint that preceded the Vulgate): "Then the Lord said to Cain: 'Why are you angry? Why is your face downcast?' Nonne si recte offeras, recte autem non dividas, peccati [If your offering follows the rules, but not the way you make it, have you not sinned?]"—and not, as in the

107. *Panel 7, Cain's plants.*

Vulgate: "If thou do well, shalt thou not receive? But if ill, shall not sin forthwith be present at the door?" (Gen 4:7).

This does not seem accidental to me, for Augustine developed his exegesis of the episode of the brothers' offerings based on the *Vetus latina*. Moreover, he suggests it in the *City of God*, the treatise that Bernward used in conjunction with *De Genesi ad litteram*, whose commentary goes no further than the expulsion from Eden:

> In this admonition or warning which God offered to Cain, it is not clear why or for what reason He said, "If thy sacrifice is rightly offered, but not rightly divided, hast you not sinned?" The obscurity of this passage has given rise to many different interpretations. . . . A sacrifice is indeed "rightly offered" when it is offered to the true God, to Whom alone sacrifice is due. But it is not "rightly divided" when we do not rightly choose the places or times of sacrifice, or the thing offered, or whom to offer it to, or those to whom what has been offered is distributed for eating. . . . [This is what is done by] all those who follow their own will, and not the will of God; that is, who live with a perverse and not a righteous heart, and yet offer gifts to God. They suppose that they are by this means purchasing God's help, not in healing their base desires, but in fulfilling them. And this is the way of the earthly city." (*De civitate Dei,* Book XV, 7, 643–644)

Bernward's choice of the *City of God* as the source for his theological development is crucial to the narrative's configuration, beginning with the episode of Cain and Abel. This change of literary reference had been prepared in panel 6, in keeping with the ecclesiological orientation the visual discourse was then taking. After having used *De Genesi ad litteram* to explain human nature*,* what interested the bishop of Hildesheim next was not so much what Old Testament history anticipated or announced would occur with the coming of Christ. Rather, his purpose was to explain how this salvific coming was prepared, in the most concrete meaning of the term, by a proto-ecclesial community.

The purpose of *De civitate Dei* is precisely to describe and study the history of two human communities coexisting throughout world history: the City of the Righteous, also called the City of God, founded by Abel, and the City of Men, founded by Cain, of which the Roman Empire is the last epigone. The history of this double foundation is told in the last panel of the bronze door's left wing.

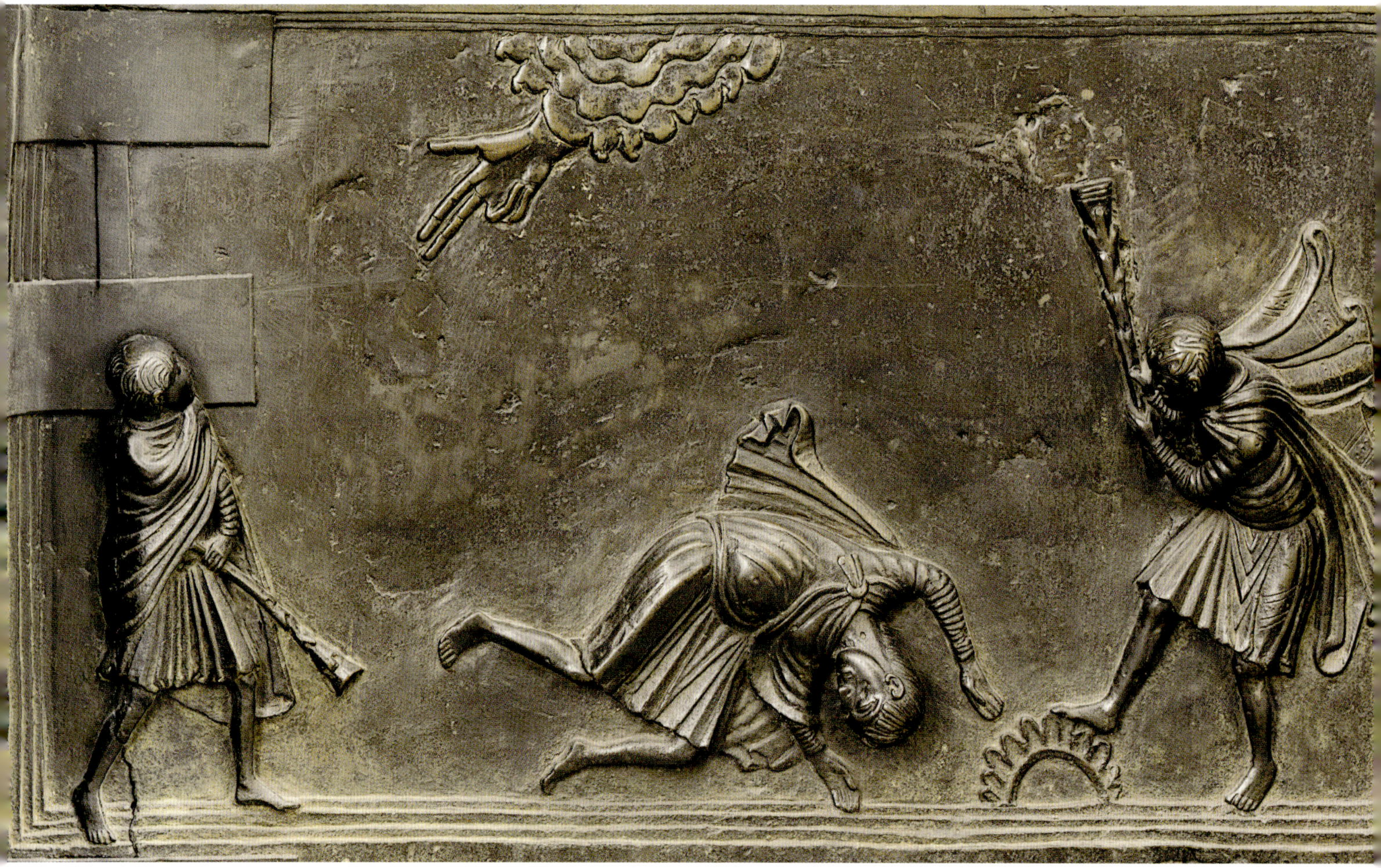

Panel **8**

FOUNDATION

In the center of the last panel of the left wing, against a plain background without any vegetal or architectural element, a man collapses headfirst to the ground, his inverted posture proclaiming both the end to which he was destined and the closing of the Old Testament narrative (fig. 108). Abel dies, the first person in history to do so. Standing in front of the door, the viewer looks down: the line on the ground toward which the body falls is also the ground under the faithful's feet. Abel's death tells of all future deaths, the nothingness into which the whole of humanity is plunged.

The panel's plastic restraint contrasts with a complex staging, linked to the intertwining narrative strands of a composite story, which is not so much a narrative as a sequence of dialogues:

> And Cain said to Abel his brother: Let us go forth abroad. And when they were in the field, Cain rose up against his brother Abel, and slew him.
>
> And the Lord said to Cain: Where is thy brother Abel? And he answered, I know not: am I my brother's keeper?
>
> And he said to him: What hast thou done? the voice of thy brother's blood crieth to me from the earth. Now, therefore, cursed shalt thou be upon the earth, which hath opened her mouth and received the blood of thy brother at thy hand. When thou shalt till it, it shall not yield to thee its fruit: a fugitive and a vagabond shalt thou be upon the earth.
>
> And Cain said to the Lord: My iniquity is greater than that I may deserve pardon. Behold thou dost cast me out this day from the face of the earth, and I shall be hidden from thy face, and I shall be a vagabond and a fugitive on the earth: every one, therefore, that findeth me, shall kill me.
>
> And the Lord said to him: No, it shall not be so: but whosoever shall kill Cain, shall be punished sevenfold. And the Lord set a mark upon Cain, that whosoever found him should not kill him.
>
> And Cain went out from the face of the Lord, and dwelt as a fugitive on the earth, at the east side of Eden. And Cain knew his wife, and she conceived, and brought forth Enoch: and he built a city, and called the name thereof by the name of his son Enoch. (Gen. 4:8–17).

108. *Panel 8.*

Cain is represented twice in the panel. Weapon raised and right foot pressing against a small mound, he appears to the right of Abel's body as a murderer. He reappears to the left of the body, wrapped in his cloak, his weapon lowered, retreating from the divine hand, and assuming a guilt-ridden posture. This double representation of a character in high relief and in frontal position is unprecedented in the bronze door. However, one should not underestimate its link with the wing's very first panel: standing on the right, Adam watched God give life to humanity; here Cain on the left sees himself or is at least conscious of having given death to humanity, although he denies it.

The figures appear noticeably separated from each other against the panel's stark background. (The two

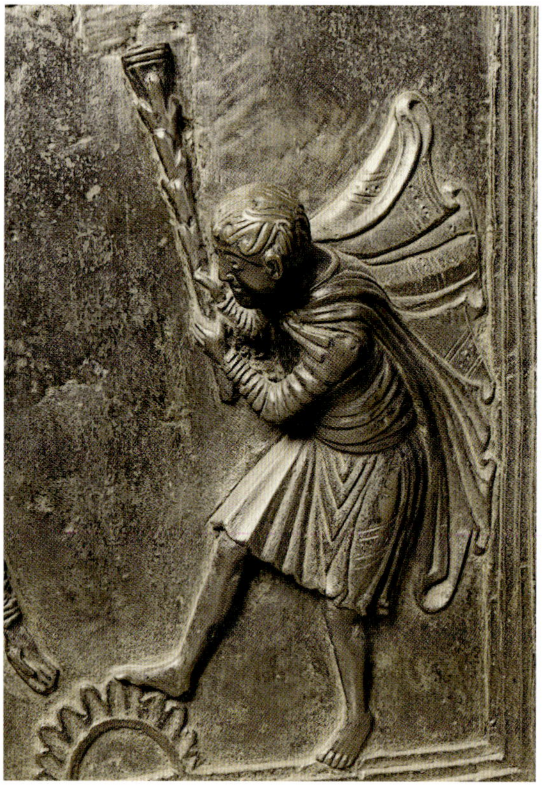

109

patches on the left are the result of restoration work.) The construction of the visual utterance rests neither on a marked proximity of the actors nor on a clear definition of spaces. Rather, it comes from the rational and directional interplay enriched by numerous analogies with the preceding panels. These associations establish a genealogy of the murderer, of the murder weapon, and of the crime itself, while at the same time causing the latter to resonate throughout the left wing.

Cain's movement echoes Adam's laborious effort in panel 6, his body stooped and unbalanced, his left leg lifted and the right one supporting him (cf. fig. 89). The son is heir to the earthly and sinful body of the father, whose mortal condition rebounds on murderer and victim alike.

Cain keeps to the right retaining the same vertical position he occupied in the previous panel (cf. fig. 99). He no longer wears a beard, the traditional mark of birthright that has no value in the hierarchy that is about to be established. He exhibits nevertheless the same inner turmoil, the same gaze fixed on the object of his emotional drives, holding the weapon with two hands as he did before with the sheaf of wheat (cf. fig. 106). Even if the weapon does not touch Abel's body, unlike the offering placed in contact with the mandorla, an iconographic detail indicates that the murderer's attitude is just as sacrilegious. With his right foot Cain leans on a small hemispherical mound placed on the panel's frame and encircled by a festoon.

Cain's garment has changed. The double lines—life channels seen in the previous panel—are now aligned with lines of dots: chisel marks (fig. 109). These chisel marks appeared for the first time in panel 3 as marks of life's destructive poison (cf. fig. 55); framed by parallel lines, they covered with arid volutes the rocky mound on which Eve was seated in panel 6 (cf. fig. 90). In panel 8, sin has atomized the body's structure, thus devitalizing, even fossilizing Cain, since by murdering his brother, the assassin has radically destroyed himself. Furthermore, and in a symptomatic manner, the realistic elements of the murderer's attire compose an ornamental system that imitates—although omitting of course the lattice-work-with-cross motif—the formal model of the light's iridescence on God's garments in panel 2 (cf. fig. 39). By taking his brother's life, Cain raises himself to the rank of the antitype of the Creator who is life's principle. He thus literally incarnates the Evil/Death he personifies: "Do not imitate Cain, who was possessed by evil [*ex maligno erat*] and who killed his brother. And why did he kill him? Because his actions [*opera*] were dictated by evil [*opera eius maligna errant*] and his brother's were righteous [*justa*]" (I John 3:12, author's translation).

Like the criminal, the murder weapon was chosen for being in continuity with the left wing. The biblical text does not identify it; artists have imagined it either as an animal's jaw, an agricultural tool, or as here, a club. The latter tradition seems to have grown out of rabbinical commentaries and is often found in Italo-Byzantine images [Kirschbaum 1970, LCI, *Abel und Kain*]. However, it is of little importance in this case to say that this weapon differs from that in the Moutier-Grandval Carolingian Bible or that it is similar to the one figured in the *Caedmon Genesis*. The viewer of the door has no way of identifying an artistic tradition. However, he or she can easily establish a link between this dry, bristly club, and the Tree of Life in panel 4 where, desiccated and covered with thorns, it represented the transmission of original sin and, consequently, of death (cf. fig. 61).

Let us pause for a moment to consider this club. On the left wing, the story of humans and of the Tree of Life are interdependent. Humans have eaten of the magnificent and forbidden plant; they have poisoned it, depriving it of its immortal sap, as they did with their own body. Furthermore, Cain has broken the bond between body and soul, disintegrating the latter by allowing evil urges to flow within it. Contrary to appearances, Cain's Tree of Life is indeed depicted

109. *Panel 8, Cain, right.*

in panel 8, where it assumes the shape of his weapon. This criminal cudgel is the ultimate version, atomized and radically disfigured, of the succession of metamorphoses undergone by the original Tree of Life from the first panel.

The pointing hand of God seems to accuse or punish Cain for his heinous crime as the murderer steps back in the image's lower left corner, the lowest part of the door (fig. 110). Such a common reading is sound but incomplete. Without knowledge of the narrative's sequel, it reduces Cain's behavior to fear, thus failing to take into account the characteristics of God's hand, quite different from those in panel 7.

The murderer's attitude betrays the inner turmoil gnawing at him. Appearing to shield himself from the divine wrath by drawing his cloak around him, the young man raises his right hand to his chin in a conventional gesture of suffering that we will find again with Salome, the woman standing in the center of panel 10 (cf. fig. 126).

Cain steps back, his eyes fixed on the light that confounds him. Just as Eve left Eden, on perceiving the clear image of what she was leaving behind (cf. fig. 78), the vision of truth looming over the murderer prevents him from henceforth imagining himself similar to God. The illusion of a physical mimesis has come to an end: there is no more "ornamentation" on Cain's clothes.

Stretched to the breaking point, the stiffly pleated draping of the cloak molds a garment clinging to his

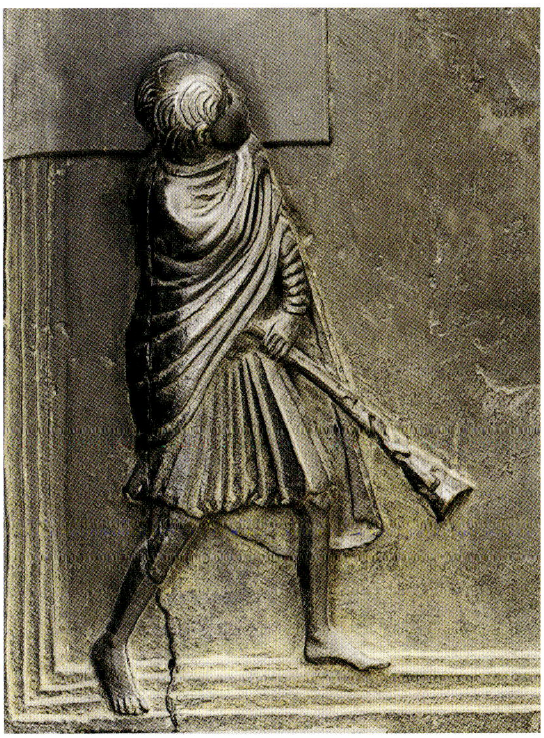

110

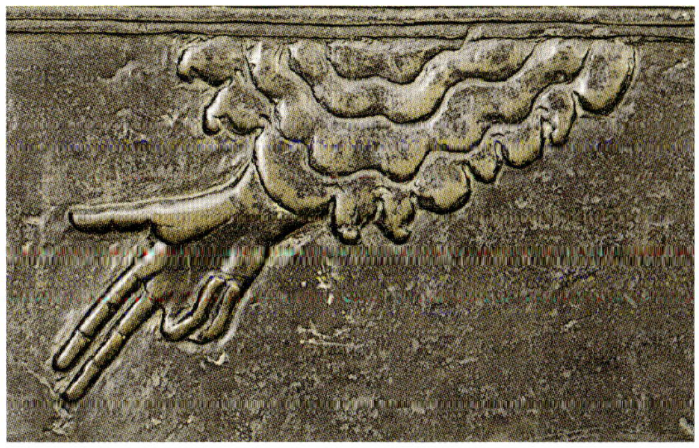

111

body in imitation of the thorny bark surrounding the club's devitalized wood. The hair has changed too. Composed of striated bands of metallic appearance, it has the shape of a helmet covering the young man's head. Just as Cain continued his father's sinful violence by bringing it to a close with his brother's murder, his body as death's prison in panel 8 brings to an end the process of building the earthly tomb that Adam initiated in panel 5 (cf. fig. 81). Cain has become identical to his weapon/Tree of Life: a mass of dead flesh agitated on the surface. Only his left hand escapes this sclerosis; it holds the murder weapon at the level of the groin, a possible reference to the deadly vitality that God granted to his progeny: animal sexuality ("And Cain knew his wife, and she conceived, and brought forth Enoch: and he built a city" [Gen 4:17]).

The mandorla of fire has disappeared and the divine hand descending from heaven now appears on the panel's empty background, emerging from a theophanic cloud mass whose residual luminosity is evidenced by the little flames surrounding it (fig. 111). The placement of the mandorla on the same background as that of the other protagonists is of great importance. Far from being the flaming mandorla that traced an intermediary sacred place between heaven and earth, it now states that God penetrates the space occupied by humans in order to address them.

The position of God's fingers—thumb straight, index and middle fingers extended and pressed together—is identical to the gesture with which the angel addressed Adam in panel 6 (cf. fig. 95). There it signified, or so I tried to demonstrate, the categorical application of the Law of time to the earthly world, a Law appearing both as a fatality, since each cycle ends in death, and as a blessing, since its cycles govern the growth and regeneration of earthly life. The divine Hand pointed toward Cain in panel 8 seems to me of the same nature, taking up the same kind of utterance but this time concerning territories. Did

110. *Panel 8, Cain, left.*

111. *Panel 8, Hand of God.*

not God put a mark on Cain, so that he could settle in a new city and there protect his life and that of his progeny?

The historiographical tradition that has focused on panel 8 was unaware of the importance of this biblical text and identified the scene on the left solely as a punishment/expulsion: it saw only the wrath, whereas the Law was also at work. From the very first panel of the bronze door, Bernward never represented God as an avenger, as the source of suffering to be imposed on humanity. On the contrary, the divine gestural motions have always manifested themselves in their performative and hermeneutical qualities. Performative in that they applied to the precepts of the Law of Life, established at the very beginning of Creation, to the functioning of the world; hermeneutical in that God's gestures unveiled the logical and automatic consequences of human actions regarding this Law. This rejection of all anthropomorphizing (even psychical) of the divine body allows Bernward the theologian to disengage God from all connections with evil, an evil conceived within the door, not as an element exogenous to the relationship between God and humans but as an alteration of the primal bond of love. Evil is shown as a defect in humanity's love for God but never as a defect of his love for humanity. Panel 8 testifies to this in a powerful way, thus cementing the two wings of the Old and New Testament.

What territory does God give to the murderer and his descendants? Cain does not stand on the ground of the panel's edge (fig. 110). His left foot leans on the border's first strip and his right foot descends even lower, thus resting on the wing's large frame, a hapax in the visual narrative. To put it another way, Cain stands on the edge, within the framework of the door containing the panels-narrative space, and not within the narrative space. Is this an invitation to ponder the conditions of human life?

The back edge of Cain's cloak reaches down to the calf of his left leg. Lying flat along the body, it isolates the figure from the panel's stark bronze surface. Two territories are articulated here, topographically intermingled but separated from each other by the abyssal substantial otherness that distinguishes Cain's flesh from the divine Hand. The first space, the panel's surface occupied by God, has received Abel's dead body. The second, the frame of the door, an infrastructure encircling it without affecting it, is the other space within which Cain's body/prison evolves. These two territories are equally earthly, yet profoundly different; one contains the other, which somehow remains on its surface and is resolutely heterogeneous to it. Within the biblical narrative of the bronze door as conceived by Bernward, I argue that one of these two territories describes the City of Man, the other the City of God.

"Now Cain was the first son born to those two parents of the human race, and he belonged to the City of man; the second son, Abel, belonged to the city of God" (*De civitate Dei*, Book XV, 1, 635).

"I have already said that two cities, different and inimical to one other, have arisen because some live according to the flesh, and others according to the spirit. It can now also be said that some live according to man, and others according to God" (*De civitate Dei*, Book XIV, 4, 587).

The point cannot be stressed enough: these two cities are superimposed on each other in the time and space of history. Since humanity lives in a body of flesh, the City of Man, even if cut off from God, constitutes the framework of material life for all humans to come, including the future members of the spiritual, immaterial, and temporary city that will be built on Abel's legacy:

> Nonetheless it is thanks to God that you are still alive: to God Who, in sparing you, warns you to correct yourselves by repentance. . . . Let these answers, and others, if more fruitful and fitting ones can be found, be made to their enemies by the redeemed families of the Lord Christ and by the pilgrim city of Christ the King. Remember, however, that among those very enemies are hidden some who will become citizens; and do not think it fruitless to bear their enmity until they shall come to confess the faith. On the other hand, while she is a pilgrim in this world, the City of God has with her, bound to her by the communion of the sacraments, some who will not be with her to share eternally in the bliss of the saints. . . . In this world, the two cities are indeed entangled and mingled with one another; and they will remain so until the last judgment shall separate them." (*De civitate Dei*, Book I, 34–35, 48–49) [cf. Brugger 1994, 90–92; Congar 1968, 66–69]

Let us turn our attention to the City of Abel. The young man, clubbed to death, occupies the center of the image. His inexpressive visage and his closed eyes (fig. 112), like those of Christ on the cross in panel 14 (cf. fig. 170), give him a peaceful appearance in contrast to the violence of the crime.

Arms forward, legs and shoulders pinned against the panel's background, the corpse plunges toward the ground but is stopped at the level of the frame's first edge, lightly brushed by the fingers of his left hand. In fact, this cadaver appears as a countermodel

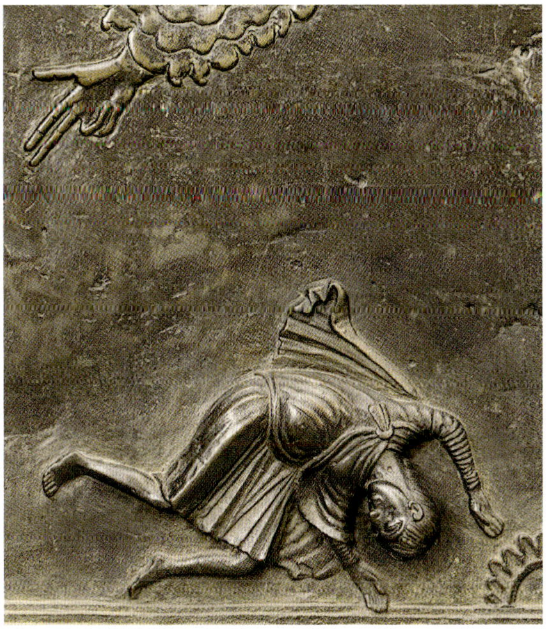

112

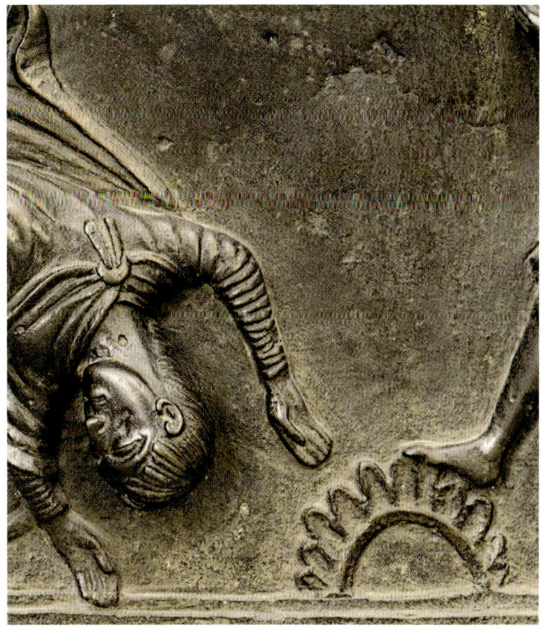

113

112. *Panel 8, Abel.*

113. *Panel 8, Voice of Abel's Blood.*

of Cain's body. Positioned under the hand of God, Abel's body does not leave the image's inner area and is totally flattened against the background (fig. 112). Were it possible to reconfigure the space surrounding him by lowering the bottom of the panel horizontally, the young man would appear to be lying on the ground. Accepted as an offering by God, who hovers over it, Abel's body would then delineate a new territory.

Cain has already moved away from the corpse. The contact he establishes with his brother is mediated by the scalloped semicircle on the ground on which he presses his foot and toward which Abel stretches his right arm (fig. 113). I suggest considering it as a fourth character in the narrative.

Contrary to several earlier representations, the image evokes the dialogues after the murder, not the murder itself: first, the exchange between God and Cain, which we have already studied, then the exchange between God and Abel, because, even if dead, the first Righteous Man is heard by his Creator: "What hast thou done? The voice of thy brother's blood [*vox sanguinis fratris tui*] crieth to me from the earth. Now, therefore, cursed shalt thou be upon the earth, which hath opened her mouth [*os suum aperuit*] and received the blood of thy brother at thy hand" (Gen. 4:10–12).

The semicircle is not rigorously hemispheric but rather leans slightly toward the hand of God and is as supple as the divine mandorla of the previous panel (fig. 108). Just like the mandorla, its incompleteness and its placement in the panel create the impression that it emerges from elsewhere, not from the highest celestial spheres but rather from the lowest depths of the earth—we are here at the viewer's ground level. Finally, just like the mandorla, this semicircle is shimmering and composite: its hemispheric shape outlines an area, in this case surprisingly empty, whereas its surface appears as animated matter.

In early medieval iconography there is a tradition of depicting the "voice of Abel's blood." Although quite rare, it was known and first developed in rabbinical commentaries and was later depicted in a small body of Italo-Byzantine images, as in Santa Maria Antiqua in the Roman Forum. Bernward might well have known about it through Theophano's Byzantine entourage or even seen it at the time of his Roman excursions (even though Santa Maria Antiqua was in ruins when Bernward was in the pontifical city). In this tradition, the "voice of Abel's blood" may assume, in addition to other aspects, the shape of a silhouette with outstretched arms enclosed in a little grotto or represented above it [Brugger and Christe 1994].

Hollowed-out spaces resembling the semicircle are found in the last panel of the bronze door (cf. fig. 186). They thus represent the caves of Hell that the resurrected Christ dominates while brandishing the cross-staff of his victory over death. Bernward thus invites the viewer's gaze to rise from the lowest point of the door up to the end of the path to salvation. What he wants to signify by this pertains to the door's general composition: as we remember, the reading sequence descends on the left wing for the Old Testament and ascends on the right wing for the New Testament, at whose threshold we now stand.

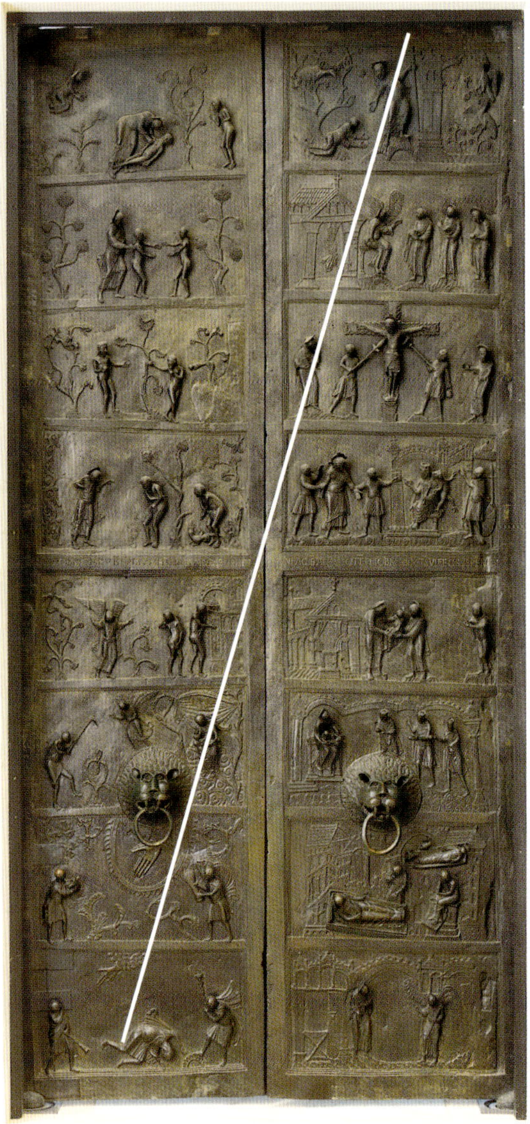

114

In panel 16, Christ extends his right hand toward Mary Magdalene, whom he is going to free from her mortal condition, an echo of the divine Right Hand with which God chose Abel in panel 7 (cf. fig. 186 and 99); the palm with extended thumb is open in the same way and inclined on the same axis. In addition, the Savior's visage, whose very high relief is underscored by the oblique position of the cruciferous halo, exhibits the same criteria of visibility and domination as the face of God in the very first panel (cf. fig. 12). True, Christ speaks to the Magdalene, but his gesture spans the entire door to include the faithful below, implying an open invitation.

If now we carefully consider the general diagonal delineating this very important gesture, we realize that it extends from the upper part of the door to its geometric center, reaching Abel's falling body (fig. 114). This diagonal axis—a geometric figure which, we will recall, visualizes the divine principle of vitalization from the first panel onward—is probably the most important feature in the historiated narrative. It transcends the narration, annulling the time of the story and testifying to both Divine Providence and the love God has for the Righteous by freeing them from death in the depths of the earth. The narrative on the right wing is, in short, the exegesis of this announced assumption.

Indeed, the scalloped cavity that Cain tramples prefigures the sepulchral grotto from which Christ will release the Righteous at the end of time. By the unusual position of his fall, Abel takes on its curved shape, so that what occurs in the image is a metonymic transfer of the cadaver into the cavity presumed to hold him after his death. The arched grotto then comes to represent a corporeal territory, a space similar to the one Cain built around himself with his mantle of flesh. Here the opposition becomes radical: whereas Cain's body of flesh is a temple of death, Abel's dead body foreshadows the temple of eternal life. It must not be forgotten that for Christians, the chosen ones will resurrect at the end of time with their bodies of flesh transfigured into eternal, spiritual bodies as participants in the body of Christ. This is what panels 14, 15, and 16 will reveal; we will understand all this at the end of the narration.

For the moment, this body/place is still closed since it prefigures that underworld from which all the Righteous will rise at the end of time. Yet an audible word emerges from it. What else, if not the scalloped edge, could better evoke this new element, the word itself? The substance comprising it has never yet been represented on the bronze door; visually, it appears to combine the silhouette of a hollow foliage and a geometrized pyric form. Vegetation is the substance incarnating the vital impulse from the first panel. It can therefore be deduced that Bernard wanted to show that this word is indeed alive. Its form is quite interesting because it tends to suggest structure rather than matter, thus giving it the function of interface similar to the role of light in the divine mandorla. As may have become clear, I suggest that it represents the *vox sanguinis* itself, a word of truth emanating from the Righteous because they have within themselves the image of the Word, having renewed their covenant with God. This living, transmissible, and prophetic Word announces the new Law that Christ will bring, precisely the Word that will allow Abel to exit his tomb. This messianic announcement will resonate through the centuries, from Righteous to Righteous, until it will become whole and salvific in the body of Jesus in the next panel. And it is in this Word, the New Law of Life,

114. *Diagonal of the full door.*

and no longer in the Tree of Life, that humanity's destiny will unfold.

In order to make visible this messianic and then incarnated Word, Bernward visually inscribes it in the territory founded by Abel, the City of God, displaying the original grotto through metamorphic architectural constructions (in this case, they could even be qualified as topological), evoking characters no longer characterized as individuals but as communities.

The world into which the viewer will enter on the right wing is based on a new reading grid, symmetrical but not superimposable on the one operating in reading the left wing. The architecture will no longer be an object in itself but a way to represent, to signify, to give voice to the City of God, in the same way as the Tree of Life gave form and language to the vital principle. Like the plant, this architecture will function both as subject and as hermeneutical principle unveiling the ontological dimension of the biblical *historia*. And just like the image of the Tree of Life cited at the beginning of Genesis, the buildings, arches, columns, and walls structuring the panels' areas will correspond to biblical sites, interacting with the characters. At the same time, just like the leaves, trunks, branches, and roots of the Tree of Life, the stones will signify certain essential qualities of the protagonists and give shape to abstract theological principles. Indeed, stones have the same plastic assets as plants: a readable geometric structure, a vast range of formal modulations, multiple possibilities of combinations, a dynamism deriving essentially from the interplay of balance and imbalance, span and thrust, and ultimately and understandably, a considerable potentiality for spatial depth, particularly adapted to the figuration and qualification of spaces.

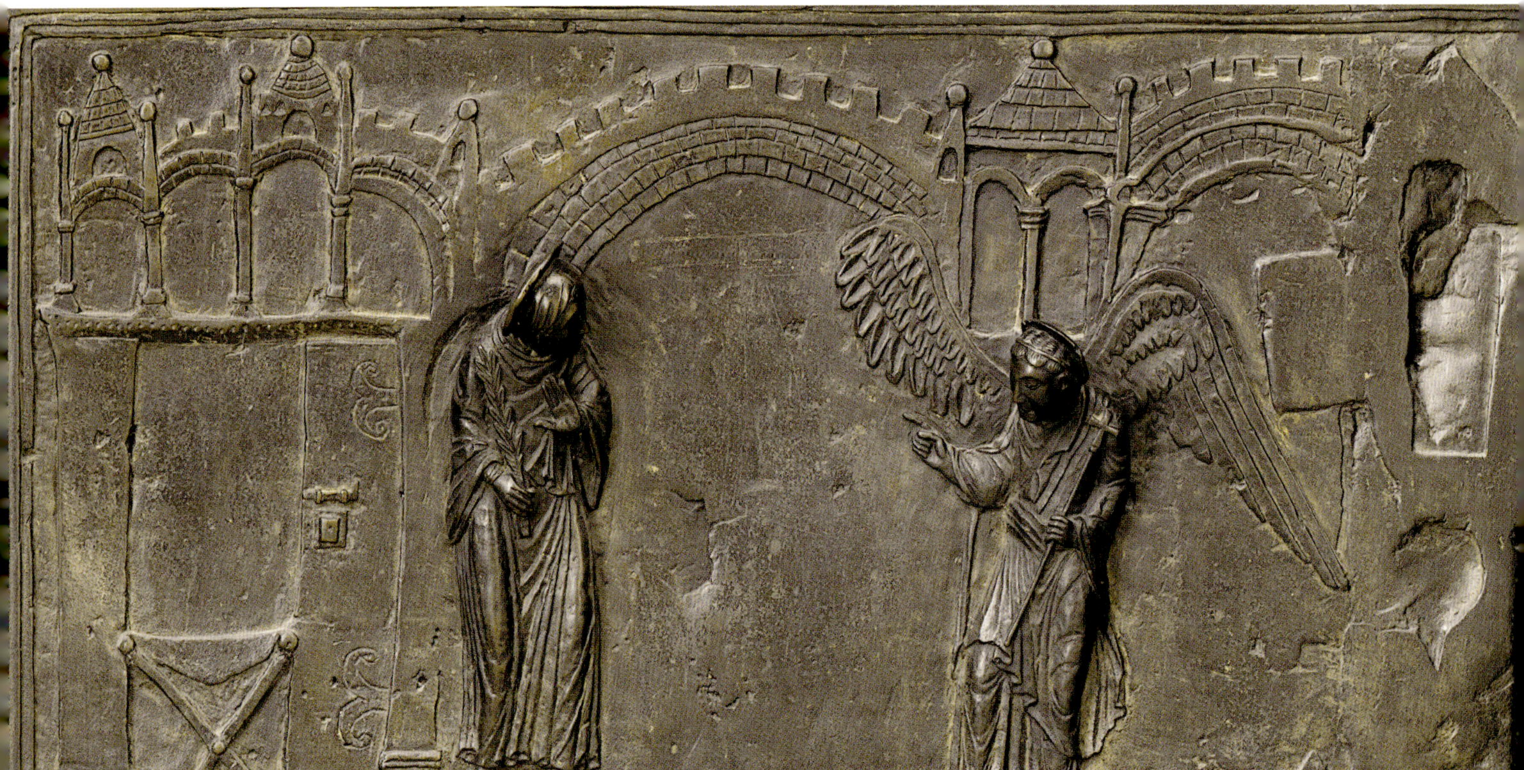

Panel 9

GOSPEL

The Annunciation to Mary inaugurates the wing of the New Testament and the rise of humanity to heaven. Gabriel stands on the right side of the panel, at a respectful distance from the young woman (fig. 115). He is represented with the same attributes as the angel in panel 6: his head haloed and circled by a diadem, his wings outstretched, and his left hand clasping the cross-staff cross, a frequent attribute in Carolingian and Ottonian iconography of the Annunciation. As in panels 6 and 16, this cross is a sign of the divine incarnate Word, dead and resuscitated.

Mary stands on the left side of the panel, facing Gabriel. Wearing a veil and a loose garment with wide sleeves, she is turned toward the angel, who is addressing her and to whom she responds with a hand gesture. Panel 5 also depicted a face-to-face encounter between a woman and an angel (cf. fig. 78). There, Eve was smaller than the guardian of Eden, and only the angel's inclined head implied a specular relationship between the two protagonists. In panel 9, the rapport between the two figures has changed: Mary's body is larger than that of the divine messenger and is elevated on a small mound, reaching the height of the angelic wing. In addition to her size, Mary is characterized by two particularly signifying attributes in the context of panel 9 (fig. 116).

The first is the halo, the disc appended at the back of her head representing a nimbus of divine light. This attribute is so commonly associated with Mary in Christian iconography that no one has questioned its presence on the bronze door. In fact, before Mary no other human being had been provided with it, not even Abel, the great prophetic figure of the left wing.

115. *Panel 9.*

Mary's second attribute is the little branch pressed against her chest. As far as I know, this branch is not found in earlier representations of the Annunciation, which generally show the young woman seated, her hands empty or holding weaving tools or, more exceptionally, a book [Schiller 1966–91, I, 48; Coatsworth 1998]. What does this little branch signify?

The lower part of the branch, by which it is held, is woody and bare; in contrast, the entire upper part is covered with opposing leaves. Because of its leaves, this branch cannot be identified with a *virga*, a small and slender stem ending with a floret that traditionally evokes Wisdom in Christian iconography, especially in early medieval Anglo-Saxon images. Nor does its ligneous appearance permit associating it with one of those flowers that much later came to symbolize Mary's virginal purity in Christian images. Vertical, slender, and symmetrically covered with leaves, it actually recalls a palm, hence the Tree of Life at the beginning of the left wing. In the absence of a known precedent for the representation of the Annunciation, Bernward has perhaps drawn his inspiration from the vast tradition of early Christian and medieval images that place in the hands of the Righteous elected to Paradise a palm recalling both their martyrdom and their glorious resurrection. Above all, it should be remembered that among other forms assumed by the Tree of Life, the second panel exhibits the palm tree whose homonymy with the phoenix has symbolized longevity and rebirth since antiquity [Deproost]. In addition to resembling the palm, the branch held by Mary, cut but still living, functions as an antonym

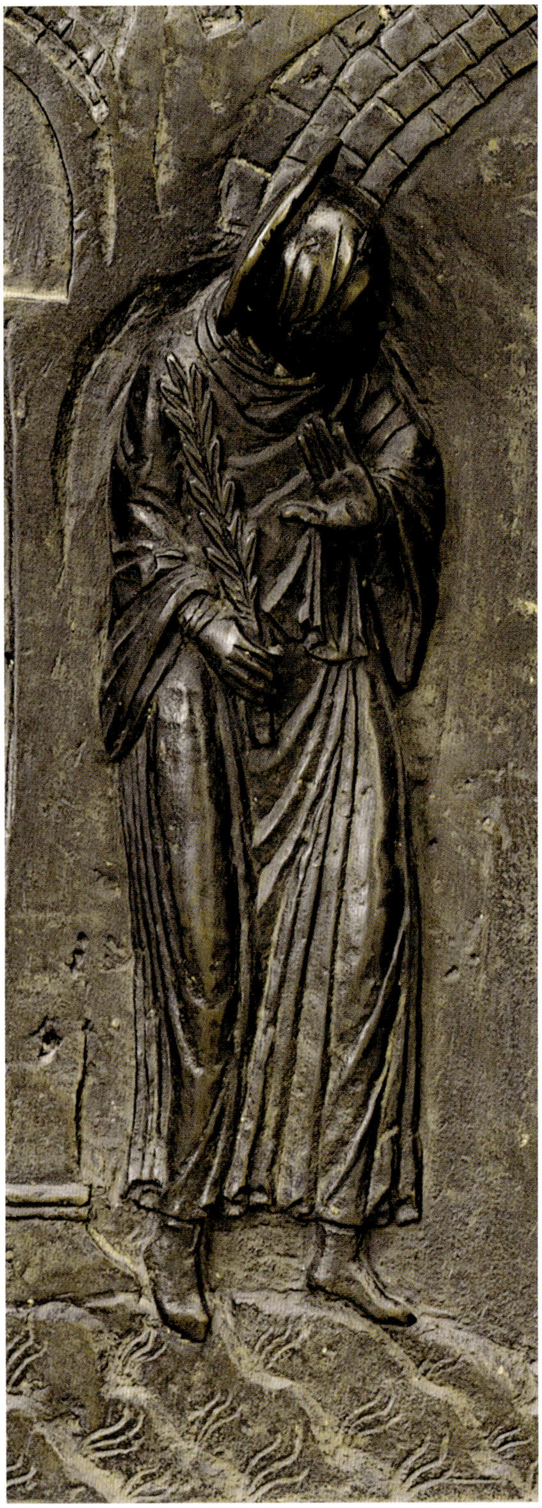

116

The whole scene, insofar as the panel's lacunae permit us to affirm, rests on an undulating ground in marked relief. Similar protrusions will reappear in the right wing but are absent on the left wing, with the exception of the panel of original sin, where, placed at the center of the image (cf. fig. 55), they represent the Garden of Eden poisoned by men.

It is precisely panel 3 that we must revisit in order to understand the ground of panel 9. In panel 3, Eve stepped down from the Edenic heights; here Mary is elevated above the ground level. The nature of the mounds' substrata turns out to be diametrically opposed: in panel 3, the garden contaminated by sin was made of mineral spirals indicating its aridity and death; in the Annunciation panel the base of the image, like a fertile carpet, is covered with slender wispy blades of grass arranged in groups of three. This vegetal configuration is identical to that of the little plant engraved in the bronze between Eve and the Tree of Knowledge of Good and Evil in panel 3 (cf. fig. 56). There the plant functioned as the sign, as discreet as it was fundamental, of the divine order's structural resistance to human destruction, constituting a promise of renewal, of a possible rejuvenation of the world. The vigorously undulating grass covering the soil in panel 9 fulfills this prophecy. It echoes the sanctified fertility of Mary's body and, more than that, it reconnects with the initial context of Creation by showing the Incarnation as the beginning of the restoration of the earthly paradise such as it appears in panel 16, as we shall see.

We still must understand more precisely where this new Tree of Life comes from—Cain had reduced the old one to sexual drive—and to do so, we must reexamine the first Marian attribute, the nimbus. The index finger that Gabriel points toward Mary is not directed at Mary herself but rather at the aureole dominating her (fig. 115). In doing so, he calls attention to the divine light. Bernward had a wide freedom of choice in an iconographic tradition that had no fixed rules for angelic gestures (Gabriel may bless Mary, point at heaven, or point at the womb destined to bear the Savior). Coherent with his syntax, the bishop has chosen to follow the biblical text by inscribing the event into the role it plays in the programmatic continuity of the bronze panels. The episode represented here is found in the Gospel according to Luke:

> And the angel being come in, said unto her [Mary]: Hail, full of grace, the Lord is with thee: blessed art thou among women. Who having heard, was troubled at his saying, and thought with herself what manner of salutation this should

to the murdering club in the previous panel and is placed in axial symmetry with the cross-staff, victorious over death, that Gabriel holds against his shoulder (fig. 115).

A final, topographical argument supports identifying Mary's branch with the Tree of Life (fig. 116).

116. *Panel 9, Mary.*

> be. And the angel said to her: Fear not, Mary, for thou hast found grace with God. Behold thou shalt conceive in thy womb, and shalt bring forth a son; and thou shalt call his name Jesus. He shall be great, and shall be called the Son of the most High; and the Lord God shall give unto him the throne of David his father, and he shall reign in the house of Jacob forever. And of his kingdom there shall be no end. And Mary said to the angel: How shall this be done, because I know not man? And the angel answering, said to her: The Holy Ghost shall come upon thee, and the power of the most High shall overshadow thee. And therefore also the Holy which shall be born of thee shall be called the Son of God. (Luke 1:28–35)

As mentioned earlier, Eve was illuminated by the light of God in panel 2, who stood behind her while presenting her to Adam; humans were able to recognize their Creator by looking at their fellow creature, that is, by recognizing themselves as creatures. In panel 9, the divine light irradiates again, but this time starting with Mary herself, so that God is recognizable no longer just through humans, but he becomes visible *in* humans. The event, the Incarnation, spectacular in itself, primarily attests to this paradigm shift, thereby underscoring the depth of the caesura between the Old and the New Testament.

If the halo is the manifestation of this paradigm shift, the branch clarifies its function. In panel 9, Mary repeats the gesture with which Adam received the eternity of the Tree of Life in the first panel: left hand on the heart, palm open (cf. fig. 13). The difference between these two figures comes from the fact that Adam's life source was external to him, whereas Mary's palm, held against her torso, appears to be one with her body. The halo and the branch are thus much more than signs of election: they announce the birth of the God—a new Tree of Life in human flesh but also, consequently, the future inscription of the vital principle of eternity in human bodies. The central scene of the right wing's first panel depicts a re-creation of humanity, a counterpart to the institution of life in the left wing's first panel, while modifying one of its fundamental laws: exteriority becomes *interiority*.

The architecture behind Mary and Gabriel encourages the viewer to understand this new genesis. A vast architectural complex composed of arcades, openings, aedicules, and crenellations unfolds in the background. These constructions seem to cover the entire width of the image, even though we cannot be certain, given the damage in the right side of the panel (probably because the molten bronze did not reach the desired temperature and volume). We can perceive only the vague shape of a tower with a triangular roof, similar to the one behind Gabriel (fig. 115).

Like the vegetation, architecture acts first through its natural capacity to organize the image's area. In this panel, two side structures frame a wide central arch whose pillars are emphasized by the figures of Mary and the angel. However, the quality of the architecture, as noted at the end of the previous panel, is due above all to the fact that it adds a third dimension to the two-dimensional geometric space that served as an organizing grid to the world of the Old Testament. Thus, in panel 9, and for the first time in the door, this three-dimensionality is emphasized by a succession of receding planes: the characters and the curule seat are placed in the foreground; a very large composite mass appears behind Mary; the framing line running across the whole panel constitutes the third plane; and last, the far distance perceived through the opening of the great central arch.

One may justifiably wonder if this spatial construction is interrelated with the Incarnation itself, inasmuch as the refoundation of the world is enacted by a Word inscribed into the materiality of the earthly world. We shall return to this question in the second part of the analysis; for the moment, and for clarity's sake, we will try to identify and understand how the different constructions of the image are structured.

The building behind Mary is of parallelepipedal shape, contrasting with the templelike edifices before which the Virgin is usually represented in medieval Annunciations, including the Ottonian ones (fig. 117). As often is the case, this building is physically connected with the young woman, who partially conceals it. This superimposition is even underscored by a kind of arch engraved in the bronze around Mary's shoulders. As the iconographic analysis will confirm, this building is Mary's home.

The lower part of the building is easily identifiable. It is the framing of a door showing the discretely ornate upper lintel as well as the two doorposts consisting of two pillars, slightly misaligned due to the unevenness of the ground. The door of the house has two casements. One of them is hung behind the right pillar by hinges. The second one is not visible because it recedes into the depth of the opening. It clears a passage paradoxically blocked by the curule seat, which we will discuss later. The lock evokes a similar ambiguity between opening and closing. In fact, this high-end mechanism appeared in the tenth century, comprising a lock and raised lock-case that can be used to both open and close [Linlaud 2014, 106–108, 189–192]. Although schematically represented, the

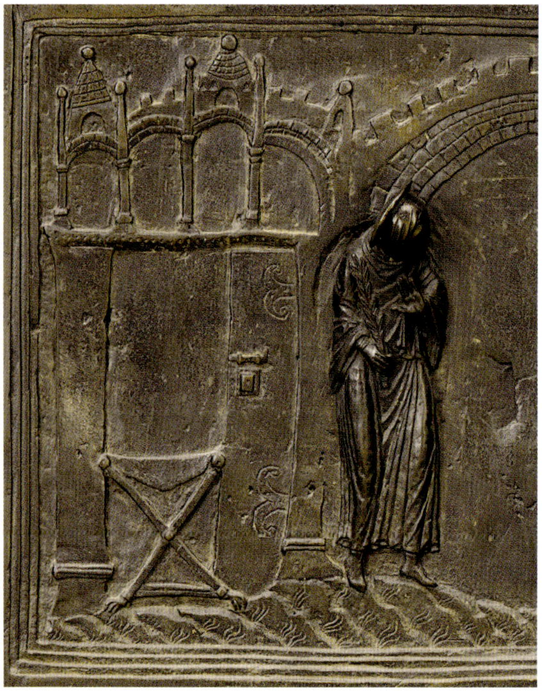

117

lock recalls Bernward's expertise in ironwork and demonstrates the careful technical attention given by the bishop to artifacts and their modernity. The quality of this lock is but the first manifestation of what was foretold by Adam's industrious hand in panel 4 (cf. fig. 79) as well as the promethean angel of panel 5 (cf. fig. 95). All subsequent artifacts will have to be examined in relation to perceptible reality and for their own intrinsic qualities. For Hildesheim's learned bishop, as for his contemporaries, the future of humanity is interwoven with the spiritual intelligence of Revelation and the scientific intelligence of the ontological explanations of the world and of history.

A very elaborate structure surmounts the door's lintel. It consists of a series of four arches with a double row of stones standing on pillars with capitals. On top of the superstructure is a row of crenellations, vertical masonry extensions ending with a ball that are placed along the pillars' axes, and two aedicules pierced by a bay and protected by a roof crowned with a ball. This complex construction uses the lintel as a base of support, but if it is visually part of the building's door, does it really constitute a part of it?

The arches and pillars that make up the arcade are not of the same height but follow a generally curved line. It is unlikely that they were intended as bays placed on an upper floor, nor even a colonnade that would require a horizontal entablature. None of this then would elucidate the role played by the crenellations and the aedicules. In fact, no known elevation scheme corresponds to what we see, suggesting that the arcade is placed behind the structure: it seems to dominate it because of a perspective raised in the plane which is unfamiliar to our eyes: in ancient or medieval scenes, what is perceived as behind or in the distance is often placed higher up in the image.

This suggestion of spatial reading is supported by observing that the row of arcades is inscribed into the visual and architectural continuity of the central arch, from which it is separated by a small conical structure surmounted by a ball, found again at the junction between the central arch and the one on the right (fig. 118). All these elements contribute to emphasizing the structural unity of the buildings extending across the panel's width. Transcending the scale whose value is more symbolic than perspectival in medieval iconography, the four little arches are thus associated with the two larger ones, constituting one and the same construction.

The combination of the continuity of the structure, the superimposition of the stone layers, the crenellations (conventional attributes of city representations), and the regular scansion of the whole by what looks like towers, naturally leads the viewer to identify it as a wall reinforced by defensive structures, and the place as Nazareth, the city of Mary: "And in the sixth month, the angel Gabriel was sent from God into a city of Galilee, called Nazareth" (Luke 1:26).

Bernward the architect has set the places—the neo-Edenic land, Mary's house, and the city of Nazareth—in a three-dimensional and topological

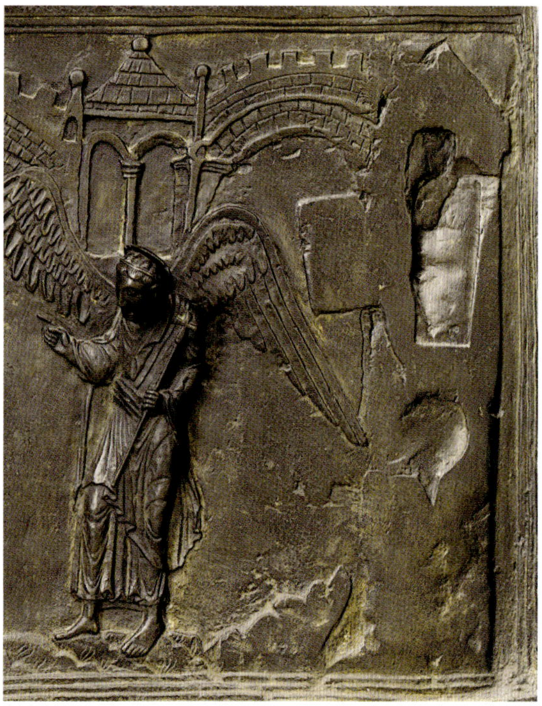

118

117. *Panel 9, building behind Mary.*

118. *Panel 9, building behind Gabriel.*

space, taking into consideration the relationships of continuity and the morphological articulations between places rather than their dimensions. Through his structuring of the building and the spatial depth, he has shown that, as an architect/engineer, he respects the rules of the art, which will be decisive in understanding panel 15. Let us now consider a more symbolical approach to the architecture in panel 9.

In the middle of the panel, the great arch imposes its powerful frontality (fig. 119), comparable to the triumphal arches of antique and early medieval churches, on which the Annunciation is frequently represented. Their function is to create a hierarchy in levels of sacredness, thus articulating a connection between the nave and the choir's apse.

In panel 9, the arch delineates a large opening in the depth of the image whose center corresponds to the geometric midpoint of the panel (fig. 115). The contradictory play between full and empty spaces becomes more evident, while at the same time an unusual vanishing point is created, albeit not visually supported by perspectival elements. It is all the more remarkable because the architecture of the following panel will establish a compact bronze setting designed according to other vanishing points (cf. fig. 126). We shall return to this point later.

In the absence of discernible pillars, the figures of Mary and Gabriel constitute the visual supports for this great arch open onto the distance. By their assimilation to supporting elements, the two characters play a metaphorical role analogous to that which the Epistle to the Galatians attributes to the apostles when it compares them to columns (Gal. 2:9). This analogy was widely used in medieval exegesis, iconography, and architecture [Bandmann, 74–83]. It is only one of the numerous structural connections that Christian scholars and artists have established between major figures of the ecclesial community and the architectural function of constitutive components of ecclesial buildings. The association of Mary, a representative of the Church if ever there was one, with religious constructions is a constant feature in Christian iconography, in the East as well as in the West. As for the arch, it is in essence the bearer of the idea of *connection*, a symbolic quality echoing the first sign of the covenant that, in the Bible, God gives to humans coming out of Noah's ark: "And God said: This is the sign of the covenant which I give between me and you, and to every living soul that is with you, for perpetual generations. I will set my bow in the clouds, and it shall be the sign of a covenant between me, and between the earth" (Gen. 9:12–13).

Quite logically, the Incarnation, as a re-creation of humanity, is first of all a renewal of the covenant

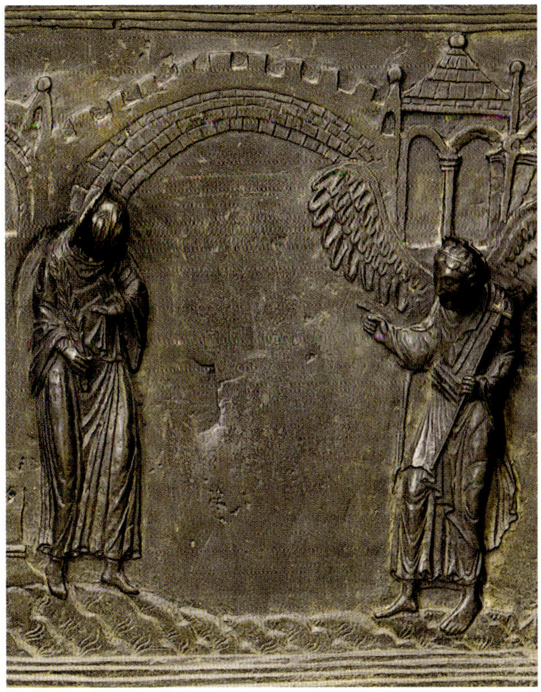

119

119. *Panel 9, triumphal arch.*

between God and his creatures. This idea of covenant is present in Luke's text: "Hail, full of grace, the Lord is with thee" (Luke 1:28), and it is rendered universal in the verses devoted by Matthew to Joseph announcing the Savior's birth: "Now all this was done that it might be fulfilled which the Lord spoke by the prophet, saying: 'Behold a virgin shall be with child, and bring forth a son, and they shall call his name Emmanuel, which being interpreted is, God with us'" (Matt. 1:22–23).

Destined to become a major motif in the right wing, the arch in panel 9 has a double function. Just as the churches' triumphal arches open onto the apse behind them, the arch in panel 9 opens onto the Nativity scene in panel 10 and, subsequently, onto the entire narrative of the New Testament (cf. fig.1). It is possible that the hollowing of the metal groove surrounding Mary at the descent of the arch (fig. 119) may be a manifestation of the way in which the Spirit penetrates the world's matter, thus making the Marian body its entrance point, and the wing's metallic background the site in which the Word acts out its theophany in images, that is, in form and substance.

At the same time the triumphal arch points to a path leading back to the Paradise represented in the door's last panel. The visual means that Bernward uses to suggest and qualify this ascending movement comes from a very effective iconicity. Using a banal principle of visual cognition (the viewer's projection into the depth of the images), Bernward creates a dynamic opening at the panel's center, under the arch placed at the door's lowest point, so that the opening appears as a door within the door. It opens onto a vertiginous ascent, since the viewer first plunges their gaze toward the earth before dramatically turning it toward heaven, that is, toward Christ placed vertically at the height of 4.7 meters: the Savior appears in the act of raising up Mary Magdalene, Abel, and with them all the Righteous in history (cf. fig. 114).

Contrary to what I have suggested so far, the passage under the arch is not empty. It contains a vast and smooth metal surface full of promises elucidated by the symmetrical relationship with panel 8 (fig. 120). Indeed, the plain bronze area delineated under the arch is located where Abel's curved body was; in addition, it takes on the hemispherical shape and the apparent emptiness of the sepulchral grotto from which issued the prophetic utterance. Better yet, in panel 8 the fingers of the divine hand designate the place that Mary, the Savior's matrix, will occupy in panel 9. Christ's body will replace Abel's as the sacred territory of the covenant, just as his Word—his utterances and actions, namely the Gospel/New Testament—will replace the Old Testament of the community of the Righteous.

After the great arch, the most readable architectural structure in the panel is Mary's house (fig. 117). As we have seen, it is very unusual compared to the buildings that traditionally frame Mary in Carolingian and Ottonian iconography. In this image, the house represents two different yet complementary things.

The first and most conventional comes from the fact that the house, being an intimate and private space, suggests the young woman's body. In a paradoxical and eminently significant manner, the passage, freed by the door's opening, is at the same time obstructed by the curule seat, an ambiguity, as we have seen, echoed by the type of lock chosen by Bernward.

By its crosslike shape and its position, the curule seat testifies to a prohibition: no man, not even Joseph can physically cross the threshold (Luke 1:34). The house door remains open, however, to God and to the Holy Spirit, who fertilizes the Virgin (Luke 1:31–32). The miracle of this spiritual fertilization stands out even more when we consider that the program in the left wing of the bronze door tries to show that the original sin was transmitted through sexual generation beginning with Adam and Eve.

Christians identify the prophecy of Marian virginity in a vision of Ezekiel (Ezek. 44:2), and it was established as a dogma from the earliest councils, reaffirmed in scriptural commentaries, and constantly exalted in poetry and liturgy. It is not surprising, therefore, that visual signs of the ambiguity present in the Marian body, both open and closed, are found in medieval iconography. The better known of these traditions, widespread at the end of the Middle Ages, is the representation of a permeable column separating Mary from Gabriel [Arasse 1999, 55]. Mary's virginity is made specific in panel 9 by its inscription in a double visual heritage.

The first is sin. The structure containing the Marian body is, in fact, framed by a band studded with chisel marks: quite different from the late dogma of Mary's immaculate conception, this contamination shows that the virginal womb inherited a mortal and poisoned flesh.

The second is royalty. Ancient and medieval chairs exhibit the degree of power and dignity of those who sit in them. In this case the curule seat placed before the house entrance signifies the *imperium,* a royal power recalling that the Virgin and her son come from royal lineage, and that the infant himself is promised royal dignity: "The Lord God shall give unto him the throne of David his father; and he shall reign in the house of Jacob forever. And of his kingdom there shall be no end" (Luke 1:32–33).

The third symbolical signification that I suggest associating with Mary's house is much less common

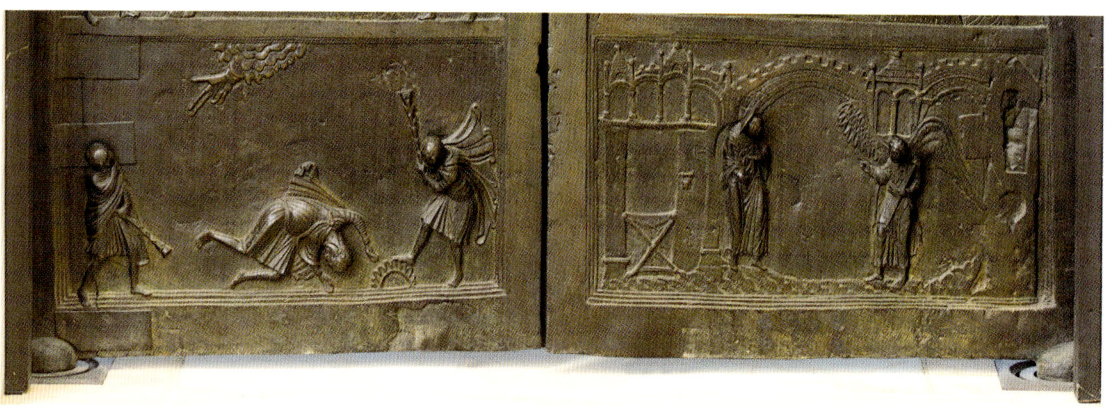

120

120. *Panels 8 and 9.*

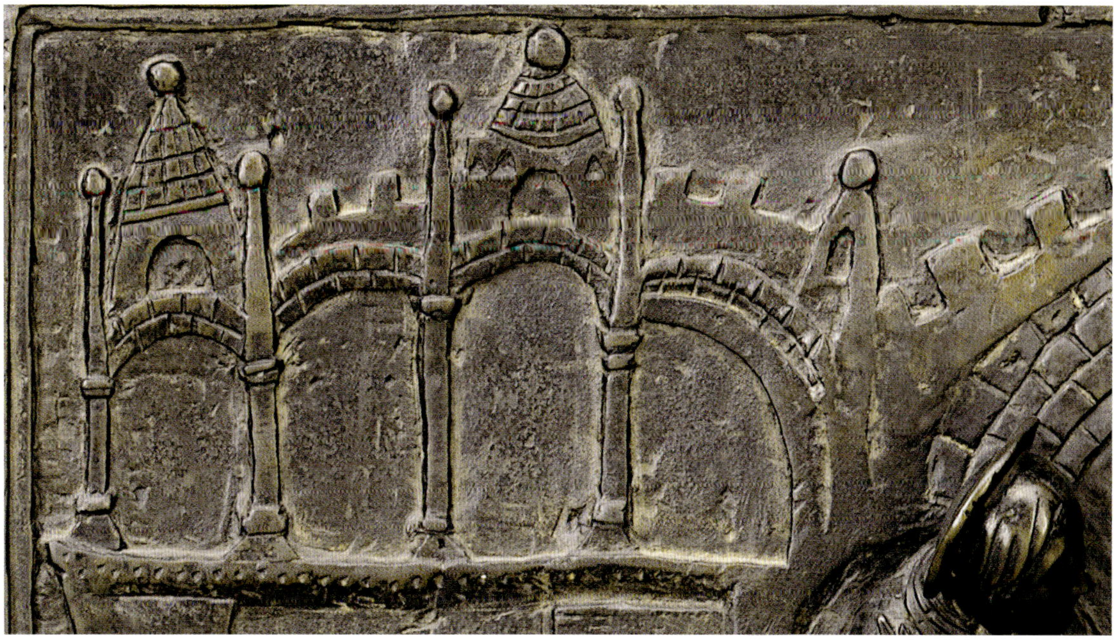

121

121. *Panel 9, upper portion of building behind Mary.*

and will be developed at length. As explained previously, the building is part of the arcade above it, but the two constructions must be considered as receding levels (fig. 121). Inasmuch as it is a rational compound of forms (architectural organization) and considering what it signifies through its deformations and interactions with its surroundings (topology), the double functioning of the architectural object is a syntactical rule that we will have to manipulate in examining the right wing as a whole. In itself, it is not very different from the double functioning of the plants in the left wing: a naturalistic one when the laws of sensible reality are integrated in the symbolical element, an expressive one when the plants are modified and interact with their surroundings through their positions and movements.

Bernward is an architect, and he perfectly handles the principles of construction. (The Church of St. Michael is a masterly achievement.) Some details of the arcade of panel 9 do not match with a fortified enclosure. As mentioned earlier, its four arches are of varying height, although together they form a generally arched shape. In addition, they rest on posts prolonged by pillars with no bearing function and whose summit comprises small spheres. Of all the possible constructions to which this building could refer, a bridge best corresponds to its structure and arrangement: a deckless bridge, thus emphasizing the arches, on which would be represented a parapet, as well as aedicules for either permitting or forbidding entrance. In order to evaluate the relevance of this suggestion, it is necessary to prolong the theoretical considerations begun in the study of the door opening onto the earthly world in panel 5.

The rare medieval representations of bridges prior to 1015 are Byzantine and depict them as a series of evenly spaced arches supporting a humped-back apron sometimes accompanied by a parapet (for example, in the Ms. BnF Grec 510, f 409v and 440). Despite some similarities, Bernward does not follow this tradition.

Some details appear particularly worthy of attention (fig. 121). The high pillars rising along the axis of the bridge-piers are not an architectonic component of the construction but an ornamental feature sufficiently original to warrant identifying them.

We do not know what the bridge over the Treibe at the foot of the episcopal city of Hildesheim looked like, and it is very unlikely that such an important stone bridge existed at that time in the Germanic world, nor could it have been built during the early Middle Ages; medieval bridges were built of wood until the twelfth century. Nevertheless, the construction in panel 9 resembles a stone bridge, a legacy from the world of antiquity and still extant in the Middle Ages, particularly in Rome. As attested by the *Memorabilia Urbis Romae,* the most ancient descriptions of the wonders of Rome are supposed to have been written during the Ottonian period [Accame and Dell'Oro 2004, 18–19]. Like gates or sacred sites, bridges were the object of considerable attention and admiration. Among Roman bridges, only one has both the shape and ornamental elements represented in the image: the Pons Aelius or, if we prefer

122

the present name, the Ponte Sant'Angelo, whose baroque sculptures of angels give it an outline similar to the one it had in antiquity. Built by Hadrian on the axis of his mausoleum, we know how it looked at the time thanks to a contemporary coin (fig. 122). (Concerns that it was an early modern pastiche were unfounded.)

How can the validity of this hypothetical identification be evaluated?

As the *Memorabilia Urbis Romae* attests, the Pons Aelius, together with the Pons Milvius (Milvian Bridge), was the most famous Roman bridge during the Middle Ages. It was also one of the last bridges still in use in the year 1000. Like all those pilgrims who reached Rome from the North, Bernward must have seen and used it. The bishop and his fellow pilgrims began their tour from the Leonine City (the Vatican), site of St. Peter's Basilica, before reaching the city itself by crossing the bridge—at least this is what an anonymous traveler from Einsiedeln says in a well-known ninth-century text [Wray 1949].

We do not know how Hadrian's bridge looked in the eleventh century, but we can reasonably imagine that it had been deprived of the pagan statues that were initially placed on pedestals in the axis of the bridge-piers [Galliazzo 1994–95, II, 1]. These slender supports were still visible, or had been reconstructed, at the time of Giulio Romano [D'Onofrio, fig. 91].

Moreover, the prominence of this bridge in the life of the Roman city was due to the fortified gate on the Tiber's left bank and to its battlements described by the Anonymous of Einsiedeln, in a word, to its military function. The gate came to be called the *Castellum Crescentii* after Otto III's aristocratic enemies [D'Onofrio, 47]. This detail could explain the aedicules on top of the bridge in the bronze door even though, as we shall see, their presence also derives from their symbolic potential.

Lastly, it should be mentioned that the fortified gate defending the Pons Aelius on the city side was renamed after the apostle of Rome as early the eighth century. The St. Peter's Gate was so important that it appears at the beginning of the Anonymous of Einsiedeln's description of the Aurelian walls. Nor does the author fail to mention a second gate located at the other end of the bridge on the side of the Leonine City that controlled access to the defensive passage built in front of Hadrian's mausoleum. This second gate, named St. Peter's Gate in Hadrianio, was also called Porta Aenea because of the two bronze door wings taken from the mausoleum, which remained in place until 1495 [D'Onofrio, 47]. It is worth mentioning—and this could be important for our iconographic inquiry—that even though the name is of common use, the gatehouse protecting the bridge over the Treibe, the river flowing at the base of Hildesheim's fortified walls, was also called St. Peter's Gate.

Let us now suppose that Bernward's bridge is indeed a reference to the Pons Aelius. The question would then be whether the bishop actually cites the bridge or whether he is merely inspired by it, as any architect looking for a monumental reference would be. In the syntactical logic of the bronze door, the viewer is expected to identify the bridge in panel 9, which does not imply that the viewer necessarily recognizes it as the Pons Aelius. (How many people actually traveled to Rome?) There are two plausible hypotheses.

The first is that reading and understanding the door relied in practice on the mediation of a learned explanation given to visitors by scholars, monks, or canons. I have often referred to the possibility of this kind of assistance, which I consider quite plausible.

However, and without being contradictory, we should note that Bernward—because he conceived his door as a plastic expression of the divine Word—aimed at a considerable autonomy of the visual utterance, one that unfolded through an equally considerable syntactic coherence. As such, the bridge had to refer clearly to the viewers' world, acquiring a historical identity. Consequently, it seems logical to first consider the contemporary culture of Hildesheim, rather than external sources, when explaining the cognitive mechanisms involved in understanding the architecture.

As the founding text of St. Michael's Church attests, Bernward's contribution to the construction-expansion of the Church of Christ, which he viewed as salvific, is mediated through his work as a founder and builder following in the footsteps of the great biblical figures, in particular Solomon, this great sinner, he says, who built the Temple of Jerusalem. In order to successfully carry out the urban and monu-

122. *Pirro Ligorio, drawing of a coin representing Hadrian's bridge, Naples, BN, ms. BXIII.*

mental development of his city of Hildesheim, Bernward drew inspiration from antique and medieval Roman architecture. Upon his return from Italy in 1001, he had the existing walls of the episcopal village extended and strengthened with large stones and protruding round towers [Kruse 1997, 111]. St. Michael's Abbey, as Bernward conceived it, shares some features with Roman Constantinian basilicas, and this inspiration goes as far as repeating very specific geometric ratios [Beseler and Roggenkamp 1954, 146–152]. Bernward also imitates, albeit in reduced format, one of ancient Rome's most prestigious political manifestos, the Trajan column, whose spiral narrative he adopts to illustrate Christ's public life. This column, placed behind the altar of the Holy Cross in the nave of St. Michael's Church, was used in the liturgy, especially during Processions of Flagellation [Gallistl 1990]. This is only one of the many Roman citations of the liturgy deployed by Bernward in Hildesheim [De Blaauw 2012]. Last, as we have seen, the bronze door itself is bound to recall Roman monumentality, such as the bronze doors of the Pantheon with their Constantinian and early Christian transformations; the wooden door of Santa Sabina, the only one that survives; the silver door of St. Peter's; or that of St. Paul Outside the Walls, both of which were replaced by Byzantine doors a little later during the eleventh century.

By inscribing these Roman images in his episcopal city, Bernward publicly testifies to the expansion of Christ's Church, a historical transference going from Jerusalem to Rome, then from Rome to his Saxon village, one of the last places where Latin Christianity spread. Recall that Hildesheim was founded as a Christian outpost in Carolingian times. Such a claim is commensurate with the *translatio imperii* of which the Ottonians, even more than the Carolingians, wished to associate with themselves politically because of their hold on Italy. There is therefore no reason, it seems to me, to discard the possibility that Bernward may have extended this system of architectural citation to the bronze door.

This approach, neglected for a time following the important work of Richard Krautheimer [1942] and Gunther Bandmann [1951] on the significance of architecture in images, resonates with more recent studies, such as those of Bernhard Schütz [1994] or Jennifer Kingsley [2014] on the references to St. Michael's Church and its liturgy in the illuminations of Bernward's Gospel Book. Following on from this work, I will argue that the door was not an isolated phenomenon but was inscribed in a network of ideological motifs, building programs, toponyms, and signifying images that participated in its understanding. The architecture represented there, supported by these local focal points of memory, resonated with the great architectural tradition of Roman Christianity.

Let us return now to our iconographic analysis, setting aside for the moment the possibility of a reference to the Pons Aelius, as well as the related question of the discursive function of such an identification. It is a bridge, then, that arises behind Mary's house, while at the same time being associated with it. This bridge is composed of arches structurally similar to the great arch linking Mary and Gabriel. It is inhabited, if the aedicules it supports are indeed houses. On top of the pillars and roofs there are little balls arranged in a triangle. It cannot be ignored that they may be conventional—they also appear on the roofs of buildings depicted on Bernward's bronze column—but they also recall the symbolical orbs that evoke domination over the world, in particular those surmounted by a cross that served as an attribute of imperial power for the Ottonians [Schramm 1958]. The number and arrangement of these orbs is intriguing, especially since they appear on the turret behind Gabriel. Last, it should be noted that the bridge is positioned against the left side of the panel, facing panel 8; its placement in height puts it at the same level as the hand of God when he answered Abel with the foundation of the City of God. That promise was realized by the Incarnation that takes place in panel 9 (fig. 120).

Let us now bring together all these elements of Mary's house. The word for house in classical Latin is *domus*, a term that also means family, inasmuch as the shared home is emblematic of the persons occupying it. This meaning would be broadened in the Middle Ages, expanding to also cover the idea of Mother House for religious communities and of dynasty for aristocratic lineages. It is even used in Luke's Gospel to evoke the ancestry of Joseph, Mary's spouse, and consequently that of Christ, according to Hebrew law: "Ad virginem disponsatam viro cui nomen erat Joseph de domo David [betrothed to a man whose name was Joseph from the house of David]" (Luke 1:26–27).

The line of Christ's royal descent is quoted twice in the Bible. The Gospel of Mathew, the first of the Gospels according to the biblical canon, opens with an enumeration of Jesus's ancestors going back to Abraham, which exegetes call a natural genealogy (or family genealogy): "The book of the generation [*generatione*] of Jesus Christ, the son of David, the son of Abraham. Abraham begot Isaac. And Isaac begot Jacob. And Jacob begot Judas and his brethren [. . .] Jesse begot David the king. And David the king begot Solomon, of her that had been the wife of Urias

[. . .]" the list continues until "And Jacob begot Joseph the husband of Mary, of whom was born Jesus, who is called Christ" (Matt. 1:1–17). In the image, this genealogy is represented by the House of Mary.

The second list of Christ's ancestors appears in the Gospel of Luke. It is longer than the previous one but also more spiritual and universal because it goes back as far back as Seth, Adam, but also God, since Adam is called "son of God" (Luke 23:38). Theologians consider it a "divine genealogy." I suggest that it is represented by the bridge placed behind and in contact with Mary's house, as many stages of a filiation that is no longer familial but spiritual, and which is identified with the history of the City of God founded by Abel. The choice of a bridge to represent this genealogy is not surprising, since it connects two sides, in this case the two wings of the bronze door, Abel and Christ, the Old and the New Testament. As for the possible choice of the Pons Aelius as an architectural reference, it would have the merit of calling attention to the passage between life and death. Besides the fact that Bernward knew it as the major bridge of Christian Rome, the bridge connects the city of the dead—the Leonine City, now the Vatican and its necropolis containing the tombs of the most important Christian martyrs, among them St. Peter—and the city of the living—the pontifical Rome situated on the Tiber's opposite shore, on the side of the Lateran, the geographic heart of Latin Christendom.

In any event, this opening on life through the Church of Christ, independent of the precise identification of the bridge, likely lies at the origin of the panel's general infrastructure.

In the *City of God*, Augustine actually unifies Christ's two genealogies within a single system of world history that distinguishes between the City of Man, namely Greco-Roman history to which he devotes the first eleven books, and the City of God, the subject of the last eleven books. Augustine concludes the history of this City of God, which merges with the biblical narrative, with a summary of its division in five acts:

> The City of God of which we speak is that to which the Scriptures bear witness: the Scriptures which, excelling all the writings of all the nations in their divine authority, have brought under their sway every kind of human genius, not by a chance motion of the soul, but clearly by the supreme disposition of providence. (*De civitate Dei*, Book XI, 1, 449)

> The first "day" is the first age, extending from Adam to the Flood; the second extends from the Flood to Abraham. . . . From Abraham down to the coming of Christ there are, as the evangelist Matthew reckons it, three ages, in each of which are listed fourteen generations: one age extending from Abraham to David, the second from David to the exile in Babylon, and the third from the exile to the nativity of Christ in the flesh. Thus, there are five ages in all. The sixth age is now in being. . . . After this age, God will rest, as on the seventh day, and He will give us, who will be that seventh day, rest in Himself. (Book XXII, 30, 1182)

As the reader may have observed, the bridge consists of four arches (as many as the number of generations between the end of Adam's epoch and the coming of Christ), leading to a fifth archway, precisely the one under which Christ arrives, whereas a sixth archway begins on the panel's right side. Although in this case we are penalized by the lacunae in the image's right side, we can hypothesize that the two arches structurally connected to the bridge are their signifying continuation on the background of the image and that they represent the stages of a topological history of the City of God.

The two rudimentary aedicules on the bridge and the one topping the tower placed behind Gabriel have a roof covered with tiles topped by an orb; they are framed by ornamental pillars and have frontal bays (fig. 123). They differ in that the roof of the bridge's second aedicule is retracted to make room for chisel marks (fig. 121), perhaps underscoring the time of the Babylonian captivity. In addition, the upper part of Gabriel's tower is an architectural combination of the two previous constructions, with tiles carefully placed in staggered rows and inscribed in a strict triangle. Its walls are vertical, higher, and more recessed due to the transformation of the uneven bay of the previous buildings into a great dual-arched opening. The impression of lightness given by the construction is enhanced by the visual relationship established between the twin bays and the two wings of the angel that seem to both reveal it and carry it.

The twin bays will reappear on the right wing on three occasions and under very specific narrative conditions since it will be systematically associated with a cross. In the panel under scrutiny, it is the archangel's cross-staff; in panel 12 it is a cross placed on the orb topping Solomon's temple; in panel 15, a cross dominates the Holy Sepulcher; in the last panel it is the cross-staff of Christ who reopens access to the Garden of Eden (cf. fig. 118, 156, and 185). In

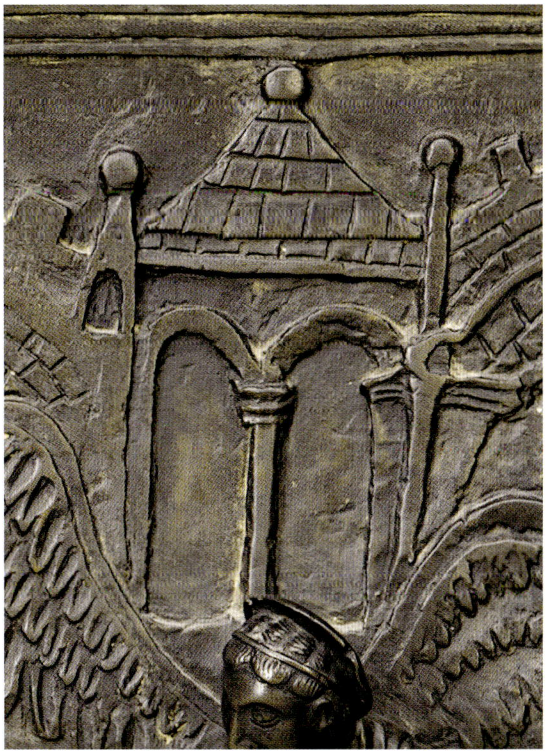

123

addition, it should be noted that the position of the cross in the panels changes according to the panel's height/level in the wing: it ends by encroaching on the edge of the frame in panel 16. We shall discuss all these issues later.

To understand the connection between the cross and the twin openings, I suggest that we consider the latter as meaningful shapes, as we did with Mary's house and the bridge. In this instance, since they are joined together, the twin bays constitute one and the same architectural entity; although being double, they are One, the simple and effective expression of two natures, human and divine, unified in Christ's person. As for the capitaled column on which the arches rest, it is the element that actualizes this unification. It represents axiality and will reappear all along the right wing, in particular when placed perpendicular to Mary's womb in the Nativity scene in the following panel (cf. fig. 127). It thus functions as the geometric paradigm of a new divine dynamic within shapes, an integrative dynamic (centripetal and vertical) and no longer an emancipatory one (centrifugal and diagonal) as was the case with the first Creation. We shall return to this matter later.

Placed under the light of the Incarnation, Gabriel's tower takes on a new relief. It is very similar in format and structure to the tower that gives access to the Garden of Eden in panel 16, in whose axis it is perfectly aligned within the right wing (cf. fig. 187). The vertical connection between the two buildings can only arise from a prophetic announcement, thus defining them both as places of transition (cf. fig. 1). Unadorned and fragile, the tower in panel 9 certainly appears much simpler than the Edenic door: it lacks its flat and bright sections, its thick pillars, its smooth roof, polished and brilliant like precious metal. Nothing can rival the beauty and monumentality of the entrance to Eden, but there is no reason why its humble human precedent should not be depicted in panel 9. In all likelihood, the twin structure "lifted" by the angel's wings represents the place where Christ comes into the world in his double nature; that is, Mary's womb inseminated by the Spirit of God. It announces the place where Christ and Christians after him will be born again in their double nature, divine and human, this other womb that is the body of Christ instituted in the Church, to which we will return at length.

For the time being, let us only note that this transitional place of birth is no longer disfigured by the chisel marks of evil, unlike the representation of Mary' house on the left of the panel. The Holy Spirit has purified the virginal womb, so that when Christ sacrifices himself in panel 13, he will literally take on himself a sin, which is foreign to him.

The representation of the Marian womb under the form of a circular architectural shape is part of a vast tradition of early Christian origin associating the anastasis, Christ's rebirth after his death, to his first birth in the Virgin's body. Life and death are linked in a drama centered on places of passage. Beside Mary's womb, this analogical series includes the Rotunda of the Holy Sepulcher, which marks the Resurrection, and the baptisteries where humanity is purified by a sacrament that is both the reception of the Holy Spirit and the admission to an ecclesial body through which rebirth to eternal life takes place. All these stages are represented in the right wing. This tradition makes the Virgin, the Savior's mother, a *mater viventium*, that is, a mother Church of the children she shelters and to whom she opens the way to eternity.

The first stage of this return journey is perhaps represented by the third tower of panel 9, the one on the image's right side, which might correspond to the world's "modern" history that continues up to the viewers' time (fig. 124). Much damaged, the shape of this tower is like the others and connected to Mary's tower through a large beveled pilaster laying against it but heterogeneous to the structure on which the arch, made with thick blocks, rests. In the lower part of

123. *Panel 9, aedicule above Gabriel.*

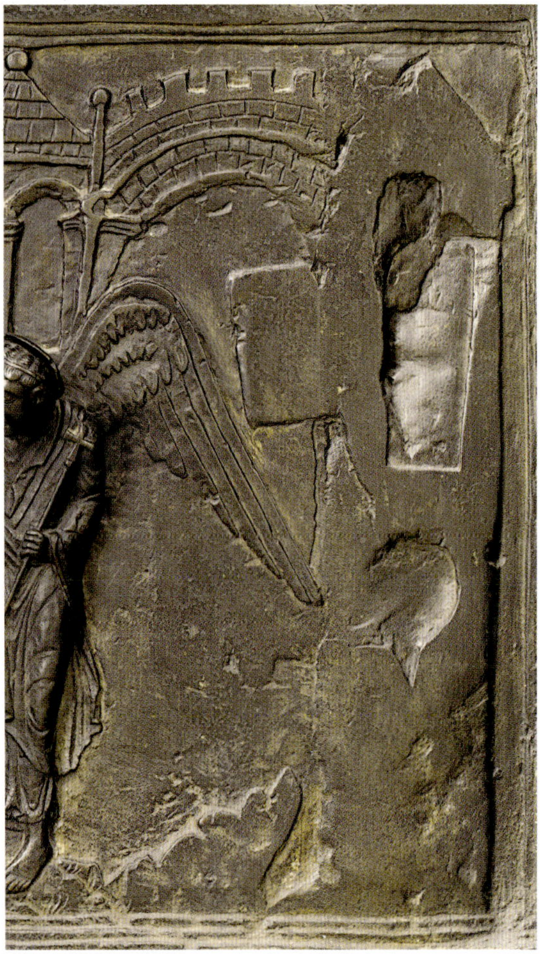

124

the tower, a circular bay can be discerned, an oculus characteristic of human constructions. The door to the earthly world built by Adam in panel 4 had one, on the first floor (cf. fig. 81). In the upper part of the tower, we can make out the residual tracing of a rectangular bay, which will be found again, accessible this time, at the bottom of the door to the Garden of Eden in panel 16 (cf. fig. 187). Its deteriorated state prevents us from continuing the analysis, but I believe that this tower must be a proto-figuration of the Ecclesia, the first stage or synthetic announcement of the succession of metaphorical and substantial transformations that will affect the City of God in the right wing, an echo of the metamorphic and substantial transformation of the Tree of Life in the left wing.

124. *Panel 9, right-hand portion of panel.*

125. *Panel 9, Gabriel.*

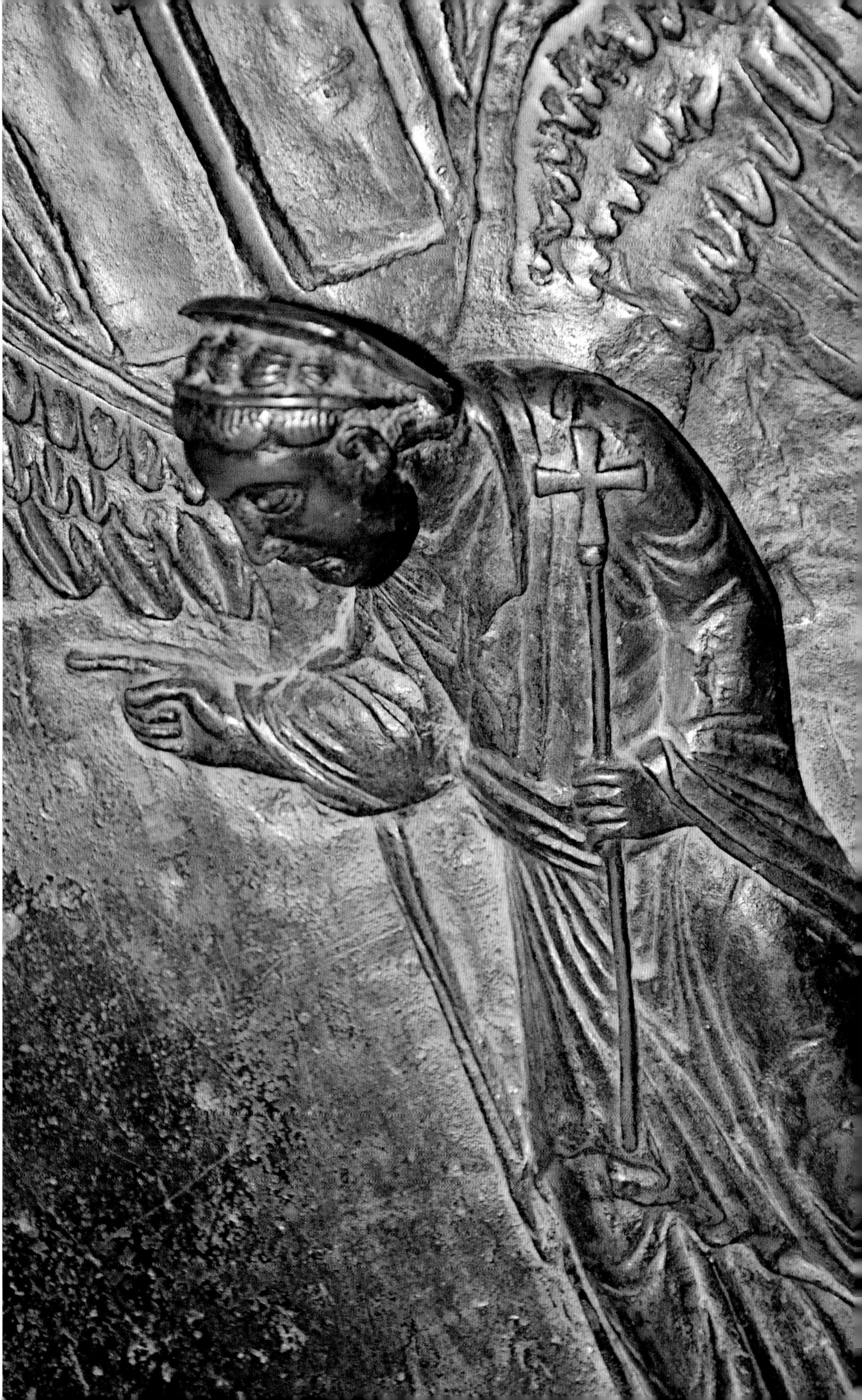

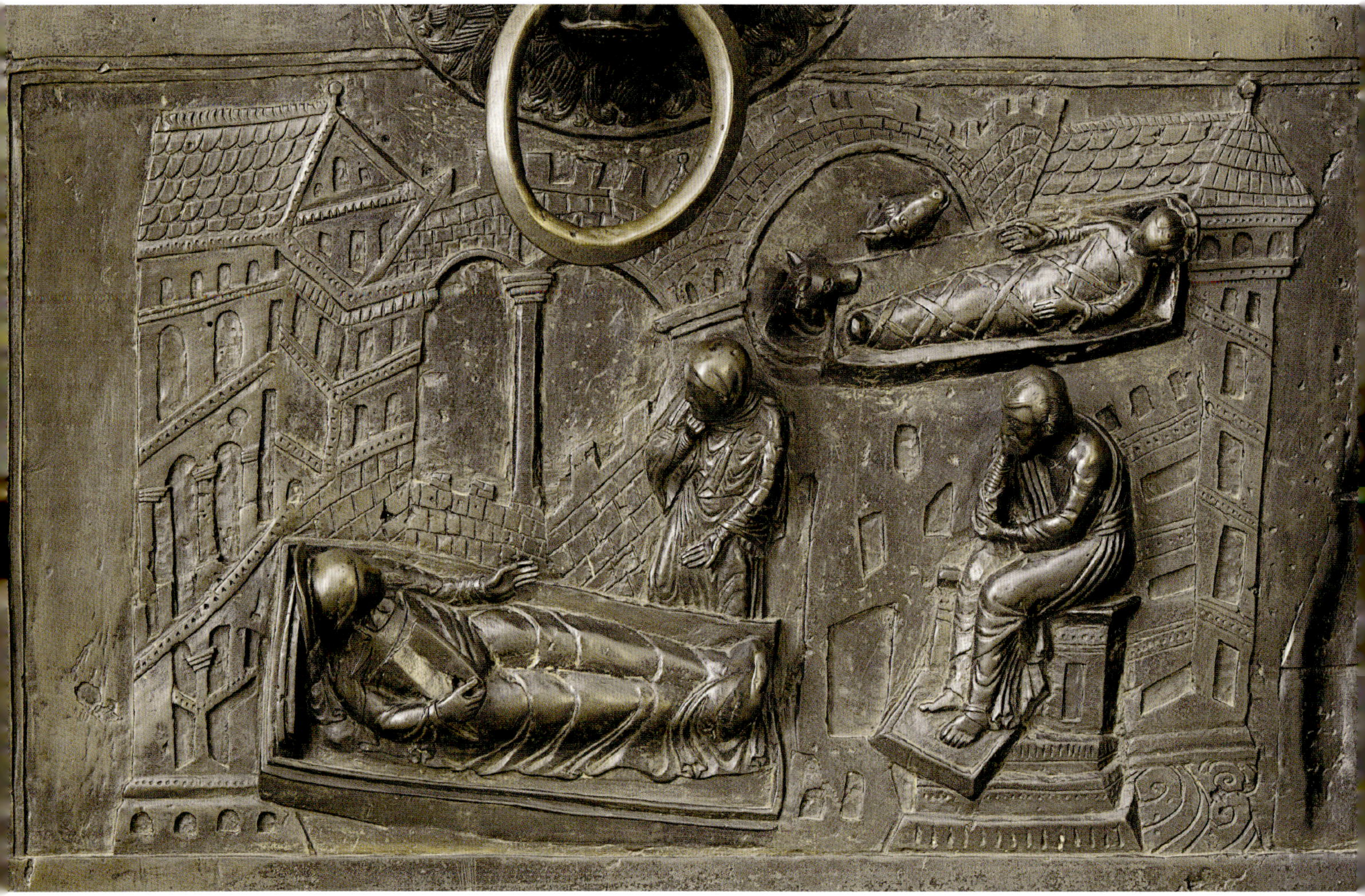

Panel **10**

CONVERSION

The tenth panel of the bronze door represents the Nativity (fig. 126). It follows immediately after the Annunciation with which it is paired, like the two episodes of Cain and Abel in the left wing (cf. fig. 1).

The architecture in the image is concentrated into a compact block clearly separated from the panel's lateral frame. Within this setting, two monumental buildings face each other. Linked together by a series of crenellated arches, both have five stories, a peaked roof, and a triangular pediment. Yet the first impression of architectural orderliness disappears as soon as the gaze tries to understand the organization of its details, a mix of hollow and solid spaces, attempts at perspectival effects, and incomprehensible architectural connections. In addition, a section of the panel's background, gouged by distorted and enigmatic quadrilateral forms, appears to have been botched even though there is no evidence of any problem in molding or casting. It is equally unlikely that this was a clumsy mistake on the part of the wax modeler, especially since the artisan was able to produce, on an even surface, extraordinary finishing touches to the building on the left: regular bays and finely designed columns with their bases and capitals are clearly visible. In analyzing this image, we have to consider the deliberately allusive initial design, playing on both the geometric deformation and the architecture's extreme precision. For the time being, let us keep in mind that panel 10 gives a double impression of order and disorder, revealing a perceptible tension between the general and the particular, structure and detail.

Four human figures and two animals are depicted in the image. To the right, a man sits on a high seat; his feet rest on a *scabellum* (stool) and he lifts a hand to his cheek. This is Joseph, represented, following tradition, as bearded, calling attention to his mature age. His presence next to the Virgin and the infant Jesus is stated in the Bible:

126. *Panel 10.*

> Joseph also went up from Galilee, out of the city of Nazareth into Judea, to the city of David, which is called Bethlehem: because he was of the house and family of David, to be enrolled with Mary his espoused wife, who was with child. And it came to pass, that when they were there, her days were accomplished, that she should be delivered. And she brought forth her firstborn son, and wrapped him up in swaddling clothes, and laid him in a manger [*praesepio*], because there was no room for them in the inn. (Luke 2:4–7)

The space does not have the rusticity of a stable, but the infant Jesus, wrapped in swaddling clothes, is clearly shown in a manger. Veiled and haloed as in the previous panel, Mary is represented at some distance from her child. She is lying on a rectangular bed in a weary posture particularly favored by the iconographic tradition of Byzantine origin that was adopted by the Carolingians in the ninth century. The coming of the Savior she carries has been announced in the writings of the Old Testament, as attested by the open book she holds for the viewers to see. Placed on the Virgin's belly, it is also a metaphor for the divine infant to come: he will subsume the messianic prophecy by realizing it as incarnated Word.

Bernward demonstrates remarkable originality in the arrangement of his models and in the inventiveness of his adaptations. Jesus is not only depicted alone and far away from his mother, he seems excluded from the panel's central scene because the other characters in the image turn their backs to him or, at least, do not have any visual contact with him. In addition, no angel or shepherd attends the newborn infant. This absence is surprising, since the theme of the birth's celebration, whether it be the spreading of the Good News or the adoration of the Child, appears very often in Ottonian images—Bernward himself depicts it in the more conventional illustration of his own Gospel Book (Hildesheim Dom Bibl., DS 18, f 18).

The panel shows neither adoration nor celebration, rather it focuses on a marginal historical episode magnified by the bishop for the purposes of his visual discourse. A veiled woman stands in the center of the panel. She holds a hand to her face, extending her other hand toward the Virgin lying in bed. In early Christian Eastern iconography, this woman is known as Zelomi/Salome. She is found in Byzantine and Carolingian images but, to the best of my knowledge, she does not appear in Ottonian art [LCI/*Geburt Christi*]. No biblical passage mentions a woman at Mary's side in the Nativity scene, nor is there any biblical evidence for the presence of a donkey with a prominent snout or a horned ox, both placed next to the infant Jesus in the panel's upper section. The source of these figures is apocryphal.

Few religious scenes have given rise to a greater proliferation of variations and picturesque details than the Nativity. The source of this creative freedom lies in the very brevity of the Gospels, which were not quite eloquent enough about the birth of Christ for popular taste. As mentioned above, Luke briefly describes the context; Mark and John make no reference to it; Matthew recounts the angel's apparition to Joseph (Matt. 1:20–23), and reports that the infant Jesus was born in Bethlehem (Matt. 2:1). Aiming to fill this silence, apocryphal narratives began to appear from the second century onward, especially in the Middle East. The Proto-Gospel of James is among these texts. Despite its exclusion from the canonical corpus, it influenced early Christian and Byzantine iconography. It is the first text to mention the presence of a midwife, Salome, next to the Virgin [Pérez-Higuera, 14–15]. However, it is another apocryphal text that will leave its mark on the West, an eighth- or ninth-century compilation called the Gospel of the Pseudo-Matthew. This text reorganizes and completes previous legends narrating the youth of Mary and Jesus; it tells of the donkey and the ox as well as the story of Salome, taken from James's Proto-Gospel. In addition to its influence on religious iconography, several literary adaptations attest to its importance in early medieval Germanic culture, such as that of Paschasius Radbertus in the ninth century, or that of the poet Hrosvitha of Gandersheim, who composed a versified transposition in the 950s.

The narrative of the Pseudo-Matthew is interwoven with the supernatural and abounds in miracles. It begins by telling the story of the Virgin's parents, Anne and Joachim. This is followed by Mary's childhood, as well as the circumstances of her marriage to the elderly Joseph. Setting aside all the fanciful details that came to enrich the iconographic tradition, what is most striking in the text is the development of the evangelical episode of Joseph's dream. In the Bible, Joseph doubts Mary's virginity and considers repudiating her when an angel appears to him in a dream, announcing that the child to be born is the son of the Holy Spirit (Matt. 1:20–25). In the Pseudo-Matthew, Joseph's doubt takes on a more dramatic turn, the traces of which can be found in liturgical theater. His initial disbelief is underscored by the priests and the people of Nazareth, who believed that spouses should be considered as such only if validated by probatory rituals (ch. XII). Hrostvita gives a lyrical version of this passage: "Nor is there any need to convey in verse / the great pain and immense grief of Joseph's heart; / for no reason he was tormented deep in his heart / when he learned by chance that such a girl was pregnant" (*Historia nativitatis laudabilisque conversationis intactae dei genitricis,* v. 531–534, *Opera Omnia*, W. Berschin ed., Monachii et Lipsia, 2001, 22, author's translation).

The place given to doubt in this popular tradition reflects an underlying mystery the emotional power of which focuses less on the Incarnation, a concept difficult to grasp, and more on the miracle of a virginal motherhood, leading to faith in the divine filiation of the child and the sanctity of the mother. To believe in Christ is first to recognize him as the son of God, as the second act of faith of the Credo affirms: "We believe in one Lord, Jesus Christ, the only Son of God." To doubt it means excluding oneself from the Gospel and refusing to be part of the chosen ones.

Doubt reappears in the next chapter of the Pseudo-Matthew, this time embodied by Salome, the Jewish midwife from Bethlehem, who refuses to believe the assertion about Mary's virginity. In this episode, the skeptical Salome asks Mary for permission to verify her virginity. The gesture is implied, but it subtly refers to the hymen's condition. As soon as the examination is over, Salome's hand withers, resulting in intense pain. In her acute suffering, the midwife complains saying she has "always feared the Lord," and has always done her utmost to do good

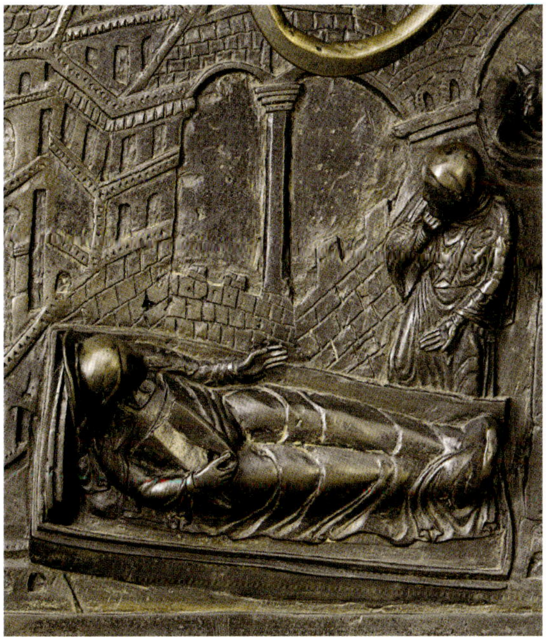

127

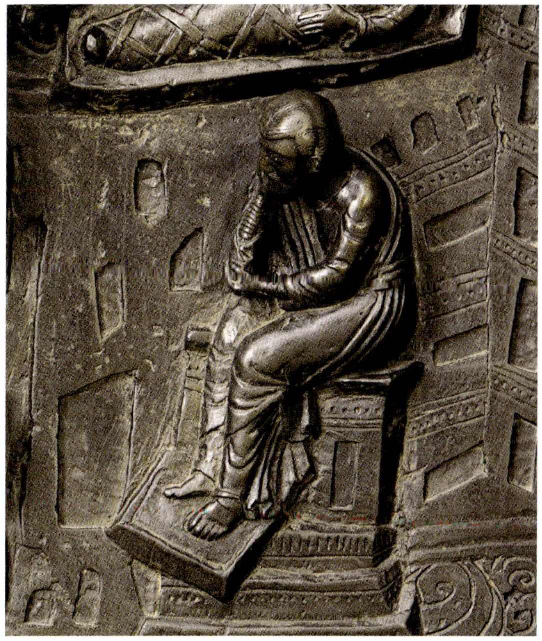

128

to others. When she acknowledges having wrongly doubted Mary's virginity, an angel appears inviting her to approach the infant, worship him, and touch his swaddling clothes. A second miracle takes place: her hand is healed.

In the image under scrutiny, Salome lifts a closed fist to her chin, a gesture initiated by Cain in panel 8; Mary repeats it, identically, in panel 14 at the foot of the cross (fig. 127). This gesture belongs to a very long iconographic tradition going back to early Christian times. The midwife shows her suffering by holding her wounded hand with her able one, a posture that the Carolingian artists from Metz gradually modified in the ninth century until it assumed the gesture on the bronze door [Toubert 1966, 329–333].

In panel 10, Salome's wounded hand hangs motionless before her, palm visible, particularly telling evidence of the pain tormenting her. However, it should be noted that this hand also interacts with Mary. It is held out along the axis of the Virgin's womb, while at the same time nodding to Salome's own womb, since it is placed by the lower part of the midwife's abdomen. Thus, the wounded hand summarizes and explains the narrative sequence: if Salome doubts Mary's virginity, it is first of all because she knows the natural law inscribed in her own body.

The insistence of the iconographic system on the sacrilegious dimension of Salome's doubt takes us back, by an analogy of great immediacy, to Cain's and Abel's symmetrical offerings in panel 7. It is even possible that the wish to establish this typological relationship may have contributed to the unusual development of the story of the two brothers and to the choice, equally unusual for Ottonian culture, to represent Salome at the panel's center.

On the right, Joseph sits on a high seat and gazes at the scene without intervening (fig. 128). He rests his cheek on the palm of his hand, holding his elbow with his left hand as if to support his arm. A reading conditioned by centuries of iconography of the Holy Family could lead one to believe that the character is meditating on the mystery of the infant Jesus's birth but that is not the case. The figure of Joseph is quite insignificant until the late fourteenth century when monks and clerics such as Bernardino da Siena or Jean Gerson, in order to support the establishment of a model Christian family, brought Joseph to the forefront of Christian devotion and iconography. It was not until 1479 that Pope Sixtus IV established a St. Joseph's feast day [Villasenor Black 2006, 22–24; Vezin 1950, 40]. Ancient iconography therefore grants little space to this character, and the Nativity scenes represent him in a marginal position and overwhelmed with doubt [Pérez-Higuera, 82; LCI, *Geburt Christi*].

Joseph is not very different in the bronze panel. His eyes open—the opposite would have meant that he was dreaming—he appears in the conventional position of meditative affliction [Garnier 1982–89 II, 120]. As he has no source of distress other than the weight of the shame overwhelming him, he represents yet another version of the lack of faith in Mary's virginity. Unlike Salome, whose miraculously healed hand functions as a sign of conversion, nothing in Joseph's behavior indicates that he has sought the path to Revelation. In addition, his position on an elevated

127. *Panel 10, Mary and Salome.*

128. *Panel 10, Joseph.*

seat isolates him from the space where the Virgin admits the midwife. The two figures of Salome and Joseph are not redundant but complementary in that they reveal the evolution of the state of consciousness of two members of the People of the Synagogue amid the messianic accomplishment.

The differentiation in the placement of the two figures is underscored by the relation they have with the architectural elements (fig. 126). In the panel's visual configuration, Joseph is dominated by the mass of the infant in swaddling clothes, stretched along the heavy stone manger. The pained posture of his stooped shoulders highlights the impression of his being crushed. As for Salome, she is placed under the base of the two crenellated arches connecting her on one side to the cradle, and on the other to the column placed on the axis of Mary's womb. Salome and Joseph are both dominated by the architecture, but in Joseph's case it appears as a burden immobilizing him—a sign of his blindness about Jesus's divine nature—whereas Salome, physically in touch with the elements surrounding her, and because of the power of the miracle that touched her, is enjoined to contemplate the truth.

The conversion process represented in panel 10 thus enfolds from right to left, and involves both the figures and the architecture surrounding them.

Until the eighth century, Western clerics distinguished between an *Ecclesia ex circumcisione* and an *Ecclesia ex gentibus* as a dual source, Hebrew and pagan, of the universal community of God's people [Thérel 1965, 150]. This vision was modified at the beginning of the Carolingian epoch when two feminine allegories representing *Ecclesia* and *Synagoga* were introduced into Christian treatises and images. The two religions became distinguished not so much by the differences opposing them in the present world (we must wait for the time of the crusades for that) but by their succession in history. As Wolfgang Seifert (in chapters 1 and 2) explains in his fine work, the two figures of the Church and the Synagogue are necessarily consistent for the simple fact of the existence of a typological relationship between the Old and the New Testament. At the same time, they are quite different. Whereas salvation could not be found in the Torah, because the Old Covenant was imposed as a yoke on the sinful Hebrews, it became possible with the Gospels, the New Covenant accepted by faith and lived in newfound freedom.

This historical shift in perspective constitutes the central theme of panel 10, as the metamorphic configuration of the architecture universalizes the individual conversion process incarnated by Joseph and Salome.

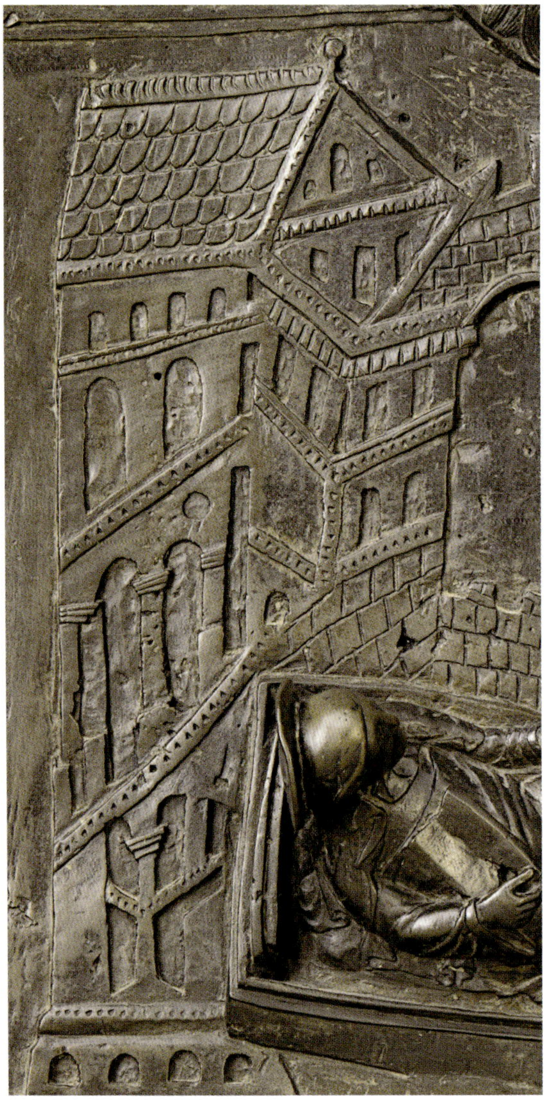

129

129. *Panel 10, left-hand building.*

The two buildings on either side of the panel are symmetrically positioned because of their basilica-type shape, their height, and the materials used in their construction. It should be noted that each of the levels of these buildings is outlined by a horizontal band punctuated by chisel marks. The motif of the small, incised triangle does not have a different meaning than before; this is supported by the fact that there is no trace of it in the construction levels above the Crucifixion panel. These two buildings therefore decidedly belong to the material world and are bearers of sin.

The building on the right behind Joseph is dominated by a tiled roof (fig. 130). The roof and the story immediately below it are represented in flattened perspective. Although seen in profile, they are pushed forward as if to present a frontal view. Both the façade and the body of the other five stories, however, are arranged diagonally, thus creating a visual impression

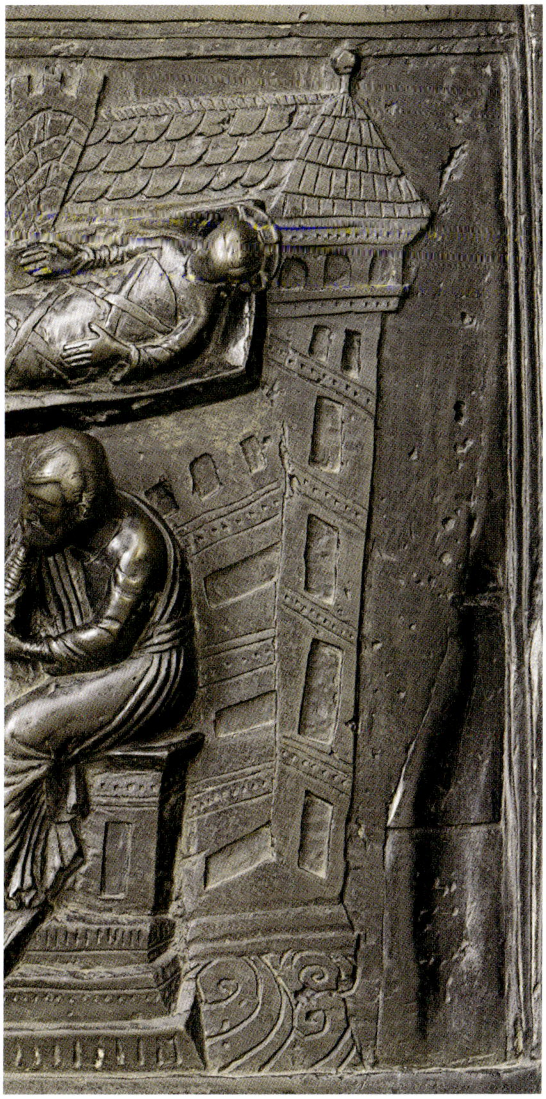

130. *Panel 10, right-hand building.*

of depth. To depict this, Bernward used a technique inherited from classical antiquity that historians call herringbone perspective: the vanishing lines, somewhat parallel, do not converge on a vanishing point but rather on a central vertical axis.

The architecture behind the Virgin consists of two distinct constructions and is much more complex (fig. 129). Parallel to the panel frame rises a first building, a tall quadrangular construction surmounted by a tile roof. Its façade, showing a pediment with openings, is represented in flattened perspective, but its mass is extended in a linear perspective which, although approximate, is much more sophisticated. Bernward may have conceptualized this device from reading Vitruvius's definition of *scenographia* (*De Architectura,* Book I, 2, 2), which explains the seeming distortion of a building presented from different angles.

Above the Marian bed and in front of the basilica-type building is a second construction. It is represented in a herringbone perspective, and its structural autonomy is shown by the discontinuity of its stories compared to those of the basilica-type building, as well as by a vertical hollowing of matter separating it from the adjoining building (cf. fig. 131). This construction consists of two walls, or rather, of two narrow buildings placed at right angles; they are pierced by windows and emphasized in the upper part by a small overhang covered with parallel tiles. This tile overhang calls attention to a large, striated band under the pediment, so that while the overhang is clearly independent of the nave, the band is associated with the building's façade, with which it forms an inner courtyard enclosed on three sides. The courtyard's fourth side is not represented, and the freed space is filled with the improbable base of a masonry arch.

This incongruous arch is the first of a series of four large crenellated arches whose size and orientation change in the panel's layout resulting in their resembling sections of walls, particularly the one in circular shape around the manger and resting against the large building on the right (fig. 132).

What do these architectural elements represent?

The symbolic association between the form of a building and its function is certainly as old as architectural art itself. It was implemented by Christians from the earliest centuries of their history [Armstrong 1974]; we have already identified its use in the visual discourse of the bronze door in the scenes of the expulsion from Eden and of the Annunciation (cf. fig. 72 and 115). The differences in elevation and architectural language between the two buildings of panel 10 are thus organized in a dialectic relation. Each one of these terms must now be addressed.

The first four stories of the building situated behind Joseph are more or less the same height, and

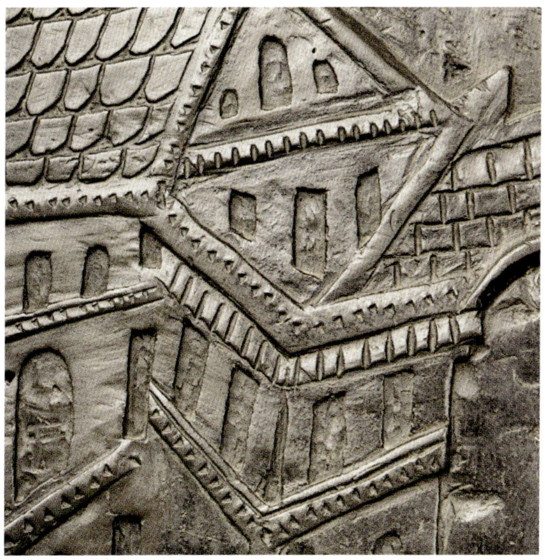

131. *Panel 10, avant-corps of left-hand building.*

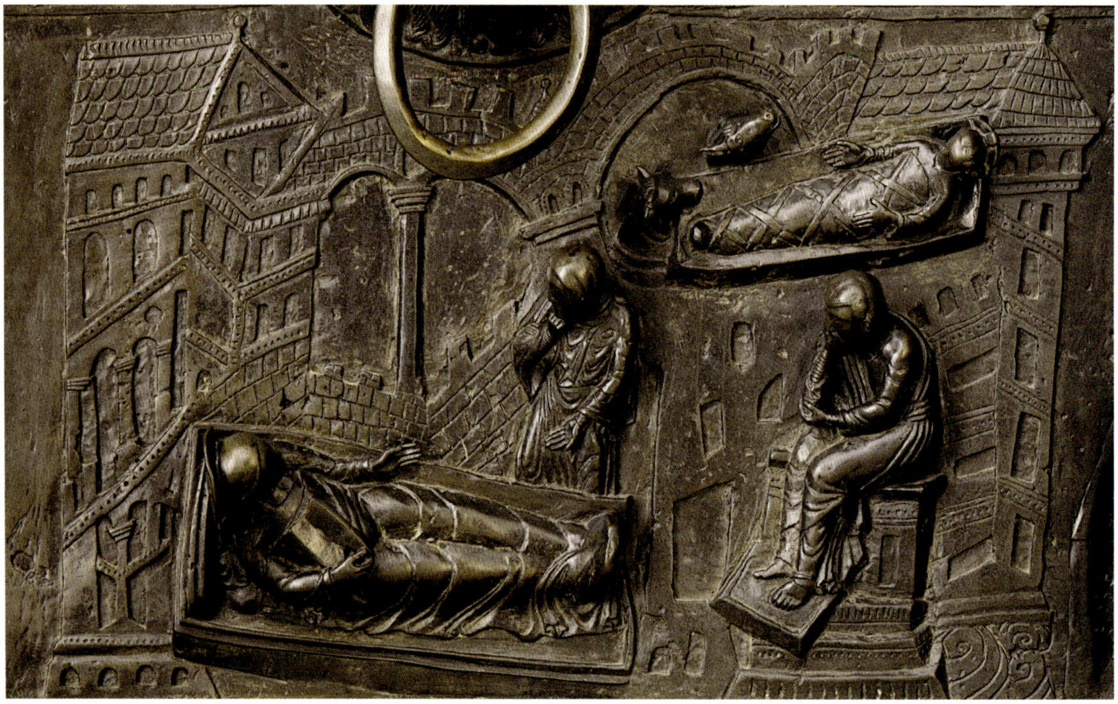

132

each one has a large quadrangular opening. The fifth and sixth stories are smaller and pierced by two and three openings. There are three more bays on the building's side, but only on the fourth story, the three lower stories showing merely an indefinite hollowing of matter. In fact, the remaining part of the building nave dissolves into the background, behind the figures of Jesus and Joseph. A structural discordance adds to this asymmetry. The elevation levels of the nave do not correspond to those of the façade, as if some sort of clumsiness had imposed its own dysfunction on the general arrangement. Realized with care but visibly imperfect, the simplicity of the building on the right corresponds to its very traditional herringbone perspective, appearing as humble as the stone block on which it stands.

This building's configuration does not recall any known construction in the bronze door. It is neither a tower, nor a door, nor an urban or palatial wall; no visual element suggests any resemblance to a religious edifice. Perhaps the bishop was inspired by early Christian paintings or mosaics, in which case he may have imitated tall basilicas, while simplifying them and eliminating their monumental door. Another hypothesis is that he remembered the big tenement buildings (*insulae*) he had seen in Italy and of which there are still traces in contemporary Rome: made of bricks, their elevation could easily support six floors.

The building behind the Virgin on the panel's left side differs considerably from the previous one. We have already seen that the perspective was more sophisticated and that it was associated with a projecting structure. The elaborate craftsmanship of its representation finds its counterpart in the architectural vocabulary employed. The masonry base sets the tone for the whole building, just like the stone block does for the building on the right: this structure displays a strong individualization of elevation levels, an ample use of arches, openings, columns, and ornamental elements.

On the building's pediment, the semicircular arched bays form a trio. This motif, known since antiquity, was widely used by Christians because of its Trinitarian reference. Immediately below, three more rectangular bays mirror the bays above: they are similar to those of the building on the right and of the projecting structure.

The building's nave consists of four stories the height of which decreases from the ground up, all the bays being semicircular. A series of four bays can be seen under the roof. Below, there are two more important semicircular arched openings, pierced into the wall, without any support, which suggests that the building has a slanted roof. At the lower level, there are again two bays with oculi, but they are higher than the previous ones and framed by columns with molded capitals; they evoke the regular scansion of an arcade in a nave, at ground level.

Bernward's architectural expertise is demonstrated by the precision of a language that differentiates and hierarchizes the levels of the edifice's elevation. Certain parts of the building are represented just as they

132. *Panel 10.*

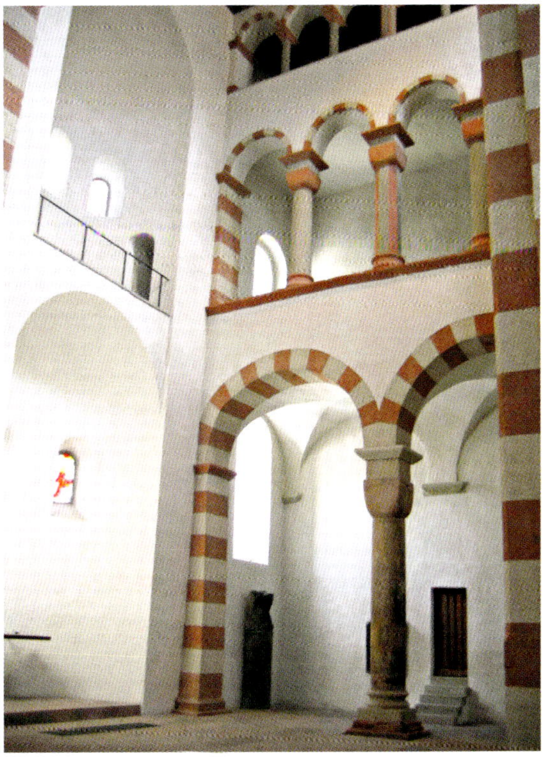

133

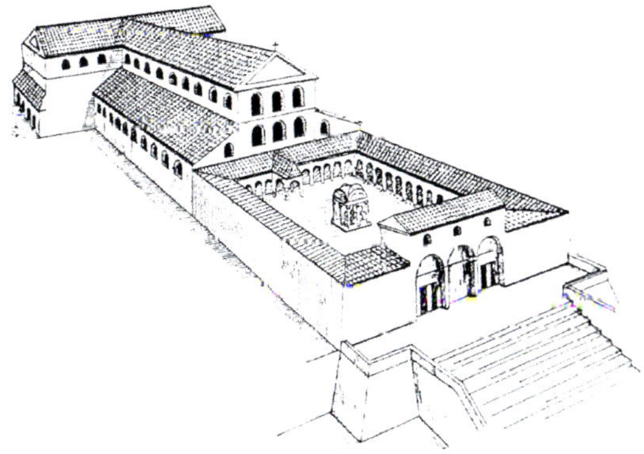

134

are perceived from outside the building, whereas others are shown in cross-section. The two visions merge in a synthetic representation, familiar to medieval artists for whom the exterior of an artifact should reveal its internal organization.

At the building's lower level, just above its base pierced by niches that we shall leave aside for the moment, there are some irregular forms hollowed into the bronze. In the middle, one can make out a stylized form topped by a capital, suggestive of both a tree and a cross, from which emerge two vault bases. It could be a column or a supporting pier and the level itself could be identified as a space for supporting structures, or in clearer terms, as a crypt.

To sum up, with its projecting body creating a courtyard and functioning as an atrium, with its hierarchized elevation, its columns with capitals, its semicircular arched openings, its pediment and its crypt, the building displays traits characteristic of Christian basilicas (fig. 134).

Could this identification be carried even further, as we did with the previous architectural forms? We can at least try, keeping in mind two important things. First, that early medieval representations are not naturalistic (mimetic), even though they are made to look realistic (referring to the world as it is). Beyond cultural conventions such as perspective and scale, the architectural representation differs from perceptible reality in order to become intelligible. We will also be attentive to the fact that in images an archeological citation has meaning only if it is articulated within a discourse to which it contributes.

As with the bridge in panel 8, the potential sources for the building behind the Virgin can be of only two kinds: contemporary or Roman. Ottonian edifices, beyond their specificity, belong to an averred filiation with Constantinian basilicas, which does not simplify things (fig. 133). Insofar as the edifice is associated with the Virgin, it is quite natural to connect it with the Constantinian Church of the Nativity in Bethlehem, or even with the first great Western Marian basilica of Santa Maria Maggiore in Rome, which enshrined the prestigious relic of Christ's cradle. Artists took such care in representing biblical topography nominally that the explicit evocation of these sanctuaries is not rare in images [Krautheimer 1942; Underwood 1950]. Furthermore, we should remember that Bernward was profoundly inspired by Roman liturgy for his Saxon town [De Blaauw 2012; Nees].

In this instance, the edifice displays some characteristics that allow for it to be compared with St. Michael of Hildesheim (fig. 135). The church is covered with a wooden roof frame, not with the vaults that became popular in the eleventh century. At the transept level, therefore quite close to the crypt, its elevation shows three levels of semicircular arched openings. This massive crypt, whose altar is dedicated to the Virgin, is on the same level as the nave, under the raised western floor. There is an intriguing detail, perhaps suggestive of an architectural citation: between the crypt and the arcade in the building in panel 10, a little bay appears along the demarcation line, which, in St. Michael, could be the door connecting the crypt and the nave.

Whatever the case, as in panel 9, a new referential system emerges here, bringing the historia up to the present time, into the space of the viewers' lives.

In the panel, the crypt is positioned in such a

133. *St. Michael's of Hildesheim, eastern transept.*

134. *Reproduction of the Early Christian St. Peter's Basilica in Rome.*

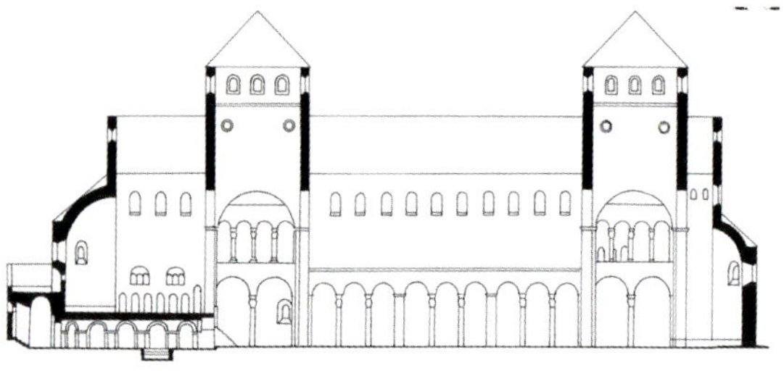

135

way as to correspond to the height of Mary's bed. It stands out as an extension, indeed like a character in the narrative. If the column in the crypt attracts attention by its aspect of tree-cum-cross and its intriguing ambiguity, it is quite another matter for the second and monumental column of the panel, placed perpendicularly to the Virgin's body, from which it seems to arise. Isolated and clearly visible, this column supports the massive walls with their crenellated arches that structure the entire upper part of the bronze panel. The first arch falls to the atrium on the left. The second one initiates a wall that starts on the right, rebounds again from a mass behind Salome, and delimits a curvilinear wall bent toward the interior and encircling the manger; the same arch then gives rise to a new curved wall abruptly butting against the roof of the building on the right. As in the crypt, the column imposes itself as a load-bearing element, unifying the entire architectural sequence.

By its position above Mary's body, its structuring function, and its connection with the bronze column that Bernward had made for St. Michael's, this column, just like the one in the crypt, undoubtedly evokes Christ. The analogy is not original, it comes from a long tradition of generic representations of the column [Bandmann 1970; 2005, 74–83], but in the discourse of the right wing, it takes on a much more precise meaning, which will be revealed in the next panel.

In the image, the Christ-evoking column is surmounted by an arched door with a chisel-marked contour (fig. 136). This door must be understood in connection with the two other little doors appearing above the mass in front of which Salome stands. This duplication qualifies the midwife's conversion as a voluntary act, a choice leading her to recognize the door to Christ's column as the sole door to salvation. At the contact point of the two arches, the presence of a curved roofing, like those of the bridge in panel 9, visually inscribes the series of arches in continuity with the arches of the previous panel, thus making conversion a supplementary stage in the earthly history of the *City of God*, which becomes the Church.

If the building on the panel's left represents the Church, we can reasonably infer that the edifice on the right is the Temple of the Synagogue; its structure is as modest and discreet as medieval synagogues could be [Krinsky, 8–12], and its historical precedence is underscored by the architectural language and a more cursory perspective. Now, what about the atrium?

Unified in its upper part by arches-walls, the lower portion of panel 10 is divided into sections. On the left, behind Mary and Salome, at the base of the Christlike column, a wall appears, built of evenly spaced bricks. There is no construction to the right, but the panel's background is marked by irregular bays appearing botched or unfinished, as we noticed at the beginning of the inquiry (fig. 137).

The caesura between these two spaces corresponds to the panel's symmetrical center, which is the precise position of the hand that Salome extends toward the Virgin. Thus, the miracle that converted the midwife compares an irregular, irrational "before" (placed on the side of the Synagogue) with a solidly constructed "after" structured around Christ's column, placed next to the Church. Faithful to the syntax he has put in place since the left wing, Bernward probably makes the absence of geometrical order between Salome and Joseph into a sign of the inner disorder engendered by doubt and blindness—but not only that.

Just like Salome, Joseph is straddling two places with different, albeit coordinated characteristics. The stool on which he is seated clearly displays a structural and ornamental continuity with the building of the Synagogue of which he appears to be an appendage: just like the Virgin, Joseph is represented in front of but also inside the building.

On his immediate right there is the bronze wall, roughly hollowed by irregular quadrilateral shapes. Behind him is the lateral wall of the Synagogue the stories of which, shifted in comparison to those of the façade, seem to converge toward him. The phenomenon is particularly noticeable at shoulder level, where the small, diagonally arranged rectangular

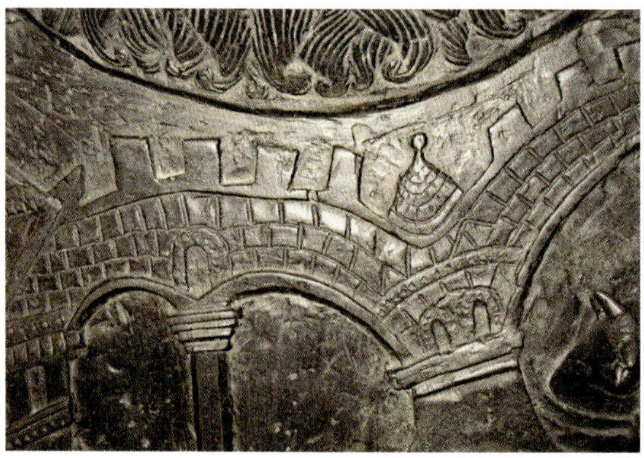

136

135. *St. Michael's of Hildesheim, cross-section.*

136. *Panel 10, architectural elements underneath the ring.*

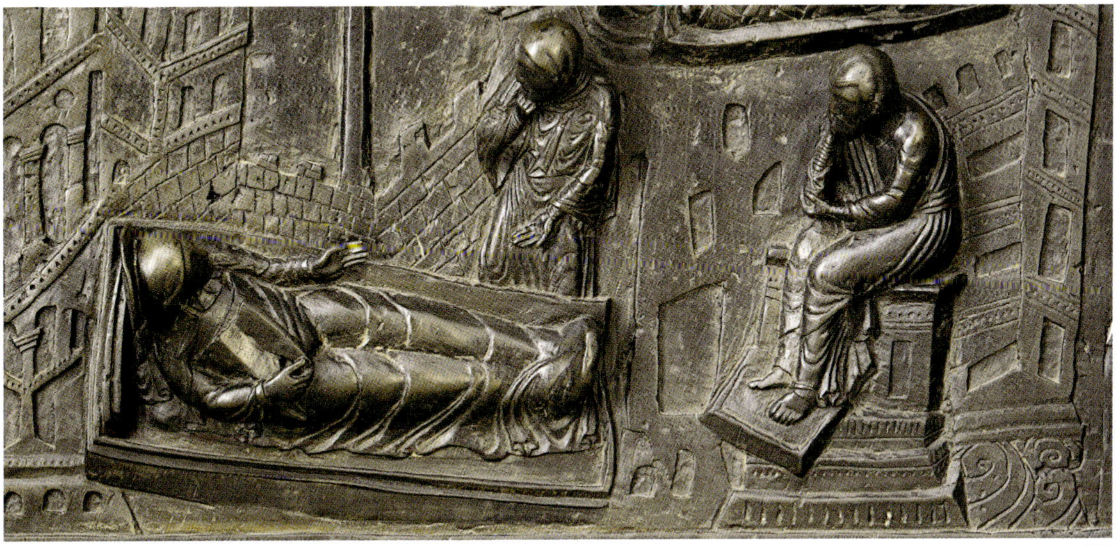

137

bays descend behind the figure. These openings, of the same shape as those of the Synagogue, seem to extend in front of Joseph. Viewed from right to left, the architectural elements associated with him progressively lose their coherence: the rules presiding over the façade's rational elevation are mangled on the building's side, then reduced to an allusive, restructured expression facing the figure.

I suggest considering this process of geometric transformation as a visual metaphor for an inner turmoil, but only insofar as the process itself is the consequence of a referential anchoring to the building on the right, that is, the Hebrew world represented by the Synagogue. The disorder arises from this confrontation: it does not annul the ancient reference points, but it transforms and attenuates them, thus paving the way for reception of Revelation. Therein lies, I think, the extreme subtlety of the discourse.

As already mentioned, for early medieval theologians, Church and Synagogue are not in opposition but are interconnected. In this panel, their shape is symmetrical, their size identical, and the Synagogue, as shown by the orb on the rooftop at the edge of the frame, is also a sacred place in relation to the sky. Their fundamental distinction, at the origin of their architectural language, comes from the way they are set on the ground.

The temple sits on a high plinth covered with mineral scrollwork studded with chisel marks, a mound similar to the one under Eve in panel 6 (cf. fig. 90). If this elevation is a biblical citation, it can only refer to Mount Zion in Jerusalem on which the Temple of Solomon was built, as seen in panel 12 (cf. fig. 153). At any rate, the edifice still belongs to those ancient times when the election of the Righteous did not obliterate the death-bearing sanction.

137. *Panel 10, carved shapes in the panel background.*

The place of the sterile Old Testament covenant is balanced by the masonry base pierced by four little niches under the church's crypt. This base has no architectural logic and can only be understood symbolically in opposition to the rocky prominence. It exhibits an unprecedented and very visible quaternity. Its presence, mirrored by the number of the semicircular arched bays under the roof, reveals the ecclesial edifice's earthly foundation. However, the base defines this locus of existence no longer according to the ways of the poisoned world but in all likelihood according to the living Word of Christ that the four Gospels transmit, thus delineating the new communal territory of God's people.

Between the Hebrew mountain and the Christian *diatessaron* (the harmony of the four Gospels), at ground level between Joseph's feet and Mary's bed, stand two little bays that can be considered as reading keys for the entire architectural complex. The one on the right is rectangular, the one on the left roughly delineates a semicircular curve. Like those around Joseph, the architectural elements are deformed but only in order to be reformed. Architecture, like the Tree of Life, is metamorphic. And it is the series of crenellated arched walls inscribed, as we have seen, into the continuity of the arches in panel 9, that has the function of describing the process of transformation from Synagogue to Church.

To the right of the series of arches, therefore preceding Salome's conversion, the infant Jesus is represented in swaddling clothes and wearing a cruciform halo (fig. 138). This human and divine body, whose sacrifice has been announced, joins the Temple, the crenellated walls, and the Church in the distance. His cradle is superimposed on the Temple's nave, reminding us that the infant was born within the

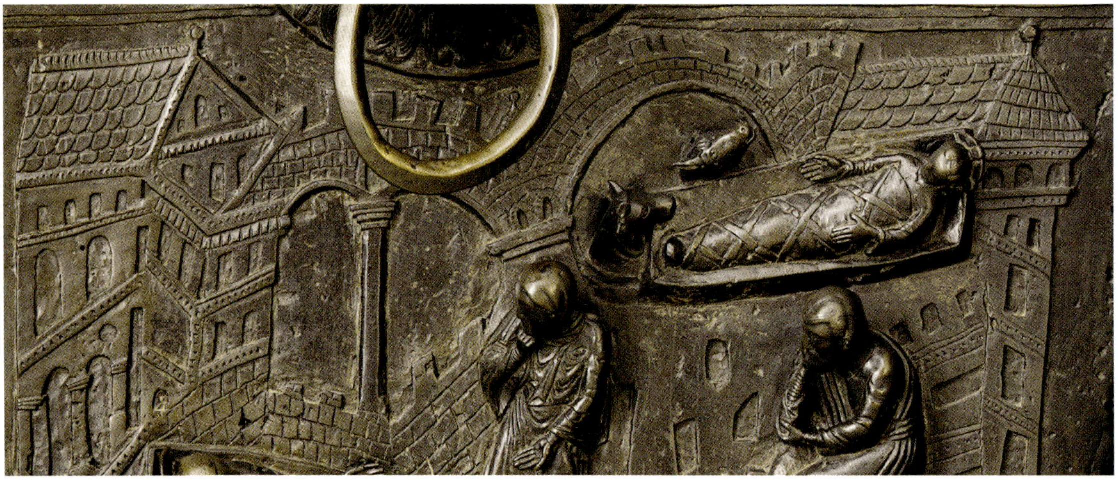

138

Synagogue's community. His right hand, palm open, is extended in the direction of the Church. What he offers is indicated by the gesture of the other hand, next to his body on crisscross strips of cloth. Last, at the level of his cruciform nimbus, an incongruity of the utmost importance appears on the Temple's façade: whereas each of the Temple's levels has rectangular windows, on the building's pediment are three semicircular openings, found as well on the pediment of the ecclesial basilica in a slightly different format. The Temple of the Synagogue—that is, the City of God founded by Abel—contained within itself, without knowing how to grasp its significance, the Trinitarian model of the Church and of the faith. In other words, Jesus's mortal body *had* to originate from the Synagogue in order to accomplish its salvific mission.

The role of Jesus, the divine child born Jewish, is reaffirmed through architecture, since it is on the base of the column that represents him in his organizing and mediating function that the continuity of the arches is concretely established with respect to the basilica-type church, but also to the atrium preceding it (fig. 131).

If this atrium seems open on its right side, this is only an optical illusion because its fourth side consists of the arch-wall plunging into it and whose starting point is the back of the Temple's roof.

Confirming the connection between the atrium and the Synagogue, we also notice that the bays of the narrow buildings surrounding the atrium are rectangular like those of the Temple, whereas its rear wall with its three bays constitutes the Church's façade: they are rectangular below and semicircular on the pediment. In other words, the atrium is part of both the Synagogue and the Church.

I suggest here that, through a fundamentally topological and highly inventive visual formulation, Bernward used the atrium to represent the back wall of the Synagogue's building. The series of arch-walls, supported and oriented by Christ, actualize the transfer of matter between the two buildings by shifting the back side of the Synagogue's nave as far as the atrium facing the Church, both materially in space and figuratively in time, just as the people of the Old Covenant preceded the people of the New Covenant. The Synagogue is thus represented as the prefiguration of a Church that it had announced and prepared and in which the Synagogue has the mission of transforming and subsuming itself.

The long investigation and the intellectual peregrinations necessary to understand the architecture represented in the image finally allows the viewers to reconnect with the organic dynamism intuitively perceived at first sight. The mechanism is not new; indeed, it constitutes a constant cognitive element in the bronze door.

As mentioned earlier, rather than a clear and obvious dogmatic utterance, Bernward prefers a laborious, albeit rewarding, unveiling process the layers of which I am trying to elucidate in my detailed analyses. In doing so, the bishop reminds us that early medieval Christian theology is not a simple assertion of statements or of rules to be followed but an ontological system as coherent and rational as the logos that produced it for the good of humanity. In this system, where no one will ever question God's existence, everything is intellectually comprehensible, save a major exception requiring an act of faith: the recognition of Jesus as incarnated God. This is what panel 10 represents, this free adhesion, this voluntary acceptance of Christ, marking the historical transfer from Judaism to Christianity, sealing the birth of the Church.

In conclusion, we may wonder how the idea of using architecture as a metaphor for the conversion

138. *Panel 10, upper arcade.*

of the people of God came to Bernward's mind. It undoubtedly came about quite naturally through the encounter between his technical knowledge as an architect, his theological erudition as a pastor, and his almost alchemical ability as a metal caster and goldsmith. As for the building metaphor, it is almost consubstantial to the notion of Church. In this context, the community and its meeting place together designate the constituted body of believers, itself identified with the body of Christ, through which alone salvation is possible. Its origin is already inscribed in the prophecies of the Old Testament and in the affirmation that the Church of Christ will be built of stone ("You are Peter and upon this rock I will build my church," Matt. 16:18). Few authors have developed it as clearly as Augustine in his *City of God,* and with good reason:

> This house of God is greater in glory than was that former one, built of wood and stone and other precious materials and metals. Thus the prophecy of Haggai was not fulfilled in the restoration of that former temple. For after it was restored, it cannot be shown to have had at any time a glory as great as that which it had had in the time of Solomon. On the contrary, the diminished glory of that house is shown first in the cessation of prophecy, and then by the great calamities which befell the nation itself, down to its final destruction, which was accomplished at the hands of the Romans, as the events described above attest. But this house of ours, which belongs to the new covenant, certainly is greater in glory, in that its "living stones" are more precious; for it is constructed of those men who believe, and who have themselves been created anew. Yet this new house was prefigured in the restoration of that temple; for the restoration of that building itself signifies, as by a prophetic utterance, the second covenant, which is called new. Therefore, when God said, through the prophet named above, "And I will give peace in this place," the word "place" is a symbol, and by it we are to understand that which it symbolizes. And so the rebuilding "in this place" stands for the Church which was to be built by Christ. (*De civitate Dei*, XVIII, 48, 894–895)

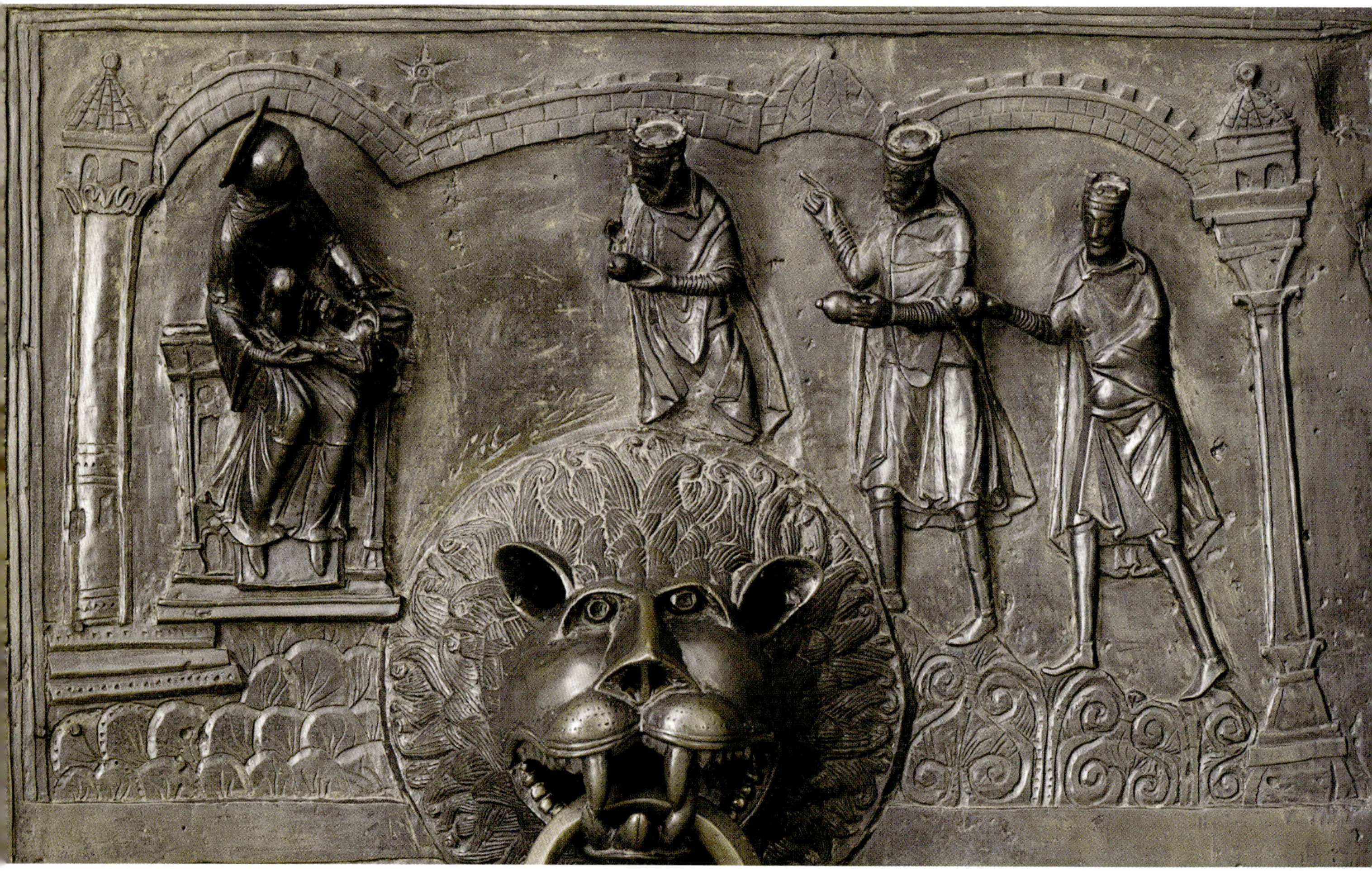

Panel **11**

LAW

After panel 10's visual complexity, panel 11, which depicts the Epiphany, is choreographed with tranquil clarity (fig. 139). The figures, framed by a simple and comprehensible architecture, stand out against a neutral background, their gestures underscored by the high relief.

On the right, three kings from the East are headed toward Jesus, whom the Virgin, seated on a throne, holds on her knees. They bring to the infant gifts contained in small, sealed bottles, pyxides full of gold, incense, and myrrh (Matt. 2:11). The scene has not particularly attracted the attention of historians, perhaps because the theme was widely used in Ottonian art or because its place in the door's program seemed assured by the typological symmetry between Eve and Mary (cf. fig. 91).

However, by combining certain traits of early Christian imagery he could have seen during his travels together with some typically Ottonian innovations, Bernward produced, as usual, an effective and unprecedented theological discourse. Contrary to the method used so far, we shall approach the study of the eleventh panel through this double source of iconographic inspiration.

In the panel the Virgin and Child are decentered, whereas the kings are aligned corresponding to a mode of Hellenistic representation found both on sarcophagi and on the wooden door of Santa Sabina. This figural arrangement is based on representations of the ritualistic worship of Roman emperors performed by representatives of distant nations [Vezin 1950, 39–40]. This is probably what appealed to the Ottonians, given the theme's relative decline in Christian art [Trexler 1997, 53], even if the scene as it appears on the bronze door is more directly linked to early Christian art than to Germanic tradition.

139. *Panel 11.*

Except for those of the Fulda Sacramentary, late tenth- and early eleventh-century miniatures depict Mary and Jesus isolated in front of or under their own aedicule. In the bronze panel, as in many older representations, all the characters are inscribed in a unified perimeter, in this case within a triple arcade resting on two vertical supports. The panel's spatial unification is all the more noticeable in contrast to the scattered figures in panel 6 on the left wing. Eve and her child are isolated on an arid mound under a cloth hanging between two trees; the angel, superior and distant, stands on the lion head, while Adam digs the soil in the panel's left side (cf. fig. 88). Therefore, two scenes and three spaces are juxtaposed, with the divine messenger acting as a figure of authority uniformly applying the harsh earthly law to the entire panel.

Panel 11 responds to the fragmentation of panel 6 with a continuous narrative that integrates all the characters in the image. The three kings are very similar. Contrary to the numerous medieval Epiphanies where they differ in age, attire, and later in ethnic origin, here they have the same stature, the same silhouette, the same clothing, they even offer the same gift.

A final scenographic element links the panel to early Christian tradition: the attitude of each visitor. In Ottonian miniatures, the visitors exhibit the same devotional posture: either the first one bows while the other two wait behind him before approaching the Child, or the three personages stand piously together. In this kind of representation, the biblical

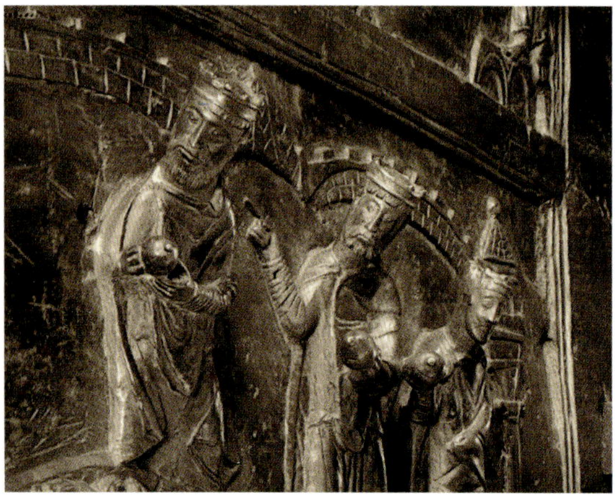

140

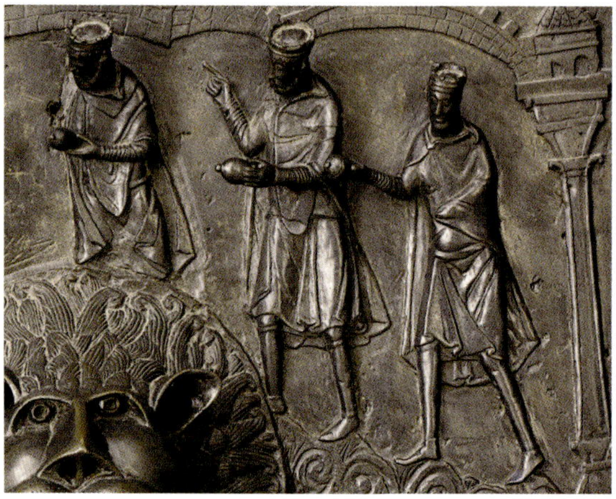

141

narrative is condensed to its conclusion: the meeting with Jesus. In panel 11 the kings each display a very different posture and different figural gestures. These variations are indeed a subtle and customary way of introducing diversity into uniformity, yet here they are arranged in a coherent sequence that takes up the narrative option favored in ancient images.

In fact, the scene unfolds in time, not by quoting from the past as in Egbert of Trier's Gospel Book, circa 980 (Trier, SB., Ms. 24, f 17), but by developing narrative through three different stages, successively embodied by each of the characters (fig. 141).

The action begins with the king on the far right, the third in the procession who is also in the lowest position; the journey toward Jesus is envisioned as an ascent. His face is turned three-quarters toward the viewers in such a way that he can see neither Virgin and Child, nor the star dominating the scene (fig. 140). Nevertheless, the intention is clear: extending his pyxis in the direction of the divine pair, he steps forward, right leg in vertical position, left leg pushing from behind. He wears a coat fluttering in the wind, and he has rolled a section of the garment around his left arm. This king is beginning his journey; he knows the reason for his quest but not yet his destination.

The king in the middle points his index finger to the star, not the one that suddenly appeared in the faraway East, described at the beginning of Matthew's narrative and in the apocryphal Gospels, but rather the sign that guides the travelers from Jerusalem to Bethlehem, the place where the child is to be found (Matt. 2:9). This king has slowed his step. The front part of his foot disappears behind the lion head serving as the wing's handle. He is on the threshold of a new space and a new time, no longer those of the prophecy but those of the Epiphany. By pointing to the star while gazing at Jesus, an unusual combination in Epiphany imagery, the king implicitly associates the two actions communicating the apparition (the Greek meaning of epiphany) of the Messiah as a light and guide.

The king closest to the Virgin and Child has reached the end of his journey. He has entered the perimeter covered by the lion head, where he occupies an ambiguous position, placed at the same time on the circle and behind it. Unlike his companions, he holds his pyxis with both hands close to his body, extending his offering toward Jesus with a restrained, deferential motion, which constitutes the high point of narrative tension (fig. 141). This gesture is not only prepared by those of the journeying kings but is also a synthesis of them: the pyxis is held at arm's length in the right hand of the first king, in the left hand of the second, and in both hands of the third. What is even more striking is that by holding his offering close to his body, the king, in Jesus's presence, bridges the distance that separated Abel from his lamb in panel 7 (cf. fig. 102). Without yet understanding the reasons, we can deduce from this that, from now on, the conditions of the covenant and the qualification of the sacred are modified.

Like all the figures on the door, the kings are defined by the clothes they wear, which requires distinguishing between two interpretative levels. The first considers garments as attributes characterizing the action or the status of the figures; this aspect has been taken into account all along in the study of the panels (thickness of fabric, shape, ornamentation, relation to the body, etc.). The second interpretive level, generally overlooked because it recurs too frequently, is the type of garment, namely their cultural code. In this instance, Bernward garbs his characters with the antique clothing that had been the norm from the beginning of Christian iconography: togas for the divine, angelic and prophetic figures; tunics for laboring men, robes and veils for women. The actors of the Holy Scripture possessing a specific social function, such as Herod, Pontius Pilate, and even soldiers, wear

140. *Panel 11, three kings.*

141. *Panel 11, three kings.*

the insignia and attributes of their status. The kings of panel 11 belong to this last category.

Described in the Gospels as *magi ab oriente* (Matt. 2:1), they are not Jews but pagans from faraway lands. The apocryphal Gospels, especially that of the Pseudo-Matthew, explicitly underscore this aspect. The kings' foreign appearance immediately places panel 11 in an ecclesiological perspective different from the one developed by the typological metamorphosis from Synagogue into Church in panel 10, which is not surprising. Christian exegetical tradition identifies the Epiphany as the moment Christ is revealed to non-Jews (a tradition founded by Augustine and continued by Fulgentius, Caesarius of Arles, Gregory the Great, and later by Sedulius Scottus, Heiric of Auxerre, and Otfrid of Weissenburg [cf. LLT-A]).

In most Epiphany imagery up until the eleventh century and even much later, the details of the kings' attire, such as Phrygian caps, luxurious clothing, ample shirts, and bouffant pantaloons, confirm their foreign provenance. This attire, already seen in the famous mosaics of the Basilica of Sant'Apollinare Nuovo in Ravenna, also brings a hint of the exotic to the illumination of the Epiphany of Bernward's Gospel Book (Hildesheim DS 18, f 18). However, the bishop of Hildesheim makes a radically different choice for panel 11: the kings wear only plain tunics covered with coats made of simple pieces of rectangular material fastened at the shoulder.

These garments are quite naturalistic, thus accentuating their drabness. The fold of the collar falls on the shoulder, whereas the thick material, probably wool, adheres to the body in large overlapping pleats. Footwear is also carefully represented. The king on the right seems to have bare legs; the second king's legs are covered by short, clinging pants tied under the knees, unless they are gaiters. (Calceological studies tend to undermine the possibility that we may be looking at knee-high boots [Goubitz et al. 2001].)

These sartorial attributes, which could apply just as easily to antiquity as to the eleventh century, qualify these three kings, engaged in a collective journey, merely as travelers. By muddying the waters of tradition, Bernward provides viewers with a significant piece of information. Although they arrive from afar, these men do not really come from the unknown, a paradox that we will try to clarify later in our analysis.

There is an incongruous element in this panoply of travelers. No one will have failed to notice that the three men all wear a crown, an object previously found nowhere in the door. The magi were designated as kings by Christian patristics from very early on, first and foremost by Caesarius of Arles. The bishop found in the royal attribute the possibility not only of exalting the episode's solemn character, but also of inscribing it into a typological perspective that evoked, in particular, verse 30 of Psalm 67: "From thy temple in Jerusalem, kings shall offer presents to thee" [Trexler 1997, 35]. It was not until late tenth-century Anglo-Saxon and Ottonian images that the crowns became a visual attribute of the Epiphany's kings [Deshman, 378].

By bestowing these *regalia* on the visitors who came to pay homage to Jesus, Bernward adheres in this instance to contemporary iconographic tradition without forgetting the syntactical rules of his door. The magi's crowns actually have the shape of large headbands, topped by evenly spaced crenellations. They do not look at all like the elaborately wrought headgear exhibited by Herod Antipas, Tetrarch of Galilee, in panel 13 (cf. fig. 163). Neither can they be ascribed to the tradition of Germanic royal headpieces, nor to semicircular crowns, nor to the diadems with fleurons that Percy Schramm studied in Carolingian and Ottonian imagery. Finally, their geometric simplicity distances them from the tiara shaped crowns decorated with pearls or little balls worn by the magi in contemporary illuminations. Bernward takes up the signifying attribute of sovereignty or power, but he plays with the symbol by conferring on it a quite unusual sobriety, enhancing the characters' humility by making it paradoxical. The same simplicity is found in their garments, very different from the luxurious attire worn by Herod and Pilate in the panel about Christ's trial (cf. fig. 160). They are not embellished by fur, embroidery, or set stones and the only visible clasp, on the king on the right, is extremely simple.

Bernward thus borrows certain attributes from tradition while neglecting others, linking them together. He sets up a discursive strategy that testifies to his mastery of both previous conventions and contemporary customs. This semiotic manipulation serves to reconsider the figures through echoes or discrepancies resulting from this approach. However, this is probably not its primary function, as it is difficult to presume that the inhabitants of Hildesheim had full knowledge of such visual conventions. Rather, such a manipulation elucidates the method used by the bishop to increase the potential of signs. To their strictly denotative function (this is a king, this is a traveler, this is or is not a Roman), he adds certain connotations (the meaning of royalty, the significance of accomplishing a long journey, the implications of belonging to this or that community). Unlike the attributes, these connotations contribute to elaborating a second level of discourse, which is

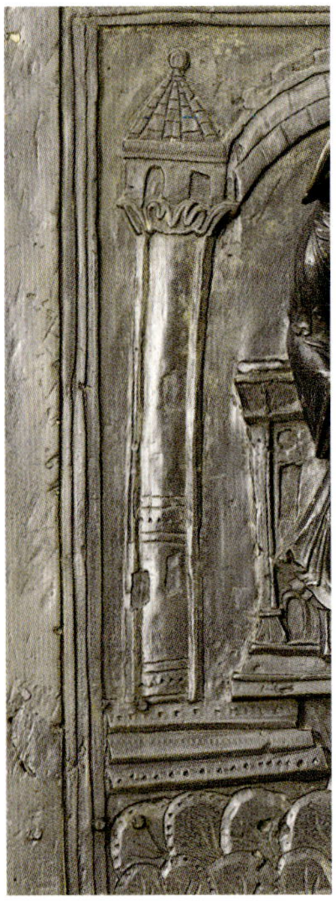

142

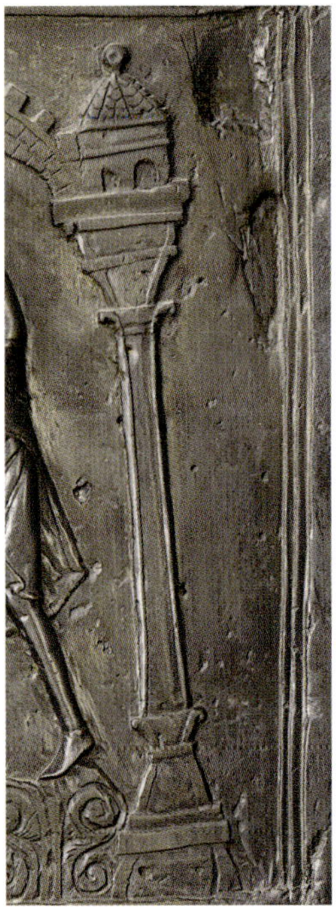

143

no longer about the identifying and expounding the narrative but rather about its ontological significance.

The crowns are indeed emblems of royal power in Ottonian images, and if Bernward portrays his magi wearing them, it is because a long literary tradition and a more recent iconographic practice authorized him to do so. Yet by conflating the riches of the distant East, not with the crown of the magi but with that of Herod, depicted exercising his political power, I would argue that Bernward reminds us that the power revealed by the attributes of the Tetrarch of Galilee come from vain, earthly glory, whereas the magi's power is primarily spiritual. In the same way, the traveling garments worn by the magi respect the biblical historia in that they evoke the travelers' journey toward the infant Jesus, but their journey is not only geographic. Progress toward the infant is accomplished not from the outside in but from within a proto-community to which the kings had belonged ever since they accepted the prophecy. It is by embracing Christ's divinity that one becomes a believer. The magi set forth: the journey they accomplish—three kings in one journey, presenting the characters in motion as just one generic believer—can be understood only through a careful study of the architecture surrounding them.

The triple arcade rests on two lateral columns, with the result that the structure appears both as an encircling wall and as a covering vault from which the intermediate pilasters are missing (fig. 139). The left column leans slightly toward Mary, whereas the right column, placed behind the magi, leans toward the panel's interior at an angle of about fifteen degrees in relation to the vertical frame on the right (fig. 143). In this instance too, it is impossible to assume that a problem in molding or casting explains these imbalances because the cross section of the columns does not vary, nor do the proportions of the capitals and the aedicules surmounting them.

Other than their symmetry and the proximity of their silhouettes, the two columns do not have the same composition. The slender and precisely rendered column on the right is architecturally accurate, even well crafted (fig. 143). Its capital is composed of an astragal, an echinus, an abacus, and an entablature. Its base has the unusual shape of an upside-down capital and is encircled by a band from which emerge two little leaves also found, less surprisingly, on either side of the shaft in the manner of a Corinthian capital. Finally, the base rests on a small hemispherical mound, which is rather incomprehensible from an architectural viewpoint.

The left column is much more sculpted but has neither base nor capital (fig. 142). Its shaft is surmounted by a crown of living matter recalling the Voice of the Blood of Abel (cf. fig. 113) but in a vegetal, less geometric design. Deprived of a base, this column rests on a podium with three plinths, two of which are covered with chisel marks, while the median one is free of them. Finally, whereas the shaft of the right column is smooth and represented as one piece, the shaft of the left column displays some graphic elements that partition it: in the lower part, two double horizontal lines framing a row of dots, call attention to a middle section on which two small quadrangular bays are affixed.

The ground under the column on the left differs from that of the column on the right. On the left side (fig. 142), the podium is set on a layer of well-arranged, small mounds of earth, covered with triple grass sprigs, but partially chiseled around the edge. They form a regular pattern identical to the one in the panel depicting original sin, in accordance with the divine promise of the restoration of the world (cf. fig. 56). On the right of panel 11 (fig. 143) is a mineral motif composed of regular scrollwork decorating the hilly perimeter on which the magi advance. All these features—position, internal structure, ornamentation, supports, growth pattern—confer to the columns certain specific qualities that will help in identifying them.

The imbalance of the right column is the architectural detail that attracts the most attention in the panel (fig. 143). By haptic projection, the viewer interprets its cause and consequence: if the column

142. *Panel 11, left-hand column.*

143. *Panel 11, right-hand column.*

sways it is because it has been forced to do so by the curvature of the small, rounded mound that it has somewhat flattened by its weight. This unbalancing movement, restrained by the counterthrust of the wall and the rocky mass, exercises an almost threatening pressure toward the right. The viewer associates this pressure with the first king moving away from the column's potential falling point. From a narrative standpoint, the little mound is therefore the first cause of a journey to which it gives its momentum, thus bestowing on it a great importance. We have encountered a similar hemispheric form only once in the door, in the last panel of the left wing, the one that gives a precise account of the foundation of a spiritual city by the death of the first Righteous Man. Of the same size and identically set within the panel's frame, it represented the trampled sepulchral cave of Abel from which issued the voice asking for and obtaining justice beyond the end of time (cf. fig. 113). Indeed, in the Bible the Eastern star of Epiphany corresponds to the star of Jacob announced by Balaam's fourth oracle: "I shall see him, but not now: I shall behold him, but not near. A star shall rise out of Jacob and a scepter shall spring up from Israel" (Num. 24:17). We find a response to this Old Testament text in the Gospel of Matthew's "Magi from the east came to Jerusalem and asked, 'Where is he that is born king of the Jews? For we have seen his star in the east and are come to adore him.'" (Matt. 2:2). The small mound that sets the column in motion and triggers the magi's progression toward Christ is most certainly the visual synthesis of the transformation of the prophetic word into the Gospel's Word: Bernward here represents the constitution of a universal City of God, which the non-Jews, having heard the call of Christ and seen His light, have come to join.

The left-hand column's powerful podium is just as forceful as the little mound, eventually revealing a stability that does not depend on its shape but on the system of the optical adjustment ruling it; this nuance has a certain importance (fig. 142). The highest plinth is strictly horizontal and aligned with the pedestal of the Virgin's throne, but the lower ones are on a slight diagonal. This masonry, adjacent to the panel's frame, is sufficient to offset the visual imbalance introduced by the irrational adherence of the throne to the structure. The stability of the base is such that it supports both the column's shaft, attached to the first layer, and the Marian throne. The plastic force of these plinths is matched by a force of another nature coming from what constitutes it ontologically: how not to see in the plinth free of chisel marks an image of Christ made flesh of the poisoned world? Or how can one not recognize in the lower section of the shaft the quadrangular bays of the Synagogue in the previous panel? Or how is it possible not to identify the foliage emerging from the shaft's upper part as Christ's Word, giving life in all its plenitude to the newly saved community? It is on the body of Christ, human and divine, that the new City of God with its universal calling is founded.

However, it would be rash to deduce from this that the two columns of panel 11 are schematic figurations of the Synagogue and Church in the previous panel. The syntactical logic Bernward imposed on the bronze door makes such a redundancy unlikely; at this stage, the only thing we can suggest is that the left column shares the same nature as the perfected Church in panel 10 and that it is the fruit of the same historia. But the most convincing argument comes from the fact that such spiritual communities are represented elsewhere in the panel. Two aedicules are placed on top of these columns. They are similar to those framing the "Old Testament bridge" in panel 8 (cf. fig. 121), where they established the historical continuity of the City of God up to the birthplace of Christ and of a new humanity, namely the womb aedicule with double entry placed above Gabriel (cf. fig.123).

In panel 11, the two aedicules surmounting the columns exhibit an identical detail, placed in axial symmetry: an arched bay, sign of the new Church, and a parallelepipedal bay, sign of the Old Temple (fig. 144 and 145). These two communal aedicules, although not superimposable, are identical places of fusion/transformation; the metamorphosis taking place in the image does not concern them as such, rather, it applies to the columns supporting them.

The two columns of panel 11 have been prefigured by those in the previous panel: one, the axis of the world, supported the conversion of Synagogue into Church; the other, in the crypt, was the basement of the complete ecclesial building (cf. fig. 126). In panel 11, the columns fortify and raise communal edifices. They conform to their telluric substratum and have attributes permitting their identification. The column on the left, slender and curved, whose lively corolla recalls the large, innervated leaves on the ground, is almost swaying, resembling a tree trunk (fig. 142). By contrast, the column on the right, set on a rocky base and placed on the cave from which came the Voice of Abel's Blood, is rigid and mineral (fig. 143). The rare vegetal elements it contains are subject to strong pressure, since they are located at the points of contact between the shaft and the two capitals framing it. What can be deduced is that the plant as vital principle is present in the structure yet maintained in an embryonic state by the aridity and

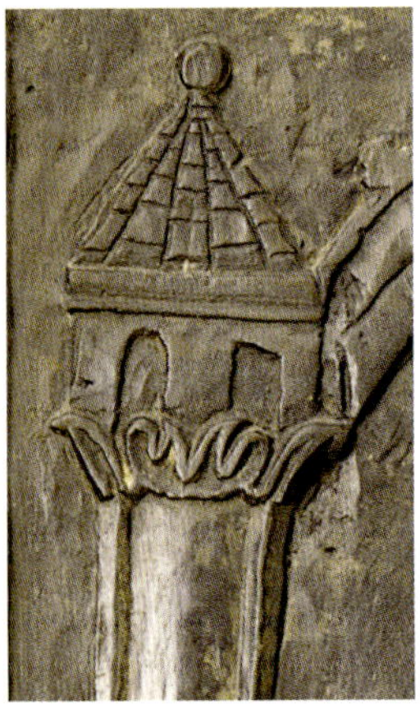

144

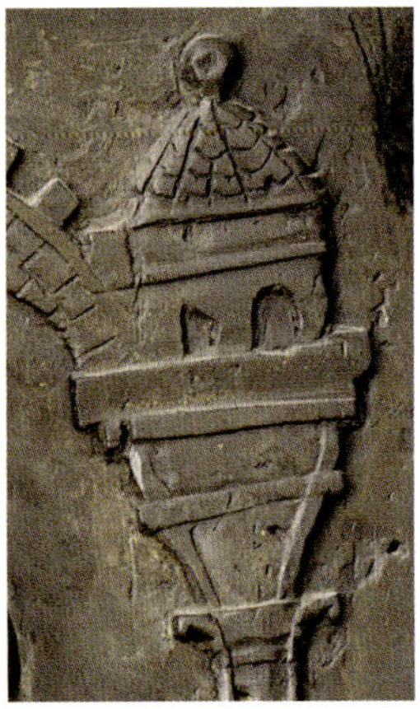

145

144. *Panel 11, aedicule on left-hand column.*

145. *Panel 11, aedicule on right-hand column.*

constraint of the architectonical elements. This infertility will be removed by the disappearance of the weight and spatial fixity generated by the capitals, so that life will blossom at the top of the left column's shaft. Somehow the right column has turned on its axis to become the left column, the Voice of Abel's Blood at the bottom being transformed into the Gospel, the living Word at the top, thus removing the constraint of the capitals.

The same mechanism is at work in the transformation of the ground. If we observe carefully, we notice that the mineral volutes, much more organized than the ones in panels 6 and 10 (fig. 93 and 130), bear the mark of fine streaks representing blades of grass, calling attention to the ground placed symmetrically under the Virgin and Child (fig. 146). It should also be noted that these volutes are arranged in pairs and placed symmetrically along vertical axes that resemble stems. Even their size increases from right to left. Vitality is therefore present in the column as well as in the ground on the right, but it is held back by the stone imposing its order, its geometric reason. In other words, the minerality which, on the right, prevents the fulfillment of a potential vitality, is removed by the vegetal power of the left column.

I suggest we recognize the action of the first law, the natural law in the lifeless stone's inherent capacity to contain and limit the vital impetus through pressure. Source of both life and of death, it had been enacted by the angel when men entered the earthly world in panel 6, placed exactly opposite the Epiphany scene (cf. fig. 96). Bernward visualized this law of the world in the narrow and slender form of a column intentionally. Its formal paradigm is the Tree of Life, the axis of symmetry of which is a trunk, and the Tree of Life behind God already had the vertical shape of a column in the panel of the condemnation of Adam and Eve (cf. fig. 68).

This law changes considerably in the left-hand column where it becomes a vital impulse supporting and irrigating the Church. It is precisely the story of this transformation/revelation of divine law in the course of history that is told in panel 11. The law evolves without dissolving, in the same way in which Synagogue was transformed into Church, as affirmed by Matthew's Gospel: "Do not think that I am come to destroy the law, or the prophets. I am not come to destroy, but to fulfill. For amen I say unto you, till heaven and earth pass, one jot, or one tittle shall not pass of the law, till all be fulfilled" (Matt. 5:17–18).

These progressive transformations/revelations are visualized in the image by powerful signs that unfold with the progression of the magi (or rather of the believer) toward the infant Jesus.

The first stage concerns the magus on the right and marks the passage between the column and the pyramidal form to which the latter is connected through the crenellated arcade (fig. 146). What is the meaning of the pyramidal form that is consistent with the initial natural law, the one that caused Abel's death? This form has greatly puzzled scholars and has generally been identified as a roof. The herringbone design covering it contradicts this hypothesis, which at any rate does not hold up under any comparison in the bronze door. Associated with the wall, whose material and curve it shares, this pyramid ensures the arcade's visual continuity. At the same time, it distinguishes itself by constituting a heterogeneous and autonomous iconic unity. It is in fact placed behind the outer wall and is visible only because a portal, emphasized by two small pillars, has been set into the wall .

Placed in the background of the panel, the pyramidal form has the silhouette and height of a distant mountain. At the same time, it is dominated by an orb calling attention to its universality. This mountain and the star that follows it in the diachronic unfolding of the metamorphic historia delineated by the arcade have the same function: they designate certain sites as sacred because they were where humans were permitted to see the signs of God. The star marks the site of Bethlehem, where Jesus reveals himself to the faithful; as for the mountain, I suggest that it recalls a sacred site in the Old Testament.

There are several possible interpretations. The mountain may be Mount Zion, though it is more likely that it represents Mount Sinai, where Moses received the Tablets of the Law. In support of this identification, recall that Mount Sinai is the only mountain indicated in the oldest preserved map of the medieval ecumene (the totality of inhabited

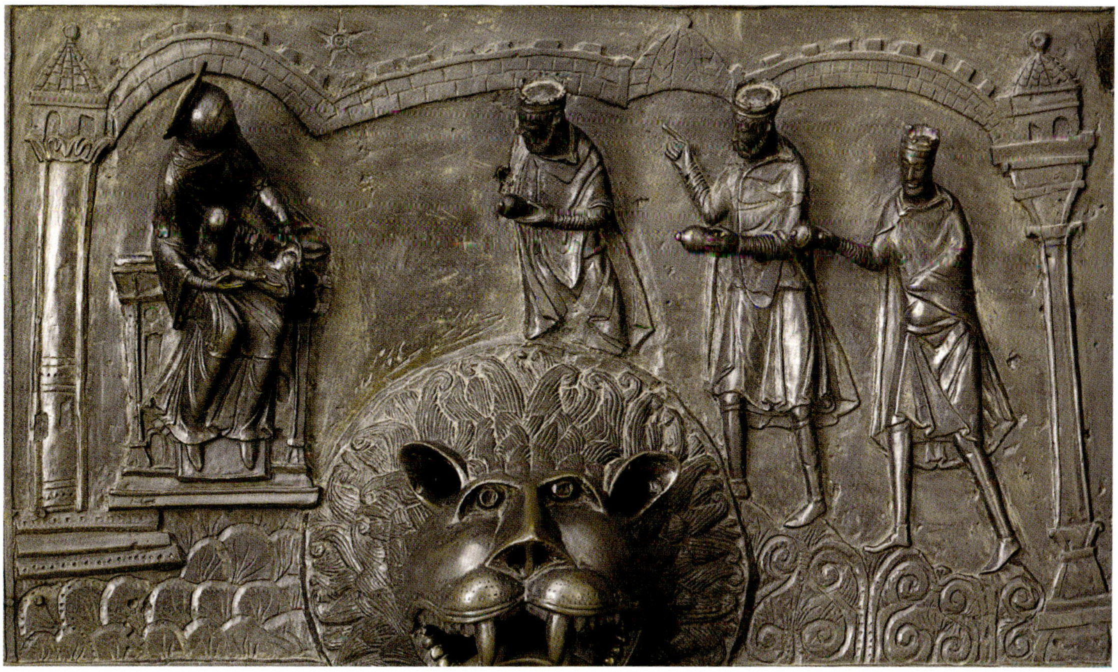

146

146. *Panel 11.*

lands), the Visigothic *Mappa mundi* of Albi [Von den Brincken and Szabo 2008, 595], where it is represented in the shape of a triangle. A second hypothesis, complementary to the first, takes into consideration a prophecy of the Old Testament that evokes the future Law of the new covenant. In Isaiah's formulation: "And in the last days the mountain of the house of the Lord shall be prepared on the top of mountains, and it shall be exalted above the hills, and all nations shall flow unto it. And many people shall go, and say: Come and let us go up to the mountain of the Lord, and to the house of the God of Jacob, and he will teach us his ways, and we will walk in his paths for the law shall come forth from Sion, and the word of the Lord from Jerusalem" (Isa. 2:2–3). This complementary interpretation has the merit of representing an Old Testament God who addresses himself to non-Jews, as is the case of the Eastern magus.

As for the principles of order and the functioning mode of this Hebraic law, the vegetal/mineral ground offers a remarkable plastic metaphor. As Christian literature unanimously explains, the ancient law is presented as an external constraint, a yoke—here the stone—imposing on human life a structure they cannot choose but that allows them to be respectful of divine precepts.

Therefore, it is the call of a Law to come that has sent the magus on his journey. Following a transfer model, found again in the progression of the three Holy Women toward Christ's tomb in panel 15 (cf. fig. 177), the magus on the right begins a process of conversion that will bring him face to face with the infant Jesus. This magus is the only one wearing a visible fibula, that is, a sign of connection attached to his garment (the Holy Woman on the right in panel 15 wears another, square and equally significant clasp, cf. fig. 178). The section of the coat wrapped around his left hand is crossed by a long, continuous, parallel, double line (fig. 147). Anticipated by the motif of circulating sap in the plants, evoked by an atomized and chaotic format on Cain's body on the left wing (cf. 115), this spiritual channel of life/animation guides his hand, while underscoring his progressive movement in the ascending diagonal. The magus has embarked on his journey toward Jesus because he is guided internally by a new force, his faith in the Revelation (and not because of some sort of external impetus).

The first quality of the new Law in the world, beyond its universal perceptibility, is its capacity to organize, to direct the body's movements toward true life. In fact, it is one thing to be alive, sustained by the *anima*; but it is a different thing to live life in truth, supported by the *spiritus*. To hear the call of the Spirit means to allow oneself to be guided by it. Or, looking ahead, it means to enter life's Law, placing oneself in this ascending diagonal, which is reminiscent of the vital impetus of the first panel on the bronze door (cf. fig. 14). Divine will is thus accomplished *in* humans.

The second stage of the revelation of Christ's Law is signified by the distance between the mountain and the star. It concerns the central magus. The traveler's

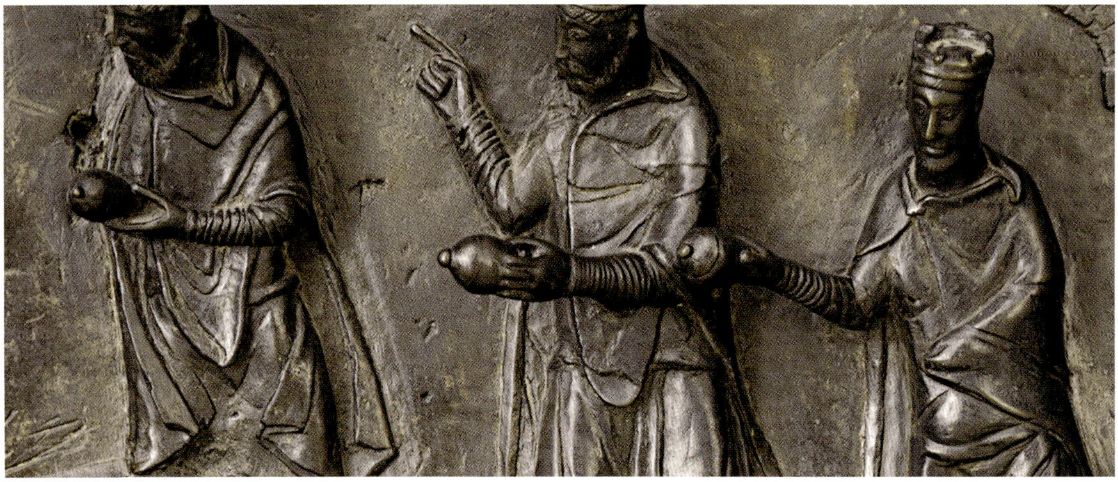

147

index finger pointing toward the star is positioned just under the mountain from which he turns away as he chooses light. If the first magus identifies the call, the second one sees and understands the light offered to him. "If you do not believe [*credideritis*], you will not understand [*intelligetis*]," writes Augustine, quoting Isaiah in the Septuagint translation [Gilson 1987, 39]. On the left side of his oval shaped cloak are pleats arranged in a star shape that converge toward the heart (fig. 147). The believer has converted the external light into internal light and looks to the infant Jesus as the source of divine knowledge. He has replaced the ancient external law by a new Law that he has understood and internalized.

For Christians, this evolution of the Law and of the kind of covenant it establishes between God and humans is announced in Jeremiah's prophecy:

> Behold the days shall come, saith the Lord, and I will make a new covenant with the house of Israel, and with the house of Juda, not according to the covenant which I made with their fathers. . . . I will give my law [*legem meam*] in their bowels [*in visceribus eorum*], and I will write it in their heart [*in corde eorum*] and I will be their God, and they shall be my people. And they shall teach no more every man his neighbor, and every man his brother, saying know the Lord, for all shall know me from the least of them even to the greatest, saith the Lord, for I will forgive their iniquity, and I will remember their sin no more. (Jer. 31:31–34)

The third stage of the unveiling of the Law is associated with the magus who stands on the lion head in front of the Virgin and Child. This phase articulates the passage between the light, which is the reception of the inner truth, and the covenant, which is its consequence. As we have seen, in terms of his positioning, his respectful posture, and his holding the pyxis with both hands, this magus is reminiscent of the figure of Abel in panel 7. Here, however, the figure is no longer isolated from the theophanic space by a fiery mandorla but is placed in the immediate presence of God. It is no longer necessary to isolate the offering from a sacrilegious contact because there is no longer any heterogeneity of substance between the believer and God in the flesh, toward whom he turns. Indeed, by offering his gift, the magus offers himself to Christ. He announces his celestial union with God, as Augustine describes it:

> For it was commanded under the old Law that the animals chosen as victims were to be immaculate and entirely free from blemish. This was because they signified holy men, free from all sin; but only one such man, Christ, has ever yet been found. At the judgment, however, those who are worthy of such purification will be purified even by fire; and, thereafter, there will be found in all the saints no sin at all. In this condition, then, they will offer themselves in righteousness. . . . For, then, there will be in the flesh and minds of the saints that purity which was prefigured in the bodies of those victims. (*De civitate Dei*, Book XX, 26, 1032–33)

This anticipation is made clear by the very special relationship between the magus and the circular handhold (fig. 148). Whether or not the figure is kneeling, his legs have disappeared under the disc, so that he is standing in a non-naturalistic place raising him above the ground; this positioning gives him completeness and stability, inscribing him into a dynamic equilibrium that no longer derives from the transference in space but from the movement in situ. The permeability of this place is confirmed by the magus's foot inserted under the edge of the lion head;

147. *Panel 11, kings' offerings.*

its earthly quality is evidenced by the superimposition of the base of Mary's throne on the lion's mane.

On the left wing, Bernward had integrated the handhold into the elaboration of his visual discourse: in panel 6, the circular shape established the celestial perimeter from which the natural law was imposed on the earthly world (cf. fig. 96); in panel 7, the hand of God's justice emerged from the high spheres (cf. fig. 99). On the right wing, reading direction has changed, now going from bottom to top. The disc, whose lower part encroaches on panel 10, somehow condenses the architectural compound of the Nativity scene showing the establishment of the community on Christ. In panel 11, it delineates a place that no longer comes from heaven but from earth, although without sharing its matter. This territory, whose circular dynamic is celestial, is the City of God placed in and above the world, within which the new divine Law is at work.

The first magus, impelled by natural law, felt the Spirit acting in him and leading him toward the messianic Law; the second magus, inscribing the divine Law in his heart, understood the Christlike nature of the renewed Law; the third one literally holds himself within God's Law and is no longer under its yoke.

His coat is made up of successive layers of cloth, incompatible with the naturalism of a one-piece garment (fig. 147); in addition, the garment's large, superimposed pleats have been reconfigured in order to exhibit an unprecedented geometric sequencing, enveloping the body of the figure on which the pleats are folded. Finally, and paradoxically, the pleats of the lower part of his cape are extremely fluid, like those of angelic tunics.

It is a new garment, different from the two previous figurations of magi: it is the garment of a new man standing on the sacred and earthly territory of the covenant with Christ. We will understand better what all this means by studying the next panels, but for now we will quote St. Paul: "There is now therefore no condemnation to them that are in Christ Jesus, who walk not according to the flesh. For the law of the spirit of life, in Christ Jesus, hath delivered me from the law of sin and of death" (Rom. 8:1–2).

We have just understood the different historical stages and the effects of the divine Law on the City of God of which it constitutes the foundation and the axis. The figure of the Virgin and Child, with which we will conclude this study, will unveil its nature more precisely.

In early Christian representations of the Epiphany, Mary and her child are depicted frontally when they are in central position, and in profile when they are off center; in Ottonian illuminations they are usually

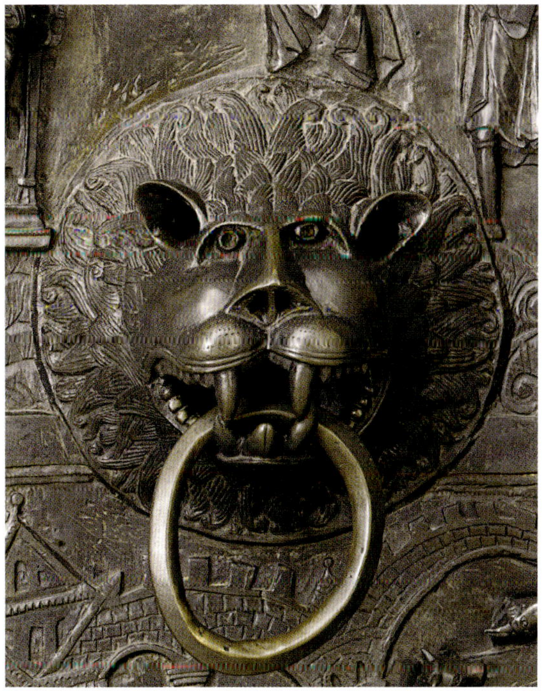

148

148. *Panel 11, ornamental fixture.*

represented in three-quarter view. This is similar to what Bernward proposes, but he chooses a plastic format that makes it possible for the spectator to see the figures from two different angles, thus offering two complementary levels of understanding.

The bust of Mary and the infant Jesus, both sculpted in the round, are clearly turned to the right so that they are placed within the magi's axis of movement (fig. 149). The three-dimensionality and dynamism of the figures considerably strengthen their quality as living presences, that is, of devotional statues. It should be noted that, in order to see their faces (which everyone unfailingly does when facing this panel placed at the viewer's height) one must adopt the magi's lateral viewpoint and consequently identify with them by taking place in the cortege.

Whereas Eve enfolds the infant Abel in her embrace in panel 6 (cf. fig. 90), making the two figures appear as one, here Jesus is stretched out on Mary's lap, fully visible to the viewers (fig. 150). In Carolingian and Ottonian Epiphanies, Mary lifts or extends her right hand in a welcoming gesture. In this panel, Bernward has given her an unusual figural movement. With her left hand holding her son tenderly on her knees and her thumb in contact with the book, Mary becomes a throne from which Christ is presented to the world. With her right hand she underscores the welcoming motion made by her son. This gesture of accompaniment is identical to the one by which God, stepping back, introduced Eve to Adam in the door's second panel (cf. fig. 36).

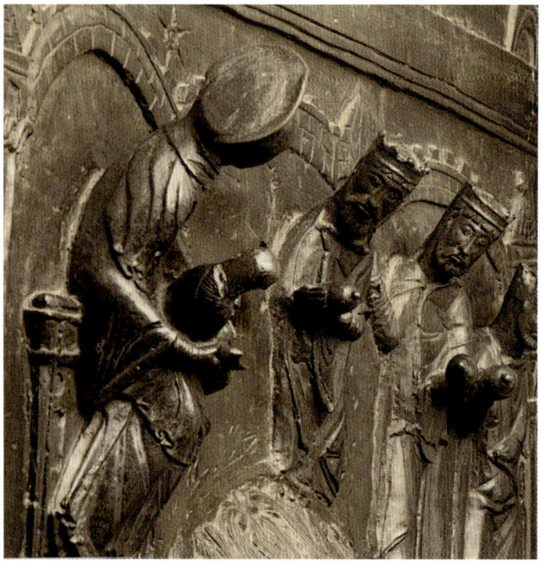

149

By withdrawing in the same manner, Mary offers to the eyes of the world the one whom she designates as the locus of a divine light located, this time, *in* a human body.

The child welcomes the visitors, offering them a covenant, his hand open and lying on his body: he is already giving himself to those he welcomes (fig. 150). He wears no halo, which is even more surprising since he was wearing a large cruciform nimbus in the previous panel (cf. fig. 130). Without developing this complex aspect of the analysis, I suggest three possible solutions to this incongruity. Inasmuch as the child's cranium is flattened and his hairline interrupted in the place where the halo should have been, previous scholars have suggested that the nimbus was lost: the problem is that there is no trace of breakage. On the other hand, it is possible that the wear of the nimbus may have led, at an undetermined time, to an attempt at a restoration by binding it together with a loop, the result of which has not survived. It is also possible that the nimbus, made of a more precious and brilliant metal that would have been ideal for this theophany, was initially placed on Jesus's head before disappearing.

However, I would like to suggest a last explanation: perhaps the nimbus did not exist at the beginning, a deficiency that may have been "corrected" later (we do not have any historical records of the door's restorations) by filing down Jesus's head and adding a halo, which has now disappeared. Although very rare, this type of configuration exists on certain early Christian sarcophagi (like those of the Lateran and the Museo Nazionale of Rome). In addition to a few early medieval crucifixions, it is found in two Germanic Epiphanies of the second half of the eleventh century: on the altar of Melk Abbey and on the portable altar from the same church, now in the Dumbarton Oaks Museum in Washington, DC. Although it cannot be verified, the inspiration for these representations might have been suggested by the Hildesheim door. According to this hypothesis, the reason for the absence of a nimbus could have been a way to distinguish between a profoundly human Jesus and the divine infant in panel 10, destined to be crucified. In addition, the absence of a halo would have been consistent with the very original presence of the book that Jesus holds on his knees.

The book is an attribute found in most Ottonian Epiphanies, whenever it is not replaced by a scroll as in the *Pericopes of Henry II*. The book is an explicit reference to the Word, as discussed in the study of panels 2 and 4. It may refer to Christ's role as a teacher (it is through his Word that he instructs men), to his function as a judge (his message and his omniscience are the measure of Judgment), but the book may also call attention to the second person of the Trinity, the Word endowed with infinite wisdom through which the Father created the world.

Unlike the illustrated codices of Ottonian tradition, as well as those the Creator holds on the door's left wing, Jesus's book is offered to the magus's view, frontally but closed. Jesus's hand is on the upper edge, not as one would hold a book but as one would present a tablet, in a probable allusion to the historical horizon in which it is inscribed: the transformation of the old law into the new.

Other details support this hypothesis. The book has the same oblong format as the divine codex in the Presentation of Eve to Adam (cf. fig. 38), which we know is closely related to panel 15, but there the binding looked like a tablet framed by a large well-wrought border. In panel 11, Jesus's book is simpler, even though the small but visible marks were perhaps applied at some time. In addition, it has two little reels, one under Jesus's hand that may qualify as a roll, and one on the right-hand side, corresponding either to the spine or to the book's closing clasp; at any rate, it characterizes it as a parchment manuscript bound between two covers. Jesus's codex, then, has all the historical properties of textual transmission, such as cover, scroll, and manuscript, bringing about within itself the same kind of synthesis as the *Ecclesia* in panel 10.

Aligned along the axis of Jesus's body, and in the continuity of the child's arm, parallel also to the right hand of the Savior as he offers himself, this book is not an attribute but a textual equivalent of Christ himself, the fulfillment, through his future life, of all the laws imposed or followed by humankind in

149. *Panel 11, Mary and three kings.*

the course of history. Consisting of the Gospels—the sum of the acts of Jesus's public life, his truths, and his teachings—this book is assimilated into a spiritual nourishment given by Christ, received by the Virgin-Church who offers it to her children in place of the milk with which Eve nourished Cain in the symmetrical panel (cf. fig. 91). This sustenance—meditated, imitated, understood, assimilated—will guide Christians toward their salvation: "As newborn babes, desire the rational milk [*rationale* in Latin, *to logikon* in Greek, namely the milk of the Word-Logos] without guile, that thereby you may grow unto salvation" (1 Pet. 2:2).

Paradoxically, the literal content of this Law, more moral than ontological, is not represented on the door but rather on the bronze column that Bernward had cast for St. Michael's Abbey. From bottom to top, in imitation of Trajan's Column, all the scenes of Christ's public life are depicted there, with the exception of the two episodes of his childhood and the four episodes of his Passion, which are illustrated on the right wing (fig. 151). Contrary to what earlier scholars have argued, this is not a complementary narrative but a hermeneutic construct inscribed at the heart of the liturgical space of St. Michael's Abbey, functioning as a network of humans and artifacts [Marchesin 2017]. The importance of the bronze column can only be understood in light of the exegesis of the "column" as Law, Tree of Life, and axis of the world offered on the bronze door. Conversely, the spiritual benefits of the discourse of the door can be assured only by accepting the Law inscribed on the bronze column, which must serve as an inner guide to a Christian life.

The definition we have just given of the Law renewed by Christ as the sum of his actions and his words is not yet complete. As we saw at the beginning of this analysis, the Virgin and Child are given a frontal view in consideration of the viewer's natural position when facing the door. In addition to the fact that this viewpoint makes it possible to see Christ's body in its entirety, as well as his book and the subtle articulation of his gestures, it also integrates the throne with the mother-child couple in order to redefine it (fig. 150).

Majestic, framed by two high columns and set on a base connected both with the foundation and the disk, this throne is pierced by five bays incorporating all the shapes represented on the bronze door: arched bay, rectangular bay, door, oculus, and irregular quadrilateral bay (cf. fig. 126). Although this referential accumulation makes Mary the path transcending all others, it also qualifies the throne as a sort of visual grammar—a kind of sketchbook—

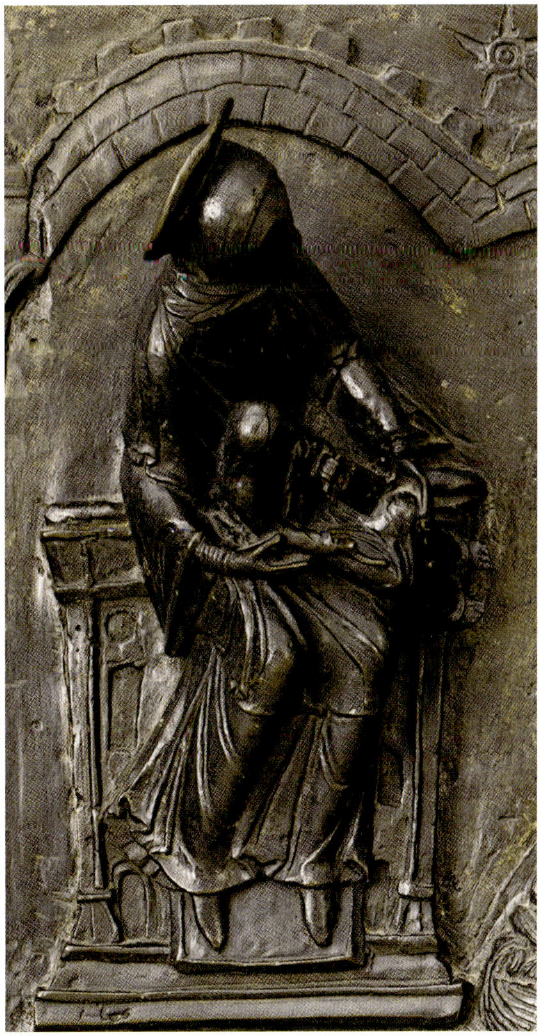

150

150. *Panel 11, Mary and Jesus.*

making it possible to read the entire system. These geometric figures are so subtle that no scholar, to the best of my knowledge, has ever noticed them. Is it fortuitous that it was precisely these figures that reoriented my approach to studying the architectural elements of the door?

We may remember that panels 6 and 11 are placed at eye level, displaying the most obvious typological relationship between the Old and the New Testaments: Eve and Mary. The rules of the architectural arts also form a system of laws. I am arguing that these two panels also provide the visual keys allowing for the understanding both of natural law and of Christ's Law. The promethean advice given to Adam by the angel in panel 6 is answered here by the path to knowledge proposed by the Word through the understanding of what he builds in the world. Prophecies and realizations, paradigms, analogies, taxonomic arrangements of forms, modifications of substance, types of movements, topological territories: human wisdom, illuminated by light and placed in the pres-

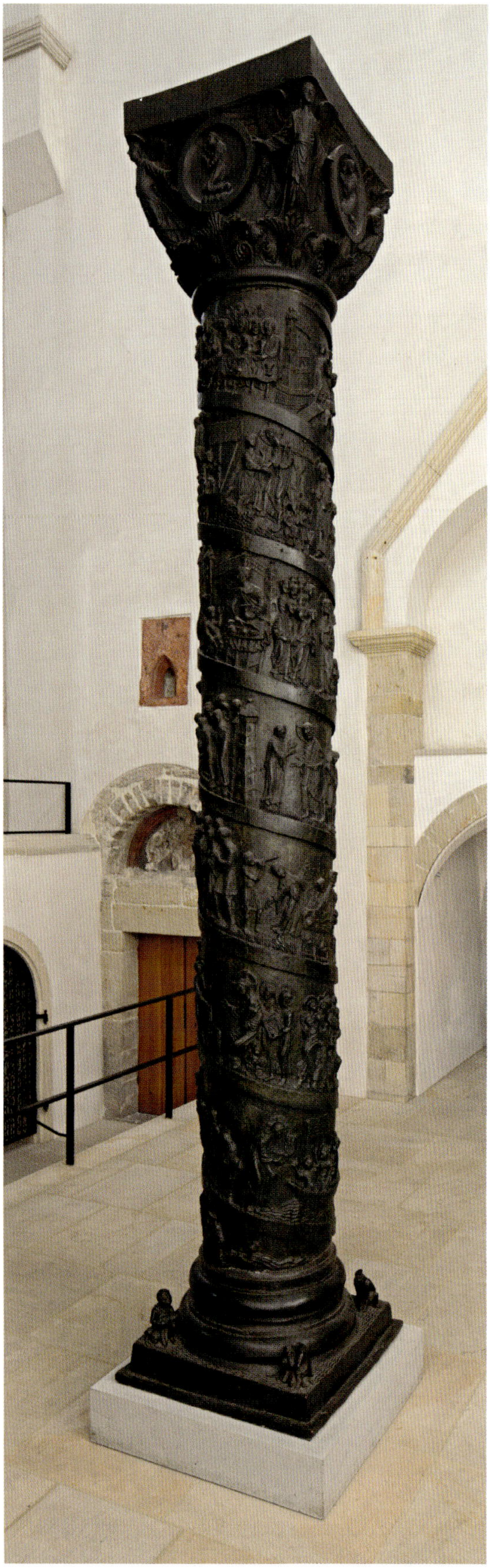

151

ence of the Word, from now on incarnated according to human measure, may accede to divine Wisdom. The seat of the Virgin and Child on the bronze door is not only a throne of Majesty but also a throne of Wisdom, a *Sedes sapientiae*, according to the denomination proposed by Ilene Forsyth [1972].

"But someone may contend that the 'days of the tree of life' of which the prophet Isaiah speaks are the present times of the Church of Christ, and that Christ Himself is prophetically called the tree of life because He is the Wisdom of God, of which Solomon says, 'It is a tree of life to them that lay hold upon it'" (Augustine, *De civitate Dei*, Book XX, 26, 1032).

151. *Bernward's column.*

(facing)

152. *Panel 11.*

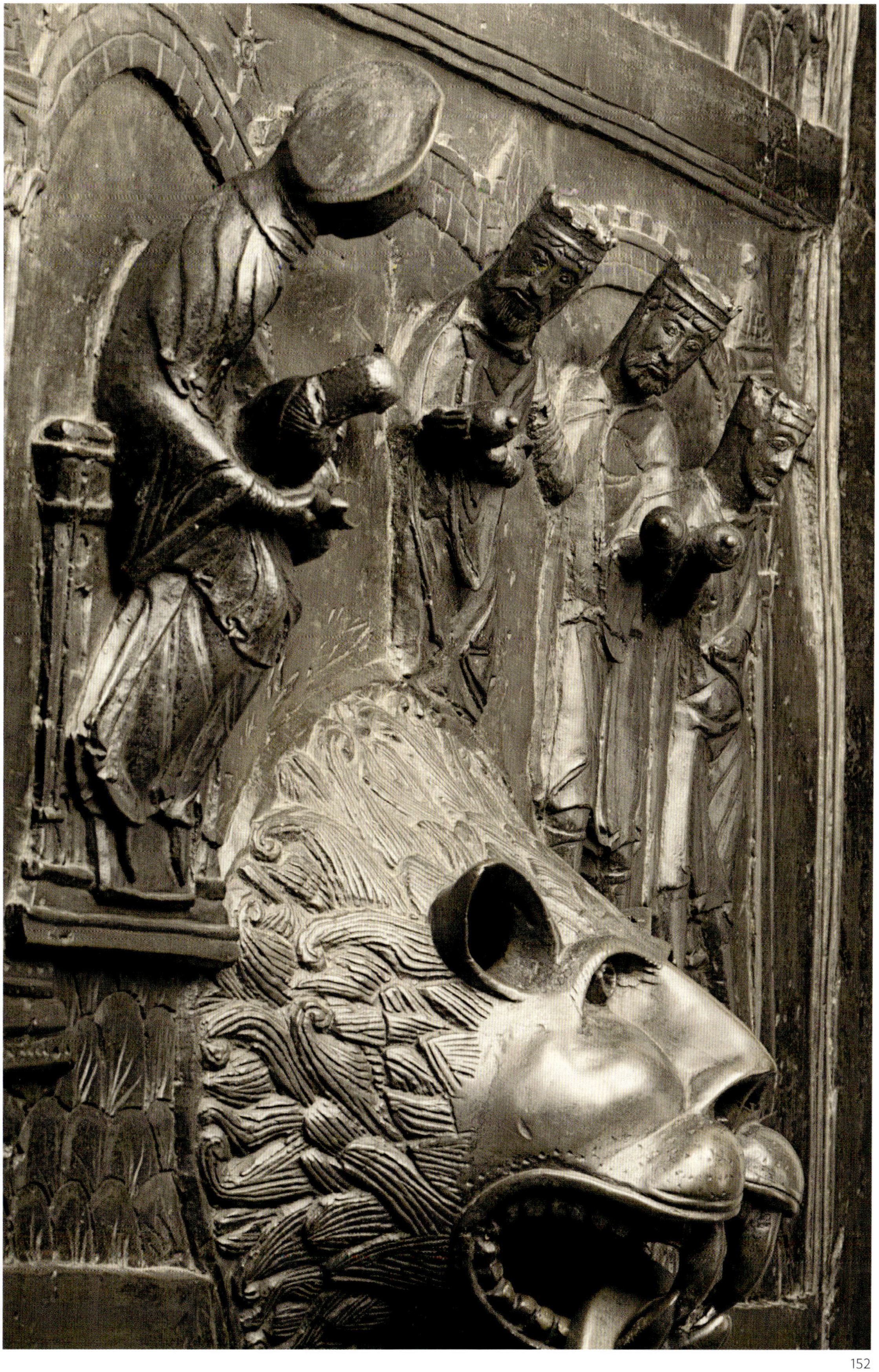

152

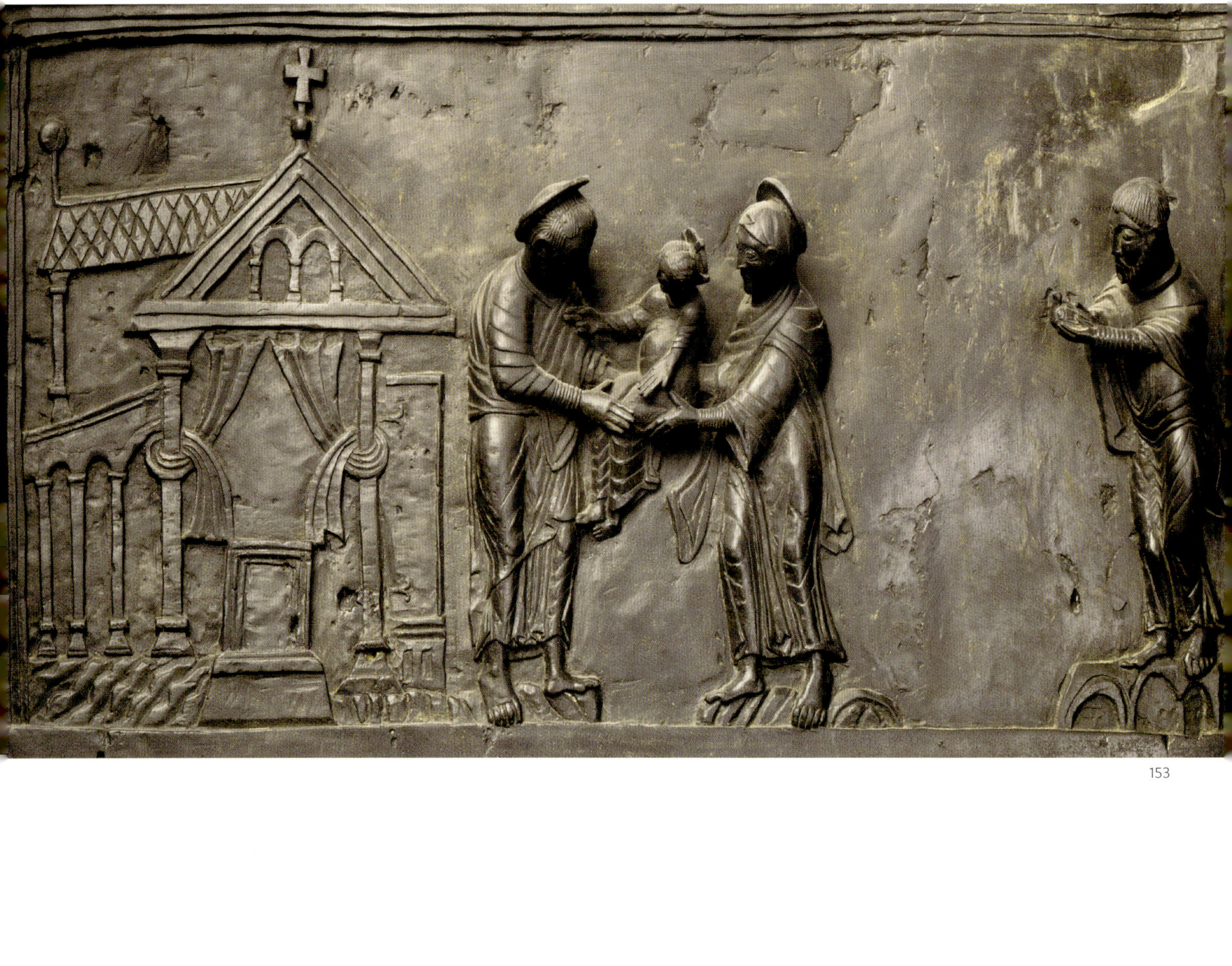

Panel **12**

LITURGY

Panel 12 closes the cycle of Jesus's infancy. Symmetrical to the scene of the expulsion of Adam and Eve from Paradise which closes the Edenic cycle, it is organized around the same underlying theme: a change of condition correlated to a change of place. However, it is also proposed as antithesis: whereas humans were driven from Paradise by the angel, Jesus is taken to the Temple of Solomon to be presented to God (fig. 153).

The identification of the figures poses no difficulty because the scene follows the biblical text almost to the letter:

> And after eight days were accomplished, that the child should be circumcised, his name was called Jesus, which was called by the angel, before he was conceived in the womb. And after the days of her purification, according to the law of Moses, were accomplished, they carried him to Jerusalem, to present him to the Lord, as it is written in the law of the Lord, every male opening the womb shall be called holy to the Lord, and to offer a sacrifice, according as it is written in the law of the Lord, a pair of turtledoves, or two young pigeons. And behold there was a man in Jerusalem named Simeon, and this man was just and devout, waiting for the consolation of Israel; and the Holy Ghost was in him. And he had received an answer from the Holy Ghost, that he should not see death, before he had seen the Christ of the Lord. And he came by the Spirit into the temple. And when his parents brought in the child Jesus, to do for him according to the custom of the law, he also took him into his arms, and blessed God, and said: Now thou dost dismiss thy servant, O Lord, according to thy word in peace, because my eyes have seen thy salvation, which thou hast prepared before the face of all peoples, a light to the revelation of the Gentiles, and the glory of thy people Israel. And his father and mother were wondering at those things which were spoken concerning him. (Luke 2:21–33)

153. *Panel 12.*

In the middle of the panel Mary presents her child to Simeon, whose back is to the temple. On the right, Joseph holds the sacrificial bird at arm's length, holding it delicately between his hands. The Temple of Solomon, a large edifice with triangular pediment, represented frontally as well as in profile, occupies the left third of the panel. Its monumental door is framed by two columns, both with a capital made of an astragal topped by a carved echinus. Isolated and without any visible interaction with the protagonists of the narration, the temple attracts attention because of its depth, revealed by two curtains drawn away from the façade. It addresses the viewer, much more so than the figures in the image, who function in a closed system.

The structure is represented as described in the Book of Kings and in the Chronicles. Its two frontal columns open onto a square sanctuary (2 Chron. 3) preceded by a courtyard on the same level as the space occupied by the figures. The Altar of the Holocaust, a quadrangular stone block (1 Kings 8:64 and 2 Chron. 8:12), takes center stage. A large cross surmounts the building. Its visibility is enhanced by its position on an orb modeled in very high relief with a diameter much larger than in the previous panels.

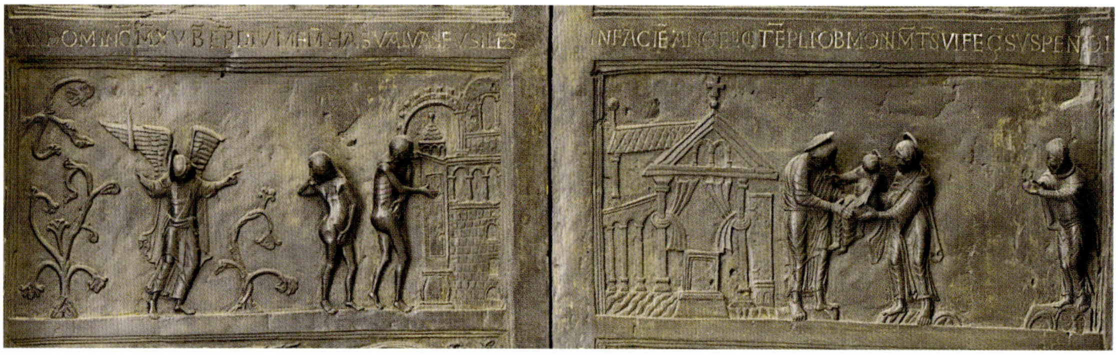

154

The orb calls attention to the universal significance of the sign dominating the temple of God.

By its very presence this sign breaks with the rigorous historicity that had been the rule so far. No other building, not even the Church in panels 10 and 11, had been designated by the cross of Christ. Biblical figures, even when caught in the mesh of historical heritages or prophetic attributes, were all represented within the framework of their historical existence, that is, in the time and place assigned to them by the biblical historia. The Temple of Jerusalem, although identified as such in Luke's text, can no longer be the Temple of Solomon *stricto sensu* in panel 12 because the cross transforms it.

In the previous panels the cross assumed two major functions, first as attribute, then as formal paradigm. It was associated either with the divinity, his messenger, or his message, thus functioning as an attribute of the creating and enunciating Word. Or the cross could be the paradigmatic imprint given by the Word to created beings and things.

Indeed, in panel 12 the cross functions as a *signum* emanating from God, modifying the nature of the Temple of Solomon and signifying it. In Christianity, signs with this double power are called sacramental signs [Rosier-Catach 2004, 471–491]. They give access to an invisible reality, transforming and revealing the connections uniting the earthly and heavenly worlds: they change "natural" constraints by reconfiguring them in order to sanctify the world and humans.

The term *signum* is frequently used in the Bible, but it should be pointed out that, in a convergence that does not seem to me coincidental, the biblical narrative of the Presentation at the Temple specifically designates Jesus himself as a sign: "Behold this child is set for the fall, and for the resurrection of many in Israel, and for a sign which shall be contradicted [*signum cui contradicetur*]. And thy own soul a sword shall pierce, that, out of many hearts, thoughts may be revealed" (Luke 2:34–35). The violence spawned by the affirmation of the universal dominance of the cross is depicted in the following panel, which shows Christ's trial. Precisely in what way is Solomon's temple transformed by the cross?

The edifice is inscribed into a system of orthonormal visual correspondences perceived almost immediately by the eye (fig. 155). Vertically, its general configuration, despite significant variations to which we shall return, announces Christ's tomb (panel 15). Horizontally, it is also correlated with the gate of the earthly prison opposite it in panel 5 (fig. 154). In retrospect, this connection even explains the representation of a door in panel 5, since the rare images of the "gate to Paradise" do not adopt the format of a building. In this respect, it should also be pointed out that locutions such as "gate to Paradise" and "Temple of Solomon," although quite medieval (*porta paradisi*, for example, is inscribed in Bernward's Gospel Book), are not used in biblical passages illustrated by the bronze door. Genesis speaks of a *paradisus* to which access is henceforth forbidden; Luke evokes only the temple in Jerusalem. It seems to me that the particular interpretation of the two episodes given by Bernward is inserted precisely in this space: the text prevails in that it states, to the letter, a truth that he returns to the visual hermeneutics of unveiling.

The analogy between the door of the earthly prison and the Temple stems not only from their symmetrical placement but also from the structural similarity of the elements composing them. They are identically constituted of two superimposed stories; they have a nave, arcades, and a door with hinges of similar shape. Furthermore, and this is unique in the entire architecture of the bronze door, the two buildings are literally joined to the lateral frame of their respective panels. The frame that cuts off the building in panel 5 thus constitutes the back of the building in panel 12, whose nave it supports. All this adds to the permeability between the two scenes.

It is possible to organize the comparison—elucidation and opposition—between the two struc-

154. *Panel 5 and 12.*

tures on this common basis. As we saw in the analysis of panel 5, the door of the earthly prison, enclosed in a small tower, was depicted as still locked, its bay inaccessible and topped by a dome evoking a sepulchral rotunda. The latter was extended by a crenellated arch that fell like a yoke—the yoke of the flesh—on the stooped shoulders of Adam, condemned to a life entrapped in "two dimensions." The rotunda, the inaccessible bays, and the arch represent subjugation to the old law.

The Temple responds to the crushing threshold of the earthly prison in two ways: by its opening and by its inclusion in the heritage of Synagogue and Church in panel 10 (cf. fig. 126).

A triple arcade on the left side of the building is reminiscent of the one found in the small tower and above the great wall of the earthly prison. In the Temple of panel 12, the arcade descends to ground level, exhibiting a new accessibility. This accessibility is underscored by the Temple's open door and the monumental entrance magnified by the separation of the curtains draped around the columns, an ancient ornamental tradition found in early medieval manuscripts.

Some of the elements that make up the Temple belong to the legacy of the Church represented behind the Virgin in the Nativity scene. To begin with, it should be noted that its façade is frontal, but its body is extended to the left in a linear perspective, the same that appears in the building in panel 10. This comparison calls attention to the similarity between the triple arcade on the left of the temple and the arcade of the ground level in the Church's nave.

This three-dimensionality is antinomic to the perspectival flattening of the gate of Eden, which, as I suggested, was deliberate, emphasizing the building's prisonlike dimension. Indeed, it is also antinomic to the frontal flatness of the right side of the Temple of Solomon, which constitutes a signifying microsystem (fig. 156). Under the hinged door that is identical in shape and ornamentation to the door of panel 5, there is a small wall, contiguous to the base of the right column of the monumental entrance. This small wall supports two rectangular bays that recall those of the Synagogue. Indeed, the new Temple has incorporated the imprisoning door as well as the useless door of the ancient Temple, replacing them with its monumental entrance.

Despite their proximity, the Temple of Solomon and the Church in panel 10 exhibit notable differences, particularly when it comes to their triangular pediment (cf. fig. 129). The three semicircular bays of the church become twin bays, a visual formulation of the double nature of Christ already present in

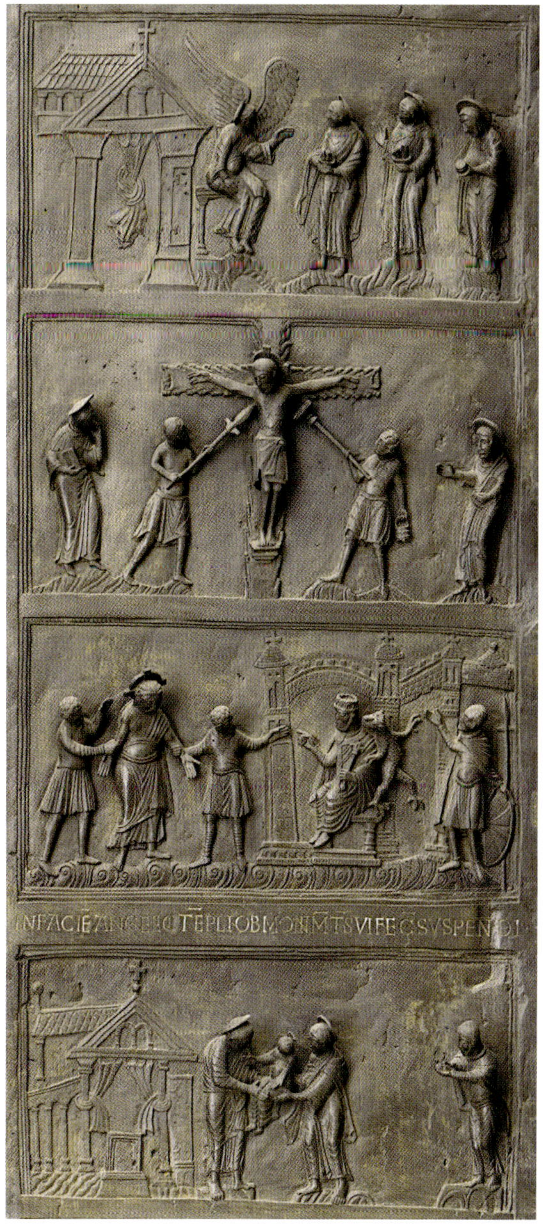

155

155. *Panel 12, 13, 14, and 15.*

panel 9 (cf. fig. 123) and perfectly articulated with the cross on the pinnacle. Similarly, both Solomon's temple and the church contain an isolated column, but whereas this column was in the crypt of the church in panel 10 (cf. fig. 129), it is now placed on the upper story of the Temple in panel 12—an ascensional process destined to continue—where it supports the roofing, also dominated by an orb (fig. 156). It is noteworthy that, unlike the bases of the columns in the Temple's lower part, the base of the isolated column supporting the roof has no chisel marks and therefore, for the first time on the bronze door, appears completely exempt from the poison of evil and from death.

However, this "column of the Law" has not

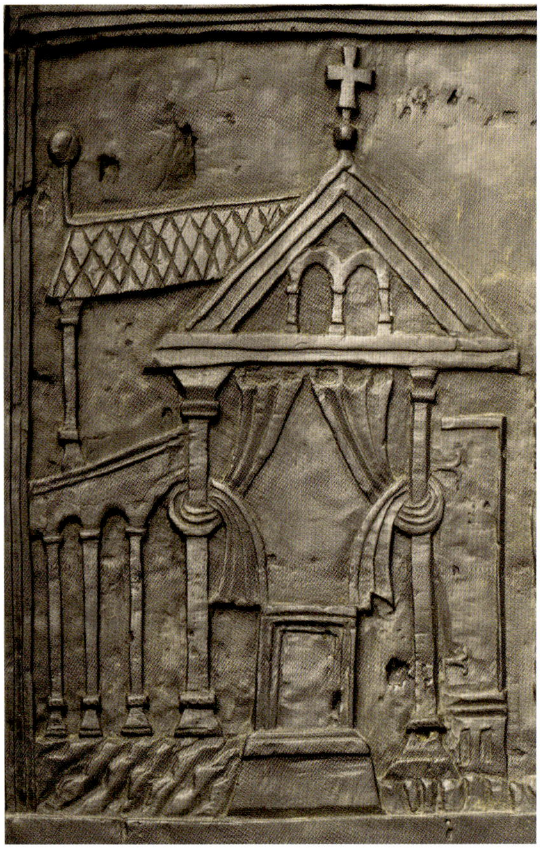

156

changed its function because the roofing it supports becomes in turn a community image. Instead of the rounded tiles of the previous buildings, the roof is built with diamond shaped tiles/slates flawlessly joined. Their model is probably the *opus reticulatum* of Roman constructions. This model gives to the community of believers supported by the column a perfectly homogeneous crisscross arrangement, one already announced by the similar interlacing of the swaddling clothes covering the body of the infant Jesus in panel 10 (cf. fig. 138). In other words, the City of God, upheld by the column of the Law *above* the sacred but earthly place that is the Temple of Solomon, can be superimposed on the very body of Christ (John 2:18–22). The reader has undoubtedly foreseen that this integrative turn prepared by panel 12 is going to happen precisely in panel 15. Only here, in this soilless place, will all traces of the poisoning of the world disappear.

At this stage of the inquiry, Bernward's theological demonstration is convincing and reassuring for Christian viewers, but it is still incomplete. How did the ancient Temple morph into the new Temple? Panel 12 introduces a reversal in the reading paradigm of the door. So far, the meaningful shapes of figures, plants, or architectural elements have clarified the holy story; now it is the historia that serves as exegesis of the quasi-sacramental action accomplished by the cross/sign in the image. It will unveil the fruits of the new covenant.

Because of its numerous Old Testament citations, the episode of the Presentation at the Temple narrated by Luke is not easily intelligible. It appears under several headings in historiography ("Meeting with Simeon" or *Hypapante*, "Purification of the Virgin," "Presentation at the Temple") and has given rise, if not to multiple interpretations, at least to differentiated liturgical practices that have influenced its understanding. It is necessary to mention it here especially because Bernward was acquainted with Byzantine scholars at the Ottonian court and may very well have had a keen awareness of these differences. A religious feast was associated with this biblical episode as early as the fourth century in the Middle East, a little later in the Latin world, where the oldest known representation is a mosaic in the triumphal arch of Santa Maria Maggiore in Rome. At the beginning this feast was organized around the main figures of Simeon and Jesus. As attested by the traditional candle-light procession in the West, it later gave rise, at least as early as the seventh century, to the celebration of the Purification of the Virgin. This wording prevails in the sacramentaries from the first decades of the eleventh century [Palazzo and Johansson 1996, 23; Schorr 1946].

This liturgy and the iconography it influenced—early Christian, Roman-Byzantine, and Ottonian, although virtually unknown in the Carolingian and Insular world [Schiller 1966–91, 100]—can only be understood in light of a typological reading of Luke's passage. The Evangelist quotes the Old Testament three times. Although the addressee remains obscure in the original text and was contested by the Church Fathers, the mention of purification ("after the days of her purification") has been associated with the Virgin Mary in connection with a passage in Leviticus describing the ritual of animal sacrifice to which a woman who has just given birth is submitted (Lev. 12:6–8). The second Old Testament ritual quoted by Luke is a prescription from the book of Exodus, established at the heart of Hebrew law after the tenth plague of Egypt killed all first-born males ("Sanctify unto me every firstborn that openeth the womb among the children of Israel, as well of men as of beasts: for they are all mine" [Exod. 13:2; cf. also Exod. 12–13 and Exod. 34:19–20]). The third Old Testament citation from Luke's passage concerns the price assigned to the redemption of the first newborn male ("a pair of turtledoves or two young doves"), indicated in Leviticus as the price set by the law for the atonement of sin (Lev. 5:7).

156. *Panel 12, Solomon's temple.*

Was Bernward's interpretation of the episode we call Presentation at the Temple (in conformity with the most neutral terminology of modern historiography) influenced by the liturgical content of earlier celebrations, and if that is the case, by which one?

The position of this episode in the narrative of the bronze door offers part of the answer. It cannot be dated with precision by reading the New Testament: Luke does not mention the magi, nor does Matthew say anything about the Presentation at the Temple. By placing the latter after the Epiphany, we might at least infer that Bernward proposed a chronology contrary to that of the Pseudo-Matthew and the majority of biblical concordances. Instead, it respects the chronology that Hrosvitha of Gandersheim introduced in the versified and slightly rearranged version she gives of the apocryphal text [Goullet 1996, 465]. In addition, this order of succession corresponds to the liturgical calendar, where the Epiphany is fixed on January 6 and the Presentation at the Temple on February 2. This sequence is also found in the cycle of Jesus's infancy of the earliest Ottonian evangeliaries, pericopes, and sacramentaries, probably inspired by Byzantine manuscripts [Mayr-Harting, 75]. Like them, Bernward must have preferred a liturgical time, already established by the Incarnation, to the linear but uncertain time of the biblical narrative. One might plausibly suggest that the bishop, in his attention to historicity, must have been aware of the rupture that this chronological sequence introduced in the narrative of the bronze door, and would certainly have used it to reinforce the strictly liturgical dimension of this panel.

It remains now to uncover the specific ritual to which the depiction refers. The central presence of Simeon receiving Jesus from the Virgin's hands, the Hypapante, seems to weaken the hypothesis that it is the Purification of Mary, even if the ritual was favored in the early eleventh century. Yet things are not so simple. Bernward undoubtedly reutilizes all the iconographic elements he received from previous Western and Eastern traditions to give a novel typological function to each character.

Simeon is the key figure in the scenes of the Presentation at the Temple. He receives the Child, either from Mary's hands, or more exceptionally, from Joseph's, as in the *Hitda Codex* [Darmstadt, Hessische Landesbibl. Cod. 1640 f 23; first half of the eleventh century]. In panel 12, the old man wears a nimbus, which proves that "he came by the Spirit into the temple" but also that his eyes "have seen [his] salvation" (Luke 2:27 and 30). His body weakened by age, he bears witness to the literal fulfillment of the angel's prophecy by meeting the gaze of the infant Jesus (fig. 153). Isolated, without nimbus, Joseph stands on some mounds at the far right of the panel, whereas Simeon and Mary, placed in contact with the Child's body they share, are already inscribed into the elective process of salvation.

The nature of the ground corresponds to the role of each protagonist (fig. 157). Represented with great care, the individualized bedrocks underscore each character's relationship with the Messiah. Two well-defined caves appear under Joseph's feet. The one on the left is accentuated by the design of an inner arch, perhaps the memory of the ancient covenant God had established with Abel. Joseph seems to be unaware of it, once again refusing to advance toward truth. The one on the right is a double cavity that will be seen in the last panel (cf. fig. 186): it represents the underworld, namely death. Indeed, Joseph stays within the bounds of the ancient law, performing the ritual of animal sacrifice.

It seems to me, however, that Bernward's objective is not to stigmatize Joseph's incredulity once more but instead to use him as a point of departure to evoke the new sacrificial ritual that will efface the old one. This continuity is shown by the fact that

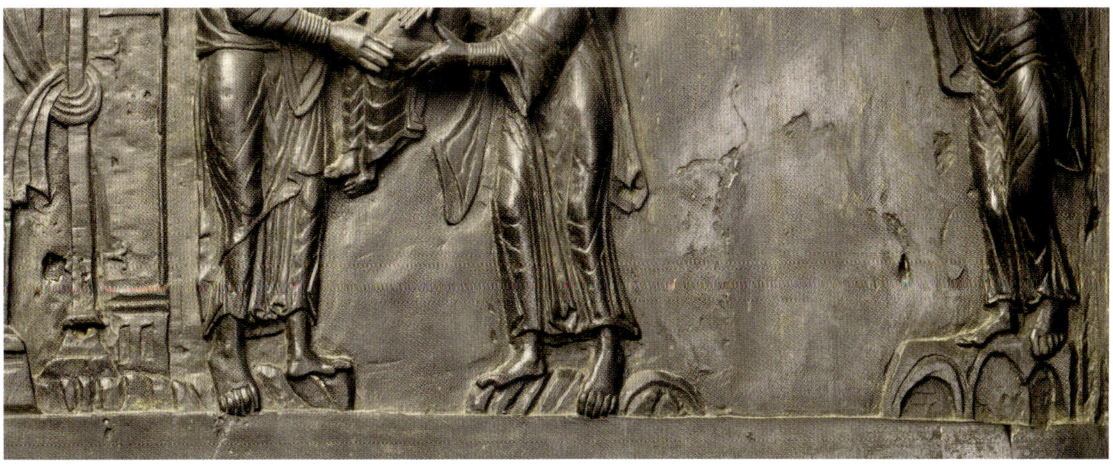

157

157. *Panel 12, ground, right.*

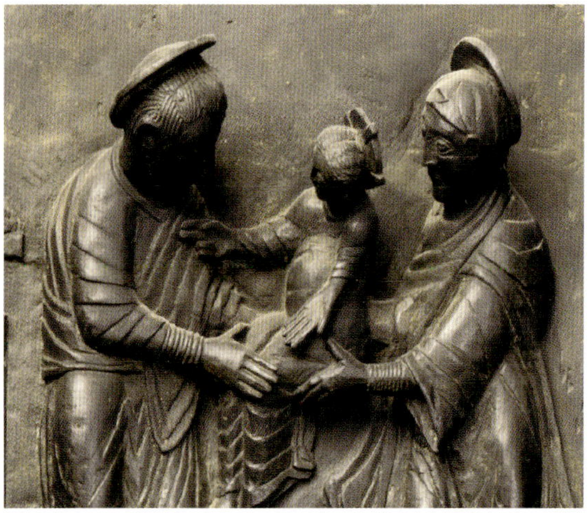

158

the garments of the three protagonists are depicted in the same way, with regular pleats very similar to those of the Child's tunic. Joseph holds only one of the two birds required for the ritual (whether for the atonement of the first born or for the purification of the mother). To the best of my knowledge, this is the only example of such a representation in Ottonian culture. In fact, his "incomplete" offering, one bird, will be completed by the one playing out in Solomon's temple. But before examining it, I suggest recalling what animal sacrifice represents in Hebrew culture.

Like all holocausts in the Old Testament, Joseph's sacrifice is a gift to God. It is offered in a spirit of penitence and adoration, acted out in blood and fire, but above all it concerns the human heart and its connection with God. For the Hebrews, this expiatory dimension was refocused around the notion of the covenant at the time of Moses's ascent to Mount Sinai. After the enunciation of the Decalogue and the formulation of the prescriptions derived from it (Exod. 19–23), Moses ratified the bond established between God and the Hebrew people, liberated from the yoke of the Pharaohs, by sprinkling his brothers with the blood of sacrificial animals (Exod. 24). The ritual of liberatory purification through blood seals the covenant between God and his chosen people. As such, it participates in the providential progression of holy history announcing, for Christians, the sacrifice of Jesus and the new future covenant (Heb. 9:19–22).

An imaginary horizontal line, drawn along the base of the Temple's pediment, connects Joseph's bird to the right hand that the Child lays on Simeon's heart (fig. 153). Yet with his other hand, shown with an open palm, Jesus gestures toward the Temple's altar on which he knows he is to be sacrificed. Reversing the terms of the first ritual immolation in the Holy Scripture, that of Isaac, here the Child takes the animal's place. His sacrifice will be the last (Heb. 9).

Arms extended, Mary holds Jesus away from her body, giving him to Simeon, who receives him without using the veil that Abel had placed over his offering, and with which the old man often appears in previous and contemporary Presentations at the Temple (fig. 158). By taking the Child in his hands, Simeon completes the triangular pattern delineated by the three hands on the Child's thighs. The gift of the body of Christ takes on a Eucharistic dimension, all the clearer because it bonds Mary and the old man, and because Mary embodies the Church.

The detail is striking: at the precise place where the Child lays his blessing hand on Simeon, the material of the toga has thickened, forming a pattern of flat parallel folds, visible as well on the Child's left arm and on the lower part of his tunic. There is more: in historical depth, these parallel folds recall the pattern of large, regular pleats on the sleeve of the divine Hand in panel 7 (cf. fig. 101). As previously mentioned, Cain tried to mimic their appearance, but his agitated flesh and garments were covered with atomized life channels. In the act of murdering his brother in panel 8, these channels bore the triangular

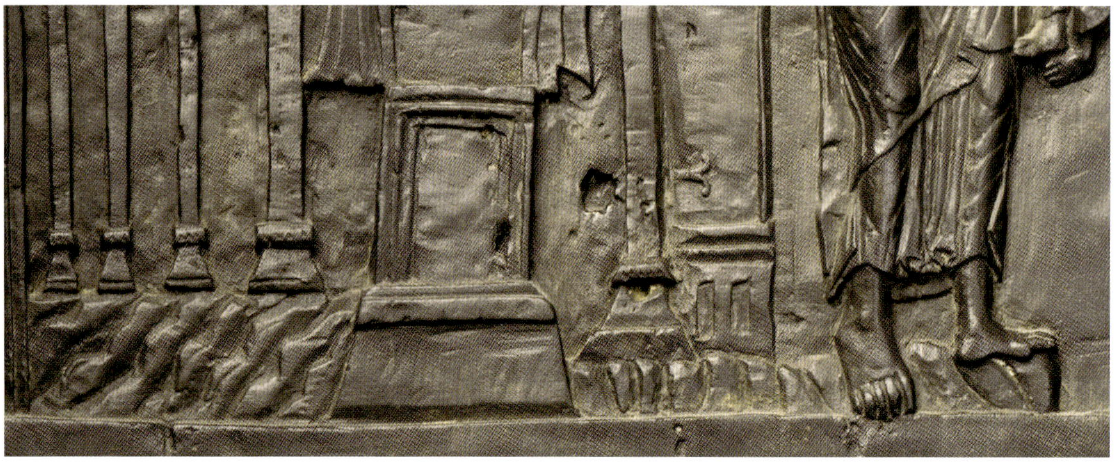

159

158. *Panel 12, Simeon, Jesus, and Mary.*

159. *Panel 12, ground and building, left.*

chisel marks of the perpetrated evil (cf. fig. 106). The act of blessing is fundamentally a divine gift that brings about a divine transformation in its beneficiary. In panel 12, the sacrificial gift that Jesus makes of himself transforms Simeon's body. The old man's specific connection with the divine image grants him purification through the sacrificial blood, and later through the body of Christ, which we will come to understand fully in the following development of this analysis.

Two distinct bedrocks are represented under the Virgin's feet (fig. 157). The curved one under her left foot includes two converging channels that cannot penetrate the crust surmounting them. They are similar in shape to the ones enclosed by the dry riverbed at the center of Eden in panel 3, the panel of original sin (cf. fig. 55). However, the bedrock under Mary's right foot is flat and crossed by thick parallel lines. They are also found in reverse orientation under Simeon's feet, with the Child's body serving as a sort of symmetrical center (fig. 157). The thick, fluid diagonals carved into the matter depict the channels reopened in the earth and destined to receive the divine substance that flows out on the left side of the panel, namely a geomorphologic equivalent of the life channels of the human body, structured to receive the Spirit.

The bedrock on which Simeon stands extends under the building that subsumed the earthly prison and the Synagogue. It comes to rest against the Altar of the Holocaust placed at the Temple's entrance (fig. 159). Tumultuous waves creating deep furrows surge from the left of the altar. The image is undoubtedly connected to a vision of Ezekiel: "He brought me again to the gate of the house, and behold waters issued out from under the threshold of the house toward the east" (Ezek. 47:1). The prophetic tradition begun with this vision is attested many times in the Acts of the Apostles and summarized in a spectacular conclusion by the apocalyptic vision of St. John: The angel "showed me a river of water of life, clear as crystal, proceeding from the throne of God and of the Lamb" (Rev. 22:1). The liquid flowing from the Altar of the Holocaust is the innocent blood of Christ, the lamb of God, announced by Abel's offering in panel 7 and sacrificed on the cross. This last sacrifice enacts the purification of the world: "In that day there shall be a fountain open to the house of David, and to the inhabitants of Jerusalem for the washing of the sinner, and of the unclean woman" (Zech. 13:1); "every living creature that creepeth whithersoever the torrent shall come, shall live . . . all things shall live to which the torrent shall come" (Ezek. 47:9).

The closed channels placed under Joseph are reopened under the Virgin and Simeon. They receive the purifying flow of the blood of Jesus. The area covered by this purification is the same as the one above which is positioned the perfectly configured roofing of the City of God, a community refounded by Christ. It is only in the bosom of this community, the Church as womb of a new life, that the conditions for the spiritual reconfiguration and purification of bodies are established. This is what the Crucifixion in panel 14 will show, having warned the viewers beforehand in panel 13 of the profound nature of this purification and of the evil the Crucifixion must confront.

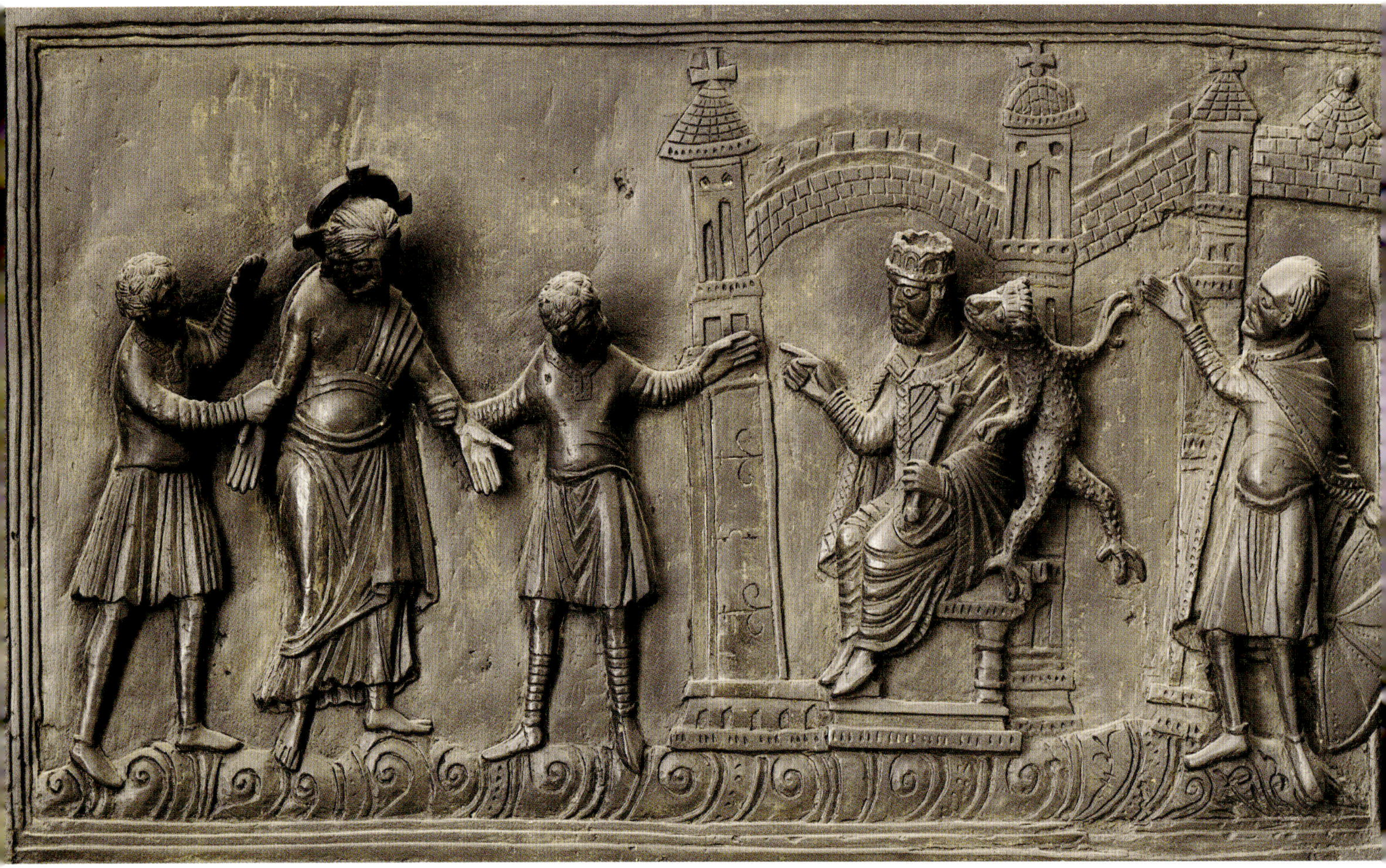

Panel **13**

EVIL

160. *Panel 13.*

With the main episodes and miracles of Christ's public life depicted on the nearby bronze column, the right wing takes up the narrative thirty years after the Presentation at the Temple when Jesus, betrayed and then arrested, is led by two men before a king in order to be judged (fig. 160).

The Son of God is represented for the first time as an adult in the same register that characterized his Father as a person in panel 4 (cf. fig. 1). In addition to the theophanic power of the depiction, it is important to note that the two divine *personae* appear in the upper half of the door, above the height of the viewers; their close proximity reminding us that the Son is there to replace a missing Father, and is positioned as his exact equivalent. They are interchangeable in this perfect substantial sameness, as established by the first Council of Nicaea in 325.

As usual in early medieval art, Jesus physically resembles the God of Genesis; his large stature dominates the panel's other characters. The Son is represented with the beard and cruciform nimbus that his father had in the left wing, the only difference being that the cross behind Jesus's head is much larger than that of the outraged God in panel 4. In addition, the halo and the arms of the cross are sculpted with a particularly signifying ornamental motif: small circular marks, regularly spaced, are visible on the rim of the disc, between each arm of the cross (fig. 161). They contrast with the triangular chisel marks of evil, particularly numerous in this panel: they cover the ground, architectural structures, garments, objects, as well as the demonic beast clinging to the side of the accusing king. Conversely, the rows of circular points are similar to the pearl ornamentation of the binding on the book that God holds tightly to his chest in panel 2 while introducing Eve to Adam in the light of divine love (cf. fig. 39). Christ's cruciform nimbus in panel 13 derives its shape not only from the cross—divine visibility—but also from the principle of union established in panel 2. This level of intelligibility of Christ is an additional stage in re-creating the covenant between God and humans.

Let us examine this body that Bernward presents as the instrument of mediation chosen by God in order to establish salvation. Unlike the Father, portrayed with long flowing garments in the opposite panel, Jesus is represented in a thick toga clinging to his body, its antique style exposing a partially bare torso (fig. 161). This nudity, absent from the scenes of the Nativity and the Epiphany, is emphasized in the Crucifixion panel (cf. fig. 169), and then concealed again in panel 16 (cf. fig. 186). Jesus's nakedness implies many concomitant, or rather converging, significations.

Conventionally, this symbolic usage appears as early as Carolingian times [Marchesin 2002]. Nudity calls attention first of all to the character's humility and submission by virtue of self-effacement before God, as witnessed by several passages in the Old Testament, particularly those concerning David (2 Sam. 6:14–16). At the same time, like the hard working and suffering Adam in panel 6 (cf. fig. 88), whom Christ comes to replace as a new Adam, nudity reveals the vulnerability that comes from God becoming human flesh.

Symmetrical to the bare shoulder in panel 13, panel 4 displays the Book of Natural Law that the Father holds to his chest and which, by the very fact

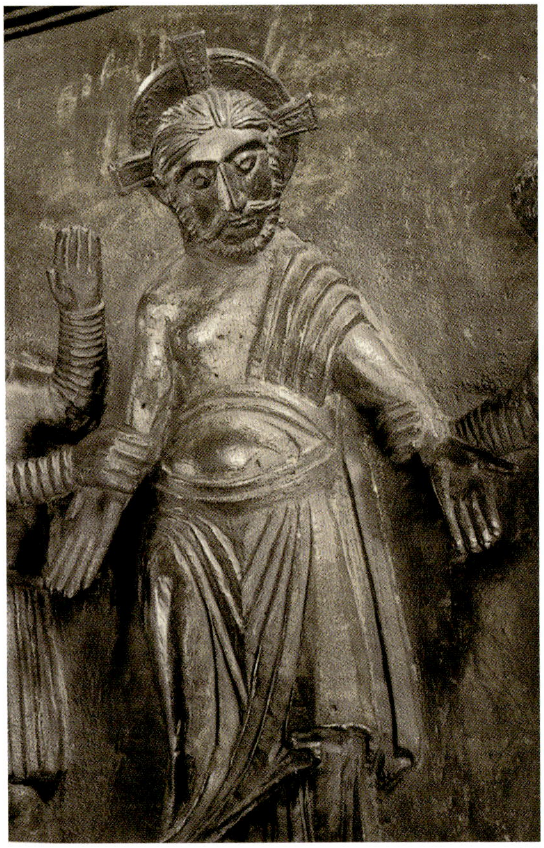

161

of its existence, explains the death to which Adam, Eve, and their descendants are destined (cf. fig. 58). The body of Jesus replaces this ancient law, having the power to convert it into the Law of eternal life. This oxymoron, at the heart of Christianity, is dramatized by Jesus's gestures. By appearing frontally and not in profile like God in panel 4, Christ exposes his body to the spectators' gaze, turning away from that of his judges. His refusal to defend himself is one of the most troubling aspects of the narrative of his appearance before Herod and Pontius Pilate: "Then Pilate asked him, 'Do you not hear the testimony they are bringing against you?' But Jesus made no reply." (Matt. 27:13–14). "Then he [Herod] questioned Him with many words, but He answered him nothing" (Luke 23:9). In the door, Jesus does not respond to the accusing finger of the earthly king but to the one God points at Adam and Eve in panel 4. He obeys only the father. Head bowed, arms hanging, palms open in total abandonment and acceptance of a sin that is not his, he redeems Adam's first sin: "Therefore, as by the offence of one, unto all men to condemnation; so also by the justice of one, unto all men to justification of life. For as by the disobedience of one man, many were made sinners; so also by the obedience of one, many shall be made just" (Rom. 5:18–19).

The program of the rest of the panel becomes the exegesis of this salvific gesture, playing on certain typological contrasts between panels 4 and 13 when set horizontally. God, the accuser, has become the accused, whereas humans, the accused, have been transformed into God's accusers. This hierarchical subversion of creatures and Creator is of the same nature as original sin, which such subversion prolongs. In the same way, in the two symmetrical panels evil is transmitted and shared, as shown by the articulation of collective gestures. In panel 4 God accused Adam, who accused Eve, who deflected the blame onto the serpent who in turn passed it on to the woman's womb. In panel 13, the hands of the protagonists, including the demonic figure between the king and the soldier, are interconnected, thus producing a long chain of fallacious accusations (fig. 160).

In spite of, or rather because of, this parallelism, the comparison between the two images brings out a major difference between them. In panel 4, God stood outside the chain of transmission of sin/condemnation to death formulated in accordance with his Law but from which he was excluded. Panel 13 proposes a human chain of which Christ is now an active participant because of his incarnation. Contrary to what Adam and Eve did, he, the Righteous One, acknowledges a sin he has not committed and takes evil on himself. As a man charged with the sin of men as well as a Son in the perfect image of God the Father, Jesus prepares himself for the redeeming sacrifice to be carried out in the next panel. His tortured body will become the paradigm for the body of the *homo novus*, the New Man. His almond shaped abdomen, emphasized by the folds of a toga tied at the hips, is already swollen with the breath of life, the same breath that animated the immortal Eve of the very first panel, visible also on the infant Jesus in the previous panel (cf. fig. 12 and 158). In addition, it is worth noting that the unexposed part of his torso is covered with the thick and superimposed pleats that, in the previous panel, characterized the modification of a body to which divine blessing had conferred the divine order (cf. fig. 158). Christ is fully a man but a man fully realized in God's image.

Surrendering to the will of the Father and assuming sin are not on the same scale as the sacrifice in the following panel. The silent battle waged by the incarnated Word in panel 13 is of another kind. To the best of my knowledge, there is no iconographic tradition likely to have supplied Bernward with a model for the staging of Christ's trial, which presents the historia not only in its divine and providential dimension but also in its felt historicity. By associating St. John's approach to sin (Jesus is the path leading

161. *Panel 13, Christ.*

back to God) with St. Paul's moral warnings (humans remain prone to sin), Bernward calls attention to the complexity of the human condition and reveals the arcane power of evil as well as the means to fight against it: "For we know that the law is spiritual, but I am carnal, sold under sin. For that which I work, I understand not. For I do not that good which I will, but the evil which I hate, that I do" (Rom 7:14–15); "I myself, with the mind [*mente*] serve the law of God; but with the flesh, the law of sin" (Rom 7:25). (For clarity's sake, I use "sin" to refer to original sin and "evil" to refer to human temptations inherent in the corrupted flesh.)

The panel presents a two-part composition in which the architectural elements are present only in the right half (fig. 160). The arrangement of the figures is symmetrical as well: Christ, placed between two guards, is positioned as counterpart to the demonic animal appearing between the king and the soldier. This split and contradictory structuring represents the combat waged by Christ not against sin, meaning the death he accepts, but against the evil of the City of Man.

The animal's shape displays a troubling morphological ambiguity for which I have found no previous occurrence (fig. 162). Its snout, with no visible teeth and with dilated nostrils, is framed by two little protruding eyes; two round ears emerge from a crest of bristly hair. The snout is soft, large, and fleshy like that of a sheep, perhaps in competition with the lamb, the traditional emblem of Christ as sacrificial victim. At the same time, the animal inherits certain traits that marked out sin on the left wing. It has the same coat flecked with regular chisel marks as the winged serpent that slithered between Eve's legs in panel 4 (cf. fig. 60); its reptilian nudity is no longer a sign of purity but rather a mark of the world's stain. The demonic animal's snout has numerous points in common with the winged dog/serpent's muzzle represented on the left tree in the panel of the original sin (cf. fig. 52). It has its rounded and protruding ears, its forelock, and its elongated nose. Deprived of its wings and serpent's tail, the clawed predator stands upright in panel 13, its fallaciously gentle appearance mimicking a human figure whose posture it usurps. In this respect, the animal twists its body in the same manner as Eve did in panel 2. The demonic creature is thus the synthesis of all the evil forms and substances of the bronze door.

In my analysis of the panel of the original sin, I suggested that the hybrid was the symbolic portrayal of the carnal bond uniting Adam and Eve, a concupiscence/self-love engendered by the two sinners that, as the first expression of evil, replaced the love for God. In panel 13, the hybrid—the fruit of sin—has become autonomous in order to incarnate a poisonous simulacrum of Christ, namely, Antichrist. During his life as a man, Jesus must struggle against this personified evil, whom the Evangelists call Tempter, Devil, or Satan, and who manifests himself for the first time by his seductive lies in the episode of the retreat to the desert (Matt. 4:10–11). The hybrid is also evil incarnate, the violence of hatred that the iniquitous vow against the Righteous One, the hatred that falsehood pits against truth, and that Bernward sets up as an antonym of Christ's love. Indeed, the Tempter remains endogenous to humanity; or to put it another way, he is powerless without the weakness of humans who yield to his seduction by re-engendering Evil within themselves.

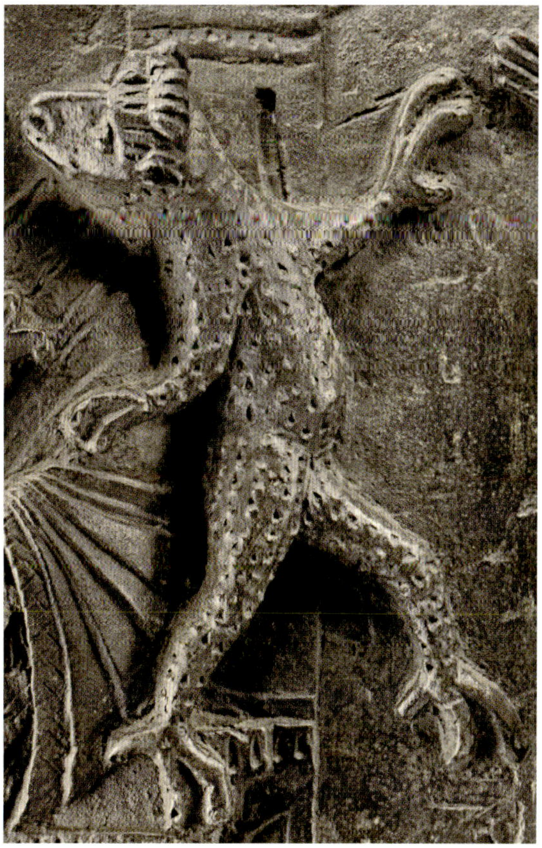

162

162. *Panel 13, demonic hybrid creature.*

In panel 13, evil acts through the king who judges Christ and who is identifiable by his sumptuous clothing and the insignia of his function, the scepter and crown (*regalia*) (fig. 163). Over his tunic he wears a very thick coat that—the eleventh century being a little early for a fur coat—we can assume is made of wool, emphasizing its animal origin. It is midlength, sleeveless, and fastened on the right shoulder by a rectangular fibula as seen in contemporary mantles or capes; this obviously medieval garment, just like

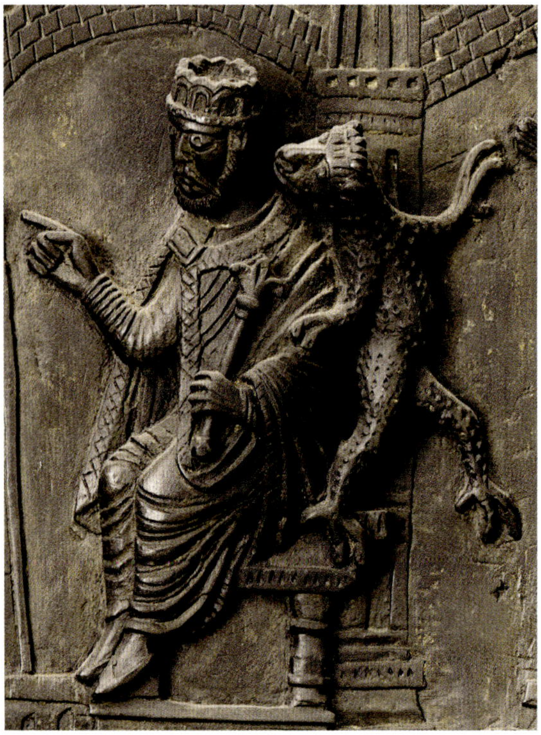

163

the fine leather sandals the king wears, has the same archeological quality as the magi's humble clothes in panel 11.

But everything here is a sham and an illusion. The collar and rim of the coat are bordered with trimmings whose interlacing imitates a cross, thus evoking the incarnated God whom the king refuses to recognize. Together with the mustache, the beard remains structurally identical to that of Christ; however, it is composed of stiff strands of hair similar to those "crowning" the Tempter's head, and to those characterizing the sacrilegious Cain in panel 7 (cf. fig. 106). The scepter's tip is a fleuron whose vegetal essence sustains the confusion between what is truly life and who gives it. The crown is shaped like an arcade, namely an architectural figure of transmission, but what the king personifies is not the transmission of the City of God but rather the earthly city founded by Cain. Although the ruler bears the signs of the *imperium,* he is not seated on a curule seat but on a stool with four legs, a chair or cathedra. The viewer cannot miss this detail because Bernward placed a curule seat in front of Mary's house in panel 9 (cf. fig. 117), using it as a sign announcing the kingdom of Christ. The king's false royalty and his false justice are presented as an outrageous mockery of true royalty and true justice.

This staging of the maleficent illusion is the New Testament replica of Eve's relationship with the serpent in the panel of the original sin (cf. fig. 41 and 42). Here the king is under the sway of the demonic animal with which he shares the throne. With its right back paw, the Tempter, emboldened by the legitimacy conferred on it by the column behind the seat, has taken hold of the seat's base. The animal is positioned on the axis of the column, symbol of the iniquitous law of the corrupted city. The Tempter whispers deceitful words into the ruler's ear, while at the same time grasping and guiding with its clawed paw the arm holding the scepter, the symbol of power. More than simply just an evil instigator, the Tempter occupies the very space of royal authority of which it is the dynamic element.

The same falsehood is spread throughout the architecture of the city ruled by the deceitful and wicked king (fig. 164). In a blatantly provocative way, three crosses dominate the turrets of the city walls and, with brazen hubris, two of them rise high enough to reach the panel's upper frame. But these crosses are merely incomplete simulacra: two of them have no base, and the lower arm of the third is replaced by a sphere. In addition to their irregular bays, expanded to look like a crack, the towers and the walls look unstable and disproportioned; moreover, the walls differ: arched, oblique and crenellated, without crenellation. The roofs are also all different. The most implausible is represented as a pseudo-roof in the shape of a net topped by an orb at the extreme right of the image. It is placed directly on a segment of wall, without any support and appearing as if held up by the soldier's spear. The end of the weapon takes on the shape of a cross and, we should note, both the wall and the spear's base rest against the last of the panel's three borders, thus making obvious the continuity established between this city and that of Cain in panel 8 (cf. fig. 110). The column of evil, that is, the law that supports and rules this city of men ever since history's first murder, is the law of violence.

From that moment on, the major struggle in the panel is between the poison of evil temptation and the salvific response. The latter conforms to the divine Law, as evidenced by the structure of the ground on which the entire scene is set.

The soil is made up of a composite and dynamic platform (fig. 165), easily identifiable here as the mineral volutes brought about by original sin, signifying the sterile and dried out soil of death. However, these scrolls are no longer covered with chisel marks, as they previously were. The poison, singled out as a substance other than stone, is confined to large vertical bands extending from the panel's frame to the ground's surface. Placed under the torturers' feet and under the supporting elements of the city of evil (gate, throne, and column), these studded bands are

163. *Panel 13, Herod.*

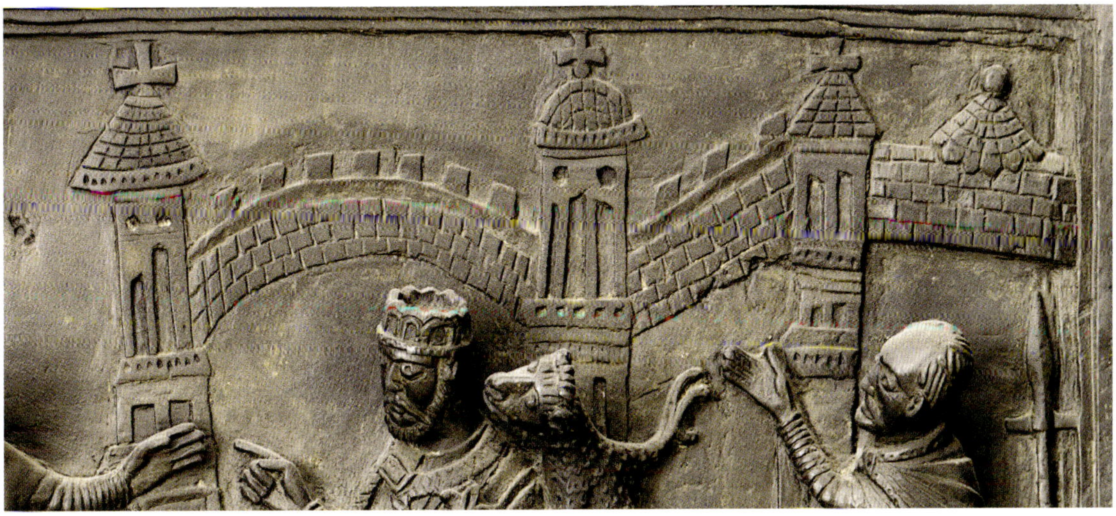

164

framed—we could even say contained—by the life channels represented by double parallel lines. Here again we find the design of the ornamental motif that covered the cape of the murderer Cain in panel 8 (cf. fig. 106). The conspicuous difference between the two derives from the fact that these life channels can now be filled with purifying blood, as explained in the previous panel. On the sterile soil of panel 13 we witness the confrontation of two territories, topographically interconnected but substantially separated: the City of God and the City of Man. An extremely important fact is that the life channels are open all along the panel's telluric substratum, a reminder that eternal life will be equally offered to all, that all bodies made of flesh, those of the righteous as well as those of the unrighteous, will be resurrected at the end of time: "Therefore, as by the offence [*delictum*] of one, unto all men to condemnation; so also by the justice [*justitia*] of one, unto all men to justification of life [*justificationem vitae*]" (Rom. 5:18). Nevertheless, as developed in the panel's right side, before that time comes, everyone is free to let the Holy Spirit or the poison of evil, which will save them or condemn them, flow within themselves.

The configuration of the soil under the feet of the armed soldier (fig. 166) is modified in a particular way. It is possible to make out, schematically traced, a little vegetal form with two bars, a zone studded with chisel marks, and a cluster of randomly curved lines composing as many mineral volutes as vegetal sprigs, namely a negation of the matrix memory left by God in his Creation, a flow of the poison of evil, and a trampling of the potentially reinvigorated soil.

As Bernward never ceased repeating throughout the left wing, the futures of the soul and of the body are interdependent, but it is one thing to resuscitate bodies by purifying the flesh from the mortal poison that polluted it and another to save souls by reforming them in God's image: "But now put you also all away: anger, indignation, malice, blasphemy, filthy speech out of your mouth. Lie not one to another: stripping yourselves of the old man with his deeds, and putting on the new, him who is renewed unto knowledge, according to the image of him that created him [*secundum imaginem ejus*]" (Col. 3:8–10).

In my opinion, the most puzzling personage in the narrative of the trial is the one who tramples underfoot the salvation that Christ offers: Pilate. This identification is not unanimous in the historiography. Based on the presence of a crown, Franz Dibelius and those inspired by his work identify the king in panel 13 as Herod Antipas, the son of Herod the Great, the king, or more precisely, Tetrarch of Galilee, Jesus's native province [Dibelius 1907, 61–62]. Conversely, Francis Tschan and others have suggested that the man on the throne is Pontius Pilate, the Roman prefect of the province of Judea between 26 and 37 CE [Tschan 1951, 210]. Their arguments are convinc-

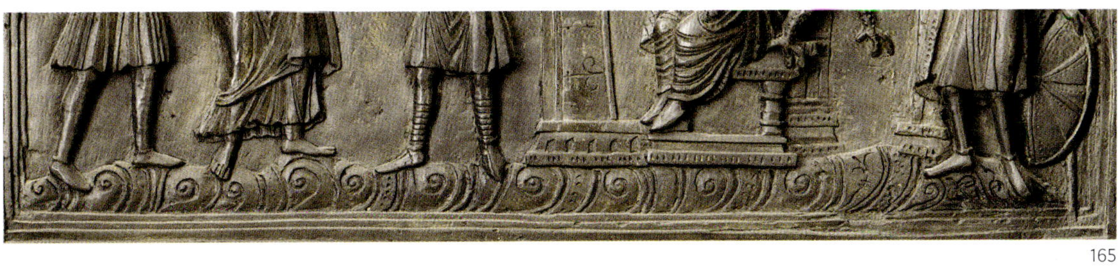

165

164. *Panel 13, city walls.*

165. *Panel 13, ground.*

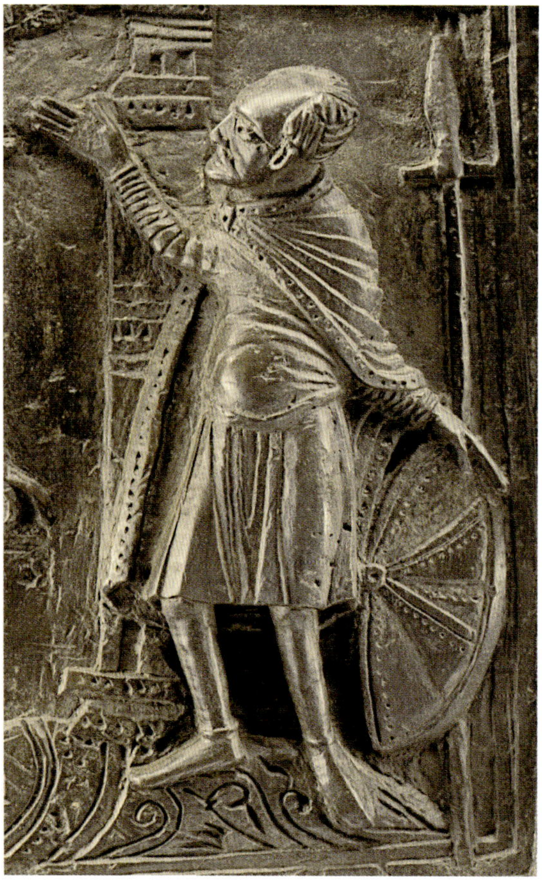

166

ing. Herod is a minor figure in the New Testament, mentioned only in Luke's Gospel and the tetrarch has elicited very few exegetical commentaries. The case of Pontius Pilate is more complex. Not only is he cited in the four Gospels and therefore more widely commented on, but he is actually mentioned in the liturgy, most prominently in the *Credo*: "Crucifixus etiam pro nobis sub Pontio Pilato, passus et sepultus est." In addition, Pilate appears very early in Christian iconography, whether receiving Christ or sending him away while washing his hands (Matt. 27:24), as on the wooden door of Santa Sabina or in the magnificent mosaic of Sant'Apollinare Nuovo in Ravenna. The presence of Herod Antipas occurs later and much less frequently. He does not seem to appear before the ninth century (the Stuttgart Psalter [Württembergische Landesbibliothek Stuttgart, Bibl. fol. 23]) and in quite an exceptional way, perhaps under Byzantine influence, since he is also found in some Greek manuscripts.

And yet, it is Herod whom I propose to identify in the royal figure judging Christ, and Pilate in the soldier on the right. I will explain why. If I have presented the possible identifications based on the biblical text, it is because I believe that Bernward himself wanted to raise these questions in the minds of the viewers—learned men or believers guided by knowledgeable men—in order to show them another dimension of evil, as well as the existence of a tool enabling them to confront and understand it: language.

Devoid of animal features, the wickedness of the soldier on the right is signified by the border of his cape, punctuated all over by chisel marks. On the other hand, we have suggested that the king's garments made of animal matter establishes his intimate association with the Tempter. The king's animality resonates in several passages of the Bible and quite specifically in the very words that Christ utters speaking of Herod, in the Gospel of Luke: "The same day, there came some of the Pharisees, saying to him: Depart, and get thee hence, for Herod hath a mind to kill thee. And he said to them: Go and tell that fox, Behold, I cast out devils, and do cures today and tomorrow, and the third day I am consummated" (Luke 13:31–33). Popular culture had already turned the cunning and deceitful fox into a trickster, as emblematized by Aesop, even before the negative symbolism of the evangelic text and its appropriation by the exegetes. The fox is the very image of the wicked kings in the City of Man, as Augustine states in his commentary on the psalms, *Enarrationes in psalmos*, the most important and the most widely read of the Latin commentaries of this book during the early Middle Ages: "Uulpes dicit reges saeculi [foxes are the kings of the century]" (*Enarrationes in psalmos*, LLT-A, CPL 283/SL, ps. 62, par. 19).

This fox king, seated on a throne and prompted by a demonic Tempter, is the antonym of the psalmist inspired by the Holy Spirit, as described in the first verse of the first psalm, and precisely as he is depicted in a widespread tradition of psalmic representations since the ninth century. An important clarification is in order: the Book of Psalms is the most important and the most commented on prayer book in the Bible and is the basis for all medieval literary education—reading, grammar, and the first steps at Christian exegesis. There are two extant Latin versions of the first verse of the first psalm: St. Jerome's translation beginning with the Septuagint, which is largely superior to the *Juxta Hebraicum* (from which the alternate underlined text is taken): "Blessed is the man who hath not walked in the counsel of the ungodly, nor stood in the way of sinners, nor sat in the chair of pestilence/*of mockers*" (Ps. 1:1). For Latin exegetes, and consistently since St. Jerome (*Tractatus in psalmos*, LLT-A, CPL 592, ps. 1), this text raises the crucial question of pernicious doctrines and falsehoods presented as truths. St. Augustine describes their deadly effects very forcefully: "The seat of pestilence may be more appropriately understood of hurtful doctrine;

166. *Panel 13, Pilate.*

whose word spreads as a canker" (*Enarrationes in psalmos,* ps.1, par. 1).

The exegesis of the beginning of the second psalm evokes the pairing of Herod and Pontius Pilate in the Christian tradition: "The kings of the earth stood up, and the princes met together, against the Lord and against his Christ" (Ps. 2.2). All commentaries agree, from Hilary of Poitiers (*Tractatus super psalmos,* LLT-A, CPL 428/SL 61, ps. 2, par. 8) to Ambrose of Milan, who calls the two men *usurpatores justitiae* (*Expositio Evangelii secundum Lucam*, LLT-A, CPL 143, book 5), to Carolingian authors: kings must be understood in relation to Herod and princes in relation to Pilate. Indeed, the pernicious doctrine is, first, a discourse anchored in sin and spread by evil in the course of history through the words of wicked princes who are opposed to Christ's truthful Word: "Pilate therefore said to him: Art thou a king then? Jesus answered: Thou sayest that I am a king. For this was I born, and for this came I into the world; that I should give testimony to the truth. Every one that is of the truth, heareth my voice" (John 18:37).

I am suggesting that at this point Bernward leads the viewers' search for identification away from the interpretative rules governing visible signs that he had used so far in his inquiry toward those governing verbal discourse. He no longer utilizes the biblical text as a mere narrative containing the truths of the historia but as the archetypal form of an utterance that imposes a learned, enlightened reading, and that calls for an exegetic revelation inspired by the Spirit of God. If I am not mistaken, here the bishop associates Christian hermeneutics with the capacity of discrimination applied to the sensible world, as the other fundamental source of the divine truth that allows for rendering evil visible and for fighting against falsehood. In other words, the Christ's silence in panel 13—that is, his acceptance of death—paradoxically holds all the strength of the truth formulated in the Gospels (his four *voces*/voices).

The clothing of the soldier represented on the panel's right—spear, shield, and a military cape reaching his knees (the *clamyde*)—has led some to believe that he was a guard, like those that accompany emperors' portraits in Carolingian and Ottonian miniatures and ivories. Historians who have identified him as Pontius Pilate have based their conclusions solely on his military appearance and his difference from Herod. I agree with this identification, but what is most important is not what it affirms but how it is determined.

In the Gospel of Luke (Luke 3:1) Pontius Pilatus, the military governor of Judea, is cited by his full name: *Pontius* is his *nomen*, a name designating his *gens*, whereas *Pilatus* is his *cognomen,* or surname, thus distinguishing him from his ancestors. *Pilatus* is an adjective derived from *pilum* (spear, javelin), therefore designating someone "armed with a spear, a javelin," as shown in the image.

Indeed, the soldier's face contains certain morphological characteristics that are too distinctive not to be meaningful, especially when compared to the very regular molding of the other visages appearing on the bronze door and the importance Bernward gives to facial hair. In fact, Pilate's cranium is quite elongated and shaped like a half-egg. His advanced baldness is also distinctive and underscores the diverging direction of the remaining strands of his hair (fig. 66). Moreover, the etymological root of *pilatus* can be connected to terms other than spear.

The first is *pilus* (hair) whose derived adjective, pilatus, means both disheveled and bald. The second is *pil(l)eus*, derived from the Greek, which refers to a conical cap found in depictions of Castor and Pollux. The term denotes a male headdress in classical Latin and Christian literature but is also associated with very specific customs. In Tertullian, it is a symbol of freedom and therefore of the reward due a brave gladiator (*De spectaculo,* LLT-A, CPL 6, c. XXI). In Christian authors, such as Isidore of Seville and Bede (*De tabernaculo* LLT-A, CPL 1345, book 3:1.948), it is the headgear of Jewish or pagan priests. Isidore of Seville describes the *pilleus* twice, first by stating that it is the hemispherical linen headdress that covers the heads of Jewish priests (*Etymologies,* LLT-A 1186, XIX, 21, 3). A little further on, he includes it among the headgear worn by pagan priests, basing his etymology on the skin, *pellis*, of sacrificial victims from which the covering was made (*Etymologies* XIX, 30: 3 and 5). A similar association may be found between the *pilleus* and the *Flamines* (major priests) in the twelfth century, both in Durandus (*De rationale divinorum officium,* LLT-A, CM 140, book II, 1) and in the *Decretum Gratiani* (LLT-A, pars 1, dist. 21, canon 1).

Supposing that the shape of Pilate's cranium suggests it, this cap would resemble the headgear of the false priest, thus corresponding to that of the false king, and making him appear as a minister of Satan. Furthermore, in Isidore of Seville *pilum* also means a pestle, the instrument used to crush something in a mortar (*Etymologies*, IV, 11, 5), which could then be likened to Pilate's action of trampling underfoot the vegetation reborn from Christ's blood. It is evil's attempt to destroy good.

Isidore's work and his attention to the nuances of the sacred language that is Latin had a profound impact not only on medieval Christian exegesis but also on cultural life at the learned courts of the Carolingian and Ottonian world. The consideration given to the visible forms and sounds of words, between which are woven analogies as numerous as those of the sensible world, invites us to plunge into a whirlwind of etymologies and possible assonances; at times it is very difficult to determine which ones predominate in the visual discourse. Available solely to learned clerics or monks, the etymologies and assonances concerning Pilate's attributes—his spear and shield—resonate throughout the panel.

The Roman officer's two weapons appear together just as often in medieval iconography as in literature, but they are designated by different terms. The formula "hasta et cli(y)peus," frequently found in the Latin Bible (1 Sam. 17:45, 2 Chr. 25:5, Job 39:23 and Ezek. 38:4), is also found in Bede and Gregory the Great. "Hasta et scutum," a more poetic formula, is found in Virgil as well as in Jerome and Venantius Fortunatus. "Lancea et scutum" is rarer, appearing only in the Bible (Neh. 4:16). The spear/javelin is also designated by the Latin words *pilum* (already cited) and *telum.*

As previously mentioned, Pilate's spear bears the weight of the pseudo-roofing placed on the wall (fig. 164). If *pilum* designates a throwing weapon, the javelin of the Romans, in medieval Latin *pila* could also mean pier or column. The pseudo-roofing, set on the wall in a very artificial fashion, takes on the bizarre and unprecedented shape of a scalloped parasol with concentric spokes. Now if *telum* describes a lance, *tela* also signifies something woven, a net, particularly a spider's web. Perhaps the term *tegulum* (tile), but also thatch or wooden covering, has influenced this incongruous configuration. It is worth noting that the pseudo-roofing is placed near the tops of the Tree of Life on the left wing; the term *hasta* could also lead to such an association because its primary meaning is that of a long wooden pole to which a metal point is attached. Furthermore, Isidore of Seville describes the spear's point surmounting the pole as a *cuspis*, a term that he claims derives from *cespes*, meaning bud or shoot, precisely the sort of vegetation that Pilate tramples underfoot (*Etymologies,* XVIII, 7:11).

The shield, *cli(y)p(p)eus* or *scutum*, is set on the ground next to the soldier, which is not surprising since this is the iconographic formula found in early medieval depictions of imperial guards, such as those in the *Gospels of Otto III.* The round shield, which must have been made of wood or leather, is here reinforced with concentric metal spokes and emphasized by triangular chisel marks. The radiating and carefully crafted shape, while unexceptional, recalls the radiant, gold-plated nimbus of Christ as it appears in the same image. *Clypeus*, besides meaning the shield on which Roman emperors were triumphantly lifted, can also designate the grandiose circular shapes of the celestial vault or the orb of the sun. The term *scutum,* often associated with oblong shields, takes on the semantic quality of protection rather than of shape. It is in this sense that St. Paul uses the term in his Epistle to the Ephesians. This usage is largely adopted by Christian patristic writing (Tertullian, Jerome, Augustine, or even Ambrose of Milan): "In all things taking the shield of faith [*scutum fidei*], wherewith you may be able to extinguish all the fiery darts of the most wicked one. And take unto you the helmet of salvation, and the sword of the Spirit [*gladium Spiritus*], which is the word of God" (Eph. 6:16–17). From false pretention and violence to the true protection of the Word of God as divine light, the two circular forms, because of their multiple analogies, appear as the climax of the spiritual struggle for truth enacted in panel 13.

We end our inquiry with the *umbo*, the central part of the shield, which, by synecdoche, can also signify the shield itself (fig. 166). In the image we see that the *umbo* is hollowed out in the middle, contrary to traditional representations where it is always prominent. Indeed, it is because of this form that *umbo* shares its root with *umbilicus*, the navel, as Isidore of Seville likes to recall, insisting not only on the shape and position but also on the analogy between the point at which the shield is fastened and the umbilical cord linking the child to its mother (*Etymologies* XI, 1, 99). One last suggestion regarding analogies between the shield's hollowed-out central part and its association with the navel: it could take us back to Pilate's abdomen, made more prominent by the folds and pleats of the tunic. The accentuated stomach recalls Christ's abdomen, swollen with life and enhanced in the same way by his clothing in panel 13. In this instance, a swollen abdomen may very well be the sign of the presence of the breath of the Spirit of life, or of pestilential flatulence such as the pride of those (*inflati*) whom St. Paul reprimanded in his first Epistle to the Corinthians (1 Cor. 4:18), or even the vain but much more dangerous breath of foul spirits (*spiritus immundus*, Mark 8:28 *ff.*); the demonic spirits (*daemones*, Matt. 8:28 *ff.*) that Christ in the Gospels expels from the bodies of the possessed.

Of all the figures in panel 13, two remain to be studied: the two guards who bring Christ before Herod (fig. 167). If the king were Pilate, they would be two Jews sent by the high priests and the Elders of the Sanhedrin (the Court), who accused Jesus of blasphemy but could not condemn him to death without contravening Hebrew law (Matt. 27:1–2; Mark 14:63

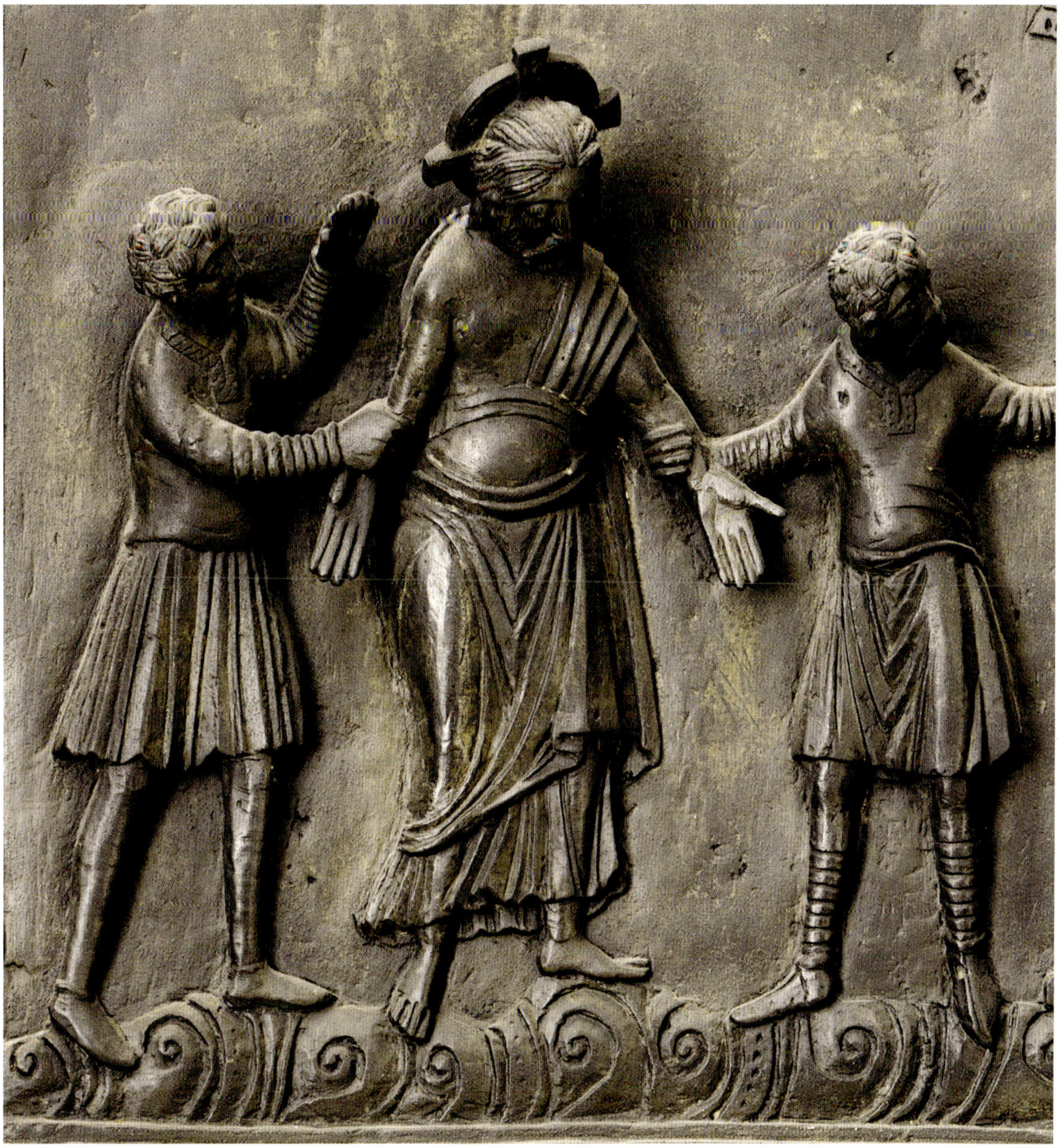

167

and 15:1; Luke 23:1; and John 18:28). On the other hand, if the king is, as I believe, indeed Herod, the two guards are Romans sent by Pilate (Luke 23:7). In the image, this ambiguity, which can be removed only by solving the complex identification of Herod and Pilate, is certainly deliberate: Romans and Jews are in fact summarily and uniformly condemned, as shown by the necklines of the two figures' shirts: one exhibits crisscross patterns as in the garment worn by Herod, the other the chisel marks covering Pilate's clothing. In addition to these analogies with the henchmen of evil, the two men have the same head of hair with short and curly strands, unprecedented in the door and very close to the canons of Roman sculpture of late antiquity, particularly of the era of the Antonines (and therefore, perhaps, an archeological citation). Let us not forget that the City of Man, described at length by Augustine, Bernward's reference book, is the Roman Empire.

167. *Panel 13, Christ and guards.*

At the same time, we cannot help but notice that the two guards are strongly individualized. They wear different shoes, one with sandals on his bare legs, the other with pleated chausses. One wears a tunic with straight and narrow pleats, the other a tunic with angled pleats. One is clean-shaven, the other has a pointed beard, perhaps meant as a characteristic of Judaism, although I have found no other confirming examples. These differences confer on them a virtual reality as strong as that of the historical personages in the panel. In other words, each believer or nonbeliever, each human figure is individually involved in this battle against evil. And just like Herod and

Pilate, the two guards take on certain traits of Christ, and more precisely those of the lower part—the most impure—of his body: the tunic of the man on the left has the same pleats as the lower part of Christ's tunic, whereas the tunic of the guard on the right repeats exactly the motif of the angled pleats. Their own mimetic relation to Christ comes from the fact that they see in Jesus a human being identical to themselves, which is the most banal and the gravest of delusions, that of Adam and Eve and then of Cain.

Panel 13 explains that to fight against evil is to focus on truths threatened by both visual deceptions and verbal manipulations. This evil is endogenous, omnipresent in the City of Man. It reproduces itself, identically engendered in the flesh, for so many generations that only by knowing Christ through visual means and sacred texts can we identify evil and fight against it. This attainment of vision and knowledge is precisely what the Church teaches, as the next chapter will demonstrate.

168. *Panel 13, Herod.*

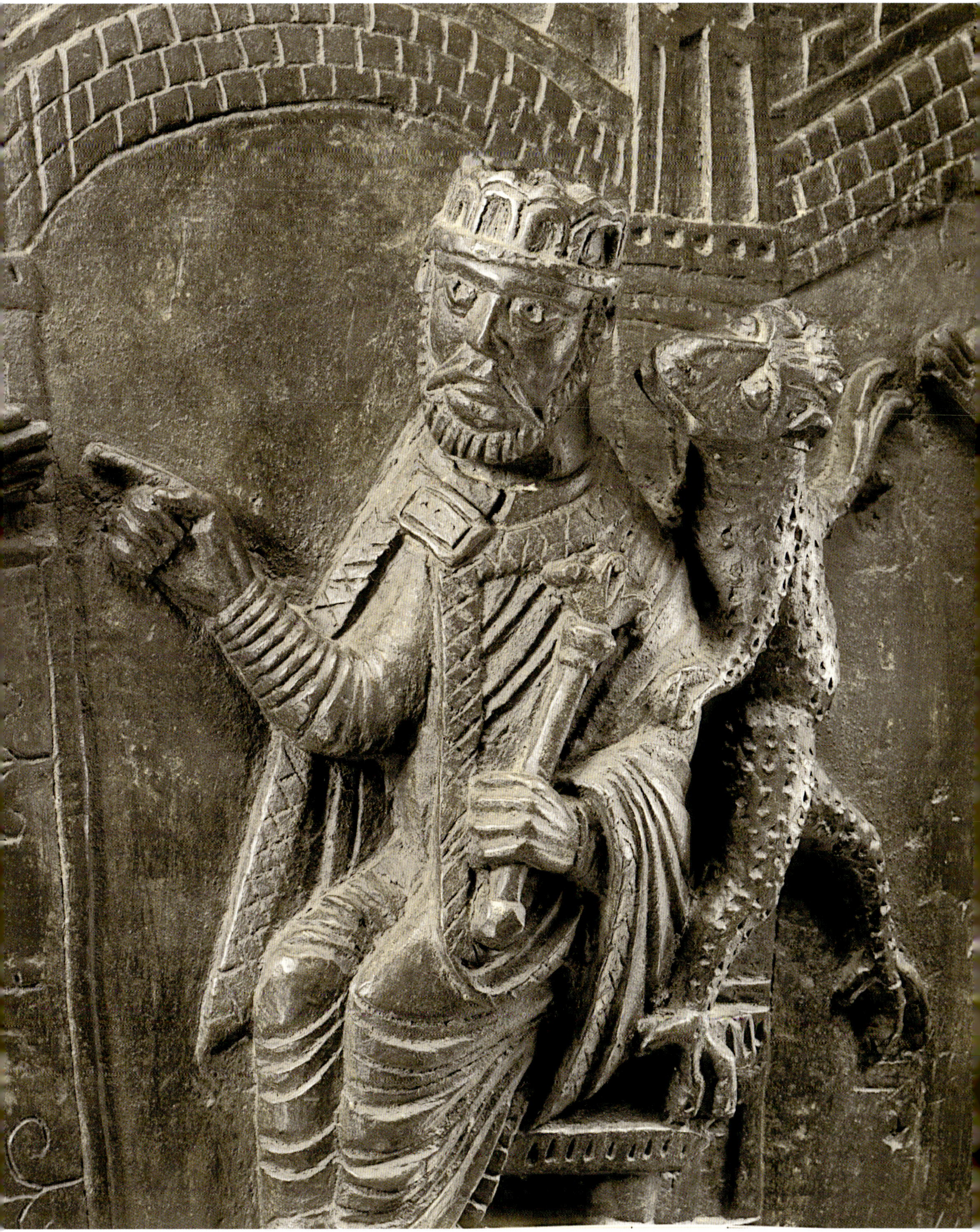

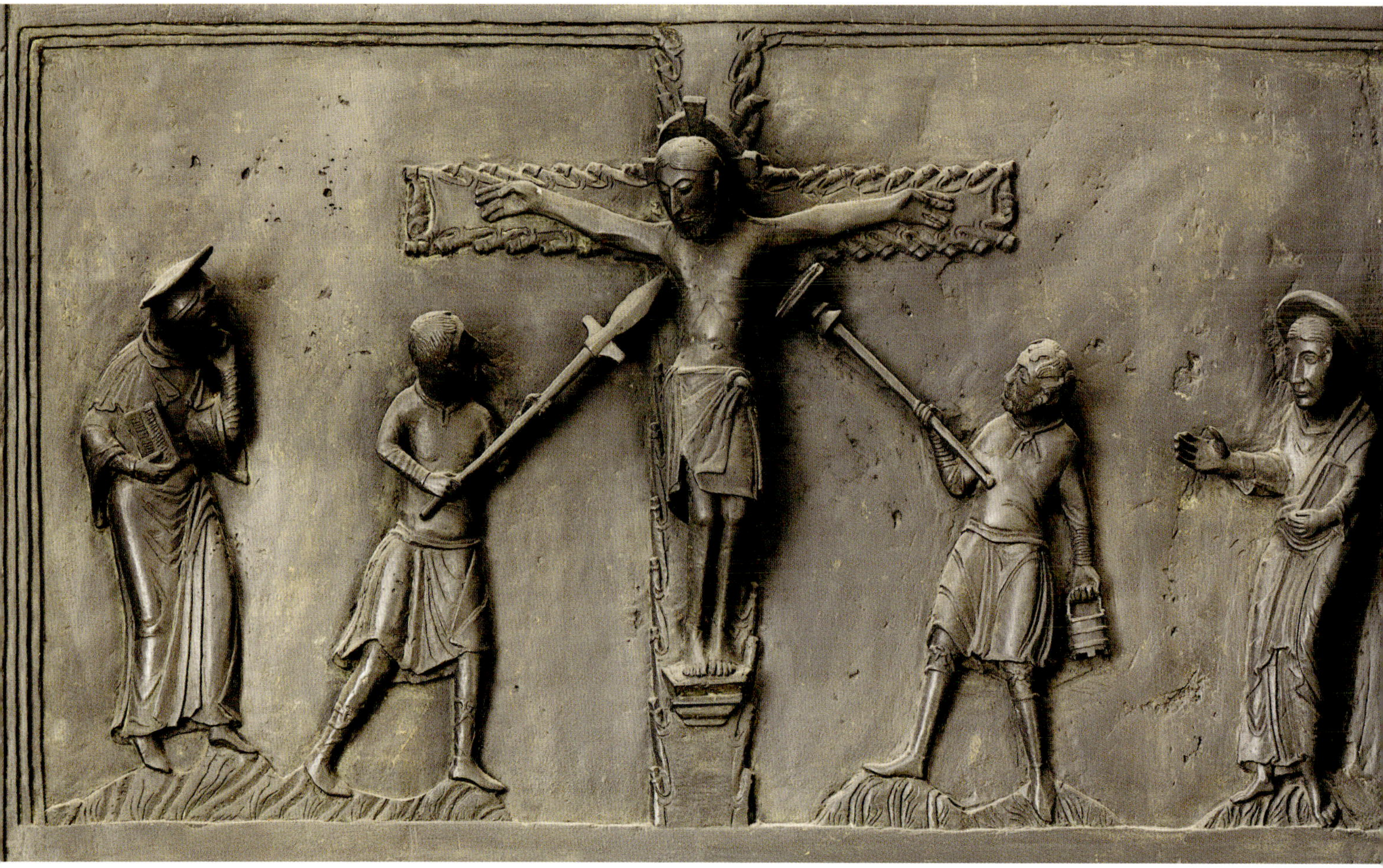

Panel **14**

REBUILDING

Jesus's Crucifixion, austere, without any perspective or structure, except for its orthonormal symmetry, is placed opposite the panel of the original sin, thus closing the history of the destruction of the world brought about by humanity's disobedience. Stripped of dry branches, reborn to life [Alibert 1990], here the sacrificial cross takes the place of the Tree of Life destroyed in the Edenic garden (fig. 169). Compared to the other panels, the image says little, but it tells the essential: much more than a visual discourse, it is a presence that imposes its literariness, its formal and substantial domination on the world.

Eyes closed, head bent, Jesus is depicted as dead—Jesus said, "It is consummated. And bowing his head, he gave up the ghost [*inclinato capite tradidit spiritum*]" (John 19:30). This is confirmed by the presence of the soldiers at the foot of the cross. In addition, John the Evangelist mentions the spear thrust into Jesus's side only after the narration of his death (John 19:31 ff). As far as I know, this lifeless Christ is possibly the first Western interpretation of an iconographic motif of undoubtedly Byzantine origin [Kirschbaum 1970, LCI, II, 613–614]. Bernward's choice raises questions.

Christ's nimbus in panel 14 repeats the largest format given to it on the bronze door, but it is completely stripped of any ornamentation. It is no longer a question of the light of the Word incarnate but rather of a sacrificed and sanctified body. Revealed to the point of near nudity—only his genitals are covered with a very thin loincloth (*perizoma*) tied to the hip—the body is emaciated, showing the same suffering imprinted on Adam's body in panel 6 (cf. fig. 89). The flattened thoracic cage has been emptied of the breath it contained; below it, a very visible navel establishes Jesus's place in Adam's lineage. This death is the true death of a man: "One of the soldiers with a spear opened his side, and immediately there came out blood and water" (John 19:34). Paradoxically, whereas it is omnipresent in previous iconography and even intimately correlated to Byzantine representations of the dead Christ on the cross, no blood appears on the corpse. There is no trace of abuse or wound, not even on the hands where the nails have been driven or on the side into which the spear has been thrust (fig. 170). Nor is there any blood on the cross. The redemptive flow is evoked in another, more essential way. A few strands of Christ's long, fine, tightly combed hair fall over his shoulders, like a liquefaction that also affects the short beard covering the lower part of the face, thus replacing the mustache and the collarlike beard in the previous panel (cf. fig. 161). The impression of flow is more evident on the perizoma, particularly in the double parallel lines—spiritual channels spreading from the knot of the wrapping. This motif is found, as well, on the tunics of the two Romans placed at the foot of the cross.

Christian exegetes often distinguished the two fluids coming out of Christ's side by connecting water analogically to baptism, and blood to the Eucharist. Bernward's approach appears quite different. He does not seem to associate them in his image, undoubtedly because he always considered the vitality of nature as bound up with water, and the vitality of human bodies as bound up with blood. It may perhaps even be argued that the ontological level at which the bishop conceives and describes life as universally given by

169. *Panel 14.*

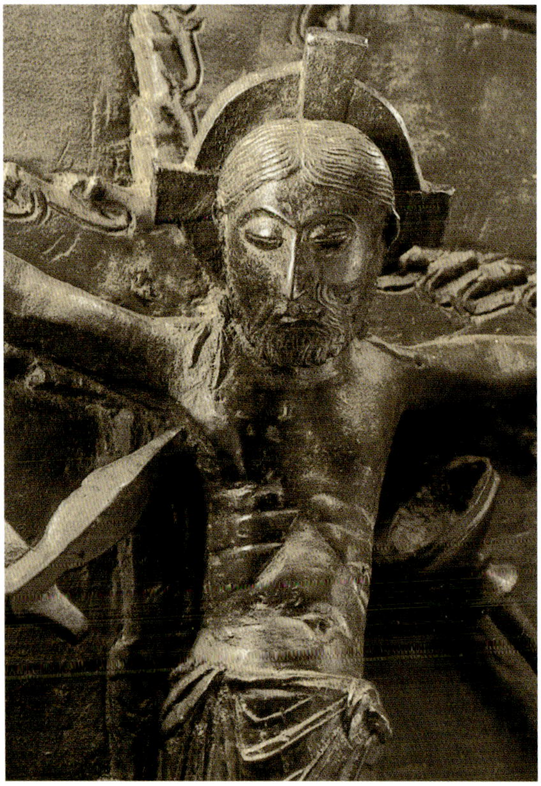

170

170. *Panel 14, Christ.*

God is based on the very correlation of the two vital, purifying fluids coming out of Christ's side.

In panel 14, the revitalizing purification appears also on the ground, in the form of life channels evenly spaced on the small mounds within and around which fine grassy stems grow; most of them are placed in three strands (fig. 169), as seen under the feet of the Virgin in the Annunciation panel (cf. fig. 117). The flowering of the Marian body inseminated by the Sprit is extended to the whole earth, thus replacing the poison of evil still visible in the previous panel.

All the characters in the panel, without exception, are touched by this purification. Contrary to the claims of some of my predecessors, there is no need to summon the apocryphal Gospels to identify the characters or to understand the staging of the panel.

Her head covered, Mary stands to the left of the cross, while St. John is to its right. This type of composition is related to a very old iconographic formula stemming from the biblical description of the two figures on Golgotha (John 19:26–27). In fact, it can be found in the Syriac *Rabbula Gospels* (Florence, ML Library, cod. Plut. I, 560, f 13, 6th cent.), and it appears in several Carolingian manuscripts, such as the *Gospels of François II* (Paris, Ms. 257, f 12v). If, indeed, this schema remains as a subtext in Ottonian crucifixions, the latter add to it some complementary visual elements (stars, the Deposition), thus reinscribing the scene in an earthly temporality absent from the more silent and contemplative Crucifixion of panel 14. (See, for example, the *Gospels of Otto III* [Munich, Staatsb. Clm 4453, f 248v] or the *Pericopes of Henry III* [Bremen, Staatsb., Ms. B 21].) Once again, Bernward's choice raises questions.

Two Roman soldiers mentioned in the synoptic Gospels are placed on either side of Christ. Like Mary and John, their mirrored gestures inscribe them in the orthonormal order delineated by the cross. Associated with the crucified body, the cross thus forms a square recalling the altar and the structure of Solomon's Temple in panel 12 (cf. fig. 171).

Contrary to custom, the two men are not represented in their military clothing. Only their footwear—one pair worn to mid-calf, the other below the knee—places them in their historical temporality (fig. 172). Their hair differs, but what they have in common is that they flow in long, smooth strands, as opposed to the thick, curly hair of the two guards who are handing Christ over to his henchmen in panel 13 (cf. fig. 167). In both panels, the men framing Christ are generic and particular at the same time. The iconography insists on their becoming individualized, and emphasizes the ontological freedom of those who, freed from sin, can choose their own path. The two men at the foot of the cross already belong to the community of the Lord: "The centurion who stood over against him, seeing that crying out in this manner he [Jesus] had given up the ghost, said: Indeed this man was the son of God" (Mark 15:39).

The change of corporal paradigm implied by the circulation of the Spirit of truth in the guards takes place at all levels of their garments. As we have seen, the lower part of their tunics is marked by the life channels that recall the relief of Christ's perizoma, just as the tight and angular pleats of the clothes in the previous panel evoked those of Christ's human form (cf. fig. 184). The collars of their tunics continue this sequence of mimetic attributes. While the collars of the two guards who led Christ to his henchmen recalled, in one case, Herod as usurper of royalty (the crisscross motif) and in the other, Pilate as servant of evil, the collar of the Roman holding the spear takes on the shape of a simple slit, a possible allusion to the wound on the side. In the case of the Roman holding the chalice, the slit at the neck is closed by a knot. This link-knot is of great importance: it is found again, larger, on Christ's loincloth and, even more imposingly, in front of the entrance to the tomb visited by the Holy Women in the next panel (cf. fig. 177). It is premature to de-

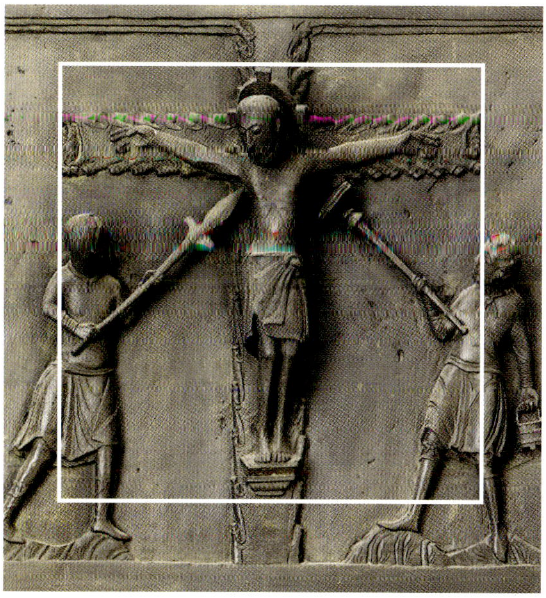

171

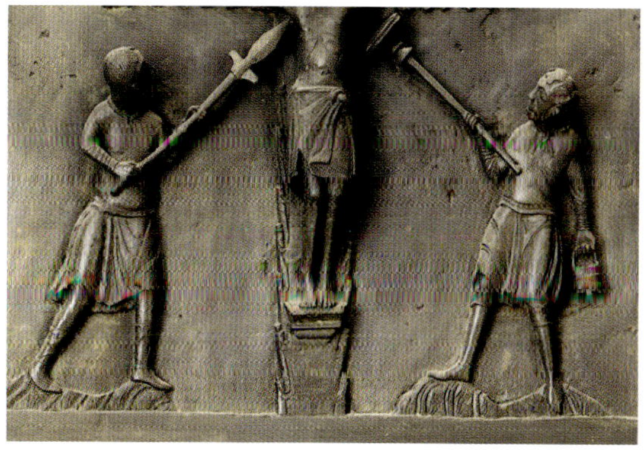

172

clare this, but I suggest that the knot announces the union of the flesh and the spirit in a final fusional transformation of corporal and spiritual substances in the body.

Let us consider, for the moment, that all the signs of mimetic transformation worn by the Romans are tangible proofs of the bodily reconfiguration/rebirth to eternal life following Christ's sacrifice.

Of the two Romans quoted in the Gospels, one thrusts the spear into Jesus's side, the other gives him vinegary water to drink soaked in a sponge (John 19:29; Matt. 27:48; and Mark 15:36). The two actions, undertaken before the Savior's death, assume, in the image where Christ is already dead, an ahistorical and universal dimension. The sponge is not represented in the panel, but the pail filled with vinegary water can be seen being held by the soldier on the right, as in all the Crucifixions illustrating this passage (fig. 172). Here Bernward introduces a variation, perhaps inspired by a tradition that was still marginal but which would become significant in the future, and which seems to have been initiated as early as the Carolingian epoch. In the Drogo Sacramentary (Paris, BnF, Ms. Lat. 9428, f 43v) two allegorical representations of the Church and the Synagogue frame the cross, and the Church gathers Christ's blood in a chalice. It is this chalice, and not the vinegary sponge, that the soldier holds up to Christ. The gesture is perfectly symmetrical to that of the spear that brings forth the divine substances that irrigate the world.

By playing on the significance of the container attached to the end of the pole and on the centripetal dynamics of the two men, one of whom thrusts his spear into Christ's body, Bernward establishes a double movement of gift and countergift, which is the quintessence of the covenant. If the Romans can gather Christ's blood, it is first of all because they give themselves to him as spiritual beings, according to the archetypal model of the just offering made to God. "I beseech you therefore, brethren, by the mercy of God, that you present your bodies a living sacrifice, holy, pleasing unto God, your reasonable service" (Rom. 12:1–2).

More broadly, the two men represent the community of believers that constitutes Christ's metabody, within which are finalized the formal principles that the Word has inscribed in the world since its creation. The panel's living cross is here a new Tree of Life around which humanity is going to live. It is this cross that now gives its measure to the world, filling the setting from one end to the other and in all its height by covering the triple border of the panel's framing: "For as the body is one, and hath many members; and all the members of the body, whereas they are many, yet are one body, so also is Christ. For in one Spirit were we all baptized into one body, whether Jews or Gentiles, whether bond or free; and in one Spirit we have all been made to drink" (1 Cor. 12:13).

Mary and John are not placed at the same level as the two Roman soldiers who embody the community of believers purified by the baptismal blood of Christ. As the biblical text literally states, they act as witnesses. Just after the water and the blood have flowed out of Christ's side, John's Gospel is quite precise: "And he that saw it, hath given testimony, and his testimony is true. And he knoweth that he saith true; that you also may believe" (John 19:35). In this respect, Mary and John attest to the truth of the Crucifixion, just as later, in panel 15, the Holy Women will confirm the disappearance of Christ's body from the sepulcher, and Mary Magdalene his Resurrection. But this truth is even deeper and does not only concern the death on the cross.

171. *Panel 14, structure of the Crucifixion.*

172. *Panel 14, ground and Roman soldiers.*

(Overleaf spread)

173. *Panel 14, Mary.*

174. *Panel 14, St. John.*

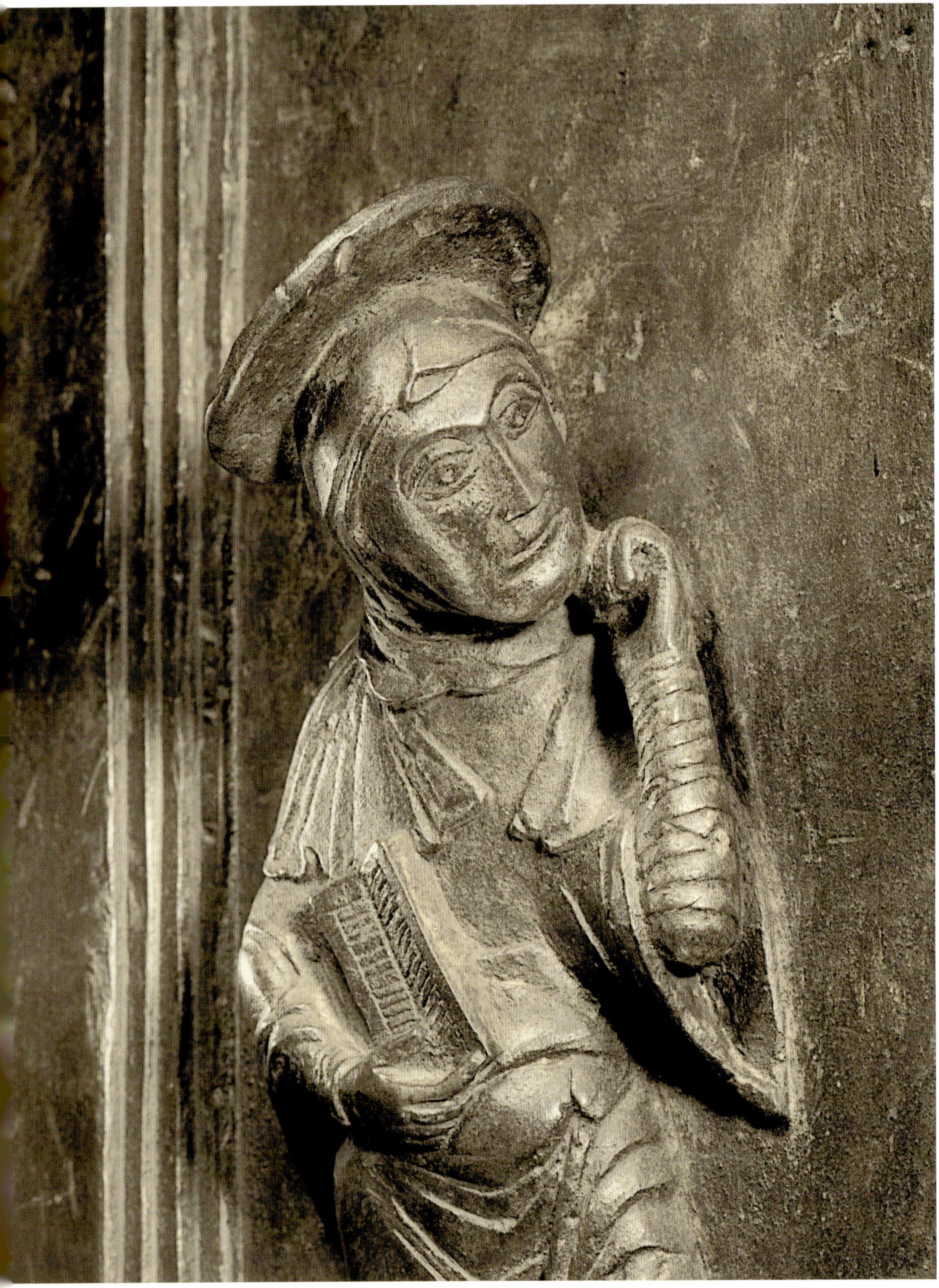

173

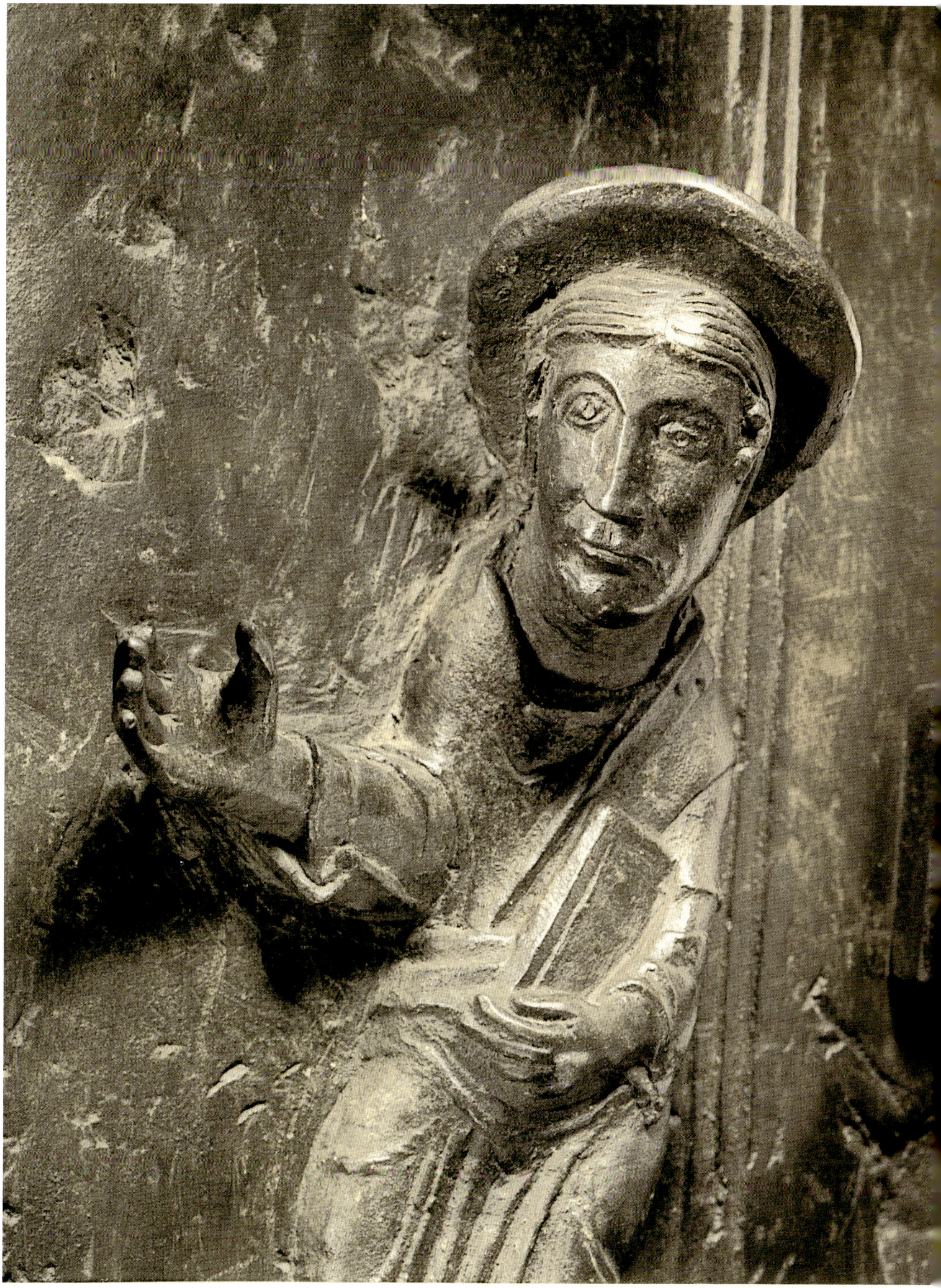

174

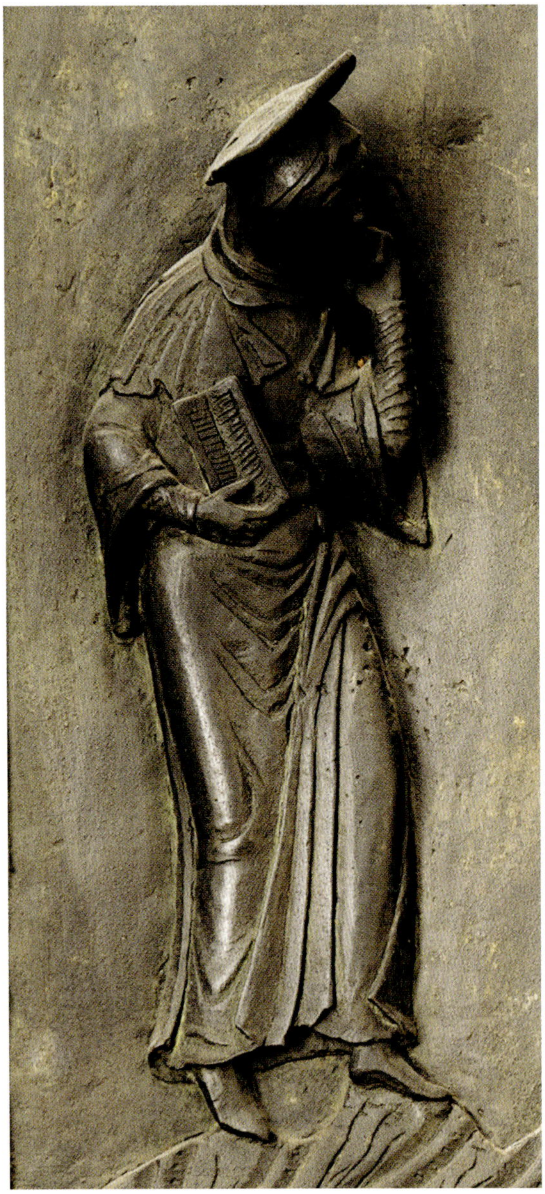

175

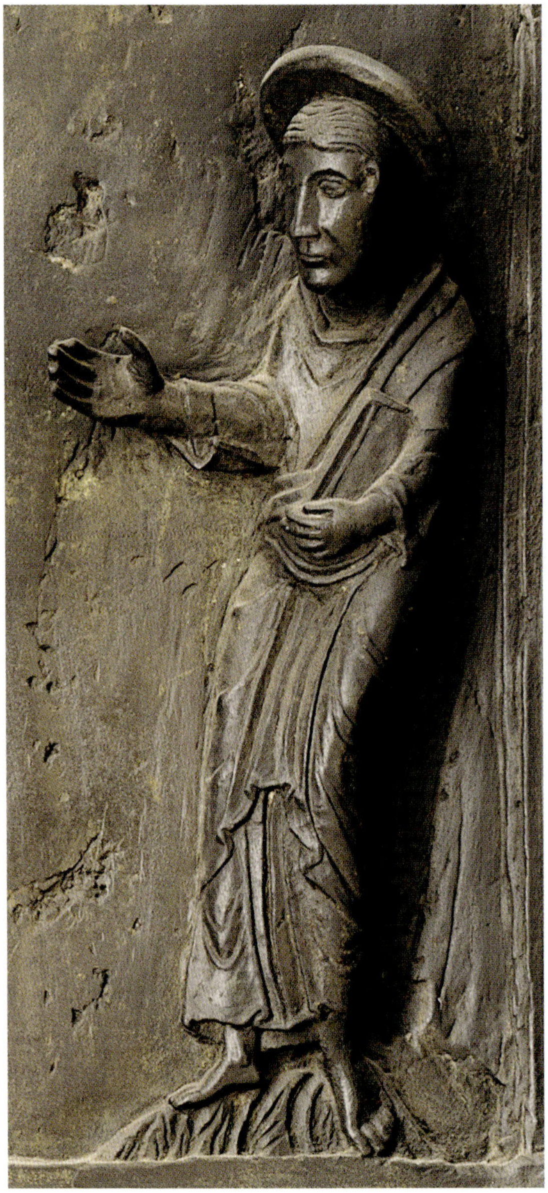

176

175. *Panel 14, Mary.*

176. *Panel 14, St. John.*

In contrast to Mary's face, one detail of John's visage, depicted in three-quarter view on the panel's surface, attracts attention for its oddness (fig. 174). Unless caused by a mistake in the casting (which we can legitimately doubt), his two eyes are strongly asymmetrical: the left eye is half closed, while the right eye is dilated, as if struck by what it sees. If we study the respective pupils of Mary and John, we realize that the Virgin gazes high up at the left (fig. 173), whereas John stares at two places at once: in front of him, toward Christ, in whose direction he extends his hand, and into a sort of ecstatic emptiness. The two characters do not see the same thing.

Mary, wearing the shoes and the veil that Bernward had attributed to her since panel 9, raises her hand to her cheek as a sign of grief (fig. 175). She holds an open book against her chest, the same one she held in the Nativity scene. While it previously represented the injunction to recognize the infant Jesus as the Messiah of the book, in panel 14 the book has become a self-referential object. It is covered with lines of writing, showing itself for the precise text it is, an utterance and no longer just a prophetic impulse. And after the verse about those who will bear witness of truth, the Gospel of John adds: "For these things were done, that the scripture might be fulfilled: You shall not break a bone of him [Exod. 12:46]. And again another scripture saith: They shall look on him whom they pierced [Ps. 33:21]" (John 19:36–37).

The veil that Mary wears on her head and shoulders, which is particularly conspicuous due to the crease it forms on her forehead, is quite unprecedented in its arrangement. It is draped around her neck, like the curtains wrapped around the columns of the Temple-Church in panel 12 (fig. 173). Perhaps this is not fortuitous. As I have explained, these coilings of antique origin constitute the conventional ornamentation of the Canon Tables in early medieval Gospels, specifically the system of ornamentation (and sacralization) of textual correspondences between the Holy Scriptures. In addition, Mary's gesture of affliction is exactly the same as that of Salome, a figure of the ancient Synagogue, converted and subsumed into the new community of believers in panel 10 (cf. fig. 126).

Placed at the crossroads of historical temporalities, Mary here affirms the providential retrieval of the ancient testimony by the new one: bringing the entire biblical past to the present time of the Crucifixion and revealing, in the light of the ancient scriptures and of what is happening, the celestial becoming that she indicates with her gaze. In a way, she represents the Church as a repository of memory and as a mediator of the divine Word.

Represented in parallel to Mary on the image's right side, St. John is inscribed into the depth of the future (fig. 176). He shares the fine, wavy hair of Christ. The Spirit of life, in the same way as the Tree of Life nourished Adam, moves his body. As slender as a rod, his body is aligned on a vertical axis which is waving, according to the flow of the life-water that fills it. As a replacement for the Tree of Life that Adam had placed on his heart with his left hand (cf. fig. 19), John holds a closed book. This book is inscribed in the undulating movement, in the continuity of the pleats of the fine tunic covering the saint. What animates him, what makes him live in his own state of visionary comprehension is the Christ-Word that resides in him from now on. His hand extended in an oratorical gesture, he will bear witness through his inspired writings, through the truth he sees in his ecstatic vision that he will unveil in his Gospel, Epistles, and Apocalypse, the last Revelation (in the Middle Ages, all these texts are attributed to the same author). Light of the present and witness of the future, the book of John is the new testimony; it extends Mary's vision to a prophetic vision of the heavenly Jerusalem:

> That which was from the beginning, which we have heard, which we have seen with our eyes, which we have looked upon, and our hands have handled, of the word of life: For the life was manifested; and we have seen and do bear witness, and declare unto you the life eternal, which was with the Father, and hath appeared to us: That which we have seen and have heard, we declare unto you, that you also may have fellowship with us, and our fellowship may be with the Father, and with his Son Jesus Christ. And these things we write to you, that you may rejoice, and your joy may be full. (1 John 1:1–4)

Jesus dies but he delivers life to the world at the same time by the baptism and by these two books that are born one from the other and are superimposed. Ancient and new testimonials merge, becoming the Word, this time incarnated in the pages of the Holy Scriptures [*Divina pagina*] in their entirety. They testify to the double vision of Mary and John, expanding into the depths of past and future. The sacrifice on the cross appears as an eternal present, acted out at each elevation of the host on the altar, not only as a renewal of the world but also as a renewal of the time that, in the end, will be annulled by death, as it is here. Indeed, the dead Christ remains the living Word within the community established in him.

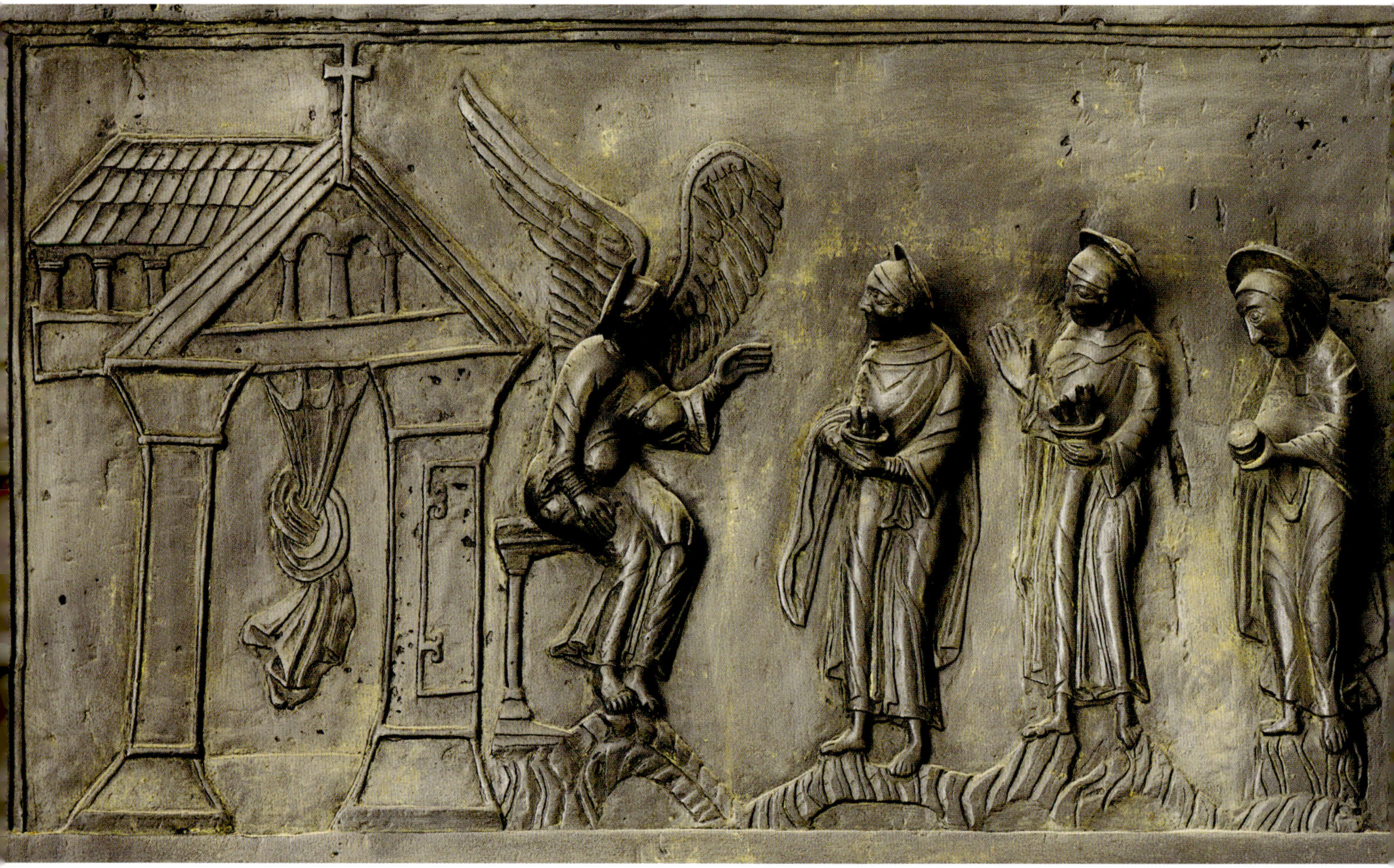

Panel **15**

LIGHT

Panel 15 represents the visit of the Holy Women to Christ's tomb. Rigorously aligned, barefooted, and veiled, the figures are approaching the angel who greets them in front of the Holy Sepulcher, a basilica-type building with columns and triangular pediment (fig. 177).

The Gospels do not name or enumerate these women in the same way. Matthew mentions Mary of Magdala and Mary, mother of Jacob and Joseph (Matt. 28:1–8); Mark adds a third woman, Salome (Mark 16:1), traditionally identified as the "mother of the sons of Zebedee," whom Matthew mentions in another passage (Matt. 27:56); while John mentions only one woman at Christ's sepulcher, Mary of Magdala, the Mary Magdalene who appears on the door's final panel.

Following an ancient tradition attested in Ottonian iconography [Bloch 1963], Bernward depicts the three women with halos as they approach the sepulcher holding small pyxides containing aromatic oils (Mark 16:1 and Luke 24:1). The magi's peregrinations toward the infant Jesus in panel 11 (cf. fig. 139) prefigure the event depicted in panel 15. In an identical way, this scene exploits the precise similarity and linear placement of the figures, suggesting that they blend into one person caught in three discrete moments while approaching the tomb. Each of these feminine figures embodies a stage of the most intimate encounter with God. Depending on the discursive necessities, Bernward leads his viewer to think either in terms of a sequence of moments or of a single one. Ultimately, this scene will come to be seen as the fulfillment and recasting of the earlier love encounter on the bronze door: panel 2, placed symmetrically to panel 15, where Adam recognizes Eve in divine light (cf. fig. 1 and 24).

Unlike Adam and Eve and the magi from the distant East, the two figures of the Holy Women on the right of panel 15 appear completely motionless, their feet at right angles. The third figure, facing the angel, is more dynamic. She has displaced her left foot by slightly lifting the heel as if to begin walking. This initial movement lifts her, rather than carrying her forward. Her right foot, identical to that of her companions, is raised on a small step carved into the ground. Unlike her antetypes in panel 11, the Holy Woman in panel 15 seems to change position without physically moving, a visual oxymoron whose full meaning will be clear only after unveiling the theological reasons for her inner evolution. This will be achieved through analyzing her gestures, the pyx she is holding, her clothes, and as usual, the shape and substance of the ground.

The beginning of the sequence starts on the right. The Holy Woman holds a closed pyx with both hands, whereas the other two containers of aromatic oils are open, displaying a very animated matter. Eyes fixed on her vessel, she is unable to see either the angel or the tomb on the left (fig. 178). In terms of visual syntax, the closed pyx enables Bernward to emphasize the subsequent opening of the little container. At the same time, this pyx is at the intersection of two converging symbolic constructions. The biblical passage represented here is organized around the theme of the opening/closing of the Holy Sepulcher. Furthermore, in medieval Christianity the

177. *Panel 15.*

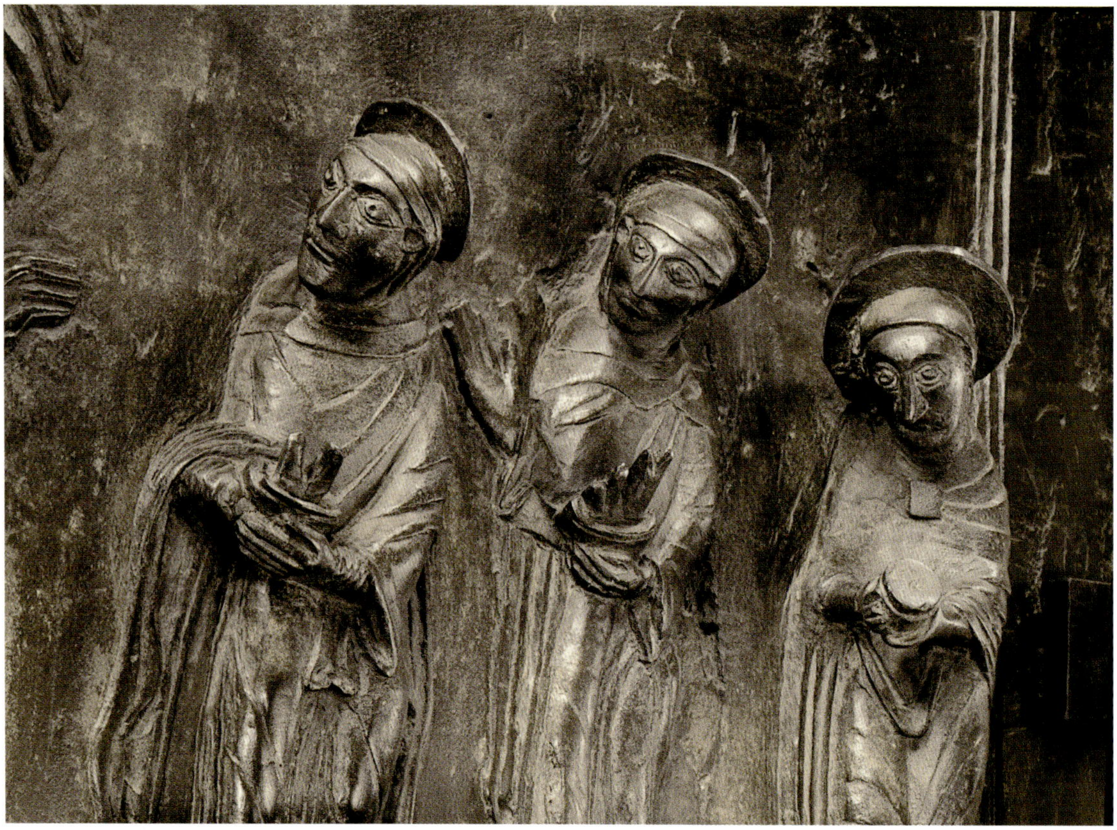

178

antique pyxides became a central piece of liturgical furnishing where the hosts, whose substance was transformed into Christ's body during the Eucharist, were kept. I therefore suggest (and this hypothesis will be corroborated in the course of this analysis) that the small, closed vessel held by the Holy Woman on the right signifies the condition of the sepulcher as she imagines it, namely closed, since she has seen neither the open door nor the angel who will explain to her the reason for this mystery: "And when the sabbath was past, Mary Magdalen, and Mary the mother of James, and Salome, bought sweet spices, that coming, they might anoint Jesus. . . . And they said one to another: Who shall roll us back the stone from the door of the sepulcher?" (Mark 16:1–3).

Just as the magus on the right in panel 11, turned toward the viewers, could not see the star or the Virgin and Child, the Holy Woman has become animated solely through her love for Christ. Like the magus, she has already gone beyond her peregrination in the City of God, founded anew and purified by Christ's blood. This community is represented by the socle onto which she has stepped, a squared-off block, a geometrized corner stone corresponding to Christ on the cross: "And I say to thee: That thou art Peter; and upon this rock I will build my church, and the gates of hell shall not prevail against it" (Matt. 16:18). This stone rests on a small mound and both are identically irrigated by life channels as prescribed by the action of the Spirit, without chisel marks, and within which the purifying blood flows (fig. 177). It should be noted, however, that, as a starting point in the evolution delineated on the ground, the squared-off stone and the irrigated soil, although substantially identical, are formally differentiated in the image: their respective channels do not meet.

The motif of the square reappears in the fibula holding together the Holy Woman's cape, a modest yet very visible clasp that does not appear on the other two figures (fig. 178). Just like the cut stone whose shape it replicates, the square fibula is worn as a sign of identity, of belonging, and yet it does not duplicate the figure's topographical position. It designates the woman's body itself as sacred ground, configured at the level that Christ established in the previous panel.

The second representation of the Holy Woman, in the middle of the group, has leaned forward and inclined her head over the body in front of her in order to see the angel seated before the tomb. With her raised hand, she responds to the welcoming gesture with which the messenger leads her to Christ's burial place (fig. 178). This second stage in the spiritual peregrination echoes that of the magus in panel 11 who, with a different gesture pointed at the star illuminat-

178. *Panel 15, Holy Women.*

ing the place where the infant Jesus would be found. The feet of the Holy Woman, still at a right angle, but further apart than before, now straddle two distinct mounds, separated by a fault (fig. 177). These mounds do not exhibit the geometric rationality of the previous socle, but they have not lost all traces of sequencing. Their silhouettes, very close together, suggest that they belonged to the same morphological unity split in two, torn apart by a brutal fracture in the ground. In addition, they are hollowed out by two openings.

In terms of historia, this topographic fault can be associated with the great earthquake that, by divine manifestation, was triggered at the moment of the angel's apparition at Christ's tomb: "Et ecce terrae motus factus est magnus [And behold there was a great earthquake]" (Matt. 28:2). By his death Christ created an opening in the ground.

At the same time, this opening refers to the first and only other break in the ground represented on the bronze door: the one in the socle of the Edenic garden that had opened under Adam's feet at the moment of original sin (cf. fig. 55). It is from this fracture, represented under the Holy Woman, that Hell was born, and it will reappear, almost identically, under Christ's feet in panel 16 (cf. fig. 186).

If the earthly movement depicted in panel 15 recalls the fracturing of the world and the birth of Hell, the place of death that resulted from it, its primary purpose is to present itself as its antonym: redemption. Substantially removed from the mineral crystallization of the poisoned Paradise, the double mound on which the Holy Woman stands is irrigated on both sides by life channels, allowing Christ's salvific water-blood to now flow into the sepulchral caves. Life will obliterate death.

What, actually, is happening?

The liberation from death is made explicit by the open pyx held by the Holy Woman. When closed, the little cylindrical vessel represents Christ's tomb as Jesus's female disciple envisaged it, believing it to be closed. When open, the pyx is a testament to the way in which the words of truth, pronounced by the angelic messenger she gazes on, have been heard and understood: "Why seek you the living with the dead? He is not here, but is risen" (Luke 24:5–6, but also Matt. 28:5–6, and Mark 16:6).

I would argue that the living matter emerging from the pyx (fig. 178) represents this Resurrection of the flesh. The three-dimensional relief that Bernward has given to this matter is unprecedented on the bronze door, yet its formal structure obviously recalls the scalloped edge representing the Voice of Abel's Blood asking for justice, demanding his return to life from his sepulchral grotto (fig. 113). Several times on the door, in particular in the case of the Edenic plants, Bernward had announced Christlike realizations through their graphic and schematic prefigurations. In the same way, it seems to me, the bishop turns Abel's voice into the matrix of an eternity announced—indeed, reified—in the true meaning of the word, by the substance emerging from Christ's resurrected body in the pyx. The crucified man is living and all the dead after him will as well. The divine promise has been fulfilled.

The Holy Woman, standing on the two mounds with her open pyx, has not changed place—she remains in the same community of believers—but she has profoundly changed her state of *consciousness*. At the very moment when she realizes that Christ's body has resurrected, she understands that Hell has reopened and that her own mortal body could become eternal, like her soul. Indeed, under her feet, the two mounds, however purified and spiritual they might have been, maintain the trace of the initial fracture of the Garden of Eden, a sign of division. It is not in this earthly garden that she will live her eternity.

The last phase of the encounter with Christ is realized in the third representation of the Holy Woman. Now she faces the angel, whom she uses as a normative and intellective model. This new mirrored relationship includes the first dramatic confrontation in panel 5, between the angel and Eve expelled from Eden. While Eve saw her death in this encounter, the Holy Woman now sees the life that is offered to her.

Although the celestial being does not belong to the earthly world, he is present and visible on earth (fig. 179), his wings underscoring his intermediate position. The right wing is curved in welcome toward the Holy Woman. The powerful movement by which he has descended toward the tomb has left its mark on the left wing, as if he were still in flight. The angel remains in an intermediary space, an in-between area not previously seen on the bronze door.

Seated before the Holy Sepulcher, he lifts one hand, signaling his intention to speak; the other rests on his thigh. Like the infant Jesus in both the Nativity panel and in the panel depicting the establishment of the new Law (cf. fig. 138 and 150), he presents his own body as a paradigm.

The configuration of the throne on which he is seated underscores this mimetic injunction. Only one column is visible; it rests on a socle irrigated by undulating life channels and adjoins the entry pilaster of the Holy Sepulcher. Associated with the symbolic quality of the column itself as a sign of the Law on the right wing of the door, the throne underscores the angelic message announcing the tomb's emptiness and

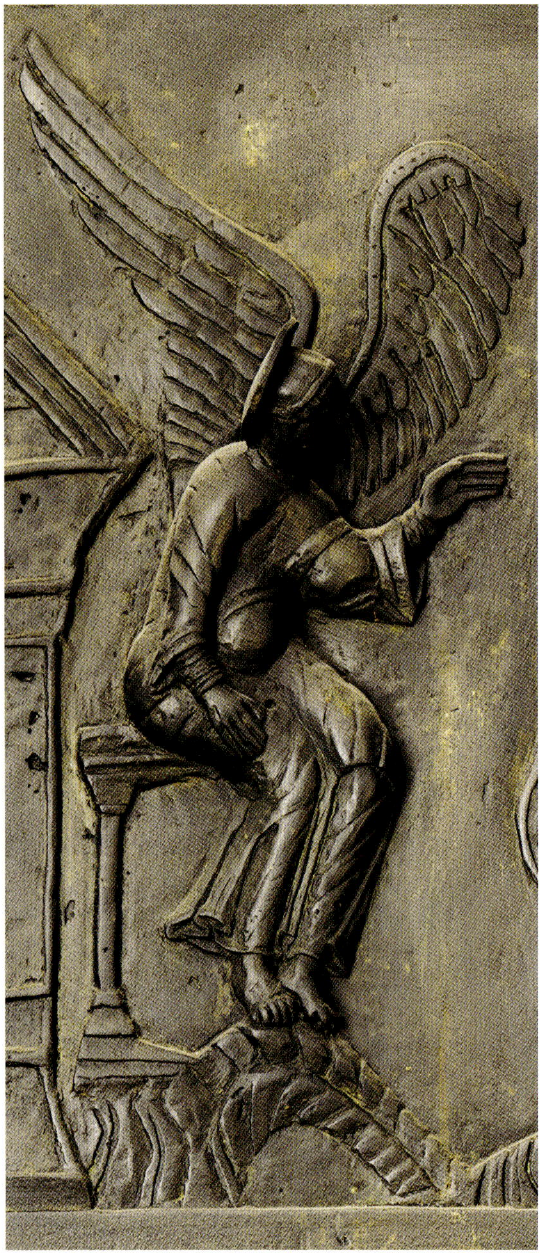

179

the Resurrection of Christ's body, namely the essence of the new Law authorizing eternal life. Furthermore, in the same way in which Mary and Gabriel took the place of certain architectural elements in panel 9, the angel's bent legs serve as the counterpart to the visible column in such a way as to clarify the terms of this new Law.

Let us elaborate on this point. The angel's feet rest on a hollowed-out mound on which there is no trace of life channels. Instead, rivulets of living water flow freely on the ground without constraint or planned direction. They show that the water's spiritual substance is of such an immaterial purity (without any earthly component) that there is no need to insert a meta-structure to channel it. The Spirit itself has no need of channels to guide and reinvigorate a substance with which it blends. In addition, we notice with some surprise that the mound placed under the angel is composed of two layers of superimposed substances, perfectly joined. Between them, the circulation lines are precisely aligned, which is not the case for the soil or the square socle represented on the panel's right. What does this mean?

The angel's garments are quite different from the ones he wore in the previous panels. Two layers of cloth cover him, clinging so tightly to each other that they are rendered visible only by an incongruous opening of the outer garment on the lower legs. As noted in the study of panel 6 and developed in the subsequent panels, the clothes that Bernward has chosen for the figures of the bronze door are highly significant. The angels in panels 5, 6, and 9, those who present themselves as God's emissaries to men, are dressed in the same way as the Creator. That was not the case for the celestial creature in the very first panel. That angel, God's witness and participant, was inscribed in the life-diagonal of the well-ordered figuration of the world's Creation (cf. fig. 20). He wore a flowing toga attached to the shoulder, a long fluid tunic reaching his feet, but also a third garment, worn very close to the body; a pleated sleeve appeared on the right forearm, which can be qualified as a *camisile* in Latin (*chainse* in Old French).

The angel seated in front of Christ's tomb in panel 15 no longer wears a flowing toga. He appears instead in the same tunic and *camisile* with pleated sleeves worn by the angel in panel 1, who thus becomes his direct antetype in the visual discourse. However, the texture of the materials has been considerably modified. The diaphanous fluidity and the pleats carved in bronze, which were the conventional attributes of the angelic and divine garments on the door, appear exclusively on the lower part of the angel's *camisile* in panel 15. They suggest the shape of his celestial body, the shape taken by the exclusively spiritual substance of which he is made.

The angel's outer tunic, on the other hand, is much thicker. It does not correspond to any other angelic or divine garment on the door and can only be compared to the spiritual human clothes, striated with fine lines, worn by the Righteous since the depiction of Abel in panel 7 (cf. fig. 102). This material tunic, unlike the immaterial camisile, speaks of the corporeal form the angel has taken in order to make himself visible to the Holy Women: "Entering into the sepulchre, they saw a young man sitting on the right side, clothed with a white robe and they were astonished" (Mark 16:5); "It came to pass, as they

179. *Panel 15, angel.*

were astonished in their mind at this, behold, two men stood by them, in shining apparel" (Luke 24:4).

Several details in the image call attention to the intense iridescence of this visible bodily sheath. The edge of the right sleeve and the middle of the tunic's left sleeve are underscored by a decorative border dotted with small ornamental circles similar to those found on God's book and sleeves in panel 2 (cf. fig. 39), and on Christ's halo in panel 13 (cf. fig. 161). The same dotting follows the curve of the diadem, which thus assumes the status of those worn by the angels depicted in Edenic spaces (panels 1 and 5); yet it is distinct from the unornamented diadems worn by divine messengers appearing on Earth (panels 6 and 9). Last, and in an entirely different fashion, the angel's diadem in panel 15 is emphasized by an arched motif, probably inspired by ancient headdresses. The light plays on the full and empty spaces, making the metal shine. Visually this frontal ornament appears as the organized and geometrized extension of the luminous radiance. Its light is less intense than that radiated by the Creator in panel 2, but it is reflected by the angel in the same way in which it illuminated Eve and made it possible for Adam to see and receive in God the companion destined for him.

And Bernward is quite precise about the nature and quality of this received and reflected light. Two parallel lines, aligned along the ornamented edges of the tunic's sleeves, diagonally cross the angel's abdomen, inflated with the breath of life. This double luminous line is no longer merely a life channel structured by the Spirit but is an axis aligned, as in the first panel, along the image's large diagonal (cf. fig. 14). Even though it appears as a material entity, the celestial figure is included by the bishop in the axis of primordial life established by God in his Creation. In other words, the Holy Spirit permeates and fills the angel's body in its entirety because the celestial figure is in the right position to participate in the divine light.

The inclusion of the angelic body in God's light has a major consequence. It qualifies the unprecedented ground on which he is positioned, an intermediary place between heaven and earth, as a place of unification. The ground's two strata, recalling the two layers of clothing, one entirely spiritual, the other corporeal (although pervaded by divine light) are here coordinated and unified: they intermingle, one flowing into the other.

We understand this as a metaphor for rethinking the relationship between the soul and the human body, which had been divided by sin, a separation that was the origin of death (cf. fig. 73). Shifted from the paradigmatic angel to the New Man, this assertion sanctions the possible reunification of the spiritualized carnal body and the soul of the Holy Woman. The Holy Spirit has the power to link the two; humans can now benefit from it if they position themselves in the right way. This is one of the Holy Spirit's major interventions in Creation. Indeed, the Spirit unites the Father and the Son in the Trinity, just as he allows for the hypostatic union of Christ's two natures, human and divine. In the background of panel 15 we see the implicit reference to a state of the human body as reported by the Bible—undoubtedly the most striking one in Christ's earthly life—the luminous body in which Jesus ap-

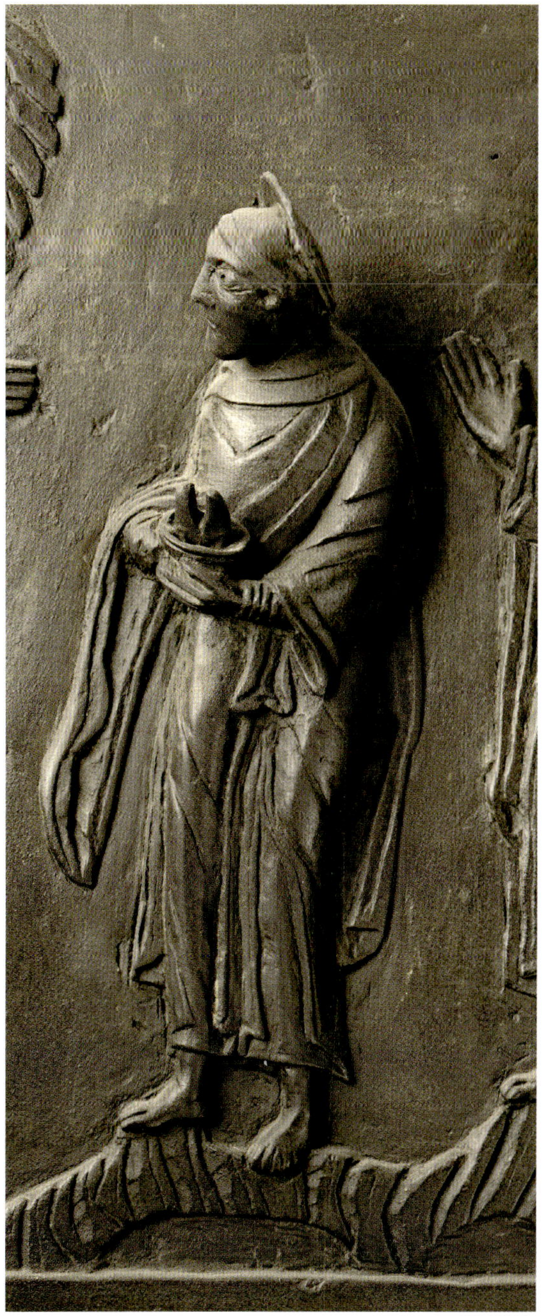

180

180. *Panel 15, Holy Woman, left.*

peared at the moment of his transfiguration: "And he was transfigured before them. And his face did shine as the sun: and his garments became white as snow" (Matt. 17:2; see also Mark 9:2–4 and Luke 9:29). It is this model of transfiguration into divine light that the Holy Woman is invited to follow (fig. 180).

From the pyx that she holds at the threshold of the tomb, two symmetrical flames arise, identical in substance and form to the fire of the divine mandorla in panel 7 (cf. fig. 99). I suggest that these two flames stand for the symbiotic state of the two unified components of the New Man, transfigured by divine light and inscribed into the sacred space he shares with God.

But in order to reach this last stage, the Holy Woman, following the angel's example, must have brought about within herself a substantial and intellective transformation whose course we must now retrace. Her external transformation is demonstrated by the evolution of the garments covering her; her intellective transformation is conveyed by the change in the nature of her vision, meaning the evolution of the processes of her soul [on the implication of noncorporeal senses in Bernward's Gospel Book, see Kingsley 2014].

We shall begin by studying her clothes (fig. 178). In her first representation, on the far right, the Holy Woman wears a thin veil simply arranged around her head. In her second representation, in the middle, this veil acquires an additional fold, becoming a shawl covering her veiled head and shoulders. This added cloth replaces the square fibula's holding function and it is this cloth that from now on will keep the garment together. In the third and last of the Holy Woman's representations, on the far left, the veil covering her head and shoulders has acquired thickness by a supplementary fold. This added fabric, giving to the headdress the shape of rigorously parallel flat pleats, had been foreshadowed by the divine sleeve in panel 7 and by the toga worn by Christ in panel 13 (cf. fig. 101 and 161); it also served as a model for the edge of Simeon's cape on which the infant Jesus apposed his hand of blessing in panel 12 (cf. fig. 158).

The same cumulative process determines the evolution of the Holy Woman's clothes from right to left (fig. 177). On the right, she wears a thin piece of cloth serving as a cape over a long, apparently sleeveless, tunic, since it shows her naked arms. To the central figure is added a cape, pushed back to reveal a tunic with wide sleeves resembling those of the angel's. In the third figure, the very ample cape has become thicker and appears to flutter, particularly at the level of the pyx from which it seems to flow. At the same time, we see the pleated cuffs of an undergarment, imitating the angel's specific garment, which reveals the shape of his celestial body.

While the evolution of the holy figures' garments in the door's right wing had consisted in reducing the material to signify the progressive spiritualization of the bodies of flesh, now the substantial transformation of the bodies of the Righteous is expressed by adding layers of cloth once the body has entered the divine light. For the first time since original sin, human bodies, united with their soul, can fully receive the Spirit who guides them and fills them with his divine nature. Purified by Christ's blood, made immortal by the Resurrection, and placed in such a way as to be within celestial light, they then become temples of God:

> Know you not, that your members are the temple of the Holy Ghost, who is in you, whom you have from God; and you are not your own? For you are bought with a great price. Glorify and bear God in your body. (1 Cor. 6:19–20)

What happens to the soul? Simultaneously to the transformation-relocalization of her integrally spiritualized body of flesh, the Holy Woman modifies her intellectual activity. Many early medieval exegetes expanded the Augustinian meditation on the workings of the soul and studied the biblical texts, in particular the Apocalypse, in order to question the nature of vision and the extent to which it brought into play sight's corporeal organ, as well as the actions of the soul and its inner images [Klein 1998a; Guglielmetti 2011]. According to my work on the Trier Apocalypse, medieval illuminators seem to have followed the theologians in this inquiry from very early on, at least since Carolingian times [Marchesin 2010]. Bernward's approach is not quite of the same order, because what is at stake in his discourse remains internal to the bronze door, though he clearly drew his inspiration from this theoretical substratum. On this basis he established the visual signs indicating the cognitive workings appropriate to the characters he represented, as we will see now.

We concluded the analysis of panel 14 with the prophetic figures of Mary and St. John, both of whom brought the trajectory of past and future times up to the present. This double experience—Wisdom from Holy Scripture and ecstatic meeting with God—prepared and established the definitive terms of the evolving gaze of the Holy Woman visiting the tomb.

The feminine figure on the right of panel 15 focuses her attention exclusively on her pyx. What she sees—the lock on the vessel—is not what is but what was and is no more: the tomb was indeed sealed af-

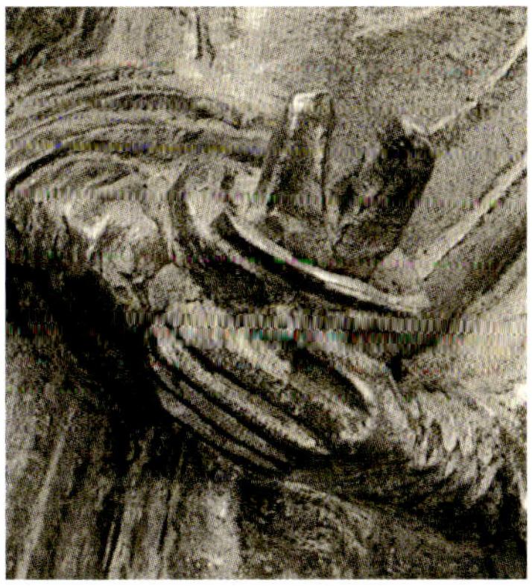

181

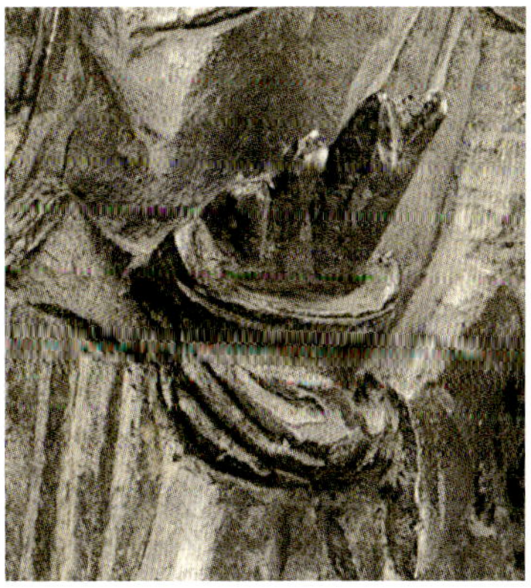

182

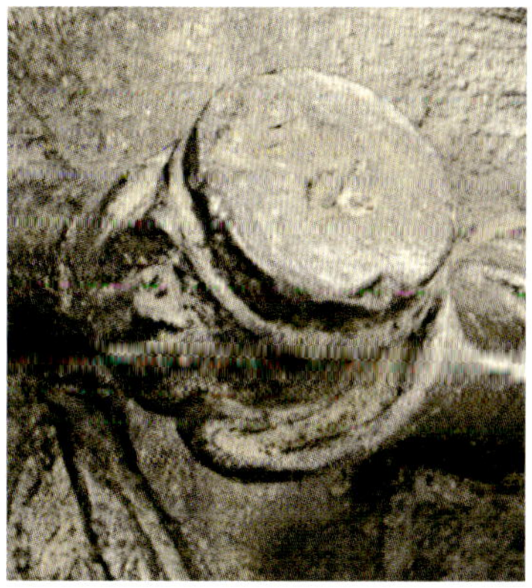

183

ter the inhumation of Christ's body but the stone closing it had already been removed in order to open up the entrance by the time the Holy Women set out on their journey (fig. 183). What the woman contemplates in panel 15 is not actual reality but the fruit of her imagination, meaning an image produced solely by her soul and made possible by the existence, within the soul itself, of referential images established after sensorial experiences: her vision is "spiritual," according to Augustinian nomenclature [Gilson 1987, 74].

As noted before, the feminine figure at the center of the group has leaned forward slightly in order to see the angel and the empty tomb. Her vision is explained by the open pyx from which emerges the substance in motion, evoking the Resurrection of Christ's body (fig. 182). What she sees is no more a vision of actual reality than the previous one. Had this been the case, the pyx would be empty, like the sepulcher from which the body is absent. Two observations can be drawn from this. The Holy Woman in the center also produces an image from her inner soul. However, unlike the previous vision, this image produced by the soul no longer refers to anything experienced, memorized, or known in the material universe. At this stage of the narrative, no one has yet encountered the resurrected Christ; as for the Holy Woman, objectively, she sees only an absence. How can she then identify the substance emerging from her pyx?

The image composed by her soul is the formal shaping of the intellectual comprehension she has elaborated, beginning with the angelic utterances and light. The fruit of her vision, detached from the physical world and its images, is simply the result of seizing divine truth through the intellect. It corresponds to the soul's cognitive faculty that Augustine qualifies as "intellectual vision." This vision happens only when the divine radiance sheds light on the soul's faculties from within: "It is an inner vision through which the thought perceives the truth revealed to it by divine light" [Gilson 1987, 57; Kessler 2000, 174–175]. In other words, it is solely because she has freed a space within herself where God sheds light on her comprehension that the Holy Woman understands the meaning of the Resurrection.

The vision that the Holy Woman has while facing the angel carries her even further in her ability to understand and penetrate the world (fig. 181). Being equal in substance and form, the two parts/flames emerging from her pyx represent the two parts of the New Man, transfigured and unified by divine light. But what does the pyx itself represent? Christ's tomb?

In addition to the Holy Woman's evolution, the form of the pyx becomes modified in the course of the spiritual conversion. When closed, as on the panel's right, it is perfectly cylindrical (fig. 183). In the center, as it opens to reveal the figure of Christ's resurrected body, it becomes oval (fig. 182). If we look carefully, we see that the substance of Christ's resurrected body has not only emerged from its receptacle. It has spread out vigorously along the pyx's longitudinal axis, while at the same time spreading in a thick layer of matter over the whole surface. Indeed, Christ's resurrected body transforms its receptacle while emerging from it, reshaping it by making it oval, thus bringing to mind the formal likeness of the extended mandorla in panel 7, the place where God already was. The sacred area, which had remained forbidden since original sin, is now shared between humans and God because it is, in the most literal meaning of the word, defined by the body of the resurrected human/divine Christ.

The pyx of the Holy Woman facing the angel retains its oval shape, but the articulation between receptacle and content has changed (fig. 181). Whereas the substance of the Resurrection had previously spread over the surface of the receptacle and determined its shape, a second, smaller oval rim is now delineated inside the ointment vessel. The second layer of matter spread on the surface represents the mate-

181 *Panel 15, pyx, left.*

182. *Panel 15, pyx, center.*

183. *Panel 15, pyx, right.*

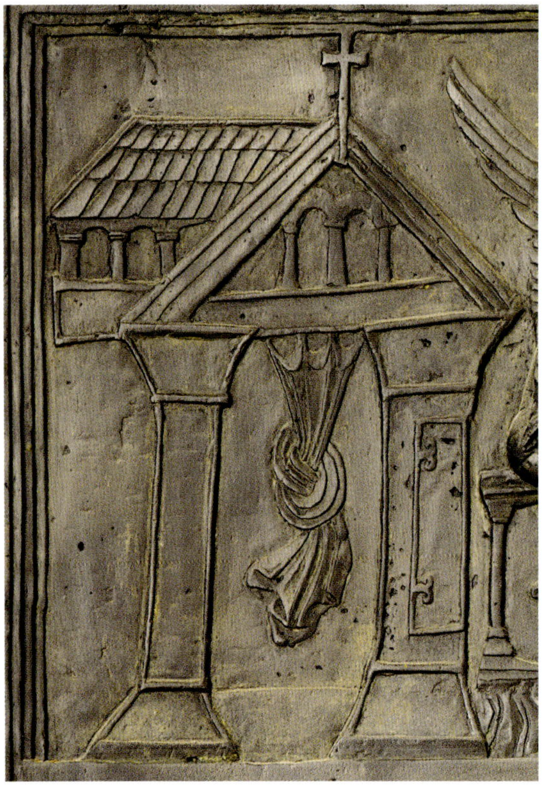

184

rial extension of the being's two parts/flames, unified in the divine light. This extension corresponds to the pyx's preexisting shape without covering it. The second layer represents the New Man, inscribed (again literally) within the sacred and luminous area that is Christ's resurrected body. The Holy Woman sees herself *inside* the body of Christ. Her actions, specifically the oval shape of her two hands holding the pyx, are also conditioned by this articulation with the holy area where the union of the human and the divine takes place.

The last oval pyx thus appears as the topological equivalent of the life-diagonal where the celestial being appears, having taken human form: a place of transformation and transubstantiation, immovable yet dynamic, allowing the growth of life inherent in it.

Although still living on earth, the Holy Woman from this point on has raised herself to an extraordinary level of awareness. Her third and last vision differs from the previous ones. It is activated by an image that is unified and re-created according to a strict resemblance to God, as well as by the inner luminous space delineated by Christ's dead and resurrected body. This last stage of the understanding of God through direct participation is a noetic understanding, like that of the angel in the first panel. The Woman's vision is thus enlightenment, human wisdom embedded in divine Wisdom [Gilson 1987, 111–122].

The Holy Woman can now advance toward the Holy Sepulcher, enter it, offer herself to God, and take the place of Abel's lamb because nothing in her nature is heterogeneous to the holy place she wishes to reach. She will thus be able to unite with Christ; the mystical nuptials match the very first meeting of Adam and Eve in panel 2, whose union will be consummated in the following panel.

The sepulcher is the earthly place of the dead and resurrected body of Christ. It shelters all those who, remaining in the divine light, constitute the ecclesial community inscribed in the divine body itself, the house of God:

> Now therefore you are no more strangers and foreigners; but you are fellow citizens with the saints, and the domestics of God, built upon the foundation of the apostles and prophets, Jesus Christ himself being the chief corner stone: In whom all the building, being framed together, groweth up into an holy temple in the Lord. In whom you also are built together into an habitation of God in the Spirit. (Eph. 2:19–22)

On a theological level, the tomb is nothing but an emphatic echo of the pyx, a sort of harmonic resonance demultiplying the individual to evoke the community of believers (fig. 184). On the semiotic level, it is much more than that. Through the configuration he has chosen to give to the Church-Body of Christ, Bernward has elaborated a theory of representation and mediation with which we shall conclude our analysis.

As mentioned earlier, the tomb of panel 15 belongs to the morphological heritage of Solomon's temple, transformed into the City of God, caused by Christ's Law in panel 12 (cf. fig. 153). The differences between the two structures are equal to the transformation that the Resurrection has brought about in the community of believers. This transformation is announced in panel 15 by the configuration of the throne on which the angelic messenger is seated. Only the structure remains of the complex Marian throne in panel 11 (cf. fig. 150): a vertical column and a horizontal seat. All the contingent elements, all the material traces of the historia (arched bays, rectangular bays, doors, oculus, irregular bays) behind the foundation of the community have disappeared.

Christ's tomb is structured in the same way as the temple in panel 12, of which it is a sketch or blueprint (fig. 184). The general shape remains, but the plastic element adopted for the visual treatment of the architecture has modified its entire texture. The building is no longer in relief but rather outlined on the panel's

184. *Panel 15, Holy Sepulcher.*

surface. Without any vanishing line, it has lost all its depth, as well as all the elements that established its three-dimensionality: the thickness of the columns, triangular pediment and roof, the roundness of the orbs, even the altar placed at the entrance. However, it is not schematized and its geometric irregularities, especially on the horizontal level, lend it a lightness suggesting its vital animation.

The three major components of Solomon's temple, the entrance, the Altar of the Holocaust, and the body of the lateral building (the basilica-type nave) have been transformed. The two large pillars at the tomb's entrance have morphed into pure geometric outline. The little open door evoking the ancient access to Solomon's temple has been flattened and incorporated into the right pillar, thus becoming a residual attribute; the traces of history, that is to say the passage of time, have been subsumed into the structure.

The Altar of the Holocaust has likewise disappeared, annulled by the last sacrifice, that of Christ. The socle, from which flowed the purifying blood of Christ, however, has permeated the bases of the pillars at the entrance. Between them, the schematic form of the fluvial valley of Eden (cf. fig. 55) is visible. The valley is now completely empty because the world's ever-changing matter, being heterogeneous, is extraneous to the Church-Body of Christ. The lower part of the lateral building has also been eliminated from the representation of the Holy Sepulcher. The three great columns that stood on the ground in the Temple of Solomon have been raised to the pediment's level. They have morphed into three little columns placed horizontally, equivalent to the twin bays symbolizing Christ's double nature already seen in panel 9. They support the roof.

In this case, just as the roof of Solomon's temple showed a lattice work whose design recalled the swaddling clothes of the infant Jesus, thus constituting the prophetic basis for the inscription of the faithful into the Church, the roof of the Holy Sepulcher is covered with long tiles which, like funerary slabs, represent the way in which every single body of the faithful comes together in a single homogeneous Christlike body. And if one still doubts the attention Bernward paid to church roofing, one should recall that he had his monogram stamped onto the tiles of the Hildesheim Cathedral [Kruse 1999].

A cross reaching the panel's frame surmounts the roof. The cross elevates the holy community toward celestial heights in an ascending movement that will extend Christ's victorious cross to the panel's upper edge (cf. fig. 186). In this respect, beyond time and beyond the world, on its way toward the Creator, the Church as Christ's living body is a prefiguration of the Heavenly Jerusalem.

However, the cross is not simply placed on the structure; without any orb or relief, the cross descends straight through the pediment, becoming part of the building and marks it, in a certain way, as a new world in itself. At the same time, the cross establishes a connection that could not be more tangible between the structure standing on the earthly ground and the panel's frame it reaches. The entire building, from the bases to the cross, cover the height of the panel and stands as an intermediary space. Everything can circulate in this space of mediation, like the angel between heaven and earth. This Church, which is at the same time in the world and above the world that she is destined to lead to salvation, is represented here in its mediating function.

Let us now consider the appearance of the structure as a whole. Regardless of the complexity of the architectural edifices and the connecting devices of their constitutive elements, Bernward had, until now, always respected the rules of the architectural art that he knew so well. For the first time since the beginning of the bronze door, a tall building structure stands with no means of support in a kind of unrealistic levitation. The appearance of the Holy Sepulcher is not linked to natural laws anymore, other than the materials with which it is built or the absence of perspective in which it is seen. The Church—Christ's living body—although earthly, does not follow the laws of the secular world; moreover, we should note that the two orbs crowning Solomon's temple have disappeared.

In order to communicate this disengagement from the material world through visual representation, Bernward abandons all previous mimetic artifices. The tomb's matter (pure glowing light reflected by the large bronze surfaces), its design (graphic elements taking precedence over the masses), its inscription into space (a weightlessness applied to the surface by the tomb's connection to the Christian pediment and its abutment to the frame) are strictly iconic. Their mission is not to represent the physical world for what it is but to translate an image of the invisible world into visible forms.

This image is arguably the equivalent of the pyx, because now the artist's freedom is equal to his own illumination; what he communicates is what he sees in his own enlightened psyche, precisely like the Holy Woman. The Church is indeed an *imago*, an inner vision: fixed, complete, perfectly created to convey its perfection. The artist's point of reference is the essence/ontology of the world, and its full comprehension is revealed to the soul by God himself.

However, this Church, Christ's body, contains yet another element—too striking to be overlooked—that belongs to the historia: the large, knotted drapery placed at the entrance of the Holy Sepulcher. Foreshadowed by Christ's perizoma on the cross in panel 12, this *sudarium involutum* is the shroud that Joseph of Arimathea and Nicodemus used, according to Jewish ritual, to swathe Jesus's body after his descent from the cross (John 19:40). More precisely, it is the cloth wrapped around Christ's head that Mary Magdalene and Peter found when they entered the empty tomb (John 20:7–8). Bernward borrows the mode of representation from Byzantine and Ottonian art, but the place he gives to it is unprecedented. Everything converges to make it an exceptional object within the semiotic system of the bronze door. As a cloth, the shroud replaces Jesus's sheath of flesh that has departed the earth. It therefore stands in the middle of the tomb as a sign both of the absence of Christ's body and of the Savior's invisible presence among humans: it is the metonymic sign of the sepulcher itself.

"Jesus answered, and said to them: Destroy this temple, and in three days I will raise it up. The Jews then said: Six and forty years was this temple in building; and wilt thou raise it up in three days? But he spoke of the temple of his body. When therefore he was risen again from the dead, his disciples remembered, that he had said this, and they believed the scripture, and the word that Jesus had said" (John 2:19–22).

Iconographically, the shroud recalls the two hangings at the entrance to Solomon's Temple in panel 12; now tied together, these two material hangings obstruct the access to the immaterial, sacred space, while at the same time appearing as the doorway giving access to the eternal Church, Christ's living body.

In fact, the knot functions in the image as the new womb through which the believer must pass in order to unite with Christ and resurrect with him and in him. Formally, it takes up and effaces the demonic and then sinful knot that appeared with original sin as the sign of ultimate death. In the crucible of a death that is a rebirth, the knot describes the matter's reversal on itself, the journey that takes it to a reconversion toward what it was ontologically before entering the earthly world—that is, a component of light as a part of the Creator.

A sign of the incarnated and resurrected Word, the knot of the Holy Sepulcher thus constitutes the geometrically paradigmatic model of the future Edenic life—eternal fusion in God—to which the Righteous are destined. It replaces Christ's orthonormal cross that was, in turn, the womb of the Word acting in the "first" Creation, the Creation of an earthly world destined to be destroyed at the end of time.

> Know you not that all we, who are baptized in Christ Jesus, are baptized in his death? For we are buried together with him by baptism into death; that as Christ is risen from the dead by the glory of the Father, so we also may walk in newness of life. For if we have been planted together in the likeness of his death, we shall be also in the likeness of his Resurrection. . . . For he that is dead is justified from sin. Now if we be dead with Christ, we believe that we shall live also together with Christ. (Rom. 6:3–8)

185. *Panel 15, Holy Woman, right.*

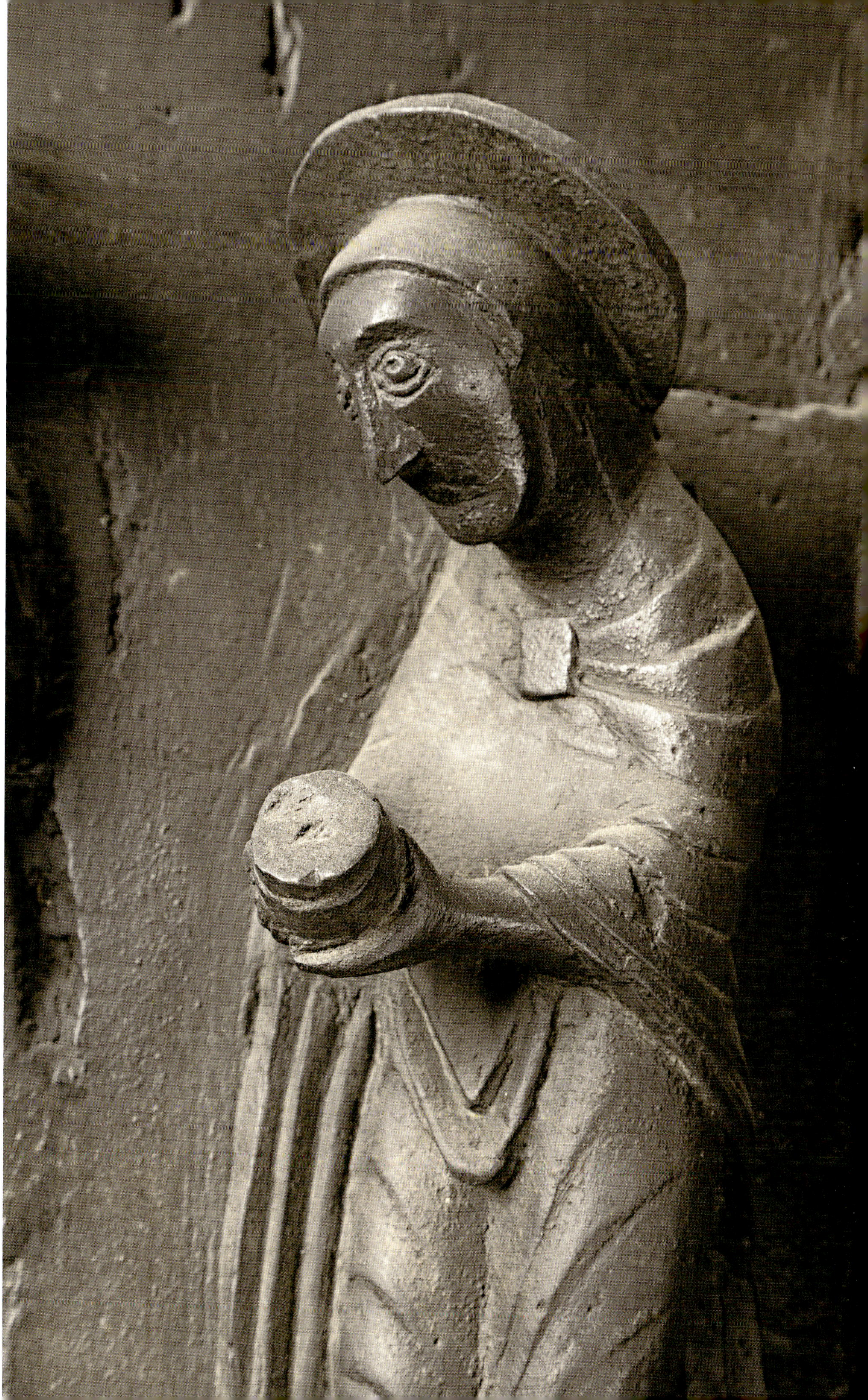

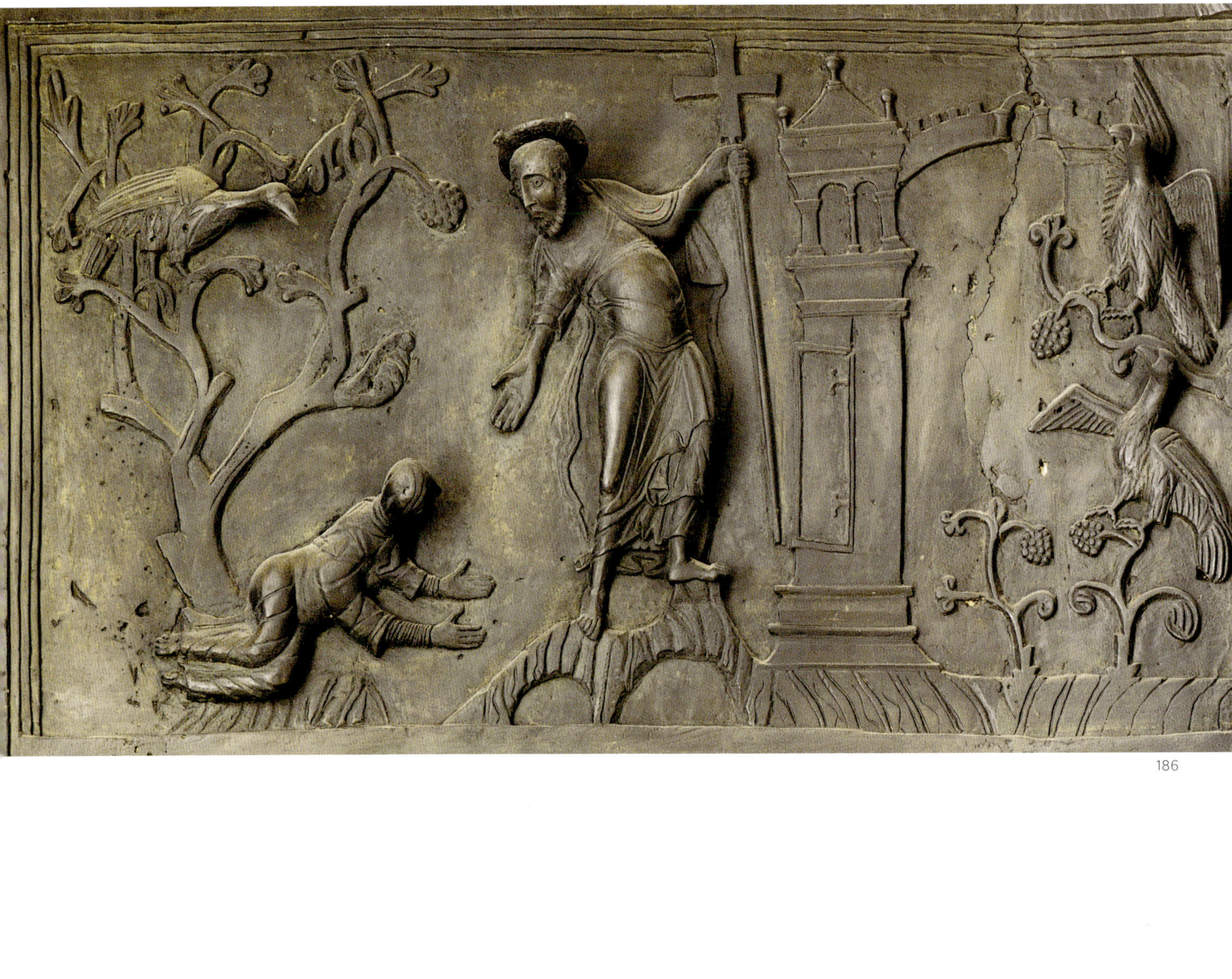

Panel **16**

COMMUNION

"Rhetoric may be defined as the faculty of observing in any given case the available means of persuasion" (Aristotle, *Rhetoric*, trans. W. R. Roberts [Dover, 2004], I: 2, 6). By using the two "books" that God gave to humanity, the Bible and Nature, and by inserting them as tangible and intelligible proofs into a discourse on form and substance whose coherence is the reflection of the Wisdom of divine Creation, Bernward demonstrated the ontological reasons for the Fall and for Christian Salvation. This discourse now comes to an end: "There are two kinds of peroration [which some call the completion and others the conclusion], for it may deal either with facts or with the emotional aspect of the case" (Quintilian, *Institutio Oratoria*, trans. H. E. Butler [Heinemann, 1921] VI, 1.1).

The scene depicted in panel 16 is a continuation of the historical narrative (fig. 186). Christ, resurrected and returned from Hell, extends his hand toward Mary Magdalene, who according to John's Gospel, turns from the empty tomb in tears and sees a man whom she first mistakes for a gardener before recognizing him as her Lord. Christ asks her not to touch him because he has not yet ascended to his Father (John 20:11–17). (On the exegesis and the cult of Mary Magdalene, see [Saxer 1959].)

In addition to being the closing scene, panel 16 is unique in that it includes all the actors of the discourse on the bronze door: God and humans, animals synthesized in the form of three birds, all the kinds of known ground (sepulchral grottos, battered earth, ground purified by life channels); vegetation (a tree and three bushes); as well as several architectural structures that had appeared in the course of the world's history (a tower/gate giving access to a garden, a crenellated enclosure, and pillars/columns).

186. *Panel 16.*

Every one of the constituent units of the door's visual message corresponds to the metamorphoses that have occurred in the course of time, serving as an epilogue, a concluding synthesis, and ultimate renewal of the Law of the world. This conclusion mirrors the magisterial overture of the bronze door in panel 1, displaying the principles of divine Creation. Of all the symmetrical panels on the left and right wings, the first and the last develop the most powerful analogical connections, closing the narrative's cycle before elevating humanity to a higher level than that of its initial condition (cf. fig. 1).

The diegetic structure of the first and last images are parallel. In panel 1, the Creator raises Eve lying at his feet while breathing life into her. In panel 16, Christ, ascending toward the Father, raises Mary Magdalene: by drawing her to him, he leads her to Heaven where she will be entitled to eternal life in God. A topographic symmetry is added to the analogy between the characters. A walled in garden serves as a counterpart to the Tree of Life and to the vivified ground on which Adam stands. What does this garden represent?

The tower/gate allowing access to the garden is inscribed in the verticality of the prophetic tower with twin bays. Placed behind Gabriel in panel 9, the tower announced that Christ's incarnation opened the way to salvation, the way of returning to the Father (cf. fig. 119). Unlike its two historical antetypes—the Christlike tower in panel 9 and the antonymous door in panel 5 (cf. fig. 72)—the monumental entrance and the garden enclosure in panel

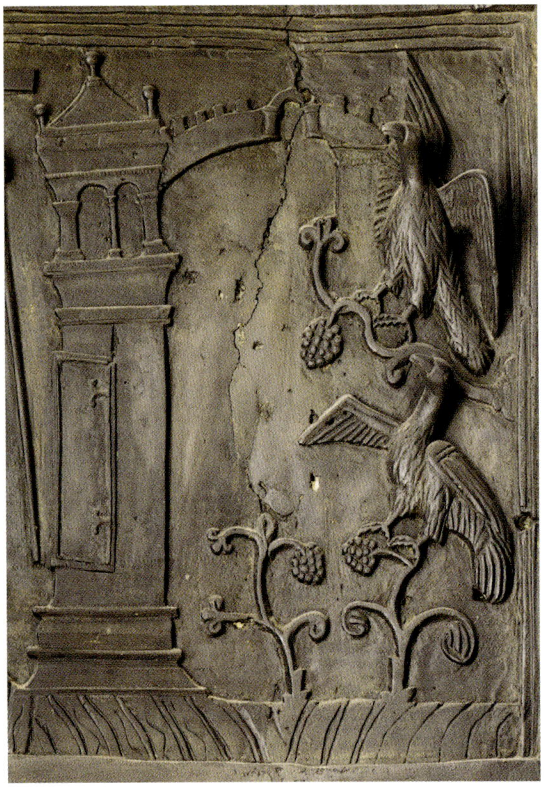

187

16 are not built with tiles and stone blocks (fig. 187). Slightly leaning, like the column of the Law in panel 11 (cf. fig. 142), the tower/gate to Paradise in panel 16 has the same lightness and energy. Its architectural components are precisely delineated and uniformly covered by a surface of smooth metal, similar to the texture of the Church-Body of Christ in panel 15. Nevertheless, one cannot help but notice that its roofing has lost its tiles and that the building has a weight and a density absent from the sepulcher in panel 15 (cf. fig. 184). The disappearance of the roof's tiles, which on two occasions symbolized the believers' inclusion into Christian unity, could indicate either that the bodies of Christians have disappeared, or that they have lost their individuality, blending into the mass containing them. (We shall return to this point.) As for the tower/door itself, it is included in the heritage of the Church as Christ's living body through which a Christian must pass in order to be saved. However, here the tower/gate is no longer an image with smoothly delineated contours: it has regained the prominence and materiality of tangible objects, in particular those of the knot of the *sudarium involutum* in the previous panel, just as its roof displays the three orbs, the triple sign of dominance over the world.

The garden on which this tower/door opens is surrounded by a crenellated wall, thus placing it in direct continuity with the representation of earthly cities on the right wing: the City of the Righteous in panel 9, then the Church, beginning in panel 10. Furthermore, it should be noted that in this case these walls were absent from the representation of the image of the Church-Body of Christ in panel 15, from which all signs of earthly ground had disappeared as well. Finally, under the door—just as under the garden—the soil is irrigated by the world's vivifying water, a clearly earthly matter. Nothing indicates that the garden in panel 16 could be found anywhere but on earth or that, in continuity with previous cities, it could represent anything other than a human community, even a highly spiritual one.

In *De civitate Dei*, Augustine had not foreseen or even imagined a theocratic destiny for the Church, nor did he suggest the possibility of a political incarnation of the City of God. In order to understand this city, earthly and Edenic at the same time, it does not seem judicious to me to evoke what historians have qualified as "political Augustinianism." This is a misapplication of the meaning of Augustine's book by which certain scholars of the early Middle Ages defined a Christian political project placing the emperor in charge of the faithful's salvation [Arquillière 1934]. Never on the bronze door have the contingencies of human history been considered other than on an ontological level—the City of Man. While selecting biblical figures for his door, Bernward never chose a powerful man as vicar or prefiguration of Christ—quite the contrary. Next to Mary, whom he mainly presented in her quality of *theotokos* (God's mother) and mother of the believers, as did Ottonian artists generally [Russo 1966, 223], the personages whom the bishop chose to embody piety, faith, and light are among the humblest: Abel, Salome, Simeon, Mary Magdalene, right down to the magi, whom he represented modestly attired in opposition to Herod.

On the other hand, it is quite possible that the specificity of the Ottonian religious culture to which Bernward belonged influenced some of his choices. Indeed, the considerable place he gave to women in the history of the Fall and Salvation (Eve, Mary, Salome, and Mary Magdalene) can be understood only by considering the influence and authority of Ottonian aristocratic women, and especially the exemplary character of their piety. Four of the five Ottonian queens were canonized, and Germanic women's *vitae* are almost more numerous than men's; one can speculate that sanctification was mainly women's work for the Ottonians [Leyser 1979, 49, 63–64].

In the same way, the establishment of an earthly ecclesial community with a dominant divine status in the world is not so much a theocratic ideal as a

187. *Panel 16, garden, right.*

dream of Christian pacification and unity broadly shared in the empire, particularly by Pope Sylvester II (Gerbert of Aurillac) and Emperor Otto III. In this instance, I do not think it is fortuitous to find the same prominent literary sources (Paul's Epistles, the *City of God*, the corpus of liberal arts studies) and the same cosmological background of an Augustinian *pax ecclesiae* (with different political stakes) in the *Life of the Archbishop Bruno of Cologne*, redacted by Ruotger around 968–69 [Hoffman 1957]. Like Bernward, Bruno anchored the legitimacy and the purpose of his ministry in the same passage of the Paul's Epistle to the Ephesians:

> To me, the least of all the saints, is given this grace, to preach among the Gentiles, the unsearchable riches of Christ, and to enlighten all men, that they may see what is the dispensation of the mystery. . . . For this cause I bow my knees to the Father of our Lord Jesus Christ, of whom all paternity in heaven and earth is named. That he would grant you, according to the riches of his glory, to be strengthened by his Spirit with might unto the inward man, that Christ may dwell by faith in your hearts, that being rooted and founded in charity, you may be able to comprehend, with all the saints, what is the breadth, and length, and height, and depth, to know also the charity of Christ, which surpasseth all knowledge, that you may be filled unto all the fulness of God. Now to him who is able to do all things more abundantly than we desire or understand, according to the power that worketh in us, to him be glory in the church, and in Christ Jesus unto all generations, world without end. Amen. (Eph. 3:8–21)
>
> I therefore beseech you. . . . Careful to keep the unity of the Spirit in the bond of peace. One body and one Spirit, as you are called in one hope of your calling. One Lord, one faith, one baptism. One God and Father of all, who is above all, and through all, and in us all. (Eph. 4:1–6)

I suggest by way of conclusion, and in distancing myself from the historicist trend of identifying connections with contemporary events in medieval religious images, that the discourse on the bronze door is actually the result of a specific cultural context, but that its interest in present time is relative only to its filiation with the universal. The garden represented on the right of panel 16, the counterpart of the earthly Paradise in panel 1, epitomizes precisely this universal: God's kingdom on earth, the same community reunited in the holy body of Christ as

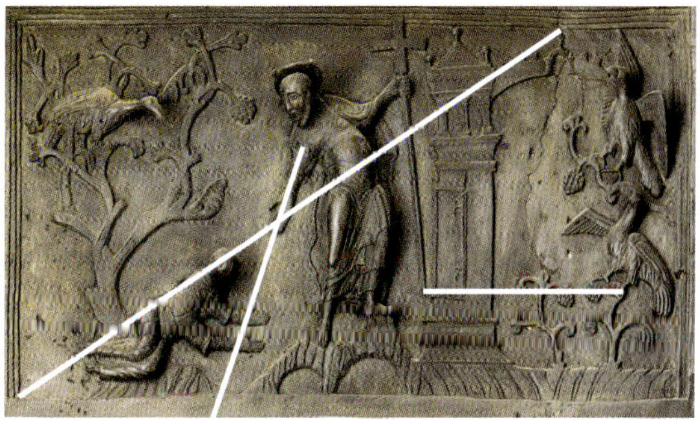

188

188. *Panel 16, panel structure.*

was depicted in panel 15, but this time qualified in its function as demiurgic crucible. As such, it allows for the actual participation of all of humanity in the new reality of the body and blood of the dead and risen Christ. Panels 1 and 16 share the same theme, the gift of eternal life, as well as a similar location, an earthly Edenic garden. Their correspondence is underscored by the fact that the gift of life proceeds from both in identical fashion, according to the divine principles linked to the Trinity's three hypostases.

In panel 1, a great diagonal revealed the process of the growth and fructification of a life engendered by the Father according to the formally orthonormal schema of the Son; the breath of the Holy Spirit, which is also light, guided and led that life to its fullness in the majestic completion of the Tree of Life (cf. fig. 14). In panel 16, this diagonal still exists, albeit in residual fashion, in the axis of Mary Magdalene's torso (fig. 188). In this instance, starting from the panel's lower left corner, it continues along the back of the Holy Woman, encountering the hand with which Christ motions the woman to rise; then it seems to join the orb surmounting a little arched doorway placed at the very end of the Edenic garden, a most intriguing detail that we will examine later.

This diagonal is the first dynamic axis in the image. Two more, complementary to it, make the action of the Father and the Son visible and intelligible, already distinguished from that of the Spirit of life in panel 1. One axis is internal to panel 16, and its paradigm is the cross-staff that Christ raises as he climbs higher in order to reach Heaven where his Father calls him. The cross is extended high enough to spill over two of the three edges (fig. 189). This suggests that the area of the ascension is beyond the panel's narrative space; in other words, the cross-staff is the matrix only of what is visible on the bronze door. We will understand why later.

The place where the cross-staff rests is higher than the feet of Christ himself, represented in ascending motion. It determines the position of the door inscribed in the entrance tower adjacent to the Edenic garden, as well as the perch of the lower bird standing

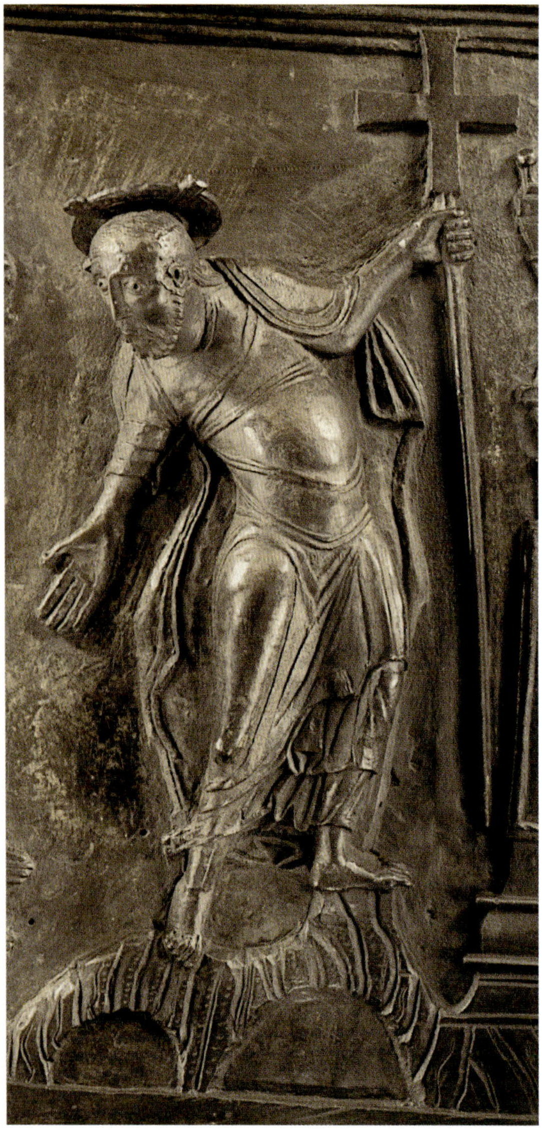

189

on it (fig. 188). The cross-staff is at the same height as the two winged figures, placed one above the other. A *signum,* certainly, but one of historical significance: here the cross-staff is no longer a universal sign but the call coming from the Father to his Son and to his children.

The last of the three dynamic axes in panel 16 has already been mentioned in the analysis of panel 8. This axis crosses the wings diagonally in the lengthening of the hand that Christ extends toward Mary Magdalene; it then passes through the geometric center of the door, descending to the lowest point of the left wing to raise Abel, the first of the Righteous (cf. fig. 114 and 188). This long diagonal must be understood in relation to the two hollows appearing under Christ's feet: they represent Hell, from which Christ has returned, victorious over death (fig. 189).

The theme of the Harrowing of Hell is implicitly evoked in the New Testament in a passage from the Epistle to the Ephesians, which says of Christ: "Now that he ascended, what is it, but because he also descended first into the lower parts of the earth?" (Eph. 4:9). Developed in Nicodemus's apocryphal Gospel, the theme frequently appeared in patristic texts and in Eastern images, particularly in Alexandria before being spread to the West by Augustine and Gregory the Great [Turner 1966, 174–178]; a vast iconographic tradition was then established beginning with the Carolingian epoch [Kirschbaum 1970, LCT, *Höllenfahrt Christi*]. From this literary and iconographic tradition, Bernward inherits the format he gives to the Harrowing of Hell with the additional meaning of the ascent to the father. But I would argue that, at the same time, the bishop poses the central question regarding the beneficiaries of the preaching in Hell and, consequently, of Christ's salvific mission. The presence of two hollows, suggesting the Jewish Sheol and the Latin Hades, seems to confirm that for Bernward the only condition necessary for salvation is to follow the universal path to liberation proposed by Christ, as developed by St. Augustine in the *City of God* (Book VII, 32 and, particularly, Book X, 25).

In essence, it is the door in its entirety—that is, Creation in its entirety as begun in the first panel—which Christ brings back to himself in order to become the mediating body of its ultimate ascension and return to the Father. Between the beginning and the end of the bronze door, the direction of the movement has been reversed: it no longer starts from the Creator and spreads out into the world, but it begins from the world and converges toward the Creator.

In panel 16, this return is embodied by the figure of Mary Magdalene (fig. 190). Through her topological connection with Eve in the first panel (cf. fig. 1), Mary Magdalene belongs explicitly to the human lineage she represents. She can also be identified with the Holy Woman in panel 15: she wears the same veil with three flat folds, and the same luminous shirt with pleated sleeves (cf. fig. 180). She becomes the essential figure of illumination and because she is inscribed into the light of God she can see and recognize the resurrected Christ.

At the same time, as I mentioned in my analysis of the first panel, Mary Magdalene's tunic has the same texture of the flowing garment worn by the angel at the very beginning of the bronze door, whose posture she also assumes (cf. fig. 20). Even so, this obvious analogy between the angel and Mary Magdalene is insufficient to allow for the superposition of the two figures: the Holy Woman is on earth whereas the angel is flying in the sky. This difference of location is very significant: in panel 1, Adam's position, fixed to

189. *Panel 16, Christ.*

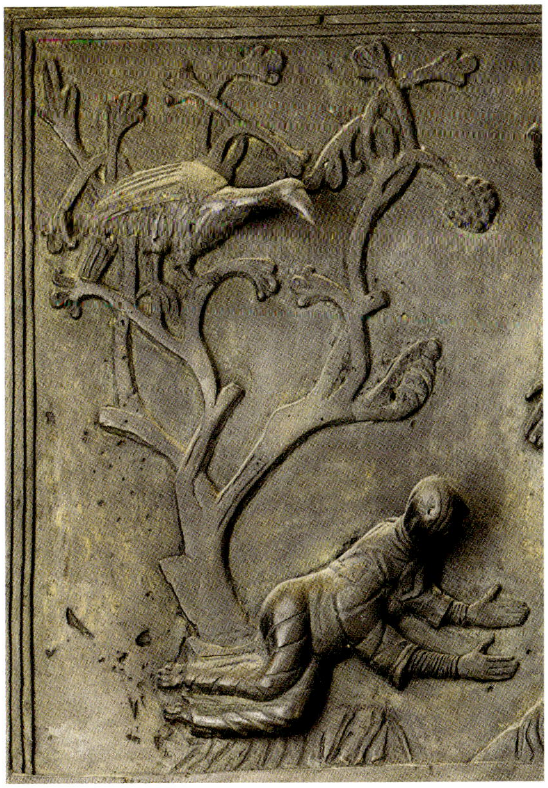

190

190. *Panel 16, Mary Magdalene and her tree.*

the ground by the imperious necessity of keeping in contact with the Tree of Life, functions as a counterpoint to the location of the celestial being (cf. fig. 1).

The iconography plays precisely on the contrast between Mary Magdalene's floating posture and her implausible earthly position on the ground. Although the mass constituted by her bent legs keeps her body attached to the soil, she is on the verge of tipping over, being positioned not on but above and in front of a socle marked by life channels whose supporting function is purely iconic (fig. 190). Placed in God's light, Mary Magdalene is a spiritual body moving above the earth, to which she remains connected by the reality of her earthly existence. The tree standing behind her becomes the exegesis of this intermediary condition, holy and imperfect at the same time.

Indeed, the placement of this tree is as ambiguous as the figure of Mary Magdalene. It does not appear to be rooted in the earth, instead it seems to have emerged from the body of the Holy Woman herself, in minuscule undulations of matter. While Adam in panel 1 stood at the foot of the plant on which his eternity depended, the tree in panel 16 by a complete reversal of perspective implies that the Holy Woman's purified body has itself become the fertile ground of eternal life. The tree trunk rises from it just as Christ's column rose from Mary's sanctified body in panel 10 (cf. fig. 126).

Formally, this plant is the first tree on the right wing. Fully grown (as evidenced by its size) and autonomous, just like the Tree of Life in the first panel, it does not, however, assume the same shape. With its two branches tied to form a heart, the first tree showed that the bipartition of humanity (like that of all living creatures) between masculine and feminine was the necessary condition for its fructification (cf. fig. 19). The plant's morphology in panel 16 is no longer bipartite but rather tripartite: three large branches rise above the trunk and then are subdivided into three boughs ending in three leaves. A new Tree of Life, this plant displays a trinary structure, encountered before only in the depiction of the soul separated from the body in panels 4 and 5 where it gave its structural model to the plant/spiritualized body of Abel opening up to God in panel 7 (cf. fig. 104). Thanks to the informative content of panel 15, we understand that this previous formal type has been fully realized in Mary Magdalene, since her soul and her spiritualized body have become reunited.

Let us expand the analysis of the tree. The paradigm of the shrubs representing the soul was not the great Tree of Life in panel 1 but the cross-shaped plant that preceded it in the image (cf. fig. 16 and 191). This shrub was the second of the three stages visualizing the formal and substantial laws of life, thus confirming the establishment of a trinary orthonormal order, naturally inscribed into the life-diagonal. It was only later on, after the creation of human beings and the flowering of the great Tree of Life destined for humanity, that Adam received his place at its roots together with his companion. By its trinary structure and its reference to the second bush of panel 1, Mary Magdalene's Tree of Life reveals the new essence of a body inscribed in the heritage of a paradigm preceding sexual distinction, namely the model used for the creation of the angel and not of humans. This new asexual body is no longer subject to the injunction of fructification because it no longer belongs to the animal realm, to the world of the flesh: it falls within the domain of the bodies of light.

If the characteristics of this unprecedented tree are explained by the differences that distinguish it from the great Tree of Life in panel 1, they are further underscored by the distance separating it from the intermediary bush in panel 1 (cf. fig. 16). The cross-shaped structure, orthonormal but rigid, that rigid bush is profoundly different from the profusion of matter organized according to a homothetic structure in Mary Magdalene's tree. Or, to put it another way, the tree's structure in panel 16 is similar to that of a fractal object (fig. 192): it results from the reduction, at different scales, of a basic geometry unit that corresponds to the shape of the object itself. Obviously,

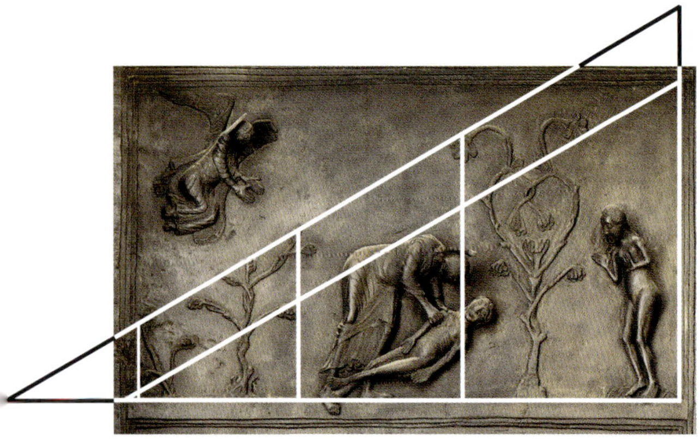

191

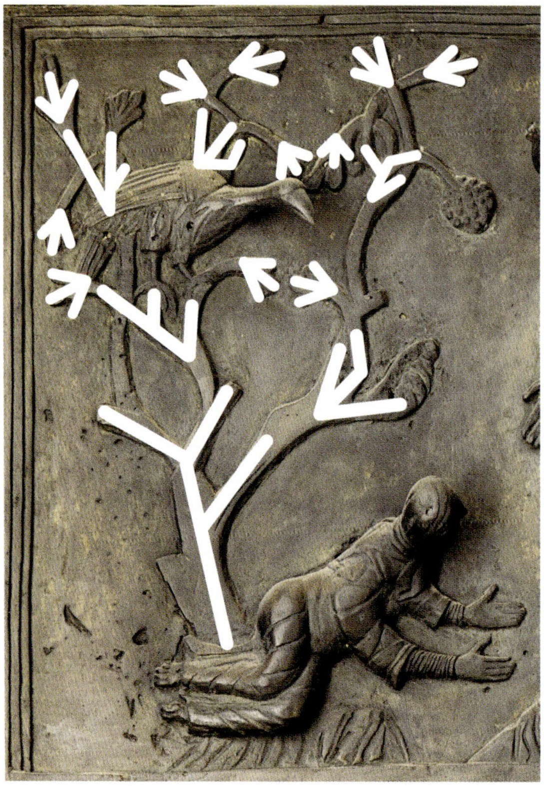

192

this original sequencing does not exactly correspond to Mandelbrot's mathematical model, but it refers to the most geometric, the most elaborate, and the most perfect geometric distribution found in nature; it can be seen in certain plants, such as ferns, whose branches seem to have been used precisely as models for the configuration of the door's first bushes.

Symbolically, these two modes of elaborating the completed form—the axial symmetry and the fractal organization—are quite different. In the first panel, the growth principle of the plant had imposed on its form a development in space and time in a coordinated fashion, according to a diagonal and regular order, that is, proportional (fig. 191). Such a mathematical order falls under the laws of the most remarkable of geometric figures, the triangle, and more precisely of the triangle whose properties are most astonishing: the Pythagorean right triangle. There were two right triangles in panel 1. The first one was an inner triangle, whose hypotenuse was the diagonal of the panel (that we named the vital impetus or diagonal of life). The second one was a bigger triangle, whose hypotenuse overlapped the growth driver of the Tree of Life (God's formal plan). If the diagonal of life was entirely visible, none of the three-line segments of the main triangle could be perceived in their entirety, no more than the proportional relation of the successive height of the three plants, in this case recalling Thales's theorem. The plant's growth was at the same time perfectly rational, perceptible by sight but not intelligible, precisely because it was the result of an order imposed from outside the scope of the visible.

Conversely, in panel 16 the mode of the tree's geometric generation proceeds from the multiplying of a visible internal module (fig. 192). Because the tree's source module and growth engine are within the completed system, they are now entirely knowable.

The possible sources of this distinction between two modes of engendering forms are numerous. Euclid's *Elements*, a major referent of scientific thought and the primary basis of these images, was little known in the West during the early Middle Ages. That was not the case for *De nuptiis Philologiae et Mercurii* [*Marriage of Philology and Mercury*], of which Books VI and VII are dedicated to Euclidean geometry and arithmetic, which were found in Ottonian culture as often as in Carolingian culture [McKitterick 1992; Riché, 51]. Furthermore, it is important to recall at this point that Bernward owned an annotated manuscript of Boethius's *De institutione arithmetica*, found also in the libraries of Hersfeld and Lorsch; Pope Sylvester II sent a copy of the manuscript to Otto III [Guillaumin 1995, XXXII and LXXII], which confirms the central place of this text in the educational program of the liberal arts [Mayr-Harting 2007, 110]. In *De institutione arithmetica,* Boethius presents the specific characteristics of the figures in Euclidean and Pythagorean geometry in their function as ontological qualities external to the world's matter. However, the essence of his treatise is the study of numbers as a proportional system based on modules, occurring especially in his exposition of the laws of music.

> [Arithmetic] is prior to all because God the creator of the massive structure of the world considered this first discipline as the exemplar of his own thought and established all things in accord with it; or that through numbers of an assigned order all things exhibiting the logic of their maker found

191. *Panel 1, proportional structuring of the panel.*

192. *Panel 16, fractal structuring of the tree.*

> concord, but arithmetic is said to be first for this reason also, because whatever things are prior in nature, it is to these underlying elements that the posterior elements can be referred. (Boethius, *De institutione arithmetica* [*Boethian Number Theory: A Translation of the de Institutione Arithmetica*, trans. M. Masi, 1983], Book I, 1.8, 74)

> [The second book] concern[s] quantity constant of itself, which is considered in geometric figures, and in which is a common element of all magnitudes. (Boethius, *De institutione arithmetica*, Book II, 2.4, op. cit. 119)

In addition to the sources cited above, we should note the significant similarity that may exist between the geometric structuring of the spiritual body placed in God's light and the Neoplatonic theories of divine emanation. These theories can be considered as part of the heritage of Calcidius's commentary and of the Carolingian and Ottonian commentaries of Plato's *Timaeus* [Mayr-Harting 2007, 50]. They follow, perhaps even more directly, the annotated versions of the *Marriage of Philology and Mercury*, redacted by Remigius of Auxerre, or even Notker the Stammerer, a monk from St. Gall. According to these authors, the way in which God has made the world and, in particular, souls, is in conformity with the luminous emanation starting from the unity-source that he himself constitutes; the greater the proximity to the Creator, the more intense this light is in the creature.

In summary, in the very last panel of the door God repeats the demiurgic process of the first panel, but Bernward changes its orientation after the middle bush. He excludes the last stage of the process, namely the sexual characterization of the Tree of Life, whose two branches tied together symbolized the complementarity of masculine and feminine and the source of human vitality (not to be confused with its eternity). In panel 16, God gives life a new orientation, a new model of conformity to divine Law, which Bernward explains by way of a fern's natural development—which attests, moreover, that the new path taken by Creation was already incorporated in the initial providential plan. That path will raise man to a higher level than the one he had been given originally.

A bird is perched on Mary Magdalene's Tree of Life (fig. 190). It occupies the same spot as the angel in the first panel, but because of its position it also ties together the plant's left and middle branches, as did the monstrous hybrid placed astride the two sexualized branches of the carnal tree in panel 3 (cf. fig. 52). The bird of prey in panel 16, placed at the angel's level in panel 1, is the antithetic figure to the monstrous hybrid representing, as I have suggested, the first evil creation of humans, their absence of devotion to God, and their carnal concupiscence regarding the world. Like the hybrid, the bird of prey belongs to the domain of the fantastic, but its morphological coherence and its substantial characteristics transform it into an actor in the divine plan. It is the phoenix, the bird that rises from its ashes, a luminous and marvelous being associated with the sun by ancient writers [Hubeau and Leroy 1939, 3–40]. The earliest Christians saw it as a figure of resurrection and, as such, it reappears as a symbol of Christ in medieval bestiaries [Deproost].

The phoenix's presence in Mary Magdalene's Tree of Life, in addition to underscoring its eternity, places the plant in direct continuity with the Palm of Judea. The *Phoenix dactylifera* mentioned by Theophrastus and Pliny is cited by Bernward in the second panel, the representation of the union of Adam and Eve in divine light, when humans loved humans in God and humans loved God in humans (cf. fig. 24). By replacing the hybrid as link, the phoenix retrieves and cancels carnal concupiscence as a bond among humans, replacing it with pure love whose paradigm is the love for Christ:

> Master, which is the greatest commandment in the law? Jesus said to him: Thou shalt love the Lord thy God with thy whole heart, and with thy whole soul, and with thy whole mind. This is the greatest and the first commandment. And the second is like to this: Thou shalt love thy neighbor as thyself. On these two commandments dependeth the whole law and the prophets. (Matt. 22:36–40)

Or, again,

> As the Father hath loved me, I also have loved you. Abide in my love. If you keep my commandments, you shall abide in my love; as I also have kept my Father's commandments, and do abide in his love. These things I have spoken to you, that my joy may be in you, and your joy may be filled. This is my commandment, that you love one another, as I have loved you. Greater love than this no man hath, that a man lay down his life for his friends. (John 15:9–13)

The divine love that bonds in brotherhood all those who keep themselves within the City of God is a necessary but insufficient stage for the complete and perfect fulfillment of the new eternal life. The tree's left and middle branches, linked together by the phoenix, display a formal incongruity which, for clarity's sake, I have not yet mentioned, involving the trinary and fractal structure of the plant (cf. fig. 192). Each branch extends into three smaller branches, all ending in a cluster of leaves. In five cases each cluster is composed of three leaves, except for the sixth, which has four. After all that we have observed about the considerable care that Bernward gives to the visual elaboration of his visual discourse, it would be inappropriate to consider this a mistake.

In the bronze door the number four has always been a sign of the earthly as opposed to the heavenly. It signifies that the world to which the tree belongs—no matter how orderly and spiritualized it may be—contains a residual imperfection, which is also reflected in the ground of the panel. This imperfection is absent from the oblong and homogeneous substratum on which Mary Magdalene seems to float, but it does appear under Christ's feet, in the socle representing the earth that the Savior is about to leave after having reemerged from the two sepulchral hollows he has reopened in panel 15 and closed again after the Harrowing of Hell (fig. 189).

The socle's composition has considerably changed in relation to the previous panel. Now the life channels traversing it alternate with lines of chisel marks, just as in panel 13 where Christ's iniquitous trial is represented (cf. fig. 165). Although the matter has been vivified by the purifying blood and has therefore been removed from the mineral sheath of the volutes in panel 13, the message contained in these alternating life channels and chisel marks is implacable: the eradication of death does not mean the elimination of evil, which remains at work in the world.

How can this be?

The answer lies in the configuration of the junction between the two infernal hollows (fig. 193). Their irrigation continues; Christ has filled the fracture separating them, a consequence of original sin and a rupturing factor between body and soul. The earth preserves the scar of its ancient wound. It remains studded by the chisel marks of evil, injury and suture at the same time. God redeems and amends, but he cannot annul the traces of the destruction that humans have inflicted on the earth, nor can he eradicate the evil consubstantial to that part of humanity that rejects salvation. Does not Christ urge his apostles to pursue the combat he has engaged in the world? (Luke 10:9). Only the disappearance of the earth itself, at the end of time, will make possible God's complete victory over evil. Apocalypse, the revelation of this ultimate triumph, is not portrayed on the bronze door but the iconographic program presages it, showing how to act on the body in order to enable it to extricate itself from the perishable world.

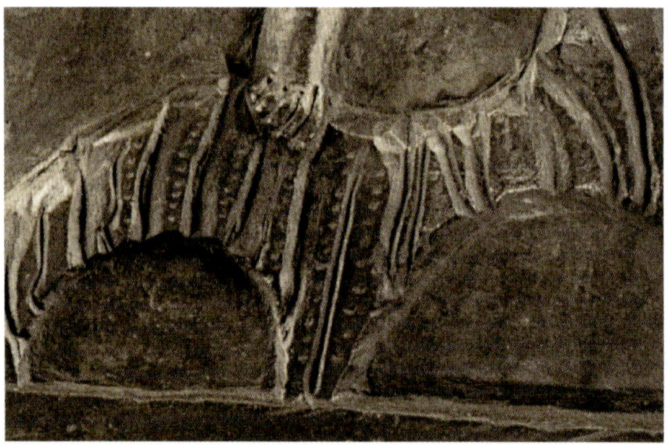

193

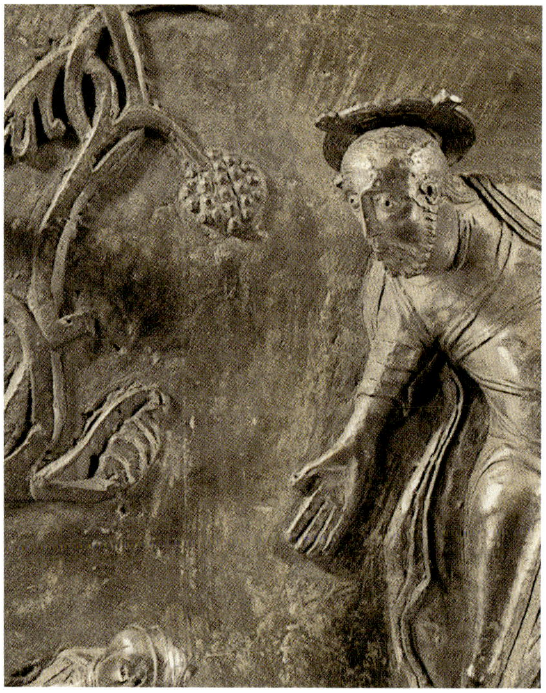

194

The discarding of the old shell is shown in two phases. The first describes the conditions of the loving encounter between Mary Magdalene and Christ; the second explains, in very concrete terms, the modalities of engendering the divine fruits from their union, which will be allowed to rise toward the Father and enter the kingdom of Heaven.

The encounter between Mary Magdalene and Christ involves the great right branch of the Tree of Life (fig. 186). Ample and majestic, it occupies the same position in the tree as the small erect branch of the sexualized Tree in panel 3 (cf. fig. 46). In a way, it prolongs its once aborted life. This branch is developed on two levels. On the lower level, a large leaf is added and, on the upper level, a granular fruit hangs from a stem. The leaf and the fruit are placed respectively along the vertical line at the edge of the two socles on which Mary Magdalene and Christ are positioned. The fruit added to the Tree of Life

193. *Panel 16, infernal hollows.*

194. *Panel 16, means of unifying the panel.*

is a cluster of grapes, easily recognizable from the accumulation of its seeds. It is found in a more oblong shape on the two small vine stocks, as well as on the tall grapevine represented in the Garden of Eden on the right. The distinctive roundness of the granular fruit and the cup-shaped leaf reaching out to receive it are explicit citations of the poisonous seed and its leaf-receptacle in panel 3 illustrating original sin. Connected by the demonic hybrid of carnal concupiscence, they represent the union of Adam and Eve (cf. fig. 47 and 48). What is this union of a new gender that supersedes the sexed generation to create a new human lineage?

The vine represents Christ himself: "Ego sum vitis vera et Pater meus agricola est" [I am the true vine; and my Father is the farmer]," says Jesus in John's Gospel (John 15:1). It is a true vine, in the sense that it yields wine, as opposed to the wild vine (*labruscum*) described by the prophet Isaiah:

> I will sing to my beloved [*delecto meo*] the canticle of my cousin concerning his vineyard. My beloved had a vineyard on a hill in a fruitful place. And he fenced it in, and picked the stones out of it, and planted it with the choicest vines [*eam electam*]. He built a tower in the midst thereof and set up a winepress therein. And he looked that it should bring forth grapes, and it brought forth wild grapes [*labruscas*]. (Isa. 5:1–2)

Isaiah then laments:

> And now, O ye inhabitants of Jerusalem, and ye men of Juda, judge between me and my vineyard. What is there that I ought to do more to my vineyard that I have not done to it? And now I will shew you what I will do to my vineyard. I will take away the hedge thereof, and it shall be wasted: I will break down the wall thereof, and it shall be trodden down. And I will make it desolate. . . . For the vineyard of the Lord of hosts is the house of Israel: and the man of Juda, his pleasant plant: and I looked that he should do judgment, and behold iniquity: and do justice, and behold a cry. (Isa 5:3–7)

The way of representing Christ's vine in the Tree of Life of Mary Magdalene, which is clearly not a vine, was probably suggested to Bernward by an agricultural practice going back to late antiquity: symbiotic climbing. This technique was broadly practiced in Italy, both in antiquity and in the Middle Ages, and less frequently in Germanic areas [Mane 2006, 188–189]. The growth of the climbing vine closely resembles the natural development of the bush in the wild as described by Isidore of Seville (*Etymologies* XVII, 5.2 and 5.11). It consists of making the vine climb a master-tree, becoming its symbiotic growth. It then mixes its grape clusters with the branches of its supporting tree to such an extent that Virgil says that the vine and the tree are bound in marriage [Mane 2006, 189].

In panel 16, Bernward celebrates the spiritual nuptials of God and Mary Magdalene, sealing the renewed covenant between humanity and God, this exclusive and mutual love having been established as the Law of the world in the second panel of the bronze door. In this union, the cluster of grapes of Christ, the new Adam, replaces the poisonous and deadly seed of the old Adam in panel 3: it inseminates the Tree of Life-body of Mary Magdalene, who thus becomes the new Eve. What will Christ and Mary Magdalene transmit to their common lineage?

As noted, in panel 4 Bernward took great care to show that, thanks to the configuration of the root blocks of the two trees associated with Adam and Eve, the maternal womb transmitted to the child its carnal matter whereas the father's seed was at the origin of the progeny's form (cf. fig. 64). In that panel's lower right corner (cf. fig. 65) this death-bearing flesh appeared to be churning, atomized, and dispersed. In panel 16, the large leaf of Mary Magdalene's Tree of Life is quite different (fig. 194). Perfectly unified, its position in space is determined by the branch bearing it, which in addition follows the same diagonal alignment as Mary Magdalene's upper body. It is because the leaf is placed along the light's diagonal axis that it makes itself receptive to divine fecundation. This positioning is indeed the leaf's only active part in the spiritual union. The leaf is receptive because it requests it, just as Mary Magdalene enters the luminous diagonal only because she prostrates herself before Christ, extending her arms toward him from the depth of her condition: "Ask, and it shall be given you: seek, and you shall find: knock, and it shall be opened to you. For every one that asketh, receiveth, and he that seeketh, findeth, and to him that knocketh, it shall be opened" (Matt. 7:7–8).

Substantially compatible with the divine seed, placed in the Spirit's light and imploring her Lord's love in all humility, here Mary Magdalene represents an enlightened, loving, maternal, and fertile Church, ready to engender divine children. As a feminine principle receiving Christ's seed, she will transmit to her progeny the very matter that formed her: Christ's resurrected body, his spiritual and eternal substance.

If the Holy Woman-Mother Church is destined to transmit her spiritual substance to her children,

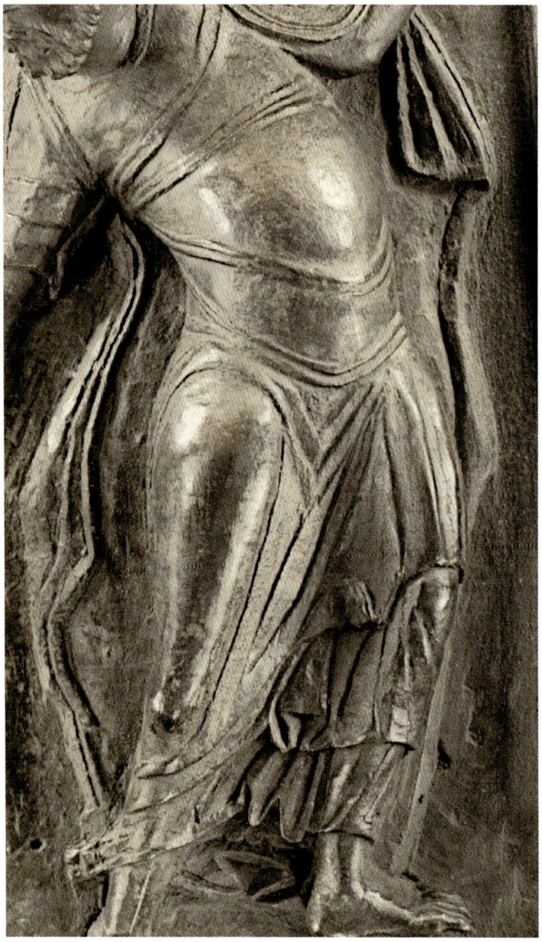

195

can it be deduced that Christ represents a masculine principle bestowing its form on them? This does not mean that the differentiation of the sexes remained relevant in the new life, but rather that the divine Law to which the animal generation conformed—the combination of the two principles permitting the articulation of forms and substances—is still at work in the world. Furthermore, in the demiurgic schema of the first panel, did not the orthonormal Word already play the role of a geometric matrix of Creation?

In panel 16, the Savior engages in his union with Mary Magdalene with a very special body, a resurrected body. Paradoxically, Christ's face had never appeared as expressive as in this panel (fig. 194), where he mirrors the ravaged bodies and faces of Adam and Eve at the time of their expulsion from Eden (cf. fig. 78). The contours of the eyes are especially emphasized, as is their round, deep-set sockets. The plastic relief gives the Savior as intense and penetrating a gaze as that of the Father on the left wing, albeit imbued with a kind of astonishingly compassionate benevolence. Christ sees and loves Mary Magdalene as a man loves a woman.

Christ's resurrected body is as lively and expressive as his face. In contrast to the emaciated body on the cross in panel 14, the sheer and close-fitting tunic reveals fleshy thighs, a prominent knee, and a well-rounded abdomen (fig. 195). His garments, overlapping in signifying layers, like those of the angel in the previous panel (cf. fig. 179), reaffirm, as does its very human plasticity, that the body of the resurrected Christ is an entirely spiritualized body of *flesh*: "See my hands and feet, that it is I myself; handle, and see: for a spirit hath not flesh and bones, as you see me to have" (Luke 24:39). Indeed, the life channels are set in strategic places, precisely where the three-dimensional volume of the torso is delineated and modeled: the Spirit's channels that constituted the material spaces within which life could flow and light can radiate have here become formal matrixes. The channels do not confer their divine substance to Christ's body; they are indeed the very form of the divine substance. This new formal sheath enfolds the two substantial layers that previously composed, as in every human being, the body of the incarnated Christ: the shape of the flesh and the shape of the soul. As in panel 15, Bernward plays with the overlapping layers of the garments. He has placed not two, but three tightly juxtaposed layers of fabric, the third partially covering the other two, on Christ's left leg, in contrast to the perfectly smooth and rounded right thigh.

This ultimate form-substance constitutes the deified, resurrected body and is the matrix of the fusion of the two others, that of the body and that of the soul. This ultimate form, delineated against the panel's background by an airy cape, is the body of glory, the celestial body that Christ and, after him, all humans will assume in order to ascend toward the Father:

> But some man will say: How do the dead rise again? or with what manner of body shall they come? . . . It is sown in corruption, it shall rise in incorruption. It is sown in dishonor, it shall rise in glory. It is sown in weakness, it shall rise in power. It is sown a natural body, it shall rise a spiritual body. If there be a natural body, there is also a spiritual body, as it is written: The first man Adam was made into a living soul; the last Adam into a quickening spirit. . . . Therefore as we have borne the image of the earthly, let us bear also the image of the heavenly. (1 Cor. 15:35–49)

The conditions of the union between Christ and Mary Magdalene are now set out. They involve a Church-Body of Christ (sanctified Mary Magdalene) transmitting its substance of eternity to its progeny,

195. *Panel 16, Christ's clothing.*

while Christ-father bestows on his children the glorious form of his celestial body. But when and how does this union take place?

Christ's seed is a vine. Of all the symbolic qualities linked to wine in the Bible, the first and the most natural is its close association with sacrificial blood, widely emphasized by exegesis. Wine, fruit of the true vine, acts in this world of both good and evil, by transforming itself into Christ's blood during the elevation of the species:

> And whilst they were at supper, Jesus took bread, and blessed, and broke and gave to his disciples, and said: Take ye, and eat. This is my body. And taking the chalice, he gave thanks, and gave to them, saying: Drink ye all of this, for this is my blood of the new testament, which shall be shed for many unto remission of sins. (Matt. 26:26–28)

> Then Jesus said to them . . . : Except you eat the flesh of the Son of man, and drink his blood, you shall not have life in you. . . . He that eateth my flesh, and drinketh my blood, abideth in me, and I in him. (John 6:54–56)

The fecundation of Mary Magdalene as Church by the wine-blood of Christ is nothing other than the Eucharist's sacramental agency. True union of humanity and God, the Eucharist replaces the first generation, creating a new life, a New Man, according to a metamorphic process whose modalities are described in the Edenic garden. Their representation pertains to the vast poetic and iconographic corpus of what historians have called the mystical wine press [Alexandre-Bidon], but the inventiveness and originality of this depiction, to the best of my knowledge, is not equaled anywhere else.

In the Edenic garden, three vine stocks have replaced Mary Magdalene's Tree of Life. Two of them are rooted in the soil and the third one is attached to the image's right frame (fig. 196).

The substratum of the Edenic garden, composed of earthly elements, as explained earlier, is modified in three phases strictly coordinated with the placement of the first vine stock, and then of the second. On the left, we see life channels where trickles of thin liquid flow. Contrasting with the poisoned soil visible under the Savior returning from Hell, this ground has been hitherto unseen. It shows the channels and the fluids flowing within. This soil continues up to the first vine stock, then the orientation of the channels is abruptly reversed at the foot of the bush while, at the same time, the water-blood trickles disappear. As we will soon understand, this blood is no longer represented in the soil because it has already passed into the plant, which still has four branches.

The soil changes again under the second vine stock. This time, the channels disappear, replaced by just one curved line ending in a narrow residual groove on the right. After the blood, this formal divine matrix disappears because it has passed into the plant as well. The plant no longer has four branches, but three, having acquired a conformation identical to that of the Trinitarian God.

Bernward represents the transfer of Christ's blood (the substance) and of Christ's form (the body of glory) in the two vine stocks as an extension of the botanical metaphor that he used for the articulation of Mary Magdalene's large leaf and Christ's grape cluster.

The first vine stock, placed at the junction of the channels' change of orientation, is attached to a substratum to which the intersection of the diagonals confers the shape of a triangle. Analogical to this telluric triangle, a sort of geometrized arrow thrust into the ground is superimposed on the bush's base, seen again at the base of the second vine stock. The way in which the plant is inserted into its substratum covers and cancels the triangles in the root blocks of the sexed plants in panel 4 (cf. fig. 64 and 65). At that

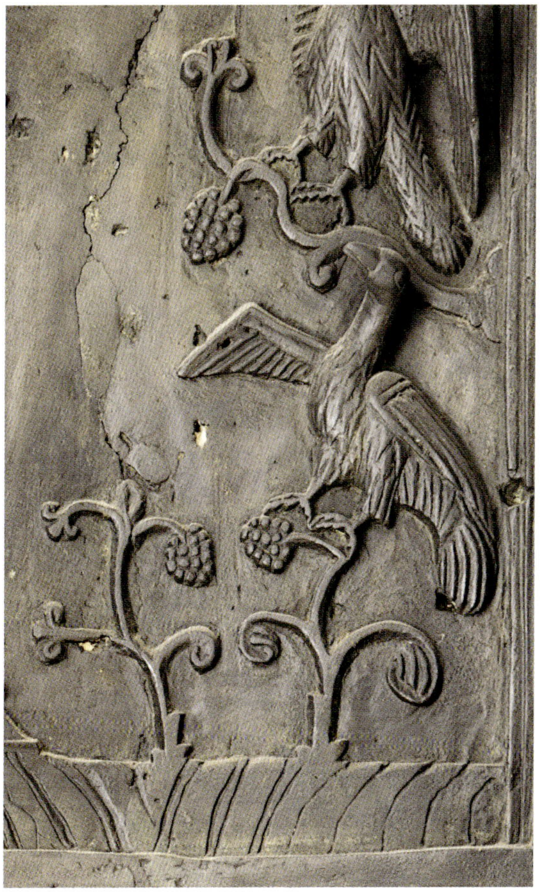

196

196. *Panel 16, ground and vines of the garden.*

time, I suggested that the triangles explained the actual mechanisms of engendering by mortal flesh: the first triangle revealed the form that the male principle gave to the animal body, the second showed the womb-substance, impure and in motion, brought by the woman to the process of sexed engendering. In panel 16, the geometrized arrow is oriented in the opposite direction of the two previous triangles. In addition, the arrow is not rooted into the soil so much as it adheres to the stem of the vine against which it is placed, while the stem itself is slightly embedded in the ground from which it derives its divine qualities.

Let us extend St. John's citation designating Christ as the vine:

> I am the true vine; and my Father is the husbandman. Every branch in me, that beareth not fruit, he will take away: and every one that beareth fruit, he will purge it, that it may bring forth more fruit. Now you are clean by reason of the word, which I have spoken to you. Abide in me, and I in you. As the branch cannot bear fruit of itself, unless it abide in the vine, so neither can you, unless you abide in me. I am the vine: you the branches: he that abideth in me, and I in him, the same beareth much fruit: for without me you can do nothing. If anyone abide not in me, he shall be cast forth as a branch, and shall wither, and they shall gather him up, and cast him into the fire, and he burneth. If you abide in me, and my words abide in you, you shall ask whatever you will, and it shall be done unto you. In this is my Father glorified, that you bring forth very much fruit, and become my disciples. (John 15:1–8)

Let us complete it with a passage from the Epistle to the Romans:

> For if the first fruit be holy, so is the lump also: and if the root be holy, so are the branches. And if some of the branches be broken, and thou, being a wild olive, art ingrafted in them, and art made partaker of the root, and of the fatness of the olive tree. Boast not against the branches, but if thou boast, thou bearest not the root, but the root thee. Thou wilt say then: the branches were broken off, that I might be grafted in. Well, because of unbelief they were broken off. But thou standest by faith, be not highminded, but fear. . . . And they also, if they abide not still in unbelief, shall be grafted in, for God is able to graft them in again. (Rom 11:16–23)

As previously mentioned, Bernward's representational choice is based both on divine Word and on his knowledge of nature. The Palm of Judea, which was used in panel 2 to describe the conditions of sexed generation, is a dioicous plant, its fertilization based on exchanges between male and female flowers, just like the wild vine. Conversely, the cultivated vine has hermaphroditic flowers, hence neither male nor female [Lachiver 1988, 21–22]. If the gardener allowed it to reproduce itself or if he planted its seeds, which he never does, the planted vine would degenerate, becoming wild again, just as the olive tree does [Mane 2006, 191].

The only way to preserve it as a true vine, namely a wine-producing vine, is by reproduction through participation or emanation from a first vine stock, according to techniques that varied according to the times and regions but all based on the same cloning principle. The simplest medieval technique was by taking cuttings, which consists in laying the year's vine shoots on the ground. The closest technique to the vine stocks in panel 16 is marcotting, a reproduction technique through rhizogenesis, by which lowered vine shoots are planted at the root of an old vine from which they take root [Mane 2006, 191–192].

Symbiotically joined to the mother-vine stock, which is Christ's body and with whom it shares divine substance and form, the vine stock is the Tree of Life of the New Man, engendered in the Church and through Christ. Henceforth, it will no longer need any soil because the vine stock lives inside the vital principle, as shown by the progressive fading of the graphic signs delineating the ground of the Edenic earthly Paradise.

The third vine in the Edenic garden is set high, attached to the panel's right frame (fig. 197). It emerges from a sort of small cloud, resembling the cloud from which Christ's paradigmatic cross appeared in panel 7 (cf. fig. 105), unless a casting problem altered its shape. In that panel, representing the establishment of the covenant between Abel and God, the Christ plant exhibited the orthonormal form that was used as a model for the shaping of the earthly matter, in particular for the body of the Righteous. In panel 16, the Christ plant is a vine and a liana at the same time. It assumes the single stalk shape of the divine, undulating tree appearing behind the Father in panel 4 (cf. fig. 68). On the day of paschal Resurrection represented in panel 16, the Son ascending to Heaven has again become identical and equal to the Father who has called him.

No vine shoot appears on this divine stem rising toward the kingdom of Heaven. Indeed, none could. No one, called like Christ to join the Father, has

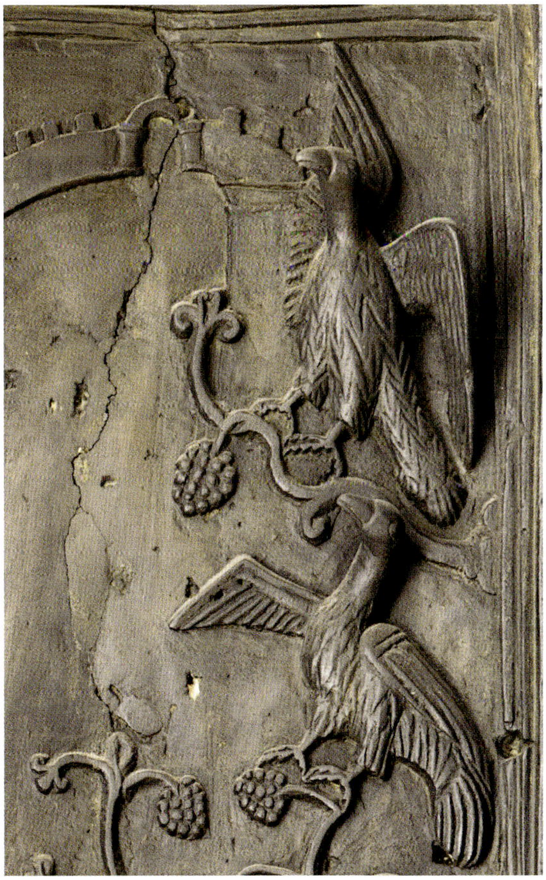

197

yet gone from life to death. For this to occur, the Christian will have to await the end of time and the resurrection of the body. However, through Eucharistic communion, a Christian can briefly participate in this future world and catch a glimpse of his celestial destiny. Is it not repeated in liturgy and in Christian hymns that the Eucharist is "the bread of Heaven" and "the bread of the angels" (Ps. 77:24–25)?

I do not know whether Bernward believed in the existence of the phoenix or whether he chose this bird precisely because it did not belong to nature such as he knew it, but the mythical winged animal takes on this brief eschatological vision, embodying the stages of the return journey toward the Father. The bird appears three times, like the Tree of Life in panel 1, the pilgrim magus in panel 11, and the Holy Woman in panel 15. These three phases correspond to the very specific motions characterizing the vertical flight of birds of prey: closed wings, open wings, wings raised behind the body (fig. 186). The flight's three moments recall the ascending axis of Christ's cross-staff, corresponding to the three moments of the metamorphic sequence that will make humanity equal to the angel. First, motionless, in its rightful place in Mary Magdalene's tree; then, wings spread above the vine stalk connected with Christ and deified in him; finally, ascending in a rigorously vertical line, holding on to the divine stem that functions as a mediation support.

197. *Panel 16, door of the kingdom of Heaven.*

The conclusion of the journey represented in panel 16 is found at the end of the luminous diagonal in which Mary Magdalene is inscribed. It is a small arched door, surmounted by an orb that specifies its universal dominance and opens into the Edenic enclosure, at the very end of the garden (fig. 197).

The climax and grand finale of the narrative begun fifteen panels earlier, this door is as small as it is significant. Its architectural monumentality recalls the great arch placed at the lowest point of the right wing, whose piers portray Mary and Gabriel, the woman and the angel inscribed in prophetic symmetry. As mentioned earlier, that arc defined the sacred space delineated by the dead body of Abel, the first Righteous Man and founder of the City of God, who had fallen at the bottom of the left wing.

The little door cut into the enclosure is the third door represented in the Edenic garden. As we have seen, the first door is inscribed in the entrance tower and gives access to the Church-Edenic garden as the Savior's resurrected body (fig. 187). A second door appears in the garden: rectangular, it is placed at the end of the crenellated arch, just in front of the phoenix's breast, its shape without hinges and underscored by a finely drawn line is barely visible. On a vertical axis, perfectly smooth and almost immaterial, this door is also a pier, a celestial column showing Christ's resurrected body as the path to Heaven. The little door at the very end of the garden is the last of the three doors. What it tells us is not depicted in the panel but projected outside the story, as narrated by the Bible and told to us by Bernward: it is the door of the kingdom of Heaven, the threshold of access to the Father through which only Christ can pass. It is the announcement of a beatific encounter that only he could have witnessed, had he wished to do so.

Christ said nothing of what followed. With a last reflective gesture, Bernward acknowledges that the meeting with the Father does not belong to the realm of representation because it does not belong to what is knowable. Here the Christian pastor imposes his limits on the artist. His initiation into the mysteries, his mystagogical catechism, is now achieved. From the depths of his soul, he believes that his bronze door will disappear together with the rest of the earth but that he will rise again, like an angel, toward his Creator.

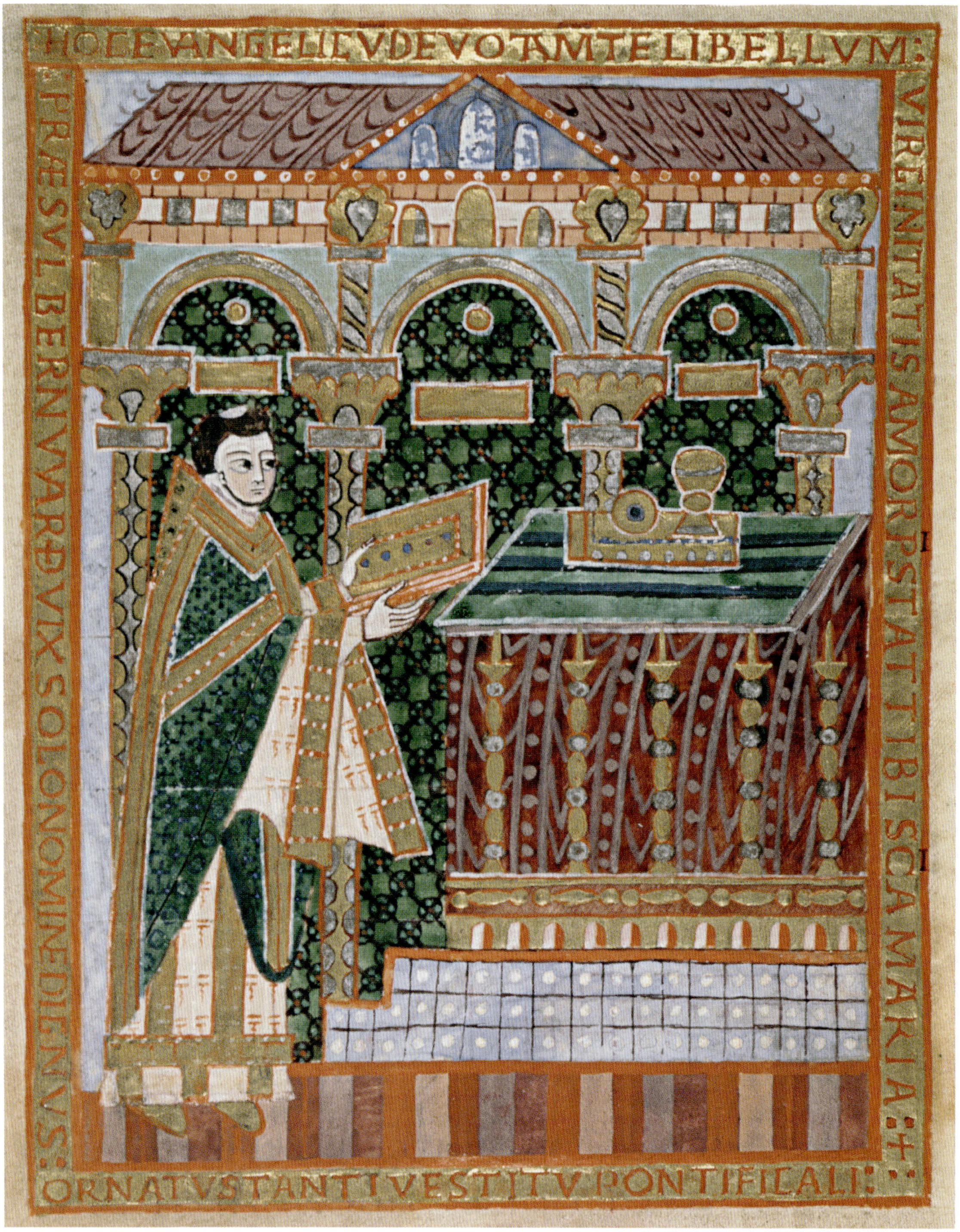

198. *F. 16v of Bernward's Gospel Book.*

CONCLUSION

God gives life, embodies its principle in a tree, and makes his love the bond that humans must establish with each other. Blinded by ignorance of their true nature, these humans engender the evil that destroys them at the same time it destroys the world's order. Incompatible with the divine, reduced to the mortal flesh of which they are made, humans enter the kingdom of suffering, led by an angel who does not abandon them, and loved by a God who prepares their redemption. Some humans, the Righteous, feel the presence of a model of an inner order, the cross of the Word, which can dominate their flesh and reestablish the covenant with God. Others, on the contrary, seek the answer to their condition in illusory appearances, yielding to the chaos imposed on them by their animal body. Death is consummated. The Righteous One, Abel, engenders a spiritual lineage of humans awaiting the foretold salvation; the others become lost at the margin of a violent and corrupted city.

God becomes incarnate. The earth turns green again. The community of the Righteous, the City of God, evolves subsuming the ancient Synagogue and recasting itself as Church on a renewed column-Law, which the Righteous embrace as guide of their conduct and as source of understanding the divine. The sacred ground they constitute together has washed away the poison of sin with the water-blood of the sacrificed Christ. The bodies-temples, whose soul and spiritualized flesh are perfectly united and brought together by the Eucharistic fusion, become comparable to the angels and, like them, participants in the divine essence.

The discourse on the door can be told in a few lines. The theological content, however, is the creation of a Christian prelate, in this case an accomplished humanist, and the objective of the sixteen bronze panels is much more ambitious. Bernward builds a journey, a visual path, a path of consciousness and understanding. Its rigor, subtlety, and ingenuity uplift those who accomplish it, and tests their comprehension each step of the way. The door is propaedeutic for the believers, but it is also an extraordinary cosmology, bringing the spectator face to face with the principles and laws of life itself.

A journey cannot be condensed or concluded. Each individual is free to choose and pursue it at will. For art historians, I would like to add two observations.

The first is that the door is part of a much wider system of signification, integrating all of the bishop's building program and the entire liturgical space of St. Michael of Hildesheim. The bronze column illustrating Christ's public life addresses the tropological part of the New Testament narrative at a level of sermonizing, which is deliberately excluded from the program of the historiated door, in favor of ontology. The narrative of the door, on the other hand, omits the most important episode in the New Testament—the Last Supper—even though the sixteen biblical episodes prepare believers for its liturgical celebration. This communal sharing is represented, embodied elsewhere in the church by the very figure of the priest standing at the nave's center, facing the altar of the Holy Cross next to the base of the bronze column, at the heart of a building whose access is sublimated by a monumental door. A medieval Christian church is sacred ground, unified and alive, built by the combined actions of humans, objects, and images.

The second observation is my belief that Bernward's genius makes him one of the most remarkable artists and one of the greatest semioticians in the history of Western art, even though there are only very few elements—motifs, signs, principles, modes of plastic expression—appropriated by him that had not already been adopted or attempted in works before his own. Because of his immense biblical, scientific, and artistic knowledge, the bishop of Hildesheim is unparalleled: he understood the wholeness of everything, channeling its totality into a holistic system.

Beyond clarifying Bernward's visual discourse, as well those of prior and subsequent artifacts, it is my hope to have helped increase interest in the ontological significance of early Christian images and to broaden the realm of what is possible in visual communication.

BIBLIOGRAPHY

Primary Sources

For the editions of the ancient and medieval texts cited, except where mentioned below, reference should be made to the Library of Latin Texts online published by Brepols (LLT-A), to the Patrologia Latina Database (PL), and Editions des Belles Lettres (EBL).

Augustine, *The City of God against the Pagans* [*De civitate Dei*], ed. R. Dyson, Cambridge: Cambridge University Press, 1998.

Augustine, *The Literal Meaning of Genesis* [*De Genesi ad litteram*], in *On Genesis*, trans. Edmund Hill, O.P., New City Press/Augustinian Heritage Institute, 2002, p. 168–506.

Calcidius, *Commentaire au Timée de Platon*, B. Bakhouche, Paris: Vrin, 2011.

Cur deus homo, Book I, chaps. 3–4; PL 158.364–65; trans. B. Davies and G. R. Evans, Oxford, 1998, p. 268–69.

The Holy Bible: Douay-Rheims Version, www.drbo.org, accessed January 2023.

Thangmar, *Vita Bernwardi*, MGH, SS. IV, 758–785.

Secondary Sources

Bernwardische Kunst, Symposium 10.10 bis 13.10 1984, eds. M. Gosebruch and F.N. Steigerwald, Göttingen: Goltze, 1988.

Bernward von Hildesheim und das Zeitalter der Ottonen, Dom- und Diözesanmuseum Hildesheim, Roemer-und Pelizaeus-Museum. Katalog der Ausstellung, Hildesheim, 15. August —28. November 1993, dir. T. Giessman, A. Eggebrecht, and M. Brandt, Hildesheim: Bernward Verlag und Mainz, Ph. von Zabern, 1993, 2 t.

Cieli e terre nei secoli XI-XII: Orizzonti, percezioni, rapport; atti della tredicesima settimana internazionale di studio, Mendola, 22–26 agosto 1995, Milano: Centro di studi medioevali, Vita e Pensiero, 1998.

Marie. Le culte de la Vierge dans la société médiévale, eds. D. Iogna-Prat, E. Palazzo, and D. Russo, Paris, 1996.

La réception des Éléments *d'Euclide au Moyen Âge et à la Renaissance*, Revue d'histoire des sciences, t. 56, 2, PUF, 2003.

Topografia urbana e vita cittadina nell'alto Medioevo in Occidente, 26 aprile—1 maggio 1973, Spoleto, Centro italiano di studi sull'alto Medioevo Settimane di studio, 21, 1973.

1000 Jahre St. Michael in Hildesheim. Kirche—Kloster—Stifter, eds. G. Lutz and A. Weyer, Göttingen: M. Imhof Verlag, 2012.

Accame M. and Dell'Oro E. (dir.), *I Mirabilia urbi Romae*, Rome: Tored, 2004.

Adamski H.J., Wehmeyer H. (phot.), *Die Christussäule im Dom zu Hildesheim*, Hildesheim: Bernward Verl., 1990.

Agaësse P. and Solignac, A. (eds. and trans.), Augustine, *De Genesi ad litteram, La Genèse au sens littéral, La Genèse au sens littéral en douze livres*, 2 vols., Institut d'études augustieniennes, 1970.

Ahlqvist A., "Gli animali nell'arte funeraria Paleocristiana. Il disegno iconografico," *Atti dell'Istituto Veneto di Scienze, Lettere ed Arti, Classe di Scienze Morali*, 1996, 2, p. 333–423.

Algermissen K. (dir.), *Bernward und Godehard von Hildesheim. Ihr Leben und Wirken*, Hildesheim, 1960.

Alibert D., "Images d'arbres et de vignes dans l'art médiéval," *Le pressoir mystique. Actes du colloque de Recloses*, dir. D. Alexandre-Bidon, Paris, 1990, p. 27–42.

Anderson G., Stone M., and Tromp J. (eds.), *Literature on Adam and Eve. Collected Essays*, Leiden: E. J. Brill, 2000.

Angliviel de la Beaumelle L., "Ève à l'épreuve des Pères," Ève et Pandora. La création de la première femme, dir. J.-C. Schmitt, Paris: Gallimard (Le temps des images), 2001, p. 69–87.

Arasse D., *L'annonciation italienne. Une histoire de perspective*, Paris: Hazan, 1999.

Armisen-Marchetti M., "Le corps de la terre dans la littérature scientifique latine: l'exemple de la circulation des fluides," *Le corps dans les cultures méditerranéennes*, dir. P. Carmignani, Presses Universitaires de Perpignan, 2007, p. 29–42.

Armstrong Gr. T., "Constantine's Churches: Symbol and Structure," *Journal of the Society of Architectural Historians*, 33 (1974), p. 5–16.

Arnold B., *Medieval Germany, 500–130. A Political Interpretation*, University of Toronto Press, 1997.

Arnulf A., *Versus ad Picturas. Studien zur Titulusdichtung als Quellengattung der Kunstgeschichte von der Anitke bis zum Hochmitelalter*, Berlin, 1997.

Arquillière H.-X, *L'augustinisme politique. Essai sur la formation des théories politiques du Moyen-Âge*, Paris: Vrin, 1934.

Aurell M., "La parenté en l'An mil," *Cahiers de Civilisation médiévale*, 43 (2000), p. 125–142.

Bagatti B., "L'iconografia della tentazione di Adamo ed Eva," *Studii Biblicii Franciscani*, 31 (1981), p. 217–230.

Balogh J., "*Voces paginarum*. Beiträge zur Geschichte des lauten Lesens und Schreibens," *Philologus*, LXXXII, 2 (1926), p. 84–109 and 202–240.

Bandmann G., *Early Medieval Architecture as Bearer of Meaning*, trans. Kendall Wallis, New York: Columbia University Press, 2005.

Bandmann G., "Früh—und Hochmittelalterliche Altarordnung als Darstellung," *Das erste Jahrtausend. Kultur und Kunst im werdenden Abendland an Rhein und Ruhr*, ed. V. H. Elbern, I, 1962, p. 371–411 and 407–411.

Barthes R., "L'ancienne rhétorique. Aide-mémoire," *Communications*, 16 (1970), p. 172–223.

Baschet J., "Âme et corps dans l'Occident medieval. Une dualité dynamique, entre pluralité et dualisme," *Archives de sciences sociales des religions*, 112 (2000), p. 5–30.

Baschet J., "Inventivité et sérialité des images médiévales. Pour une approche iconographique élargie," *Annales. Histoire, Sciences Sociales*, 51, 1 (1996), p. 93–133.

Baschet J., "Une série ample. Ève est-elle née," *L'iconographie médiévale*, Paris: Gallimard, 2008, p. 298–314.

Baud A. (dir.), *Espace ecclésial et liturgie au Moyen Age, colloque international, Nantua, Ain, nov. 2006, Lyon, Maison de l'Orient et de la Méditerranée*, Paris: Boccard, 2010.

Bauer G., "Bemerkungen zur Bernwardstür," *Niederdeutsche Beiträge zur Kunstgeschichte*, 19 (1980), p. 9–35.

Baxandall M., *L'oeil du Quattrocento. L'usage de la peinture dans l'Italie de la Renaissance*, Paris: Gallimard, 1985.

Benoit J., "Survivances païennes à Hildesheim autour de l'an Mil," *Gazette des beaux-arts*, 110, 1427 (1987), p. 191–202.

Benoit P. and Boismard M.-E., *Synopse des quatre Évangiles en français avec parallèles des Apocryphes et des Pères*, Paris: Cerf, 1965.

Berger B.-D., *Le drame liturgique de Pâques. Liturgie et théâtre, théologie historique*, Paris: Beauchesne, 1976.

Bergmann U., "Prior Omnibus Autor, an hochster Stelle aber steht der Stifter," *Ornamenta ecclesiae. Kunst und Kunstler der Romanik in Koln. Katalog zur Ausstellung des Schnutgen-Museums*, Cologne, 1985, 1, p. 117–148.

Bériou N., Caseau B., and Rigaux D. (eds.), *Pratiques de l'Eucharistie dans les Églises d'Orient et d'Occident (Antiquité et Moyen Âge)*, 2 vols., Paris: Institut d'Études Augustiniennes, Collection des Études Augustiniennes—Moyen Âge et Temps Modernes, 2009.

Bertram A., *Die Thüren von St. Sabina in Rom, das Vorbild der Bernwards-Thüren am Dom zu Hildesheim*, Freiburg: Friesenhahn, 1892.

Bertrand P.-M., "La Fortune mi-partite. Un exemple de la symbolique de la droite et de la gauche au Moyen Âge," *Cahiers de civilisation médiévale*, 40 (1997), p. 373–379.

Beseler H. and Roggenkamp. H., *Die Michaelskirche in Hildesheim*, Berlin: Mann, 1954.

Binding G., *Bischof Bernward als Architekt der Michaeliskirche in Hildesheim*, Köln: Veroffentlichung der Abteilung des Kunsthistorischen Instituts der Universitat, 1987.

Binding G., "Bischof Bernward von Hildesheim—architectus et artifex?" *Bernwardische Kunst*, op. cit., 1988, p. 24–47.

Binding G., *Der früh- und hochmittelalterliche Bauherr als* sapiens architectus, Darmstadt: Wissenschaftliche Buchgesellschaft, 1998.

Bischoff B., *Manuscripts and Libraries in the Age of Charlemagne*, Cambridge University Press, 1995.

Bloch P., "Das reichenauer Einzelblatt mit den Frauen am Grabe im Hessischen Landesmuseum Darmstadt," *Kunst in Hessen und am Mittelrhein*, 3 (1963), p. 25–43.

Blumenkranz B., *Le Juif médiéval au miroir de l'art chrétien*, Paris: Études Augustiniennes, 1966.

Bock N., Kurmann P., Romano S., and Spieser J.-M. (dir.), *Art, cérémonial et liturgie au Moyen Âge, Actes du colloque de 3e Cycle Romand de lettres Lausanne-Fribourg, 24–25 mars, 14–15 avril, 12–13 mai 2000*, Rome: Viella, 2002.

Bonnassie P. and Toubert P. (eds.), *Hommes et sociétés dans l'Europe de l'an mil, colloque international, Conques, 19–21 mai 2000*, Presses de l'Université Toulouse-Le-Mirail, 2004.

Bonne J.-Cl., "Les ornements de l'histoire (à propos de l'ivoire carolingien de St. Rémi)," *Annales. Histoire, Sciences Sociales*, 51, 1 (1996), p. 37–70.

Bonne J.-Cl., "Relève de l'ornementation celte païenne dans un Évangile insulaire du VIIe siècle (les Évangiles de Durrow)," *Ideologie e Pratiche del Reimpiego nell'Alto Medioevo*, Centro Italiano di Studi sull'Alto Medioevo, Spoleto, 1999, p. 1011–1053.

Bonnet-Cadilhac C., "L'anatomo-physiologie de la génération chez Galien," thèse de doctorat, EPHE, IVe section, 1997.

Boockmann H., "Fruhstadtische Siedlungen in Hildesheim des 11. und 12. Jahrhunderts," *Bernward von Hildesheim und das Zeitalter der Ottonen*, op. cit., 1993, Bd. 1, p. 283–289.

Boquet D., "Le libre arbitre comme image de Dieu," *Collectanea Cisterciensia*, 65 (2003), p. 179–192.

Brandt M. (dir.), *Der Hildesheimer Dom. Studien und Quellen*, Hildesheim, Zürich: G. Olms, 1996.

Brendel O.J., *Symbolic of the Sphere. A Contribution to the History of Earlier Greek Philosophy*, Leiden: E. J. Brill, 1977 (Études préliminaires aux religions orientales dans l'empire romain, 67).

Bretin-Chabrol M., "Le sexe des plantes. Analogie et categories du genre chez les agronomes romains," *Le Corps dans les cultures méditerranéennes*, P. Carmignani (dir.), Presses Universitaires de Perpignan, 2007, p. 15–28.

Brincken A.-D. von den and Szabo T. (eds.), *Studien zur Universalkartographie des Mittelalters*, Göttingen: Vandenhoeck & Ruprecht, 2008 (Veröffentlichungen des Max Planck-Instituts für Geschichte, Bd. 229)

Bröckner W., Haack U., Leveque J., and Klemens D., "Archaometrische Untersuchungen und Blei Isotopenverhaltnismessungen an Bernwardtur und Bernwardsaule von Hildesheim," *Archaologisches Korrespondenzblatt*, 26, 3 (1996), p. 347–356.

Bruderer-Eichberg B., *Les neuf choeurs angéliques. Origine et évolution du thème dans l'art du Moyen Âge*, Poitiers: CESCM, 1998.

Brugger L., "La 'voix du sang' d'Abel comme réalité escatologique du salut," *Arte cristiana* N.S. 82 (1994), p. 87–100.

Brugger L. and Christe Y., "La 'voix du sang' et l'ensevelissement d'Abel," *Arte cristiana* N.S., 82 (1994), p. 75–86.

Brunet R., *Marie-Madeleine (Ier-XXIe siècle). De la pécheresse repentie à l'épouse de Jésus: histoire de la réception d'une figure biblique*, Paris: Cerfe, 2004.

Bruns B., *Die Bernwardssäule: Lebensbaum und Siegessäule*, Hildesheim: Bernward Verl., 1995.

Bruns B., "Das Epiphaniebild im kostbaren Evangeliar des hl.Bernward," *Diozese Hildesheim in Vergangenheit und Gegenwart*, 61 (1993), p. 11–19.

Bührer-Thierry G., "Unter dem Blick des Herrschers. Blick, Augen und Sicht im Früh- und Hochmittelalter," *Verwandtschaft, Freundschaft, Bruderschaft. Soziale Lebensund Kommunikationsformen im Mittelalter*, Symposium 2007, éd. G. Krieger, Trèves: Akademie Verlag, 2009, p. 221–228.

Bührer-Thierry G., Évêques et pouvoir dans le royaume de Germanie. Les églises de Bavière et de Souabe (*876–973*), Paris: Picard, 1997.

Capponi C. (dir.) *L'altare d'oro di Sant'Ambrogio*, Milan: Silvana, 1996.

Capriotti G. "Le città di Maddalena: iconografia di una leggenda," *Guardate con i vostri occhi . . . Saggi di storia dell'arte nelle Marche*, dir. A. Montironi, Macerata: Saggi Lamusa, 2002, p. 233–264.

Cardon D., *La draperie au Moyen Âge. Essor d'une grande industrie européenne*, Paris: CNRS, 1999.

Carruthers M., *The Craft of Thought. Meditation, Rhetoric, and the Making of Images, 400–1200*, Cambridge University Press, 1998.

Casagrande C. and Vecchio S., *I peccati della lingua. Disciplina ed etica della parola nella cultura medievale*, Rome: Istituto della enciclopedia italiana, 1987.

Castellani M.-M. and Prungnaud J. (eds.), *Architecture et discours*, Éditions de l'Université Lille 3, 2006.

Cavallo G., *Le biblioteche nel mondo antico e medievale*, Bari: Laterza, 1988.

Chazelle C., *The Crucified Theology and God in the Carolingian Era Art of Christ's Passion*, Cambridge University Press, 2001.

Cleary J.-J., *Aristotle and Mathematics. Aporetic Method in Cosmology and Metaphysics*, Leiden: E. J. Brill, 1995.

Coatsworth E., "Cloth-making and the Virgin Mary," *Anglo-Saxon Literature and Art. A Memorial Tribute to C. R. Dodwell*, eds. G. R. Owen-Crocker and T. Graham, Manchester University Press, 1998, p. 8–25.

Cohen A. S. and Derbes A., "Bernward and Eve at Hildesheim," *Gesta* 40, 1 (2001), p. 19–38.

Congar Y., "Ecclesia ab Abel," *Abhandlungen über Theologie und Kirsche, Festschrift für Karl Adam*, Düsseldorf, 1952, p. 79–108.

Congar Y., *L'ecclésiologie du haut Moyen Âge*, Paris: Cerf, 1968.

Congar Y., "Civitas Dei et Ecclesia chez St. Augustin. Histoire de la recherche, son état présent," *Revue des études anciennes*, 3 (1957), p. 1–14.

Corbet P., *Les saints ottoniens. Sainteté dynastique, sainteté royale et sainteté féminine autour de l'an mil*, Sigmaringen: Thorbecke, 1986.

Christe Y. (dir.), *De l'art comme mystagogie. Iconographie du Jugement dernier et des fins dernières à l'époque gothique, colloque Genève 13–16 février 1994*, Poitiers: CESCM, 1996.

Crivello F., "Bernoardo di Hildesheim. Il committente come artista in età ottoniana," *Artifex bonus. Il mondo dell'artista medievale*, dir. E. Castelnuovo, Rome: Laterza, 2004, p. 42–49.

Crossley P. "Medieval Architecture and Meaning. The Limits of Iconography," *Burlington Magazine*, vol. 130, 1019, Special Issue on English Gothic Art (1988), p. 116–121.

Curtius E. R., *Europäische Literatur und lateinisches Mittelalter*, Bern: A. Francke, 1948.

Cutler A., Dell'Acqua F., Kessler H. L., Shalem A., and Wolf G. (eds.), *The Salerno Ivories. Objects, Histories, Contexts*, Berlin, 2016.

Dahan G., "L'exégèse de l'histoire de Caïn et Abel du XIIe au XIVe siècle en Occident," *Recherches de théologie ancienne et médiévale*, 49 (1982), p. 21–89.

D'Alverny M.-T., "Les anges et les jours," *Cahiers archéologiques*, 9 (1957), p. 271–300.

Davids A. (ed.), *The Empress Theophano: Byzantium and the West at the Turn of the First Millennium*, Cambridge University Press, 1995.

Davy M.-M., Renneteau J.-P., Abecassis A., and Mokri M., *Le thème de la lumière dans le judaïsme, le christianisme et l'islam*, Paris: Berg International, 1976.

De Blaauw S., "Hildesheim und Rom. Architektur und Liturgie," *1000 Jahre St. Michael in Hildesheim*, op. cit., 2012, p. 66–76.

De Bruyne E., Études d'esthétique médiévale, 1946, repr. 2 vols., Paris: A. Michel, 1998.

Del Lungo S., *Roma in età carolingia e gli scritti dell'anonimo augiense*, Sociéta romana di storia patria, XLVIII, Rome: Bibl. Valicelliana, 2004.

De Lubac H. *Exégèse médiévale. Les Quatre sens de l'Écriture*, 3 vols., Paris: Aubier, 1959–64.

Deproost P.A., "*Formatur . . . Limatur* . . . . Le corps d'Adam et Ève dans la poésie latine chrétienne," *Le corps dans les cultures méditerranéennes*, dir. P. Carmignani et al., Presses Universitaires de Perpignan, 2007, p. 105–125.

Deproost P. A., "Les métamorphoses du phénix dans le christianisme ancien," *L'oiseau: entre ciel et terre, Actes des Journées universitaires de Hérisson, été 2004*, eds. M. Mazoyer et al., Paris: L'Harmattan, 2005, p. 112–137.

Deremble C., "Les premiers cycles d'images consacrés à Marie Madeleine," *Mélanges de l'École française de Rome. Moyen Âge, Temps modernes*, 104, 1 (1992), p. 187–208.

De Rosa A., Sgrosso A., and Giordano A., *La geometria nell'immagine. Storia dei metodi di rappresentazione,* Vol. 1, *Dall'antichità al Medio Evo*, Torino: UTET, 2000.

Deshman R., "Another Look at the Disappearing Christ: Corporeal and Spiritual Vision in Early Medieval Images," *Art Bulletin* 79 (1997), p. 518–546.

Deshman R., "*Christus Rex* and *magi reges*. Kingship and Christology in Ottonian and Anglo-Saxon Art," *Frühmittelalterliche Studien*, 10 (1976), p. 367–405.

Desrosiers S., *Soieries et autres textiles de l'Antiquité au XVIe siècle. Catalogue du Musée national du Moyen Âge-Thermes de Cluny*, Paris: Réunion des musées nationaux, 2004.

De Wit H. C. D., *Histoire du développement de la biologie*, vol. 1, Lausanne: Presses Polytechniques et Universitaires Romandes, 1992.

Dibelius F., *Die Bernwardstür zu Hildesheim*, Strasbourg: Heitz und Mündel, 1907, p. 5–13, 37–41.

D'Onofrio C., *Castel S. Angelo*, Rome: Cassa Di Risparmio, 1971.

D'Onofrio G. (dir.), *Storia della teologia nel Medioevo*, 3 vols., Casale Monferrato: Piemme, 1996.

Donovan R. B., *The Liturgical Drama in Medieval Spain*, Toronto: Pontifical Institute of Medieval Studies, 1958.

Drescher H., "Einige technische Beobachtungen zur Inschrift auf der Hildesheimer Bernwardstür," *Bernwardische Kunst*, op. cit., 1988, p. 71–78.

Drescher H., "Zur Technik bernwardinischer Silber-und Bronzegüsse," *Bernward von Hildesheim und das Zeitalter der Ottonen*, op. cit., 1993, Bd. 1, p. 337–351.

Dronke P., *Women Writers of the Middle Ages. A Critical Study of Texts from Perpetua (dead 203) to Marguerite Porete (dead 1310)*, Cambridge University Press, 1984.

Dufour-Kowalska G., *L'Arbre de vie et la croix*, Genève: Tricorne, 1985.

Dunand F., Spieser J.-M., and Wirth J. (eds.), *L'image et la production du sacré, colloque Strasbourg 20–21 janvier 1988*, Paris: Klincksieck, 1991.

Duperray E. (ed.), *Marie-Madeleine dans la mystique, les arts et les lettres, colloque Avignon 20–22 juillet 1988*, Paris: Beauchesne, 1989.

Dutton P. E. and Kessler H. L., *The Poetry and Paintings of the First Bible of Charles the Bald*, Ann Arbor: University of Michigan Press, 1997, p. 104.

Duval N., "La représentation des monuments dans l'Antiquité Tardive," *Bulletin Monumental*, 138 (1980), p. 77–95.

Duval N., "La représentation du Palais dans l'art du Bas-Empire et du Haut Moyen-Âge d'après le Psautier d'Utrecht," *Cahiers archéologiques*, 15 (1965), p. 207–254.

Eastmond A., "Narratives of the Fall. Structure and Meaning in the Genesis Frieze at Hagia Sophia, Trebizond," *Dumbarton Oaks Papers*, 53 (1999), p. 219–236.

Engemann J. and Mohnhaupt B., "Beziehungsgeflechte: typologische Kunst des Mittelalters," *Jahrbuch fur Antike und Christentum*, 45 (2002), p. 259–265.

Erdmann, C., "Studien zur Briefliteratur Deutschlands im Elften Jahrhunderts," MGH, Schriften, 1938, p. 117 sq. and 210 sq.

Erffa H.M. von, *Ikologie der Genesis. Die christlichen Bildthemen aus dem Alten Testament und ihre Quellen*, München, Berlin: Deutscher Kunstverlag, rééd. 1995.

Erismann C., *L'Homme commun. La Genèse du réalisme ontologique durant le haut Moyen Âge*, Paris: Vrin, 2011.

Esche S., *Adam und Eva. Südenfall und Erlösung*, Düsseldorf: Schwann, 1957.

Euw A. Von and Schreiner P. (dir.), *Vor dem Jahr 1000. Abendländische Buchkunst zur Zeit der Kaiserin Theophanu. Ausstellung des Schnütgen-Museums und Kunst im Zeitalter der Kaiserin Theophanu, Akten des Colloquiums*, Köln: Locher, 1993.

Exner M., "Die Wandmalereien der Krypta von St. Georg in Oberzell auf der Reichenau," *Zeitschrift für Kunstgeschichte*, 58, 2 (1995), p. 153–180.

Fehr M., *Exemplarische Untersuchungen zur Ikonographie und Erzählstruktur der Hildesheimer Bronzetüren*, Diss. Bochum, 1978.

Ferrante J., "The Education of Women in the Middle Ages," *Beyond Their Sex: Learned Women of the European Past*, ed. P. H. Labalme, New York University Press, 1980.

Ferré R.-M., "L'art et le théâtre au Moyen Âge. Jalons et perspectives," *Médiévales*, 59, 2 (2010), p. 77–89.

Fillitz H., "Ottonische Goldschmiedekunst," *Bernward von Hildesheim und das Zeitalter der Ottonen*, op. cit., 1993, Bd. 1, p. 173–190.

Fleige K., "Bischof Bernwards Weihnachtsbilder. Eine Bildbetrachtung," *Diozese Hildesheim in Vergangenheit und Gegenwart*, 68 (2000), p. 363–369.

Fleige K., "Die Bronzetur von San Zeno in Verona. Vorbild fur die Bernwardstur," *Hildesheimer Jahrbuch fur Stadt und Stift Hildesheim*, 64 (1993), p. 87–119.

Focillon H., *La vie des formes*, Paris: E. Leroux, 1934.

Foletti I., Gianandrea M., *Zona liminare. Il nartece di Santa Sabina a Roma, la sua porta e l'iniziazione cristiana*, Rome, 2015.

Folkerts M., *Essays on Early Medieval Mathematics. The Latin Tradition*, Aldershot: Ashgate, 2003.

Fontaine J. and Pietri C. (dir.), *Le monde latin antique et la Bible*, Paris: Beauchesne, 1985.

Forsyth I. H, *The Throne of Wisdom. Wood Sculptures of the Madonna in Romanesque France*, Princeton University Press, 1972.

Fournée J., "Architectures symboliques dans le thème iconographique de l'Annonciation," *Synthronon, art et archéologie de la fin de l'Antiquité et du Moyen Âge*, dir. A. Grabar et al., Klincksieck, 1968, II, p. 225–235.

Frazer M. E., "Church Doors and the Gate on Paradise: Byzantine Bronze Door in Italy," *Dumbarton Oaks Papers*, 27 (1973), p. 145–162.

Frühe U., *Das Paradies ein Garten–der Garten ein Paradies. Studien zur Literatur des Mittelalters unter Berücksichtigung der bildenden Kunst und Architektur*, Frankfurt: Peter Lang, 2002.

Funkenstein A., *Theology and the Scientific Imagination from the Middle Ages to the Seventeenth Century*, Princeton University Press, 1986.

Galliazzo V., *I ponti romani*, 2 vols., Trévise: Canova, 1994–1995.

Gallistl B., *Die Bernwardsäule und die Michaeliskirche zu Hildesheim*, Hildesheim: G. Olms, 1993a.

Gallistl B., "Byzanz-Rezeption und Renovatio-Symbolik in der Kunst Bernwards von Hildesheim," *Byzanz und das Abendland im 10. und 11. Jahrhundert*, dir. E. Konstantinou, Köln: Böhlau, 1997, p. 129–160.

Gallistl B., "Die Dombibliothek zu Hildesheim und ihre Geschichte," *Diozese Hildesheim in Vergangenheit und Gegenwart*, 64 (1996), p. 59–90.

Gallistl B., "Die Hildesheimer Bronzetur und die sakrale Vorbildlichkeit in der bernwardinischen Kunst," *Hildesheimer Jahrbuch fur Stadt und Stift Hildesheim*, 64 (1993b), p. 69–86.

Gallistl B., "La porta di bronzo di Bernward da Hildesheim: iconografia e iconologia," *La porta di Bonanno nel duomo di Pisa e le porte bronzee medioevali europee: arte e tecnologia: atti del convegno internazionale di studi Pisa 6–8 maggio 1993*, Pontedera: Bandecchi e Vivaldi, 1999, p. 107–121.

Gallistl B., "Die Tur des Bischofs Bernward und ihr ikonographisches Programm," *Porte di bronzo dall'antichita al secolo XIII*, dir. S. Salomi, Rome: Istituto della enciclopedia italiana, 1990a, p. 145–181.

Gallistl B., "Die Urgerstalt der Hildesheimer Christussaule. Eine liturgiegeschichtliche Studie zur Bernward Stiftung St. Michaelis," *Archiv fur Liturgiewissenschaft*, 32, 1 (1990b), p. 27–46.

Gallistl B., "Das wiedererlangte Paradies. Zur Bedeutung der Maria Magdalena auf der Bernwardstur," *Diozese Die Hildesheim in Vergangenheit und Gegenwart*, 52 (1984), p. 19–38.

Gallistl B. and Muller W., *Die Bronzeturen Bischof Bernwards im Dom zu Hildesheim*, Freiburg: Herder, 1990.

Galonnier A. (ed.), *Boèce ou la chaîne des savoirs. Actes du Colloque international de la Fondation Singer-Polignac, Paris 8–12 juin 1999*, Louvain-La Neuve: Peeters, 2003.

Garnier F., *Le langage de l'image au Moyen Age*, 2 vols., Paris: Le Léopard d'or, 1982–1989.

Garrison E. B., *Studies in the History of Medieval Painting*, Florence: L'Impronta, 1953–1962.

Gatti Perer M. L., "La dimora di Dio con gli uomini" (Ap 21,3)," *Immagini della Gerusalemme celeste dal III al XIV secolo. Catalogo della mostra*, Milano: Vita e Pensiero, 1983.

Gauthier M.-M., "Images ou modèles d'architecture," *L'architecture en representation. Catalogue d'exposition*, Paris: Ministère de la culture, 1985, p. 199–205.

Gell A., *Art and Agency. An Anthropological Theory*, Oxford: Clarendon Press, 1998.

Gerstinger H., *Die Wiener Genesis*, Vienna: B. Fester Verlag, 1931

Giese W., "Zur Bautätigkeit von Bishöfen und Äbten des 10. Bis 12. Jahrhunderts," *Deutsches Archiv für Erforschung des Mittelalters*, 38 (1982), p. 388–438.

Gilson E., *Introduction à l'étude de Saint Augustin*, Paris: Vrin, 1987.

Glass A., "A Medieval Bronze Lion," *Gesta*, 1, Pre-Serial Issue (1963), p. 1–3.

Gosebruch M. and Steigerwald F. N. (eds.), *Symposium 10.10 bis 13.10 1984*, Göttingen: Goltze, 1988, p. 71–78.

Götz U., *Die Bildprogramme der Kirchentüren des 11. und 12. Jahrhunderts*, Phil. diss., Tübingen, 1971.

Goubitz O., Van Driel-Murray C., and Groenman-Van Waateringe W., *Stepping through Time. Archaeological Footwear from Prehistoric Times until 1800*, Zwolle: Stichting Promotie Archeologie, 2001.

Goullet M., "Hrotsvita de Gandersheim, Maria," *Marie. Le culte de la Vierge*, op. cit., 1996, p. 441–470.

Grabar A., "L'iconographie du ciel dans l'art chrétien de l'Antiquité et du haut Moyen Âge," *Cahiers archéologiques*, 30 (1982), p. 5–24.

Grabar A., *Les origines de l'esthétique médiévale*, Paris: Macula, 1992.

Grabar A., *Les voies de la création en iconographie chrétienne. Antiquité et Moyen Âge*, Paris: Flammarion, 2008.

Grant E., *The Foundations of Modern Science in the Middle Ages. Their Religious, Institutional, and Intellectual Contexts*, Cambridge University Press, 1996.

Greenhill S., "The Child in the Tree. A Study of the Cosmological Tree in Christian Tradition," *Traditio*, 10 (1954), p. 343–349.

Groszmann D., "Kloster Fulda und seine Bedeutung für den frühen deutschen Kirchenbau," *Das erste Jahrtausend. Kultur und Kunst im werdenden Abendland an Rhein und Ruhr*, ed. V. H. Elbern, Düsseldorf: L. Schwann, Bd. I, 1962, p. 344–370.

Guerreau-Jalabert A., "'Aimer de fin cuer.' Le coeur dans la thématique courtoise," *Il cuore, Micrologus*, XI, SISMEL, Edizioni del Galluzzo, 2003, p. 343–364.

Guglielmetti R. (dir.), *L'Apocalisse nel Medioevo. Atti del convegno Internazionale dell'Universtà degli Studi di Milano e della Società Internazionale per lo Studio del Maedioevo Latino, Gargnano 18–20 maggio 2009*, Firenze: SISMEL—Edizioni del Galluzzo, 2011.

Guglielmo M., *Le chiese di Roma dal IV al X secolo*, coll. Roma cristiana, vol. 3, Rome: Cappelli Editore, 1962.

Guillaumin J.-Y. (ed. and trans.), *Institution arithmétique de Boèce*, Paris: Les Belles Lettres, 1995.

Guldan E., *Eva und Maria. Eine Antithese als Bildmotiv*, Graz: H. Böhlaus, 1966.

Günther F. (ed.), *Der Egbert Codex, das Leben Jesu: ein Höhepunkt der Buchmalerei vor 1000 Jahren, Handschrift 24 der Stadtbibliothek Trier; Ausstellung in der Schatzkammer der Stadtbibliothek Trier, 27. April 2005–8. Januar 2006*, Stuttgart: Theiß, 2005.

Gy P.-M., "Églises doubles et groupes d'églises du point de vue de l'histoire de la liturgie," *Revue de l'Antiquité tardive*, 4 (1996), p. 51–54.

Harf-Lancner L., Mathey-Maille L., and Szkilnik M. (eds.), *Ovide métamorphosé. Les lecteurs médiévaux d'Ovide*, Paris: Presses Sorbonne-Nouvelle, 2009.

Harvey J., *The Mediaeval Architect*, London: Wayland, 1972.

Heck C., *L'échelle céleste dans l'art du Moyen Âge. Une image de la quête du ciel*, Paris: Flammarion, 1997.

Heitz C., *L'architecture religieuse carolingienne. Les formes et leurs fonctions*, Paris: Picard, 1980.

Heitz C., "Cluny II—Saint Michel d'Hildesheim. Une comparaison," *Cahiers de Saint Michel de Cuxa*, 20 (1989), p. 61–76.

Heitz C., "L'église porche/Westwerk. Naissance et diffusion d'un type architectural aux VIII et IXe siecles," *Studien zur Sachsenforschung*, 8 (1993), p. 55–67.

Heitz C., *La France préromane. Archéologie et architecture du haut Moyen Âge du IVe siècle à l'An Mil*, Paris: Errance, 1987.

Heitz C., "Jardins carolingiens," *Traverses*, 5–6 (1976), p. 63–67.

Heitz C., *Recherches sur les rapports entre architecture et liturgie à l'époque carolingienne*, Paris: S.E.V P.E.N., 1963.

Heslop, T.A, "St. Anselm, Church Reform and the Politics of Art," *Anglo-Norman Studies, Proceedings of the Battle Conference for 2010*, Woodbridge, 2011, pp. 103–126.

Henderson G., "Cain's Jawbone," *Journal of the Warburg and Courtauld Institutes*, 24 (1961), p. 108–14.

Herzog E., *Die ottonische Stadt. Die Anfänge der mittelalterlichen Stadtbaukunst in Deutschland*, Berlin: Mann, 1964.

Hillgarth J. N., *L'influence de la Cité de Dieu de Saint Augustin au Haut Moyen Âge*, Dordrecht: M. Nijhoff, 1985 (Sacris Erudiri, 28).

Hiscock N., *The Wise Master Builder. Platonic Geometry in Plans of Medieval Abbeys and Cathedrals*, Aldershot: Ashgate, 2000.

Hoffmann, H., "Politik und Kultur im ottonischen Reichskirchensystem: zur Interpretation der Vita Brunonis von Ruotger," *Rheinische Vierteljahrsblätter*, 22 (1957), p. 31–55.

Hohmann S.B., "Tradition und Neubeginn in der ottonischen Kunst," *Das Münster*, 54 (2001), p. 194–208.

Hoogland Verkerk D., "Exodus and Easter Vigil in the Ashburnham Pentateuch," *Art Bulletin*, 77, 1 (1995), p. 94–105.

Hope T., *Costumes of the Greeks and Romans*, New York: Dover, 1962.

Hubeaux J. and Leroy M., *Le mythe du phénix dans les littératures grecque et latine*, Paris: E. Droz, 1939.

Hughes C., "Visual Typology: An Ottonian Example," *Word and Image*, 17 (2001), p. 185–198.

Huschner W., *Transalpine Kommunication im Mittelalter. Diplomatische, kulturelle, und politische Wechselwirkungen zwischen Italien und dem nordalpinen Reich (9.-11. Jahrhundert)*, Hannover: Hahnsche Buchhandlung, 2003.

Hutter I. (dir.), *Byzanz und der Westen. Studien zur Kunst des europäischen Mittelalters*, Wien: Verlag der Österreichischen Akademie der Wissenschaften, 1984.

Iogna-Prat D., Palazzo E., and Russo D. (eds.), *Marie. le culte de la Vierge dans la société médiévale*, Paris: Beauchesne, 1996.

Iogna-Prat D. and Picard J.-C. (eds.), *Religion et culture autour de l'an Mil. Royaume capétien et Lotharingie; actes du Colloque Hugues Capet, 987–1987, la France de l'an Mil, Auxerre, 26 et 27 juin 1987, Metz, 11 et 12 septembre 1987*, Paris: Picard, 1990.

Isenberg G. and Scholkmann B. (eds.), *Die Befestigung der mittelalterlichen Stadt*, Köln: Böhlau, 1997.

Jacquart D., "La médecine au Xe siècle," *Gerbert l'européen. Actes du colloque d'Aurillac (4–7 juin 1996)*, eds. N. Charbonnel et J.-E. Iung, Aurillac, Société des lettres, sciences et arts "La Haute-Auvergne," 1997, p. 219–231.

Jacquart D. and Thomasset C., *Sexualité et savoir médical au Moyen Âge*, Paris: PUF, 1985.

Jaeger, C.S., *The Envy of Angels. Cathedral Schools and Social Ideas in Medieval Europe, 950–1200*, Philadelphia: University of Pennsylvania Press, 1994.

James-Raoul D. and Thomasset C. (dir.), *La montagne dans le texte médiéval. Entre mythe et réalité*, Paris: Presses de l'Université Paris-Sorbonne, 2000.

James-Raoul D. and Thomasset C. (dir.), *Les ponts au Moyen Âge*, Paris: Presses de l'Université Paris-Sorbonne, 2008.

James-Raoul D. and Thomasset C. (dir.), *En quête d'utopies*, Paris: Presses de l'Université Paris-Sorbonne, 2005.

Jantzen H., *Ottonische Kunst*, München: Münchner Verlag, 1947.

Jensen R.M., "The Fall and Rise of Adam and Eve in Early Christian Art and Literature," *Interpreting Christian Art*, eds. H. J. Hornik and M. C. Parsons, Macon: Mercer University Press, 2003, p. 25–52.

Jeremias G., *Die Holztür der Basilika Saint Sabina in Rom. Unter Verwendung neuer Aufnahmen von Franz Xaver Bartl*, Tübingen: E. Wasmuth, 1980.

Jolly P. H., *Made in God's Image? Eve and Adam in the Genesis Mosaics at San Marco, Venice*, Berkeley: University of California Press, 1997.

Kahsnitz R., "Der christologische Zyklus im Odbert-Psalter," *Zeitschrift für Kunstgeschichte*, 51, 1 (1988), p. 33–125.

Kahsnitz R., "Bronzetüren im Dom. Bernward und die Reliquien," *Bernward von Hildesheim und das Zeitalter der Ottonen*, op. cit., 1993, Bd. 2, p. 503–512.

Kantorowicz E. H., "The 'King's Advent' and the Enigmatic Panels in the Doors of Santa Sabina," *Art Bulletin*, 26, 4 (1944), p. 207–231.

Karkov C. E., *Text and Picture in Anglo-Saxon England. Narrative Strategies in the Junius 11 Manuscript*, Cambridge University Press, 2001.

Kaspersen S., "Cotton-Genesis, die Toursbibeln und die Bronzetüren. Vorlage und Aktualität," *Bernwardische Kunst*, op. cit., 1988, p. 79–103.

Kehrer H., *Die heiligen Drei Könige in Literatur und Kunst*, 2 vols., Leipzig, 1908–09, repr. Hildesheim: G. Olms, 1976.

Keller H., *Ottonische Königsherrschaft. Organisation und Legitimation königlicher Macht*, Darmstadt: Wissenschaftliche Buchgesellschaft, 2002.

Kemp W., *Christliche Kunst. Ihre Anfänge. Ihre Strukturen*, Munich: Schirmer-Mosel, 1994.

Kendall C.B., "The Gate of Heaven and the Fountain of life. A Speech-Act Theory and Portal Inscription," *Essays in Medieval Studies, Proceedings of the Illinois Medieval Association*, 10 (1993), p. 11–128.

Kessler, H., *"Aliter enim videtur pictura, aliter videntur litterae"*: Reading Medieval Pictures, *Scrivere e leggere*, Settimana di studio LIX, 2011, Spoleto: CISAM. 2012, pp. 701–29.

Kessler H., *Illustrated Bibles from Tours*, Princeton University Press, 1977.

Kessler H., "Hic Homo Formatur. The Genesis Frontispieces of the Carolingian Bibles," *Art Bulletin*, 53, 2 (Jun. 1971), p. 143–160.

Kessler H., *Spiritual Seeing. Picturing God's Invisibility in Medieval Art*, Philadelphia: University of Pennsylvania Press, 2000.

Kessler H., "An Unnoticed Scene in the Grandval Bible," *Cahiers archéologiques. Fin de l'Antiquité et Moyen Age*, 17 (1967), p. 113–120.

Kieffer R. and Bergman J. (dir.), *La main de Dieu/Die Hand Gottes*, Tübingen: Mohr, 1997.

Kingsley J., *The Bernward Gospels. Art, Memory, and the Episcopate in Medieval Germany*, Penn State University Press, 2014.

Kingsley J., "UT CERNIS and the Materiality of Bernwardian Art," *1000 Jahre St. Michael in Hildesheim*, op. cit., 2012, p. 171–184.

Kirigin M., *La mano divina nell'iconografia cristiana*, Rome: Pontificio Istituto di Archeologia Cristiana, 1976.

Kirschbaum E. (ed.), *Lexikon der christlichen Ikonographie*, 8 vols., Freiburg: Herder, 1970.

Klein P. K., "From the Heavenly to the Trivial. Vision and Visual Perception in Early and High Medieval Apocalypse Illustration," *The Holy Face and the Paradox of Representation. Papers from a Colloquium Held at the Bibliotheca Hertziana, Rome, and the Villa Spelman, Florence, 1996*, eds. H. Kessler and G. Wolf, Bologna: Nuova Alfa Editoriale, 1998a, p. 247–278.

Klein P. K., "Zur Nachfolge der karolingischen Bilderbibeln: die touronische Vorlage des Bernward-Evangeliars in Hildesheim," *Zeitenspiegelung zur Bedeutung von Traditionen in Kunst und Kunstwissenschaft. Festschrift für Konrad Hoffmann zum 60. Geburtstag*, dir. P. K. Klein und R. Prange, 1998b, p. 33–45.

Klemke G. and Mehler H. (eds.) *Hildesheim und seine bauliche Entwicklung*, Wiesbaden: Verl. Architektur, 1984.

Kopp S., "Der liturgische Raum in der westlichen Tradition," Ph.D. diss., Berlin: LIT Verl., 2011 (Ästhetik, Theologie, Liturgik, Bd. 54).

Koshi K., "Der Adam und Eva Zyklus der sogenannten Cottongenesis-Rezension. Eine Übersicht über mögliche Mitglieder der verzweigten Cottongensis-Familie," *Bulletin Annuel du Musée National d'Art occidental*, Tokyo, 9, 1975, p. 46–55.

Kracher A. (comm.), *Millstätter Genesis und Physiologus Handschrift*, facsimile ed., Graz: Akademische Druck- u. Verlagsanstalt 1967.

Krause-Zimmer H., *Bernward von Hildesheim und der Impuls Mitteleuropas*, Stuttgart: Verl. Freies Geistesleben, 1984.

Krautheimer R., "The Constantinian Basilica," *Dumbarton Oaks Papers*, 21 (1967), p. 115–140.

Krautheimer R., "Introduction to an 'Iconography of Mediaeval Architecture," *Journal of the Warburg and Courtauld Institutes*, 5 (1942), p. 1–33.

Krinsky C. H., "Representations of the Temple of Jerusalem before 1500," *Journal of the Warburg and Courtauld Institutes*, 33 (1970), p. 1–19.

Krinsky C. H., *Synagogues of Europe: Architecture, History, Meaning*, Cambridge: Massachusetts Institute of Technology Press, 1985.

Krücke A., "Über Einige Angebliche Darstellungen Gott-Vaters im Frühen Mittelalter," *Marburger Jahrbuch für Kunstwissenschaft*, 10, 1937, p. 5–36.

Krug A., "Antike Gemmen und das Zeitalter Bernwards," *Bernward von Hildesheim und das Zeitalter der Ottonen*, op. cit., 1993, Bd. 1, p. 161–172.

Kruse K. B., "Zur Bautätigkeit Bischof Bernwards in Hildesheim," *1000 Jahre St. Michael in Hildesheim*, op. cit., 2012, p. 29–40.

Kruse K. B., "Die Bernwardsmauer in Hildesheim. Grabungsvorbericht," *Diozese Die Hildesheim in Vergangenheit und Gegenwart*, 55 (1987), p. 21–29.

Kruse K. B., *Fruhe Dachziegel aus Hildesheim, Festschrift fur Gunther Kokkelink*, Hannover: Institut fur Bau und Kunstgeschichte, 1999.

Labande E.-R., "Mirabilia mundi. Essai sur la personnalité d'Otton III," *Cahiers de Civilisation Médiévale*, 6 (1963), p. 297–313, 455–476.

Lachiver M., *Vins, vignes et vignerons. Histoire du vignoble français*, Paris: Fayard, 1988.

Lacoste J.-Y. (dir.), *Dictionnaire critique de théologie*, Paris: PUF, rev. ed. 2007.

Ladner G. B., *God, Cosmos, and Humankind. The World of Early Christian Symbolism*, Berkeley: University of California Press, 1995.

Ladner G. B., "*Homo Viator*. Mediaeval Ideas on Alienation and Order," *Speculum*, 42, 2 (1967), p. 233–259.

Ladner G. B., "Vegetation Symbolism and the Concept of Renaissance," *De artibus opuscula. Essays in Honor of Erwin Panofsky*, ed. M. Meiss, New York University Press, 1961, p. 303–322.

Laging W.D., "The Methods Used in Making the Bronze Doors of Augsburg Cathedral," *Art Bulletin*, 49, 2 (1967), p. 129–136.

Lamirande E., *L'Église céleste selon Saint Augustin*, Paris: Études augustiniennes, 1963.

Lammers W., "Ein karolingisches Bildprogramm in der Aula regia von Ingelheim," *Festschrift für Hermann Heimpel,*

Veröffentlischungen des Max Planck Institut für Geschichte, 36/3, Göttingen, 1971.

La Plante M. F., "The Perception of Sanctity in Ottonian Germany. The Case of St. Bernward, Bishop of Hildesheim, 993–1022," *Studies in Medieval Culture*, 12 (1978), p. 35–41.

Lasko P., "The Tomb of St. Bernward of Hildesheim," *Romanesque and Gothic. Essays for George Zarnecki*, Woodbridge: Boydell Press, 1987, p. 147–152.

Lauras A. and Rondet H., "Le thème des deux cités dans l'oeuvre de Saint Augustin," Études augustiniennes, 1953, p. 97–160.

Lawrence M., "City-Gate Sarcophagi," *Art Bulletin*, 10, 1 (1927), p. 1–45.

Ledit J., *Marie dans la liturgie de Byzance*, Paris: Beauchesnes, 1976.

Le Goff J. and Schmitt J.-C. (dir.) *Dictionnaire raisonné de l'Occident médiéval*, Paris: Fayard, 1999.

Lehman K., "The Dome of Heaven," *Art Bulletin*, 27, 1 (1945), p. 1–27.

Leisch-Kiesl M., *Eva als Andere. Eine exemplarische Untersuchung zu Frühchristentum und Mittelalter*, Köln: Böhlau, 1992.

Leisinger H., *Romanische Bronzen. Kirchentüren im mittelalterlichen Europa*, Zürich: Europa Verl., 1956.

Lejbowicz M., "La géométrie de l'angle au XIe siècle latin et la tradition euclidienne," *Langages et philosophie. Hommage à Jean Jolivet*, dir. A. de Libéra, A. Elamrani-Jamal and J. Gallonier, Paris: Vrin (Études de philosophie médiévale), 1997, p. 31–38.

Lemoine M. (dir.), *L'image dans la pensée et l'art au Moyen Âge. Colloque organisé à l'Institut de France le vendredi 2 décembre 2005 par l'Association Rencontres médiévales européennes*, Turnhout: Brepols, 2010.

Lemoine M., "Le Timée latin en dehors de Calcidius," *Langages et philosophie. Hommage à Jean Jolivet*, dir. A. de Libéra, A. Elamrani-Jamal and J. Gallonier, Paris: Vrin (Études de philosophie médiévale), 1997, p. 65–78.

Lepelley C. (ed.), *La fin de la cité antique et le début de la cité médiévale, de la fin du IIIe siècle à l'avènement de Charlemagne. Actes du colloque tenu à l'Université de Paris X-Nanterre, les 1, 2 et 3 avril 1993*, Bari: Edipuglia, 1996.

Leyser K. J, "Ritual, Ceremony and Gesture: Ottonian Germany," *Communications and Power in Medieval Europe. The Carolingian and Ottonian Centuries*, ed. Timothy Reuters, London: Continuum, 1994.

Leyser K. J., *Rule and Conflict in an Early Medieval Society. Ottonian Saxony*, London: E. Arnold, 1979.

Linlaud M., *Serrures médiévales, VIIIe-XIIIe siècle*, PUR, 2014.

Lobbedey U., "Ottonische Krypten. Bemerkungen zum Forschungsstand an Hand ausgewählte Beispiele," *Herrschaftsrepräsentation in Ottonischen Sachsen*, ed. G. Althoff and E. Schubert, Siegmaringen: Thorbecke, 1998, p. 77–102.

Luttikhuizen G. P. (ed.), *Eve's Children. The Biblical Stories Retold and Interpreted in Jewish and Christian Traditions*, Leiden: E. J. Brill, 2003.

Maddalo S., *In figura romae. Immagini di Roma nel libro medioevale*, Rome: Viella, 1990.

Maguire H., "The Iconography of Symeon with the Christ Child in Byzantine Art," *Dumbarton Oaks Papers*, 34/35 (1980/1981), p. 261–269.

Mane P., *Le travail à la campagne au Moyen Âge. Étude iconographique*, Paris: Picard, 2006.

Manns F., *Les enfants de Rébecca. Judaïsme et christianisme aux premiers siècles de notre ère*, Paris: Mediaspaul, 2002.

Marchesin I., *L'image organum. La représentation de la musique dans les psautiers médiévaux, 800–1200*, Turnhout: Brepols, 2000.

Marchesin I., "La mise en réseau des hommes et des artefacts dans l'église Saint-Michel d'Hildesheim," *Visibilité et présence de l'image dans l'espace ecclesial. Byzance et Moyen Âge occidental*, eds. S. Sulamith Brodbeck and A.-O. Poilpré. Paris: Éditions de la Sorbonne, 2019, p. 257–276.

Marchesin I., "Ontologie et fonctions du visible et de l'audible dans les premières images de l'Apocalypse de Trier (Stadtbibliothek Cod. 31)," *L'Apocalisse nel Medioevo. Atti del convegno Internazionale dell'Universtà degli Studi di Milano e della Società Internazionale per lo Studio del Maedioevo Latino, Gargnano 18–20 maggio 2009,* Firenze: SISMEL—Edizioni del Galluzzo, 2011, p. 181–206.

Marchesin I., "Temps et espaces dans le frontispice du Psautier de la Première Bible de Charles le Chauve," *Die Methodik der Bildinterpretation*, dir. A. von Hülsen-Esch and J.-C. Schmitt, Göttingen: Max Planck Institut für Geschichte, 2002, t. II, p. 317–353.

Mariaux P.A., "L'image selon Grégoire le Grand et la question de l'art missionaire," *Cristianesimo nella storia*, XIV, 1 (1993), p. 1–12.

Martianini-Reber M., "Tentures et textiles des églises romaines au haut Moyen Âge d'après le *Liber pontificalis*," Rome: Mélanges de l'École française de Rome, 1991, p. 289–305.

Mayr-Harting H., *Church and Cosmos in Early Ottonian Germany*, Oxford University Press, 2007.

Mayr-Harting, H., *Ottonian Book Illumination. An Historical Study*, London: Miller, 2 vols., rev. ed. 1999.

Mayr-Harting H., "Ruotger. The Life of Bruno and Cologne Cathedral Library," *Intellectual Life in the Middle Age. Essays Presented to Margaret Gibson*, ed. L. Smith and B. Ward, London: Hambledon, 1992, p. 33–60.

McKitterick R., "Continuity and Innovation in Tenth-Century Ottonian Culture," *Intellectual Life in the Middle Age. Essays Presented to Margaret Gibson*, ed. L. Smith and B. Ward, London: Hambledon, 1992, p. 15–23.

McKitterick R., "Ottonian Intellectual Culture in the Tenth Century and the Role of Theophanu," *Early Medieval Europe*, 2, 1 (1993), p. 53–74.

McKitterick R., "Ottonische Kultur und Bildung," *Otto der Grosse, Magdeburg und Europa. Eine Ausstellung im Kulturhistorischen Museum Magdeburg vom 27. August-2. Dezember 2001, Katalog*, dir. M. Puhle, 2001, p. 209–224.

McKitterick R., *Perceptions of the Past in the Early Middle Ages*, University of Notre Dame Press, 2006.

Mende U., *Die Bronzetür des Mittelalters*, Munich, Hirmer Verlag, 2nd ed., 1994.

Mentré M., "L'apocalypse dans les cloîtres romans du Midi," *Cahiers de Saint-Michel de Cuxa*, 1 (1976), p. 103–121.

Mentré M., "L'image de la Jérusalem céleste dans l'iconographie des XIe et XIIe siècles," *Jérusalem, Rome, Constantinople. L'image et le mythe au Moyen Âge, colloque du département d'études médiévales de l'Université de Paris IV—Sorbonne*, ed. D. Poirion, Paris: Presses de l'Université Paris-Sorbonne, 1986, p. 17–31.

Messana VI., "L'esegesi tropologica presso i padri e le bibliche figure di Abele e di Caino in Ambrogio ed Agostino," *Seventh International Conference on Patristic Studies, Oxford 1975*, Berlin: Akademie Verlag, 1984, p. 185–195.

Metzger M., *Histoire de la liturgie. les grandes étapes*, Paris: Desclée de Brouwer, 1994.

Michel P.-H., "L'iconographie de Caïn et Abel," *Cahiers de Civilisation Médiévale*, I (1958), p. 194–199.

Miedema N.R., "Medieval Images of the Eternal City. Rome Seen through the Mirabilia Romae," *The Power of Imagery: Essays on Rome, Italy and Imagination*, dir. P. Van Kessel, Rome: Apeiron, 1993, p. 203–211.

Mohnhaupt B., *Beziehungsgeflechte. Typologische Kunst des Mittelalters*, Peter Lang, 2000.

Morton A. G., *History of Botanical Science. An Account of the Development of Botany from Ancient Times to the Present Day*, London: Academic Press, 1981.

Nebbiai-Dalla Guarda D. and Lombardi G. (dir.), *Livres, lecteurs et bibliothèques de l'Italie médiévale (IXe-XVe siècles). Sources, textes et usages: actes de la table ronde italo-française (Rome, 7–8 mars 1997)*, Paris: Ed. CNRS, 2001.

Nelson A. H., "Mechanical Wheels of Fortune, 1100–1547," *Journal of the Warburg and Courtauld Institutes*, 43 (1980), p. 227–233.

Niehoff F., "Umbilicus mundi—Der Nagel der Welt. Jerusalem und das Heilige Grab im Spiegel von Pilgerberichten und- karten, Kreuzzügen und Reliquiaren," *Ornamenta Ecclesiae, Katalog zur Ausstellung des Schnütgen-Museums*, Cologne: Schnütgen-Museum der Stadt, 1985, p. 53–173.

Nilgen U., "The Epiphany and the Eucharist. On the Interpretation of Eucharistic Motifs in Mediaeval Epiphany Scenes," *Art Bulletin*, 49, 4 (1967), p. 311–316.

Nilgen U., "Roma e antichità romane nelle raffigurazioni medievali," *Roma antica nel Medio Evo: mito, rappresentazioni, sopravvivenze nella 'Respublica Christiana' dei secoli IX-XIII, Atti della quattordicesima Settimana internazionale di studio, Mendola, 24–28 agosto 1998*, Milano: Vita e Pensiero, 2001, p. 449–467.

Nordenfalk C., "Noch eine turonische Bilderbibel," *Festschrift Bernhard Bischoff zu seinem 65. Geburtstag*, Stuttgart, 1971, p. 153–163.

North, W. and Cutler, A., "Ivories, Inscriptions, and Episcopal Self-Consciousness in the Ottonian Empire. Berthold of Toul and the Berlin Hodegetria," *Gesta*, 42, 1 (2003), p. 1–17.

Novótny V., *Cur homo? A History of the Thesis of Man as a Replacement for Fallen Angels*, Prague: Karolinum Press, 2014.

Nowak G., "Studien zur Bernwardstur in Hildesheim," *Diozese Die Hildesheim in Vergangenheit und Gegenwart*, 49 (1981), p. 7–17.

Obrist B., *La cosmologie médiévale textes et images. Les fondements antiques*, Florence: SISMEL-Ed. del Galluzzo, 2004.

Obrist B., "Le diagramme isidorien des saisons, son contenu physique et les représentations figuratives," *Mélanges de l'Ecole française de Rome. Moyen Âge*, 108, 1 (1996), p. 95–164.

Oexle O.G., "Bernward von Hildesheim und die religiosen Bewegungen seiner Zeit," *Bernward von Hildesheim und das Zeitalter der Ottonen*, op. cit., 1993a, Bd. 1, p. 355–360.

Oexle O. G., *Memoria als Kultur*, Göttingen: Vandenhoeck & Ruprecht, 1995.

Oexle O.G., "Les moines d'Occident et la vie politique et sociale dans le haut Moyen Âge" *Revue bénédictine*, 103 (1993b), p. 255–72.

Östling C., "The Ploughing Adam in Medieval Church Paintings," *Man and Picture: Papers from the First International Symposium for Ethnological Picture Research in Lund, 1984*, Stockholm: Almqvist and Wiksell, 1986, p. 13–20.

Ousterhout R., "Architecture as Relic and the Construction of Sanctity: The Stones of the Holy Sepulchre," *Journal of the Society of Architectural Historians*, 62, 1 (2003), p. 4–23.

Ousterhout R., "The Temple, the Sepulchre, and the Martyrion of the Savior," *Gesta*, 29, 1 (1990), p. 44–53.

Overesch M. and Alfhart G., *Himmlisches Jerusalem in Hildesheim. St. Michael und das Geheimnis der sakralen Mathematik vor 1000 Jahren*, Göttingen: Vandenhoeck & Ruprecht, 2009.

Pabst B., "Ideallandschaft und Ursprung der Menschheit: Paradieskonzeptionen und -lokalisierungen des Mittelalters im Wandel," *Frühmittelalterliche Studien*, 38.2004 (2005), p. 17–53.

Palazzo E., "Art, Liturgy and the Five Senses in the Early Middle Ages," *Viator*, 40, 2010, p. 25–56.

Palazzo E., "La liturgie de l'Occident médiéval autour de l'An mil. État de la question," *Cahiers de Civilisation médiévale*, 43 (2000), p. 371–394.

Palazzo E., "Le 'livre-corps' à l'époque carolingienne et son rôle dans la liturgie de la messe et sa théologie," *Quaestiones Medii Aevi Novae*, 2010, p. 31–63.

Palazzo E., "Marie et l'élaboration d'un espace ecclésial au Haut Moyen Âge," *Marie. Le culte de la Vierge*, op. cit., 1996, p. 313–325.

Palazzo E., *Les sacramentaires de Fulda: Étude sur l'iconographie et la liturgie à l'époque ottonienne*, Münster: Aschendorff Verlag (coll. Liturgiewissenschaftliche Quellen und Forschungen, Band 77), 1994.

Palazzo E. and Johansson A.-K., "Jalons liturgiques pour une histoire du culte de la Vierge dans l'Occident latin (V[e]–XIe)," *Marie, Le culte de la Vierge*, op. cit., 1996, p. 15–43.

Pang A. A, "Augustine on Divine Foreknowledge and Human Free Will," *Revue Augustinienne*, 40 (1994), p. 417–431.

Panofsky E., *Die Deutsche Plastik des 11. bis 13. Jahrunderts*, 2 vols., Munich, 1924.

Panofsky E., *La perspective comme forme symbolique et autres essais*, Paris: Les Éditions de Minuit, 1975.

Parisse M., "Bernward in Frankreich (1007)," *Bernward von Hildesheim und das Zeitalter der Ottonen*, op. cit., 1993, Bd. 1, p. 133–144.

Pastoureau M., "Bonum, Malum, Pomum. Une histoire symbolique de la pomme," *L'arbre. Histoire naturelle et symbolique de l'arbre, du bois et du fruit au Moyen Âge*, Paris, Le Léopart d'or, 1993, p. 155–199.

Payne B., Winakor G., and Farrell-Beck J., *The History of Costume*, 2nd ed., New York: Harper Collins, 1992.

Pépin J., *Théologie cosmique et théologie chrétienne (Ambroise, "Exam" I, 1, 1–4)*, Paris: PUF, 1964.

Pérez-Higuera T., *Chronos. Die Zeit in der Kunst des Mittelalters*, Würzburg: Echter, 1997.

Pérez-Higuera T., *La Nativité dans l'art médiéval*, Paris: Citadelles Mazenod, 1996.

Pettorelli J.-P., "La vie latine d'Adam et Ève. Analyse de la tradition manuscrite," *Apocrypha*, 10 (1999), p. 195–296.

Pevsner N., "The Term 'Architect' in the Middle Ages," *Speculum*, 17, 4 (1942), p. 549–562.

Picard J.-C., *Le continent apocryphe. essai sur les littératures apocryphes juive et chrétienne*, Dordrecht: Kluwer Academic, 1999.

Piccolo Paci S., *Le vesti del peccato. Eva, Salomè e Maria Maddalena nell'arte*, Milano: Àncora, 2003.

Pierce S., *The Essential Peirce. Selected Philosophical Writings*, vol. 1, eds. N. Houser and C. Klosel, Bloomington: Indiana University Press, 1992.

Pierce S., "The Mausoleum of Hadrian and the Pons Aelius," *Journal of Roman Studies*, 15 (1925), p. 75–103.

Pigeaud J., "Coeur organique, coeur métaphorique," *Il cuore, Micrologus*, XI, SISMEL, Edizioni del Galluzzo, 2003, p. 9–36.

Pinto-Mathieu E., *Marie-Madeleine dans la littérature du Moyen Âge*, Paris: Beauchesne, 1997.

Pochat G., *Zeitgestalt und Erzählstruktur in der bildenden Kunst von den Anfängen bis*, Vienna: Böhlau Verlag 1996.

Pognon E., *L'an mille. Œuvres de Liutprand, Raoul Glaber, Adémar de Chabannes, Adalberon, Helgaud*, Paris: Gallimard, 1947.

Poulle E., "Gerbert homme de science," *Gerberto d'Aurillac—Silvestro II linee per una sintesi, atti del convegno internazionale Bibbio, 11 sett. 2004*, dir. Pietro Nuvolone, 2005, p. 95–124 (Archivum Bobiense, V).

Rädle F., "Calcidius und Paulus begründen ein Vermächtnis: Zu Bernwards Dotationsurkunde für St. Michael in Hildesheim," *Latin Culture in the Eleventh Century. Proceedings of the Third International Conference on Medieval Latin Studies, Cambridge, Sept. 9–12, 1998 (Publications of Journal of Medieval Latin)*, eds. M. W. Herren, C. J. McDonough, and R. G. Arthur, Turnhout: Brepols, 2002, p. 328–349.

Rast-Eicher A. and Windler R. (dir), *NESATIX. Archäologische Textilfunde-Archaeological Textiles, Braunwald, 18–21 Mai, 2005*, Ennenda: Archeo Tex, 2007.

Relaño F., "Cosmographia arithmetica: le monde, ses parties et la numérologie médiévale," *Le Moyen Âge*, CIX (2003/1), p. 113–127.

Renna T., *Jerusalem in Medieval Thought 400–1300*, Lewiston: Mellen Press, 2002.

Ribémont B., "Isidore de Séville et les Mathématiques," *Discours et savoirs. encyclopédies médiévales*, eds. B. Baillaud, J. de Gramont and D. Hüe, Presses Universitaires de Rennes, 1998, p. 23–43.

Riché P., *Les Carolingiens. Une famille qui fit l'Europe*, Paris: Hachette, 1983.

Riché P. (dir.), *L'Europe de l'An Mil*, Saint-Léger-Vauban: Zodiaque, 2001.

Riché P. and Lobrichon G. (dir.), *Le Moyen Âge et la Bible*, Paris: Beauchesne, 1984.

Robertson D. W. Jr., "The Doctrine of Charity in Mediaeval Literary Gardens: A Topical Approach Through Symbolism and Allegory," *Speculum*, 26, 1 (1951), p. 24–49.

Rokseth Y., "La liturgie de la Passion vers la fin du Xe siècle," *Revue de musicologie*, 31, 89/92 (1949), p. 1–58.

Rommevaux S., "La réception des Éléments d'Euclide au Moyen Âge et à la Renaissance. introduction," *Revue d'histoire des sciences*, 56, 2 (2003), p. 267–273.

Ronk-Vaandrager M., "Tabernacle, temple et Jérusalem celeste "premier, deuxième et troisième temple?" Étude d'iconographie biblique de la peinture du IXe au XIIe siècle," Thèse de doctorat, Paris IV, septembre 1996.

Rosier-Catach I., *La parole efficace. Signe, rituel, sacré*, Paris: Seuil, 2004.

Rottlander R. C. A., "Zur Entwurfskonstruktion von St. Michaelis in Hildesheim," *Diozese Hildesheim in Vergangenheit und Gegenwart*, 58 (1990), p. 7–16.

Rudolph C., "In the Beginning: Theories and Images of Creation in Northern Europe in the Twelfth Century," *Art History*, 22 (1999), p. 3–55.

Ruggero P., *L'occhio e l'idea. Storia e fisiologia della visione*, Torino: Bollati Boringhieri, 1981.

Russo D., "Le Christ entre Dieu et homme dans l'art du Moyen Âge en Occident, IXe-XIVe siècles. Essai d'interprétation iconographique," *Le Moyen Âge aujourd'hui, Actes de la rencontre de Cerisy-la-Salle*, dir. J. Le Goff and G. Lobrichon, Paris: *Les Cahiers du Léopard d'Or*, 7, 1997a, p. 247–279.

Russo D., "Iconologie et ecclésiologie médiévales. Une question d'histoire de l'art," *Perspective. La revue de l'INHA*, 2008–1, p. 129–133.

Russo D., "La Madeleine pénitente. Iconographie et retables peints pour les femmes en Italie centrale, XIVe-XVe siècles," *Femmes, art et religion au Moyen Âge, actes du colloque international, Colmar, 3–5 mai 2001*, dir. J.-C. Schmitt, Presses Universitaires De Strasbourg, Colmar: Musée Unterlinden, 2004, p. 102–113.

Russo D., *Marie, Vierge à l'Enfant et Mère de Dieu. Recherches sur la formation et les développements de l'iconographie mariale en Occident, du IIIe siècle au milieu du XIIIe siècle*, 2 vols., thèse d'habilitation à diriger les recherches, Paris: Université Paris-Sorbonne Paris IV, 1997b.

Russo D., "Les représentations mariales dans l'art d'Occident. Essai sur la formation d'une tradition iconographique," *Marie. Le culte de la Vierge dans la société médiévale*, op. cit., 1996, p. 173–291.

Salomi S. (dir.), *Le porte di bronzo dall'antichità al secolo XIII*, Istituto delle Enciclopedia italiana, Rome, 1993.

Sansterre J.-M., "Miracles et images. Les relations entre l'image et le prototype céleste d'après quelques récits des Xe-XIIIe siècles," *La performance des images*, eds. A. Dierkens, G. Bartholeyns and T. Golsenne, Bruxelles: Éditions de l'Université de Bruxelles, 2009, p. 47–57 (Problèmes d'histoire des religions, 19).

Sansterre J.-M., "Vénération et utilisation apotropaïque de l'image à Reichenau vers la fin du Xe siècle. Un témoignage des 'Gesta' de l'abbé Witigowo," *Revue belge de philologie et d'histoire*, 73 (1995), p. 281–285.

Sansterre J.-M. and Schmitt J.-C. (eds.), *Les images dans les sociétés médiévales, pour une histoire comparée, Actes du colloque international organisé par l'Institut historique belge de Rome, en collaboration avec l'École française de Rome et l'Université libre de Bruxelles, Roma, Academia belgica, 19–20 juin 1998*, Rome: Institut historique belge, 1999.

Saxer V., *Les origines du culte de Marie Madeleine en Occident*, Paris: Beauchesne, 1959.

Saxer V., *Sainte-Marie-Majeure. Une basilique de Rome dans l'histoire de la ville et de son église (Ve-XIIIe)*, Rome: École Française de Rome, 2001.

Saxer V., "L'utilisation par la liturgie de l'espace urbain et suburbain. L'exemple de Rome dans l'Antiquité et le haut Moyen Âge," *Actes du XIe congrès d'archéologie chrétienne, Lyon, Vienne, Grenoble, Genève et Aoste, 21–28 septembre 1986*, Rome: École Française de Rome et Pontificio Istituto di archeologia cristiana, 1989, t. II, p. 917–1031.

Schade H., "Das Paradies und die *Imago Dei*," *Wandlungen des Paradiesischen und Utopischen. Studien zum Bild eines Ideals. Berlin*, 1966 (Probleme zur Kunstwissenschaft, 2), p. 79–182.

Schade H., "Hinweise zur frühmittelalterlichen Ikonographie, I. Adams grosses Gesicht," *Das Münster*, 11/12 (1958), p. 375–80.

Schapiro M., "Cains' Jawbone That Did the First Murder," *Art Bulletin*, 24 (1942), p. 205–212.

Schieffer R., "Ein Bischof vor tausend Jahren," *Hildesheimer Jahrbuch fur Stadt und Stift Hildesheim*, 64 (1993), p. 13–26.

Schild-Bunim M., *Space in Medieval Painting and the Forerunners of Perspective*, New York: Columbia University Press, 1940.

Schiller G., *Ikonographie der christlichen Kunst*, 5 vols., Gütersloh: G. Mohn, 1966–1991.

Schilling M., "Rota fortunae. Beziehungen zwischen Bild und Text in mittelalterlichen Handschriften," *Deutsche Literatur des späten Mittelalters. Hamburger Colloquium 1973*, eds. W. Harms and L. P. Johnson, Berlin, 1975, p. 293–313.

Schmitt J.-C. (dir.), Ève et Pandora. La création de la première femme, Paris: Gallimard, 2001.

Schorr D., "The Iconographic Development of the Presentation on the Temple," *Art Bulletin*, 28 (1946), p. 17–32.

Schrade H., "Zu dem *Noli me tangere* der Hildesheimer Bronzetür," *Westfalen*, 39 (1961), p. 211–214.

Schramm P. E., *Die deutschen Kaiser und Könige in Bildern ihrer Zeit 751–1190*, Munich: Prestel, 1983.

Schramm P. E., *Herrschaftszeichen und Staatssymbolik. Beiträge zu ihrer Geschichte vom dritten bis zum sechzehnten Jahrhundert*, 3 vols., Stuttgart: A. Hiersemann, 1955.

Schramm P. E., *Sphaira. Globus Reichsapiel. Wanderung und Wandlung eines Herrschaftszeichens von Caesar bis zu Elisabeth II ein Beitrag zum "Nachleben" der Antike*, Stuttgart: A. Hiersemann, 1958.

Schuffels H.-J., "Bischof Bernward von Hildesheim," *Das Kostbare Evangeliar des Heiligen Bernward*, eds. M. Brandt, R. Kahsnitz, and H. J. Schuffels, München: Prestel, 1993, p. 8–17.

Schulz-Mons C., *Das Michaeliskloster in Hildesheim. Untersuchungen zu Gründung durch Bischof Bernward (993–1022)*, 2 vols., Gerstenberg: Hildesheim, 2010.

Schütz B., "Zum ursprunglichen Anbringungsort der Bronzetur Bischof Bernwards von Hildesheim," *Zeitschrift fur Kunstgeschichte*, 57, 4 (1994), p. 569–599.

Seiferth W., *Synagogue and Church in the Middle Ages. Two Symbols in Art and Literature*, New York: F. Ungar, 1970.

Séné A., "Les équerres au moyen âge, remarques sur la forme inattendue d'un outil simple," *Actes du 95e Congrès national des sociétés savantes, Reims, 1970, section d'archéologie et d'histoire de l'art*, Paris: BnF, 1975, p. 525–548.

Sepière M.-C., *L'image d'un Dieu souffrant (IXe-Xe siècle). Aux origines du crucifix*, Paris: Cerf, 1994.

Settis S., "Von auctoritas zu vetustas: Die antike Kunst in mittelalterlicher Sicht," *Zeitschrift fur Kunstgeschichte*, 51, 2 (1988), p. 157–179.

Shelby L. R., "The Geometrical Knowledge of Mediaeval Master Masons," *Speculum*, 47, 3 (1972), p. 395–421.

Shelby L. R., "Medieval Masons' Tools. Compass and Square," *Technology and Culture*, 6, 2 (1965), p. 236–248.

Simek R., *Erde und Kosmos im Mittelalter*, Munich: C.H. Beck, 1992.

Sinding-Larsen S., *Iconography and Ritual. A Study of Analytical Perspective*, Oslo: Universitetsforlaget AS, 1984.

Skubiszewski P., "Ecclesia, Christianitas, Regnum et Sacerdotium dans l'art des Xe-XIe siècles. Idées et structures des images," *Cahiers de Civilisation Médiévale*, 28 (1985), p. 133–180.

Somfai A., "The Brussels Gloss. A Tenth-century Reading of the Geometrical and Arithmetical Passages of Calcidius' *Commentary* (circa 400AD) to Plato's *Timaeus*," *Scientia in margine. Études sur les Marginalia dans les manuscrits scientifiques du Moyen Âge à la Renaissance*, ed. D. Jacquart and C. Burnett, Geneva: Droz, 2005, p. 138–167.

Somfai A., "The Eleventh-Century Shift in the Reception of Plato's 'Timaeus' and Calcidius' 'Commentary,'" *Journal of the Courtauld and Warburg Institute* 65 (2002), p. 1–21.

Spieser J.-M, "Liturgie et programmes iconographiques," *Travaux et mémoires*, 11 (1991), p. 575–591.

Staats R., "Die Pilatuskrone in der Bernwardstür und die Reichskrone. Eine auffallende Parallele," *Das Münster*, 46, 3 (1993), p. 219–226.

Stahl H., "Eve's Reach. A Note on Dramatic Elements in the Hildesheim Doors," *Reading Medieval Images*, ed. E. Sears, Ann Arbor: University of Michigan Press, 2002, p. 163–175.

Stahli M., "Die Handschriften des Hildesheimer Domschatzes," *Diozese Die Hildesheim in Vergangenheit und Gegenwart*, 50 (1982), p. 83–94.

Steinen W. Von Taen, "Bernward von Hildesheim über sich selbst," *Deutsches Archiv für Erforschung des Mittelalters*, 12 (1956), p. 331–362.

Storm U., *Die Bronzetüren Bernwards zu Hildesheim*, Phil. diss., Berlin: Ernst-Reuter-Gesellschaft, 1966.

Stratmann M., "Zur Rezeption Hinkmars von Reims durch Bernhard von Hildesheim und Bernold von Konstanz," *Deutsches Archiv fur Erforschung des Mittelalters*, 44, 1 (1988), p. 170–180.

Talley T., *Les Origines de l'année liturgique*, Paris: Cerf, 1990.

Taton R., *La science antique et médiévale*, Paris: PUF, 1957.

Teviotdale E. C. and Cohen A. S., "The Getty Anglo-Saxon Leaves and New Testament Illustration Around the Year 1000," *Scriptorium*, 53 (1999), p. 63–81.

Thérel M.-L., *Les sources et l'évolution de l'iconographie du thème symbolique Marie-Église*, thèse de doctorat, Paris: EPHE, 1965.

Thomasset C., "Ce corps étrange," *Histoire des femmes, Le Moyen Âge*, dir. G. Duby, Paris: Plon, 1990, p. 56–70.

Toubert P., *L'Europe dans sa première croissance. De Charlemagne à l'an mil*, Paris: Fayard, 2004.

Toubert H., "Les représentations de l'Ecclesia dans l'art des XIe et XIIe siècles," *Musica e arte figurative nei secoli X-XII, convegno Todi, 1973*, repr. in *Un art dirigé. Réforme grégorienne et iconographie*, Paris, 1990, p. 37–63.

Toubert H., "La Vierge et les sages-femmes," *Marie. Le culte de la Vierge*, op. cit., 1996, p. 327–352.

Trexler R. C., *The Journey of the Magi: Meaning in a Christian History*, Princeton University Press, 1997.

Tronzo W., "The Hildesheim Doors. An Iconographic Source and its Implications," *Zeitschrift fur Kunstgeschichte*, 46, 4 (1983), p. 357–366.

Tronzo W. (ed.), *St. Peter's in the Vatican*, Cambridge University Press, 2005.

Trotzig A., "L'apparition du Christ ressuscité à Marie Madeleine et le drame liturgique: étude iconographique," *Revue de Musicologie*, 86, 1 (2000), p. 83–104.

Tschan F. J., *Saint Bernward of Hildesheim*, vol. 1, *His Works of Art*, University of Notre-Dame Press, 1951 (Publications in Medieval Studies).

Turner R. V., "*Descendit ad inferos*. Medieval Views on Christ's Descent into Hell and the Salvation of the Ancient Just," *Journal of the History of Ideas* 27, 2 (1966), p. 173–194.

Ulrich A., "Kain und Abel in der Kunst. Untersuchungen zur Ikonographie und Auslegungsgeschichte," Ph.D. diss., Bamberg, 1981.

Underwood P., "The Fountain of Life in Manuscripts of the Gospels," *Dumbarton Oaks Papers*, 5 (1950), p. 43–138.

Untermann M., "St. Michael und die Sakralarchitektur um 1000. Forschungsstand und Perspektiven," *1000 Jahre St. Michael in Hildesheim*, op. cit, 2012, p. 41–65.

Van Der Ploeg K., "The Altar and the Column. Symbolism in St. Michael's Church at Hildesheim," *Media Latinitas: A Collection of Essays to Mark the Occasion of the Retirement of L. J. Engels*, dir. R. Nip, Turnhout: Brepols, 1996, p. 309–315.

Van Dijk A., "The Angelic Salutation in Early Byzantine and Medieval Annunciation Imagery," *Art Bulletin*, 81, 3 (1999), p. 420–436.

Van Ginhoven H. J., "Le miniaturiste du Pentatheuque de Tours et sa méthode de travail," *Cahiers archéologiques*, 42 (1994), p. 65–74.

Vasiliu A., *Du diaphane. Image, milieu, lumière dans la pensée antique et médiévale*, Paris: Vrin, 1997.

Vergnolle E., "La colonne à l'époque romane. Réminiscences et nouveautés," *Cahiers de Civilisation Médiévale*, 41 (1998), p. 141–174.

Vezin G., *L'adoration et le cycle des mages dans l'art chrétien primitif*, Paris: PUF, 1950.

Vileisis B., "The Genesis Cycle of Santa Maria Antiqua," Ph.D. diss., Ann Arbor: University of Michigan, 1979.

Villasenor Black C., *Creating the Cult of Joseph: Art and Gender in the Spanish Empire*, Princeton University Press, 2006.

Villette J., *La maison de la Vierge dans la scène de l'Annonciation. Étude d'iconographie dans la peinture italienne du XVe siècle*, Paris: H. Laurens, 1940.

Vinge L., *The Five Senses: Studies in Literary Tradition*, Lund: C.W.K. Gleerup, 1975.

Vinken P., *The Shape of the Heart*, Amsterdam: Elsevier, 2000.

Vogel C., *Introduction aux sources de l'histoire du culte chrétien au Moyen Âge*, Spolète: Centro italiano di studi sull'alto medioevo 1963 (Biblioteca degli studi medievali, 1).

Vogtherr T., "Bischof Bernward von Hildesheim nach 1000 Jahren: Bemerkungen uber Nutzen und Ertrag der Bernward Ausstellung 1993 und ihrer Begleitpublikationen," *Hildesheimer Jahrbuch fur Stadt und Stift Hildesheim*, 1993, p. 27–53.

Voisenet J., "L'animal et la pensée médicale dans les textes du Haut Moyen Âge," *Rursus*, 1 (2006), https://doi.org/10.4000/rursus.50.

Warland R., "Frühbyzantinische Vorlage und mittelalterliche Adaptation. Die Szenenfolge zur Kindheitsgeschichte Christi auf einer der Ciboriumssäulen von San Marco in Venedig," *Zeitschrift für Kunstgeschichte*, 56, 2 (1993), p. 173–182.

Warner D., "Saints and Politics in Ottonian Germany," *Medieval Germany: Associations and Delineations* (Claremont Cultural Studies), ed. N. Van Deusen, Ottawa: Institute of Mediaeval Music, 2000, p. 7–28.

Wehmeyer H. (phot.) and Saul W., *Die Bernwardstür, Tor zum Leben*, Hildesheim: Bernward Verl., 1994.

Weil M. S., *The History and Decoration of the Ponte St. Angelo*, University Park: Pennsylvania State University Press, 1974.

Weinryb I., *The Bronze Object in the Middle Ages*, Cambridge University Press, 2016, pp. 70–73.

Weinryb I., "Materiality, Maker, and Ornament in the Middle Ages," *Gesta*, 52, 2 (2013), p. 113–132.

Werckmeister O. K., "The Liturgical Locality of St. Michael's at Hildesheim 'in Some Place, Suitable for Wild or Brutish Beasts," *The Metamorphosis of Marginal Images from Antiquity to Present Time, International Conference of Tel Aviv University, January 1999*, eds. N. Kenaan-Kedar and A. Ovadiah, Tel Aviv: The Yolanda and David Katz Faculty of the Arts, 2001, p. 139–146.

Wesenberg R., *Bernwardische Plastik. Zur Ottonischen Kunst unter Bischof Bernward von Hildesheim*, Berlin: Deutscher Verein für Kunstwissenschaft, 1955.

Wilpert J., *I sarcofagi cristiani antichi*, 4 vols., Rome, Città del Vaticano: Pontificio istituto di archeologia cristiana, 1929–36.

Wolff U., *Bischof Bernward—Leben in der Jahrtausendwende*, Hildesheim: A. Lax, 1996.

Wray B. M., "The Notitia and Curiosum and the Einsiedeln Itinerary. Translation of the Texts, Together with an Analysis and Comparison of Their Form and Content," Ph.D. diss., University of South Dakota, 1949.

Wu N. Y. (dir.), *Ad quadratum. The Practical Application of Geometry in Medieval Architecture*, Aldershot: Ashgate, 2002.

Wulf C., "Bernward von Hildesheim, ein Bischof auf dem Weg zur Heiligkeit," *Concilium Medii Aevi*, Bd. 11 (2008).

Young K., *The Drama of the Medieval Church*, Oxford: Clarendon Press, 1933.

Zahlten J., *Creatio mundi. Dartellungen der sechs Schöpfungstage und naturwissenschaftliches Weltbild im Mittelalter*, Stuttgart: E. Klett-J.G. Cotta, 1979.

Zaitsev E.A., "The Meaning of Early Medieval Geometry. From Euclid and Surveyors' Manuals to Christian Philosophy," *Isis*, 90, 3 (1999), p. 522–553.

Zimmermann B., *Wiener Genesis im Rahmen der antiken Buchmalerei. Ikonographie, Darstellung, Illustrationsverfahren und Aussageintentionen*, Wiesbaden: Reichert, 2003.